CW00969392

# THE JOURNAL OF WILLIAM DOWSING

Portrait in oils, said to be of William Dowsing. See pages 324-6.

# The Journal of William Dowsing

*Iconoclasm in East Anglia
during the English Civil War*

Edited by
Trevor Cooper

The Ecclesiological Society

The Boydell Press

First published 2001

The Boydell Press, Woodbridge
in association with
The Ecclesiological Society

ISBN 0 85115 833 1

The Boydell Press is an imprint of Boydell & Brewer Ltd
PO Box 9, Woodbridge, Suffolk IP12 3DF, UK
and of Boydell & Brewer Inc.
PO Box 41026, Rochester NY 14604-4126, USA
website: http://www.boydell.co.uk

The Ecclesiological Society
c/o The Society of Antiquaries of London,
Burlington House, Piccadilly, W1V 0HS, UK
website: http://www.ecclsoc.org

A catalogue record for this title is available
from the British Library

This book is printed on acid-free paper

Printed in Great Britain by
St Edmundsbury Press Ltd, Bury St Edmunds, Suffolk, UK

Thus far, Gentlemen, I have gone seriously to, and now according to the Mode of dispatching business in our Parish, lets go to the Tavern, and merrily discourse what all of us can say farther about this matter. There may possibly be some amongst you of that tender-natur'd, simpathizing humour as to be a little heated at sight of this poor Image [St Michael] in Flames, and ready to quench them with compassionate Tears... Let such Gentlemen take their Course.

(Edmund Sherman, *The Birth and Burning of the Image called S. Michael... All Saints, Barkin London... set up Anno 1659/60, burnt 1680/81, 1681*.)

Publication of this volume has been made possible by grants from:

The Marc Fitch Fund

The Scouloudi Foundation in association with
the Institute of Historical Research

# Contents

# Plates

*Frontispiece:* A possible portrait of William Dowsing, held by Christchurch Mansion, Ipswich. This painting is discussed in appendix 2.

*Plates 33– 48 will be found between pages 232 and 233*

*Acknowledgements for permission to reproduce illustrations*

Permission to reproduce items in the keeping of the following institutions and individuals is gratefully acknowledged for the following plates: 18a, Ashmolean Museum, Oxford; 8a (1608/1098), 8b (1477.b.31), 17a (G4099), 17b and 17c (599 A19), 18b (G4099), 55 (Add MS 4969, fol. 91) by permission of the British Library (shelfmarks or manuscript number in brackets); 32d, 35a (detail) and 35b, 38, 39, Dr John Blatchly; 15, the Syndics of the Cambridge University Library; 19, *Country Life* Picture Library; 4b, permission to take photograph and reproduce kindly given by the Director on behalf of the Trustees of Dr Williams's Library; 11a, the Fraternity of the Friends of St Albans Abbey; frontispiece and 10, Ipswich Borough Council Museums and Galleries; 4a, Maggs Bros. Ltd., London; 21b, 21c, 22, 25, 26, 27, 28, 29, 30, 40, 47, 50, 51a, 63, 64, © Crown copyright. NMR.; 9b, by courtesy of the National Portrait Gallery, London; 13, © Crown copyright. in the custody of the Public Record Office, PRO SP 16/498/87; 23, RIBA Library, Drawings Collection; 5, 6, 7, Suffolk County Director of Libraries and Heritage and Headmaster of Ipswich School; 1, 12, 14, 16b, Suffolk Record Office, Ipswich; 58, Suffolk Record Office, Bury St Edmunds; 28b, 35a, 36, Philip Whittemore.

# Figures in the text

The title-page to the Journal, at page 149, is modelled on Loder's 1786 edition of the Suffolk portion of the Journal.

# Maps

## General maps

## Maps showing Dowsing's progress chronologically in 1644

A series of maps charting Dowsing's progress chronologically will be found in the body of the Journal, the first on page 206.

# Tables

# Contributors

DR JOHN BLATCHLY, FSA, was Headmaster of Ipswich School 1972–93. He has been President of the Suffolk Institute of Archaeology and History since 1976, and Chairman of the Suffolk Records Society since 1988. He is the author of numerous articles and books on Suffolk matters, including *The Topographers of Suffolk* (Ipswich, 5th edition, 1988), *Eighty Ipswich Portraits* (Ipswich, 1980), *David Elisha Davy's Journal of Suffolk Excursions 1823–1844* (Woodbridge, 1983), and *Ipswich Town Library: a History and Catalogue* (Woodbridge, 1989).

TREVOR COOPER read Physics at Oxford. After a period as a schoolmaster, he is now a management consultant. He has a long-standing interest in church buildings and their use, and is a member of the Council of the Ecclesiological Society.

PROFESSOR JOHN MORRILL, FBA, is Fellow and Vice Master of Selwyn College Cambridge and Professor of British and Irish History. He is the author and editor of numerous books about the seventeenth century and has a special interest in Puritanism in general and Oliver Cromwell in particular. The refurbished and revised edition of his *Revolt in the Provinces: the English People and the Tragedies of War 1634–1648* (Longman, 1998) provides a full context for the themes in this volume.

DR S. L. SADLER lectures at Anglia Polytechnic University. Dr Sadler's doctoral thesis was on aspects of allegiance in Cambridgeshire during the English Civil Wars.

ROBERT WALKER has worked as a conservation officer in Cambridgeshire for twenty years and is currently the Conservation Manager for South Cambridgeshire District Council. He has been a member of the Ely Diocesan Advisory Committee since 1985 and was a founder member of the Cambridgeshire Historic Churches Trust.

# Foreword

*by the Secretary of the*
*Council for the Care of Churches*

It is sound British irony that the Secretary of the Council for the Care of Churches should be invited to write an introduction to Dowsing's Journal. My Council is committed to the proper treatment of church buildings and furnishings whereas William Dowsing has become notorious as a byword for official vandalism.

Although this book is the first to combine a coherent edition of Dowsing's Journal with a summary of all that is known of the man, his name has been familiar for generations. The Journal seems to have been copied around a number of antiquaries not long after it was sold to a London bookseller in 1704. Despite, or rather because of, its tale of destruction, it became welcome evidence for conservative historians, who could use it to demonstrate how Parliamentary or Whiggish principles would lead to the destruction of both Church and State. A century later Dowsing was as useful to ecclesiologically-minded clergymen, who could show that much of the Catholic past had survived the Reformation, only to be removed by the orders of a rebel officer. For them the diaries proved that the second, Puritan, Reformation was not the result of a popular longing to purify churches from corrupting images but the wanton destruction of ancient works of art in the face of local opposition.

The publication of the complete Journal is not simply a convenience for the reader but a major contribution to understanding the text. Putting the whole picture together reveals the extent of Dowsing's labours and hints at the plan behind them. We can now reconstruct the journeys Dowsing made, and track them on a map to show where he concentrated his efforts and where and why he seems to have called in deputies.

The result is that, instead of a cartoon character of an iconoclast, we can make out William Dowsing as an individual. Thanks to the diligent and imaginative detective work of John Morrill, John Blatchly and others, it is possible to reconstruct his life in some detail, his two marriages and his successive homes in Laxfield, Coddenham and Stratford St Mary. Above all, it has been possible to reconstruct his library and decipher the marginal comments he made on some of his volumes.

Dowsing was not a failure in life, turning through disappointment to revolution, but a propertied yeoman. Although he himself does not appear to have been to university, he was well educated and sent his son to Cambridge. His biography helps to explain the particular shape of iconoclasm during the English Civil War. It was not always the work of a mob of zealots incited by agitators but could be a legalistic, almost pedantic process of removing evidence of Popery. In a sense, it was not anti-artistic but non-artistic; the process did not recognise objects, such as screens or stained glass, as having an aesthetic aspect. That there could be a conflict is shown by Dowsing's parson at Coddenham, Matthias Candler or Gillet. 'He never was forward for conformity', joining in the protest at Bishop Wren's visitation of 1636 and serving during the Interregnum as a minister in the Suffolk 'classis'; but he was an enthusiastic antiquary and herald, preparing manuscript collections for a history of Suffolk.

Perhaps the most significant achievement of this book is that it restores Dowsing from a freak and extremist among extremists, into his true position as an unexceptional member of the winning side in the Civil War, who worked within his society not against it. Although he did have the ultimate threat of muskets to support his commands, most of the time he operated according to the situation he found in the different communities. If readers have, like the present writer, an East Anglian background, they may become curiously fond of Dowsing, as he pursues his well-meaning but lonely task across his native countryside, undramatic in itself but the setting for destruction.

Thomas Cocke

# Editor's preface

William Dowsing's Journal is unique. It records his activities in late 1643 and 1644, when he visited some 100 parish churches in Cambridgeshire, and about 150 in Suffolk, smashing stained glass and other 'superstitious' imagery, ripping up monumental brass inscriptions, destroying altar rails and steps, and pulling down crucifixes and crosses. He dealt just as vigorously with the chapels of the Cambridge colleges. Thus his Journal, with its notes on what he did at each church, is fascinating to those who love East Anglian churches. It is also a prime source of information about state-sponsored iconoclasm during the Civil War.

The need for a reliable edition of the text of the Journal has long been recognised. This book provides that, for the first time recombining the long-separated Cambridgeshire and Suffolk sections; but it is also much more. Every one of Dowsing's churches has been examined, and the remnants of his activity identified. Furthermore, to make better sense of Dowsing's entries, extensive use has been made of churchwardens' accounts and a range of other records. The interior arrangements of the college chapels during the 1630s and 1640s, in place for only a few years, have been recreated from accounts and unpublished contemporary descriptions. There are maps and photographs to illustrate Dowsing's various expeditions.

In addition the introductory chapters break much new ground. In chapter 1, Professor Morrill's seminal essay on Dowsing (here much enlarged and revised) serves as an introduction to the whole book. Chapter 2 is unashamedly local, showing us Dowsing's homes and introducing us to one of his acquaintances. The following four chapters deal with Dowsing's activities in Cambridgeshire and Suffolk, including Robert Walker's assessment of the Cambridgeshire expeditions, Dr Sadler's discussion of Dowsing's lively argument with university men, and Dr Blatchly's account of how Dowsing divided up Suffolk amongst his deputies.

Chapters 7, 8 and 9 deal with damage to parish churches in the neighbouring counties of East Anglia; they ask how Civil War iconoclasm can be recognised, and then use this to look at Norfolk, Essex, Huntingdonshire, Lincolnshire and Hertfordshire. Then follow the history of the Journal and a note on the text, before the Journal itself with its full commentary.

The appendices provide the bedrock of detail; different appendices will, of course, attract different readers. The book closes, in appendix 16, with a list of some of the questions which are raised in its pages, and explains how we may be contacted with any new information, or with corrections to what has been said. One means is via the website for this book, which contains the Journal online and links to other sites: **www.williamdowsing.org**.

## Acknowledgements

This book is the work of several hands. My first thanks as editor and convenor are thus due to my fellow contributors, whose enthusiasm, effort and expertise have taken the project further than I imagined, and added considerably to its pleasure. In addition to their own substantial work, they have also commented upon drafts of each other's chapters, helping greatly to make the book coherent.

Many other people have assisted us in one way and another, and they are thanked individually in the notes to each chapter. It will be seen that in a number of cases the help given was extensive.

I am in debt to Dr Thomas Cocke, Secretary of the Council for the Care of Churches. Not only has he kindly written the foreword, but I have benefited much from discussion with him on matters East Anglian and seventeenth-century.

My thanks are also due to Mary Ann Kernan, Michael Bundock, and Graham Chainey, who read the book in typescript from the point of view of the interested layman, and passed many improving comments. I am grateful for this act of friendship. Professor Diarmaid MacCulloch also read an earlier draft, as did Dr Margaret Aston (with whom I have enjoyed much invigorating debate): I am indebted to both for rescuing me from many errors. The remaining faults are, of course, my responsibility.

Acknowledgements to the various organisations who allowed illustrations to be reproduced will be found in the list of plates.

This project has been a spare-time activity carried out in the interstices of a busy professional career. Those who have done such a thing will know how it affects one's family. So my final thanks are to my wife and children. They too have suffered at the hand of Dowsing. I am grateful for their forbearance.

Trevor Cooper

# Note to the reader: dates and prices

## *Dates*

For Dowsing and his contemporaries the norm was to regard the change of year as occurring not on 1 January, but on 25 March (Lady Day). Thus, for example, dates which to us lie between 1 January and 24 March 1644, would by Dowsing have been regarded as falling at the tail end of 1643.

In giving dates, we have used the modern calendar convention, that the year starts on 1 January, and have converted year numbers accordingly – to 1644 in this case. However, when we quote documents *verbatim*, we have followed the convention of giving both contemporary and modern year numbers, separated by a slash. For example a date quoted in a document as 4 February 1643/4 falls within our modern 1644, but to Dowsing would have been in late 1643.

Churchwardens' years typically ran from Easter to Easter.

## *Prices*

A short note on wages will be found at the beginning of appendix 8, and a discussion of the cost of reglazing in appendix 12. Dowsing's annual income is explored on page 3.

# Outline chronology

*This outline chronology is intended to help the general reader get his bearings. Some minor events are shown where they help put Dowsing's iconoclasm in context.*

| | | |
|---|---|---|
| 1596 | | Birth of William Dowsing |
| 1625 | | Accession of King Charles I |
| 1629 | | Beginning of the King's 'personal rule' (eleven years without Parliament) |
| 1633 | | Laud made Archbishop of Canterbury, supports widespread changes to church discipline and practice ('Laudianism'), e.g. railing in of communion table |
| 1637 | | New Prayer Book introduced into Scotland: provokes uproar |
| 1639 | | First war against the Scots |
| 1640 | Apr 13 | 'Short' Parliament summoned (three weeks) |
| | June | King's army beaten by Scots, King has to sue for peace |
| | Nov 3 | 'Long' Parliament (20 years) meets |
| | Dec 18 | Archbishop Laud impeached for high treason |
| 1641 | Oct 23 | Rebellion breaks out in Ireland |
| | Sep 28 | House of Commons orders removal of 'Laudian' innovations in churches |
| | Dec 7 | First reading of Militia Bill (placing military appointments under Parliamentary control) |
| 1642 | Aug 22 | King raises his standard at Nottingham |
| | Oct 23 | Battle of Edgehill (Royalist victory) |
| 1643 | July 26 | Fall of Bristol (Royalist victory) |
| | Aug 10 | Earl of Manchester appointed to command the army of the Eastern Association (East Anglia) |
| | Aug 28 | Parliamentary Ordinance for demolishing of monuments of idolatry etc. |
| | Dec 19 | Based on the Ordinance, William Dowsing receives commission and starts work |

| 1644 | Jan 22 | Ordinance for regulating the university of Cambridge and for removing of scandalous ministers in the counties of the Eastern Association |
| | Feb 2 | Parliament orders Solemn League and Covenant to be taken by all men over the age of eighteen |
| | April | Many college Fellows ejected by the Earl of Manchester from Cambridge for not taking the Covenant |
| | May 9 | Second Parliamentary Ordinance for demolishing of monuments of idolatry etc. |
| | July 2 | Battle of Marston Moor (Parliamentary victory) |
| | Oct 1 | William Dowsing's final Journal entry |
| | Oct 27 | Second Battle of Newbury (Royalist victory), Earl of Manchester's star wanes |
| 1645 | Jan 10 | Laud executed |
| | Mar 5 | Directory of Worship adopted, Book of Common Prayer not to be used |
| | June 14 | Battle of Naseby (Parliamentary victory) |
| 1646 | | Charles I surrenders to Scots |
| 1649 | | Charles I executed |
| 1653 | | Cromwell made Lord Protector |
| 1658 | | Death of Cromwell |
| 1660 | | Restoration of the monarchy |
| 1668 | | Death of William Dowsing |

# Abbreviations

| | |
|---|---|
| Add. MS | Additional manuscript in the British Library |
| BL | British Library |
| Bod. | Bodleian Library |
| *CJ* | *Journal of the House of Commons* |
| CRO | Cambridgeshire Record Office |
| CUL | Cambridge University Library |
| *DNB* | *Dictionary of National Biography*, (L. Stephen and S. Lee (eds.), 63 vols., 1885–1900) |
| ERO(CO) | Essex Record Office, Colchester |
| ERO(CH) | Essex Record Office, Chelmsford |
| HERO | Hertfordshire Record Office |
| HURO | Huntingdonshire Record Office |
| HLRO | House of Lords Record Office |
| Journal | This edition of the Journal of William Dowsing; entries are referred to by number |
| LA | Lincolnshire Archives (previously Lincolnshire Record Office) |
| MS | Manuscript |
| NRO | Norfolk Record Office |
| *OED* | *The Oxford English Dictionary*, second edition |
| RCHME | The Royal Commission on Historical Monuments (England) |
| Soc. Antiq. | Society of Antiquaries of London |
| SRO(B) | Suffolk Record Office, Bury St Edmunds |
| SRO(I) | Suffolk Record Office, Ipswich |
| SRO(L) | Suffolk Record Office, Lowestoft |
| *TLS* | *Times Literary Supplement* |
| VCH | The Victoria History of the Counties of England (county series) |
| W&C | Willis R. & Clark, J. W., *The Architectural History of the University of Cambridge and of the Colleges of Cambridge and Eton*, 3 vols., Cambridge, 1886 |
| WD | William Dowsing, the iconoclast |

# I

# William Dowsing and the administration of iconoclasm in the Puritan revolution
## *John Morrill*

You shall make you no idols nor graven image neither rear you up a standing image, neither shall you set up any image of stone in your land, to bow down unto it: for I am the Lord your God. [And if you will not be reformed by me in these things]… I will destroy your high places and cut down your images and cast your carcasses upon the carcasses of your idols.
  (*Leviticus* xxvi. 1, 30)

Then shall it come to pass, that those that ye let remain of them shall be pricks in your eyes, and thorns in your sides, and shall vex you in the land wherein ye dwell.
  (*Numbers* xxxiii. 55) ★

WILLIAM DOWSING IS KNOWN for what he did, but not for what he was.[†] The Journal he kept of his destructive visits in 1643–44 to the churches of Cambridgeshire and Suffolk has been frequently reprinted, although always – until now – in misleading and inadequate editions.[1] He has been constantly held up as the model of Puritan vandalism in the Civil War era, as

★Two of the five mottoes referred to at the head of William Dowsing's Journal describing his iconoclasm in Cambridge in December 1643, according to an early eighteenth-century transcript. See note 1.
[†]This is a revised version of an essay which was originally published under the title 'William Dowsing: the bureaucratic Puritan' in Morrill, Slack, and Woolf, *Public Men and Private Conscience in Seventeenth-century England.* This version is heavily modified,

the grim reaper of wooden angels on roof-beams, stone saints and stained-glass cherubs.[2] This essay seeks to suggest that he is actually a much more interesting and even sympathetic figure than the bleak and unthinking iconoclast of legend. This introductory essay to the (surely definitive) edition of his Journal will seek both to find new ways of analysing his account of his iconoclastic activity and to reconstruct something of his social milieu and of his mental world. We will examine in turn the fragmentary evidence of his life as farmer and Puritan activist; the retrievable fragments of a most interesting personal library; and the details of his brief career as commissioner for the destruction of 'monuments of idolatry and superstition' on the authority of the second Earl of Manchester as Captain General of the Parliamentarian armies of East Anglia, between December 1643 and the autumn of 1644.

## I

William Dowsing (1596–1668) is a man whom we see from time to time throughout his life as he scuttles out of the shadows through a well-lit room and then back into the shadows.[3] He has proved an elusive quarry, especially as he is hard to find in the tax records.[4] He was born in Laxfield in north-east Suffolk, the younger son of a prosperous yeoman-farmer,[5] and moved to Coddenham about fifteen miles to the south and west, in the very heart of Suffolk, no later than the early 1620s, the date of his marriage to Thamar Lea, daughter of a minor Puritan gentleman who resided in Coddenham.[6] He acquired copyhold land there, presumably from his father-in-law. By 1637 the last six of his ten children by Thamar had had their births recorded in the Coddenham parish register[7] and he appears under that parish in a militia list for the autumn of 1638.[8] He and his family then disappear from the parish and the death of Thamar in the spring of 1640 is not recorded.[9] In 1642 we

with substantially new sections IV and V on the background to Dowsing's appointment and remit, major revisions to section VI on iconoclasm in neighbouring counties, and many small changes throughout the other sections. These seek to take into account the research reported in other parts of this volume. In preparing the original essay, I recorded my thanks to John Blatchly, Frank Bremer and Paul Slack for their comments on drafts; to Arnold Hunt for passing on much information about the current location of books once owned by Dowsing; and to Tim Wales, for tireless and sensitive archival retrieval and excellent advice on what could and could not be relied on. For this version, I need to record special thanks once again to John Blatchly and to Trevor Cooper, both of whom were penetrating critics of the earlier version and enthusiastic spurrers-on to fresh research.

find him signing a petition of the godly in Essex and by then, and, if not, certainly by 1643,[10] he was resident in Stratford St Mary on the Suffolk side of the River Stour.[11] This may seem to be an odd move since the Lord of the Manor of Stratford was a convicted Catholic recusant, Sir Edward Sulyard,[12] and the vicar, Dr Samuel Lindsell was a Laudian and a ceremonialist.[13] But Stratford lies just across the Stour from Dedham, whose lecturer, Matthew Newcomen, we will find was just one of many friends there. It would seem that he remained in Stratford until his death in 1668;[14] and it seems clear that if he signed petitions by gadding across the border to append his name to those of his friends in Dedham,[15] he is likely to have gadded to sermons and divine worship there throughout the period.

Although his letter of appointment as the Earl of Manchester's visitor describes him as a gentleman,[16] he looks much more like a typical yeoman. His will tells us that he possessed freehold and copyhold lands in Brundish and Wilby parishes (contiguous with his birthplace-parish, Laxfield), in Coddenham, and in Stratford. By his will, the Coddenham lands were to be sold for an estimated capital sum of £300 (suggesting an income to Dowsing of c.£15–20), which was to be divided between four of his daughters. The Brundish and Wilby lands were to provide annuities worth £11.50 a year for the children of his second marriage and to be the main inheritance of his only surviving son by his first wife. His Stratford lands were to provide for his wife during her lifetime and then for the son of his second marriage.[17] His house in Coddenham was a traditional yeoman's house, longitudinal in shape, three rooms upstairs and three downstairs, with a large fireplace between two of them.[18] His house in Stratford had five hearths, according to an assessment made in 1674.[19] It would be surprising in view of all this if his income was below £50 p.a.; or if it was much more than £80 p.a.

There are hints of a godly background. His grandfather's will of 1614 contains a classic 'puritan' preamble.[20] He married into a family which used Old Testament names for the children, his wife Thamar bearing the most distinctive and striking.[21] Despite his knowledge of both Latin and Greek,[22] he does not appear to have been to university himself (although his nephew and his namesake (godson?), with whom he has usually been conflated, and later his own eldest son, Samuel, were sent to Emmanuel, academy of the godly).[23] More important is his signature on an Essex petition to the House of Commons presented on 20 January 1642. The petitioners thanked the House for its 'great care and extraordinarie endeavour to settle our religion and peace', but apprehended 'a great stopp of reformation in matter of religion' and a threat from 'papists and other ill-affected persons… ready to act out the parts of those savage bloodsuckers from Ireland'. It called for the exclusion of the bishops from the House of Lords and other effectual measures of reformation. William Dowsing's distinctive holograph is to be found about two-thirds through the accompanying list of more than five thousand signatories, in close proximity to those of Matthew Newcomen, of three inhabitants of Dedham who were to appear in Dowsing's will, and of many other inhabitants of that town.[24]

In the almost complete absence of personal correspondence, details of his private life have largely to be derived from his long but formal will (Plate 1b). This contains hints of tensions between the children of his two marriages, and precautions about his wife short-changing her godchildren. But once again the evidence merely tantalises. The will also contains no religious preamble and no bequests to charitable uses. But he willed small sums to a group of men and women in Dedham who can he identified with leading supporters of reformation there in the 1640s and as members of a semi-separatist congregation there in the 1660s and to the deprived minister who served them.[25] The most important of this group was probably Bezaliel Angier,[26] a prominent clothier. Bezaliel, the brother of the prominent Lancashire dissenter John Angier, had been born in Stratford but spent all his adult life in Dedham. His godliness is confirmed by Oliver Heywood in his exemplary life of John Angier.[27] His name appears in close proximity to those of Dowsing and Matthew Newcomen, the Dedham Lecturer, in the Essex Puritan petition of 20 January 1642;[28] he was an elder for Dedham in the classis set up in 1646, and a long-standing governor of Dedham School;[29] he was left ten shillings by Dowsing in his will and was asked to see the will fully performed. In his own will, made in October 1678, he left £5 for distribution amongst 'some faithfull ministers of the Gospell or the widdows of deceased ministers that are lowe in their estate', and ten nobles for the poor of Dedham, 'which is all I give because I had twentie nobles taken from me and given to the poore in my liftyme', a reference to fines under the Conventicle Act.[30]

It can be speculated that Dowsing's decision to move to the Stour Valley in about 1639 was related to his desire to place himself in an area where, over successive generations from the 1550s, there was a steadfast witness to the 'hotter sort of Protestantism'.[31] His personal links with godly ministers can be seen in his only surviving letter, which he wrote to Matthew Newcomen in 1643 with messages for Harbottle Grimston MP and for his 'interest in parliament men'. We will see how this 'interest' probably extended to the Earls of Warwick and Manchester.[32]

Dowsing's will also contains references to his library. We will find it to be a collection of several dozen works in English with a strong evangelical Protestant bias. This is something to which we must return.

All the straws are blowing in the same direction; and they come together to produce that historiographical straw man – the godly middling-sort Puritan: a man of comfortable means, uncertain social status (younger son, connected to minor gentry), educated, well read, with indirect and third-hand contacts with powerful and influential leaders of the godly coalition in the 1640s.

## II

William Dowsing was a yeoman-farmer with a substantial library; and it is unusual for the historian to be able to find out as much about such a man's reading habits as we can about Dowsing's. He bequeathed his library to his eldest son, and on that son's death 35 years later it was sold to a London bookseller, Mr Huse.[33] He in due course sold it piecemeal. Fortunately Dowsing was an inveterate and meticulous annotator. Thus he wrote his name on the title page of everything he owned. He even had volumes rebound with his own monogram (Plate 4).[34] I have been able to recover 23 of his books in ten libraries in Britain and the United States. In addition, his annotations contain cross-references to other works in his collection, and these add a further 25 titles to the list.

His taste was eclectic. It contained some works of biblical exegesis, usually from a safe Calvinist stable. Thus he possessed Gervase Babington's *Comfortable Notes upon the Five Books of Moses*[35] and Joseph Caryll's multi-volume commentary on the Book of Job.[36] The library contained far more controversial theology, and here he did not confine himself to works he approved of. Thus he owned Pocklington's Laudian contribution to the altar controversy[37] and an unnamed work of Bishop Bilson's.[38] He possessed a work he refers to as *Laws of Church Policy*, perhaps Parker's *De politeia ecclesiastica*.[39] But he owned much more Puritan and anti-Catholic polemic including Tyndale's *Obedience of a Christian Man*,[40] Heinrich Bullinger's *A Most Sure and Strong Defence of the Baptisme of Infants*,[41] Thomas Clarke's *The Pope's Deadly Wound*,[42] George Walker's *The Manifold Wisedome of God, in the Divers Dispensations of Grace by Iesus Christ*,[43] John Robinson's *The People's Plea for the Exercise of Prophesie*, and two works by the Pilgrim Father Thomas Dighton.[44] One striking volume in this part of the collection is a copy he acquired in 1638 of John Bale's parodic edition of Princess Elizabeth's translation of Margaret of Angoulême, *A Godly Medytacyon of the Christen Sowle*.[45] A third major part of the collection consisted of works on classical and modern history (Plutarch,[46] Livy[47] and Josephus;[48] Ralegh's *History of the World*,[49] Bacon's *History of Henry VII*[50] and possibly Hayward's *History of Edward VI*[51]). He also owned three different editions of Foxe's *Acts and*

*Monuments*.[52] A fourth part consisted of works of political theory: most notably an edition of Polybius which he acquired in 1651,[53] and one of the major republican answers to the *Eikon Basilike*[54] (which he purchased alongside a copy of *A Narration of the Title, Government and Causes of the Execution of Charles Stuart, King of England*).[55] His annotation of these books is especially detailed and agitated, suggesting deep concern about recent political events. Finally, there are a number of works which are more difficult to classify. In 1640 he bought a copy of *A Diamond Most Precious*, a guide for masters and servants published in 1577.[56] He spent 25 December 1643 in Cambridge, having just begun his work as an iconoclast. His reading that day was Francis Quarles's *Divine Fancies: Digested into Epigrammes, Meditations and Observations*, a book he annotated in a way that showed that he had very mixed feelings about it.[57]

The largest single cluster of works in his collection, however, is the collection of 158 sermons preached to the Long Parliament which he had bound together into six fat volumes.[58] The collection consists of most, but not all, of the sermons preached at the monthly Fasts before the House of Commons up to the middle of 1646;[59] a much smaller number of the monthly sermons preached before the Lords at their monthly Fasts;[60] and 28 sermons preached before one or both Houses on other special occasions (the death of Pym, the signing of the Covenant, the victories at Marston Moor and Naseby, etc.).[61] He annotated and argued with the texts of these sermons more than with almost any of the books in his collection which I have seen.

All his books are carefully annotated. He began by writing his name on the title page, frequently followed by the date on which it was purchased and the date on which it was first read. It is clear from this that he acquired the sermons piecemeal, often many months in arrears, and that he then read them quite quickly, often within a few days, usually within two or three weeks, although he was occasionally in such a hurry that he had to add a written reminder to himself to return later for a fuller study.[62] He received many fairly soon – within a month – after they appeared, but many more much later.[63]

Amazingly, given the haphazard manner of purchase, he eventually acquired a nearly complete set of the monthly sermons to the Commons. He was like a schoolboy of a more recent age keenly collecting a complete set of cigarette cards. As he read the sermons, he then and there (with the precision of the business man on Southern Region working his way through a crossword puzzle in his daily newspaper) went through the text completing or providing the biblical references. He either knew the bible by heart (including the chapter and verse of every saying) or he went through everything he read with a concordance at his elbow. In a sample of ten sermons, I counted the addition of 194 references to 26 books of the Bible. Sometimes this would lead him into a fierce exegetical riposte to the preacher: when Samuel Rutherford used *Acts* to argue against the magistrate granting liberty of conscience, Dowsing wrote in the margin:

> Whereas you say they preach not against sins of 2 Table, what did Christ, Acts 24:26... and if you had well minded vers 23 of the same chapter you might have found he had there spake against brib[e]s.[64]

Beyond this compulsion to add biblical references (and an almost equal compulsion to add cross-references to Foxe's Acts and Monuments),[65] Dowsing's annotation was inconsistent. Frequently, he added to the title pages of books and sermons an index of items that were of particular interest to him;[66] frequently he scored the margin with varying degrees of emphasis;[67] and less usually he summarises a passage in the margin or engaged in argument with the author.

His habits of reading suggest an obsessively tidy mind; a man sufficiently meticulous to go through a text manually making corrections included in an erratum slip on which he then scrawls 'mended'.[68] His method of reading was calm, methodical, purposeful; but this belied, as we shall see, an intensity of feeling that lay behind that calm manner.

Dowsing's marginalia tell us much about his convictions and obsessions. We have evidence of his purchases from 1620 until 1651, and we can trace his commitment to godly reformation through the 1620 and 1630s to a high point in the early 1640s before something of a collapse of self-confidence becomes evident around the mid 1640s.

In 1620 Dowsing acquired and read a series of tracts published in Leyden on behalf of the Pilgrim Fathers. Two of them, by William Euring and John Robinson, were lightly annotated, although they show evidence that Dowsing knew the works of Cartwright. However, he took much more interest in two works by Thomas Dighton – *Certain Reasons of a Private Christian against conformitie to kneelinge in the very act of receiving the Lord's Supper*; and *The Second Part of a Plain Discourse of an Unlettered Christian*. The marginalia are persistent but monotonous: 'all persons that desire life ar tied to the Worde & not to carnall Reason'; 'what is not waranted & grounded on God's Word is sin'; 'all that conforme without warrant from the word are not of the truth'; 'every ceremony is evill'; 'antichrist the ordeyner of ceremonies that belong to God'; 'faith founded only on scripture'.[69] In the other tract purchased in 1620 – *A True Modest and Iust Defence of the Petition for Reformation* – Dowsing was less in an endorsing than in a confrontational mood, meeting the conformist arguments head on: on ceremonies in the Church of England –

'the popish use of practice & government that are still retayned I would also be removed'; he denies one familiar argument – 'the office of B[ishop] & presbiter ar one by the word of God'; he rejects an argument against popular participation in worship – 'this is but a popish distinction taken from *John* 7.48,49 that the common people were cursed. See Cowper on *Romans* 8.9';[70] 'your argument have no ground from scripture therefore your conclusion is false'.[71] This was a man with fire in his belly. He was not content with the Church as it was, and yearned to purify it. He was willing to listen to and endorse the protests about the corruptions of the Church he found in the writings of radical separatists if not to join them in their howling wilderness. By 1640, however, he had moved to the Stour Valley, into the heartland of passive disobedience to Laudianism, into an area that was a terminal for the New England Ferry. His reading, and, it would seem, his contact with SMECTYMNUUS,[72] were designed to keep his hunger for reformation very keen.

In the early 1640s, Dowsing had no doubts of what *had* to be done: '11 evils to be reformed' he noted at the head of his copy of a sermon by Obadiah Sedgwick he read in February 1642, and he took note of 'the publike plots of fallow ground which need a further breaking up'.[73] The priorities were unambiguous: episcopacy was 'Babylon's love token';[74] 'the Lord's Supper polluted', he noted, as Marshall thundered against 'the promiscuous multitude everywhere, not only allowed, but even compelled to the receiving of it… multitudes wallowing in all prophaneness and licentiousness'.[75] When, in addition to a welter of such highlightings, we add his preoccupation with idolatry throughout the Church, the pressure to make this meticulous man take upon himself a key role in the battle with popery becomes easy to understand. 'The walls of Jerusalem were 70 years in finishing', the advocacy of ceremonies was a 'wicked policy', and the country was 'wallowing in blood… [on] the onely account that could be given of it, a Bishop's Rochet, a Surplice or a Cross'.[76] Shortly after noting these words, Dowsing was, as we will see, drafting what amounted to an application for the post of Iconoclast General in East Anglia.[77]

But from 1643 on, and especially from 1645, dark clouds were forming. He began to lose confidence in the two Houses and their determination to carry through the great work of Reformation. He approved Calamy's denunciation of the 'oppression, the injustice in the Parliament's committees in the Counties'.[78] 'Committees of Parliament put in and restore corrupt priests into the ministry', he wrote twelve months later.[79] He distrusted the Scots, saying of part of one of Gillespie's sermons that it was 'rather Scottish devinity or no sence'.[80] The sermons marking the signature of the Covenant on 18 January 1644 are the only ones of the 158 he did not bother to annotate.[81]

More disturbing to him, however, was liberty turning to license. 'Corrupt books crept in', he noted of a list which included *The Bloody Tenant of Persecution* and *The Compassionate Samaritan* anathomized by Lazarus Seaman in September 1644;[82] and Mortalism, Divorce, Antinomianism, and a denial of the divine inspiration of Scripture were amongst those he gloomily noted as 'blasphemous errors' after reading a sermon in February 1645.[83]

Two things preoccupied him throughout 1645–46: the role of the civil magistrate in religion and the extent to which liberty should be extended to tender consciences. Nothing throughout the recoverable parts of his library was so intensively annotated as those sermons which addressed those issues. Initially, he seems torn, annotating and indexing alternative points of view.[84] But gradually he seems to have come to a point of repose: he indicated his approval of preachers who call upon the civil magistrate to involve themselves in the work of reformation, to set the limits to freedom and to police those limits.[85] And after showing sympathy for those who found classical Presbyterianism too rigid, and after approving Hugh Peter's plea that 'those who held errors' be counselled rather than punished,[86] he came down firmly against Independency and separatism. In perhaps the most heavily scored and annotated of all the sermons, Thomas Goodwin's *Hope Deferred and Dashed* (which he read on 13 November 1645), Dowsing emphatically endorsed the following passionate outbursts:

> We are to have Classical and Presbyteriall meetings; let them be to us as it were little universities; let our employments in them be opening of scripture, diving into the sense of difficult places; handling heads of divinity; searching into the grounds and redressing of erroneous opinions; resolving cases of conscience, communicating the experiences of the ministry, discovering Satan's depths and such like... For these particular men ['Independents', Dowsing adds] I doe here professe I reverence their persons... [yet] under this notion of Independencie weavers and taylors may become pastors... so that one may binde his sonne prentice to a cobler and at seven yeares end he may goe at free a minister... A Christian magistrate as a Christian magistrate, is a Governour of the Church; all Magistrates, it is true, are not Christians, but that is their fault; all should be, and when they are they are to manage their office under and for Christ. Christ hath placed Government in His Church.[87]

This classic defence of non-separating Congregationalism on the New England model would afford him little practical comfort in the months and years that lay ahead. Shortly after this he recedes into the mist. He seems to have abandoned the purchase of sermons with one preached as the Civil War ended in May 1646. His last recorded date of purchase (of sermons preached in the winter of 1645–46) was in mid June 1646, and all 156 sermons were bound together as a six-volume set and dated 9 October 1646. He then sat down methodically to read them through a second time, a task which took him from 14 December 1646 to 7 March 1647. It is tempting to see this as an attempt to regain his bearings, to refocus on essentials as victory in war turned to a disintegration of hopes for the peace. Tempting but probably wrong: as he began the task, he wrote 'I beg[an] this Book Dece'b' 14 & end 28. Ps.33.1.2.3'.[88] This was an upbeat message to himself: 'Rejoice in the Lord, O ye righteous; for praise is comely for the upright'.[89]

Like many 'mainstream' Puritans, he was appalled at the trial and execution of the King and at the abolition of monarchy. He acquired Polybius's account of the virtues of 'mixed' polities with elements of monarchy, aristocracy and democracy in them, as well as some of the items in the dust-storm created by Charles I's *Eikon Basilike* and Milton's *Eikonklastes*. Many Puritans like himself simply refused to take the Engagement, the solemn, signed promise to 'be true and faithful to the Commonwealth of England as it is established without a King or House of Lords'. Taking the Engagement was a pre-condition not only to the holding of any office in church or state but also to being able to take any part in civil legal proceedings. On 19 August 1650 Dowsing, acting as administrator of the estate of his second wife's first husband, attempted to recover debts owing to him at the time of his death by Henry Harrison. The Ipswich Petty Court found that since Dowsing 'hathe not taken the Engagement… it is ordered that execution [of the writ] shalbe stood *quo usque etc*'. Most refusers took the Engagement when it was going to cost them not to do so; Dowsing was amongst the more recalcitrant if he was still refusing it in August 1650.[90]

Perhaps because of his hostility to successive Commonwealth and Protectorate regimes, he is invisible in the records of the 1650s. In the 1660s a new crisis of conscience seems to have driven him, at the very least into semiseparatism. In truth, we lose sight of him. What we can say is that when he was called to his only public duty in the winter of 1643–44, his private conscience was fully formed. His belief that God would build a New Jerusalem if only the godly would clear the site was at its height. In December 1643 his sun was at its zenith.

### III

On 6 March 1643 Dowsing drafted a letter to Matthew Newcomen, the opening of which must have made the Dedham lecturer wince (Plate 7):

Syr my kind respect to you. This is let you understand I canot but take it ille that in 2 yeeres space you returne not my booke I lent you of Church Policy.[91] I have desired you to write to Mr Grimston[92] for it & tell him it was not your owne. You told mee you would writ I heare not of it yet. I pray with out more delay, write to him & let me begett the parties absolute answ[er] betwene this and march 25 & then if god permit me with life & helth I will come or send to you for it. I had rather losse 10 s[hillings] by farr than that very book, because there are divers notes in it[93] & divers bookes cite that booke & that edit[io]n, though I feare my booke is pulled apeces by the printer that since printed it in a quarto edit[ion], for it is printed by some Parliament mens action.

The letter continues with some choice biblical reproofs.[94] Dowsing then changes tack completely and a thoroughly shaken Matthew Newcomen was given an opportunity to make amends.

Sir, I would m[en]cion you with one thing, if you have anie interest in parliament men, now we have an army at Cambridge it might be a fitt tyme to write to the Vice Chancellor of Cambridge & Mayor to pull down all ther blasphemous crucifixes, all superstitious pictures and reliques of popery according to the ordinances o' parliament. I only reffere you to that famous story in Ed[ward] 6th['s reign how] the English got the victory against the Scots in Museleborough field the same day [&] hower the reformation was wrought in London and images burnt – *A[cts]* & *M[onuments]*[95] edit[ion] last.[96]

We have just one clue as to what inspired him to write this letter. On the same day on which he wrote this he may well have had on his desk a copy of John Arrowsmith's sermon, *The Covenant Avenging Sword Brandished.* Indeed it is bound into his collection immediately before the surviving copy of his letter, copied in his hand onto the blank recto of the next sermon. On the final page of the Arrowsmith sermon is printed the following:

Acts and Monuments. Mr Fox observes, that in King Edward the sixth time the English put to flight their enemies in Musselburgh field the self-same day and houre wherein the Reformation enjoined by Parliament was put in execution in London, by burning of idolatrous images. Such a dependence hath our increase upon our obedience.[97]

We will never know whether this was a formal letter of application. It seems to have been treated as such. Within a few weeks, as the Earl of Manchester (Plate 9) took over as commander of the Eastern Association, a William Dowsing was appointed as Provost-Marshall of the army of that association. Between August and December the accounts of this William Dowsing show him attending Manchester at the siege of King's Lynn, making arrangements for prisoners of war and equipping troops who were being sent into Essex.[98] It is hard not to believe that this was our William Dowsing, although given that other men shared that name, it cannot be demonstrated.[99] The most suggestive point, perhaps, is that just before the terminal date of these accounts (28 December 1643),[100] our William Dowsing was appointed as the Earl of Manchester's commissioner for removing the monuments of idolatry and superstition from the churches of Cambridgeshire and Suffolk. It is pure speculation, but not wildly implausible, to imagine that Newcomen shared Dowsing's letter with Grimston, who shared it with his friend and mentor the earl of Warwick, who had a word in the ear of his son-in-law, the earl of Manchester. How else might this stolid yeoman have got the job?

## *IV*

Dowsing was commissioned by the Earl of Manchester to implement a Parliamentary Ordinance of 28 August 1643; so much is clear (Plate 12). By what right Manchester commissioned him is far from clear.

The Ordinance predicated itself upon the two Houses' 'serious considerations how well pleasing it is to God and conduceable to the blessed reformation in his Worship... that all Monuments of Superstition and Idolatry should be removed and abolished'. It required the removal and/or destruction of all *fixed* altars, altar rails, chancel steps, and of 'all crucifixes, crosses, and all images and pictures of any one of more persons of the Trinity, or of the Virgin Mary and all other images and pictures of saints or superstitious inscriptions in or upon all and every church'. However, having categorised the 'monuments of idolatry and superstition', the Ordinance went on to lay responsibility for this orderly iconoclasm upon all churchwardens who were to raise parish rates to cover the costs of destruction and removal and the cost of replacement and making good.[101] (It might be added here that in authorising the costs of making good, the Ordinance speaks explicitly of the cost of repair of 'windows... which shall be broken', which removes all doubts that the 'superstitious' images and words Dowsing was instructed to destroy included images in glass.) The Ordinance laid down that wherever the churchwardens were reported as having defaulted, Justices of the Peace were to undertake the work and charge all expenses incurred to the defaulting wardens.[102] It also laid down that all this was to be accomplished before 1 November 1643. Thus by the time Dowsing was appointed to enforce these measures, the deadline set in the Ordinance had passed, although the requirements remained in force ('none of the like [images] hereafter permitted').

The Ordinance does not provide for any person other than church-wardens or JPs to take responsibility for its enforcement. The Earl of Manchester's warrant to Dowsing of 19 December 1643 is thus anomalous. It begins by making direct reference to it: 'whereas by an Ordinance of the Lords and Commons…'; and it continues by paraphrasing it: 'it is amongst other things ordained that all crucifixes, crosses & all images of any one or more persons of the Trinity… be taken away & defaced'. (It is striking nonetheless that it homes in on pictures and representations of the host of heaven and passes over the leading section of the Ordinance which deals with altars, rails and raised chancels.) But having quoted and paraphrased the tasks to be undertaken, the commission continues: 'these are therefore to will & require you forthwith to make your repaier to the severall Associated Counties and put the said Ordinance in execution'.[103] Nothing in the Ordinances establishing Manchester's authority over the Eastern Association,[104] nor anything in the Association Ordinances themselves,[105] nor anything in Captain General Essex's commission appointing Manchester to be Sergeant Major General of the forces of the Eastern Counties authorised him to issue such a commission to Dowsing.[106] Shortly after this, Manchester was given specific powers to appoint others to regulate the universities and to remove scandalous men from them; but no reference is made even in that Ordinance to the enforcement of the August 1643 orders against images.[107] Although the idea itself was not new (as Speaker, he would have known that county commissioners for iconoclasm had been proposed by the House of Lords),[108] Manchester seems simply to have taken it upon himself to appoint Dowsing. It may well be striking evidence of Dowsing's dependence on the personal authority of Manchester that his work as commissioner ground to a halt just when Manchester's position as General and head of the Association was challenged in Parliament in the autumn of 1644.

All this matters because it helps to confirm that there was only one Dowsing. In no other region of England was anyone given the kind of visitorial powers conferred upon him. The patchy evidence of iconoclasm outside East Anglia suggests that such iconoclasm as took place was either the responsibility of churchwardens or local JPs or of troops on the march or on the maraud. The note at the end of the commission, 'To Will'm Dowsing gen[tleman] & to such as hee shall appoint',[109] must leave open for the moment the question of whether there were other visiting commissioners within the counties of Norfolk, Essex, Hertfordshire, Huntingdonshire (and Lincolnshire)[110] – the other counties beside Suffolk and Cambridgeshire within the Eastern Association.

Within two days, Dowsing had set to work in the colleges and parish churches of Cambridge. All seems to have gone smoothly for the first week, during which he visited a number of colleges – Gonville and Caius, Peter-house, Jesus, and (perhaps) Queen's and St Catharine's – and some city parish churches. He then became embroiled in a heated argument with the Fellows of Pembroke.[111] This eventually became a heated exchange over scriptural warrant for iconoclasm, with Dowsing unflinchingly trading bib-lical citations with the dons until the whole thing degenerated into a slanging match with Dowsing telling them 'my child preaches as well as they [do]'. But it began with a debate on the content and on the authority of the Parliamentary Ordinance. It was alleged by different Fellows that Parlia-mentary Ordinances lacking the royal assent were invalid and illegal; that by the Ordinance 'pictures were not to be pulled down'; that the enforcement of the first four commandments lay with the clergy and not with the civil magistrates; and finally and most importantly for us, it was alleged by Robert Mapletoft that 'he did not think my Lord's Covenant was according to the Ordinance, and so I durst not abide by it'. It seems fairly evident that 'my Lord's covenant' was a reference to the Earl of Manchester's commission to Dowsing; and what he is saying is that Manchester had acted *ultra vires* and therefore that Dowsing's action was illegal.

Dowsing did not stop work. Slowed down, perhaps, at Pembroke College, he appears to have arrived rather late in the day at King's, and was therefore unable to begin work on the windows. He left orders for 'the [altar] steps to be taken [up] and one thousand superstitious pictures'. This suggests that it was to be done later. The Fellows must have hesitated and perhaps, steeled by what they heard had happened at Pembroke along the road, they held off; he did not return and it saved the windows of King's from destruction.[112] (It has been suggested that since King's chapel was by its foundation a memorial to King Henry VI, it was seen by Dowsing – or strongly represented to him as – protected by the words of the August Ordinance which provided that 'this ordinance… shall not extend to any image, picture or coat of arms in glass, stone or otherwise in any church, chappel, church-yard or place of publique prayer as aforesaid, set up or graven onley for a monument of any King, Prince or Nobleman'. This is an attractive suggestion, but made more difficult by the clear instruction for the destruction of 1000 superstitious pictures.)[113]

Having averaged four churches and chapels a day hitherto, he then had a very quiet day on 27 December, visiting only the parish church of St Mary the Great and doing little himself, leaving what had to be done to the churchwardens. Perhaps he was taking stock and writing to Manchester with details of the difficulties he was experiencing. His Journal suggests he did not have the necessary time to go up to London in person to consult with the Major General; but there were regular posts and he may well have sent

off a letter. Certainly this is the most obvious explanation of the supple-
mentary commission Manchester issued on 29 December (Plate 13). This
empowered Dowsing to bring before the Earl all defaulting heads of colleges, deans and subdeans of cathedrals and all churchwardens of parishes
who obstructed his work throughout the six counties;[114] and it instructed all
colonels and captains in his army and parish constables to assist him in his
work.[115] Manchester seems to have been intent in showing that his authority
rested ultimately on main force.

Eight months after the first Ordinance – on 8 May 1644 – the Lords
and Commons approved 'an Ordinance for the further demolishing of
monuments of idolatry and superstition'. This summarised the provisions of
the Ordinance of August 1643 and expanded them, specifically adding to the
list of things to be taken away and/or defaced representations of angels,
superstitious vestments, roodlofts, holy-water stoups and organs together
with their cases and frames; and it explicitly speaks of images in stone, wood,
glass and of images on church 'plate or other things used… in the worship of
God'. Once again responsibility for enforcement was laid upon parish
officers and JPs (and deputy lieutenants).[116] No Dowsing-like commissioners are envisaged.[117]

We do not know whether Manchester issued a further commission to
Dowsing to incorporate these changes. We do know that he henceforth
began to pay much closer attention to holy-water stoups and fonts in
particular.[118]

## V

It would seem that Dowsing was unique. No similar commission for any
other county or association has survived, and there is no evidence of any
other person or group of persons undertaking a similar task. Richard Culmer
seems to have had some commission for his demolition of the windows – in
the face of a hostile crowd – at Canterbury Cathedral, but his writ seems to
have been specific to the cathedral.[119] And if Dowsing's Journal had not
survived we would still know something of his work from specific references in churchwardens' accounts[120] and from hostile royalist sources.[121]

The manuscript of Dowsing's Journal for the period from 21 December
1643 to 1 October 1644 appears to have been lost, presumed destroyed.
At some point, different people copied out many (not necessarily all) the
entries for Cambridgeshire and Suffolk. There is no reason to think that
these were originally written in different journals. On the contrary, there is
evidence that they were extracted from the same document. Subsequently
several editions of both the Cambridgeshire and Suffolk entries have been

published, but the edition here presented is the first which reunites the two halves. The erratic dating of his Cambridge visit in December 1643 suggests that he may originally have scribbled notes to himself on what he undertook or ordered to be done without specifying where he was at the time, which would also explain his confusion between Caius and Peterhouse.[122] There are several similar puzzles – such as his failure to note that there were two churches sharing one churchyard in Swaffham Prior in Cambridgeshire – which might result from careless recording or retrospective recording from flawed memory.[123] To be blunt, we just do not know what was the relationship between what he recorded and what was transcribed *by him* or by his *later* editors. But there is no internal evidence to suggest any serious interference with, or bowdlerisation of, the text. Indeed the general impression of the Journal is that it took him a few days to get himself organised and that thereafter he settled into a routine of recording (i) those things which he had destroyed or defaced and (ii) those things which he had had no time to destroy but for which he had left orders (often with named persons) to be destroyed after his departure. This may indicate that he intended to check up on whether or not his orders had been observed (a possibility strengthened by an entry noting that he had sent someone in May 1644 to check up whether orders issued during his visit to Ufford on 27 January had been carried out).[124] As time went on, however, especially after the long gap in his recorded iconoclasm between mid April and mid July, his entries become much more general. Indeed, John Blatchly has plausibly argued that many of the later entries relating to Dowsing's visits to north-east Suffolk were his own follow-up checks on churches visited by his deputies.[125]

Given this pattern, there are certain generalisations about *how* he went about his iconoclasm that we can make. For example, we know that he was at least sometimes accompanied by a deputy[126] and by soldiers.[127] His first task in each church was to make an inventory of all objects of idolatry and superstition; his second was to destroy what he conveniently could and to leave orders for the destruction of the rest. In the early weeks he tried to see everything done by himself and his party, including the levelling of chancels and the removal of crosses from spires and church gables. But he soon realised how such a policy would slow him down. Henceforth he almost always left instructions that chancels were to be levelled and crosses on roofs removed by named persons within a specified period (often 14 or 28 days). On the other hand he and his party continued to take responsibility for all offensive inscriptions and altars and for most other accessible depictions in stone, wood and glass. In Suffolk he tells us that he completed all such tasks in 113 churches, but that he left some of the work to others in twelve churches and all of the work to others in fifteen churches. Most of these last fifteen can be explained by his being in a hurry. For example, on 5 February he was journeying from home to Cambridge and he visited just three churches on his 40-mile journey – two in Bury St Edmunds and one in Kentford (presumably the two places where he stopped for refreshment).[128] In each case he made a quick inspection and left instructions but undertook none of the work himself.[129]

On a handful of occasions he records that some of the work had been done before he came (and it is clear that most of the altar rails and vestments had been taken down and got rid of in 1641–42); on a few more occasions he says or implies that he met with a warm and eager response, that is with a party eager to cleanse their church but waiting for external authority to arrive so that it could be undertaken. Equally on a few occasions he met with sullen or passive non-co-operation (keys lost, ladders missing). But the number of such instances is too small for generalisation. Perhaps more striking is the variety of officers he commissioned to undertake work after he went. In Cambridgeshire he laid the responsibility on fourteen pairs of church-wardens, seven ministers, one overseer, one sequestrator (of the living of Shingay), 'Lord North's man' (at Kirtling), the squire's widow (at Hinxton), and a 'widow Rolfe' (at Ickleton).

William Dowsing was the bureaucratic Puritan. If something was in the Ordinance, it was removed or ordered to be removed. If it was not in the Ordinance it was left behind, as the quantity of stained glass containing coats of arms or royal insignia which remains even today bears testimony. He only began to deface fonts and remove holy-water stoups after they were mentioned by name in the subsidiary Ordinance of May 1644.[130] This was no blind fanaticism; but resolute enforcement of what the Bible and Parliamentary injunction had ordered. He followed both literally and un-swervingly.

The Journal of William Dowsing is a record of his visits to more than 250 churches and chapels in Cambridgeshire and Suffolk.[131] But it is not a complete record. It is possible, on the basis of close attention to his itinerary, to suggest that he almost certainly visited more Cambridgeshire churches and may have visited more elsewhere. Table 1.1 is a record of his progress.

Laid out like this, there is no doubt Dowsing's Journal integrated his accounts of his visits to both Cambridgeshire and Suffolk. Thus between 6 and 9 January the Cambridgeshire Journal sees him leaving Cambridge and visiting parishes on the route back to Suffolk; while we find the Suffolk Journal recording his stops from the county border to his home. But there is also no doubt that there is at least one hole in the record: what was he doing between his arrival in Cambridgeshire on 6 February and his departure on 20 February? Map 1.1 provides a possible answer.

Table 1.1 *Dowsing's progress through Cambridgeshire and Suffolk*

| | | |
|---|---|---|
| Dec 21 – | Jan 3 | Cambridge colleges and city churches |
| Jan 3 – | Jan 9 | visits churches en route from Cambridge to home |
| Jan 9 – | Jan 19 | at home in Stratford St Mary |
| Jan 19 – | Feb 5 | tours within Suffolk |
| Feb 6 | | leaves Suffolk, visits a parish near Cambridge |
| Feb 6 – | Feb 20 | no entries (but see discussion below) |
| Feb 20 – | Feb 23 | visits Brinkley (Cambs) and Suffolk churches and arrives home. |
| Feb 26 – | Mar 1 | visits Suffolk churches |
| Mar 5 – | Mar 26 | visits most Cambs parishes in three sweeps from Cambridge |
| Apr 3 – | Apr 15 | visits Suffolk churches |
| Apr 15 – | Jul 16 | no evidence |
| Jul 17 | | visits Suffolk church |
| Jul 18 – | Aug 21 | no evidence |
| Aug 21 – | Aug 30 | visits Suffolk churches |
| Sep 1 – | Sep 25 | no evidence |
| Sep 26 – | Oct 1 | visits Suffolk churches |

Dowsing systematically searched Cambridge city during his first visit and the south of the county in four separate sweeps. On 6 February he entered Cambridgeshire and arrived at Chesterton on the outskirts of Cambridge. On the 20th, he left the county through Brinkley. Is it not plausible to assume that in the period in question he was sweeping through all the northern parishes, leaving via Bottisham on his way to Brinkley, which he records visiting? The evidence of churchwardens' accounts and visits to the churches today afford some though not conclusive evidence of such a sweep. The only surviving set of churchwardens' accounts for the north Cambridgeshire parishes are those of Landbeach: and there we find a record of a substantial sum (£2. 0s. 0d.) being paid 'for mendin the wendoes'. This undated entry comes between two dated entries from June and September 1644, a little late; but there are plenty of other examples of payments for the making good of Dowsing's iconoclasm many months after the event.[132] The complaint of the churchwardens at Dry Drayton in 1662, that the damage to their chancel steps and communion rails had occurred during 'the rebellion' at the hands of a 'pretended power', would also seem to point to Dowsing.[133]

Furthermore the survival rate of those monuments and inscriptions pro-scribed by the Ordinances was equally low in the Cambridgeshire parishes

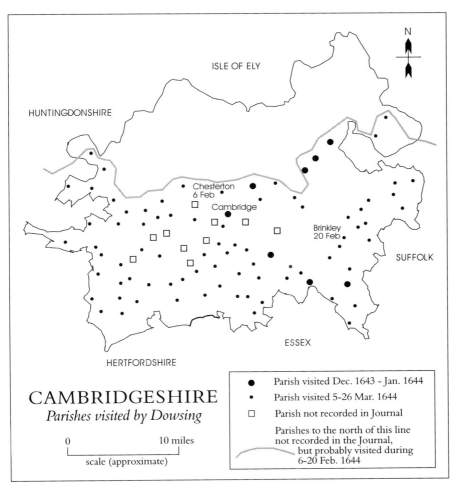

N

ISLE OF ELY

HUNTINGDONSHIRE

Chesterton
6 Feb

Cambridge

Brinkley
20 Feb

SUFFOLK

HERTFORDSHIRE

ESSEX

# CAMBRIDGESHIRE
*Parishes visited by Dowsing*

| | |
|---|---|
| ● | Parish visited Dec. 1643 - Jan. 1644 |
| • | Parish visited 5-26 Mar. 1644 |
| □ | Parish not recorded in Journal |

Parishes to the north of this line
not recorded in the Journal,
but probably visited during
6-20 Feb. 1644

0          10 miles

scale (approximate)

*Map 1.1* Dowsing's visits to Cambridgeshire, December 1643 – March 1644. The map also shows which parishes are not recorded in his Journal. See text for further discussion.

he is known to have visited and the rest. By comparison, the survival rate in the parishes of the Isle of Ely is much higher. I base this statement on a study of the meticulously recorded visits of an eighteenth-century antiquary in search of monumental inscriptions,[134] on two modern inventories of churches, and on personal visits to more than half the churches in the county and in the Isle.[135] Proscribed images and inscriptions survive in 6 of the 96 Cambridgeshire parishes he visited, and 2 of the 36 not mentioned in his Journal; but in 8 of the 25 in the Isle. Furthermore survivals in the shire are items easily overlooked in a crowded itinerary – such as a single bench-end of St Michael weighing souls on one of the poppy-head bench ends at Ickleton,[136] or an alabaster saint in a niche in a side chapel at Little Shelford.[137] One of the two parishes in North Cambridgeshire, Isleham, is remote and adjacent to the Isle, is cut off by floods for much of the winter, and is so full of surviving images it is tempting to think that this is one he did pass by.[138] There is no church in the shire which can still boast of such rich woodcarvings as survive at Wisbech St Mary, stone dragons such as on the font at Witcham, stained glass as at Wisbech or Rampton or of a reredos as at Coveney illustrating the Passion.[139] It would seem that either a couple of pages of his Journal became detached, or he never got round to writing up that part of his journey.

In Suffolk, his work takes a different form. Map 1.2 indicates the area he covered in his recorded visits. The scattered parishes to the west indicate places he alighted in as he journeyed to and from Cambridgeshire. Otherwise there is a concentration in the south and east, but only one deanery was completely unvisited.

## VI

Dowsing's Journal therefore does not include all *his* iconoclasm within Cambridgeshire. Nor does it give any representation of the extent of the iconoclasm undertaken by his deputies in Suffolk. We have seen that there is a gap in his Journal for 7–19 February when we can be fairly certain that he was at work in northern Cambridgeshire. (We can presume that this section was lost before transcriptions began in the eighteenth century.) What was Dowsing doing between 15 April and 17 July, and between 1 and 26 September? Might he have been visiting the many parts of Suffolk, that 70 per cent of the parishes not recorded in his diary? And what conclusions can we draw about iconoclasm elsewhere in the Eastern Association?

It seems that we can rule out the possibility that he was hard at work elsewhere in Suffolk. We know that in Suffolk he had a team of deputies, some of whom seem to have accompanied him (as on a journey through central Suffolk in late February), but some of whom worked independently of him. On reaching Elmsett on 22 August, Dowsing recorded that 'Crow, a deputy, had done before we came'.[140] When he appointed his deputies, he seems to have nominated the deaneries for which they were to have responsibility.[141] Parish records confirm that they were making their own visitation of parts of the county. According to the rector of Lowestoft, 'there came one Jissope with a commission… to take away from gravestones all inscriptions on which he found *Orate pro anima*… he took up in our church soe much

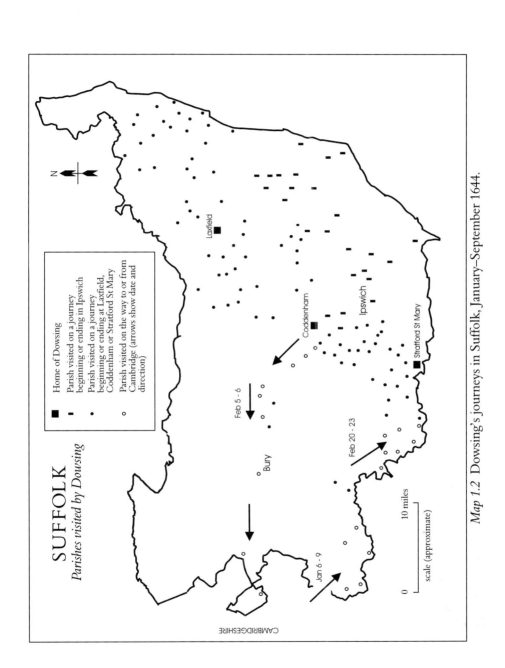

## SUFFOLK
### Parishes visited by Dowsing

**Legend:**
- ■ Home of Dowsing
- ▬ Parish visited on a journey beginning or ending in Ipswich
- • Parish visited on a journey beginning or ending at Laxfield, Coddenham or Stratford St Mary
- ○ Parish visited on the way to or from Cambridge (arrows show date and direction)

Laxfield

Coddenham

Ipswich

Stratford St Mary

Bury

Feb 5 - 6

Feb 20 - 23

Jan 6 - 9

CAMBRIDGESHIRE

N

0                    10 miles
scale (approximate)

*Map 1.2* Dowsing's journeys in Suffolk, January–September 1644.

brasses as he sould to Mr Josiah Wild for five shillings'.[142] All this is much
more fully studied by John Blatchly in the accompanying essay.[143] It can be
confidently asserted that there is no significant evidence from parish records
of iconoclastic visits which cannot be found in Dowsing's Journal or which
cannot be ascribed to one of his known deputies. Thus there is no real
evidence, as there is for Cambridgeshire, that he spent the intervals in his
diary on the stump through Suffolk. I find one other fact revealed by plotting
his itinerary on the map very suggestive. For his work in Suffolk consisted
less of the kind of week-long sweeps of twenty or so parishes he favoured in
Cambridge; rather he tended to make far more short expeditions. It is in fact
possible to divide his Suffolk work into 21 separate expeditions. Only twice,
in separate sweeps of the Suffolk coastal parishes from 22–28 January and
3–10 April, is there anything to match his long excursions through Cambridgeshire. A plotting of his routes reveals that at least fourteen of the 21
expeditions began or ended near to one of three hub villages: Laxfield (where
he was born), Coddenham (where he had lived *c.*1620–40), and Stratford
St Mary (where he was living).[144] The fact that he was still operating from
his home bases in August and September makes it likely that he had been
preoccupied with other things – his farm? – in the intervening period. The
three-week gap in September, coinciding with harvest, is particularly suggestive. Whatever he was doing during the gaps in his Journal, it seems that it
was not conducting visits to other Suffolk (or Cambridgeshire) churches.[145]

  Thus, we can be fairly sure that Dowsing appears to have reserved the
whole of Cambridgeshire to himself; that he divided Suffolk up into deaneries and allocated some to himself and others to deputies. Is there evidence
of his activity, or supervision of activity, elsewhere in the counties of the
Eastern Association? John Blatchly argues persuasively below[146] that one of
his deputies – Captain Clement Gilley, from Troston – was responsible for
extensive iconoclasm not only in north Suffolk but in south Norfolk and for
a level of activity perhaps second only to Dowsing himself, though his travels
did not reach to the north of Norfolk, where notable quantities of glass
survived the troubles. Gilley's trade-mark was a preoccupation with inscriptions on bells. After that the evidence is harder to interpret.

  As discussed by Trevor Cooper in chapter 9, there is evidence that visitors
were responsible for the 'cleansing' of churches in many parts of Essex; in
parts, and possibly the whole, of Hertfordshire; and more impressionistic-
ally in Huntingdonshire. But there is no direct evidence to suggest that
Dowsing himself was involved either as visitor himself or through deputies
appointed by him.[147] It is striking that churchwardens' accounts record the
work as undertaken either by those sent by the Earl of Manchester, or as a
result of articles sent by him. Thus the Bishop's Stortford churchwardens'

accounts speak of one shilling and sixpence paid to 'the earle of Manchester his officer' sometime before Easter 1644, an entry that comes from within a list of payments totalling almost £8 for repairs to the fabric, for glazing and for tiling of the floors;[148] while at Baldock the accounts speak more baldly of money spent 'for pulling downe the glasse in the church by Manchesters command'.[149] Much of the iconoclasm clearly was undertaken only after external intervention, and almost all of it may have been.

There are various possible readings of the surviving evidence, all equally plausible. Firstly, Dowsing may have appointed deputies in, for example, south Norfolk and north Essex, but on commissions making clear that he was acting on Manchester's authority.[150] Churchwardens inspecting the warrants of the visitors would be more taken with the Earl's name than with the yeoman's. Dowsing's commission certainly states that he had responsibilities over the whole Association as well as the authority to appoint deputies.[151] Furthermore, the gap in his draft commission to deputies where the county name would appear suggests that he had a pile of blanks intended for use in respect to several counties.[152] On the other hand, his deputies seem to have generally been men already known to him[153] – and how well would he have known men outside Suffolk? (The appointment of a Suffolk man for south Norfolk reinforces this.) Secondly, Manchester may have appointed other men with an authority equivalent to Dowsing's for other parts of the Association. Perhaps as the scale of the task became clear, Manchester supplemented the commission to Dowsing with others for other counties, reinforcing those commissions with instructions to county committees to co-operate with the commissioners.[154] The third possibility, a variant of the second, is that Manchester came up with a different solution in each county, perhaps with the added possibility that the committee in Norwich which took up the challenge did so independently of him.[155]

However, whatever the intention in December 1643, there is insufficient evidence to conclude that Dowsing himself supervised the 'cleansing' of churches throughout the Association. It remains unclear just how systematic the iconoclasm was outside Cambridgeshire and Suffolk. And no similar commission for any other county and association in England has survived, and there simply is no evidence of any other person or group of persons undertaking work in the same way. Iconoclasm elsewhere was undertaken by soldiers on the move or by local parish officers in accordance with the Parliamentary Ordinances. The former was often savagely done but covers only a small number of churches; the latter with a lighter touch, leaving less irreversible damage.[156] It was the misfortune of Suffolk and Cambridgeshire to be 'Dowsinged'.

## VII

What else does Dowsing's Journal tell us about civil-war iconoclasm? I would suggest that it tells us first about the earlier iconoclasms; that it tells us something of his priorities; and that it affords hints about the popularity of the godly reformation in its supposed heartland.

Dowsing records some things in more detail than others. His Journal entries allow us to know in considerable detail how many inscriptions there were on tombs he destroyed and in many cases exactly what the offending words were. It also tells us precisely where he reordered the east end (by the removal of rails and the levelling of chancels); it tells us about orders for the removal of crosses on spires and in chancel arches; and much less precisely, it records the removal of 'popish' or 'superstitious' images in glass, wood and stone. In only one quarter of the entries is it possible to differentiate these 'images' by location and material. Within those constraints, his visitation can be tabulated as shown in Table 1.2.

Perhaps most frustrating is his unwillingness to differentiate between 'images' in glass, on canvas, and in wood or stone. For him it was the fact of representation and not the form that mattered. The painted 'images' on canvas screens recently introduced into college chapels were amongst his targets, but by no means his only ones.[157] The churchwardens' accounts time and again record the employment of glaziers after his visits, which indicates that windows had been broken.[158] Why then did a certain amount of medieval stained glass survive in Cambridgeshire and Suffolk? The simple answer is that less certainly did so than in many other counties, certainly far less than in north Norfolk, for example.[159] But it is also clear that on some occasions the glass was *carefully* removed rather than smashed, stored away and later restored.[160] This *could* have been the situation at King's College, although I have already suggested that Dowsing left it to be done and it was left undone. H. Munro Cautley gives a number of examples of this in his discussion of *Suffolk Churches* (although mainly from elsewhere in the country),[161] and Christopher Woodforde has offered East Anglian examples from the sixteenth century.[162]

Dowsing's diary clearly indicates what the first Reformation had most effectively concentrated on and already destroyed. There is a splendid and moving passage in J. J. Scarisbrick's *The English People and the English Reformation* which makes my point for me:

> The Reformation simplified everything. It effected a shift from a religion of symbol and allegory, ceremony and formal gesture to one that was plain and direct: a shift from the visual to the aural, from ritual to literal exposition, from the numinous and mysterious to the everyday. It moved from… a

religion that sought out all the senses, to one that concentrated on the word and innerliness... The late medieval parish church had consisted of a 'mysterious succession' of semi-independent spaces cut off from nave and chancel by parclose screens of stone and wood... Here again the Reformation simplified. As the side altars and screens of guilds and chantries came down, nave and chancel were turned into a single, open auditorium in which the faithful could assemble to hear the minister proclaim the word of God, plain and unadorned.[163]

Margaret Aston's analysis of the iconoclasm of 1530–70 is as perceptive as it is detailed. Examining the statutes and injunctions of the period, she admirably captures the ambiguity of official approaches. There was a tension between a literal interpretation of the second commandment – 'they wanted to erase not simply the idols defiling God's churches, but also the idols infecting people's thoughts'[164] – and a willingness to distinguish between images which had been worshipped and those which could retain value as aids to prayerfulness – a distinction another recent historian summarised as that between abused and non-abused images.[165] I would like to suggest that those responsible for the iconoclasm of 1530–70 took this in practice to mean the difference between those images which were part of the 'devotional apparatus' of late medieval Catholicism, and those which were essentially instructional and ornamental.[166]

The first Reformation was principally directed against the doctrine of the communion of saints, the doctrine that bound together the living and the dead as a community of believers helping one another in preparation for the day of judgement. The living prayed constantly for those members of their

Table 1.2 *Analysis of Dowsing's activities*

| | Cambs ★ | Suffolk |
|---|---|---|
| *Number of parishes visited* | *98* | *147* |
| Images destroyed | 95% | 92% |
| Chancels to be levelled | 50% | 39% |
| Altar rails removed | 1% | 2% |
| Inscriptions removed | 32% | 41% |
| Crosses to be removed from | 46% | 21% |
| Holy-water stoups | 1% | 8% |
| Other iconoclasm occurred/ordered (angel roofs/wall paintings/organs) | 5% | 6% |

★ Includes *parish* churches in the City of Cambridge and throughout the county, but not Cambridge college chapels.

family and local community who had gone before them, and even enlisted them into their fraternities. They also benefited from the chantries others had founded. They looked to the saints and the host of heaven to watch over and protect the living and to intercede for them with the Father. Every *active* manifestation of that communion of the living and the dead was destroyed in the first generation of the Reformation: the side altars, the chantries, the reliquaries, the shrines, the Doom and the paintings that illuminated that theme. What was left behind for Dowsing were passive reminders of that discredited theology: the stained glass, the invocations on tombs (and more rarely in glass);[167] images in stained glass; and (as a result of early Stuart changes) the communion table presented as an *altar*, a place of sacrifice.[168] Most of the images in stone and wood which had survived were ornamental (bench-ends, roof adornments) rather than instructional. And that is what marked out Dowsing's priorities: he was first and foremost concerned with using his chisel to obliterate or lever off the invocations to prayer on the tombs of the long-dead; and he carefully itemises them:

> [St] Mary's at the tower [Ipswich], Jan. 29. We took up 6 brass inscriptions, with *Ora pro nobis*, and *Ora pro animabus*, and *Cujus animæ propitietur deus*; and *Pray for the soul*, in English.[169]

In many cases – it is hard to tell how many, because of subsequent damage – Dowsing concentrated on that invocation alone. The remainder of the inscription and most of the remaining carvings into the brass were left undamaged. It would often have been easier to destroy the whole.[170]

Second in importance was the levelling of the chancels. It seems that most chancel screens had survived down to the 1580s and 1590s and had then been mostly removed in a little remarked flurry of activity.[171] The opening up of the east end had led to a polarisation of opinion about how best to conduct the holy communion service, and had led to the 'Laudian' altar policy of the 1630s, with the railing of altars in perhaps 90% of all parish churches and the placing of 'altars' on raised daises at the east end in most churches. Dowsing's records strongly suggest that most altar rails had vanished even more quickly than they had appeared – only seven needed his attention in the 250 parishes he visited.[172] But almost half still had chancel steps. In the early weeks he and his companions dug them up themselves, but from 1 January 1644 onwards, only six chancels were levelled in the course of his visitation; in the other 101 cases it was left to (often named) individuals. At Covehithe in north-east Suffolk, he recorded that 'there was 4 Steps, with a vault underneath, but the first two might be levelled, which we gave orders to the churchwarden to do'.[173] Here his severely practical approach to iconoclasm comes through. When it came to the hundreds of images he destroyed in stone, glass, and wood, my itinerary in the company of modern inventories leaves me in little doubt that his principal targets were those pictures and images which would be a distraction to the worshipper. No complete window has survived for a church he visited; few if any reredoses or wall paintings except for those uncovered in recent times from behind their sixteenth- or seventeenth-century lime washes. What is striking is that as time wore on and Dowsing became more hardened and resigned to the limits of the possible he stopped bothering so much about purely ornamental (bench-ends, angel roofs).[174]

## VIII

Dowsing was, as his library indicates, a sincere and godly man. He undertook the work of state iconoclast because he believed that the Reformation was impeded by images that distracted the mass of the people from paying attention to the word of God; because many of the images perpetuated a false and discredited theology of Grace; and because he believed it was the duty of the Christian magistrate to enforce the second commandment, and that God might well withhold victory over the King until his graven images were destroyed. Perhaps like Samuel Ward, the Ipswich town preacher who systematically obliterated the word 'pope' from the books in his library as though it represented a kind of ectoplasm that menaced his peace of mind as he sat writing his sermons,[175] Dowsing simply felt in the presence of evil when he saw a carving of the persons of the Trinity or of the host of Heaven. He was no mindless vandal, but a man driven by personal conviction. He is very much of a piece with others whose private worlds have been opened up for us by scholars in recent years. Like the town clerk of Northampton, Robert Woodford, or the Warwick schoolmaster, Thomas Dugard, whose diary has been dissected by John Fielding[176] and Anne Hughes,[177] we sense the build up of tension, or internalised anger, amongst the godly in the years before 1642 – what I would call the coiled spring effect. Unless we grasp the bitterness of those years, of the sense that the Protestant cause and therefore God was being betrayed, then the release of pent-up energy in the early 1640s cannot be understood.

Many puzzles remain. Why should this new fervour against images have welled up in the breasts of Henry Sherfield, Richard Culmer and William Dowsing at this point? For decades, parish churches taken over by godly cliques had remained much as the first reformers had left them. In most parishes there was enough anger against the ecclesiastical authoritarianism of the 1630s to see altars and rails as expensively destroyed in 1641–42 as they had been expensively fitted a few years earlier. But in Samuel Ward's

Ipswich, in godly Cawston, and in precise Aylsham stained glass and statuary which had marked the devotion of pre-Reformation worshippers looked down untroubled on parishioners who, scrupulous over word and gesture, impassively ignored them. In part, this new fervour of *some* of the godly is to be seen as a response to Laudian idolatry, which released new passions and caused some to look to the survival of distracting images as the reason for so many men and women failing to respond to the word of God.

But each of the godly had to make his or her stand on his or her own issues. Just as the ministers of the Stour Valley and of central Essex had to decide in the late 1620s and early 1630s between exile and an uneasy struggle to sustain duty to their flocks with the strains on conscience that a partial conformity to the demands of rabid bishops required, so men like Dowsing had to work out how, in their particular and humble circumstances, they could best serve the Lord. Determined and disciplined pollution control was just one of the options. But it was the one chosen by William Dowsing.

William Dowsing was just a small farmer who emerged briefly from obscurity. But he reminds us – as we seem constantly to need reminding – that religious conviction was the motor that drove *some* (but by no means all) men to arms and hence made it possible for the Civil War to happen. His is a telling example of a life rooted in a quite remarkable biblicism. He reminds us that men of humble status were able to make independent political choices in the 1640s. Dowsing was very much a plain russet-coated captain that knew what he fought for and loved what he knew. He demonstrates that iconoclasm was a necessary part of a wider programme of godly reformation. It was not just part of an ecclesiastical reordering, but was seen as part of the reordering of the world to make it fit for the return of Christ. We see in him the central dilemmas of Puritanism in the 1640s: certainty about what to destroy, and uncertainty about what God would have in its place; a controlled self-righteousness that channelled a toxic mixture of anger and hope into a destruction of the past (ancient constitutionalism, stained glass windows) and a febrile search for a new land of Canaan. This was the bureaucratic Puritan; a man of suppressed but not repressed passion. He travelled with the Ordinances of Parliament crammed in one pocket and the Bible and Foxe's *Book of Martyrs* crammed into the other. In March 1643 Dowsing told Newcomen that God had given the armies of Edward VI victory over the Scots at Musselburgh the day the destruction of images was wrought in London, and because that destruction was wrought. He would have believed that in some measure Fairfax was given victory on 25 January 1644 at Nantwich over the troops returned from Ireland because on that day he wrought destruction of images at Orford, Snape and Sternfield. Herein lies the strength and the agony of the Puritan Revolution.

# 2

## Dowsing's homes

### *John Blatchly*

WILLIAM DOWSING was born in Laxfield, Suffolk, in 1596. He moved to Coddenham around the time of his first marriage in the late 1620s, and moved finally to Stratford St Mary, on the Essex border, before the end of 1641.[1] This chapter uses the available evidence to explore what is known of his homes in these three places, and investigates the damage at his local churches. The final section of the chapter describes Matthias Candler, Dowsing's minister at Coddenham for some fifteen years, a Puritan, and an antiquary.

#### *Laxfield: Dowsing's Farmhouse*

There is no firm evidence as to where Dowsing was born or brought up in Laxfield. There is, however, an old house, 'Dowsing's Farmhouse', which lies on the road which curls round to the north of Laxfield village.[2] The antiquity of the name cannot be accurately measured. It is however strongly probable that it was a Dowsing family home as long ago as the sixteenth century, perhaps, therefore, the home of our Dowsing and his parents.

It is much altered. Just one fact makes it remarkable. In 1983, two 8-inch wide painted planks, 70 and 24 inches long respectively, were found nailed on to rafters, slight remnants of a painted display which must have roofed the sanctuary of a chapel or chantry in the fifteenth century. They can be seen in Laxfield Museum. Sheila Fisher suggests that the iconography indicates that they roofed an altar to St John the Baptist, and wills prove that between 1374 and 1471 there was an altar to that saint in Laxfield church.[3] To take one further inductive leap, if it were a member of the Dowsing family who hid them in the house after the Reformation, might it have been Wolfran Dowsing, great-great-uncle of the iconoclast? – we know, because of his involvement in the burning at the stake of the Protestant John Noyes at Laxfield in 1557, that he was an ardent Catholic.[4]

For our Dowsing's iconoclastic activities at Laxfield church, see Journal entry 243.

### Coddenham: Baylham House

It is still possible to see Baylham House (Plate 1a) where the iconoclast lived at Coddenham during his first marriage to Thamar Lea, and a very delightful house it is, particularly in its situation on a bend of the Gipping, its nearest neighbour Baylham Mill.[5] Dowsing will have known the carved wooden door frame of the oldest part of the Mill, with male and female heads as hood mould stops. What a mercy they look entirely secular!

The house itself has been much extended in the eighteenth century and since; in Dowsing's time it had the usual longitudinal three rooms upstairs and down, with a large fireplace between two of them on each floor. There are no marks or inscriptions anywhere to indicate former occupiers, but we are helped by records of the appointments of new parish Constables, which include addresses. In 1642 Edward Ives was 'then dwelling in the house of Mr William Dowsing neere Bayleham Mill' and in 1661 Robert Hersham was 'ten't to Mr Dowsing neere to Bayleha' mill'.[6]

From here, between 1626 and 1637, William took six children to Coddenham Church to be baptised, the last four by Matthias Candler, antiquary, herald and historian of the county, and the incumbent from 1629 until his death in 1663; or by Thomas Waterhouse his curate. Both ministers were good preachers and, by all accounts, sound Puritans.[7]

The narrow lane the Dowsings would have taken to Coddenham church now leads after a few hundred yards to the mighty A14 and has become a cul-de-sac, with grass and weeds breaking up the tarmac and the carcasses of dead trees strewn at intervals. From the house, situated in the most remote corner of Coddenham parish, it would have been almost half as far to Baylham church as to Coddenham, but we know which the Dowsings chose. For one thing the minister at Baylham from 1625, John Bird, would not have been approved of by Dowsing; he was ejected from his living in 1645, partly for holding another in Bedfordshire.

How did Coddenham and Baylham churches fare in the iconoclasm? Very lightly indeed at Coddenham (Journal entry 53), and not much worse at Baylham (entry 248), though damage to the font there is eloquent witness to the work of reformation. At Coddenham we may suppose that Candler would have tried to find ways of limiting the losses by acting in advance of any official cleansing visit. Did he perhaps hide the alabaster of the crucifixion now to be found in the church? It was discovered in 1774 in the roof of a house opposite the church formerly occupied by clergy, where someone, possibly Candler, hid it for safety.[8]

## Stratford St Mary: site unknown

We do not know precisely when Dowsing moved to Stratford St Mary, on the Essex border, but it was before 1642.[9] His first wife had died in May 1640, allegedly in childbirth; thus he was a widower when he took the role of iconoclast. In June 1647, he married Mary Cooper,[10] and they produced five children.[11] In 1674 the Hearth Tax shows his widow paying for five hearths: there was one house in the parish with nine, one with eight, two with seven and six with six, and the Dowsing house was one of nine in the next category in this parish of large houses.[12] Unfortunately we cannot identify which was his, even though there exists a wonderfully detailed survey of all the properties in several manors around East Bergholt made by William Brasier in 1733; it is just too late to find a Dowsing living in Stratford, and we do not know the surnames of his married granddaughters.[13]

We know Dowsing took no part in the Committee hearings which led to the minister here losing his living in 1644 (the iconoclast was away from home).[14] We can guess that he approved of the successor, Daniel Wall, the Rector of St Mary's from 1657, because Wall was ejected in 1662. He lived on in the parish (with Dowsing's encouragement and support?) to be buried there with a eulogistic epitaph in 1667, the year before Dowsing died.

Certainly, with their home being near Puritan Dedham and the Essex border, the Dowsings would have felt confident of majority support amongst their neighbours for their views. Why then did Stratford church not appear in the Journal, and how could Dowsing have overlooked so much here that he swept away elsewhere?

For the church has English prayers for the souls of members of the Mors family (wills 1510 and 1526) in large letters in a flint flushwork frieze running from the east end to the west. There survive also the usual crowned MR and IHS devices as well as a curious and inexplicable alphabet in detached letters.[15] Furthermore, in about 1820 the brasses of Edward and Elizabeth Crane (1558), with prayers for their souls in English, were found still in excellent condition in their slab which had been buried beneath the floor of the north side of the nave. After their discovery they were detached from the stone and are now mural on a board. The only hint of iconoclasm in the church is in the centre of the nave roof, where mortice holes from figures probably removed in some cleansing were only filled with new carvings in 1878. We can surmise that not everyone in Stratford was pulling Dowsing's way.

As we have seen, Dowsing's widow Mary stayed in Stratford, and a few years later, in 1672, their son William was old enough to hold office, first as 'Overseer for the Poore', and then six years later, the year Mary died, as churchwarden. Samuel, then the only surviving son of Dowsing's first marriage, was described as 'of Stratford' on his death in 1703, and it was in his library, inherited from his father, that the manuscript of the Journal was discovered.[16]

## *Matthias Gillet* alias *Candler, the Puritan antiquary*

As we have seen, Dowsing's minister during his years at Coddenham was the Puritan antiquary Matthias Candler (who sometimes used the surname Gillet).[17] He was Vicar of Coddenham from 1629. He was not ejected in 1662, the register of the parish showing clearly that he was succeeded only after his death in December 1663.[18] The last entries in his hand are a marriage in October 1661, a burial in March 1662 and a christening in April 1663. His successor William Smith wrote in the same book in June 1664: 'What are lacking here looke for them in the Cromwelian register', so Candler had conformed enough to switch books during the Commonwealth, then back at the Restoration.[19]

However, he was said to have been admonished for 'inconformitie' at Bishop Wren's Visitation of 1636; he certainly signed the Petition of Suffolk ministers on church government ten years later, arguing for 'a form of church government, according to the word of God, and the example of the best reformed churches', which would suppress 'schismatics, heretics, seducing teachers and soul-subverting books'.[20] In 1655 he was chosen as one of the ministers to serve on the seventh division of the Suffolk classis, which was to meet at Coddenham, probably at Shrubland Hall.[21] Two of the lay members, Edmund Blomfield and Edmund Mayhew, were Dowsing deputies.[22] Much later, in 1696, John Fairfax wrote to Henry Sampson claiming that he had known Candler well, and that like Fairfax and Sampson, he was a nonconformist. Fairfax describes his old friend most engagingly:

> The Good he had done in former Times, (wherein he never was forward for conformity...) is almost beyond belief: For all, far and near, flock'd after his Ministry. Neither was he less esteem'd in those loose times, when Men having itching Ears, heap'd up to themselves Teachers according to their

Humours. He still taught them the good old savoury Truths, by which men best get to Heaven. He had one peculiar Study and Diversion that made him acceptable to Gentlemen, which was Heraldry and Pedigrees. He had really been a fit man to have wrote the Antiquities of his Country.[23]

Candler's manuscript collections for a history of the county exist in at least seven different versions in the Bodleian Library, at the Society of Antiquaries and in the British Library.[24] They consist of church and parish notes, pedigrees and notes on gentry families. They provided the basis for the family history of Dowsing and of his deputy Blomfield, described elsewhere.[25] Two excerpts will help us to judge to what extent he was torn between Puritan principles and regret for the loss of antiquities through iconoclasm. The first is a conversation with the sexton at St Nicholas, Ipswich, which is recorded in the commentary to Journal entry 79. The second is in his notes on Coddenham, where a wistfulness is betrayed in what he writes:

> There lies a stone in the chancell neare the North wall; it is not known for whom it was laid but the armes of Deynes are in the window by it.
>
> In the Chancell under a Marble lies Edmund Jermy who died 1506. I have heard Mrs Hellen Bacon say hee was her great Uncle. The brass is taken of[f] because of the superstitious inscription.
>
> In the Church under a Marble lies Thomas Barnabe a priest who died 1489. The inscription was in brasse and is taken off being superstitious. His coate armour was allso upon the stone, a lyon rampd. There be severall other Stones which seeme very antient but the yeare was not set downe. The brass of them all is now gone.[26]

All of this does raise the question why Candler had not made full notes before the spoliation. He had been incumbent for over a decade before Dowsing began his work.

Candler's most attractive dark grey marble ledger slab is fixed vertically outside the church, let into the wall of the south nave aisle. Matthias is described as 'Minister of the Gospell in this parish 33 years' and 'of his age 59'. He and his wife were 'expecting the Resurrection of their bodies'. The four lines of verse below the inscription are of the kind often placed beneath engraved portraits of the period:

Solid in divinitie

Laborious in's ministry

Heavenly in society

A mirrour of sound pietie

HERE THE WEARY BE AT REST [27]

# 3

# William Dowsing in Cambridgeshire

## *Robert Walker*

WHEN I BEGAN MY SURVEY of Dowsing's Cambridgeshire visits, I decided that I would ignore previous writers on Dowsing and try to visit the buildings with innocent eyes. I knew that the surviving manuscript sources of the Journal were not in Dowsing's own hand, and on reading the scruffy and disjointed notes I was in doubt about their veracity. The first impression was distinctly chaotic, the language seemed to be a caricature, and the claims often either excessive or trivial. Because of this I think that I set out not to verify Dowsing but to disprove him.

After visiting the churches and college chapels and examining the small number of churchwardens' accounts which survive I have, of course, reached the conclusion that the visits did take place. There is clear evidence of this in both word and stone, though in any one church exactly what damage was done by Dowsing, and what was the result of independent efforts by local zealots, collaborators, and looters, must often still be guessed at. Considerably more damage to church fabric has now been recognised than previously, and the most important examples – Comberton, Kingston, Madingley – previously overlooked, are clear testimonies to the troubles.

The Cambridgeshire Journal is probably incomplete and some parts of Dowsing's account remain puzzling, but therein lies the fascination. Truly accurate and bureaucratic accounts – like the inventories of church goods drawn up a century earlier – would be shocking but tiresome, and would, perhaps, speak less of the tumult of the times. We, in our time, probably know as much as any age about the randomness which is a facet of political terror, even where it is driven by the strongest and most single-minded dogma. We should not be surprised that chaos lurks between Dowsing's lines.

## Sources for the survey

In addition to visiting the Cambridgeshire churches, I used a number of sources extensively. An important one for understanding what Dowsing would have seen is the record of inscriptions taken by Layer only a decade before Dowsing's visits.[1] There are significant cases, which I discuss in the Journal commentary (for example Babraham, entry 35), where superstitious inscriptions have been lost since Layer's time, but which are not claimed by Dowsing. Layer's evidence provides confirmation of the Journal at, for example, Bassingbourn and Whaddon (Journal entries 161, 162) where Dowsing's wording corresponds closely with Layer's record.

The descriptions of churches made by William Cole in the 1740s are invaluable: much can happen in a hundred years, but Cole remains the best single source of information on the state of the churches following Dowsing's visits.[2] There are some pleasing threads: for example Swaffham Prior (32), and Melbourn (159), where Dowsing took the steps or rails and Cole found that the holy table was 'neither railed in nor on any ascent'.

The parish histories in the *Victoria County History* and, to a lesser extent, the litany of sequestration in *Walker Revised* provide an insight into the pastoral circumstances at each church.[3] The comprehensive programme of visits in rural Cambridgeshire indicates that churchmanship did not influence Dowsing's selection of churches,[4] but I have included some of the more interesting details in the commentary on the Journal, to give a flavour of the times.

I have examined parish records, mostly churchwardens' accounts. The rate of survival of churchwardens' accounts in Cambridgeshire for these particular years is reasonable, at around three per cent, but the surviving sets are in one respect disappointing, in that most lie either in Cambridge itself or in the south of the county, both of which figure in Dowsing's Journal, and therefore they do not help us to resolve the question of whether he visited north Cambridgeshire. Only one Cambridgeshire set (Landbeach, discussed later in this chapter) is outside the area recorded by Dowsing.

## Dowsing's progress through Cambridgeshire

Dowsing began work in Cambridge, where he visited every college chapel and every parish church. This is the most disjointed part of the whole

Journal, barely in chronological order, with no dates given for six buildings. As discussed in chapter 4, Dowsing seems to have had definite priorities for destruction in Cambridge which explain the ordering of the earlier days of his visit.

Christmas fell during Dowsing's Cambridge visit. The fact that he visited Holy Trinity – but only Holy Trinity – on 25 December 1643 is suggestive (Journal entry 25). The Puritans had for a long time objected to the observation of major Christian festivals which they saw as rooted in superstition. For them the sabbath, and only the sabbath, was to be dedicated to public prayer, and a proscription of Christmas was high on their agenda. Parliament itself sat on Christmas Day 1643. It is no surprise, therefore, that Dowsing worked on Christmas Day. But it is noteworthy that he only visited one church; he may have been unwilling to interrupt the many acts of worship taking place that day in church and chapel.[5]

Dowsing did not, of course, work on the Sabbath. During the work in Cambridgeshire the company also took Mondays off. If Dowsing was still a member of the army at this time, he may have had military responsibilities in Cambridge on Mondays, as this was the day on which a full list of soldiers was produced, showing 'how they had demeaned themselves'. In Suffolk Dowsing's weekend practice varied, but Sunday was always kept free.[6]

In contrast to his visits in Cambridge, his rural progress in the county is coherent, and there is a sensible path from church to church.[7] The apparently isolated visits to Chesterton (6 February, entry 111) and Brinkley (20 February, 112) could be the terminal dates of a two-week tour of north Cambridgeshire, the record of which has been lost (discussed in chapter 1 and below).

Dowsing's progress through Cambridgeshire is systematic, and shows no sign of a plan of selection. From what is known about churchmanship it appears that the 'godly' were visited in the same way as the Laudians and the time-servers. The few churches in the south of the county which do not appear in the Journal have nothing in their records of churchmanship which suggests a pattern of deliberate de-selection, although there are some puzzles in their fabric.

The amount of physical work undertaken by the company each day varied, both in terms of the number of churches visited and the distance travelled. One of the most uniform periods in the Cambridgeshire peregrination occurs during the period 14–23 March, which represents a gruelling programme of five or six churches every day. The simple variable in all this may be the weather, but it is also possible that the company was of shifting form. The slacker days may represent a small company and the mid-March tour a solid and well organised body of men.

As in Suffolk, the churches in Cambridgeshire show more destruction than the sum of Dowsing's claims. Some will have been carried out in the mid sixteenth century. Other work was carried out between the first instructions from the House of Commons in 1641 and Dowsing's starting work in Cambridge following the Parliamentary Ordinance of 1643. To take just two examples, rails were removed at St Mary the Great in 1641–42; and in 1642 the organ, hangings and rails were removed at Trinity College.[8]

Furthermore, as Dowsing prepared to cleanse Cambridge there may have been some immediate action in anticipation. The diary of Dr Worthington for Wednesday 20 December 1643, which was the day Dowsing began work in the city, records that

> This week pictures begun to be taken down in Cambridge, by an order from the earle of Manchester.[9]

Should the use of 'this week' as opposed to 'today' be interpreted to mean that there was a general movement in the City to remove offending pictures immediately in advance of Dowsing's arrival? If so, the same may have occurred to some extent during his rural tour. The Suffolk Journal includes examples of work done shortly before his visit, as at Ipswich, St Clement's (entry 85) where 'They four days afore they had beaten up divers superstitious inscriptions'. It is very likely that there were similar happenings in Cambridgeshire.

In addition to work done in anticipation, much destruction was done by, and at the cost of, the colleges and churches themselves as a direct result of Dowsing's visit. Indeed, the great majority of his entries state that either orders were given or that things were 'to be done'. The accounts for All Saints (entry 23), St Mary the Great (24), and Holy Trinity (25), demonstrate the expense imposed on Cambridge parishes, matching the pattern found in Suffolk.

Dowsing often made churchwardens and constables responsible for following his orders. Their task may not always have been unwelcome. Margaret Spufford has shown that in West Cambridgeshire (where the evidence survives) about one third of churchwardens of the time signed the petition against Bishop Wren and episcopacy in 1640, indicating at the very least their substantial dislike of the 'innovations' he was introducing. In addition, many of the individuals named by Dowsing gave testimony against their minister to the local Committee for Scandalous Ministers.[10] These men may well have provided Dowsing with a substantial bedrock of Puritan support within local church and parish administration. But this may not always have been the case: in Suffolk, Roger Smallage, churchwarden of

Ufford (entry 247) dragged his feet over meeting Dowsing's demands, even though he was happy to act as witness against his rector.

## The nature of Dowsing's work

Two debated aspects of the Journal concern what Dowsing meant by 'super-stitious pictures', a term which appears in at least 90% of the entries; and whether his claims for them are numerically realistic. In the seventeenth century the term 'picture' was similar to our 'image', referring to *any* two- or three-dimensional representation. It is therefore a pity that all entries are not as precise as that for South Cove (230) where 'We took down 42 super-stitious pictures *in glass*'(my italics). However in the vast majority of cases in Cambridgeshire (and Suffolk) there is not any reasonable doubt, on the evidence of churchwardens' accounts, that Dowsing was normally referring to images in glass. As pointed out in chapter 1, the Parliamentary Ordinance to which Dowsing was working specifically refers to the need to repair windows broken as a result of iconoclasm. Sometimes, however, pictures will have been in wood or stone, and in the college chapels may have been in the form of hangings.[11]

In most of Dowsing's entries there is nothing questionable about the number of pictures.[12] The few examples where the numbers are remarkably large do seem to be in suspiciously round figures, and '1000' appears excessive even in terms of King's College chapel (entry 13), but in only a few cases are the claims out of proportion to the architectural importance of the buildings. In a number of cases of large churches – for example, Bassing-bourn (162) and Guilden Morden (169) – it is not the number but the paucity of forbidden things which is surprising. It is strange, but probably of no consequence, that odd numbers rarely appear.

The Cambridgeshire portion of the Journal raises a number of points about the destruction of specific types of objects. (These should be read in conjunction with the discussion of Dowsing's destruction which will be found in chapters 1 and 7.)

First, the removal of bell inscriptions does not appear to have been systematically pursued by Dowsing either in Cambridgeshire or Suffolk, except by one of his deputies in north Suffolk and south Norfolk.[13] Bells with superstitious inscriptions survive in more than twenty of the churches in Cambridgeshire and it is highly unlikely that all of these were acquired since Dowsing's visit. At both Toft (135) and Croxton (142) a bell survives in spite of a suggestion to the contrary in the Journal (the only places in the entire Journal where bells are mentioned); and at Kingston (136) a bell with *Ave Maria* survived when the expunging of superstition in the body of the church was comprehensive. At St Botolph in Cambridge (12) and at Bartlow (188) three bells with *Orate* survive and even at King's College, where the bells were in a separate and accessible *clocher,* one with *Ave Maria* remained in the eighteenth century.[14]

Secondly, Dowsing's treatment of angels and cherubim appears to have been inconsistent. Of the visited Cambridgeshire churches, 24 retain some form of decoration with angels. The survivals are principally in stone, and form corbels for roof supports or the decoration of fonts and niches.

Finally, despite the exclusion of tombs from the Parliamentary Ordinances, superstitious *inscriptions*, which can only have been associated with tombs (in the form of brasses), make up a substantial body of items in the Journal. Nevertheless, there are some puzzling survivals in churches which were visited – for example, at Swaffham Prior and Burwell, both visited 3 January (entries 32, 33) – and there must remain a degree of doubt about the extent of Dowsing's interest in brasses: or perhaps he was simply unable, through lack of time, to drive home a thorough reformation. A hundred years later, William Cole found that the destruction of brasses was still going on, confirming – if confirmation were needed – that the Civil War cannot be blamed for all inscriptions removed, and brasses damaged, since the Reformation.[15] During the Civil War itself (and to some extent immediately before) local efforts, and damage caused by soldiers, were significant, so even during this period Dowsing cannot be held guilty for all the harm inflicted.[16] The same is true, of course, in Suffolk.

There is evidence that iconoclasts were not trusted to respect monuments. The mood of iconoclasm is reflected in the monument to Symon Folkes, who died in 1642, at Cheveley (later visited by Dowsing). It is of a common form with a kneeling figure framed by columns and a pediment. It is however devoid of any symbol of death or Christianity. Clearly the need for what we might now call political correctness influenced this design, and a study of monuments of the 1640s might well reveal a general lack of imagery. The actuality and influence of iconoclasm gives rise to a touching response far from the old Cambridgeshire in Marholm (which is in the new county) where the monument of Edward Hunter d.1646 is inscribed to the 'courteous soldier' (grassante bello civili):

> *Noe crucifixe you see, noe Frightfull Brand*
> *Of superstition here, Pray let me stand.*

A year later, in Bassingbourn, Henry Butler was commemorated with a curious, one might almost say humanistic, shrouded image and an English inscription which almost deny the intervention of God.

## *The unreported churches*

The Cambridgeshire churches not listed in the Journal are a problem (see Map 3.1). Does the lack of an entry mean they were not visited? As discussed in chapter 10, the Journal was probably put together from Dowsing's rough notes, or his memory, so a church's absence from the Journal may simply mean that Dowsing's notes of his visit were never written up, or the visit forgotten. As we will see, in the absence of other written evidence it is often impossible to prove whether or not they were visited.

As John Morrill discusses in chapter 1, the gaps in the Journal, and especially the missing fortnight in February, represent sufficient time for Dowsing to have visited all of the churches in the old county, south of the Isle of Ely; and there are no strong arguments, other than the possibility of poor weather or difficulties of travel, for his missing any deliberately. It cannot be that the campaign simply ran out of steam, because Dowsing was active in Suffolk after he left Cambridgeshire. Even if the remaining churches were frightened into doing the work themselves, a visit to confirm compliance would surely have been thought essential, as at the Ipswich church noted above.[17]

On balance, my own view – which should be read in conjunction with the discussion in chapter 1 – is that the unlisted churches to the south of Cambridge did not escape, as they are no richer in forbidden things than the churches which Dowsing claimed. Perhaps these churches were visited in the final week of March, where there is a short gap in the Journal after Dowsing leaves Cambridge (after entries 206–209). There is more than a measure of doubt about the churches on the fen side (north) of Cambridge where there are some interesting survivals, though it must also be remembered that King's College chapel was visited and the glass survives. Given the time of year, it is possible that Dowsing was prevented from travelling in these low-lying areas. Further to the north of the county there is not a particularly high rate of survival of superstitious material, and Dowsing may well have visited, though enough imagery remains to cast some doubt.

Consider first the missing churches to the south and west of Cambridge (Coton, Grantchester, Haslingfield, Barrington, Harlton, Little Eversden, Great Eversden, Arrington), lying firmly within the area covered by the Journal (Map 3.2). Arrington could easily have been visited on 15 March or the day after, but may have been deliberately omitted if the church, which is a very small and perpetually poor one, were known to contain nothing of interest (Layer had found that there were 'no armes' in the church). The others could have been visited during the missing February fortnight or

1a. Baylham House, Dowsing's second home, from a photograph taken in 1934. See pages 30–31.

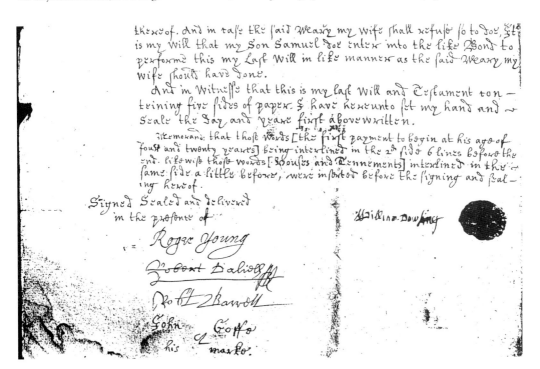

1b. The foot of Dowsing's will, showing his distinctive signature on the right.

2a. Stratford St Mary church from the north, showing the prayer for the soul of the Mors family, untouched by Dowsing. See page 31.

2b. Laxfield church, the brass to William Dowsing, grandfather of the iconoclast. See page 323.

3. Coddenham church, which Dowsing attended whilst living at Baylham House (see pages 30–31, and page 219).  3a (top).  The exterior from the north, showing the parapet with its undamaged *Orate* inscription.  3b (lower left).  A brass indent, the inscription of which was never recorded.  3c (lower right). A damaged carving on a wall post.

4. Two volumes from Dowsing's library, which is discussed on pages 5–10. Both these items are stamped with his initials, 'W' and 'D', on the cover. 4a (left). Fabian's *Chronicles*, courtesy of Maggs Bros. Ltd., London. 4b (above). Walker's *Manifold Wisedome of God*, courtesy of the Trustees of Dr Williams's Library.

5 (opposite). A title page from Dowsing's copy of the sermons preached to Parliament, showing his typical annotations and indexing. See pages 5–10 and 327–33 for discussion of his marginalia.

# Sions Memento,

## AND

# Gods Alarum.

### IN

A SERMON AT WEST-minster, before the Honorable House of Commons, on the 31. of *May* 1643; the Solemne day of their monethly Fast.

By FRANCIS CHEYNELL late Fellow of *Merton* College in *Oxford*.

Printed and published by order of the House of COMMONS.

REVEL. 19. ver. 19.20.

*And I saw the Beast and the Kings of the earth, and their armies gathered together, to make war against him that sate on the Horse, and against his army. — And the Beast was taken, and with him the false Prophet. — These both were cast alive into a lake of fire burning with brimstone.*

REVEL. 17.1.1. *Come hither, I will shew unto thee the judgment of the great whore that sitteth upon many waters, with whom the kings of the earth have committed fornication.*

LONDON,
Printed for SAMUEL GELLIBRAND, at the Brazen Serpent in Pauls Church-yard. 1643.

---

Die Mercurij, 26. Aprill, 1643.

IT is this day Ordered by the COMMONS Assembled in PARLIAMENT, That Sir *Robert Harley* doe from this House give thanks unto Mr. *Iohn Ley*, for the great paines he tooke in the Sermon he this day preached at the intreaty of this House, before the COMMONS at St. *Margarets Westminster*, (being a day of publike humiliation,) And that he desire him to Print his Sermon, And it is Ordered, that no man presume to print the Sermon of the said Mr. *Ley*, but whom he shall appoint and authorize under his hand-writing.

H. *Elsyng* Cler. Parl. D. Com.

I Appoint *Christopher Meredith* to print the fore-said Sermon.

JOHN LEY.

6 (opposite). Two of the four pages of notes in Dowsing's hand, probably of a sermon. See pages 332–3 for transcription.

7 (left). Dowsing's copy of his only known letter, made on the blank page of a printed sermon. The letter suggests that something should be done about superstitious imagery in Cambridge. See page 11.

# AN ORDINANCE

## OF

### The Lords and Commons assembled IN ~England~ PARLIAMENT,

For the utter demolishing, removing and taking away of all

# MONVMENTS

### Of Superstition or Idolatry,

Out of all the Churches and Chappels within this Kingdom of *England*, and Dominion of *Wales*,

*Before the First day of November,* 1643.

Ordered by the Commons in Parliament, That this Ordinance be forthwith printed & published: H. *Elsynge*, Cler. Parl. D. Com.

Printed for *Edward Husbands*, October 11. 1643.

---

# TWO ORDINANCES

## OF THE

### Lords and Commons

Assembled in Parliament,

For the speedy Demolishing of all *Organs, Images,* and all manner of Superstitious *Monuments* in all Cathedrall Parish-Churches and Chappels, throughout the Kingdom of *England* and Dominion of *Wales,* the better to accomplish the blessed Reformation so happily begun, and to remove all offences and things illegall in the Worship of God.

Die Jovis, 9 Maii. 1644.

Ordered by the Lords in Parliament Assembled that these Ordinances shall be forthwith printed and published. Jo. Brown Cler. Parliamentorum.

*LONDON,* Printed for *John Wright* in the Old-baily, May 11. 1644.

8a and 8b. The title pages of the 1643 and 1644 Ordinances of Parliament ordering the removal of superstitious monuments and other objects from churches. See pages 337–44.

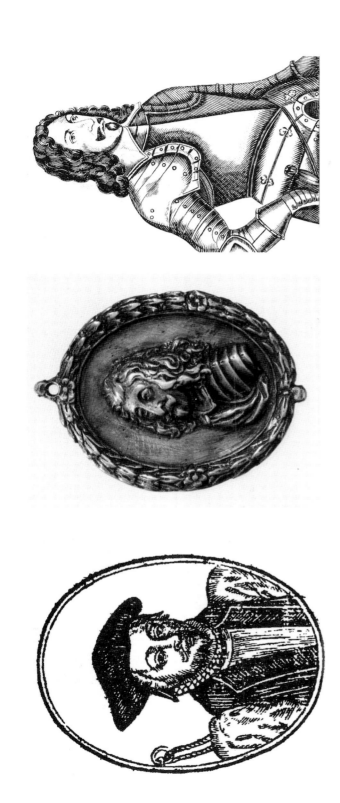

9a. Archbishop William Laud in prison with a chain round his neck. His impeachment in 1640 was followed by a reversal of many of the changes in church furnishing and arrangements which had been introduced in the previous decade. See chapter 4.

9b and 9c. The second Earl of Manchester, Commander of the Eastern Association army, and the man who commissioned William Dowsing to visit churches (see pages 12–15). Medal of 1643, drawing published in 1647.

10. Portrait, probably of John Smith of Laxfield. Previously thought to be of 'John Dowsing', due to a muddle in the 1930s. See pages 324-6.

The youth in his converted state Ætat. su 16.

Narrow is the Way that leads to life

11. Two images showing everyday clothing of the late seventeenth century. Compare with the clothes worn in the frontispiece. 11a (left). The 'Little Man' of St Albans, a carving in the Abbey generally dated to the 1680s. 11b (right). A puritan 'youth in his converted state', from Benjamin Keach's *War with he Devil*, various editions of the early 1670s.

12. A contemporary copy of Dowsing's first commission from the Earl of Manchester, dated 19 December 1643, and addressed at the foot to 'William Dowsinge gen(t) & to such as hee shall appoint'. See pages 12–15 and 349.

87

159

E Manchester

195

13. Dowsing's second commission from the Earl of Manchester, dated 29 December 1643. Note in line 7 the list of counties for which Dowsing's instructions applied. See pages 12–15 and 350.

**(16)**

on the Topp of the Steeple to the which two are over to be hanged till the Default on Saturday come fortnight at Ipswich at all the Colledys.

131. Barking. Aug. 21. 1643 was St Catherine with her whose many S.P.s were done down afore I came there was Maried on the Church Door.

132. Willesham Aug. 22. An holy water font in the Chancell. The Stepps were Levelled and I had room to one afore by a Lord Bishops Injunction and by another Lord Bishop after Commanded Testifyed to me, by him that saw it done, by one John Brownbridge.

133. Darmsden Aug. 23. Three Crosses in the Chancell on the Wall and a holy water font there and the Chancell to be Levelled by Saturday fortnight after.

14. An extract from Martin's transcript of the Suffolk part of the Journal (see pages 140–43). This life-size reproduction shows the entries for Barking, Willisham and Darmsden (pages 309–10). Notice the use of 'SP' for 'superstitious picture'.

Laudi accapell, non nobis Domine &c: & six Angells in the windower
witnesses Will: Dowsing & George Longe.

Pembroke Hall 1643. Decemb: 26

In the presence of these Fellowes Mr Weeden, Mr Mapletoft, & Mr Sterne, &
Mr Quarles, & Mr Fellow, we broke ~10 Cherubims. we broke & pulled downe ~
80: superstitious Pictures, & Mr Weeden told me he could feach a plaine Booke
to shew those pictures were not to be pulled downe; & & him feach & shew
it, & they should stand; & he & Boldero told me, the Clergy had only to do, in
Ecclesiasticall matters, neither magistrate, nor Parliament had any say to do,
& I deny & perceived, they were of Queens judgment, & told them I would ~
prove, the people had to do, as well as the Clergy, & cited the Actes 1,15,16, 23, ~
the 120 Believers had the election of an Apostle, in the tome of Judas—& & told ~
Acts & Kings & Reforming Religion, with the other good Reforming Kings of Juda,
& prove it, & for the raising downe of Images, & told them, the Book of Homelys,
did prove it, & they so much honored, valaged 2: 12, 13, &c: against the perill
of Idolatry, & the Queen's Injunctions, offers allowed them &c: & ...

15. An extract from Baker's transcript of the Cambridge part of the Journal (discussed on pages 138–40). This life-size reproduction shows part of Dowsing's record of the argument at Pembroke (pages 161–2).

The takeing of the Holy League and Covenant.

16. The Solemn League and Covenant, a test of Parliamentary allegiance taken in Spring 1644 (see Glossary). 16a (left). The signing of the Covenant. 16b (below). The signature of Francis Verdon, one of Dowsing's deputies, heading the list (an indication of his status) of those signing or making their mark at his home parish of Linstead parva, Suffolk. See pages 76-80.

and the peace and Tranquillity of Christian Kingdoms and Common-Wealths.

ffrancis Verdon

Robert Pooley

Christopher Longstaff
his marke.

Thomas R Peare.
his marke.

James ✕ Tuthill.

Abrahame Glew

Hastinges Wiffinsen Hund
his marke.

John ∧ Brundish

Richard R Robson.
his marke.

Richard ✝ Allen.
his marke.

William M Ward
his marke.

willm Smith
his marke.

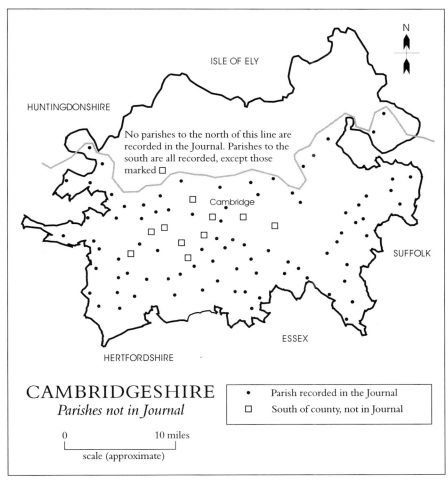

*Map 3.1* The parishes in Cambridgeshire not reported in the Journal. Most parishes in the south of the county are recorded by Dowsing. Parishes in the north of the county are not.

between 2 March and 6 March when the adjacent parishes to the west were dealt with, or perhaps during the missing few days after 26 March.

There are survivals, but none which would definitely suggest that this group of churches escaped. Barrington and Harlton retain series of roof corbels, some of which are angels, and Harlton has the magnificent Friar monument of 1631 which has some very suspect angelic imagery. Both churches have extensive graffiti with some superstitious inscriptions.[18] It is

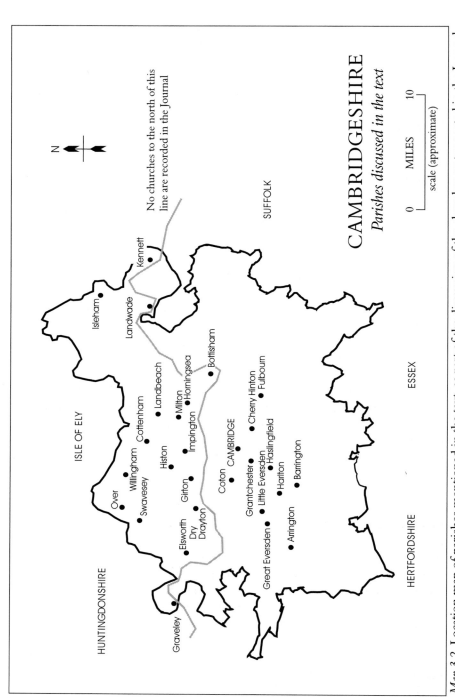

*Map 3.2* Location map of parishes mentioned in the text, as part of the discussion of the churches not reported in the Journal.

CAMBRIDGESHIRE
*Parishes discussed in the text*

N

No churches to the north of this line are recorded in the Journal

ISLE OF ELY

HUNTINGDONSHIRE

SUFFOLK

ESSEX

HERTFORDSHIRE

Graveley

Over
Willingham
Swavesey
Cottenham
Landbeach
Histon
Milton
Impington
Horningsea
Bottisham
Elsworth
Dry Drayton
Girton
Coton
CAMBRIDGE
Grantchester
Little Eversden
Haslingfield
Cherry Hinton
Fulbourn
Great Eversden
Harlton
Barrington
Arrington

Isleham
Kennett
Landwade

0    MILES    10

scale (approximate)

tantalising but still inconclusive that the church at Coton is the only one in the rural part of the county where the word *Orate* can be read on glass – twice (in the east window of the south aisle).

For this group of churches, then, the balance of evidence is probably that they were visited. The omissions immediately to the east of Cambridge are not as straightforward (Horningsea, Bottisham, Fulbourn and Cherry Hinton).

Horningsea and Bottisham are both close to the route of the first rural excursion (starting 3 January) which went to Burwell via Fen Ditton and the Swaffhams. The fabric at Horningsea has nothing to tell about a possible visit either way. Bottisham is a large and well furnished church and is surrounded by parishes which are recorded, lying close to the routes taken on both 3 January and 26 March. The fabric of the church gives no definite clues. There is a monument to two children of the Allington family which displays outrageous cherubim supporting a tester, but its survival may simply be the result of strict observance of the Ordinance. It would be a cruel Puritan indeed who could lay a destructive hand on this tear-jerker. The brass to Elias de Beckingham with its angels and *cujus anime propicietur Deus* inscription has been removed, but it appears insufficiently damaged for Dowsing's purposes, as the indent remains legible. Perhaps this was the work of a later hand interested only in the value of the metal, though something similar happened at Stoke by Nayland (47), which *was* visited by Dowsing. William Cole in the eighteenth century found some surviving saints (albeit broken) in glass, named as Sancte Nicholas and Sancte Gregorius.[19] He also found an inscription recording the reglazing and re-leading of the church in 1660, and it is possible to imagine that the reglazing was to tidy up the mess left by earlier iconoclasm and piecemeal repair. The evidence for Bottisham, then, is mixed, and no conclusions can be drawn.

Fulbourn also is surrounded by parishes which were visited. There were two churches here in the seventeenth century. The survivor, St Vigor's, has many damaged brasses, mostly with spoiled inscriptions which might, with the reservations already discussed, indicate Dowsing's hand. All that survives of All Saints' is a brass to Geoffrey Bysschop, now also in St Vigor's. It, too, had its inscription removed, though it has since been restored from Layer's record. Two panels depicting saints, which came from a former screen, are incorporated in the pulpit.[20] So the balance of evidence here is for iconoclasm, though of what period it is impossible to say.

At Cherry Hinton the meagre evidence of damaged brasses would also suggest that the church might not have escaped[21] but there is contrary evidence in that the aisles have many angels on corbels which are within easy reach. In addition, Blomefield found three *Orate* inscriptions in glass and a chancel screen painted with the Virgin and Magdalene and the praying donor, from whose mouth came the words, clearly visible, *Orate pro anima-bus...*[22] The chancel was lined with stalls which were decorated with many popish images including a man bidding his beads. This has all disappeared since Blomefield's time, but it suggests that Cherry Hinton might have escaped Dowsing's hand.

In the far east, where the border with Suffolk has shifted over the years, Kennett and Landwade are not recorded in the Journal. They are on the edge of the territory recorded by Dowsing. The former church is of modest interest and tells no helpful story, but Landwade was probably missed, or 'work to be done' was neglected. The numerous brasses damaged before the middle of the eighteenth century, when Cole visited, might suggest iconoclasm, but Cole also found that 'in almost all the windows of the church are the pictures of Angels, having each a cross on his head, very neatly done in glass'. There were also complete figures of St Margaret, the Virgin and Child, St Etheldreda and other saints. Much of this glass survives, though there is not a single angel remaining.[23]

In the far west the church at Graveley, just within the Journal boundary, is also omitted despite the record of a visit to the contiguous parish of Papworth St Agnes (entry 145). Graveley now has an eighteenth-century chancel, and no firm conclusions can be drawn from what remains.

Lying outside the area covered by the Journal, the fen churches immediately to the north of Cambridge are not particularly rich in forbidden things but the number of surviving objects must cast some doubt on whether Dowsing visited every church. Thus, at Histon a rood with supporters remains on the south transept gable apex and within the church there is a label stop at eye level depicting a praying priest in the south transept. These might be expected to have been of interest to Dowsing. On the other hand, the churchwardens complained in 1662 that 'the surplice was conveyed away at the beginning of the warre', so *something* happened here.[24]

At Impington a fine brass to John Burgoyn d.1505 remains, the four corner roundels with symbols of the Evangelists still intact, and the modest damage to the inscription apparently having occurred since Blomefield's time. Some time between 1638 and 1666 the church lost its rails and altar step, but whether this compliance with the 1643 Ordinance was prompted by visitors or was home-grown is impossible to say.[25] At Milton a very similar brass, but some half a century later, survives with similar evangelist symbols. The top line of the marginal inscription had gone by the eighteenth century: Cole guessed it was removed for being an *Orate*.[26] In contrast, an inscription in brass is upside-down – was it removed by family or friends for safety, and put back carelessly? Something similar is found at Metfield, in Suffolk (269).

At Girton six brasses with *Orate* inscriptions survived until Blomefield's day and Cole was led to conclude:

> This church is one of the few that Dowsing takes no notice of in his journal, of which I am inclined to believe he never entered, for the number of Brasses yet remaining in it, and of which no doubt he would have purged it had he known of them...[27]

Later in his description of Girton, Cole makes an observation about post-Civil-War vandalism, which must be borne in mind when heaping blame on Dowsing:

> In our time I find [the Brass] is temptation enough with some sort of people to make them commit the worst species of Theft; the robbery of the monuments of the dead: for since the year 1726 when Mr Blomefield collected the monuments in this church, out of 8 then entire and perfect as to the inscriptions no less than two are stolen away... and this is not the only church where the clerk or churchwardens have informed me of brasses lately torn away...[28]

At two further churches in this area documentary evidence is at least supportive of iconoclasm. At Landbeach, the churchwardens' accounts survive. Although they make no direct reference to a visit by Dowsing, there are modest items for building work, and, in Landbeach terms, a relatively large sum of £2 for glazing in summer 1644 which could well be the repair of deliberate damage:

> Item payd Goodman Mulldon for mendin the wendoes[29] . . . £2. 0s. 0d.

The 'mendin' of windows in summer 1644 would fit nicely with any damage caused during the missing February fortnight in the Journal, such a gap often being found between damage and repair. As discussed in appendix 10, this type of record is entirely consistent with, but cannot be taken to prove, a visit by Dowsing.

At Dry Drayton the churchwardens in 1662 used the entire repertoire of explanations to explain why church belongings had gone missing two decades earlier. They begin, 'We have only one steppe or ascent in our Chancel, no raile of wood or enclosure, both being demolished in the time of the rebellion, but by what then pretended power we know not'. The reference to a 'pretended power' doing a job which must have taken several hours sounds suspiciously like official iconoclasm, perhaps Dowsing. Later they excuse their position by complaining about specific individuals: 'A poor Communion Table carpett has been purloyne some say by James Gifford our former Clerke and a very civil and decent Hood some say by William Borne,' and further on in the paragraph guilty party number three appears, in the form of the military – 'what Braste [brass] and Sculptuer have bin pillaged were done by an unknowne company of Rambling rumagatt [runagate][30] soldiers'. The wardens' further reference to 'these late unhappy times of disorder and confusion', whilst entirely understandable, does highlight the difficulties faced by the modern interpreter.[31]

The next most northerly ring of parishes includes churches of great stature, at, for example, Cottenham, Willingham, Over, Swavesey, and Elsworth. Willingham may have been attacked, as the angels in its hammerbeam roof are all modern, but the other churches give no clear indications either way. The life-size angels on the Kempe monument at Swavesey would probably have been saved by the exclusion in the Ordinances, even if visited.

In the north-east corner of the county is Isleham, which lies just outside the Isle of Ely, close to the Suffolk border, a few miles from churches known to have been visited by Dowsing. Here about half of the brasses are damaged, including one which had a Crucifixion, and an inscription has been turned upside down; but many others remain with superstitious inscriptions intact.[32] The roof retains its splendid angels. There is a rail across the chancel which on stylistic grounds is of the early seventeenth century, thus pre-dating Dowsing (Plate 31).[33] This evidence suggests that Isleham was unvisited by iconoclasts in the 1640s, with the brass damage being done at the Reformation and in the following years.

As soon as the border is crossed into the Isle of Ely the survival of superstitious inscriptions and objects is markedly greater. To take just two examples, Wilburton has three complete brasses with inscriptions, whilst March retains the Hansart brass with two superstitious scrolls and an Annunciation and another, earlier, brass with inscription. These are in addition to the famous angel roof there which appears to be remarkably unrestored – compare this with Willingham, which is almost entirely re-angelled.[34] It seems that neither Dowsing nor his colleagues ever reached this area.[35]

# 4

## Dowsing at Cambridge University

### *Trevor Cooper*

DOWSING BEGAN with Cambridge University, where he visited every college chapel.* His only surviving letter shows how keen he was to see the University purged, and in this chapter we consider the reasons for his enthusiasm, and the events leading up to his visit.[1]

### *Laudian changes*

Much of the 'superstitious' material which Dowsing removed dated from before the Reformation. But much else had only been set up in the decade before his visit, when many of the chapels had been altered, partly to meet the increase in student numbers, but also in response to an increasing enthusiasm for well-ordered liturgy and the 'Beauty of Holiness'.

*Trevor Cooper is responsible for this chapter, whilst he and Robert Walker together wrote the Journal commentary for the University colleges, Great St Mary's, and Little St Mary's, to which this chapter forms an introduction. Both of us are grateful to those who provided advice and assistance. Dr Sadler contributed greatly by exploring sources, in particular pointing us to the work of Dr Hoyle on BL Harl. MS 7019 (discussed below). Christopher Brooke provided orientation and guidance before work started. As work progressed, Graham Chainey's advice on various points was invaluable. John Blatchly, Christopher Brooke, Graham Chainey, Thomas Cocke, Patrick Collinson, Kenneth Fincham, David Hoyle, and John Morrill commented helpfully upon earlier drafts of this chapter and the University sections of the Journal commentary. Any faults that remain are the responsibility of the author(s).

For want of a better term, we shall refer to the movement that brought about the changes in the University chapels as 'Laudian', though Laud (archbishop from 1633 until his downfall and imprisonment in 1640; see Plate 9) was not its instigator, and some of those who were devoted to its principles disagreed with the insensitive means by which he was seen to promote them.[2] To Dowsing, much of this recent reordering was idolatrous.

The new ceremonies, and the chapel interiors to accompany them, had begun to creep into the University in the late 1620s as the Laudian party grew in influence, supported by the King. The process accelerated in the following decade – 'oh the strange change in 7 years', as one unsympathetic observer exclaimed in 1636.[3] Looking back, the Puritan Sir Simonds D'Ewes recalled the Cambridge of the early 1620s as a time when

> None then dared to commit idolatry by bowing to, or towards, or adoring the altar, the communion table, or the bread and wine in the sacrament of the Lord's Supper.[4]

By 1635, according to Archbishop Laud's first biographer,

> Many things had been done at Cambridge... as beautifying their Chappels, furnishing them with Organs, advancing the Communion Table to the place of the Altar, adorning it with Plate and other Utensils for the Holy Sacrament, defending it with a decent Rail from all prophanations, and using lowly Reverence and Adorations, both in their coming to those Chappels, and their going out.[5]

The effect of reform on the college chapels could be dramatic. A plan of King's College chapel dating from about 1609, before the time of Laud's ascendancy, shows the communion table placed with its long axis east-west ('table-wise' in contemporary parlance) between the stalls.[6] (See Plate 23, and Plate 22 for a late nineteenth-century view of the chapel to put the plan in context.) Far from being richly covered, the table was draped with 'Kent canvas' purchased in 1603 for just 4s. 8d. – no surprise, then, that in 1618 a Venetian visitor to King's, used to richer trappings, commented 'the church is all bare'.[7] This arrangement, with the altar away from the east end, standing table-wise and bearing little or no furniture or adornment, was in place in a significant number of the chapels (and in parish churches too) until the Laudian movement gained ground. Here communion was taken seated or kneeling together round a *table*, itself merely a convenient piece of furniture of no sacramental importance.

By 1634 King's had a Laudian interior: the contrast would have been acute. The altar was placed at the east end, raised up on steps, turned north-south ('altar-wise'), railed in, gorgeously furnished, surrounded by hangings and covered with a canopy.[8] No plan exists for King's (or any other college chapel) in its new garb, but the inspiration for these arrangements can be traced back to the private chapel of Bishop Andrewes, a (possibly idealised) plan of which does survive (Plate 24).[9] In this plan the altar is dominant: it stands at the east, protected by a rail, and approached by steps covered with a fine carpet. There is plate – candlesticks, an alms dish or basin – permanently on the altar, and it is covered sumptuously. Behind it, not shown on the plan but mentioned in the accompanying list, are hangings and pictures. Surrounding it are subservient furnishings, each with its part to play in the communion service. For associated with this physical layout is a particular ideal for worship: ceremonial which is well-ordered, hierarchical and formal; a service which is partly or wholly choral, with choice music, supported by an organ; and acts of corporal worship – turning towards the east, bowing to the altar on entrance and exit, 'adoration' at the name of Jesus, kneeling to receive communion. The physical furnishings do not stand alone, but are the outward and visible signs of an approach to worship which the Puritan found papist and shocking.[10]

The general picture is confirmed by a letter from a Carmelite friar in England to the 'Father Generall', dated 26 July 1633:

> The Communion-tables in the churches are going out of fashion, and are gradually replaced by altars with hangings and candlesticks, but the candles may not be lighted. In the chapels of students Divine Office is chanted in latin, and I am told crucifixes are to be introduced and placed on the altars.[11]

In Cambridge, Peterhouse was amongst the first to introduce such 'innovations', with a new and richly decorated chapel built 1628–32: 'here,' it was said, 'is a little chapel but much popery' (Plate 19).[12] By the mid 1630s four other colleges – St John's, Queens', Jesus and Pembroke – had also introduced the new practices, and refurnished their chapels accordingly. To these five must be added King's, though for all its work of redecoration its services were still criticised by the Laudian party.[13]

In line with the new furnishings, choral services and choirs were being introduced at these five colleges (in addition to the older choral foundations of King's and Trinity).[14] Thus, in 1635 Dr Cosin, the Master of Peterhouse, acquired an organ for the chapel, and introduced two new college statutes which encouraged polyphonic music and provided for a small number of trained singers to supply the nucleus of a choir. Three years later four new fellowships and four new scholarships were founded, with a requirement to 'performe their parts with others that sing divine service in the Chappell'. Prayer book services were sung in Latin – a move seen as akin to popery by the opposite wing of the church.[15] At least three other colleges – Christ's,

Queens' and Pembroke – introduced organs and choral services over the next few years.[16]

Despite the headway in these particular colleges, in the mid 1630s 'in most Colledges, all things stood as they had done formerly',[17] and in May 1635 Laud determined to move matters forward by means of a formal visitation to the University. In 1636, in advance of this planned visit, a report on religious practices at the University was prepared for him, which confirms how much further his programme had to go. The five colleges in the vanguard were more or less approved of, but his informant found weaknesses at the others, either in their approach to the liturgy or in their furnishings. King's, which as we have seen, had already rearranged its chapel on the new lines, had a poor choir – 'neere one half of them mutes' – and abbreviated its services. A number of colleges (Corpus Christi, Emmanuel, Trinity, Sidney Sussex, St Catharine's) had not even taken the first step of moving their communion table to the east end.[18] In Caius (whose progress we will follow)

> The Holy Sacrament when it is administered is brought down from the Table to every Fellow & Scholler remaining in his own Seate, where the Priest strides & crowdes over some of them with the Sacred Elements in his hands not without irreverence and trouble… Some here (of which the Master is one) bow not at the name of Jesus, & other reverence is little regarded.[19]

Laud's visit never took place, but his biographer claimed that

> the bare reputation of it [the planned visit] did prevail so far, that many who were slack or fearful in embelishing their Chappels and publick Places of Divine Worship, went on more confidently than before.[20]

There was indeed a further spread of Laudian furnishings and practice after 1636. By 1641, Clare, Caius, Trinity, Christ's, and to some extent Trinity Hall had all beautified their chapels, and introduced forms of worship to match. By then, Caius, heavily criticised before, had spent more than £500 on chapel furnishings. Of the other colleges, Magdalene did the minimum and Corpus Christi, Emmanuel, Sydney Sussex and St Catharine's maintained their Protestant or Puritan tradition, though all except the last wobbled to some extent. Nor was the town neglected. Great St Mary's, the University church, and Little St Mary's, closely attached to Peterhouse, were both reordered at the instigation of John Cosin, Master of Peterhouse.[21]

The Long Parliament was alarmed at these religious developments: as part of a wider reaction, the Universities were investigated, and in May or June 1641 a report was drawn up, on 'Innovations in religion and abuses in government in the University of Cambridge'.[22] About one third of the report is devoted to a college by college assessment of churchmanship, concentrating on theological statements and attitudes. At Caius, in the five years since the previous report, matters had so far changed from those described earlier that:

> Adoration towards the East is practised by the greatest part of the Fellowes and Schollors, and this soe farre promoted, that for these late yeares none have bene admitted into Fellowship that used not that gesture.[23]

Although concentrating on theology and practice, the report does briefly describe the furnishings of each chapel. In many cases it provides the sole description of interiors which were gone within a few years, and it forms the foundation of our commentary on the University section of the Journal.[24]

## The dismantling of Laudianism

For by the early 1640s the wind had changed. Parliament's concerns were crystallised by a formal declaration of the House of Commons in June 1641, removing any obligation at the Universities for 'doing reverence to the communion-table' (that is, 'bowing and congeeing unto it'), and three months later the Commons ordered, amongst other things, the removal of the communion table from the east end, and the removal of images and altar furniture.[25]

In that year it was noted that

> Dr Bainbridge hath begun reformation in his Chapel [Christ's], he hath devastated the altar of its ornaments and hath forbid bowing towards it as also standing up at the gloria patri and singing of service. They have wholly left standing up at the Doxology at Sidney.[26]

In 1641 Caius too begun the process of undoing its recent expensive changes, turning the communion table to make it table-wise.[27] Over the next year or two other colleges followed suit, with the choral services mentioned earlier stopping by about 1642. Further warning bells must have rung when, in early 1643, Great St Mary's had its screen despoiled by soldiers, and Parliament made the wearing of surplices non-mandatory.[28]

Thus well before the Parliamentary Ordinance of August 1643 and Dowsing's visit later in the year, a number of colleges – six for certain, and probably more – had taken the precaution of removing or hiding some of their new furnishings.[29] We should assume, therefore, that much of the more portable material described in 1641 had been removed before Dowsing's arrival.[30]

No doubt the extent of these precautionary measures varied from college to college, and exactly how much of the Laudian project was still in place to

Table 4.1 *Dowsing's visits in Cambridge, in chronological order*

Colleges shown in CAPITALS, churches in Lower Case

| | | | |
|---|---|---|---|
| Dec | 20 | PETERHOUSE | |
| | 21 | ,, | |
| | | St Clement's | |
| | 22 | JESUS | *Baker omits date (for sources, see chapter 10)* |
| | | GONVILLE AND CAIUS | *Baker omits this entry* |
| | 23 | ,, | |
| | | return to PETERHOUSE | |
| | 24 | *Sunday* | |
| | 25 | Holy Trinity | |
| | 26 | PEMBROKE | |
| | | QUEENS' | |
| | | ST CATHARINE'S | *Baker gives 28 December* |
| | | KING'S | *Baker places this after Trinity Hall* |
| | | St Michael's | |
| | ? | St Andrew the Great | |
| | ? | St Andrew the Less | |
| | 27 | St Mary the Great | |
| | 28 | CORPUS CHRISTI & St Benedict's | |
| | ? | CLARE | |
| | ? 28 | TRINITY HALL | *Date mistranscribed as 2 December* |
| | 29 | TRINITY | |
| | | ST JOHN'S | |
| | ? | St Botolph's | |
| | | St Mary the Less | |
| | 30 | ,, | |
| | | SIDNEY SUSSEX | |
| | | MAGDALENE | |
| | | St Peter's | |
| | | St Giles' | |
| | 31 | *Sunday* | |
| Jan | 1 | St Edward King and Martyr | |
| | | All Saints | |
| | | return to St Clement's | |
| | 2 | CHRIST'S | |
| | | Holy Sepulchre | |
| | ? | EMMANUEL | |
| | 7 | *Sunday* | |
| | ? 7 | return to St Mary the Great | |

catch Dowsing's eye is not always easy to ascertain. Its remnants, together with surviving 'superstitious' pre-Reformation fittings, were enough to keep him busy for more than a fortnight, over Christmas and the New Year,[31] and there is some very slight evidence that later in 1644 he found it necessary to complete the work, or check that it had been completed.[32]

The only independent description of his activities in Cambridge – not flattering, and probably exaggerated – comes from a Royalist pen:

> And one who calls himselfe John [*sic*] Dowsing, and by vertue of a pretended Commission goes about the Country like a Bedlam, breaking glasse windowes, having battered and beated downe all our painted glasse, not only in our Chappels, but (contrary to Order) in our publique Schools, Colledge Halls, Libraryes, and Chambers, mistaking perhaps the Liberall Artes for Saints (which they intend in time to pull down too) and having (against an Order) defaced and digged up the floors of our Chappels, many of which had lien so for two or three hundred yeares together, not regarding the dust of our founders and predecessors, who likely were buried there; compelled us by armed Souldiers to pay forty shillings a Colledge for not mending what hee had spoyled and defaced, or forthwith to goe to Prison...[33]

Whether or not Dowsing went around 'like a bedlam', he certainly acted systematically, though this is largely masked by the disorder of his entries. Once they have been reorganised chronologically the pattern becomes plainer (Table 4.1 and Map 4.1), though some uncertainties remain because of the undated entries, and the occasional muddle created by his illegible writing.[34]

He began on Wednesday 20 December 1643 with Peterhouse, the number one target, and an opportunity for a show of strength. He continued there the next day, fitting in a church to the north (St Clement's, Bridge Street) – perhaps this was *en route* from his lodgings? The following day he went to Caius and Jesus: these two colleges are not neighbours, but colleges probably chosen because they too had a foremost position in the Laudian movement, having devoted considerable sums to rearranging and beautifying their chapels, the former college with the direct assistance of Cosin.

On the next full working day which he committed to the task (Tuesday 26 December) Dowsing concentrated on two more of the leading Laudian colleges (Pembroke and Queens'), which were close neighbours. Thus five major centres of unpuritan practice were cleared within the first few days. It is perhaps surprising that he did not include St John's in this initial sweep, but this might have been because the college had already removed those recent additions to its furniture which would have offended him. Having cleansed the worst offenders, his policy seems to have been to work with neighbouring clusters of colleges, whether or not they had introduced

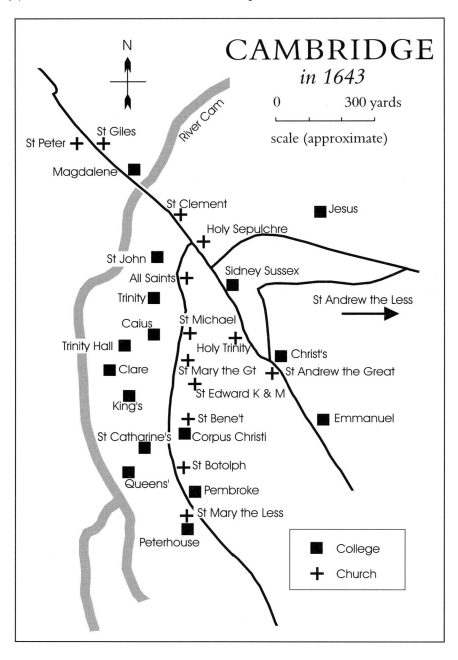

*Map 4.1* The colleges and churches of Cambridge in 1643.

Laudian furnishings, fitting in parish churches as convenient.[35] Sensibly he left the easy work, Sidney Sussex and Emmanuel, strongholds of Puritanism, until near the end.

Dowsing's work of cleansing the college chapels is only part of the picture. Liturgical practices had to be reformed, and Romish theology rooted out. The direct approach was taken: soon after Dowsing's fortnight of physical cleansing, the Earl of Manchester began ejecting Fellows, and most of those who had watched Dowsing at work were removed.

At Caius, whose progress we have been following, the Master, Batchcroft, was asked by Manchester for 'the names of all such in your College as have practised bowing at the naming of the name of Jesus, adoration towards the East, or any ceremony in divine service not warranted by law'. Replying in July 1644 – by which time eight Fellows had been ejected – he was able to say that the offending practices 'have been soe by degrees left, as there are none in our whole Society that doe use or practice any of them'. The process of reversal was complete: within eight years Caius, like much of the University, had embraced ceremonial worship, then abandoned it.[36] Manchester had rooted out the men of unsound belief. Dowsing, Manchester's agent, had erased the material signs of both pre-Reformation superstition and Laudianism.

# 5

# Dowsing's arguments
# with the Fellows of Pembroke

## S. L. Sadler

WHEN WILLIAM DOWSING undertook the work at Pembroke College chapel (Journal entry 2),[*] he had already been active for five days since receiving his commission from the Earl of Manchester to travel into East Anglia to implement 'in every particular' the 'Ordinance for the utter demolishing, removing and taking away of all Monuments of Superstition or Idolatry' where it had been neglected. It was a course of action 'much desired by both Houses of Parliament'.[1]

It was also a path Dowsing was willing and able to pursue. As a private individual, he had embraced the ways of the most godly communities of the Stour Valley. He had found there a home which could nourish and sustain his religious convictions to the full. As Provost Marshall of the Eastern Association's army he had already spent five months fighting for the cause, not as a front line soldier but in a supporting role.[2] He was experienced in providing the arms those soldiers needed, and dealing with the prisoners they captured. He had been responsible for the practical implementation of justice, having 'the power to apprehend any Soldiers whom he sees transgressing the Laws and Articles of War, from doing whereof no Officer may hinder him'. As well as acting as gaoler, he was practised in presenting his charges to the Court of War where 'that Justice may be done on them for the

[*]I am grateful for the assistance and advice offered by John Blatchly, Nicholas Cranfield, Jim Auty and John Morrill.

crimes they have committed, which he [the Provost Marshall] is obliged to specifie, and he is to be present at the execution of every sentence'. He also had a primary role in implementing the Court's decision in both a practical and symbolic sense, for 'when a Soldier is to run the Gatloupe, he is to give him the first lash'.[3] In his role in providing provisions Dowsing had been empowered to police the civilians who victualled the army as well as the men of war. Runaways and Parliamentary reprobates as well as Royalists might find themselves in the clutches of the Provost Marshall and his soldiers.

This was a man who was already used to enforcing order and if necessary striking the first blow, within the strict limits of his jurisdiction. Now the Provost Marshall had given up his role for a new task. Instead of supporting Parliament's, and God's, cause by policing the army and its captives, Dowsing turned to the churches. He would eliminate transgressions made in the house of God, he would strike the first blow where crimes had been committed against God's word. Dowsing was ready to smash the idols.

## I

The natural place to begin was Cambridge, the Eastern Association's headquarters and home of the University. The attempts of several of the colleges to send plate to the King, to print Royalist tracts, to support Royalist prisoners in the town, demonstrated the rank perversion of justice which was to be expected from those who had turned the seat of learning (or at least many of the colleges in it) into a nursery for the propagation and dissemination of Laudianism. The iconoclast had made a vigorous start, attending both to college chapels and parish churches in Cambridge. Now, at Pembroke Hall, he continued in the cleansing he had begun, noting 'broke 10 cherubims… 80 superstitious pictures'.

His iconoclasm was witnessed by the college's Fellows gathered there. In the presence of Mr Thomas Weeden, Mr Robert Mapletoft, Mr Stern, Mr William Quarles (kinsman of the more famous Francis), Mr Felton, Mr Edward Boldero, and Mr Roger Ashton, Dowsing carried out his work. They seem to have been mostly younger men, in their twenties and thirties, young enough to have been bred into the beauty of holiness. Their ages (where we know them) may have given the middle-aged Dowsing seniority, but little else did. Their formal education far outstripped that of the man before them. And whereas the iconoclast lived amongst the radical edge of an increasingly embattled Protestantism, they belonged to what in recent years had become an established arena of the King's professed religion. Their spiritual world had become central, Dowsing's had been officially pushed into the margins.

Like the man they were facing, several of them had relatively local connections in addition to their places at the college, but their positions in the outside world, as well as their place at the University, ought to have commanded greater respect than that afforded to the yeoman. Ashton was the vicar of Linton, Mapletoft until a few months previous had been rector of Bartlow (both in Cambridgeshire), and Boldero held a curacy at Ipswich. The Feltons were a Cambridgeshire family with a clerical tradition.[4] In a world held right-side up the Fellows would be accounted the iconoclast's superiors, but the balance of power had dramatically shifted by 1643 and their world was now upside-down. Laudianism was no longer in its ascendancy. The leading lights of their movement were elsewhere: Laud, Wren and Cosin had already been carted away to face the wrath of Parliament.

These were not Laudians of the first rank, but they nevertheless gathered to stand their ground. The college men would not witness the desecration of their chapel without attempting to resist. The (University) statutes, they said, did not permit such actions: Dowsing recalled how 'Mr Weeden told me, he could fetch a Statute Booke to shew, that pictures were not to be pulled down'. It was a reasonable attempt to stop Dowsing in his tracks. The University had wielded its authority successfully to demand exemption from Parliamentary decrees for military impressment and war taxation.[5]

But the bureaucratic Puritan[6] was not so easily diverted from his task, and from his previous experience as a Provost Marshal he would have been fully conversant with the place of rules in times of action. Undeterred, Dowsing 'bad him fetch and shew it, and they should stand'.

While Weedon attempted to disable Dowsing with the statutes, Boldero joined in a second line of attack, on the iconoclast's authority to deal with church matters. They told him 'The clargie had only to do in ecclesiasticall matters, neither the Magistrate, nor the Parliament had any thing to doe'. If the learning of the Fellows, on their home ground, was meant to intimidate the yeoman into submission, it failed.[7] Dowsing, uncowed, replied that he 'perceived they were of Cuzen's [Dr John Cosin's] judgment'. Cosin was more extreme than most followers of Laud in proclaiming the separation of powers between minister and magistrate, something that led to the charge that he advocated 'an English if not a Roman popery'. Government and discipline were the most important concerns of the Church, according to Cosin, and the clergy's complete control of these factors was essential to the spiritual health of the country.

But the University men did not have a monopoly on debate any more than they had sole right to control of the church, and the yeoman challenged, 'I would prove the people had to doe as well as the clergie,' and commenced to hurl scripture at his opponents. It was a point he had established in his own mind perhaps as early as 1620 and he was unlikely to have found much difficulty in presenting evidence to support his view against that of the University men.[8] He began by quoting Acts i. 15, 16, 23, when the disciples filled the space left by the dead Judas:

> And in those days Peter stood up in the midst of the disciples, and said, (and the number of names together were about an hundred and twenty)… Men and brethren, this scripture must needs have been fulfilled, which the Holy Ghost by the mouth of David spake before concerning Judas, which was guide to them that took Jesus… And they appointed two, Joseph called Barsabas, who was surnamed Justas, and Matthias.

The Scriptures clearly showed that 'The 120 believers had the election of an apostle, in the rome [room, ie place] of Judas'. Dowsing continued with a more recent authority: 'Calvin, and in his Institutions, in the poynt of ministers elections'.

Having first established against Boldero the principle of people's elections (Parliament) he next provided an example of religious reform emanating from the monarch (the Magistrate), at the same time picking up the more immediate issue. He 'told them [of] Josiah's reforming religion, (1 Kings xxii. 21)'. King Josiah had long been a biblical model of the image-reforming monarch. He came to the throne aged eight, following which 'they brake down the altars of Baalim in his presence; and the images, that were on high above them, he cut down; and the groves, and the carved images, and the molten images, he brake in pieces, and made dust of them'. He was often compared to the boy-king Edward VI, whose reign had also seen the widespread removal of images. The example of King Josiah may have held a particular resonance in the early 1640s, as it was the people, not their ruler, who showed loyalty to God and the true way, and who raised up Josiah to be king: 'the people of the land made Josiah his son king in his [Amon's] stead'. The people's intervention was vindicated by Josiah's rule, which led to a renewed Covenant with the Lord.[9]

Boldero's argument for the independence of the clergy dealt with, Dowsing continued with the theme of idolatry: 'and for the taking down of images, I told them the Book of Homilys did prove it, which they so much honored, and alledged, p. 12, 13, 14, 15, 23 against the Peril of Idolatry'. The first part of the Elizabethan Homily against the peril of idolatry, in which Dowsing's first four pages fall, uses scripture to show that 'images' and 'idols' are one and the same thing, 'wherefore our images in temple and churches be indeed none other but idols, as unto the which idolatry has been, is, and ever will be committed', and that 'the authority of God's holy word' can be brought to bear against such 'foul abuses'. The second part (in which Dowsing's reference to page 23 falls) contains a series of ancient authorities who argued and wrote against such acts. The example of Epiphanius, who tore down a cloth image, must have seemed particularly relevant: it is summarised under four points:

> First, he [Epiphanius] judged it contrary to christian religion, and the authority of the scriptures, to have any images in Christ's church. Secondly, he rejected not only carved, graven and molten images, but also painted images out of Christ's church. Thirdly, that he regarded not whether it were the image of Christ, or of any other saint; but being an image, would not suffer it in the church. Fourthly, that he did not only remove it out of the church, but with a vehement zeal tare it in sunder... [10]

The list of authorities goes on and on. Dowsing further bolstered his argument by calling on 'the Queens Injunctions'. The Injunctions of Queen Elizabeth, he claimed, showed the grounds for reforming religious practices. 'They shall not set forth or extol the dignity of any images... They shall take away all... pictures, paintings, and all other monuments of feigned miracles, pilgrimages, idolatry and superstition, so that there remains no memory of the same'.[11] In Elizabeth's time the churches had been cleansed of ceremonies and images, which were offensive because they were 'so farre abused, partly by the supersticious blindnesse of the rude and unlearned, and partly by the unsaciable avarice of such as sought more their owne lucre, than the glorye of God'.[12]

The churchmen wrested the use of scripture from him, alleging that scripture proved 'cherubims to be lawfull'. There was no doubt amongst the various protagonists that *idolatry* was abhorrent, but where devotion ended and idolatry began was less clear and the Fellows endeavoured to show Dowsing that in his zeal for reform he had gone too far.[13] But he was sure of God's requirements, referring to Deut. iv. 12:

> And the Lord spake unto you out of the midst of the fire: ye heard the voice of the words, but saw no similitude; only ye heard a voice... *16*. Lest ye corrupt yourselves, and make you a graven image, the similitude of any figure, the likeness of male or female.

God's power was without similitude, or form. The Israelites had been warned. Contamination with the lives and practices of their enemies must not be tolerated. Their idols must be destroyed.

> *Deut. vii. 5.* But thus shall ye deal with them; ye shall destroy their altars, and break down their images, and cut down their groves, and burn their graven images with fire... *xii. 2.* Ye shall utterly destroy all the places, wherein the nations which ye shall possess served their gods, upon the high mountains, and upon the hills, and under every green tree.

The danger of turning away from His laws was present in Dowsing's own time, just as it had been then. The parallel was obvious.

The Fellows claimed that both Moses and Solomon had made cherubim *without any special command from God* – essential if they wished to argue that cherubim, and other images, were normally regarded by Israel's greatest leaders as falling outside the terms of the second commandment. Dowsing 'denied it', and turned up the passage recording the Deity's instructions to Moses:

> *Exod. xxv. 18.* And thou shalt make two cherubim of gold, of beaten work shalt thou make them, in the two ends of the mercy seat... *20.* And the cherubim shall stretch forth their wings on high, covering the mercy seat with their wings, and their faces shall look one to another; toward the mercy seat shall the faces of the cherubim be... *22.* And there I will meet with thee...

The scholars tried again. They said 'Solomon did made them, without any Command'. Dowsing answered, 'He received a pattern from David'. Taking his bible he 'read to them' I Chron. xxviii. 10:

> Take heed now; for the LORD hath chosen thee to build an house for the sanctuary: be strong and do it. *11.* Then David gave to Solomon his son the pattern of the porch, and of the houses thereof, and of the treasuries thereof, of the upper chambers thereof, and of the inner parlours thereof, and of the place of the mercy seat.

and he carried on with the precise specifications, ending with verse 19:

> All this, said David, the LORD made to understand in writing by his hand upon me, even all the works of this pattern.

The Fellows, having lost ground on the Old Testament, grasped at the New to rally their cause. Thomas Weedon said, 'Reading Paul's sermons was better preaching then now is used, because it was not Script[ure]'. Dowsing countered 'God saved by foolishnes of preaching, not reading, and alleged, I Cor. i. 21': 'For after that in the wisdom of God the world by wisdom knew not God, it has pleased God by the foolishness of preaching to save them that believe'. Dowsing carried through his attack. 'I told them,' he recorded in his Journal, 'if reading was preaching, my child preaches as well as they'. He claimed victory, noting 'and they stared one on another without answere'.[14]

Dowsing may have won silence from the Fellows in their scriptural contest but they were not ready to concede defeat. He noted in his Journal, 'More, Pembroke-Hall, 1643'. The college men started another onslaught from a different direction. Putting the bible aside they turned to the laws of the land. Ashton challenged, 'Laws made in time of warr were not of force'. The iconoclast was ready and thrust the charge aside. 'I alleged Magna

Charta, made in time of warr, between Henry the Third and barrons, that was in force still, and Richard the 2d's tyme the like'. Ashton tried again: 'The Parliament could not make laws, the King being away, and so many Members'. Dowsing would not give way, and instead turned their own example against themselves. He told them, 'their practice proved it, that chose Fellowes by the greater number present'. Dowsing made no mention of those MPs who had gravitated to the King at Oxford and does not record the Fellows alluding to them. There was another more compelling reason than the habits of scholars to which he could attempt to anchor the law's legitimacy. He reminded them 'that the King had taken an Oath to seal what both Houses voted'.

The Fellows turned to the detail of the law and Dowsing's commission, and here they may finally have struck a significant blow. Robert Mapletoft 'said he did not think my Lords Covenant was according to the Ordinance, and so I durst not abide by it, but thought I would run away, and used threatning speches'. The others joined in, Dowsing noting 'This last Spech was Weedens, and Bolderas'. Dowsing, according to his Journal, brushed aside the University statutes and left the Fellows 'without answere' in his Scriptural combat, but he recorded no rejoinder to their attack on the validity of his commission from Manchester. Instead, he immediately acquired a new commission from Manchester, emphasising authority through force.[15]

## II

No military battle took place on Cambridgeshire's soil during the civil war. Spiritual battles were another matter. The debate and its consequences provide a vivid example of what a historian of iconoclasm describes as 'the interaction of learned and popular, in which the abstractions of theology had concrete meaning for the illiterate'.[16] Dowsing was hardly illiterate, but he did belong to the popular rather than the elite section of civil war society. Furthermore, the failure of the Pembroke Fellows to crush Dowsing resulted in many parishioners who were indeed illiterate witnessing the destruction of the representation of abstruse ideas, just as in earlier years they had seen the fabric of their churches altered to express them. Dowsing claimed he could prove 'the People had to doe as well as the Clergie'. Little more than a week later, Roger Ashton's flock, the parishioners of Linton, would have seen eight inscriptions taken up, three crucifixes broken, 80 superstitious pictures destroyed and the communion rails dismantled along with an order left to deface two grave stones (Journal entry 36). Some at least would have understood the significance of this, nine of them being prepared to witness against Ashton, their absentee vicar, in the ejection proceedings in the Spring.[17] In this parish the people as well as the clergy did indeed 'have to doe', though how representative these parishioners were is not clear. Robert Mapletoft's previous parish, Bartlow, was also visited by Dowsing (entry 188).

A yeoman and soldier had challenged the learned men of the University. What is more he had challenged them in their own arena, both physically and intellectually, and in doing so he challenged established channels of social order as well as spiritual ones: and in at least one area he had won. Different visions of legitimacy collided with force. It was an important collision and the timing of the event suggests its broader significance. By December 1643 it was no longer possible to believe in a short decisive war. The sword that had penetrated civilian society could not swiftly be dislodged. Parliament had set up committees and introduced new levels of taxation to arm its men. It had begun to sequester its enemies as well as fight them in the field. Many of its endeavours were coaxed through the House by the guiding hand of Pym. New allies were within view. The country was in the clutches of war in a way that might not have seemed imaginable at the beginning and the fight ahead was unlikely to bear any relation to the short decisive outcome hoped for in 1642. The prospect of a long-term war was probable and God's blessing must be earned if victory was to be secured.

The timing of the confrontation also suggests one weapon the Fellows failed to use in their attempt to defend the chapel from the iconoclast. As we shall see, the Royalists could have struck home by attacking the fissures in the religious unity of the Parliamentarians. It would have been a difficult blow to fend off. Roger Ashton had made a start by questioning the legitimacy of laws made under the pressure of war, but in Dowsing's account that argument did not really develop. Thus in Dowsing's (possibly partial) record the bulk of their argument was fought out in the spiritual and scriptural sphere rather than the political and military one.

Even so, these two dimensions were both present. For the man the Fellows were confronted with exemplified many of the currents present in the Parliamentary camp at the time. John Pym's recent death had been a body-blow to the morale of Parliamentarians, and Stephen Marshall, the minister conducting his funeral sermon, made no attempt to disguise it. Pym had been the lynchpin of the Parliamentarian cause in the House and the epitome of the 'Good Man', the Christian magistrate. Marshal told the MPs and Divines who had gathered to mourn (and through the press the wider public), 'so, doth God often times take away the most useful men, when his Church hath most need of them'.[18] Dowsing bought and read the sermon (although it is not clear exactly when)[19] and Manchester, whose commission authorised Dowsing's work, may well have heard it being delivered.[20] Marshall endeavoured to make this catastrophe explicable. Pym's death would teach them to 'let all the Church learn never to rest on men, how excellent so ever'. To afford God's servants more respect than God had allotted was itself tantamount to idolatry. Dowsing certainly paid attention to Marshall's point, writing in the margin 'observe this' and scoring much of the page. Pym's death was a timely reminder to the protagonists of God's cause not to inflict injury themselves. It was not only the Laudians who could incur His wrath. Later in the funeral sermon Marshall re-emphasised the point: 'the Lord in mercy makes us sensible of these heavie strokes before it be too late'. There was a solution. Pym's death was a timely reminder, not a sentence. 'Let therefore everyone whom God hath fitted for any service, do what their hand findes to do with all their power,' Marshal thundered

> doe it with all thy might, for there is neither worke, nor device, nor knowledge, nor wisdome in the Grave, whither thou goest; as if he should have said, thou knowest not how long God will use thee, lay not up thy Talent in a Napkin, thy Master may suddenly call thee to an account for it.

Four days after Marshall preached these words in London, Dowsing held a commission from Manchester in his hand.[21]

The religious atmosphere was charged in Parliamentarian quarters. Three days after Dowsing's confrontation at Pembroke Hall, A. Coe printed in the newspaper _Remarkable Passages_ a message directed from the Assembly of Divines to the public.[22] The message was authorised by order of the House. Members were concerned about the dangers of schism as some Parliamentarians raced towards the Reformation faster than they were able or willing to follow. The Divines put forward nine points for their consideration (Table 5.1). The first three made clear who it was who should undertake this Reformation, the second three urging the necessity of unity within the Parliamentarian ranks. The beauty of holiness which the Fellows had attempted to defend was identified by the Assembly as an idolatrous attack on the word of God and a weapon of the enemy, the Royalists who upheld idolatry. Thus one dimension of the action Dowsing undertook was to strip the chapel bare of all its idolatrous filth and move forward to a further Reformation, where others had turned back. But another facet of his actions was probably to bind fast the divergent tendencies within the religious spectrum of Parliament's supporters. It is to be wondered to what extent Dowsing would have been conscious of this. The Divines firmly connected the two, in their final three points.

Table 5.1 *The nine points of the Assembly of Divines*

1 That it belongs to the Christian Magistrate to be leaders in such Reformations.

2 That it is the duty of all people to pray for them, Joyn with them, and waite upon them.

3 That at this time God hath enclined the hearts of the Honorable Houses of Parliament, to engage themselves herein, and they have required the Assembly of Divines to make the word of God their only Rule.

4 That seeing the enemy seeks to overthrow the work of God, nothing can be more destructive to the friends of the Cause of Religion than to be divided amongst themselves.

5 That it is not to be doubted, but the Counsels of the Assembly of Divines, and the care of the Parliament will be, not onely to reform, and set up Religion throughout the Nation, but will concurre to preserve whatsoever shall appear to be the Rights of particular Congregations, according to the Word. And to bear with such whose consciences cannot in all things conform to the publique Rule, so far as the word of God would have them born withall.

6 That therefore they forbear, till they see whether the right Rule will not be commended to them in this orderly way.

7 That we do alreadie enjoy more liberty to serve God already, then ever was in England before.

8 That it is unfit and uncomfortable to set up their own way, whilest the Magistrates are about to reform the Church.

9 That if the Magistrates should not deliver the right Rule, then should they have more peace with God and their consciences to oppose it: but it is hoped there will be no such cause.

BL Thomason Tracts, E. 79 (26), *Remarkable Passages*

Yet another area with potential for disunity, which could have been used by the Fellows to attack Dowsing, was the increasing involvement of the Scots and the rigid Presbyterianism they were eager to impose on their allies. Here there were major tensions. Before his death, Pym directed his energies into stressing the common ground between the English and Scottish supporters of the cause. This was no mean feat. At his funeral sermon Marshall commented: 'Our bretheren from Scotland with their Armies, may more prejudice theirs and our successe, then the strength of the Enemies can do'.[23] Dowsing, for his part, had read Marshall's comments about the danger from the Scots, marking and noting the page, and noting at the beginning of his copy 'not to rely too much on the Scots'.

## III

That winter the Earl of Manchester (the authority behind Dowsing's commissions) by skilful political lobbying successfully manoeuvred a series of reforms through Parliament. Amongst measures to reform and improve the forces under his control the commander gained the authority to purge the University and the Eastern Association of its malignant clergy.[24] The Fellows who had resisted Dowsing would soon be facing the test of the Covenant, with William Quarles and Edward Boldero fighting against the Parliamentarian imposition by attempting to rouse the University's opposition in their contributions to the pamphlet *Certain Disquisitions*.[25] Cromwell, meanwhile, silenced the cathedral choir at Ely: God's word was not to be distorted by polyphony into a form of incomprehensible voluptuousness any more than his power should be limited by the imagery of idolatry. And Dowsing himself, undeterred by the Fellows' attempts to stop him, was seizing the moment, not waiting for the great leaders to accomplish all themselves, not relying on the Scots to undertake the work the English failed to do, but acting himself. His actions were tied to his faith in God and the Parliamentarian cause and his opportunity to serve one and promote the victory of the other.

Thus in the winter of 1643 these men were acting in concert. They were fighting together both in the field and in the churches. The timing of Dowsing's endeavours adds eloquence to his rather terse notes, giving insight into one man's need to smash the idols.

# 6

# Dowsing's deputies in Suffolk

## *John Blatchly*

IN CAMBRIDGESHIRE, Dowsing seems to have worked without deputies,[1] but in Suffolk the prospect of over 500 churches to visit must have convinced him of the need for assistance, and between 27 and 29 February 1644 he first records work done by a deputy. As discussed below, this was probably Thomas Denny of Earl Soham. Another deputy, whom we will argue was probably Francis Verdon, accompanied Dowsing on a long tour during early April.[2]

Although in the Journal deputies are recorded as working alongside Dowsing, the form of words by which he appointed them makes it clear that they had authority to act in his absence:

> February 4. By Vertue of a Warrant directed to me from the right Honourable the Earl of Manchester I do hereby depute and appoint you T. D. [Thomas Denny] in my absence to execute the sayd Warrant in every particular, within the County of _ _ _ _ according to an Ordinance of Parliament therein mentioned and power given unto me by the said Warrant as fully as I myself may or might execute the same. In witness whereof I have hereunto set my hand and seale.[3]

It must be significant that the name of the county is left blank in this form for authorisation of deputies, and it raises the question whether Dowsing used the power explicitly given him in the second commission to send men into other counties than the two for which we have his Journal, a point discussed in later chapters.[4] This one concentrates on his Suffolk deputies: as we shall see, there is ample evidence that deputies did indeed act alone, and in many cases we can name the men responsible and make a reasoned guess as to the areas they were allocated.

## Dowsing's list of deputies

The body of the Journal mentions just two deputies by name. One is Crow (entry 252), who had independently visited Elmsett church before Dowsing's arrival. The other is 'Mr Oales' to whom a fine was to be sent by the churchwardens of Occold (267). For other names we depend on a not entirely helpful list which prefaces the earliest transcript of the Journal, and which is here printed with surnames and place-names regularised, and laid out in a way which clarifies its structure:

> William Dowsing substitutes
>
> Edmund Blomfield of Aspall Stonham,
> Edmund Mayhew of Gosbeck,
> & Thomas Denny
> & Mr Thomas Westhropp of Hundon, a godly man
> and Thomas Glandfield of Gosbeck,
> Francis Verdon
> > for Wangford, South Elmham, Blything, Bosmere, Sudbury, Clare,
> > Fordham, Blackbourn, and would have had Hartismere.
> And Francis Jessup of Beccles,
> > for Lothingland and Mutford Hundred, and Bungay, Blythburgh,
> > Yoxford, and Ringshall.[5]

The places allocated to deputies do to some extent complement those visited by Dowsing and recorded in the Journal (Map 6.1). The notable exception is the north-east of the county, but, as we discuss later, it is likely that Dowsing visited this area alongside his deputy, or revisited laggard parishes already dealt with independently by the deputy.

But in other ways this list is far from unambiguous. For one thing the areas are referred to by a mixture of hundred and deanery names. The parishes in each almost coincide, but on balance it seems that Dowsing is planning to work by the latter. Secondly, 'Ringshall' is some distance from the other cluster of named parishes: might it be a mistranscription of 'Ringsfield'? (Both are shown on the map.) For reasons explained later, it will be assumed that Ringshall is meant. Finally, and crucially, does Dowsing mean that the first six men named were to divide the eight deaneries listed between them (and if so, how?); or was Verdon, who in that case 'would have had Hartsmere', intended to cover all of them on his own, with Ipswich and the twelve Suffolk deaneries not named perhaps being left for the other five men? Dowsing's allocation is unclear.

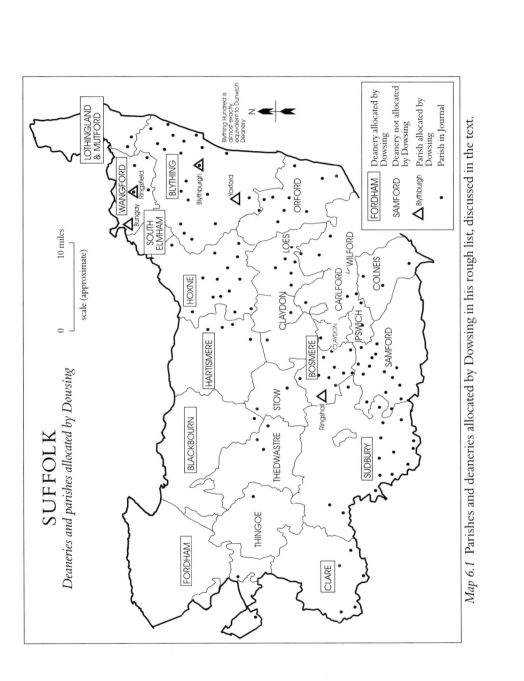

Map 6.1 Parishes and deaneries allocated by Dowsing in his rough list, discussed in the text.

The chance discovery of a most interesting post-Restoration document in the Public Record Office prompts a more radical approach to the allocation dilemma. A committee chaired by Sir Henry North of Mildenhall met in Bury St Edmunds in June 1662 to compile the evidence against people alleged to have profited during the Interregnum, for submission to the Attorney General. In a very miscellaneous list the oddest entry of all, under Gazeley (in Sudbury deanery), concerns the visits which two of the deputies named by Dowsing had carried out eighteen years previously:

> Major John [*recte* Thomas] Westropp of Hundon, an able sufficient man, with one Crow of Haverhill, did rifle this church of all the brass and was the common rifler of all the churches in these parts to a considerable value.[6]

This information gives just the impetus needed to the search for a more plausible interpretation of Dowsing's list of deaneries. It is, after all, unlikely that Verdon would have been sent to eight deaneries ranged around the edges of the county. Now we know that Westhropp and Crow were widely involved in the west. Using this fact, and other evidence presented later in the chapter, we can see that Dowsing seems to have been jotting down his thoughts about assistance along the following lines (my italics):

> William Dowsing substitutes Edmund Blomfield of Aspall Stonham, Edmund Mayhew of Gosbeck, & Thomas Denny [*of Earl Soham*] & Mr Thomas Westhropp of Hundon, a godly man and Mr Thomas Glandfield of Gosbeck. *These to be deployed.*
>
> Francis Verdon for Wangford, South Elmham, Blything. *In his own area.*
>
> Bosmere, Sudbury, Clare, Fordham, Blackbourn. *To allocate to the others.* And *they* would have had Hartismere also.
>
> And Francis Jessup of Beccles, for Lothingland and Mutford Hundred [*a single deanery*], and Bungay, Blythburgh, Yoxford, and Ringshall. *Unambiguous.*

Who were these men, Dowsing's deputies? As will become clear, they seem to fall into two distinct categories: friends and relatives, of a similar social status to his own; and men of lesser education or breeding, nonetheless useful in some places. Thus, although at least one of the deputies (Crow) was illiterate, four of those listed were important enough to be co-opted in November 1645 to be 'joyned to the Ministers' on the classis in their division of the county. The usual complement was four knights or esquires, eight ministers and between twelve and fifteen others, and the division covered a whole hundred. Blomfield and Mayhew joined the Bosmere and Claydon division, the seventh; Francis Verdon the fifth for Blything; and Westhropp was in the Risbridge group, the fourteenth.[7]

Table 6.1 *Dowsing's deputies, their social status, and the evidence for their involvement in iconoclasm*

| Name | Rel'n | Status | Evidence | | |
|---|---|---|---|---|---|
| | | | L | J | R |
| Edmund Blomfield | M | Yeoman, mother from visitation family | Y | | H |
| John Crow | | Almost illiterate | | Y | Y |
| Thomas Denny | | Above average ship money | Y | | H |
| Clement Gilley | | Son of yeoman, Captain | | | Y |
| Thomas Glandfield | ?R | Not known | Y | | |
| Francis Jessup | ?M | Uncertain (tailor) | Y | | Y |
| Edmund Mayhew | ?M | Yeoman, rose to gentleman | Y | | |
| Alexander Ouldis | | Gentleman | | Y | |
| Francis Verdon | N | At least middling status (lay member of classis) | Y | | Y |
| Thomas Westhropp | | Gentleman, Major | Y | | Y |

The column headed *Rel'n* indicates the relationship of the deputy to Dowsing. 'R' indicates a relative, 'M' connected by marriage, 'N' a neighbour.

The three columns under *Evidence* show first whether the person is named in Dowsing's list ('L'), secondly whether the person is mentioned in the Journal ('J'), and thirdly where there are any parish records ('R') or similar, indicating involvement of this person in iconoclasm (in this column, 'H' indicates involvement at the home parish only).

The table simplifies some complex evidence: for full details, consult the text.

This is as far as Dowsing's list can take us. As the Journal does not record visits by named deputies (with the exception of Crow), we are reliant on the chance survival of other records for further evidence of the extent of the activities of these men (see Table 6.1). They confirm that Verdon, Jessup and Crow did indeed carry out independent visits over a wide area, and that Blomfield and Denny tackled at least their own parishes, and may have ranged further afield. Only for Glandfield is evidence lacking.

In examining the evidence for each deputy, it is important to appreciate that, with fewer than one in twenty churchwardens' accounts surviving from the period, the evidence for iconoclasm is extremely patchy; working out what the deputies did is made even harder by the fact that churchwardens often did not record the occurrence of a visit, merely the consequences.[8] Thus lack of surviving evidence about a particular deputy by no means indicates that he was inactive – a deputy could visit forty churches without any evidence surviving. Equally, the survival of just a few pieces of evidence might indicate a large number of visits. A single surviving record of a visit might mean that the deputy visited just that church; equally, he might have visited twenty or forty or even more. This must be borne in mind when the evidence for each deputy is presented.

## Edmund Blomfield

Edmund Blomfield of Stonham Aspal happened to be churchwarden there (and only 25 years of age) when the work had to be done.[9] (See Map 6.2 for places mentioned in the following discussion.) Blomfield held office at the church throughout the changeover between the incumbency of Jeremy Holt (ejected 1645) and the more godly John Swayne, who was married to the elder sister of Blomfield's wife.[10] There is no record for this parish in the Journal – Dowsing did not visit here – and Blomfield was, in effect, the visitor:

*Stonham Aspal 1644-45*

| | | | |
|---|---|---|---|
| It' for taking down the Scandalous pictures | 0 | 11 | 02 |
| It' for our Dinners when wee tooke the Covenant | 0 | 02 | 10 |
| It' for the Glasier for the Church | 9 | 00 | 00 |
| It' to Richard Raynolds for helpinge the Glazier | 0 | 09 | 06 |
| It' to Anth'y List for Lyme & sand for the Glasier[11] | 0 | 02 | 00 |

On his will, Edmund made only a mark, odd in normal circumstances for one of yeoman's station: perhaps it was because he was ill. Many Blomfield families flourished in the parishes of Bosmere: one family at Coddenham, two at Stonham Aspal (at East End and Mowneys), and one at Stonham parva; they were all staunch Puritans and there was some inter-marriage. Candler (Dowsing's minister at Coddenham) was connected with Edmund's branch at Stonham Aspal by marriage, and recorded the family relationships in a way which no amount of consulting parish registers today could effect.[12] The Coddenham and Mowneys branches were included in the 1664 Visitation, a sign of significant social status.[13] Edmund's parents Robert and Priscilla were of the East End and Mowneys branches respectively.[14]

Both of William Dowsing's wives had Blomfield relatives (Fig. 6.1).[15] Anne, the mother of his first wife Thamar, had a brother William Blomfield, Gent., of Stonham parva.[16] Margaret Cole, the half sister of Dowsing's second wife (Mary Cooper), married in about 1641 another William Blomfield (1616–72), J.P., of Wattisham Hall, of the Coddenham branch, whose mother was Alice Lea, apparently Dowsing's first wife's sister; in his

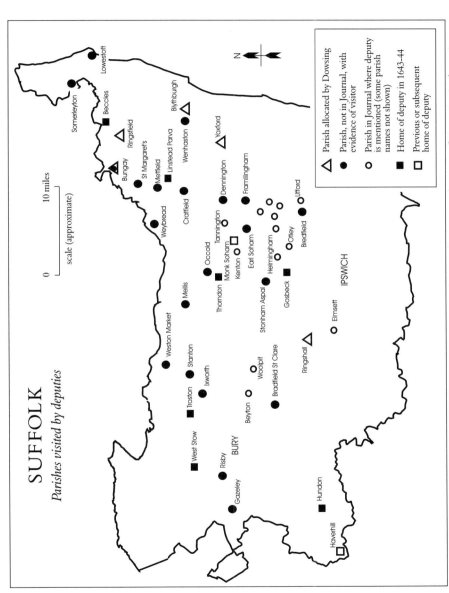

# SUFFOLK
*Parishes visited by deputies*

scale (approximate)

0      10 miles

N

Lowestoft

Somerleyton

Beccles

Ringsfield

St Margaret's

Bungay

Metfield

Linstead Parva

Blythburgh

Wenhaston

Weybread

Yoxford

Cratfield

Dennington

Framlingham

Occold

Tannington

Ufford

Mellis

Thorndon

Monk Soham

Kenton

Earl Soham

Bredfield

Otley

Weston Market

Helmingham

Stonham Aspal

Gosbeck

Stanton

Ixworth

IPSWICH

Troston

Elmsett

Woolpit

Beyton

Ringshall

Bradfield St Clare

West Stow

Risby

BURY

Gazeley

Hundon

Haverhill

|  |  |
|---|---|
| △ | Parish allocated by Dowsing |
| ● | Parish, not in Journal, with evidence of visitor |
| ○ | Parish in Journal where deputy is mentioned (some parish names not shown) |
| ■ | Home of deputy in 1643–44 |
| □ | Previous or subsequent home of deputy |

*Map 6.2*   Parishes for which there is documentary evidence of visitation by one of Dowsing's deputies.

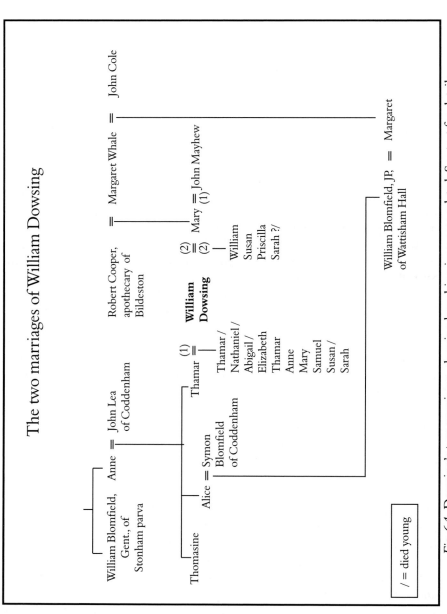

*Fig. 6.1* Dowsing's two marriages, showing how his wives were related. See text for details.

will Dowsing described this William as 'his loving kinsman', and made him responsible for disposing of some of his (Dowsing's) estate at the best available price after his death.[17] So both Dowsing's wives had links with the Coddenham side of the family, one of the two Visitation branches.

### *Edmund Mayhew and Thomas Glandfield, both of Gosbeck*

Edmund Mayhew of Gosbeck[18] may also have been a connection of Mary Cooper, Dowsing's second wife, for her first husband was John Mayhew, whom she married at Nedging in 1629.[19] Edmund was the eldest son of a yeoman, Edmund, who died in 1629, and grandson of another; he prospered by the 1660s to attain gentry status. He was witness against Theodore Beale, vicar of Ashbocking, accusing him of saying that the Houses (of Parliament) were full of Anabaptists and Brownists: Beale was ejected from his living 30 July 1644. At about this time the 'painted crucifix' in the east window came down, so perhaps Mayhew was involved in that.[20]

Apart from the evidence provided by Edmund's appearance in Dowsing's list, there is an illuminating marginal note in Martin's transcript of the Suffolk portion of the Journal. Dowsing, who had given orders the previous May to the uncooperative churchwardens of Ufford, wrote in a second Ufford entry for 31 August (entry 247), 'I sent one then to see it done and they would not let him have the key'. It is Mayhew's name which appears in the margin alongside the 'one' sent, indication that in the original his name was probably there. We can therefore associate Mayhew with work in Wilford deanery, to reach which he would have to cross only five parishes (Map 6.3 and Table 6.2).

Previous authors have claimed that a third deputy, Thomas Glandfield of Gosbeck was also a relative of Dowsing by marriage, but they give no evidence, nor has any been found.[21] Thomas and his wife Ann baptised a daughter Sarah in 1641 and two Johns, in 1644 and 1646, so if Glandfield was an active deputy, it may have been at a time when his wife was bearing their first son, who was to die in infancy. The parson of Gosbeck was the godly George Burrough, whose acceptable teaching won him the loyalty both of the two deputies in his parish (Mayhew and Glandfield) and a legacy in the will of Edmund Mayhew's brother William in 1633.

Glandfield was a witness against William Walker, rector of Winston, examined at Ipswich on 1 April 1644. Walker, it was claimed, 'is very superstitious in his practices in cringing & boweing to the Communion table sett upp at the East end of the Chancell. Both affirm his preachinge for the boweinge at the name of Jesus & Practizinge the same'. Walker was ejected that August.[22]

Apart from his appearance in Dowsing's list, there is no surviving evidence that Glandfield took part in organised iconoclasm. As we have seen, even if he had visited twenty churches, the chances of no relevant churchwardens' accounts surviving would still be quite high, so not too much must be read into this lack of evidence. We can allocate him to Carlford and Colneis Deaneries in our conjectural scheme, only Ashbocking in Bosmere standing between Gosbeck (his home) and the nearest Carlford parish, Otley.

### Francis Verdon

Also of gentle stock was Francis Verdon, of Linstead parva,[23] no distance from Dowsing's birthplace in Laxfield. There is a Verdon Lane at Linstead today, and a farm in the family name a couple of miles from Laxfield: the Dowsing and Verdon families would have known each other.

Francis was a sergeant of Sir William Playters of Sotterley Hall,[24] who was a committee man of the Eastern Association.[25] Verdon himself was a lay member of the classis for the fifth division of meeting at Halesworth, covering Blything, Dunwich and Southwold. As further evidence of his status, his florid signature heads the list of those subscribing to the Solemn League and Covenant, written in the first Linstead parva register book (Plate 16).[26] The Covenant itself is entered in the elegant italic hand of the curate, William Aldus or Aldhouse, whom Dowsing recorded in his Journal on 4 April (Journal entry 216).

Verdon was single and of Monk Soham when he married Alice Benham at her parish church of Cretingham in October 1636, but they settled at Linstead parva where their children were baptised: Ann (1637), Alice (1638) and Bridget (1640). A son Francis was baptised on 23 September 1642, but his mother Alice was buried just ten days later. So it was as a widower that Verdon undertook to visit churches; he died, still unmarried, in 1670.

His work is recorded by churchwardens at six churches. Given the low rate of survival of churchwardens' accounts, this suggests that the number of churches visited by Verdon may well have run into three figures, and might not have been very different from the number visited by Dowsing. In comparison with Verdon's six, it should be recalled that only one set of churchwardens' accounts mentions Dowsing by name.[27]

The surviving churchwardens' evidence has Verdon visiting four deaneries: three churches in Hoxne deanery (Dennington, Metfield, and Weybread), Framlingham in Loes deanery, Cratfield in Dunwich deanery, and St Margaret in South Elmham. Of these churches, Dennington and Metfield visits are recorded in the Journal (entries 269 and 270). The entries

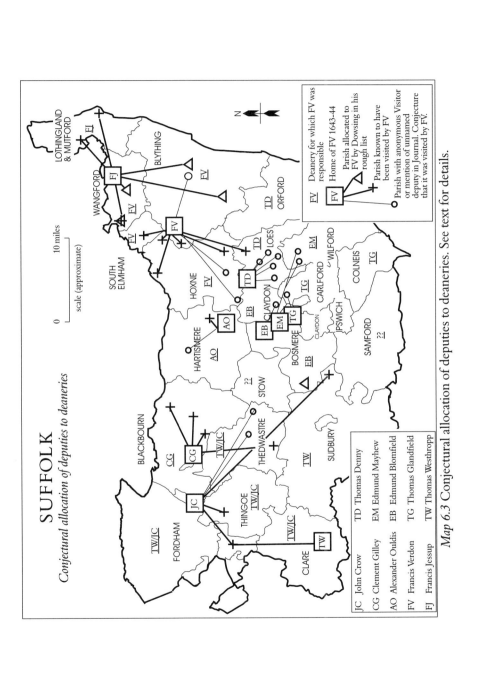

# SUFFOLK

Conjectural allocation of deputies to deaneries

scale (approximate)

0      10 miles

N

| | | |
|---|---|---|
| JC John Crow | TD Thomas Denny | |
| CG Clement Gilley | EM Edmund Mayhew | |
| AO Alexander Ouldis | EB Edmund Blomfield | |
| FV Francis Verdon | TG Thomas Glandfield | |
| FJ Francis Jessup | TW Thomas Westhropp | |

FV    Deanery for which FV was responsible

FV    Home of FV 1643–44

+    Parish allocated to FV by Dowsing in his rough list

◁    Parish known to have been visited by FV

○    Parish with anonymous Visitor or mention of unnamed deputy in Journal. Conjecture that it was visited by FV.

FORDHAM TW/JC

BLACKBOURN

CLARE TW

THINGOE TW/JC

CG

THEDWASTRE TW/JC

SUDBURY ??

STOW ??

HARTISMERE AO

HOXNE FV

SOUTH ELMHAM FV

WANGFORD FV

LOTHINGLAND & MUTFORD FJ

BLYTHING FV

ORFORD TD

LOES TD

WILFORD EM

CLAYDON EB

BOSMERE EB

CARLFORD TG

COLNEIS TG

SAMFORD ??

IPSWICH

*Map 6.3* Conjectural allocation of deputies to deaneries. See text for details.

Table 6.2 *Conjectural allocation of deaneries to Dowsing's deputies,*
*with number of visits to each deanery recorded in the Journal*

| Name | Home parish (home deanery) | Deaneries allocated | N | J | J% |
|---|---|---|---|---|---|
| Edmund Blomfield | Stonham Aspal (Bosmere) | Bosmere★ | 26 | 14 | 54 |
| | | ?Claydon | 13 | 3 | 23 |
| John Crow and/or Thomas Westhropp | West Stow (Thedwastre) Hundon (Clare) | Fordham | 18 | 1 | 6 |
| | | ?Sudbury★ | 53 | 16 | 30 |
| | | Thingoe | 21 | 2 | 10 |
| | | Thedwastre | 22 | 3 | 14 |
| | | Clare | 30 | 6 | 20 |
| Thomas Denny | Earl Soham (Loes) | Loes | 19 | 6 | 32 |
| | | ?Orford★ | 21 | 9 | 43 |
| William Dowsing | Stratford St Mary (Samford) | Ipswich | 12 | 12 | 100 |
| | | ?Samford | 28 | 14 | 50 |
| | | Stow & Hadleigh | 15 | 3 | 20 |
| Clement Gilley | Troston (Blackbourn) | ?Blackbourn | 36 | 1 | 3 |
| Thomas Glandfield | Gosbeck (Bosmere) | ?Carlford★ | 17 | 4 | 24 |
| | | ?Colneis★ | 11 | 3 | 27 |
| Francis Jessup | Beccles (Wangford) | Lothingland | 22 | 2 | 9 |
| Edmund Mayhew | Gosbeck (Bosmere) | Wilford★ | 17 | 4 | 24 |
| Alexander Ouldis | Thorndon (Hartismere) | ?Hartismere | 33 | 4 | 12 |
| Francis Verdon | Linstead parva (Dunwich) | Wangford | 21 | 5 | 24 |
| | | South Elmham | 9 | 0 | 0 |
| | | Dunwich★ | 44 | 22 | 50 |
| | | Hoxne★ | 27 | 14 | 52 |
| | | TOTAL | 515 | 148 | 29 |

★William Dowsing may have planned to share this deanery with the named deputy.

Under 'Number', 'N' is the estimated number of parish churches in the diocese (an attempt having been made to allow for churches in ruinous condition in Dowsing's time), 'J' is the number of visits recorded in the Journal to the deanery listed under 'deanery allocated', and 'J%' is the percentage of churches in this deanery recorded in the Journal.

make no mention of a deputy, and the churchwardens' accounts mention Verdon, but not Dowsing, suggesting that more than one visit may have been paid. Unfortunately the accounts bear no firm dates so we cannot tell whether Verdon came before or after Dowsing, but the fact that Verdon was paid a fee whilst Dowsing has no record of one in his Journal may suggest that Verdon was first on the scene.

*Framlingham 1644–45*
August 10th to **Mr Francis Verdyn** as halfe a fee for visiting the
     church by E: Manchesters warr. 3s. 4d. & a pint of sack 8d . . . o 04 00
Sept 4th to John Adkins for removing the organs . . . . . . . . . 1 10 00
For glew, aqua vitae & nayles 6d. & a skin to mend bellowes . . . o 01 00
to Tho. Ladd & Jo. Morrice each 2 dayes to help hym about the
     removall of the orgaines & setting them up againe[28] . . . . . . o 04 00

*South Elmham St Margaret 1644–45*
It' layd out to one **Vardinge** for the church 17th of May . . . . . o 03 04
It' to the glaser for the church windows the 6th of June  . . . . . o 16 00

*Weybread 1643–44*
Item to a sheete of Parchment and for wrighting the cove-
     nant in it . . . . . . . . . . . . . . . . . . . . . . . . . . . o 02 06
It'm to **Mr Verdin** for demolishing and taking away onlaw-
     full things upon our church windowes, and in other parts
     about our church being authorised hereunto by the Earle of
     Manchester . . . . . . . . . . . . . . . . . . . . . . . . . o 05 00

The churchwardens' accounts show Verdon operating in the year beginning April 1644. The Journal for the period 3–6 April 1644 (entry 210 onwards) takes Dowsing and an unnamed deputy from Kenton, through Bedingfield, Tannington, Brundish, Wilby, and Stradbroke in Hoxne deanery through to the Linsteads, and from there on they are always in Verdon territory. (Map 6.3 shows the first few of these.) Going through Halesworth and Beccles they end up at Covehithe. Surely this identifies Verdon as the companion for those four days, perhaps on his 'training trip'.

Verdon may have had some responsibility for the cleansing of the church at Uggeshall, not far from Sotterley where his master, Sir William Playters, was based. The rector of Uggeshall church was Lionel Playters, younger brother of Sir William. Although Sir William remained a supporter of Parliament, Lionel's sympathies appear to have lain with the Royalist cause, and he was ejected in the summer of 1644. With the connivance of the sequestrators (local men) the brasses in the chancel at Uggeshall were removed and the steps dug up, leading to the discovery and removal of the pot containing 200 gold pieces which Lionel Playters had carefully hidden in his children's grave.[29]

Overall, the evidence suggests that Verdon was allocated Wangford, South Elmham, Blything (Uggeshall lies within this hundred, which is nearly identical with the deanery of Dunwich).[30]

## Francis Jessup

If we accept the Lowestoft vicar James Rouse's verdict on the educational attainments of Francis Jessup of Beccles, we should set him down as principal of Dowsing's artisan deputies:

> In the same yeare [1644] also on the 12th of June **there came one Jissope** with a commission from the Earle of Manchester to take away from gravestones all Inscriptions on w'ch hee found Orate pro anima. A wretched commissioner **not able to read** or find out that w'ch his commission injoined him to remove; hee took up in our church soe much brasses as he sould to Mr Josiah Wild for five shillings w'ch was after-wards contrary to my knowledge runn into the little bell that hangs in the town house. There were taken up in the middle alley twelve pieces belonging to twelve severall generations of the Jettors.[31] In the Chancell one belonging to Bpp. Scroope; the words these – *Richardus* [recte *Thomas*] *Scroope Episcopus Dromorensis et huius Ecclesiae vicarius, hic jacett, qui obijt 10 may anno 1364* [recte 15 January 1491]: There was alsoe by this Jyssope taken up in the Vicar's Chancell, on the North side of the Church, a faire piece of brasse with this inscription: *Hic iacet Johannes Goodknapp hujus Ecclesiae vicarius qui obijt 40 Decembris 1442.*[32]

The bell made from the lifted brasses is still on the Town Hall and is struck mechanically: it reads 'John Brand made me. 1644'. Jessup missed at least one brass, but, according to an eighteenth-century author, was responsible for mutilating the figures on the font.[33]

Two facts give us pause in accepting Rouse's claim of Jessup's illiteracy. In the first place Rouse may have been away when Jessup came, detained at Cromwell's pleasure in Cambridge. As Rouse records below, he shared his (apparently intermittent) imprisonment with Sir Thomas Knyvett of Ashwellthorpe in Norfolk, whose letters (discussed in chapter 8) provide useful background for iconoclasm in that county:[34]

> Anno Domini 1644: Reader, whoever thou art, that shall occasion to peruse this booke [the parish register], know that by this means for these two following years it comes to bee soe imperfect as thou find'st it; on the fourteenth of March 1643 Collonell Cromwell with a Brigade of Horse and certaine foote which hee had from Yarmouth came to this Towne, and from thence carried away Prisoners Sir Thomas Barker and his brother Sir John

Pettis, Mr Knivett of Ashwell Thorpe,... which others to Cambridge and with these my selfe... the inhabitants weare inforced to procure now one and then another to baptise their children... only those few hearafter mentioned wear by myselfe baptised in those intervals when I enjoid my freedome... June 1st 1646.[35]

Secondly, the first sighting of a possible Francis Jessup is the marriage of one of that name to a Mary Whale at Wingfield in October 1628. Is it coincidental that Margaret Whale was the wife of Apothecary Cooper of Bildeston, and that it was their daughter Mary who married William Dowsing in 1646? Whale was not a common name in Suffolk, and Jessup may therefore have been a relative of Dowsing by marriage, and perhaps, therefore, of similar social status. The licence for a second marriage, on 27 March 1637, describes Francis Jessup of Beccles as tailor (and widower).[36]

No visits by Jessup are recorded in the Journal. But, as well as at Lowestoft, Jessup is recorded in parish documents at Bungay – as allocated in Dowsing's list – and Somerleyton, where he is described as 'Quarter-Master to Captain Browning' (Dowsing surely).

*Bungay St Mary 1643–44*
It'm to **Jesopp** for Veiwinge the Church by order from the
  Earle of Manchester . . . . . . . . . . . . . . . . . . . . . . . . . o 06 08
It'm to Robte Spence for stoninge the place where the grate
  [railing] was . . . . . . . . . . . . . . . . . . . . . . . . . . . . o 02 06
It'm more to him for takinge downe the Organs & makinge upp
  the place with brick & lyme . . . . . . . . . . . . . . . . . . . o 03 00

*Somerleyton (from the Journal of Sir John Wentworth of the Hall, died 1651)*
  For fynes levied we never had any, only Thomas Manby, the churchwarden, that time being, paid to **Francis Jessop**, Quarter-Master to Captain William Browning [*sic*], the sum of 6 shillings and 8 pence for [removing] certayne painted glasse, being in the church windows.[37]

Possible evidence of another visit by Jessup turned up in 1985, when part of a Norwich-made foot-inscription brass bearing the words *Orate p[ro] a[n]i[m]a Wil...* and *& Margarete ux...* was found during excavation of the ruined nave at St Bartholomew's church, Corton. It probably came from the memorial to William and Margaret Wynston (he died 1512/13).[38] As such partial damage to inscriptions can probably be dated to the early 1640s, and often to 1643–44, it seems likely that this was a piece Jessup removed and discarded as 'popish' on his visit to the area. Surprisingly, the church also possesses a very fine fourteenth-century gable cross, with the crucifixion on one side and the Virgin and child on the other, showing no signs of deliberate damage, and *in situ* until 1891.[39]

From what we know, Jessup was operating before the end of April 1644 and well into June. He seems to have been allocated the deanery of Lothingland with Mutford, and four parishes: Bungay,[40] Blythburgh, Yoxford and Ringshall. Perhaps Sir Robert Brooke of Cockfield Hall, Yoxford (who had interest at Blythburgh also) required Jessup's help in his home parishes; his Puritan inclinations are shown by his being made responsible by Dowsing for levelling the steps at Bramfield (entry 238).[41] At Ringshall, some trouble may have been expected from the incumbent, William Keeble, which would explain why Dowsing took pains to allocate the parish.[42] (It is this which suggests that it is indeed Ringshall which is meant in Dowsing's list, and not Ringsfield.)

## John Crow and Thomas Westhropp

John Crow[43] was certainly almost illiterate, for we have his painstaking signature on a receipt for his fee at Risby (Plate 58). He was, as we have seen, referred to as a 'common rifler' of many churches in the west of the county (Map 6.3).

> xxii Maij 1644
> Recd of Grigorie Woods gent Church Warden of Risbie vjs viijd allowed out of 40s Forfeited for not takeing away and demolishing of popish Pictures & Crosses in & upon the Parrish Church of Risbie aforrsayd & Chancell of the same according to an Ordinance of Parliamt the Residue of the 40s is to be distributed to the Poore of the Parrish of Risbie aforesayd.
> Iohn Crow

As recorded in the Journal (entry 252), Crow was the first to visit Elmsett, where George Carter was being prosecuted by his parishioners as a scandalous minister. Was it felt that someone of Crow's rough authority was needed here?

Additionally, as we have seen, Gazeley church was named in the 1662 certificate as having suffered at his hands, by which time it was said that he was living at Haverhill.[44] He and Westhropp, his colleague, certainly had a good haul at Gazeley, to judge by the number of empty brass indents there today. A small chalice brass, two shields (all three set very firmly in their stones) and two unoffending post-Reformation inscriptions remain, but everything else is gone. Eleven slabs and the back wall of a table tomb display the empty matrices of brasses removed. Yet there is much fine glass in several windows, particularly high up in the north clerestory. For one who wished to profit from the spoils of destruction, climbing to great heights to smash glass would have little appeal.

Though Risby and Gazeley are neighbouring parishes, they are in different deaneries: Thingoe and Sudbury respectively. The inference is that Westhropp and Crow between them covered some or all of the four deaneries: Thingoe, Thedwastre, Clare and Sudbury, and possibly Fordham also. It is highly probable that it was Crow that Dowsing referred to in his Journal as 'my Deputy' at Woolpit and Beyton on 29 February and 1 March (Journal entries 131, 132).

The 'godly man' Thomas Westhropp (as he spells his name signed rather elegantly on his will of 1675), Gent. of Hundon,[45] had much to bequeath to his wife and children on his death, and clearly was a man of substance, indicated by the epithets 'able' and 'sufficient' applied to him in 1662.[46] As Major Westhropp of Hundon he sat with the members of the Risbridge classis (the fourteenth division), meeting at Clare.

J. W. Darby transcribed the inscription on his headstone at Hundon which showed that he was born in 1616. He was therefore in his mid-twenties when called to service by Dowsing, younger than the typical deputy. Some years later, in 1652, by then about thirty-six years of age, he married Margaret Moody, six years his junior, but of similar social status.[47] She was the daughter of Samuel Moody, the powerful Puritan churchwarden at St James, Bury whom Dowsing met on 5 February (Journal entry 108). According to Candler, Moody was 'a woollen draper in Bury: Alderman [Mayor]. A man of great power in committees, justice of the peace, chosen by the Borough into several Parliaments [two in fact: 1654 and 1656]'. He was a senior member of the eleventh division of the classis.

Major Westhropp carried out no visits for which contemporary records survive (there is a shortage of surviving churchwardens' accounts in his area); but with Crow he probably covered the west of the county.

## Thomas Denny

The deputy Thomas Denny is found at work only at Earl Soham, his home parish, at which he pays five shillings Ship Money, putting him amongst the better off of his neighbours.[48] Thomas signed his name to the Solemn League and Covenant in the first column of the literate parishioners written in the register. He and his wife Margaret baptised two daughters at the church, Mary in 1626 and Elizabeth the next year. He died in November 1653.

*Earl Soham 1643–44*

laid out for nayles when the Church windows were glased . . . o oo o6
layd out for 16 pound of Iron for bares for the windows of
Church . . . . . . . . . . . . . . . . . . . . . . . . . . . . . . o o8 oo

for my [i.e. Henry Bardwell, churchwarden] work when the
    Church windows were glased . . . . . . . . . . . . . . . . . o 07 oo
to John Kame when he tooke doune the Images of the Church . . o 02 oo
and for my owne worke in defacinge & takings doune . . . . . . o 01 06
to John Kame for takinge the alter dune & my owne worke . . . o 05 oo
to **Thomas Denny** for his worke done then . . . . . . . . . . . o [torn]
layd out att Woodbrige when wee tooke the covenant . . . . . . . o 01 oo

It is worth looking at 'his worke done' *in situ*. There is a cross stump on the nave gable and a replacement cross on the chancel; the stump on the porch now supports a large worn figure which clearly does not belong there. Trinity and Passion shields in the south door spandrels are only time-worn, but every detail of the font has been mutilated. In the double hammer-beam nave roof, the upper and lower rows, perhaps of angels, are missing; but the bench end figures, mostly real and imaginary beasts, are in good order.

It is interesting that the transcript of the form of words for the appointment of deputies has 'T.D.' in the name-blank, and the date 4 February at the side.[49] If 'T.D.' is Denny (and no other known deputy has those initials) then he was appointed in time for the late February itinerary mentioned earlier,[50] and at about the time Dowsing was planning to return to Cambridgeshire.

We may perhaps infer that Denny was given the other parishes in Loes deanery; he would then be the man whose visits at Otley, Monewden, Hoo, Letheringham, Easton and Kettleburgh are dated 27 and 28 February in the Journal. (The only problem with that inference is that Otley is in Carlford deanery and Helmingham, where that tour ended on 29 February, is in Claydon, a deanery traditionally linked with Bosmere, and therefore likely to have been mainly the responsibility of Blomfield.) Denny could conveniently have taken on Orford deanery also.

## Alexander Ouldis

Maps 6.2 and 6.3 make it clear that, even where we know that visitors had been appointed, Dowsing seems not to have been able to leave what he had delegated. Although Jessup was to deal with only the one, north-eastern, deanery, Dowsing still went personally to the parishes of Mutford and Rushmere St Michael. He had given Verdon Wangford deanery but visited Beccles, Ringsfield, Ellough, Redisham and Sotterley himself. He does seem to have given Verdon a free hand in South Elmham, but in Dunwich deanery Verdon was not left much to do after Dowsing had himself tackled 22 parishes including the Linsteads, nor Westhropp and Crow in Sudbury deanery, where 16 parishes are written up in Dowsing's first person in the Journal. In Clare deanery, Dowsing visited Hundon (perhaps to spare Westhropp who lived there – or was this where he met Westhropp?), Clare church where his zeal was unsurpassed, and four other churches. He could not resist taking in Newmarket and Kentford (in Fordham and Clare respectively) on journeys to or from Cambridge. In Bosmere, very much Dowsing territory from his Coddenham days, Blomfield was left with only about half the churches to visit.

In late August Dowsing seems to have been making visits in areas to follow up what he had left to others. The evidence for this is cumulative. For some of the time he is visiting an area where we know Verdon and Jessup were very active; in two places, churchwardens' accounts record a payment to Verdon, but Dowsing does not record a payment, suggesting that Verdon visited first. There is the only case in the Journal of money being ordered to be paid to the poor as a fine, allowed for under the terms of the Ordinance, and in this case probably a response to deliberate foot-dragging after an earlier visit. There is a falling off in the Journal of mention of superstitious inscriptions (suggesting they may already have been dealt with). There is a concentration of churches which had explicitly been 'done' before or where there are indications that this is the case, and finally there is a subtle change in the style of writing, including a considerably reduced use of the first person, which gives the impression that one is reading an inventory of existing problems as much as a record of action.

The visits to Hartismere are particularly interesting in this context, as they expose another deputy. Hartismere is the deanery Dowsing did not after all include in his allocation (the one the deputies 'would have had'). By calling at Wetheringsett on 26 August he could check on whoever was covering Hartismere deanery, and next at Mickfield (where a ten shilling fine for non-compliance was administered) could examine what Blomfield or Verdon had covered in the north of Bosmere. There was still work to be done. Two days later therefore, he checked three more Hartismere churches, Eye, Occold and Rishangles, coming after the official visitor, as words like 'broken down afore' indicate. The entry for Occold (Journal entry 267) has to be read carefully; the italicised words are inserted for clarity.

> 267. Ockold [Occold], Aug [30th]. Divers superstitious pictures were broke *already*. I came, and *still* there was Jesus, Mary, and St. Lawrence with his gridiron, and Peter's keys. Churchwarden promised to send 5s. to **Mr. Oales**, before Michaelmas. 5s. p[ai]d m[emoran]d[um].

The sum of five shillings at this second visit was probably a fine, not a fee; too many 'pictures' remained following the earlier visit.[51] Mr Oales ('Mr' indicates gentle status) would be someone of importance in the deanery, and one Alexander Ouldis, our next deputy, indeed paid £1. 10s. 4d. Ship Money at Thorndon (next to Occold), when as Constable there (signing Alex. Oleis) he was collecting from the whole parish.[52] There is no other surname remotely like Oales to be found in the records of the area; the name will have been corrupted to Olds and probably further to Oles. In the Thorndon Town Book he is entered from 1635 onwards (the book has a gap after 1640) as paying rent at £7 per half year.[53] His inventory exists and shows that before he died in July 1665 he had moved from Thorndon to Hoxne in the deanery of that name, and was prosperous, leaving money and goods worth over £2000.[54] Here is another middle-ranking deputy.

It is very likely that this man was Dowsing's deputy in Hartismere. At his home church of Thorndon there has certainly been iconoclasm: a heavy hammer must have been taken to the stoup outside the south porch and to two shields in the spandrels of the west doorway, which formerly showed the Instruments of the Passion and the Trinity in a triangle, but are now cracked and impacted.

## Clement Gilley

The problem of the allocation of Blackbourn deanery, where Dowsing called only at Elmswell, brings us to important evidence which survives there and in south Norfolk. In several parishes in this deanery, and in more in Norfolk, the damage implicates one Captain Clement Gilley, a Suffolk man, whose area of iconoclasm stretched from parishes near his own home at Troston in Suffolk for about twenty miles into Norfolk. Fuller particulars of Gilley will be found in chapter 8, but we can attribute to him damage done to bells at Weston Market, Stanton All Saints and Ixworth, all near Troston, and Bradfield St Clare not too far distant. As there are three parishes in Blackbourn deanery showing Gilley's trademark, we may tentatively surmise that he was Dowsing's deputy there, as well as being sent by him into Norfolk.

## The extent of deputy activity

To complete the allocation of deaneries, more evidence would be required; all possible deductions have been made, and some suggestions have necessarily been tentative. Just two deaneries remain where nothing can be conjectured, Samford and Stow; but the former is so near Stratford St Mary that Dowsing could have covered it from home. Certainly someone thorough chiselled the English prayers on the brass to John Smythe (1534) at Stutton[55], just a few miles to the east (Plate 37). The brass, in the centre of the nave, has the underlined words *Of your charity pray for the sowle of* and *o[n] whose sowle J[e]hu have m[e]rcy* selectively damaged.[56]

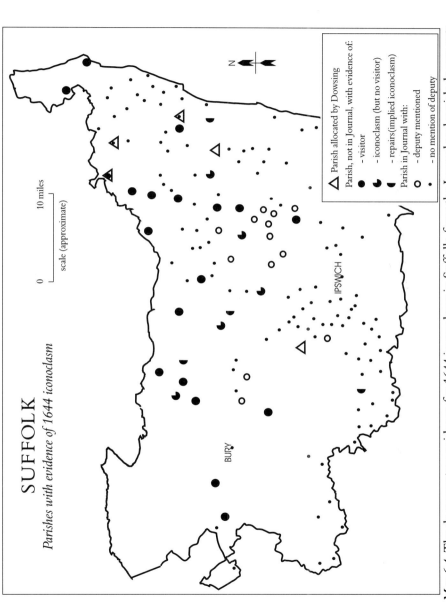

## SUFFOLK

*Parishes with evidence of 1644 iconoclasm*

0      10 miles

scale (approximate)

N

BURY

IPSWICH

△ Parish allocated by Dowsing

Parish, not in Journal, with evidence of:

● - visitor

◗ - iconoclasm (but no visitor)

◖ - repairs(implied iconoclasm)

Parish in Journal with:

○ - deputy mentioned

• - no mention of deputy

*Map 6.4* The documentary evidence for 1644 iconoclasm in Suffolk, from the Journal and parish documents.

Having established, as far as possible, the *pattern* of deputy activity, we must now briefly consider its *extent* – the proportion of churches covered by the deputies. In Suffolk whenever a church has documentary evidence outside the Journal, this always has some indication of iconoclasm, with exactly the pattern we would expect if *all* the churches had been visited (see appendix 10). Unfortunately the surviving churchwardens' accounts are largely from the east of the county (Map 6.4), but there are enough of them to confirm that, in this part of the county at least, iconoclasm and probably visitation were certainly common and possibly universal, whether or not churches are mentioned in the Journal.[57] This is borne out by the general impression that few churches have much left in the way of glass or superstitious objects.

Probably, then, the majority of churches in Suffolk were dealt with. As has been shown, those who ensured this widespread destruction of superstitious images and inscriptions formed part of Dowsing's network of friends and relatives amongst the godly. These men, well established in their communities and mostly of some social standing, were organised by him with delegated authority to enforce the efficient cleansing of their county.

# 7

## Brass, glass and crosses: identifying iconoclasm outside the Journal

*Trevor Cooper*

The breaking of Church-windows, which time had sufficiently defaced; pulling downe of crosses, which were but civill, not Religious markes; defacing of Monuments, and Inscriptions of the dead, which served but to put posterity in mind… are the effects of popular, specious, and deceitfull Reformations…

*Eikon Basilike*, page 84

IN THIS CHAPTER we move outside the geographical boundaries of the Journal, to look at the nature of iconoclasm throughout East Anglia during 1643 and 1644. In particular we consider whether iconoclasm of this period leaves a unique fingerprint on church fabrics, one which can be distinguished from earlier damage and later modifications. The two following chapters then examine the evidence for those counties of the Eastern Association not recorded by Dowsing – Essex, Hertfordshire, Huntingdonshire, Lincolnshire, and Norfolk.

In the absence of a Journal for these counties, more or less the only documentary evidence for 1640s iconoclasm is to be found in churchwardens' accounts. In addition to the records of expenditure, which we analyse below, the comments which churchwardens make about their visitors are revealing. The taking down of stained glass was very high on the agenda. In Suffolk, Verdon is described as 'viewing o[u]r church windows', or 'demolishing and taking away onlawful things upon our church windows, and in other parts about our church', or as coming to 'search for scandalous pictures' (the word 'pictures' could indicate a representation in any medium). The unnamed visitor at Wenhaston was there 'to breake downe the pictures in the glasse windowes'. In Norfolk, Captain Gilley is seen as being interested in 'Imagerie Glass', as coming to 'view the Church windowes', or as being responsible for 'abollishing superstitious pictures'. In Cambridge, churchwardens describe Dowsing as 'overseer of the windowes' and as 'him that had order for the glasse windows'. In Essex, William Aymes arrived with a commission to 'demolish Idolatrous pictures etc'.[1]

Glass is highest on the agenda, but inscriptions on brasses are also on the wanted list, together with crosses. Dowsing's visit to Walberswick is succinctly summarised as 'about takinge downe of Images & Brasses of grave stones'. Jessup was seen as coming 'to take away from grave stones all Inscriptions on w'ch hee found orate pro anima'; elsewhere he charged a church for 'certayne painted glass'. In Hertfordshire, the man 'came to take up the popish sentences from of the graves and windows'.[2] Risby parish church paid a fine to Crow for being guilty of 'not takeing away and demollishing of popish Pictures & Crosses'.

The pattern is the same at those churches where no visitor is mentioned and the churchwardens refer directly to the authority of the Earl of Manchester. At Baldock in Hertfordshire, the wardens recorded that they were 'pulling downe the glasse in the church by Manchesters comand'; we do not know whether this command manifested itself in the person of a visitor or was promulgated by some other means. At Hornchurch in Essex the parish paid for 'taking Downe the crosse of the Steeple by comand from the Earle of Manchester' and for 'taking up of Sup'stitious inscripcons of brasse and beating downe other things [glass, presumably] according to an order from the Earle of Manchester'.

Consistently, then, regardless of county, regardless of whether there was a visitor or who it was, those on the ground thought of the authorities as wanting to remove glass, brass inscriptions, and (to a lesser extent) crosses. This shopping list matches Dowsing's commission, and John Morrill's analysis in chapter 1, above, confirms that it was indeed these three remnants of a papist past on which Dowsing spent his energy. These priorities correspond also to the damage complained of in *Eikon Basilike,* the Royalist *apologia*, quoted at the head of this chapter.

In addition, as we discuss below, Dowsing had three other concerns: he frequently did down roof angels, ordered the levelling of chancel pavements (many of which had been introduced in the previous decade), and, after they were included in the Parliamentary Ordinance of May 1644, he also dealt with fonts on a systematic basis.[3]

All this raises two questions. First, whether such damage can be distinguished from earlier reformation or later good taste and can thus *by itself* indicate iconoclasm of this period at an individual church. Secondly, does the converse hold – does the lack of such destruction indicate the absence of iconoclasm, that is, that there was no attempt to remove any superstitious objects at a particular church in the 1640s? We will discuss each type of damage in turn.

### Imagery in glass

Much medieval glass survived the Reformation and its aftermath.[4] In the 1630s, judging from the accusations against them, some Laudian ministers were thought to be incorporating surviving east window crucifixes into their worship. This is perhaps not surprising: where previously the communion table might have been lengthwise in the centre of the chancel, with communicants gathered round, under Laudian reforms it was moved permanently to the east end, directly under the east window, with (in many cases) communicants facing eastwards as they knelt. The dominant presence of an east window crucifix must have made itself felt for the first time in decades. Thus the accusers of the curate at Castle Camps in Cambridgeshire said that he read the communion service 'towards the east window'.[5] At Anstey in Hertfordshire it was claimed that the vicar 'used bowings and cringings' before a 'great Crucifix and Picture of the Virgin Mary in the East window over the… Table', and at Matching in Essex 'there being a Crucifix in the window over the altar, [the vicar] useth to bow towards it, and would not suffer it be pulled downe, notwithstanding the Order of Parliament for it'.[6] At one of the parish churches of which he was parson, Edward Martin, Laudian president of Queens' College, was accused of 'falling downe upon his knees before it [the altar], with his eyes on a crucifix, being in the East window over it'.[7] When the rails and glass at Much Hadham in Hertfordshire were broken, a local wag asked 'whether he [the rector] would bow to the holes'.[8]

Seth Chapman, the rector of Hasketon in Suffolk, was even more deliberate in his re-use of old material. According to those who testified against him,

> he caused a piece of glasse painted to be removed from the south window in the Chancell, to the likeness of Christ nailed upon the Crosse, to be sett & placed in the East window of the Chancell over the alter there, & said that it was fitting it should stand there to putt playne people in remembrance of Christ; & that he himselfe did idolize it in boweinge reverence… That when the said Seth Chapman did come into the Chancell he always kneeled

downe upon his knees with his face towards the picture and held upp his hands towards it as though he had worshipped it.[9]

This new lease of life for old glass was not a welcome development to the Puritan, and it is perhaps not surprising that during 1643 and 1644 most churches in at least six counties of the Eastern Association had their medieval glass knocked out.[10] This can be seen from the churchwardens' accounts (Table 7.1). Of the 67 sets of available accounts, 47 have payments explicitly recording iconoclasm (they mention visitors, or payments for damage). Of this 47, some three-quarters explicitly refer to glass (36 sets), and another 8% (4 sets) mention images or pictures, probably in glass. Of those accounts which do not have payments explicitly recording payments for damage (the 20 other accounts which make up the total of 67), all but three show money spent on *repairs* to windows, presumably after damage.[11]

As John Morrill points out, Dowsing records the taking down of 'pictures' or 'images' in more than 90% of the churches he visited. But he rarely identifies the medium, so the churchwardens' accounts are important in confirming beyond a shadow of doubt not only that it was indeed glass which Dowsing was destroying, not only that he ensured it was destroyed in the very great majority of churches he visited (in the remainder, it may have already been dealt with by compliant parishioners), but that this poking out of windows and hiring of glaziers to do repairs was the norm across the six counties of the Eastern Association, *even where Dowsing did not visit.*

What was this glass, which had survived all previous purifications? – and where in the building was it? Neither of our sources specifies the location of the glass very often.[12] Nor are the accounts of any help with the subject matter; but here the Journal does contain considerable detail, though it may be selective – Dowsing may, for example, have been more inclined to mention certain images than other. Nevertheless, the results are of some interest. The Virgin Mary is mentioned in about 6% of Dowsing's parish churches (Plate 42 shows an example), God the Father in around 8%, and a figure of Christ, not associated with a crucifix, in about 10%. The Apostles or Evangelists are almost as frequent as Mary, whilst the Holy Ghost and the Lamb of God make a few appearances each. Most importantly, in 20% of churches an interior crucifix is mentioned; this, it is fair to assume, will usually have been the surviving medieval east window.[13] It seems that, in the mid seventeenth century, a fair amount of medieval imagery remained in parish churches.

How much glass was smashed? Dowsing often counts the number of pictures he has broken down, and this gives us one estimate. An alternative approach is to look at the expenditure on new glass recorded in churchwardens' accounts. These approaches give similar results: in the majority of

Table 7.1 *Frequency of various types of destruction shown in churchwardens' accounts (only those accounts showing a visitor or damage)*

| In Journal? | Visitor or Damage?[1] | No. of c/w accounts | Number of accounts mentioning specific types of object destroyed | | | | |
|---|---|---|---|---|---|---|---|
| | | | Glass | Image/Picture[2] | Brass | Cross | Steps |
| Yes | Visitor | 6 | 5 | 0 | 1 | 1 | 2 |
| Yes | Damage | 5 | 3 | 1 | 0 | 2 | 2 |
| No | Visitor | 20 | 15 | 1 | 2 | 8 | 2 |
| No | Damage | 16 | 13 | 2 | 2 | 4 | 0 |
| | *TOTAL* | *47* | *36* | *4* | *5* | *15* | *6* |

The table only includes churches where damage or visits are explicitly shown; it excludes churches where the accounts merely show repairs.

1 Was a visitor recorded, or merely damage?
2 Note that objects recorded as 'Image/picture' will very often have been in glass.

churches, the amount of glass removed would have occupied a few windows, or a rather special east window; and in something like a quarter of churches, rather more – sometimes much more – than this.[14]

The near universality of glass-smashing across the Eastern Association, and the amount taken down in each church, means that where glass does survive in a particular church the parish may have escaped iconoclasm in this period; the exception to this rule is armorial glass, which, following the Ordinance, seems for the most part to have been left alone (see for example Wrentham, Journal entry 264). Elsewhere in this volume the pattern of surviving stained and painted glass has been used to argue that the churches of north Norfolk were not visited, and similarly for the Isle of Ely; and the lack of glass supports the idea that Dowsing did visit north Cambridgeshire, but that those pages of his Journal were never written up or have been lost.[15] Unfortunately, although overall patterns of survival are probably helpful, the test is not foolproof for individual churches: in some cases (for example, Madingley, entry 133) a church which is known to have been visited retains its old glass, and it is known that glass was sometimes taken out to be returned when times were quieter.[16] Dowsing himself caught one parish in the attempt (Barton, entry 176). Nevertheless, the presence of a substantial quantity of old glass should make one alert to the possibility that a church was passed over in the 1640s.

## Angels and cherubim

From his very first visit, Dowsing waged war on angels and cherubim, attacking members of the heavenly host on numerous occasions (Plate 32).

What does he mean by 'cherubim'? He usually orders cherubim to be taken down by others rather than doing it himself (implying that it is a time-consuming activity), on two occasions he suggests a ladder is needed (so the cherubim were high up), and he typically records an even number of cherubim, implying symmetry. This would suggest that he usually reserves the word either for roof angels or for small angels in the head tracery of a window (or both). There is evidence that it is normally roof angels to which he refers: they are often about twenty in number, he sometimes says they are made of wood or stone, and in a good number of cases there is a good match between the number of cherubim he records and the surviving roof structure.[17]

His use of 'angel' is rather less consistent. Some of his 'angels' were in the roof (he says so). Many of them were probably in glass. On a few occasions he notes their position elsewhere – on a pulpit, on the 'steeple end', painted on the wall, in a private pew.

Dowsing dealt with cherubim (roof angels) quite frequently, in about one in eight of the parish churches which he visited.[18] In a few cases he overlooked them, probably through haste or bad lighting (which is no doubt also the explanation for the brasses he left untouched).[19] He destroyed other angels in a further dozen or so parish churches.

At a good many churches he does not mention cherubim, but they have none the less suffered damage. When did this occur? Our only documentary evidence for such a case is at Walberswick (entry 233), where the cherubim were taken down (by the carpenter, so clearly these were roof angels) the day after Dowsing's visit, despite his not recording any order for this. It is just possible that the churchwardens suffered a fit of unnecessary enthusiasm as soon as he went, but given that cutting down the cherubim cost the parish 6s. 10d., it is more likely that Dowsing did request their removal, but simply forgot to record the fact. In general, we do not at present know whether removal of cherubim ever occurred before 1640, and until this is established one way or another cherubim will be of no use as an indicator of 1640s iconoclasm.

Dowsing's anti-angelic activity is surprising. Angels, in whatever form, were not on his list of forbidden images as laid down by Parliament in August 1643. They were added in May 1644 but by that time Dowsing had done most of his damage. As discussed in chapter 1, for the most part

Dowsing stuck to the letter of the law, but here he seems to have been acting well in advance of what was permitted.[20]

However, it might be that he only took down cherubim and angels when they were decorated with crosses and other unacceptable symbolism. This hypothesis would be an alternative explanation as to why at a few of his churches he did not request the destruction of angels.

Certainly, on a few occasions Dowsing does mention that there were symbols on the breasts of the angels, so it is just possible that this was his criterion for destruction.[21] Even this would not acquit him of acting beyond his instructions, because in one case the image which annoyed him was 'stars on their breast', and stars were not on the list of proscribed items either.

The hypothesis that he only destroyed angels bearing superstitious decoration is sustainable, but he mentions this sort of decoration so rarely that it is difficult to avoid the impression that he regarded angels themselves as fair game. His note of 10 'mighty great angels in glass' which he then broke down does not give the impression of a man cold-bloodedly assessing each of the images for the presence of illegal symbolism about its person.[22] On one occasion he mentions 'angels and saints' in the same breath,[23] so perhaps it was simply that in his mind the heavenly orders were lumped in with the generality of saints, which he was fully entitled to remove. Perhaps Old Testament prophets suffered the same guilt by association, for he was also happy to destroy images of the patriarchs, though they, too, were not proscribed.[24]

How did other visitors behave towards angels? We have rather little to go on. Our corpus of churchwardens' accounts do not mention angels being taken down by his deputies. But this may mean nothing, for neither are angels recorded in the accounts even where we know roof cherubim were definitely taken down on Dowsing's orders, confirming the limitations of this form of evidence.[25] Nor have we systematically inspected those churches known to have been visited by deputies, to see whether they routinely show damage to roof cherubim. We do know, however, that at two churches Dowsing's local appointees did *not* find it necessary to pull down cherubim, and this might suggest that he was unusually purist in this regard.[26]

Dowsing ignored or overlooked cherubim in a few churches, and in a few others his instructions were disobeyed or the angels were later restored, so an angelic presence today is no indication that a church escaped iconoclasm. Conversely, we do not know how many roof angels were taken down in the century before Dowsing, nor the extent to which they were sawn off in later centuries – at Bildeston church, for example, (the place of Dowsing's second marriage), the chancel angels were apparently taken down and burnt as idolatrous in the late eighteenth century, under the influence of George Whitefield.[27] So damage to roof angels is not a definite sign of 1640s iconoclasm.

All this needs further research, but the presence or absence of angels in a particular church today is certainly not indicative of what happened in the 1640s. Unusually for heavenly messengers, they tell us nothing.

## *Fonts*

What of fonts? The deliberate injury of fonts is often assumed to be 'Cromwellian' (that is, of the 1640s). Certainly, under the second Parliamentary Ordinance of 1644 the use of fonts was forbidden and they were ordered to be defaced. In many churches fonts were replaced by a basin and frame, and sometimes the font was turned out of the church forcing either a new one to be purchased at the Restoration, or the old one to be recovered and perhaps refurbished (as at Ipswich, St Clement's, Journal entry 85).[28] Thus at Kelsale the church paid 3s. 6d. 'for a bason', and 6d. to 'Robert Moose for takeinge downe the Font' in the year ending Easter 1645. At Hartest it seems that the churchwarden was forced to pull down the font 'out of fear & by the colour of an Order of some of the Earl of Manchester's soldiers lying then in and about Hartest'.

Some churches had not waited on legality: as early as 1642, at Norwich, St Peter Mancroft, one Ducket was paid 1s. 0d. 'for takeing downe images at the font'. At Chelmsford, in 1644, an even more thorough refurbishment took place:

*Chelmsford 1644*

It' pd Johnson to white the church, and remove and take off
    pictures from the Funt . . . . . . . . . . . . . . . . . . . . . . . 0 07 00
It' pd for glewing the Funt . . . . . . . . . . . . . . . . . . . . . . . 0 05 00
It' pd for paynting the Funt in oyle . . . . . . . . . . . . . . . . . 0 11 00

After the May 1644 Ordinance, Dowsing was not shy of removing superstitious decoration from fonts (as at Linstead parva, entry 216), though the majority of his churches (some 90%) were visited before this date, and at these churches fonts are not mentioned.

Our commentary to the Journal confirms that font defacement is widespread in Dowsing's churches. Such damage is to be found in about forty of the churches in his Journal; many of the other fonts were too plain to attract attention. What is puzzling is that the majority of such defacement occurs in churches where Dowsing does *not* record this type of spoliation in his Journal (for an example, see Plate 39).

Does this mean that fonts were damaged by Dowsing, but the work was not recorded by him? Or were they defaced by the churchwardens some time after his visit, in response to the subsequent Parliamentary Ordinance? Or had they had been dealt with before Dowsing arrived? If so, how long before – earlier in the 1640s, or many years earlier? Our corpus of church-wardens' accounts for 1643 and 1644 is of little help, payments for mutilating fonts occurring very infrequently in this period (though the replacement of fonts by basins is not uncommon). Hammering a font need not have cost much, but given the highly professional chiselling flat of some font imagery one would have expected to find expenditure recorded in a proportion of churchwardens' accounts.

A recent discussion of the defacement of seven sacrament fonts concludes that it is likely that in East Anglia this particular group (with their highly-charged imagery) had been damaged in the sixteenth century.[29] But the argument rests heavily on the mood of the times: there are no known documented examples of font damage in this period.[30]

The font at Cratfield, Suffolk was removed from the church in 1567; it has been damaged at some time, probably deliberately, and quite possibly at the time it was removed.[31] Additionally the restorer of the font at St Peter Mancroft, Norwich, believed that this was first defaced as early as the 1560s; this font was further damaged to install a wooden platform in 1623 (though this was indifference, not iconoclasm), and, as we have seen, it was certainly deliberately defaced in 1642.[32] But this seems to be the limit of our knowledge of East Anglian font damage before the 1640s. [33]

Thus we know fonts were damaged in the 1640s. They may well have been deliberately disfigured before this. Font defacement in a particular church may therefore indicate iconoclasm of the 1640s, but, as matters stand, no certainty is possible. Further work needs to be done looking for documentary evidence at all periods after the Reformation.

A final difficulty with the use of fonts as reliable markers of 1640s iconoclasm is that an undamaged font does not necessarily mean that a church avoided iconoclasm: there are more than a dozen churches which Dowsing visited where there is font imagery in good condition. In some cases this may be because unacceptable carvings were simply covered with plaster rather than being chiselled flat.[34]

### Steps and rails

The Parliamentary Ordinance made churchwardens responsible for seeing that chancel steps were removed. However the cost of the work was to be borne by the person responsible for the upkeep of the relevant part of the church.[35] In the case of the chancel this was customarily the parish minister,[36] and the churchwardens would therefore not expect to foot the bill for taking down the steps. This explains why the levelling of chancels appears routinely in the Journal (in more than 40% of Dowsing's entries) but much less frequently in churchwardens' accounts (just 6 of the relevant 47 accounts).

Dowsing's practice matches these legal requirements. At Halesworth, for example (Journal entry 219), there is a clear example of a division of labour: the churchwardens are to remove the steeple cross, but the 'parson of the town' is to deal with the steps. On numerous other occasions Dowsing specifies that it is the minister (or the farmer of the rectory) who must 'level the chancel'; at other times he merely notes the names of the churchwardens or constables, no doubt seeing them as generally responsible for ensuring that a variety of matters were dealt with (including, in a very few examples, their being given explicit responsibility for steps).

Churchwardens were indeed prepared to take action. This is confirmed from the chance survival of complaints against ministers for deliberately blocking them. For example, at Girton (in north Cambridgeshire, and thus not in the Journal) it was said of the minister William Ling, who had been one of the first to introduce rails into Cambridgeshire, that

> when the Churchwardens had procured workmen to Levell the Chancell the said Wm Ling soe disturbed the workemen with his threats against them that they went away and left the worke.[37]

Churchwardens carrying out the work on their own initiative would perhaps expect the minister to foot the bill. No doubt the confusion of the times sometimes meant they could not recover their money; then the expenditure would appear in their accounts. There is one example amongst the four sets of accounts for churches where we know Dowsing had the steps removed. At Metfield (269) and Kelsale (61), where he ordered the steps down, there is, as expected, no record of a payment for the work; but at Stowmarket (103) the accounts do include the expenditure on steps incurred by the churchwardens when his order was complied with. Rather surprising is Cambridge, St Botolph's (21): here Dowsing and his colleagues did the work themselves, but the churchwardens still had to find a shilling to pay for it.

A further complication with churchwardens' accounts is that expenditure on steps may be hidden inside other items – for example, at Ipswich, St Peter's (76) the expenditure on tiles might be for making good the chancel floor, as might the payment to the mason at Ipswich, St Clement's (85), and the 15s. 6d. 'laid out for Brick & masons worke' at Boxford (not visited by

Dowsing). In this case, the Journal is invaluable in providing a possible context for general building expenditure.

In summary, then, despite the statistics mentioned at the beginning of this section, there is no reason to suppose that altar steps were more frequently dealt with by Dowsing than by other visitors. The presence or absence of chancel steps today is, of course, of very little practical value in identifying iconoclasm, given the multiple reorderings which most churches have experienced since the 1640s (but see Burstall and Kingston, Journal entries 91 and 136, the latter illustrated in Plate 45).

The survival of pre-1640 altar rails would seem a more promising indicator of lack of 1640s iconoclasm. Rails were in place in most parishes in Cambridgeshire and Suffolk by the late 1630s.[38] Parliament ordered their removal in 1641, and as pointed out in chapter 1, most had been removed before 1644 when Dowsing visited so their survival might indicate a church where iconoclasm was somehow avoided.[39]

In practice, matters are not clear cut. To begin with, for the survival of rails to be useful in any way, one must be certain that rails predate 1640, and this can be problematic, few rails being dated.[40] Secondly, altar rails could be transferred from one church to another, as at Ware, Hertfordshire, thus muddying the evidence.[41] Thirdly, it is possible that rails which had been in place for many years were allowed to stay, following the spirit though not the letter of the Ordinance, which allowed altar steps to remain if they were twenty or more years old.[42] Finally, and crucially, rails could be hidden by churchwardens, and later replaced.[43]

The problems are made concrete at Chediston, Suffolk. This church today contains communion rails which are stylistically of the early seventeenth century, and appear to have been made for the church (Plate 31). It was visited by Dowsing (Journal entry 218), but he makes no mention of rails. It is hardly credible that they were in the church and overlooked by him: either the dating is wrong,[44] or he was persuaded that they had been there many years, or they were somewhere else – in another church, or hidden in a loft or outhouse. More than that we cannot say.

For all this, the survival of pre-1640 rails may occasionally be useful. For example, one authority claims that the rails at Lingwood and Burlingham St Edmund (both in Norfolk) are of the appropriate date; these are outside the area dealt with by Captain Gilley, so these two churches may well not have been visited.[45] Elsewhere in this volume John Blatchly considers the rails at Wilby, Norfolk, whose date is fairly firm, and whose survival may perhaps indicate that Captain Gilley did not visit every church in his patch.[46]

*External crosses*

As regards external crosses, the Journal and the accounts are largely in agreement, showing the removal of crosses from gables and steeples in approximately a quarter of cases (Plates 33 and 34). In the City of London, too, the removal of steeple crosses a few months earlier was commonplace, probably part of a campaign by the authorities following demolition of Cheapside Cross in 1643 (Plate 17).[47] Crosses (as against crucifixes) do not appear in the 1641 Order of Parliament, but are explicitly included in the 1643 Ordinance, whether they are 'in' or 'upon' the building, or are in the churchyard.[48] In 1644, Richard Culmer, the incumbent of Minster in Kent, felt strongly enough about the procrastination of his churchwardens over the matter to climb his own church spire by moonlight to put ladders in position so that the crosses could be removed.[49]

Was the removal of gable crosses a new form of iconoclasm, invented in the 1640s, or did it have a long history? The question does not previously seem to have been discussed. It could be argued that if this activity were new, and deemed necessary, then more or less complete coverage would have been found in the accounts, as with glass. But in many churches the necessary expenditure may be hidden under general works, and in others there may have been enthusiastic young men who relished the opportunity to swing a hammer on the nave roof, charging nothing for the privilege. At Kelsale, for example, the cross was ordered down by Dowsing (entry 61), and has come down, but the accounts show no expenditure on this (at least, not in the early 1640s).

Further work is needed, but it may well turn out that damage to gable and steeple crosses is a useful indicator of iconoclasm during 1643–44. If so, this will need care in practice as, with the encouragement of the nineteenth-century ecclesiologists,[50] many mutilated and missing crosses have long since been replaced (for an example, see our commentary on Sudbury, Journal entry 40). Additionally, the order to remove a gable cross may sometimes have been ignored as, for example, at Orford (entry 57). Or the cross may have been overlooked, as at Blythburgh (235), where Dowsing did not notice a figure of the Deity on the chancel gable, still there today. Something similar probably happened at Corton, where a fine gable crucifix of medieval date survives at a church which was almost certainly visited.[51] So, whereas damage to a gable cross may indicate iconoclasm of our period, lack of damage may not mean that the church escaped.

## Brasses

The destruction of brasses was not purely a 1640s phenomenon. As early as the fourteenth century, Langland satirised friars who were happy to remove old monuments to make way for new:

> And in beldyng of toumbes, They travaileth grete
> To chargen ther cherche flore, And chaungen it ofte.

There is ample evidence not only of the sale of brasses during the upheavals of the 1540s and 1550s, but of neglect and wilful damage throughout the next few centuries.[52] Where brasses are well-documented, such as those in the Cambridge colleges, this pattern of continual erosion is very obvious and should make one hesitate before automatically assigning losses to the Reformation or the Civil War, or indeed to religious motives.[53]

An example of brasses being removed because of their 'superstitious' nature is recorded at Coventry in the sixteenth century. Sir John Harington, writing in the early seventeenth century, noted that

> the pavement of Coventry church is almost all tombstones, and some very antient; but there came in a zealous fellow with a counterfeit commission, that for avoiding of superstition, hath not left one penny-worth nor one penny-bredth of brasse upon the tombes, of all the inscriptions, which had been many, and costly.[54]

This incident probably involved the removal of all the brass. In contrast, the 1643 Ordinance, to which Dowsing was ultimately working, targeted superstitious *inscriptions* in the list of items to be removed, and the Journal mentions their being taken up (mostly from brasses) in more than a third of churches.[55] Outside the Journal, expenditure on such activity is recorded by the churchwardens at Hornchurch, and something similar may be referred to at Chelmsford, where there is a payment for 'mending the foote work of the Brasses in the middle Ile'. Yet brasses figure rather infrequently in our churchwardens' accounts (in just over 10%), probably because there was little expenditure involved – in fact, some profit could be made, though probably not enough to motivate removal.[56] If we had to rely on expenditure in these accounts alone, the very considerable systematic damage to brasses which occurred at this time would to some extent have been concealed. This is another area where the Journal is crucial to our understanding of events.

The target was inscriptions, and sometimes their removal was carried out very precisely, leaving the remainder of the brass intact. Examples include Orford (57), Weston Colville (194), and Nettlestead (249). However, our commentary on the Journal leaves the strong impression that often the whole brass was lifted, although in the generality of instances this cannot be

Table 7.2 *Parishes in the counties of the Eastern Association with brasses with the opening or closing prayer clause on the foot inscription obliterated or excised*

| County | Number of parishes | List of parishes, with references |
|---|---|---|
| Cambridgeshire | 3 (all in Journal) | Cambridge, St John's College (Jnl 12); Cambridge, King's College (Jnl 13); Linton (Jnl 36) |
| Essex | 8 | List in Table 9.2 |
| Hertfordshire | 25 | List in Table 9.3 |
| Huntingdonshire | 0 | — |
| Lincolnshire | 0 | — |
| Norfolk | 6 | Ashwellthorpe; Hoe; Norwich, St Andrew (2); Norwich, St Stephen; Poringland; Wells; (see pp. 112–14, *passim*) |
| Suffolk | 5 (3 in Journal)★ | Corton (p. 81); Ipswich, St Mary le Tower (Jnl 81); Letheringham (Jnl 127); Metfield (Jnl 269); Stutton (p.86). |

Some of the examples are from the corpus of rubbings at the Society of Antiquaries of London of inscriptions, or brasses, which have since been lost.

proved, because the gap between Dowsing's visit and that of the next passing antiquary gave plenty of time for local vandals or impecunious churchwardens to remove what had been left. Furthermore, once the inscription had gone, the brass became anonymous, and thus perhaps more prone to removal in future years.

At Ashwellthorpe in Norfolk we have an eyewitness account of the business, apparently with entire brasses being lifted, as the lady of the big house writes to her husband:

> I must tell you our superstitious glas in the church windows and the brase upon the graves are going up most vehemently, the visiting captain said he never came into a church wher he saw so much.

It is not certain who would normally profit from the metal in these instances. We know that at Walberswick the churchwardens sold it off some months after Dowsing removed the inscriptions (entry 233), and a similar total clearance must have occurred at Saffron Walden in Essex:

*Saffron Walden 1643–44*
Received of John Pam[m]ent for the brasses that were taken of
    the grave stones by an Ordenaunce of Parliament, which
    wayd 7 score 18lb . . . . . . . . . . . . . . . . . . . . . £2.  19s.  0d.

The disappearance of an entire inscription is, however, no proof of 1640s iconoclasm, as these independent pieces of metal can disappear at any time. Nor, it is worth noting, does the presence of an inscription show that the church was free of iconoclasm. Both these points are exemplified at Stow cum Quy (entry 207), where an inscription overlooked by Dowsing remained until the eighteenth century, but has since disappeared. As a further complication, inscriptions in Norman French were also regularly ignored by Dowsing (as, for example, at Brundish, entry 213), by at least one of his deputies (Letheringham, entry 127) and by others operating at the time,[57] probably because the language was a mystery to them.

The presence or absence of a complete inscription is therefore not a useful indicator of iconoclasm of the period in an individual church. However, it is possible that the geographical pattern of missing inscriptions might prove helpful in identifying the extent of iconoclasm over an area, and some initial results of this type are reported in appendix 13. In Suffolk, Cambridgeshire, Essex and Hertfordshire a very high proportion of pre-1540 inscriptions, of the order of 65% to 80%, disappeared between the early 1600s and the early to mid 1700s. In Suffolk, where we have the necessary data, about 50% of inscriptions had gone by 1660, the remaining 30% disappearing over the following seventy or eighty years. This rate of loss post-1660 may also have been true of the other counties, implying that Dowsing and his contemporaries damaged about one half of the existing brasses, leaving the others alone either through oversight or because they did not contain prayer clauses. In Norfolk the results are tentative, but it would appear that in the north of the county perhaps 75% of inscriptions in place in the early seventeenth century *survived* to the eighteenth century, with a lower rate of survival in the south, tending to confirm that much of the county was not visited in the 1640s, as discussed in chapter 8.

However, in an individual church, neither the removal of an entire brass nor of an entire inscription is evidence of 1640s iconoclasm: both are common, and can occur in any period.[58] A third type of brass damage is much less common, consisting of the scratching out or careful cutting out of the prayer clause of a foot inscription, leaving the remainder behind.[59] This form of damage is widespread, but unusual (see Plates 26, 36, 37 and 38 for examples).

A strong case can be made that this particular type of mutilation was peculiar to the 1640s. There are a number of examples within Dowsing's Journal (see Table 7.2), but this form of damage will only be useful for our purposes if people other than Dowsing carried it out, and only in the 1640s. We first need to demonstrate that it never occurred before or after the 1640s, and here the most that can be said is that no cases are currently known to us; such argument from silence will, of course, collapse if any are in future discovered.* Secondly we need to show that partial destruction of inscriptions definitely was carried out during the early 1640s, and with this we are on firmer ground, with no fewer than six documented examples.[60] Five of these are from London:

> *St Michael Wood Street, 1641*: 'pd for a pinte of sack to the man that cutt the Brasse'; 'pd to the man that cutt the letters out of the Brasse'.[61]

> *St Dunstan-in-the-West, 1643–44*: Edward Marshall, 'stone-cutter', was paid 40s. for 'altering the inscriptions in brasse upon div[er]s gravestones'.[62]

> *All Hallows, Barking-by-the-Tower, 19 March 1643/4*: one Shurlan was 'paid to erase the superstitious letters from brasses'. Four brasses have been thus treated. For example, the brass to Andrew Evyngar, citizen and salter of London (1533), and his wife Ellyn has the following words erased: *Of your Charite praye for the Soules* and *wyffe on whose Soules Jesu have m'cy Amen.*[63]

> *St Helen Bishopsgate, 1644*: a man was paid £1. 2s. od. for 'defacing the super-stitious inscriptions'. A number of brasses have had inscriptions partially damaged, probably also by Shurlan, given the similarity in the way the work was carried out.[64]

> *St James Garlickhithe, 1644–45*: money was paid for 'cutting out superstitious words'.

The final example is from Hertfordshire, at St Albans, St Peter's where we have seen that the visitor arrived 'to take up the popish sentences from of the graves and windows' and where Samuell Ellement was paid 6d. 'to helpe him to cute them of'. In that church the now lost brass to William Victor, 1486, and his wife Grace, did indeed have the closing clause removed.[65]

In addition to these six firmly documented examples of known mutilation in the early 1640s, there is the suggestive expenditure at King's Lynn in 1645 on 'defacing superstitious Epitaphs' (see appendix 8); and the surviving example at Ashwellthorpe, Norfolk, discussed in chapter 8, which was prob-ably carried out in 1644.

*See note at the end of this chapter.

It is possible that prayer-clause obliteration may sometimes have been carried out by relatives willing to sacrifice a small part of their ancestor's memorial in order to preserve the rest from the hands of potential visitors. We are not aware of any firmly documented examples, though the Ashwell-thorpe brass may well have been sterilised by the family, who had plenty of warning that the church would be visited.[66] It is noteworthy, however, that in all six of the accounts quoted above, the prayer clauses were removed at the behest and cost not of individuals, but of the parish. On the other hand, the survival of relevant documentary evidence is weighted towards parish rather than individual expenditure, and the possibility of a relative acting in-dependently must therefore be borne in mind: mutilation of this kind would then indicate the fear of iconoclasm at a particular church, but would not prove that the church actually suffered in any way. Two interesting cases are Linton in Cambridgeshire (entry 36) where it seems that an influential recu-sant family may have persuaded Dowsing to remove just the prayer clauses from some of the family brasses, and Metfield in Suffolk (entry 269), where, after an initial refusal to co-operate, Thomas Jermy may have arranged for limited defacement of his ancestors' brass.

If it is accepted that selective prayer clause damage of this type is limited to the early 1640s, then we have a useful tool for identifying churches which suffered iconoclasm in that period (or were under distinct threat of it, if some cases are thought be the result of preventative cleansing by relatives). A number of cases of this type of mutilation are known in East Anglia, and there are almost certainly more to be discovered (Table 7.2).[67] Our commentary on the Journal includes several examples in churches visited by Dowsing, and other chapters in this volume deal with other counties of the Eastern Association. In one county, Hertfordshire, the number of examples and their extent is valuable in understanding the scope of iconoclasm.

★ ★ ★

In summary, it has been suggested that the survival of roof angels tells us nothing of 1640s iconoclasm; whether their destruction was limited to the 1640s has not been explored. Nor is the defacement of fonts necessarily indicative of iconoclasm of the 1640s. The survival of altar rails and stained glass may be helpful in identifying churches which were unscathed, but caution is needed.

More positively, two useful pointers to 1640s iconoclasm are probably damaged gable crosses and deliberate mutilation of prayer clauses in brass, the former perhaps being more common in the period immediately after 1643. We make cautious use of these latter conclusions in the next two chapters: they need thorough testing before being regarded as anything other than tentative.

### *Further note on the mutilation of prayer clauses*

Four weeks before this book went to press (and some two or three years after the above was written), I discovered a counter-example to the hypothesis that deliberate prayer-clause mutilation occurred only during the 1640s. In the introduction to his *Ancient Funerall Monuments*, published in 1631, Weever says (my italics):

> I conclude the Epitaphs and Funerall inscriptions in this booke as I finde them engraven, with a cuius anime propitietur Deus: or with God pardon his soule; which some may say might have beene as well left oute of my booke, *as they are in many places scraped out of the brasse*:…

It follows that prayer-clause mutilation is *not* a safe pointer to 1640s icono- clasm, which it now seems was occurring before this date. Currently our only documented examples are from the 1640s, as laid out earlier in the chapter, and it will be interesting to see if earlier documentation emerges. Given the late discovery of this counter-example, I have not attempted to make any changes to the text of the book.

It will be seen that in chapter 9 I have used the exceptional extent of prayer-clause mutilation in Hertfordshire to argue that the whole county was probably visited in the 1640s (as supported by other evidence). The restriction of this particular form of spoliation to one administrative area continues to suggest central direction, and the evidence from St Albans, St Peter's would support the suggestion that it was all done in 1644. But the argument for this is, of course, weakened by the discovery that the work could have been carried out before this date.

# 8

# In search of bells:
# iconoclasm in Norfolk, 1644

## *John Blatchly*

IN HIS FINE BOOK, *Norfolk in the Civil War*, Ketton-Cremer described something of Dowsing's work in Suffolk and Cambridgeshire, ending: 'But there seems to be no record of how the horrid work was carried out in Norfolk, or who was entrusted with the task'.[1] A search through the surviving churchwardens' accounts of the period, and other sources, has gone some way towards explaining just how and by whom 'the horrid work' was perpetrated, and how far it penetrated into the county.

### *Iconoclasm in rural Norfolk*

Our starting point is Bressingham in south Norfolk, where the churchwardens' accounts, now lost, were quoted by Blomefield in the eighteenth century (see Map 8.1 for places mentioned in this chapter). They name a visitor, and mention an unusual form of iconoclasm – bell-damage.

*Bressingham 1644–45*
Item paid vij of May to **Captaine Gilley** by the towne for the
   viewing of the church for abollishing superstitious pictures . . o o6 oo
Item paid to John Nun for 2 dayes work and for taking down of
   glas and pictures about the church and **the letters about the
   bells** . . . . . . . . . . . . . . . . . . . . . . . . . . . . . . . . . o o3 o4

The damage done to the inscriptions on the first and second bells at Bressingham, at Captain Gilley's instigation, was not thorough enough to

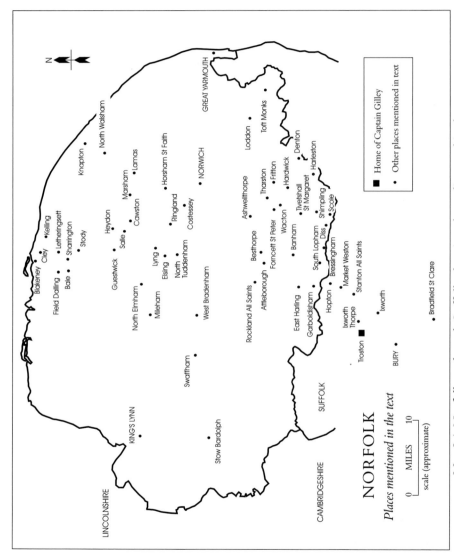

*Map 8.1* Norfolk, and north Suffolk, showing places discussed in the text.

render them illegible, but nothing at all remains on the third.[2] Blomefield went on to relate that the reglazing of the windows after this 'reformation' came to £2. 6s. 0d., and that, although several windows were lost, some were preserved and put up in the windows of the Hall, such as the emblem of the Trinity, St John the Evangelist, St Catharine, the Virgin, and St Margaret, together with the arms of Verdon and others. This glass came back to the east window of the church at the expense of Humphry Clayton, rector when Blomefield was writing (1736), and there are today remnants of old glass in the east window.[3] The church suffered much, for in 1664, £54. 11s. 8d. had to be raised by rate to put it in order, and to replace the ornaments it had lost.

Who was Captain Gilley? It was Dr Paul Cattermole who first published extracts from the Banham churchwardens' accounts which give the crucial information that Gilley was from outside the county, 'of Hopton in *Suffolk*'.[4]

*Banham 1643–44*
It' to Thomas Rawth for a boshill of lime and bringing of it from
    Thetford for sand to fasten the panes of glass in the church
    windows . . . . . . . . . . . . . . . . . . . . . . . . . . . . 0 01 04
It' to Cracknell of Diss for glasing work at the Church when the
    Imagerie Glass was taken downe by order from the Parlia-
    ment, by the view and apointment of **Mr Gillie of Hopton
    in Suff being imployed by the Parlt. for the same pur-
    pose** . . . . . . . . . . . . . . . . . . . . . . . . . . . 2 13 01
It' given to the glaser and his man to drink when they began and
    when they mad an end of glasing . . . . . . . . . . . . . . . . 0 00 08

It is interesting that, because Gilley was implementing a Parliamentary Ordinance, the Banham churchwardens assumed that he was directly employed by Parliament. At this church something prevented him from getting up the tower, or his orders were neglected, for the inscriptions on four pre-Reformation bells are still in perfect order.

The Bressingham entry linking Gilley to bell-damage is extremely important, as both these churches lie amidst an extraordinary cluster of churches which have had bell inscriptions removed. There are four of these churches in Suffolk, eleven in south Norfolk (see Table 8.1 and Map 8.2).[5] There is just one other known case of bell-damage in the churches of the counties of the Eastern Association;[6] Dowsing himself mentions bells twice in his Journal but even in those two churches they were not touched.[7] When this bell-damage is plotted on a map, the evidence for a localised form of iconoclasm is obvious (Map 8.2), and this rare form of damage must surely indicate the work of a single guiding hand, that of Gilley.

Almost all of the bell-damaged churches lie close to roads running south from Norwich into Suffolk. The significance of this will become apparent

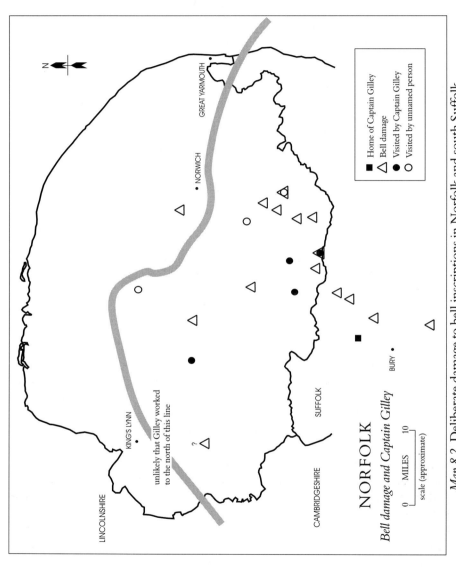

Map 8.2 Deliberate damage to bell inscriptions in Norfolk and south Suffolk.

LINCOLNSHIRE

N

KING'S LYNN •

unlikely that Gilley worked
to the north of this line

GREAT YARMOUTH

NORWICH •

CAMBRIDGESHIRE

SUFFOLK

BURY •

NORFOLK

*Bell damage and Captain Gilley*

0     MILES     10

scale (approximate)

■ Home of Captain Gilley
◁ Bell damage
● Visited by Captain Gilley
○ Visited by unnamed person

Table 8.1 *Parishes with bell-damage in Norfolk and Suffolk*

| County | Parish | Comment |
| --- | --- | --- |
| Suffolk | Bradfield St Clare | – |
| .. | Ixworth | Home of Gilley's forebears (Plate 62) |
| .. | Stanton All Saints | – |
| .. | Market Weston | – |
| Norfolk | South Lopham | – |
| .. | Bressingham | Churchwardens' accounts name Gilley |
| .. | Shimpling | – |
| .. | Tivetshall St Margaret | – |
| .. | Hardwick | Churchwardens' accounts mention unnamed visitor |
| .. | Wacton | – |
| .. | Tharston | – |
| .. | Rockland All Saints | – |
| .. | Stow Bardolph | Damage is of a different nature, may not be Gilley |
| .. | West Bradenham | – |
| .. | Costessey | Bell bought second-hand in 1800, source unknown |

Parishes are listed by location, most southerly first

when Gilley's home is identified below. Shimpling, Tivetshall St Margaret, Wacton, and Tharston are to the west of the Scole to Norwich road, with Hardwick to the east. Interestingly, at nearby Forncett St Peter, a parish adjoining both Wacton and Tharston, an inscription on the parapet of the porch, similar to those on bells, has been damaged: *Saints Petur and Pawle patronnys of yis place Praye to Ihu i[n] heven yt I may see his face*.[8] Market Weston, Stanton, and Ixworth lie on the road dropping south from Garboldisham, and further up this road towards Norwich lie Banham and Ashwellthorpe, with East Harling just to the east, places which will be encountered later. Bradfield St Clare lies just off an old route running south from Ixworth.[9] Bressingham and South Lopham lie off the east-west Diss to Thetford road, running along the county boundary. Outside this group is a damaged bell north-west of Norwich at Costessey, but this was bought second-hand in 1800 and came from a church which cannot be identified. Farther afield is Stow Bardolph, but bell-damage at this church is of a rather different kind, and perhaps not part of the same series. The only significant exceptions to the north-south distribution are Rockland All Saints and West Bradenham.

At Ashwellthorpe, up the road from Banham and just three miles from bell-damaged Tharston, the patron, Sir Thomas Knyvett, well aware of the Ordinance, tried to anticipate the actions of the expected visitors to the parish church, which served also as the family chapel. A declared Royalist, he was aware that Manchester was seeking an order to sequestrate his property, but remained concerned for the church, and wrote from London in March 1644 asking his wife to send for a cousin with heraldic knowledge to copy the family arms in glass in case an overzealous cleansing took place – under the terms of the Parliamentary Ordinances this glass should have been safe. Two months later he suggested that Roger Gallard the incumbent should take prompt action to save the family glass:

*11–14 May 1644*
I have sent you an ordinance concerning mon[u]m[en]ts & church windowes. I wish Mr Gallyerd would cause the church wardens to take downe the superstitious things in the windowes According to this ordinance, & preserve the coats of Armes by vertu of the same command, else perhapps thay may suffer together by violence.

Katherine Knyvett answered her husband's letter in terms which support the idea that it was 'Captaine' Gilley who came here. There are no early bells here today, and may not have been any then, so he was not able to leave his trademark.

*16 May 1644*
I must tell you our superstitious glas in the church windows and the brase upon the graves are going up most vehemently, the visiting captaine said he never came into a church wher he saw so much. 'Twill cost you a good sume the new glasing your chaple which truly shalbe let alone till winter; poor Mr Gallard grones at that which fales to his share to reforme; the ordinance of parliament which you sent downe hath preserved the steps att the altar which were sentenced to be taken away. Now tis time to lett you know I am Dear boy thy faithfull loveing wife K K[10]

One brass was left, that to Jane Knyvett, who died in 1561, in Elizabeth's reign. The last four lines of her brass provide the expected panegyric, but the sting is in the tail:

Gentle, just, quiet, voyde of debate & strife
   Ever doing good, so thus she led hir life
Even unto the grave where earth on earth doth lye
   On whose soule god graunt of his aboundant mercye.

Table 8.2 *Iconoclasm in rural Norfolk recorded in churchwardens' accounts*

| Parish | Evidence shows: |
| --- | --- |
| Ashwellthorpe | Unnamed visitor – 'the visiting Captain' |
| Bale | No record of iconoclasm |
| Banham | Gilley as visitor |
| Besthorpe | Expenditure on glazing; articles |
| Bressingham | Gilley as visitor |
| Denton | Iconoclasm |
| Elmham, North | Unnamed visitor |
| Fritton | Expenditure on glazing; articles |
| Garboldisham | No record of iconoclasm |
| Harleston | Iconoclasm. |
| Harling, East | Gilley as visitor |
| Swaffham | Gilley as visitor |
| Walsham, North | No record of iconoclasm |

Today the final line is scored through, done some time after it was recorded by Weever, who published in 1631 (Plate 37). Gilley's work? – Or did Katherine Knyvett sacrifice the offending line of her husband's ancestor's memorial in order to preserve the rest?[11]

Gilley's name, variously spelt, is mentioned as visitor also in the accounts of two other Norfolk churches (Table 8.2): at Swaffham, and at East Harling, where extensive armorial glass was left untouched, and the 'superstitious' glass was taken to the great house, later to be returned (Plates 63 and 64).[12] He may well also have been the unnamed visitor recorded in the churchwardens' accounts at North Elmham, though we cannot point to damage of his usual kind there. At Banham he dealt with the 'imagerie glass' before Easter 1644 (21 April);[13] he was at Bressingham on 7 May, East Harling on 9 May, and on 16 May Katherine Knyvett wrote to her husband about the work at Ashwellthorpe. His activity may have been restricted to a short period, or this may be a false impression given by the chance survival of the evidence.

In the records of four parishes we have the variants Gelle, Gilley, Gillie, Gylly, all similar enough. In Suffolk, if Dowsing had left no Journal, we should have had to consider whether Dowson and Browning were the same person, throwing in the possibility that Dewden at an Essex church was another sighting. His Christian name and identity would never have been discovered. It is an interesting chance that in contrast Gilley's name is given so often in Norfolk, written down by people who probably only met him once.

The man responsible for all this, Gilley, sometimes Captain, is probably Clement Gilley of Troston, despite his description as 'of Hopton' at Banham (Hopton and Troston are close). There are no Gilleys in the records of Hopton, but a Clement Gilley paid Ship Money in 1639–40 at Troston and Ixworth Thorpe, and he heads the list of 'able men' in the 1638 militia muster list.[14] He was the eldest son of John Gilley, yeoman, of Troston (died 1630) and Amy his wife (1638).[15] The Gilleys had been millers at Ixworth since the sixteenth century. As for 'Captain' Gilley, there was no-one of that name and rank in the Suffolk Regiment.

At Troston, Gilley's home, the bells were recast in 1868, but Thomas Martin in about 1740 had no difficulty in recording the pre-Reformation inscriptions on three bells, one a prayer to Katherine and another to Mary Magdalene. The porch, too, has four flushwork panels along its parapet which ought to have given offence, each crowned: an elaborate T (for Trinity perhaps?); IHS; *merci*; and MR. It looks as though Gilley passed over his own parish church rather as Dowsing seems to have ignored inscriptions at Stratford St Mary, his home parish. Davy's collections for Gilley's home deanery (Blackbourn) yield no more instances of iconoclasm, except extensive damage to the font at Badwell Ash.[16]

It is important not to concentrate on bell-damage to the exclusion of the destruction of images in glass: as at Bressingham, both tasks would have been carried out, side by side. There are indications, however, that Gilley seems not to have been as vigilant for the far more accessible inscriptions on monumental brasses: the illustrations in Cotman's *Norfolk Brasses* provide no examples of inscriptions trimmed of the *Orate pro anima/animabus* and *cuius anime/quorum animabus* parts, so easily accomplished on the marginal fillet on which they are often included.*A recent search has found just three parishes outside Norwich, in addition to Ashwellthorpe, which have the erasure of opening prayer clauses on foot inscriptions, a far smaller proportion of parishes than in neighbouring counties.[17]

Dowsing's commission gave him freedom to act throughout the counties of the Eastern Association, and included the power to appoint deputies. Gilley seems, on the evidence of bell-damage, to have operated in two counties, perhaps working first in a few parishes close to his home in

*Since this was written, further work has been carried out which tends to confirm Dr Blatchly's supposition. See appendix 13.

Suffolk, later moving up into Norfolk with a commission from Dowsing to cover a good deal of that county. The surviving churchwardens' accounts in the south of the county support this general picture, the only puzzle being the accounts at Garboldisham, right in his path, which record nothing to suggest iconoclasm.[18] But nearby is Wilby, where the communion rails are of similar appearance to other woodwork in the church dated 1637 and were probably erected shortly after the church caught fire in 1633: if these are genuinely pre-Commonwealth, they are an unexpected survival to find in the middle of Gilley's territory, and (combined with the negative evidence of Garboldisham) may indicate that he was not as thorough as he might have been.[19]

How far did Gilley range into Norfolk? It is under twenty miles to Denton, Ashwellthorpe, West Bradenham and Swaffham, the furthest outposts of bell-damage, or his name recorded as visitor. Further afield the northernmost mention of a visitor (anonymous) is at North Elmham which is within range of Swaffham and the Bradenhams. This suggests that Gilley dealt with a wide swathe of south Norfolk, but that he did not penetrate to the north of the county.

Unfortunately it is difficult to confirm this hypothesis, as almost all the surviving churchwardens' accounts in rural Norfolk for this period are from the south; there are two exceptions, North Walsham and Bale, both near the north coast. At the former, a grand town church, the accounts are ambiguous, but would suggest damage to the glass well before 1643 and 1644, the period when Dowsing and his colleagues were at work: there is no significant medieval glass today. In the accounts at the latter church, Bale, there is no iconoclasm recorded and no sums of a size to indicate repairs after iconoclasm, and here there is still a large window made up of medieval glass of the highest quality and interest.

Bale is not unique in this respect: it is noteworthy that similar substantial survivals are found elsewhere in and close to the Hundred of Holt, as at Stody, Salle and Wighton, with significant remains also at Blakeney, Field Dalling, Cley and Kelling (Map 8.3).[20] At Letheringsett, the medieval glass now in the church came from the summer-house in the Hall gardens, suggesting how the church windows may have survived iconoclasm. At Sharrington, next to Bale, Dr Edmund Newdigate reported remarkable glass still entire in 1735. Overall, of the 27 remaining churches in Holt Hundred, medieval glass can be seen today in six churches, and antiquarian notes of the 1730s (which for this hundred are easily accessible) show that there were then superstitious displays in glass or wood in a further six.[21]

Further to the east, at Heydon, Cawston, Lammas, and Marsham, Blomefield described glass remaining in the eighteenth century, albeit not all in

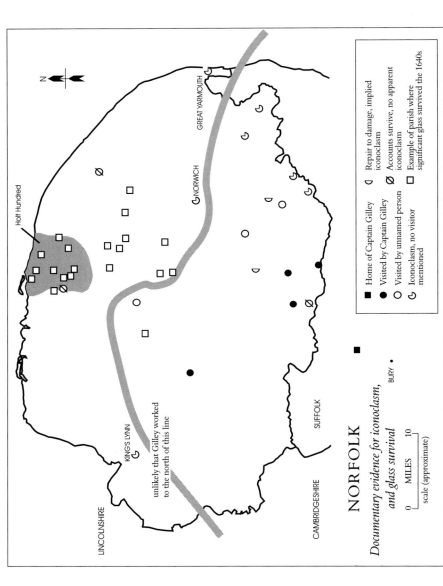

NORFOLK

*Documentary evidence for iconoclasm,
and glass survival*

| | | | |
|---|---|---|---|
| ■ | Home of Captain Gilley | ᕱ | Repair to damage, implied iconoclasm |
| ● | Visited by Captain Gilley | Ø | Accounts survive, no apparent iconoclasm |
| ○ | Visited by unnamed person | □ | Example of parish where significant glass survived the 1640s |
| ᕱ | Iconoclasm, no visitor mentioned | | |

LINCOLNSHIRE

Holt Hundred

KING'S LYNN

unlikely that Gilley worked
to the north of this line

NORWICH

GREAT YARMOUTH

SUFFOLK

CAMBRIDGESHIRE

BURY ●

0   MILES   10

scale (approximate)

*Map 8.3* Documentary evidence for 1644 iconoclasm in Norfolk, and examples of glass which survived the period.

perfect order, but it had escaped destruction. At about the same time, a little to the south, Martin recorded good glass at Ringland, much of which has since disappeared, as also at Guestwick; at Elsing he commented that 'the East Window has been beautifully adorn'd with painting, and indeed so have all about the church which were never broken by design, but suffered to fall to ruin by the Incuriousness of the Parishioners'.[22] Good glass was also noted by him at nearby North Tuddenham just before the then incumbent removed it to allow more light into the church (what is there today may be from Lyng). Nearby Mileham retains a good west window. The incomparably fine roof angels at Knapton are original and in very good condition.

The survival of such material *in extenso* suggests that iconoclasm was patchy or non-existent in the north of the county. It would require a full study of the history of the glass in each parish in the county to *prove* that iconoclasm was more uneven in the north than the south, though one recent handlist of surviving Norfolk glass certainly gives that impression.[23] Further support to this view is given by plotting the survival of images of Mary in glass (for a fine example, see Plate 64). Map 8.4 shows that there is a clear preponderance to the north (and a small cluster south of Norwich).[24] It seems that, either because of a shortage of manpower or the will to carry it out, Gilley and the cleansing did not reach far north of Norwich.

No other visitor than Gilley is named in churchwardens' accounts anywhere in the county. However energetic he may have been, he would have needed assistance to cover the more than six hundred churches. In Suffolk Dowsing needed ten men to help him with just over five hundred churches. There are perhaps clues as to how the operation was performed in the accounts of two parishes which are well within the Gilley arc, which carried out iconoclasm, but where there are no records of a visitor:

*Besthorpe 1643–44*
For glasinge the Church windowes & for Irons . . . . . . . . . . o 10 08
Layd out when the townsmen w't to Norwich **to pout the articles before the Lord of Manchesters Committee** for our expencis . . . . . . . . . . . . . . . . . . . . . . . . o 03 00

*Fritton 1643–44*
Ite' for glasinge the windowes in the Church . . . . . . . . . . . 1 08 00
It' to Mr Sayer for **writinge the answers to diverse gen[er]all Art[icl]es sent by the Earle of Manchester to our towne, twise over**, and our accomptes writing . . . . . o 05 00

Perhaps in order to cover some churches for which no arrangements about visiting had been made, bureaucracy took over. Articles, it seems, had to be written in duplicate, and laid before the Norwich Committee. The

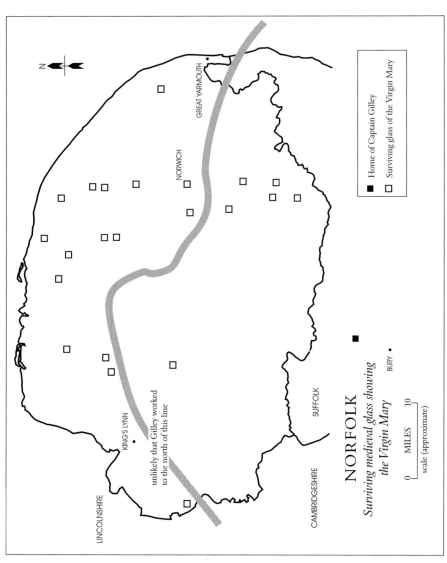

NORFOLK
*Surviving medieval glass showing
the Virgin Mary*

LINCOLNSHIRE

KING'S LYNN ·

unlikely that Gilley worked
to the north of this line

GREAT YARMOUTH ·

NORWICH

SUFFOLK

CAMBRIDGESHIRE

BURY ·

0 ____ MILES ____ 10
scale (approximate)

■ Home of Captain Gilley
□ Surviving glass of the Virgin Mary

*Map 8.4* Surviving medieval glass in Norfolk which shows the Virgin Mary (annunciation or coronation).

second copy could have been retained by the churchwardens for comparison with the office copy when, later, someone did come to see that the work had been completed as certified. (Certificates similar to this are required by the 1641 Order of Parliament, but not by the 1643 Ordinance.) At Harleston, chapel of ease to Redenhall, there is an entry in the churchwardens' accounts which might almost have been copied from the rubric of the articles:

> There be fyve things are thowght each of them to make the Inventions of men very unconvenyent & burthensome and soe not to be used.
>
> > fyrst. yf ther be noe necessarye use of them.
> > second. yf they swerve from some patterne w'h may be had in such things in scripture.
> > third. yf they be thinges have bene or are abused to superstitions.
> > fourth. yf they have significac'on put uppon them by men.
> > fyft. yf they be fraudulous in the use of them.
>
> yf any such thinge bee at pr'sent in the Church, or happen to be hereafter; avoyd the use of them w'th as much convenyency as may be vale.

## The cleansing of churches in Norwich, Yarmouth and King's Lynn

Within the city of Norwich, churches were dealt with in quite another way, as Blomefield relates from the city records.[25] Most of the churchwardens of the city churches were loyal to Parliament, particularly those who held the top offices, two sheriffs and mayor, during the Civil War and the Interregnum. Thus such churchwardens' accounts as survive make no mention of visitors; they record without comment what it cost to put things in order, including the reglazing of windows after the images had been removed.[26]

On 10 January 1644, committees to view the churches for pictures and crucifixes were appointed, it being ordered that

> sheriff Toft, Messrs Lindsey, Puckle, Sherwood and Greenwood, Aldermen; Mr Kett, John Knight, Messrs Allen, Brewster, Craske, Davy and Rye,[27] or three or four of them, shall from time to time meet together, and repair to the several churches in this city and view the same, and take notice of such scandalous pictures, crucifixes, and images, as are yet remaining in the same churches, and demolish or cause them to be demolished, and also to take the names of all such persons as can give any information of any misdemeanours of scandalous ministers, and to certifye from time to time their doings therein to the maior and the rest of the deputy lieutenants in the said city, at the councell chamber, who are agreed to sit there every Tuesday and Thursday in the afternoon, to receive their informations, concerning the same, and to proceed further therein, as the cause shall require.

Blomefield continues:

> Upon this, these new constituted reformers, relying on the support of their soldiers, began to view the churches, deface the monuments, break the windows, file the bells, dash in pieces the carved works, and reave the brasses off the stones and monuments; and in short by the forwardness of Toft, who was ringleader of the rabble, but little escaped his felonious hands, when he had once got a taste of the value of the brasses he pulled off, the cathedral affording him above a hundred; all which he seized, thereby defacing the memory of the ancestors of many of the most ancient and worshipful families in the county; pulling down the pulpit in the Green Yard, and placing it in the New-hall Green, which had lately been the Artillery Yard.

It is noteworthy that filing the bells is mentioned. The only damaged bell in a Norwich church today came, already mutilated, from a country parish.[28]

Toft, Lindsey and Greenwood were the prime movers in all that followed. Matthew Lindsey was the 'Linsey' of the committee, a grocer, who died during his mayoralty in 1650. Thomas Toft, sheriff in 1643, was another grocer, of St Clement's parish, an Independent in religion, and still conducting civil marriages as late as 1657; he was extreme in his political views and actions.[29] For his Puritan zeal he was put out of his aldermanship at the Restoration, although he had been mayor in 1654.

That the men given these responsibilities were fired with enthusiasm for the work appears by several accounts. They gave Bishop Joseph Hall a hard time even before he was expelled from his palace. He wrote and published his own account of the proceedings later, in May 1647.[30] He tells how Sheriff Toft and Alderman Lindsey, 'attended by many zealous fellows', visited his private chapel looking for superstitious pictures and relics of popery. There was argument here as fierce, but not as erudite, as Dowsing met at Pembroke College in Cambridge.

> They sent for me, to let me know that they found those windows full of images, which were very offensive, and must be demolished. I told them that they were the pictures of some ancient and worthy bishops, as St Ambrose, Austin, &c. It was answered me, that they were so many popes; and one younger man amongst them (Townsend, as I perceived afterwards) would take upon himself to defend that every diocesan bishop was pope. I answered him with some scorn; and obtained leave that I might, with the least loss and defacing of the windows, give order for taking off that offence; which I did by causing the heads of those pictures to be taken off, since I knew the bodies could not offend.

The bishop went on to describe what Toft, Lindsey and Greenwood did in the Cathedral: that story has been often told.[31] They saw the advantage of making a public show of their discharging the Ordinance. On 9 March the

Court, sitting in the Guildhall in the market, gave the order and 'seven popish pictures taken from St Swithin's church, the angel and four evangelists from St Peter's, Moses and Aaron, and the four evangelists from the Cathedral, together with some other superstitious paintings, were publickly burnt in the market'.[32] This followed a mock-religious procession, described by Joseph Hall:

> … vestments, both copes and surplices, together with the leaden cross which had newly been sawed down from over the Green Yard pulpit, and the singing books and the service books, were carried to the fire in the public market place, a lewd wretch walking before the train in his cope trailing in the dirt, with a service book in his hand, imitating in an impious scorn the tune, and usurping the words of the litany used formerly in the church. Near the public cross, all these monuments of idolatry must be sacrificed to the fire; not without much ostentation of a zealous joy, in discharging ordnance, to the cost of some, who professed how much they had longed to see that day. Neither was it any news, upon this guild-day, to have the cathedral, now open on all sides, to be filled with musketeers, waiting for the Mayor's return, drinking and tobacconing as freely as if it had turned an ale-house.

Most of the churchwardens' accounts of the Norwich churches of the time reveal something of interest (see appendix 8). Several churches needed a whole 'case' of glass to replace broken windows. At St John Maddermarket, work on the windows was phased and those 'below' cost less than the upper, perhaps because they were more accessible. The small sum for the painter at this church could have paid for a good deal of obliteration of offending images, saving the great expense of reglazing. At St Gregory's, money was spent on 'mending holes with the old painted glass', another way of dealing selectively and economically with the work. So much had been cleansed in Edwardian times at St Mary Coslany that the cost of further reglazing here was small. At St Andrew's the accounts do not survive, but two brasses have been recorded with the opening prayer phrase removed.[33] At St Peter Mancroft one of the churchwardens was the Royalist John Uttinge: he was Mayor in 1647, until in April that year his supporters blew up the Committee House in Bethel Street (damaging St Peter Mancroft in the blast) and he was exiled to his house at Brandon, then put in the Fleet. At this fine church something of a compromise must have been reached: how else should there be so much early glass left, almost enough to fill the great east window?[34] But of the crucified Christ, all but the feet had to be removed.

There was some resistance: the minister at St Laurence and St Mary Coslany chose a fast day, during the month that the committee for iconoclasm was appointed, to preach a sermon in which he 'rayled on them that were the executioners of parliamentary ordinances in demolishing scandalous pictures and said they were base domineering fellows w'ch scandalised the ministers of God and abused the temples of the Lord'.[35] Perhaps it was harder to find one scandalous who had declared himself scandalised: Charles Davill, the minister, knew that attack was the best defence. He surely had something to do with saving the twelve brasses at his church, all found loose in the vestry by Farrer a century ago.[36]

As at Norwich, so too at Great Yarmouth there was no need for Parliamentary visitors. With so many loyal to Parliament in that town there would have been no shortage of enthusiasts for the work of cleansing, though the crosses came down rather late, in the April–June quarter of 1644, and the steps between July and September. The main interest of the entries here is the full account of what was involved in 'takeing downe the steppings of the Alter' at that godly town. The brasses needed no action: they had all been sent to London in 1551, to be cast into weights and measures.[37]

At King's Lynn, the churchwardens' accounts of St Margaret's (St Nicholas was a chapel of ease)[38] tell what a financial burden the work was, since both buildings have many large windows, now mainly filled with clear glass. The sum of £100 was needed to begin the work, but the accounts do not show whether this proved sufficient, nor how it was applied. Colonel Valentine Walton, the commanding officer of the garrison, was involved twice, once in guaranteeing that no precedent was set by the order for raising the money, later in providing soldiers to accompany the assessors as they visited tax defaulters. Three years after the order was made, there were uncollected arrears of over £38. It is interesting that the epitaphs were not tackled before 1645, and then not thoroughly. The Latin marginal inscriptions of the enormous Flemish-made Attelathe and Braunche brasses are perfect still: perhaps such inscriptions were a matter of indifference to all but the most enthusiastic reformer.

Thus in Norfolk we find a spectrum of responses to the Parliamentary demands. They range from enthusiastic iconoclasm organised by the authorities (Norwich), through grudging compliance by taxpayers (King's Lynn), attempted damage-limitation by local folk (Bressingham, Ashwellthorpe), to lassitude and inactivity in the absence of external impetus (north of the county). To the south there was Captain Gilley, actively enforcing the required reformation. He must have met the full range of reactions: but to any personal authority he possessed, he could add that of the Earl of Manchester, commander of the Eastern Association Army.

# 9

# Iconoclasm in other counties of the Eastern Association

*Trevor Cooper*

DOWSING RECORDS VISITS to just two counties, Cambridgeshire and Suffolk, yet his commission allowed him to roam freely over all seven counties of the Eastern Association. Did he? And if not, were visits carried out by others under his authority ('such as hee shall appoint')[1] or assigned directly by Manchester? In the previous chapter John Blatchly discussed events in Norfolk, and in this chapter we examine the evidence for Essex, Lincolnshire, Huntingdonshire and Hertfordshire. We shall see that the signs point to considerable iconoclasm in all these counties during 1643–44, some of it – possibly most – instigated by visitors. The lack of an iconoclast's Journal must not mislead us into thinking that these were quiet backwaters outside the mainstream of organised image smashing.

However, despite a thorough trawl of the churchwardens' accounts, no sign of Dowsing's personal involvement has been found. It must be admitted that initially the failure to catch our man at work outside his Journal was something of a disappointment (though it would have raised doubts about the completeness of the Journal). This was soon overcome by the intrinsic interest of the material collected during the search. The conclusions offered here are exploratory and tentative, but it is hoped that they may serve as pointers to future work.

*Map 9.1* Places in Essex discussed in the text.

## Essex

As Bill Cliftlands has shown, Essex was a radical county.[2] As early as summer 1640, well before any Parliamentary Order, there were anti-communion-rail riots. Soldiers were 'taking it upon themselves to reforme Churches, and even in tyme of divine service to pull down the Rayles about the Communion Table'.[3] In October that year, at Halstead, one Robert Howard 'rushed up to the desk where Mr Carter, the curate, was reading the baptismal service at the font, struck the prayer book out of his hand and, with several others, kicked it about, saying "it was a popish book"'.[4] By 1642 some parishes had illegally discontinued use of the surplice, 'the Ragges of Rome' as the garment was described at Chelmsford. Cliftlands emphasises, however, how difficult it is to know how widely the Parliamentary Order of 1641 was obeyed, and whether it was welcomed with open arms even at those parishes which did carry out its requirements: so whereas at Maldon it was church funds which were used to pay for 'fagotts to burne Popishe bookes & pictures' in January 1643, at Danbury the churchwardens resisted taking action, their obstinacy being described as a 'great griffanc[e] of the people'.[5]

In this volume we are focusing on Dowsing, his deputies, and the work of other agents of the Earl of Manchester, and more generally on iconoclasm in 1643–44. There are a number of parishes in Essex with evidence of iconoclasm of this date (Maps 9.1 and 9.2; Table 9.1). One such is West Ham, where the churchwardens' accounts show the parish acting before 5 November 1643 ('Gunpowderday'), in an attempt to meet the deadline of the first Ordinance:[6]

*West Ham 1643–44*

| | | | |
|---|---|---|---|
| Paid unto the Masons for defaceing Images . . . . . . . . . . . . . | 0 | 12 | 06 |
| Paid for 3 doz. of Mr Perkin's Catechismes . . . . . . . . . . . . | 0 | 03 | 04 |
| Paid for taking up of brasse popish peices by an Order from the Parliament . . . . . . . . . . . . . . . . . . . . . . . . . . . . | 0 | 06 | 08 |
| Paid to the Ringers for ringing on Gunpowderday . . . . . . . . | 0 | 16 | 06 |
| Paid to Prentice the bricklayer for defaceing of more Images . . . | 0 | 04 | 00 |
| Paid to Thomas Wager for takeing downe of some popish pictures in the glasse windowes in obedience to an Ordinance of Parliament and for setting up new glasse in the roome thereof . . . . . . . . . . . . . . . . . . . . . . . . . . . | 1 | 16 | 00 |

Maybe this church never needed a visitor, though one might have put in an appearance to check everything was in order (as, for example, Dowsing did at Great Wenham, Journal entry 97).

At Saffron Walden, there was a visitor, but (as elsewhere) the accounts record some action *before* the arrival of Manchester's agent:

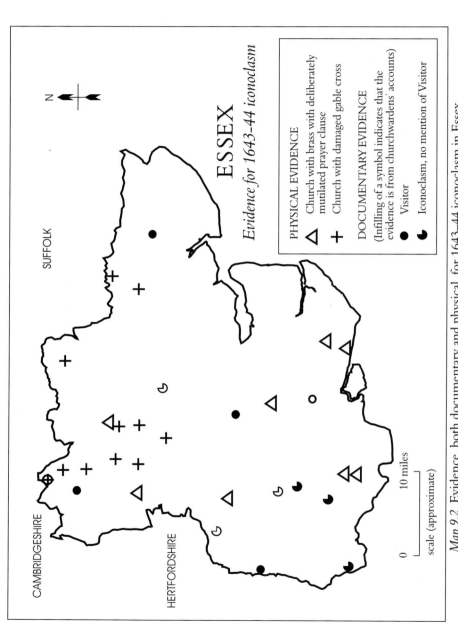

*Map 9.2* Evidence, both documentary and physical, for 1643–44 iconoclasm in Essex.

Table 9.1 *Documentary evidence for 1643–44 iconoclasm in Essex*

| Parish | Document | Evidence shows: |
|---|---|---|
| Braintree | Vestry decision | Iconoclasm |
| Chelmsford | CW accnts | Visitor |
| Great Bromley | CW accnts | Visitor★ |
| Ham, West | CW accnts | Iconoclasm |
| Hornchurch | CW accnts | Iconoclasm |
| | | |
| Latton | Letter | Iconoclasm |
| Navstock | Parish register | Iconoclasm |
| Nevendon | CW accnts | Visitor |
| Saffron Walden | Parish register | Visitor |
| Waltham Holy Cross | CW accnts | Visitor |
| | | |
| Weald, South | CW accnts | Iconoclasm |
| West Ham | CW accnts | Iconoclasm |

★Recorded as 1645, not 1644

*Saffron Walden 1644–45*
It' paid Aprill 9th to Achell Shelford for takeinge down the
    crosses and the Images in the church & to his helpe[r]s . . . . 2 17 06
It' paid to the man that came to view the Church from the Par-
    liament . . . . . . . . . . . . . . . . . . . . . . . . . . . . . 0 10 00

A visitor is not explicitly recorded at Hornchurch, although the Earl of
Manchester is seen as the authority, indicating either a visitor carrying
instructions or the publishing of a formal written order:

*Hornchurch 1642–45*
For Taking Downe the crosse of the Steeple by comand from
    the Earle of Manchester . . . . . . . . . . . . . . . . . . . . 2 05 00
Payd to John Bush the Glazier b'ys Bill due . . . . . . . . . . . 2 13 00
For taking up of Sup'stitious inscripcons of brasse and beating
    downe other things according to an order from the Earle of
    Manchester . . . . . . . . . . . . . . . . . . . . . . . . . . . 0 07 00

Over the whole county, just seven churchwardens' accounts survive for
our period.[7] Four of these record payments to a visitor, three of them during
April–June 1644.[8] None of these men is known to be associated with
Dowsing; in this county we do not have the advantage of the allocation list
which provides a link between Dowsing and his deputies in Suffolk. The

Table 9.2 *Essex brasses in which the prayer clause has been
deliberately and selectively mutilated*

| Church and brass★ | Type of damage (CC = closing clause) |
| --- | --- |
| Elsenham (I) | prayer scroll erased |
| Finchingfield (I) | CC marked out for removal |
| Hanningfield, West (I) | CC hatched and marked out for removal |
| Laver, High (I) | CC hatched |
| Leigh, near Rochford (I) | CC hatched |
| Ockendon, North (I) | CC hatched |
| Ockendon, South (I) | CC hatched |
| Rochford (I) | CC hatched |

★The roman numeral in brackets indicates which brass at the church is referred to,
cross-referencing to Stephenson, *List of Monumental Brasses*.

remaining three accounts show no payment to an external agent, but money
is spent on deliberate damage. In churches which Dowsing is known to have
visited, only one third of the surviving accounts record a payment to a visitor,
so it is not unrealistic to argue that all seven of the Essex churches were in
fact visited.[9] Indeed, to the extent that the existing churchwardens' accounts
are random survivals, the evidence suggests that a significant proportion of
Essex churches may have suffered from iconoclasm, and perhaps from
Parliamentary visitors, at this time.[10] To the churchwardens' accounts can be
added documentary evidence of the period from four other parishes, all
showing iconoclasm, and adding Nevendon to the list of those definitely
visited.[11] Unfortunately, the surviving evidence is biased to the north and
west of the county, so what happened to the south and east is unknown.[12]

   In addition to this documentary evidence, there is evidence in the fabric,
of the type discussed in chapter 7. The fonts at Althorne, Great Clacton,
Stanway and Wrabness may have been deliberately damaged, and there are
probably others. Font damage, however, is not a certain indicator of damage
of our period.[13] More usefully, there are six churches known to us where
prayer clauses have been scratched out or cut out of a brass (see Table 9.2),
and two more where the prayer clauses are marked ready for an excision
which was never executed: did the visitor do the marking and leave the rest
for the churchwardens?[14] Additionally, the stumps of gable crosses have
been recorded by the Royal Commission on Historical Monuments at a
cluster of churches in the north of the county (Ashdon, Bardfield Saling,
Belchamp Otton, Boxted, Great Bardfield, West Bergholt) and there are
damaged remains at Little Dunmow and Wimbish;[15] probably many other

churches have not even a stump left, or have had the cross replaced, as we have noted so frequently in Suffolk (for example, Layham, Journal entry 94). These excised brass inscriptions and damaged gable crosses provide further evidence of iconoclasm during the early 1640s, the crosses almost certainly of 1643–44, and the incised inscriptions probably so. Finally, in appendix 13 we show that the extent to which brass inscriptions disappeared after the 1630s is consistent with iconoclasm in the following decade.

The overall picture in Essex seems to be one of an early, not to say premature, start in 1640–41, but with many churches requiring – or, at least, receiving – a further Puritan workover in 1643–44, often encouraged by visitors. Some churches, though, may have escaped iconoclasm. The now-demolished church of Hazeleigh, St Nicholas retained its early-seventeenth-century altar rails, and Hadstock and Tilty have undamaged gable crosses; at Thaxted a gable crucifix survived.[16] None of these, however, guarantees that the church did not suffer in other ways.

## Lincolnshire

It has only been possible to scratch the surface in Lincolnshire.[17] One sign of 1640s iconoclasm is absent, no cases having been found of brass inscriptions with the opening or closing clauses removed.[18] Nor have any bells been recorded as suffering deliberate damage.[19] On the other hand, the county is by no means rich in glass, though there are hardly any reports of iconoclasm.[20] The absence of RCHME volumes makes it difficult to track other indicators of 1640s iconoclasm, such as damaged gable crosses or surviving communion rails.[21]

In the whole county we have located just one surviving set of churchwardens' accounts for 1641–44, for Louth, St James.[22] This is a large church in a central town, and the accounts are particularly full.[23] Nevertheless, their interpretation is frustrating. To begin with, there is no obvious expenditure on pulling down the communion rails, unless it was the unspecified but suggestive work carried out one day in 1641, when a man was paid 1s. 6d. 'for one dayes work about the communion Table & laying at the new bridge two peeces of wood'.[24] Also ambiguous is the significant expenditure on new glass in 1644. This would normally indicate repairs after iconoclasm, but there had been similar expenditure in 1641, so the 1644 work may be part of a rolling programme, not connected with the removal of images. Alternatively, there may have been two distinct waves of glass-smashing in the town, in both 1641 and 1644: the earlier year did see the populist breaking of windows elsewhere. There is one secure indication of iconoclasm in the 'taking downe the cross over the south porch' after midsummer 1644, but even this is weakened by the survival of a wreath of thorns as a gable cross.[25]

Eighty years later it was believed – or thought useful to claim – that significant damage had been caused during this period, the preamble to a subscription list of 1720 stating that 'the pews and seats as well as the pavement thereof were very much ruinated in the time of our unfortunate civil wars, and never since regularly mended, some or most of them being the same as they were [left] by those enemies of our place of devotion'.[26] But this sounds less like iconoclasm than rough handling on the part of the soldiery, perhaps coupled with some brass-lifting (Pevsner records no brasses today).

As things stand, we have no evidence of visitors in Lincolnshire, and precious little evidence of iconoclasm. Understanding what deliberate damage to churches was carried out during the early 1640s needs considerably more work.

## Huntingdonshire

*Robert Walker writes*: West of the old Cambridgeshire lies Huntingdonshire, home of Cromwell and Manchester.

Documentary evidence here is scarce, there being only three surviving sets of churchwardens' accounts. Two of the three show iconoclasm (the removal of images) and the third records repairs to glass. This pattern is perfectly compatible with the arrival of Parliamentary visitors, but does not prove it, and the small surviving sample would make it dangerous to generalise across the county.[27]

A broad survey of the fabric of the churches in the county is inconclusive. In the whole county there is not one *Orate* inscription or superstitious image in brass, although it is plain that many once existed.[28] The loss of brasses has been notably high in this county, with 133 lost brasses out of a total recorded number of 172.[29] Against this, there are some significant survivals of glass, notably at Wistow and Diddington, which would seem to exceed in completeness any glazing in the areas Dowsing is known to have visited; and in general the survival of images in wood is significant, whether in the form of the roof angels at, for example, Buckden, Alconbury and Ellington, or bench beasts and angels at, for instance, Godmanchester and Eynesbury. Early-seventeenth-century communion rails survive at Great Gidding.[30]

The most obvious oddity is at Kimbolton, Manchester's parish church. There survives the best painted, sainted screen in the county.

## Hertfordshire

Hertfordshire saw trouble at Rickmansworth (Map 9.3) after service one Sunday in August 1640, when Captain Aylee 'did there riotously and suddenly pull downe and breake in peeces the rayles about the Comunion Table, and... breake down and defaced part of the cover of the font', in company with a group of other soldiers. That night he spoke more freely in the White Hart than was perhaps wise, and antagonistic witnesses reported that he claimed that he had previously 'broken with his own hand' the communion rails at seventeen churches in the county. Under questioning later that week he was quick to deny this and other statements as being made in the 'heat of drinke'. Some of his drunken claims were undoubtedly wild (he claimed to have five hundred soldiers ready to do his command), and it seems unlikely that this glazier turned temporary soldier had destroyed rails in anything like the quantity he boasted about or would have liked.[31]

For the period 1643–45, there are just five sets of churchwardens' accounts (Map 9.4). Two mention a visitor, though not Dowsing. One of these (St Albans, St Peter's) is discussed in a previous chapter.[32] The other accounts are from Bishop's Stortford:

*Bishop's Stortford 1643/4*
Paid to John Pegrume for worke & stuffe to mend the church-
    wyndowes . . . . . . . . . . . . . . . . . . . . . . . . . . . . . . . . 0 11 70
Paid to John Eve for glazing the church wyndowes . . . . . . . . 1 13 04
Paid for 300 of payving tyles [for the chancel perhaps?] . . . . . 2 01 06
Paid for the charges when we went to take the covenant . . . . . 0 06 00
Paid for taking downe the crosse & for putting the wearther-
    cocke uprighte & for ironwork . . . . . . . . . . . . . . . . . 3 03 04
Paid to the Earle of Manchester his officer . . . . . . . . . . . . . 0 01 06

At this church some remains of glass survived the 'Earle of Manchester his officer', probably until 1709, when a gallery was erected and the chancel 'beautified'.[33]

Of the other three accounts, those at Baldock include expenditure of 3s. 4d. for 'pulling downe the glasse in the church by Manchesters command' (there are fragments of glass remaining in the east window of the north chapel),[34] and at Thundridge and Ashwell expenditure is recorded on glass repairs. This pattern of evidence could well have occurred if all five churches had been visited.[35] The number of examples is by itself too small to say how widespread was iconoclasm.

In appendix 13 we show that the county lost almost as many brass inscriptions between the early seventeenth and early eighteenth centuries as Cambridgeshire and Suffolk, consistent with 1640s iconoclasm. However,

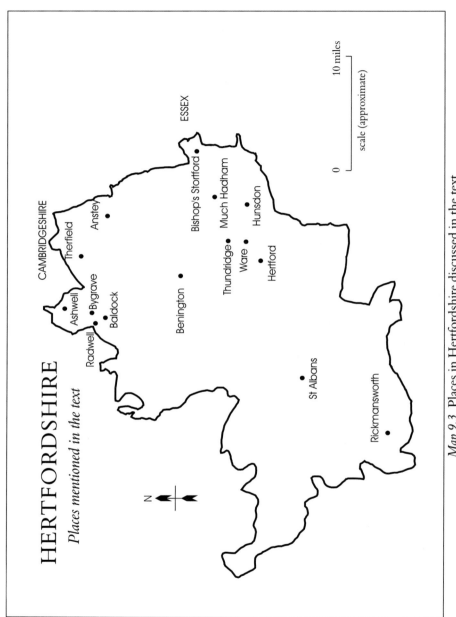

*Map 9.3* Places in Hertfordshire discussed in the text.

Hertfordshire is exceptional in one respect: based on Philip Whittemore's
initial analysis, it seems that at some 25 churches there are (or have been)
brasses which had the opening or, more usually, closing prayer clause of the
inscription deliberately removed (Table 9.3). If so, this represents one in five
churches, a quite remarkably high proportion.[36] Indeed, the number of cases
in this relatively small county is higher than the known examples in all the
other counties of the Eastern Association combined, including the giant
counties to the east.[37] In an earlier chapter we have argued that this form of
damage is almost certainly limited to the early 1640s.* But in Hertfordshire
we can go further, for such unusual uniformity of action across just one
administrative area, not spreading widely into its neighbours, must surely
indicate some form of central control rather than the dictates of fashion.
Furthermore, by great good fortune one of the few sets of churchwardens'
accounts to survive in the county (that for St Albans, St Peter's) explicitly
mentions a visitor coming to remove 'popish sentences', records payment to
help him 'cute them off', and the church contained a (now lost) brass with
part of the inscription removed. If there was central control, and a visitor was
responsible in 1644 at one of the few churches with documentation, it is
hard to avoid the conclusion that those other churches in the county which
have inscriptions partially obliterated were similarly visited.[38]

If so, were these twenty-five the *only* churches in the county to be visited,
especially selected in some way? It seems unlikely. There is no particular
geographical pattern in their distribution: they are found in countryside and
town, and across the whole county. Nor does it seem that the incumbents of
these churches were singled out for being of the opposite wing of the church
to the Puritans.[39] It is more likely that a great many churches in the county
were visited, and that these are a random sample which bear a particular type
of scar.

There is no evidence that Dowsing was involved in this. On balance it is
improbable. Three of the five Hertfordshire accounts, those for churches
lying in the north-east of the county, show damage occurring before Easter
1644 (21 April), a period when Dowsing has few gaps of any length in his
Journal. And it would be strange if an iconoclast of his professionalism and
expertise suddenly decided to make his life more complicated by insisting on
partial removal of inscriptions as a matter of routine. Of the approximately
270 parish churches and college chapels known to have suffered Dowsing's
attention, this form of damage is found in only eight,[40] the evidence suggesting that at his visitation it was more normal for the entire inscription,

---

*Chapter 7. But see closing note at the end of that chapter.

Table 9.3 *Hertfordshire brasses in which the prayer clause has been deliberately and selectively mutilated*

| Church and brass | Clause* | | Damage* | | Comment |
|---|---|---|---|---|---|
| | Op | Cl | Rem | Hat | |
| Abbotts Langley (I) | | • | • | | |
| Aldenham (VIII) | | • | • | | |
| Aldenham (IX) | | • | • | | |
| Aldenham (XI) | | • | • | | |
| Ardeley (I) | | • | | • | |
| Ardeley (II) | | • | | • | |
| Ardeley (n/a) | | • | | • | William Cortysmore (lost) |
| Aspenden (II) | • | • | • | | |
| Berkhampstead, Great (VII) | | • | • | | |
| Buckland (II) | | • | | • | Partial closing damage |
| Buckland (III) | • | | | • | Partial hatched |
| Clothall (I) | | • | | • | |
| Clothall (II) | | • | | • | Additional damage |
| Clothall (III) | | | | | Details not available |
| Gaddesden, Great (I) | | • | • | | |
| Flamstead (I) | | • | • | | |
| Hadham, Little (I) | | • | | • | |
| Harpenden (I) | | • | • | | |
| Hitchen (II) | | • | • | | |
| Hitchen (III) | • | | • | | |
| Hitchen (n/a) | • | • | • | | Nicholas Matlock |
| Ippolyts (I) | | • | • | | |
| Knebworth (I) | | • | • | | |
| King's Langley (I) | • | • | • | | |
| Mimms, North (II) | | • | | • | |
| Royston (V) | | • | • | | |
| St Albans, St Michael (IV) | | • | • | | |
| St Albans, St Peter | | • | • | | Discussed p. 104 |
| Sawbridgeworth (n/a) | | | | • | See note |
| Shephall (I) | | • | • | | |

Table 9.3 *(cont)*

| Church and brass | Clause★ | | Damage★ | | Comment |
|---|---|---|---|---|---|
| | Op | Cl | Rem | Hat | |
| Standon (I) | | ● | ● | | |
| Standon (IV) | | ● | ● | | |
| Stevenage (I) | | ● | ● | | |
| Willian (I) | | ● | ● | | |
| Wormley (I) | | ● | | ● | |
| | | | | | |
| Wormley (II) | | ● | | ● | |
| Wormley (n/a) | | ● | | ● | Richard Ruston (lost) |
| Wormley (n/a) | ● | | | ● | Edw. Sharnbrook (lost) |

★The columns headed 'Clauses' and 'Damage' indicate whether it was the opening or clos-ing prayer clause which was removed, and whether the type of damage was removal of the clause or hatching.

At Sawbridgeworth there was an effigy of a priest in academics, *c.*1480 (now lost). A small portion of the scroll remaining had a word hatched out.

or even the entire brass, to be lifted. Hertfordshire has fewer than half as many medieval churches as are in the Journal and more than three times as many partially excised brasses.

Some forbidden objects have survived. Ware, for example, retains a font full of superstitious carvings in excellent condition. Bygrave and Radwell have early-seventeenth-century communion rails, and so did Benington until they were moved to the south chapel of Ware.[41] However, as discussed in an earlier chapter, although suggestive, this type of evidence does not prove the church was untouched.[42]

Elsewhere resistance is recorded. At Hunsdon the minister explained that the failure to remove painted windows was because the 'Lord of Dover' (Henry, Earl of Dover, later buried at the church) wanted to ensure that 'the Coate armes might be preserved'.[43] Today the church has various badges and crests in the windows. Perhaps also as a result of the minister's reluctance, six apostles remain in the head of a nave window, and in the tracery of the east window an Annunciation and Adoration of 1440–50 are preserved, unusual survivals for this part of the world.[44] Although the communion rails here are post-Restoration, the early-seventeenth-century screen remains, dividing the nave from the south chapel, though this 'room-divider' may well not have offended Puritan sensibilities. That a minister could try to resist iconoclasm, at least in the early days, is also shown by John Montfort, Rector of Anstey and Therfield: when his churchwardens and a glazier

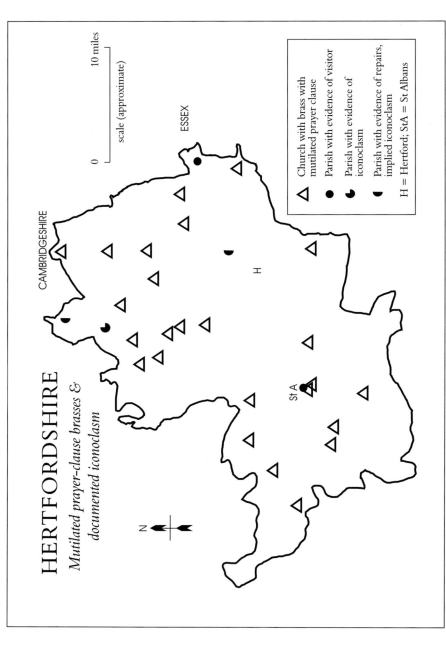

*Map 9.4* Hertfordshire, showing brasses with mutilated prayer clauses, and documentary evidence for 1644 iconoclasm.

pulled down a crucifix and Virgin Mary in the east window, he arrested them![45] And Henry Hancocks, vicar of Furneaux Pelham – a man who said that if the bishops ordered him to wear a kettle on his head, he would do it – walked the churchyard at night, sword in hand, to prevent the pulling up of communion rails.

Equally direct action was taken at Much Hadham, but by the opposite party, and before Parliament had made any Orders on the subject, when on 4 August 1640 three local men broke into the church by 'thrusting back the bar' and 'did beat downe the glasse windowe at the East end of the Chancel with a pike they found in the churche and… pulled up and sawed and beat in peeces the rales that were set about the communion table'.[46] They also used 'peeces of the said rayles' to break the glass. One local man pointedly asked what the vicar would bow to now, 'the Rales being broaken and whether he would bow to the holes'. The vicar, Thomas Paske, Master of Clare College,[47] where Laudian furnishings had been introduced into the chapel, offered to withdraw proceedings if the damage was reinstated, though with what result we do not know.[48] One's image of sturdy Puritans being valiant for truth is perhaps somewhat dented by the discovery that the miscreants were bribed to do their work. Today St Peter and St Andrew and other saints remain at the top of the east window, silent witnesses of the unlicensed thuggery of 1640, the 1641 Parliamentary Order legitimising removal of communion rails, the ejection of Thomas Paske,[49] the 1643 and 1644 Ordinances and subsequent iconoclastic visitation (if there was one), the Restoration (both of the Monarchy and of Paske), and several centuries of improvements and repairs.[50] They should act, too, as reminders of the difficulty of sorting out the history of iconoclasm in a particular church from the fabric alone, and make us even more grateful for the existence of Dowsing's Journal, which helps make sense of damage in so many churches and chapels.

# 10

# The history and nature of the Journal

*Trevor Cooper*

THE ORIGINAL MANUSCRIPT of Dowsing's Journal has been lost, and we are reliant on eighteenth-century transcripts, each of which covers just one county, Cambridge or Suffolk. This chapter describes what is known of the history of the Journal, and what can be deduced about its original form.*

## *The Cambridgeshire entries*

First to be published were the entries for Cambridgeshire, in 1739 (see Fig. 10.1 for summary). They appeared in a short book entitled *The Schismatics delineated from Authentic Vouchers* ('vouchers' here in the older sense of 'witnesses').[1] Appearing under the pseudonym Philalethes Cantabrigiensis, the writer was the Cambridge antiquary and religious historian Zachary Grey (1688–1766).[2]

In this short polemic Grey is writing against a pro-Puritan view of the Civil War and Commonwealth, and to support his arguments he includes two appendices, the second of which he describes as *The Journal of Will. Dowsing, the famed Demolisher of Superstition, in the University, Town and County of Cambridge in the Year 1643. Copied likewise from his Original Manuscript.*[3] He comments: 'Be pleased, Sir, carefully to read over the Journal of Will. Dowsing... and if his Account of the *terrible Havock he made* will not convince

*I am grateful to John Blatchly for elucidating the history of the Suffolk portion of the Journal, and to him, Michael Bundock, John Morrill and Robert Walker for comments on an earlier draft of this chapter. I remain, of course, responsible for any errors or omissions.

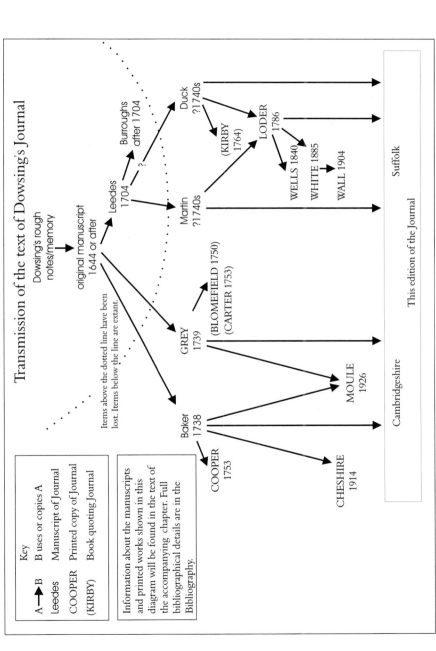

## Transmission of the text of Dowsing's Journal

Dowsing's rough
notes/memory

original manuscript
1644 or after

Leedes
1704

Burroughs
after 1704

?

Duck
?1740s

(KIRBY
1764)

LODER
1786

WELLS 1840

WHITE 1885 → WALL 1904

Martin
?1740s

GREY
1739

(BLOMEFIELD 1750)
(CARTER 1753)

MOULE
1926

Baker
1738

COOPER
1753

CHESHIRE
1914

Suffolk

Cambridgeshire

This edition of the Journal

Items above the dotted line have been
lost. Items below the line are extant.

### Key

A → B    B uses or copies A
Leedes    Manuscript of Journal
COOPER    Printed copy of Journal
(KIRBY)    Book quoting Journal

Information about the manuscripts
and printed works shown in this
diagram will be found in the text of
the accompanying chapter. Full
bibliographical details are in the
Bibliography.

*Fig. 10.1* Transmission of the text of Dowsing's Journal, showing the early split between Cambridgeshire and Suffolk portions.

you, that the *colleges* and *Parishes* (who were fined 40 shillings apiece for not repairing the Damages he had done) had reason to complain of hard usage, I don't know what will'. [4]

The manuscript of the Journal which Grey published was also transcribed by the celebrated Cambridge antiquary Thomas Baker (1656–1740)[5] at more or less the same time, in late 1738 or 1739.[6] Baker's hand-written transcript provides valuable confirmation of the accuracy of Grey's printed text,[7] though Baker deliberately omits names and other non-topographical material included by Grey.[8]

We do not know where Grey and Baker obtained their copy of the Journal, and it has since disappeared. Were they themselves working from a transcript, or had they somehow acquired Dowsing's original manuscript? Certainly Grey believed he was printing from the original. This is explicitly stated on his title page;[9] and elsewhere, in a hand-written note, he describes his copy as 'an original manuscript now in my custody'.[10] Whatever the case, Dowsing's original manuscript is now lost.[11]

Within little more than ten years, selected entries from the Cambridge-shire Journal were being used for topographical purposes by Francis Blome-field (1705–1752),[12] the great historian of Norfolk briefly straying into Cambridgeshire, and by 1753 all the parish entries from the Journal had been reprinted as part of a topography of the county.[13]

## The Suffolk entries

It was to be close to another 50 years before Suffolk historians saw their portion of the Journal printed, though their appetites must have been whetted in 1764 by the publication of the second edition of *The Suffolk Traveller*[14] which quotes from the Journal when describing Ufford and three Ipswich churches.[15] The two principal contributors to this book were Ipswich men, the Revd Richard Canning and Joshua Kirby, whom we will encounter again. It was not until 1786 that Dowsing's full record of destruction in Suffolk appeared in print, published by Robert Loder of Woodbridge.[16] This edition makes no mention of the publication of the Cambridgeshire portion of the Journal half a century earlier, and the two parts of the Journal have remained separate ever since.[17]

Fortunately the hand-written transcript on which Loder's editor based his text has survived, and it gives us important information about the early history of the Journal. The transcript[18] was made for the Suffolk antiquary Thomas Martin of Palgrave (1696–1771)[19] and is a second generation copy, based on an earlier transcript which was taken by the Revd Edward Leedes in 1704.[20] The heading, originally written by Leedes, states:

A true copy of a manuscript found in the Library of Mr Samuel Dowsing of Stratford being written by his Father William Dowsings own hand (carefully and almost literally transcribed Sept 4 1704).

At the foot of his manuscript Martin copies another note originally made by Leedes:

The MSS went no further [i.e. there are no further entries]. It was found amongst the sayd Mr William Dowsing's books sold by his son Mr William Dowsing[21] to Mr Huse a Bookseller at Exeter Change in the Strand, London Septr 1704. He let me [Leedes] transcribe it and I deliver'd the original to him at Ipswich Septr. 6. 1704.

Alongside the heading of the manuscript, Martin adds a marginal note in his own hand explaining how he obtained his copy:

This was copied [from Dowsing's original manuscript] by the Revd Mr Leedes of Ipswich from whose copy my clerk transcribed this [copy]. Note the Revd Mr Burrough[22] of Bradfield took a copy from Mr Leedes also. Query: where that is now and compare them.

Martin's transcript has six deliberate gaps where there should be proper names, no doubt left wherever Leedes' first generation copy had become illegible through age or smudging.[23] Martin probably wanted to locate Burrough's copy in order to fill in these gaps.

It is clear, then, that on the death in 1703 of Samuel Dowsing (the eldest son of the iconoclast) Samuel's library, including his father's manuscript, was sold to a London bookseller by Samuel's half-brother and executor (named William after his father). In September 1704, probably whilst Mr Huse the bookseller was staying in Ipswich after collecting the library, the manuscript was copied by the Revd Leedes, and this copy was itself copied by the Revd Burrough, and later by Thomas Martin. Burrough was an uncle of Martin,[24] and may have mentioned the manuscript to him; whatever the case, Martin arranged to have his own copy taken from the transcript made by Leedes.

Dowsing's library was later sold piecemeal, by Huse or his associates;[25] its contents are discussed by Dr. John Morrill in the introductory essay to this volume. After 6 September 1704 Dowsing's original manuscript is lost to view, unless it was the copy which Baker and Grey saw in Cambridge some thirty years later. The first-generation transcript made by Leedes, and Burrough's copy of this, have also both disappeared.

Martin's copy is thus the only early transcript of the Journal whose provenance is documented. Unfortunately, rather little can be gleaned about the likely date of this important source. We can assume that when the marginal note was written Burrough 'of Bradfield' was dead, or Martin would have known where to apply for it for comparison. Martin's copy was therefore made after 1732. There is a further, slight indication that the copy was made after 1753.[26]

Martin's manuscript was later bound up for the topographer Craven Ord (1756–1832)[27] with a copy of Loder's printed version, and it is now in the Suffolk Record Office.[28] The footnotes to Loder's edition were probably written by Ord,[29] no doubt acting as editor.

By 1786, when Loder published, it seems likely that a number of manuscript copies were in circulation, interest in Dowsing perhaps having been stimulated by the already published Cambridgeshire entries. As it happens, one such manuscript copy has survived,[30] and is now in the library of the Society of Antiquaries of London. Thanks to some exemplary detective work by John Blatchly, the copyist has been identified,[31] and his identification gives further insight into the transmission of the text.

The copyist was Edward Duck, born about 1690, or a little earlier, who in 1710 moved into the parish of St Lawrence, Ipswich. Duck, a brazier, was overseer for the parish in 1711 and churchwarden five times between 1715 and 1739. His second son, Richard was a Foundation Scholar at Ipswich Grammar school from 1719 and thus sat under Edward Leedes who, as we have seen, took the original copy of the Suffolk entries from Dowsing's Journal. The incumbent of Duck's parish was Richard Canning, whom we have already encountered as co-author, with Joshua Kirby, of the revised *Suffolk Traveller*, which quoted a few entries from the Journal in 1764. These quotations come from Duck's copy rather than Martin's,[32] so Canning had obviously seen his parishioner's transcript.

From internal evidence Duck made his transcript in the 1750s, which, as we have seen, may have been the period in which Martin's copy was made. It is notable that Gardner's important *Historical Account of Dunwich, Blithburgh and Southwold,* published at about that time, in 1754,[33] displays complete ignorance of Dowsing's Journal, despite describing the Civil War destruction at Southwold in memorable terms,[34] specifying the damage to brass inscriptions at Blythburgh,[35] and quoting both the Walberswick churchwardens' record of Dowsing's visit and the account of the visit of Jessup, Dowsing's deputy, to Lowestoft.[36] The illustrations to Gardner's book were provided by Joshua Kirby, later to be co-contributor with Canning to *The Suffolk Traveller*, and if Kirby had been aware of the Journal in 1754 he would surely have drawn it to Gardner's attention. Yet, as we have seen, ten years later Canning and Kirby are able to quote from Duck's manuscript, 'which accidentally came into our hands'. What little evidence we have seems to point to the 1750s as the period when awareness of the Suffolk portion of the Journal became widespread amongst local historians.[37]

Although there can be little doubt that Loder's published edition was based on Martin's copy, Loder must have had access to some other copy to have filled in the six deliberate blanks in Martin's manuscript. Duck's copy does not have the six blanks (indicating that it was not derived from Martin's copy), and Loder may have used Duck's copy to fill in the gaps.[38] Supporting this are a number of places where Loder's printed version agrees with Duck against Martin. Given the number of copies likely to be in circulation, it is of course possible that some other copy, now disappeared, was used to fill in the gaps: variants in this third putative version could explain the few places where the printed version disagrees with both Duck and Martin, though it is more likely that these disagreements are caused by carelessness or lack of concern on the part of Craven Ord when editing the text for Loder.[39]

Unfortunately, for some reason, Duck (or a copyist further up his chain of transcripts) decided to smooth Dowsing's rough notes into grammatically correct English, and it is therefore not possible to carry out a word for word comparison of the two texts. However there is agreement between Duck's copy and Martin's copy in virtually every matter of substance, and given their independent transmission subsequent to Leedes this must increase our confidence in the text.

## The nature and structure of the original Journal

The various copies of the Journal are charted in Fig. 10.1. The entries for both counties have been published on several occasions, but always separately. In our edition the entries have been recombined chronologically, a simple task as Dowsing spent blocks of time in each county, and did not casually cross the county boundary.[40] Entries have been kept in their original order, which is largely chronological.

When reconstructed in this way, it can be seen that in places the Journal is not simply a personal record, including as it does the formal record of 'witness George Longe', and Dowsing's comment to some reader other than himself that Crow was 'a deputy' (though that explanation might have been added by a later hand).[41] The circumstantial detail provided in the first few entries in particular gives the impression of a complete and fairly polished account written for the perusal of others, though one which is perhaps less formal than might be expected of any official document. Much of the rest of the text is in more abbreviated form, though more or less complete. In Cambridgeshire, and to a certain extent in Suffolk, Dowsing takes care to record who in each parish is responsible for carrying out his orders, giving the impression that he expects compliance to be confirmed, another indication, perhaps, that this was intended as a semi-official record.[42]

However, although complete, the Journal is for the most part unpolished, and in several respects something of a mess, with the puzzling list of deputies,[43] the stray entry at the end of the Suffolk entries,[44] and the half-completed form for authorising a deputy.[45] Although these particular rough edges might have arisen from Leedes transcribing scattered notes not forming part of the Journal proper, there are other difficulties not so easily explained.

Within the body of the Journal the dated entries themselves are sometimes not in chronological order,[46] those for Cambridge college chapels and churches being quite chaotic (surprisingly so, given the formal nature of the early entries).[47] Within an entry there are repetitions, and entries are not always complete.[48] Most striking of all, the Journal accidentally repeats the entry for five parishes; in each case the duplicate entry is similar to, but not identical with, the initial entry.[49]

All this strongly suggests that Journal entries were written up haphazardly, in batches, from memory, or perhaps from rough notes on odd scraps of paper.[50] Slips of memory would explain much, or hastily written notes may have become out of order, giving rise to misplaced dates, mistranscribed or misremembered names, and accidental duplication (an original note being used twice, expanded slightly differently the second time).[51] Whether written from notes or memory, it is probable that the Journal made extensive use of abbreviations,[52] and there is evidence that the handwriting was bad; we know that, according to the circumstances, Dowsing's hand varied from a very neat printing script to something almost illegible, and all the evidence suggests that the Journal was at the rougher end.[53]

The fullness of the first few Cambridge entries makes it just possible to be persuaded that here we have a very early draft of Dowsing's official report, together with some odd bits and pieces which he never threw away and which Leedes dutifully transcribed. Perhaps Dowsing never produced a polished version of the report, or perhaps it has been lost. But the overall disorganisation and untidiness make it more likely that what emerged from Samuel's library was a rough document created in a slapdash way at the time of the events recorded, or pieced together later, without too much care, from scribbled notes on individual pieces of paper.[54]

We know that Dowsing wrote entries for Suffolk and Cambridgeshire. Did he create separate sections reporting progress in each county or were the entries in chronological order? Did, for example, Leedes transcribe the Suffolk entries by picking his way amongst a continuous chronological manuscript containing entries for both Suffolk and Cambridgeshire (and possibly other counties)? Or had that work been done for him?

The duplicate entry for Withersfield provides the only indication as to the original structure of the Journal.[55] This shows the normal signs of being copied twice from rough notes, but is particularly interesting because it appears once in the Cambridge entries, once amongst those for Suffolk (where it belongs). The duplicates have different dates – 5 January in the case of the Cambridgeshire version, 6 January for the Suffolk version. These dates mean that the entry occurs exactly at the boundary of Cambridgeshire and Suffolk visits. Baker copied it under the impression it was a Cambridgeshire entry. Probably then he had in front of him a manuscript which included entries for both counties in chronological order, like our reconstituted text, and he copied all the Cambridgeshire entries, ploughing on until he came to the first reference to Suffolk on 6 January. In this way he accidentally included Withersfield, his sole Suffolk entry, on 5 January. This then is evidence that the Journal seen by Baker and Grey did *not* have separate manuscripts for each county, but was in chronological order.[56]

To accept this, it has to be credible that each transcriber should have chosen to copy just one county. Baker's ignoring Suffolk is easily understood: he was primarily a historian of the University and its surrounding county, and may anyway have known that the Suffolk portion of the Journal had already been transcribed.[57] Leedes made his copy in a hurry, and would naturally have concentrated on his home county. And Grey's purpose was to demonstrate the character of Puritanism, not to provide a working edition of the Journal; in general his readers were more likely to be interested in Cambridge than in rural Suffolk, and by omitting the one county he cut the length of his text by about two thirds.

No firm conclusions can be drawn, but it seems most likely that Dowsing's Journal was a single document organised chronologically. This makes it less likely that entries for other counties once existed but have been lost without trace. However, the Journal may just have included visits to other counties which were never transcribed (for example, to Essex between 10 January and 18 January, with re-entry to Suffolk recorded on 19 January).

None of these textual issues casts doubt on the credibility of Dowsing's account in the form it has come down to us.[58] Its fundamental reliability is supported in a wide variety of ways. It will be apparent to readers of this edition that even though the entries are not in strict date order, the dates are coherent, the tours make geographical sense, and the transfer from one county to another is smooth. Wherever there is independent evidence of date, place, or person, it reinforces confidence in the essential accuracy of Dowsing's record. Despite the uncertainties as to its textual transmission and its precise purpose and nature, the Journal provides a unique and trustworthy record of officially endorsed iconoclasm of the period.

# II

# The text of this edition

## *Trevor Cooper*

GIVEN THE HISTORY of multiple transcription described in the previous chapter, there is little to be gained from paying attention to the fine details of the text of the Journal. Our aim has been to provide a readable edition, with enough apparatus to track only those textual variants which change the meaning of what is being reported – for example, differences in the number of angels recorded by Dowsing – or which give some clues as to the transmission of the text.

For Suffolk we have therefore used Martin's transcript, (expanding his 'SI' and 'SP' to 'superstitious inscription' and 'superstitious picture' respectively.) We have commented where Loder and/or Duck differ significantly from Martin. It has not always been sensible to compare Duck's precise wording with the other two sources for Suffolk, because his transcription smooths out the grammar and syntax of the original; for this reason we have not always quoted Duck's variant.

For Cambridgeshire we have reprinted the Grey version, noting significant disagreements with Baker. In a very few cases we have used Baker silently to correct Grey where he has an obvious misprint.

Occasionally we have chosen one of our other sources over Grey or Martin; this is always indicated.

We have not drawn attention to those cases where one source systematically omits material. For example, Baker almost always omits bible references and the names of churchwardens, and Duck often omits the fees received from churchwardens, and we have not recorded these omissions.

We have renumbered the entries. As regards Cambridgeshire, the Baker transcript has no numbering, whilst the Grey version gives numbers to the visits to Cambridge colleges, then starts the sequence again with the town churches, then again for the rural churches, but making errors in the sequence. Grey's numbering of the town churches suggests it may possibly preserve something of Dowsing's original – the parishes are numbered sequentially in the order in order of presentation, but the number five was not used, the sequence jumping from four to six (suggesting St Bene't's, buried in the college entries, was number five in Dowsing's mind).

The three versions of the Suffolk portion of the Journal (Martin's copy, the Duck transcript and Loder's printed edition) all have slightly different numbering, due to different decisions about the isolated Sudbury entries (9 January), and a certain slipshodness on everyone's part. Duck and Martin both correct their mistakes as though bringing their numbers into line with the copy they were working from, which would mean that this itself was numbered. (This would be Leedes' copy in the case of Martin, and possibly for Duck also.)

There is, then, little evidence that the original Journal was numbered, and if it was, we have no way of capturing the numbering. We have therefore created an entirely new set of numbers.

For the sake of legibility we have modernised the eighteenth-century capitalisation, underlinings and italicisation present in our sources. We have, however, largely, though not slavishly, reproduced their punctuation and spelling, though we have silently converted 'of' to 'off' in the interests of readability. For the Suffolk entries the punctuation is almost entirely that of its first publisher, Loder, as Martin's manuscript, from which he was working, is more or less unpunctuated. The Baker transcript for Cambridgeshire does contain slight punctuation, and Grey added to this.

We have interleaved entries for the two counties in date order: the entries now numbered 39–110, 113–132, and 210 to the end are from the Suffolk transcript of the Journal, the remainder from the Cambridgeshire portion.

THE

# J O U R N A L

O F

## *WILLIAM DOWSING,*

O F *S T R A T F O R D ,*

## PARLIAMENTARY VISITOR,

APPOINTED UNDER A WARRANT FROM THE

## E A R L   O F   M A N C H E S T E R ,

FOR DEMOLISHING THE SUPERSTITIOUS PICTURES
AND ORNAMENTS OF CHURCHES, &c.

WITHIN THE COUNTIES OF CAMBS. & SUFFOLK,

IN THE YEARS 1643–1644.

Newly edited, and prepared for the Press, by *Trevor Cooper.*

With extensive NOTES, never before published, plainly shewing the
*Destruction* wreaked by the *Visitor.* The notes on SUFFOLK churches
are by *Dr. John Blatchly*—on CAMBRIDGESHIRE parish churches,
by *Mr. Robert Walker*—and on the College Chapels of the UNI-
VERSITY OF CAMBRIDGE  and its Church, *viz.,* Great St. Mary's,
(and on Little St. Mary's also), by *Messrs. Trevor Cooper & Rob<sup>t</sup> Walker.*

# Places in the Journal

Reference are to Journal entry number, not to page number.

# The Journal of William Dowsing

*20 December 1643 – 2 January 1644. Dowsing began work in Cambridge. For about a fortnight he dealt with college chapels (which he records first) and town churches. Unlike the rest of the Journal, his entries here are not in chronological order.*

*As discussed in chapter 4 (for which see a map of the town), Dowsing dealt first with four colleges whose chapels had been enthusiastically reordered in Laudian style, then with neighbouring clusters of colleges.*

A note of the colledges names in Cambridge, 1643, and the superstitious images and pictures, (Numb. xxxiii. 4, 52, 55; Lev. xxvi. 1, 30; Deut. vii. 4, 25, 26. and ii. 2 [*recte* xii. 2]; Gen. xxxi. 34.)

The Scriptural references emphasise God's abhorrence of idols and the need for them to be pulled down. Two of them are expanded at the head of chapter 1.

1. Peter-House. We went to Peter-house, 1643, December 21, with officers and soldiers, and in the presence of Mr. Hanscott, Mr. Wilson, the President Mr. Francis, Mr. Maxey, and other Fellows, Dec. 20, and 23.

We pulled down two mighty great angells, with wings, and divers other angells, and the 4 Evangelists, and Peter, with his keies on the chappell door (see Ezek. viii. 36, 37 [?*recte* vi. 3–7] and ix. 6; Isa. xxvii. 9 and xxx. 22) and about a hundred chirubims and angells, and divers superstitious letters in gold.

And at the upper-end of the chancell, these words were written as followeth: *Hic locus est domus Dei, nil aliud, & porta coeli.*

Witnes, Will. Dowsing, George Longe.

These wordes were written at Keyes Colledge, and not at Peter-House, but about the walls was written in lating, *We praise the ever*; and on some of the images was written, *Sanctus, Sanctus, Sanctus*; on others, *Gloria Dei, & Gloria Patri,* and *Non nobis Domine* on others, and six angells on the windowe.[1]

Witnes, Will. Dowsing, George Longe.

The biblical references urge the destruction of idols: '[make] all the stones of the altar as chalkstones that are beaten in sunder'; 'defile also the covering of thy graven images of silver… cast them away'. For Dowsing's first visit, to Peterhouse Chapel, these biblical injunctions must have seemed particularly apposite.

For the chapel was the flagship of ceremonial worship in the University, and John Cosin, the Master from 1635, a particular target for those of the opposite party. His like-minded predecessor Matthew Wren built the chapel between 1628 and 1632, in a mix of Gothic and classic styles intended to emphasise the essential continuity of the Church of England. Cosin fitted it out, and introduced services which were 'noted above all the Towne for popish superstitious practises' (Plate 19).[2]

The chapel was furnished from funds raised from friends and well-wishers, and large sums were spent. Embossed gilt candlesticks, plate, altar cloths, cushions, hangings and Latin service books were purchased, and the chapel was decorated with roof angels. Cosin's wife paid for marble tiles for the floor. Luke Skippon, a Fellow, donated a splendid east window based on Rubens' 'Le Coup de Lance', and £50 was donated for the west window. Yet Cosin wanted perfection and a document drawn up by him lists his *desiderata*: a marble front for the Altar, a silk pallium, painted glass for seven windows, a decorated case for the organ, and narrative painting for the walls. At least some of this he achieved. And he set up a choir, supported by scholarships and fellowships.[3]

Not surprisingly the 1641 report to Parliament on 'Innovations in Religion' devoted to Peterhouse the lengthiest and most antagonistic account of any college.

The chapel 'since Dr Cosin's arrival'

hath bene so dressed up and ordered soe cerimoniously, that it hath become the gaze of the University and a greate invitation to strangers. The pavement beneath the steps ascending the Altar is of unpolished Marble but the steps and all above are of polished Marbell, upon wch none that officiates may tread, but either a great Turkey karpet is spread first or ells they put on slippers to prevent any sully to the marble.[4]

Upon the ascent stands an Altar covered on the three sides to the grownd with party coloured [variegated] silkes, on it are placed constantly two great guilt candlesticks with tapers in them, a Bason, two bookes covered richly. At solomne tymes the furniture is changed, and the dresse altered, above the Altar is a Dove to represent the holy Ghost, above it Cherubim, upon the hangings behind the Altar are painted Angells with this Lemma [motto] *In quod cupiunt Angeli.*[5]

In the East window is a large crucifix set up and in many frames on both sides of the Chappell are divers pictures of the history of Christ, at the end of every seate is a crosse of wood.

On the dore of the outward Chappell is the Image of St Peter cut in wood with keyes in his hand.

On solomne dayes a pot of incense is set upon the steps of the Altar, and as the smoke ascends the Organs and voices in the Chappell are raised. [6]

Incurvation towards the Altar at ingresse and egresse, and all approaches towards the Altar, and returne from it is made by all, soe likewise upon all transverse and other occasionall motions.

The lords prayer and confession are sung and said by all the chappell towards the East. When the hymnes psalmes and Creedes are sung and repeated all stand with theire faces towards the East, and diverse at the Close adore towarde the Altar.

The service is sung or said in sev[er]all places, the second service at the Altar with diverse bowings and cringeings; the Letany on Sundayes and holy dayes is sung by two kneeling before the Altar. Latine service on comon dayes is used…

In the Inner chappell hang divers novel orders wch are rigourously imposed, as noe wearing of gloves in the Chappell, noo sneezing, noe blowing of noses, noe scratching of the head, noe yawning, noe spitting upon the pavement and the like… [7]

Two years later, in Spring 1643, the organ and other chapel ornaments were dismantled, payment being made to Anthony Fawkner and his labourers 'for worke about the frames for the blew hanging[?es] done in the Chapple & remooving the organ pipes'.[8] The organ, here as elsewhere, seems to have been the big worry. There were further payments for 'altering the Angells at the East end of the Chapple', and in June 1643 the accounts

Table J1 *Items from Peterhouse chapel discovered hidden*
*in the Perne Library in 1650*

One Alter Cloth of Sattin imbroydered with Gold & Silver, & bordered round
    with a Golden Fringe, with these Letters IHS. CHRS. DNS
Another of the like Sort belonging to the Altar, without Fringe, with these Letters,
    ADOREMUS DOMINUM
One cover for the Altar of red velvet, with a gold Fringe on one edge, about 4 yards
    of Length
One broad Peice Parte of Velvet with Sattin Letters interpaned with Cloth of Gold
    & Silver
One Cover for the Altar of red Taffeta, lined with Serge
A Side Cloth for the Altar of red Taffeta & Sky Colour, lined with Serge
A Border for the Edge of the Altar of the same
One large Peice for the East End with Sky coloured Taffata & red uppon blew
    Serge
One cover for the Altar of black & Purple Taffata, lined with black Fustian
One hanging for the East End of the same
One green Cotton Carpet with worsted Fringe
Eight Pieces of painted blew Broad Cloath
Five Peices of a coarser Sort of blew Broad Cloath, some greater, some lesse
One Peice of blew Perpetuano [?]
Three Peices more of the same
Some Peices of blew & red silke Fringe & four Tassells
Three window Cloths of red Cloth
The Organ Pipes of Wood & Mettall
One Picture of Gregorius

BL Add. MS 5861, p. 260 (fol. 132v), Cole's copy of the Peterhouse Register.
The list is dated 17 June.

record 2s. 6d. paid for 'carrying Queens' Coll. ladder heather and theather,
and to the workmen for removing the ladder from Angell to Angell';[9] but
the angels were still there when Dowsing arrived, so this expenditure may
simply have been on improvements or cleaning.

What happened to the furnishings after this clearance? In 1644–45 the
accounts show two Fellows buying chapel furniture, so it seems some
material was held back until it was clearer how matters would turn out: the
appointment of the Puritan Lazarus Seaman as Master in 1644 must have
resolved any uncertainty.[10] But many other items were hidden in the Perne
library, then being fitted out, the concealed material including the organ
pipes and bellows, various soft furnishings and the music books. Two
'Turkey carpet table-cloths' seem to have been found quite soon, and were

put in the hands of the new Master for his use.[11] The rest stayed hidden, until in June 1650 'upon probable information given him' the Master ordered a search to be made. The items discovered in 1650 give an idea of the colourful splendour of the chapel in its heyday (Table J1). However three service books hidden in the Library were not found then: they lay undiscovered for nearly three hundred years, until in 1926, covered with dust and cobwebs, they were found behind a panel in the library, where they had lain for nearly three hundred years.[12]

In July 1650, a month after the discovery, it was decided to send a number of items up to London so 'they may be sold to the best advantage of the colledge'. The organ was sold for £31, though there were regrets ten years later when its true value was discovered and the college took legal proceedings to reclaim it. Presumably much of the rest was also disposed of, though this may perhaps not have been for some time as it was not until April 1653 that Dr Francius, a Fellow who had observed Dowsing at work, purchased for £7 'eight pieces of blew broad cloath with pictures on them, drawne in oyle and black leade, with 5 other peices of blew broad cloath without pictures, heretofore belonging to the chapel'; presumably he did this in order to save them from secularisation.[13]

It is hard to disentangle exactly what was left in the chapel after the very thorough precautionary removals of early 1643, but it seems that a significant part of Cosin's interior – the architectural decoration, at least, if not the more movable furniture – was still in place when Dowsing arrived, for he found various sets of angels, cherubim, and apostles, and St Peter still on the door. In the 1643–44 college accounts £4. 4s. 4d. is spent 'pro deformatione sacelli', so it seems the college had the further indignity of bearing the cost of workmen carrying out the removals ordered by Dowsing.[14]

Of angels mentioned by Dowsing, his two 'mighty great Angels' were perhaps the ones painted on the hangings behind the altar. As for the 'divers other angels', these may have been the cherubim above the altar recorded in 1641 (presumably on some form of frame or reredos), though they might perhaps have been connected with the roof bays. The accounts of 1631 record payment for '8 Angells and woode to make the winges of the Angells', but do not locate them.

Dowsing also refers to 'about a hundred chirubims'. This almost certainly includes – indeed, with Dowsing's penchant for wild approximation, probably refers only to – 54 putti heads in ceiling panels, the heads placed within ovals with rayed decoration (Plate 21).[15]

Where were Dowsing's 'four evangelists'? They had been bought, ready made, in June 1638, costing £6. 13s. 4d. Their erection required two sets of scaffolding and the purchase of a small number of heavy iron cramps (presumably to hold them in place), and, most tellingly, there is reference to the workmen helping the 'carver'. So these images were statues, not in glass. They probably stood in the four large, exterior niches, two on each of the east and west façades, now empty.[16]

The 'Chappell Door' is dated 1632. It is in fact a pair, the meeting stile of the north side being fashioned as a pilaster with a capital. This wooden capital was probably the plinth for 'Peter, with his Keies'.

Dowsing's account then becomes confused. It is probably to be read as correcting himself about the location of *Hic Locus Domus...*, and then continuing to describe Peterhouse, with its various inscriptions. None of these survive, or are elsewhere recorded.

The glass in the side windows of the chapel was apparently destroyed (though one panel was unharmed and is now on display; see Plate 20) but the east window does survive.[17] It depicts the Crucifixion (as noted in the 1641 survey), and has attendant saints and apostles in the tracery lights.[18] These are pictures which must have invited destruction and Blomefield asserts that this glass was hidden during the Commonwealth:

> The East Window containing the History of Christ's Passion is very fine and whole being hid in the late troublesome times, in the very Boxes which now stand round the Altar instead of Rails... [19]

It supports this story that Dowsing recorded nothing other than six angels in the glass and completely failed to mention the dominant crucifixion scene, the main part of the glass presumably by then having been removed. Surrounding the crucifixion there still are six winged angels, four in the upper row of tracery and two in the row below. Did he not harm them, or are they replacements?

This is the only occasion in the entire Journal when soldiers are mentioned. The only other direct evidence that Dowsing was accompanied by soldiers are the churchwardens' accounts for Walberswick (Journal entry 233); the Royalist John Barwick also claimed that Dowsing was accompanied by 'armed souldiers'.[20] The number of men under Dowsing's control is not known, but three visits to Peterhouse would appear to be reasonable given its importance, and in terms of the amount done, particularly if the ceiling had to be tackled.

George Longe, Dowsing's co-signatory, has not been identified.[21] Four Fellows of the college watched Dowsing at work. 'Hanscott' is William Handscomb, made a Fellow in 1639, escaping ejection by dying three months after Dowsing's visit. He is buried next door, in Little St Mary's. John Wilson and Patrick Maxwell ('Maxey'), a Scot, were expelled, along with most of the other Fellows, in the great purge of 1644–45, a particularly sorry event for Maxwell as he had only been made Fellow the previous year, by Royal Warrant, 'having taken into our Princely consideration his many sufferings'. Uniquely amongst the Fellows of this most Laudian of colleges, Dr John Francius kept his place, and became deputy bursar, remaining a Fellow until his death in 1665.[22]

2. At Pembroke-Hall, 1643, December 26. In the presence of Fellowes Mr. Weeden, Mr. Mapthorpe, and Mr. Sterne, and Mr. Quarles, and Mr. Felton, we broak 10 cherubims.

We broake and pulled down 80 superstitious pictures; and Mr. Weeden told me, he could fetch a Statute Booke to shew, that pictures were not to be pulled down; I bad him fetch and shew it and they should stand; and he and Mr. Boldero told me, the clargie had only to doe in ecclesiastical matters, neither the Magistrate, nor the Parliament had any thing to doe; I told them I perceived they were of Cuzen's [Cosin's] judgement, and told them I would prove the people had to doe as well as the clergie, and alledged, Acts i.15, 16, 23. (Calv. on Acts i.) The 120 believers had the election of an apostle in the rome [room, ie place] of Judas. I cited Calvin, and in his Institutions, in the poynt of ministers elections, and I told them Josiah's reforming religion (1 Kings xxii. 21) with the other godly reforming Kings of Judah proved it; and for the taking down of images, I told them the Book of Homilys did prove it, which they so much honored, and alledged, p. 12, 13, 14, 15, 23 against the Peril of Idolatry [and the Queens Injunctions]. Others alledged cherubims to be lawfull by scripture (Deut. iv. 12, 16 and vii. 5, 25, 26; xii. 2) and that Moses and Solomon made them without any command. I deny'd it, and turned to Exod. xxv. 18, 22. Then they said, Solomon did make them without any order from God. I answered, he received a pattern from David, and read to them, 1 Chron. xxviii. 10, 11 to 18, 19. Weeden said, Reading Paul's sermons was better preaching then now is used, because it was not script[ural]. I told them, God saved by foolishness of preaching, not reading, and alleged, I Cor. i. 21; I told them, if reading was preaching, my child preaches as well as they, and they stared one on another without answere.

More, Pembroke-Hall, 1643. Ashton: Laws made in time of warr were not of force. I alleged Magna Charta, made in time of warr, between Henry the Third and barrons, that was in force still, and Richard the 2d's tyme the like. Ashton said, the Parliament could not make laws, the King being away, and so many Members. I told them, their practice proved it, that chose Fellowes by the greater number present; and that the King had taken an oath to seal what both Houses voted. Maplethorpe said, he did not think my Lords Covenant was according to the Ordinance, and so I durst not abide by it, but thought I would run away, and used threatning speches. This last spech was Weedens, and Bolderas.[23]

Pembroke was amongst the first colleges to introduce Laudian reforms.[24] By the early 1630's the Master, Benjamin Lany, was being praised for beautifying the college chapel, and adding dignity to services and the chapel,[25] and was one of only five to be commended to Laud in 1636. A choir and organ were introduced.[26] The 1641 report gives some information about the new furnishings, but does not make clear what were Dowsing's ten cherubim and 80 pictures:

> In this Chappell is an alter railed at the East end and upon it stand two great Candlesticks wth tapers, two bookes leane against the Back of it. The wall behind the Altar is dressed up wth hangings of Divers Colours, soe is the Altar itselfe to the ground.[27]

The eighty pictures which Dowsing 'broake and pulled down' might have been in painted or embroidered cloth, as at Peterhouse, Clare, Trinity and St John's; or – just possibly – they might have been prints (see Plate 18 for a contemporary example of Roman Catholic pictures).[28] The likelihood, though, is that they were in the windows, which were glazed in the mid fifteenth century with the four Doctors of the Church and various saints. In line with the Parliamentary Ordinance, Dowsing seems to have left alone the glass showing the arms of a fifteenth-century Master, as this was apparently still in place in the eighteenth century.[29]

A new chapel was built to the designs of Christopher Wren in 1663–65; the old chapel was converted into a library in 1690, and is now used as a meeting room. There is no remnant of Dowsing's activities.

Dowsing's argument with the Fellows is dealt in chapter 5.[30]

3. At Keies Colledg [Gonville and Caius], Dec. 22, 23, 1643. Dr. Bodycroft, Master, and Mr. Wats and other Fellows. We tooke down 68 cherubims, with divers superstitious inscriptions in letters of gold.[31]

WITNESS WILL. DOWSING.

Thomas Batchcroft (Dowsing's 'Bodycroft'), elected Master in 1626, was by inclination a low churchman (although not a party man), but he inherited a college with a tradition of fostering tolerance to different opinions: Cosin, who later became Master of Peterhouse, had been a junior Fellow.[32] According to the (partisan) 1641 survey, one Fellow 'was soe earnest for the aforesaid [Laudian] innovations that he whipped a student of the house for not observing them', and in general the report believed that

> many of the Fellowes of this house are very ill affected to the Religion established in the church of England, and great favourers of Popish doctrines, and ceremonies, some of them having crucifixes in theire chambers, and being suspected to use beades and crossinge.

In chapter 4 we have already referred to the changes in forms of worship which took place in the chapel after 1636.[33] These were accompanied by very heavy expenditure, to a total of more than £500, on the fabric and furnishings. The chapel, built in the fourteenth century, was lengthened eastwards, the windows altered (and any remains of medieval glass probably removed), and the floor new-paved. Stalls were constructed. The tomb of Dr Caius was lifted off the floor to make more room (Plate 21). Much of the motivation for these changes must have been the increase in student numbers during the previous seventy years from 62 to 180.[34] But room was also found for the rising religious fashion: a new ceiling was constructed, decorated with carved and painted 'cherubins heads', and surrounded by a frieze; Cosin gave £10 to buy a communion table, a rail was built in front of it and 'freeses, pilasters and under-freeses about the table'.[35]

The author of the 1641 report believed that in all this Batchcroft must have been carried along by the Fellows. But even by this date there are signs (the altar being turned table-wise again) that the improvements were being undone:

> The chappell of this Colledg of late yeares by the overbearing sway of the Major part [of the] Fellowes (The master being rather passive than otherwise) hath had much Cost bestowed upon it in wainscotting and gilding to the expense of some hundreds of pounds.

The East end is ascended by steps, an high erected frame of wood placed to the proportion of an Altar, but the table never placed there, because this part of the Chappell was newly taken in from an out peece of ground and was not consecrated, soe that the Table stood beneath the steps, turned formerly Altarwise by Mr Lingate Fellow of that house, but of late it hath bene turned againe table wise. In the East end there were formerly two hollow places for images, wch now at the reedifying of that part of the chappel are againe fitted for any the like purposes.[36]

That Dowsing only mentioned the cherubim and inscriptions most probably indicates that the altar rails had been removed by the time he arrived; some remnants of altar rails survive in the organ gallery which it has been suggested may be those of Dowsing's time.[37] His 'inscriptions in letters of gold' probably relate to the expensive 'wainscotting and gilding' recorded in 1641. In addition to what he records, there were damaged brasses here in the mid eighteenth century.[38] The glass in the east window is known to have survived Dowsing's visit though is now lost; it was Elizabethan, containing various coats of arms, and was thus outside the scope of his commission.[39]

Dowsing obviously got muddled between Peterhouse and Caius (probably because of their similar cherubimic ceilings (Plate 21), perhaps compounded by the link between Peter's keys and his spelling of the college name). He corrects himself to say that *Caius* had *Hic locus est Domus Dei etc* at the east end, but this is not known from other sources.

How would Dowsing have dealt with carved and painted cherubim and gilt inscriptions on the high ceilings at Peterhouse and Caius? – by hammering them flat, painting them over, or pulling down the ceiling boards which supported them? Whichever it was, although the cherubim at Peterhouse have gone for ever, those at Caius have returned, restored some time after 1660 (they are mentioned by the mid eighteenth century) and forming an angelic presence today.[40] Following various changes in the past few centuries, today's visitor will count seventy-five cherubim, and not Dowsing's (probably inaccurate) sixty-eight.[41] The Journal suggests that two days were taken for this work which appears comparable with the three visits to Peterhouse for a similar undertaking.

As well as Batchcroft, Dowsing was observed by Richard Watson ('Wats'), who was ejected from his fellowship in the following April. Already unpopular with Presbyterians for a sermon preached in Great St Mary's, he fled to Paris where 'his controversial spirit found fresh employment in disputations with the Romanists concerning the visibility of their Church'. He was reinstated at the Restoration.[42]

4. At Queens' Colledg, Dec. 26. We beat down about 110 super-stitious pictures, besides cherubims and ingravins.

And there none of the Fellowes would put on their hats all the time they were in the chappell; and we digged up ther steps for 3 howers, and broake downe 10 or 12 apostles, and saints pictures in ther hall.[43]

The year 1631 saw the arrival of a committed Laudian, Edward Martin, as president of Queens' (he had been chaplain to Laud). This coincided with the expenditure of some £80 on 'Reparation of the Chappell' (the building dated from the foundation of the college in 1448) though details of the purchases appear not to have survived. There was then a gap, perhaps because of a shortage of money, until in 1637 work started again: the communion plate was replaced and an organ introduced, and in 1638 there was further expenditure, when the altar was raised.[44] In 1641 it was reported that there was a choir ('Anthems are used instead of singing of psalmes with the organs') and a Laudian interior:

> There is an ascent at the East end of the Chappell, and upon it an Altar set covered richly. Upon the Altar are placed two candlesticks wth tapers, a guilt bason, two greate guilt pots; Behind the Altar are hangings either of Cloth embroidered with gold or ells of guilt leather.[45]

This was the chapel seen by Dowsing, still with its steps in front of the altar, and irritating him with cherubim, 'ingravins', and pictures (which may have been the pre-Reformation glass, known to have contained saints' images).[46]

At the Restoration, the chapel (in the north range of the Front Court) was refurnished, and it was substantially remodelled in the eighteenth and nineteenth centuries. After its replacement by Bodley's new chapel in 1890, it served a variety of uses, being converted to a library in 1951–52. No furniture or fittings of Dowsing's period remains there.

However, in the new chapel there are three brasses in their slabs which were removed from the old chapel. All have been damaged or had inscriptions partly or totally removed.[47] Perhaps these were the 'ingravins' in his Journal (see entry 7, St Bene't's church, for another example).

It is surprising to find Dowsing interpreting his commission to include a college hall. (The complaint of the *Querela Cantabrigiensis* that he generally included these may have been based on this single example.) He does not say where in the hall he found his 'saints pictures'. At that time the hall contained linenfold panelling of 1531–32 (now in the President's Study), surmounted by coats of arms and heads: but these are not the heads of saints,

and they show no sign of damage. Perhaps the painted canvas hangings of
1501–2, with their texts of scripture, were still there for him to criticise and
remove,[48] or perhaps he found his saints in the windows. There are today, in
the roof of the hall, carved angels of medieval appearance. Some or all of
these may be Victorian restorations or replacements, Bodley's work of 1875;
but some (or all) may be fifteenth-century originals: if medieval, did they
survive Dowsing's visit because they were unreachable; unnoticed; or
regarded as unimportant as they bore no popish symbols, merely the initial
letters of the patrons and Foundresses of the college?[49]

Why did Dowsing make the comment about hats? He must have known
that willingness (sometimes enthusiasm) to wear a hat in church was a sign
of Puritanism. Perhaps the weather was sharp, and the sight of bare-headed
Fellows in an icy chapel struck him with some force.

5. At Katharine-Hall, 1643, Dec. 26. We pulled down St. George
and the Dragon, and popish Katharine, St. to which the colledg
was dedicated. Dr Brunbricke, the B[isho]p maintained more
reverence due to a place called churche, then any other place, and
the communion cup not to be used for no other use in church and
any civil act, he said it was an error. We broake down John Baptist
there, and these words, *Orate pro anima, qui fecit hanc fenestram*; Pray
for the soul of him that made this window.[50]

Reflecting the college's mild Puritan tradition, the report to Laud in 1636
was uncertain as to the religious practices at St Catharine's, though 'of late
they were as irregular as any & most like Emanuel', and the communion
table was not then at the east end.[51] A chapel inventory of 1636 confirms this
picture: for the communion table there is merely a taffety carpet and linen
cloth, a silver chalice and two pewter flagons. An iron-branched candle-
stick, a Bible, four service books, a bell and two reading desks complete
the picture.[52] Anyone seeking to create a measurement scale for chapel
furnishings of the 1630s could well use St Catharine's and Peterhouse in
1636 to set the two extremes.

In 1638–39 the college spent over £90 'Enlarging of the Chappell and
Lodge', including a new belfry and casements, but this appears not to have
involved any change to the chapel furnishings; the accounts are unspecific,
being mostly for labour, but where chapel furnishing are mentioned they
are of no significance.[53] In 1641 the college, along with Corpus Christi,
replied to a question from Parliament that there were 'noe innovations
practiced in ther chappels'.[54] This is the only college ignored by the Puritan
report of 1641.

It seems likely, then, that the small number of the items listed by Dowsing at St Catharine's arose from a lack of forbidden things rather than a lack of time. Dowsing's work on 26 December was extensive, including the debate at Pembroke and far-reaching works at Queens' (which included three hours at the chancel steps) and it may be that he chose to finish a rather busy day with a college where not much effort would be required. The original chapel was licensed in January 1475, and it is likely that the things Dowsing did find to destroy (three saints, and an *Orate* in a window) were part of the original furnishings and fabric, rather than contemporary introductions. A new chapel was consecrated in 1704, and there are no remnants of Dowsing's visit. [55]

Ralph Brownrigg ('Brunbricke') was Master from 1635 and served two periods as Vice-Chancellor of the University. He was made Bishop of Exeter in late 1641. He had a reputation as a moderate Puritan, but tended to steer a middle course, and his comments on the special sanctity of place and object would not have pleased Dowsing. In April 1645, Brownrigg was arrested for preaching an allegedly pro-royalist sermon, but was later released and lived in retirement, dying in 1659.[56]

6. 1643. Benet Coledg [Corpus Christi], Dec. 28. Dr Love, M[aste]r. Nothing in the chapell to be amended. I Sa. i. 9. The word 'temple', he told me, was a common name given to publique places, set apart for worship, both among heathens and Christians. And they told him, in Rochell, and in the churches of Fraunce, being there when Rochell was besieged, and he told, they used not the word 'ecclesia' for a church, but the other word 'templum' for a place of worship.[57]

WITNES, WILL. DOWSING.

The chapel was Elizabethan (started in 1579) and would therefore have no hang-over of pre-Reformation imagery to annoy Dowsing.[58] Nor, under the control of the moderate Puritan Richard Love, elected Master in 1632, were Laudian furnishings introduced. Thus in 1636 it was reported to Laud that the communion table was in the nave and was 'poorly furnished' – a reflection, perhaps, of the poverty of the college, as well as its conservative Protestantism. In addition, the chapel was unconsecrated, another point of unease for the Archbishop.[59] The chapel inventory of 1640, which lists removable furnishings but not plate, confirms the general impression, recording for the communion table merely a carpet, two diaper communion cloths, and two diaper napkins. The remaining items are equally utilitarian:

there are no pictures, tapestries, or hangings, the only hint of visual drama being a brass eagle lectern. Compared to the furnishings of Peterhouse or St John's, this is simplicity indeed.[60]

The Master and Fellow's essential conservatism and resistance to extremes meant they were able to tell an uneasy Parliament in 1641 that they had introduced no innovations,[61] and the survey of that year supported this, though revealing a temporary lapse:

> Certaine new orders were introduced into this Colledge Chappell some two yeares since by Mr Tunstall[62] senior Fellow and President in the Masters absence, which were throwne out againe by the Master Dr Love presently upon his coming home.

So Dowsing found nothing to cleanse. But he found something to criticise, in the use of the Old Covenant word 'temple' (hence his somewhat gnomic reference to I Samuel i. 9, referring to Eli sitting in the temple).[63] The term 'temple' was often applied to St Benedict's church (next entry), and Dowsing may also have noticed the inscription *has sacras Aedes fieri fecit*, which used the equivalent word in recording the (not entirely sufficient) munificence of Sir Nicholas Bacon, who had part-funded the construction of the college chapel.[64] But Love read his man well and chose a telling counter-example: the 'temple' at La Rochelle, a strong-hold of Huguenot Calvinism, had been built to seat 3500 for the hearing of godly sermons.[65] Richard Love, a man clearly skilled at avoiding unnecessary confrontations, retained his Mastership throughout the following turbulent years until his death in 1661. As Blomefield commented a century later, 'this Dr Love was a Favourite of those Times, for he continued master all the Time of the Usurpation, and at the Restoration he was appointed Dean of Ely'.[66] Nevertheless, another eighteenth-century historian, though generally admiring Love for guiding the college through troubled times, was to criticise him for not using his 'interest' with Dowsing to restrain his depredations.[67]

The chapel which Dowsing saw was lost when it was demolished as part of the scheme of William Wilkins to build New Court. The furnishings were dispersed: the Restoration Royal Arms from the chapel are now in the hall above high table; and some at least of the original stalls are in the new chapel, together with four Elizabethan carved canopies, placed above the four stalls in the south side of the chancel.[68]

7. At Benet Temple [St Bene't's church], Dec. 28. There was seven superstitious pictures, 14 cherubims, and 2 superstitious ingraving; one was to pray for the soul of John Canterbury, and his wife. Mr. Russell, church-warden, he lent 100l. to the

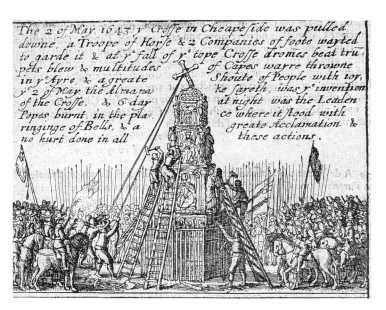

The 2 of May. 1643 ỹ Croſſe in Cheapeſide was pulled
downe, a Troope of Horſe & 2 Companies of foote wayted
to garde it & at ỹ fall of ỹ tope Croſſe dromes beat tru-
pets blew & multitudes of Capes warre throwne
in ỹ Ayre, & a greate Shoute of People with ioy,
ỹ 2 of May the Almana- ke ſareth, was ỹ invention
of the Croſſe, & 6 day at night was the Leaden
Popes burnt, in the pla- ce where it ſtood with
ringinge of Bells, & a greate Acclamation &
no hurt done in all theſe actions.

17a. A contemporary image of the destruction of Cheapside Cross,
London, a potent symbol of a more general attack on crosses, discussed on
page 100.

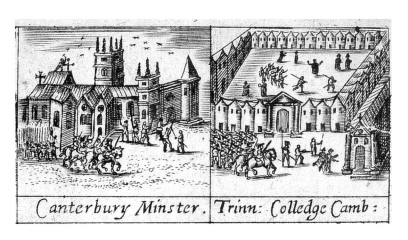

Canterbury Minster. Trinn: Colledge Camb:

17b and 17c. Two vignettes from the title page of *Mercurius Rusticus*,
published in 1647, here enlarged to about double their original size. 17b
(left). Cross being removed from Canterbury Cathedral. 17c (right).
Soldiers in Trinity College, Cambridge, a common sight from 1643 onwards
(see page 464).

The Souldiers in their passage to York turn unto reformers pull down Popish pictures, break down rayles, turn altars into Tables

18a. The destruction of chancel furniture in the early 1640s, an image first published in 1642 (discussed on page 469).

23. May. 1643. Voted that if Queene Pawning the Iewells of ye Crowne in Holland & there with buying Armes to assist the Warr against ye Parlam: & her owne actuall performances with her popish army in the North was high Treason & transmited to the Lords; jmages, Cruci- fixes papistecall bookes in Somerset and Iameses ware burnt and ye Capuchin friers sent away

18b. Destruction of the Queen's chapel furnishings in 1643, including pictures. Pictures were also introduced into the Cambridge college chapels (e.g. at Peterhouse, pages 158-9).

19. Peterhouse college chapel, looking east. Except for the altar and its surrounds, the furnishing are the original ones of the seventeenth century. This chapel was the first to be visited by Dowsing, not surprising given its notorious reputation amongst Puritans (see pages 155-61).

20. Part of an aisle window from Peterhouse chapel, on store for many years in the basement (probably following removal in Dowsing's time), now restored to view in a college meeting room. The event pictured is Christ washing the feet of his disciples, but the image of Christ has not survived (see page 160).

21a. The interior of Caius College chapel. Notice the monuments, raised above floor level in the 1630s to make more room (see page 163).

21b (top). The roof of Caius chapel.
21c (bottom). The roof of Peterhouse chapel, which probably also held cherubim until Dowsing's visit (see page 164).

22 (opposite). The interior of King's College chapel, looking east, some time between 1877 and 1897. In Dowsing's time there was a screen between the first pair of pillars, with the communion table in front (see page 179). Just beyond the choir stalls is the 'gradus chori', a step across the width of the building, which can be seen in the plan on Plate 23.

23 (below). A plan of King's College chapel of about 1609 (discussed on page 48). Notice the communion table placed lengthways ('table-wise' in contemporary parlance) between the choir stalls.

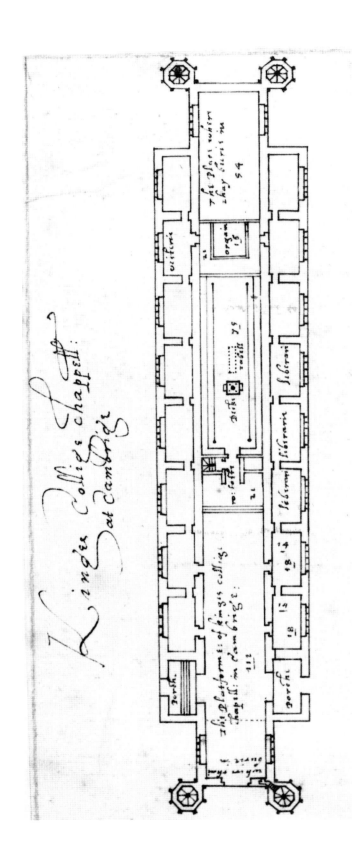

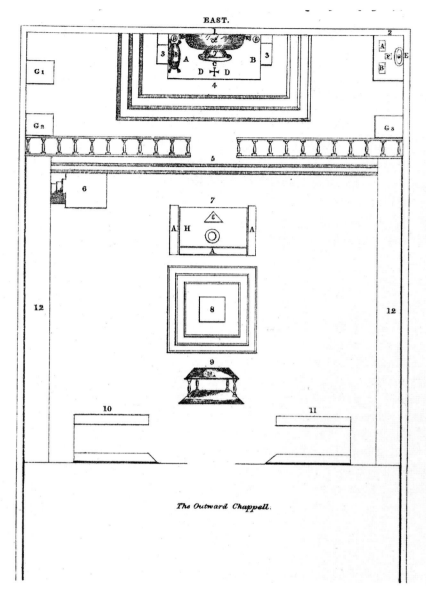

24. The plan of Lancelot Andrewes's chapel, an important influence on 'Laudian' thinking about the ideal ordering of churches (see page 49).

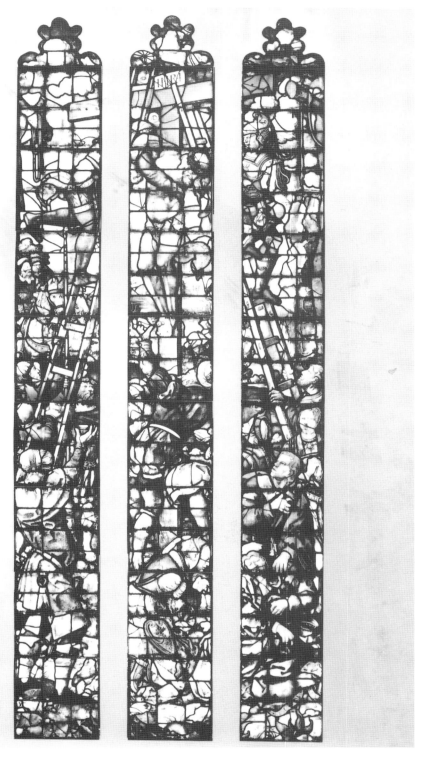

25. King's College chapel, a detail from the east window showing Christ being taken down from the cross. It was probably this image that Dowsing referred to in his cryptic notes (page 179).

26. Three brasses in King's College chapel, with various histories of damage (see page 186). 26a (above left). Robert Brassie (d.1558): the prayer scroll was left untouched by Dowsing, and disappeared later. 26b (above right). John Argentein (d.1507): the crucifix had gone by the eighteenth century, but the *Orate* remains today. 26c (left). William Towne (1496): the prayer clauses have been erased, perhaps by Dowsing.

27a (left). A thirteenth-century coffin lid in Jesus College chapel, discovered when Dowsing was digging up the chancel steps (see page 171).

27b (below). The brass to Nicholas Metcalfe in St John's College chapel, with its prayer clause defaced (see page 178).

28a. The eagle lectern in Christ's College chapel, mentioned by Dowsing (see page 188).

28b. The brass to Richard Billingford in St Bene't Cambridge, from which Dowsing removed the inscription (see page 169).

29. Laudian fonts and covers in Cambridge. 29a
(above left). Font cover in St Mary the Less (see
page 194). 29b (above right). Font and cover of
1632 in St Mary the Great (see page 203). 29c
(left). Font and case in St Botolph (see page 195).

30a. The Laudian litany desk of 1636 in Jesus College (see pages 170-71).

30b. Altar rails now in Milton church, originally from King's College chapel. These may have been the rails in use in the 1640s (see page 472).

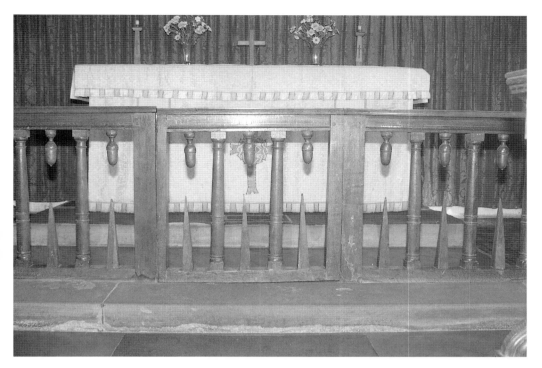

31a. The altar rails at Chediston, Suffolk, almost certainly pre-dating Dowsing's arrival, though he does not mention them (see pages 99, 289).

31b. The altar rails at Isleham, Cambridgeshire, a church probably not visited by Dowsing (see page 46). Compare their design with those above.

32. Damaged roof figures. 32a (top left). Replacement roof angel at Badingham, Suffolk (see page 319). 32b (top right). Damaged corbel angel at Kingston, Cambridgeshire (page 257). 32c (bottom left). Damaged angel on wall-plate at Comberton, Cambridgeshire (see pages 262-3). 32d (bottom right). Defaced wall-post figure of St Jude (carrying his ship) at St Margaret, Ipswich (see pages 231-2).

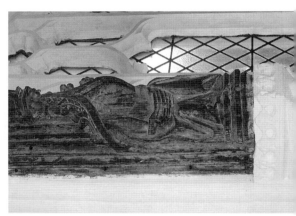

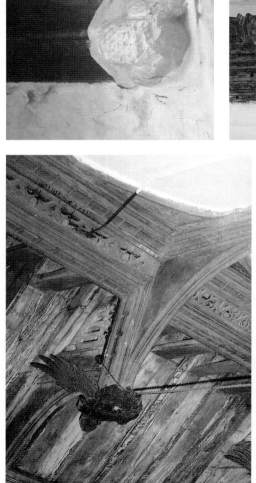

Parliament, and set forth a horse, and maintaineth him at his charge, and lent Col. Cromwell 300[£] to pay his soldiers.

And an inscription of a mayd Praying to the Son and Virgin Mary, 'twas in lating, *Me tibi-Virgo pia genitor commendo Mariæ*; A maid was born to me which I commend to you oh Mary (1432). Richard Billingford did comend this his daughters soule.[69]

A new roof was contracted for in 1452, ornamented with angels, probably fourteen of them (neatly coinciding with Dowsing's fourteen cherubim, one of the few occasions on which he appears to have counted accurately). In 1636 six new angels – perhaps replacements – were put up in the roof.[70]

John Caunterbury was clerk of the works at King's College in the latter part of the fifteenth century (died *c*.1492), and his wife Isabella was sister of Robert Woodlark, Provost of King's College, and founder of St Catharine's.[71]

Dowsing's 'inscription of a mayd praying' was probably the brass of (the entirely male) Richard Billingford, now in the south aisle (Plate 28). The kneeling figure remains but the inscription and prayer have been removed. The inscription is known to have been *Me tibi Virgo pia genetrix commendo Maria*, and was surmounted by a brass representing the Virgin and child borne by angels.[72] Dowsing's translation had some of the words right. Other indents survive, likely to be the remnants of Dowsing's cleansing.

According to Masters, the eighteenth-century historian of the college, Dowsing also removed a cross from the steeple.[73]

Other than the famous Saxon tower, the church was greatly rebuilt in the nineteenth century.

## 8. 1643, Jesus Colledg, Dec. 22. Mr. Boyleston, Fellow. We digged up the steps there, and brake downe of superstitious, of saints and angells, 120 at least.[74]

The chapel at Jesus is formed of part of the church of the medieval Benedictine nunnery of St Radegond, taken over by Bishop Alcock of Ely when he founded the college in 1497. As we shall see, some of what Dowsing found, albeit accidentally, came from the original church; but he seems to have overlooked some 'superstitious' memorabilia connected with Bishop Alcock.

There had been changes in the decade previous to Dowsing's visit. Following the appointment of William Beale as Master in 1632, Latin service books were purchased, and 'hanginges' for the chapel. In 1634 Beale moved to St John's (where a similar programme was begun) and the new

Master, Richard Sterne, a Royalist and Laudian – he attended Laud on the scaffold – continued Beale's refurbishment. In 1634 an organ was contracted for at a cost of £200, and a year later an organist appointed, his salary being provided by a tax on college members (except the more junior ones, who were instead required to blow the organ). Wax tapers for the chapel were provided by a similar tax. In 1636 the accounts show expenditure for 'the Rail, Floor, Freez, Hangings, etc., about the Altar, and for the Letany Desk', and some two years later communion plate, candlesticks and a basin were acquired for the Altar. [75]

Thus in 1641 the report to Parliament described a typical Laudian chapel:

> In the chappell of this Colledge is an Altar erected wth stepps to it and rayles before it, behind the Altar alsoe the compasse of the septum [the width of the altar rails] are hangings of blew.[76] The Altar itself is covered with cloth embroidered wth gold. At each end of the table lyes a velvet cushion.
>
> Along upon the gilt ledge to wch the hangings are fastened are placed Cherubim heads gilt. At the west end of the Chappell is a lately erected paire of organs on the back of wch are these three letters gilt I H S.[77]

In early 1643 members of the college were given leave of absence 'in view of the impending danger', and in late March or early April of that year 15s. 0d. was spent on 'taking down the organs' (to be buried, legend has it, in the Master's garden).[78] Indeed, by the time of Dowsing's visit all that was left for him to comment on were the steps, and the saints and angels.

Some of his 'Saints and Angels 120 at least' were probably the 'Cherubim heads gilt' above the hangings. Others may have been in the roofs: in 1663, when the chapel was repaired, the accounts show expenditure on 'cleaning the Cherubim and setting them up', and some demi-angels, much restored, still hover in the south transept roof.[79] Others again will have been in the medieval windows which were glazed with 'figures of the Saviour, the Blessed Virgin Mary, the Apostles, the Fathers, and all the hierarchy of heaven, executed with wonderful beauty of workmanship'. The windows also included 'the Founder's picture'. Did Dowsing destroy this memorial by accident, or did it show a kneeling donor with an *Orate*, and thus call for cleansing?[80]

Nearly a year after his visit expenditure on repairs to the chapel confirms that Dowsing had indeed 'digged up the Steps', broken windows, and left walls looking bare:

*Michaelmas 1644 – Michaelmas 1645*
For levelling the chappel, tile lime sand and labourers wages per
    billam Nov. 14. . . . . . . . . . . . . . . . . . . . . . . . . . . . . 3 02 05
To the glazier for 4 windows mending . . . . . . . . . . . . . . . . 3 16 00

For a communion to Mr Boilston [see below] . . . . . . . . . . 0 01 02

To the glazier for the other windows per billam Feb. 14 1644

   [1644/5] . . . . . . . . . . . . . . . . . . . . . . . . . . . . . 7 00 00

For colouring in the chappel at the same time[81] . . . . . . . . . . 0 07 00

Almost twenty years later the college Commemoration Book records the restoration of the chapel, a reversal of a reversal:

> The sacred place wherein we are now assembled having been in the time of the Great Rebellion much defaced and by Fanatic Outrage despoiled of the utensils and ornaments provided for decency in Divine Worship, was upon the happy Restoration of the Church and Monarchy, restored to its former comeliness by the assistance of the Benefactors following...[82]

The chapel has been much altered since Dowsing's visit; no glass of his time survives, but the 'Letany desk' of 1636 still exists (Plate 30).[83] The chapel also contains the most unlikely souvenir of Dowsing's visit: a thirteenth-century stone coffin lid, discovered in the course of the steps being dug up (Plate 27).[84] There are some interesting pre-Reformation survivals, too, in the form of four bench end finials with the figures of a bishop and Doctors of Divinity. More spectacular as a survival of numerous bouts of iconoclastic zeal is a bench end with Bishop Alcock in an architectural surround surmounted by two complete figures of priests.[85]

'Mr Boyleston', who watched Dowsing at work, is John Boilston or Birlston, a Fellow of the college, previously a Fellow of Christ's College. He was one of only two Fellows from Jesus not to be ejected by Manchester the following year. He may simply have prevaricated over taking the Covenant, for he was duly expelled in 1645 (so perhaps the communion recorded in the above accounts is his farewell service) and retired to a living in Derbyshire, dying a Canon of Lichfield Cathedral after the Restoration.[86]

## 9. 1643, At Clare-Hall, Decemb. Mr. Gunning, Fellow. Ther are steps to be made up, 3 cherebims, 12 apostles, and 6 of the Fathers in the windowes, and a crosse.

The chapel which Dowsing saw was built in 1535, replacing a fourteenth-century building. There seem to have been no burials in the chapel (and hence no brasses for Dowsing), possibly because it was unconsecrated. This chapel was pulled down in 1763, and replaced by one to the design of Sir James Burrough and James Essex.[87]

There are no accounts or chapel inventories for the period leading up to Dowsing's visit,[88] but part of his record of destruction – apostles and the Church Fathers – is elucidated by a description of the chapel from the mid eighteenth century, when William Cole reported that there are three Windows on each side of the Chapel, in which formerly were the Figures of the 12 Apostles, and 4 Doctors of the Church curiously painted; but these were broken in the general destruction of such pieces of decency throughout this county in 1643, and nothing but the lowermost half of them remain, with their names at the Feet of most of them. [89]

The 1641 report takes no notice of the glass, but does mention Dowsing's steps, and his cross ('crucifixe'):

A high Altar raised three steps higher than the rest of the Chappell, the steps and all wthin the railes being Covered wth wrought cloth[;] at the foote of the Altar there lyes a greate wrought cushion.

Over the Altar upon the wall hangs a peece of arras in wch is a Crucifixe wrought in blew between the two theives, over the head of the Crucifix is Drawne a circle full of light beames wth this superscription I N R I.

Upon the high Altar stand two great wax candles, two bookes.[90]

The cherubim mentioned by Dowsing may have been connected with the 'circle full of light beams'.

The 'Mr Gunning, Fellow' recorded by Dowsing was Peter Gunning. In 1642 he preached a sermon against Rebellion, and he cannot have been too surprised to be ejected by Manchester in 1644. Restored to his fellowship at the Restoration, he was made Master of Corpus Christi in 1661, moved on to be Master of St John's the same year, and played a major role in the introduction of Anglicanism into the University, before becoming Bishop of Chichester (1670) and then Ely (1675).[91]

## 10. 1643, Trinity-Hall, Dec. 2. Mr. Culiard, Fellow. *Orate pro anima*, on a grave stone.[92]

By 1641 Trinity Hall appears to have moved some way towards the Laudian ideal, but with nothing like the enthusiasm shown elsewhere.[93] Thomas Eden, the Master since 1626, and Member of Parliament from 1640, was no supporter of the Court,[94] and no doubt the Fellows were content to show that caution and attachment to the middle way which was to be expected from a college where many were lawyers.[95] The report of 1641 was very brief, reading in whole:

In this Colledg Chappell the Communion table is placed at the East end of the Chappell close to the wall and turned Altarwise, with rich wrought hangings upon the wall behind the table; and the table covered wth the like. At theire standing up at Gloria patri we did not discerne them to turne towards the East. [96]

Apart from the Founder's arms in glass (which Dowsing would not have touched) it is not known how many of the chapel's pre-Reformation fittings survived until Dowsing's visit; all he noted was a (presumably pre-Reformation) memorial *Orate*.[97]

The medieval chapel he saw is still in use, though much altered. It has a communion table of *c.*1600, perhaps the one referred to above. Despite Dowsing's efforts, a brass of Walter Hewke, Master (d.1517) survives intact with a cope decorated with a Majesty and the Apostles and an inscription *Sancta Trinitas unus deus Miserere nobis. Of your charity pray for the soule of Master Walter Hewke*....[98] Was it hidden, or overlooked?

'Mr Culiard', who watched Dowsing at work, must be Thomas Cullier, a Fellow from 1628–56, his non-ejection a few months later probably indicating at least a degree of sympathy with Dowsing's standpoint.[99]

## 11. 1643, Trinity Colledg, Dec. 29. Mr. Potts, a Fellow, Mr. Roods, a Fellowe. We had 4 cherubims, and steps levelled.[100]

In the report to Laud of 1636, this college, an ancient choral foundation, received the longest litany of complaint. Divine service was slackly attended, the men of the choir were 'ignorant and unskilful' whilst the day choristers 'never could... sing a note'. The services were altered and abbreviated. Nor was the layout of the chapel or the style of worship satisfactory, though reforms were said to be afoot:

> They have a large Chappell & yet the Boyes rowes of Pewes are placed just in the middle of the Chappell before & behind the Communion Table which some there are about to reforme. They leane or sitt or kneele at prayers, every Man in a severall posture as he pleases. At the name of Jesus few will bowe & when the Creed is repeated many of the Boyes by some Mens directions turn towards the West Doore. Their Surplices and song Books & other furniture for Divine Service is very mean. The Cloth that commonly leyes upn the Table not worth 14*d*.[101]

The college was indeed 'about to reforme', for in the same year, presumably in anticipation of Laud's forthcoming visit, the college commissioned 'the beautifying of the Chappell, and the decent adorning of the Communion Table'; and it was agreed on 15 June 1636

> to set our Communion-table in our Chappell as it is in Cathedrall Churches and Chappells, at the upper end, and the ground to be raysed; and that the chappell be adorned accordingly.[102]

About £500 was spent. There was a new pavement of Ketton stone and marble; the walls were wainscoted, with a gilt frieze; and new altar cloths and painted hangings were provided – London work, costing about £200.[103] The organ was painted and gilded at a cost of some £50.[104] To protect their investment, the college hired a man at the rate of 26s. 8d. per annum to 'keepe dogges out of the Chappell'.[105] As a result, there was much for the Puritan report of 1641 to condemn:

> About foure years since this Chappell received a new Dresse, an high Altar was erected ascended by many steps, and this inclosed on three sides with a Carved raile, wthin the raile the pavement is of black and white marbell Covered with blew say [fine cloth]. The Altar is trapped on the three sides wth rich hangings and in an high erected frame, behind it are coloured silkes of the same kind wth those that cover the Altar; at the hight of this frame in the middle of it is a shield placed guilded over.
>
> On the Altar stand two candlesticks wth two tapers in them and in the middest betweene them a guilt bason. The whole East end of the Chappell from the fellowes seates is taken up wth the history of Christ drawne upon blew kersey [coarse woollen cloth], this stayned cloth being raised very high and flagging three sides of the Chappell. Neere the Altar between the windowes are there foure pictures drawne at large, and very richly guilt, viz of Christ, the virgine Mary, Elizabeth, St John Baptist.
>
> The roofe of the whole Chappell is guilt very much, soe are those ledges of wainscot to wch the hangings at the East end are fastened and of late the Organs.
>
> On the South side a vestry is lately made, wherein the Altar plate and the sev[er]al suits of hangings for the Altar are laid up.[106]

The Royal stamp of approval was afforded in March 1642 when the King visited the chapel and 'seemed very well to approve all their ornaments'. Accounts for 1641–42 also include expense on 'the entertainment of Captaine Cromwell and his gentlemen Soldiers', a reminder of the difficult balancing act being performed by the colleges and university.[107]

In the following year (ending Michaelmas 1643), the accounts show that work to remove Laudian furnishings in the chapel began before Dowsing's visit.

| | | | |
|---|---|---|---|
| To Chambers for not blowing the organs a whole year | 2 | 00 | 00 |
| To M$^r$ Knuckles for whiting over the Figures and for his paines and his servants | 2 | 10 | 00 |
| To George Woodruffe for taking downe the organs and hangings | 0 | 15 | 00 |
| To Mr Jennings for taking downe the Organ pipes | 2 | 05 | 00 |
| To Mr Halfhead when the Organs, hanginges & other thinges were pulled downe | 2 | 10 | 10 |

Given to free Masons, bricklaiers, carpenters and upholsterers
    for removing the hangings and railes in the Chappell[108] . . . . 1 08 00

Other offensive items were spirited away in advance of Dowsing's arrival.
A publication of 1662 describes how the newly restored altar in the chapel
was accidentally set on fire by the candles. This altar

> was the first that was set up in Cambridge, yea, as it is believed in all England
> since the late Revolution; and the reason of it was, because Mistress
> Cumber, Wife to the former Master of that Colledge did,[109] about twenty
> years ago, out of great Piety, Zeal and Devotion, secretly convey away this
> Altar, with all its appurtenances, that it might escape those most Sacri-
> legious hands, which at that time did both in Cambridge, and everywhere
> else, destroy those Sacred Shrines, as Badges of Superstition, and Introd-
> uctions to Popery. [110]

This foresight paid off: by the time Dowsing arrived there were just four
cherubim left for destruction (where were they?) and the steps to be
levelled; no doubt the college had decided to leave those alone unless forced
to act.[111] In the mid eighteenth century Blomefield found several stones
robbed of their brasses; these could have been damaged at any time, but
might also have been Dowsing's work.[112]

A few month's later there were further incidents in the chapel with
unruly soldiers, but the use of cash incentives seems to have preserved it
from any damage; the accounts for the first quarter of 1644 record:

> To diverse souldiers at severall times that behaved themselves
>     very devoutly in the chappell  . . . . . . . . . . . . . . . . . 0 05 00
> To some of Major Scot's souldiers who defended the chappell
>     from the rudenesse of the rest [113] . . . . . . . . . . . . . . . 0 05 00

Over the centuries the chapel, erected in the gothic style in 1556–67, has
been much altered and completely refurnished and no evidence remains of
the forced oscillations of the mid seventeenth century.

Dowsing had two observers. The first, 'Rood', is probably John Rhodes
(or Roddes), expelled in 1650. 'Potts' has not been identified, unless he was
John Potts of Christ's College.[114]

## 12. 1643, St. John's Colledg, Dec. 29. Mr. Thorten, President, and Mr. Turwhit and Mr. Peche, Fellowes. 44 with *Cujus animæ propitietur deus*, and one with *Orata pro anima*; 20 former, ten last.[115]

William Beale was imposed by the King as Master of St John's in 1634,
following a disputed election,[116] and seems to have set about a programme
of Laudian reform more or less immediately, as he had at Jesus.

Up till then the chapel

retayned the ancient decency of churches and chappells, onely there was an ascent of three steps to the place where the Communion table stood, and the table placed Altarwise wch was done… by Mr John Price Senior fellow of that house, a man that for many yeares alone practised bowing towards the Altar. [117]

Under Beale's Mastership, a new organ was set up in 1634–35, and by 1636 there was a surpliced choir, though the attempt to create a nucleus of four paid, trained singers (as at Peterhouse) came to nothing.[118] Old painted glass was placed in the east window, probably pre-Reformation material preserved from the destruction of 1558–61, and a 'new window' built and glazed.[119] A couple of years later there was expenditure on raising the seats in the chapel, the purchase and renovation of 'statues' and candlesticks for the seats, and providing wainscot at the east end. The roof was painted. Sixteen 'Pictures about the Chappell' were acquired, showing the story of Christ, and frames for them, and '2 railes at the ends of the Altar', together with six candlesticks, presumably for the altar. Some thirty shillings was spent on 'angells and wings', and a few shillings more for 'plates to fasten the angels'. A 'dove of glory' was put up for twenty-five shillings. The total cost was more than £430.[120]

All this was near enough to popery not to endear itself to the Puritan mind. One (not impartial) observer commented that Beale 'caused such a general adoration to and towards the altar and sacraments to be practised, that many godly fellows and scholars of the house left their places to avoid the abomination'.[121] Another disapproving Fellow commented later that the college 'was so fermented with the old traditions… that I could not digest their sour belches against the parliament'.[122] And Dowsing's routine removal of cherubim and angels throughout his visits is surely made more comprehensible by the extravagant behaviour of men such as Price, 'a man popishly affected', who

adventured at the time of the Celebration of a Communion not long since, to turne himselfe to the pictures of the Angells, where he repeated these words in the Liturgie: Therefore wth Angells and Archangells… [123]

In the 1641 report to Parliament the chapel received one of the lengthier reports. It gives a good impression of a chapel furnished and decorated in the style aspired to by the Laudian wing of the church.

The Altar or table is covered to the ground, on the west side hangs a cloth wherein Christ taken from the Crosse and prepared for his sepulchre is painted, upon the Altar stand two gilt candlesticks with tapers in them, two service bookes covered with red velvet embossed with silver leane against a pedastall.

On the back of the Altar is an high erected frame, wch archeth over the table, in it is a large Crucifix betweene the two theives, on the head of wch are these foure letters I H R N [*sic*][124] above upon the bowing arch are many angells limmed [painted, portrayed], the limbus [border] or edge is guilt richly[;] the rest of the story of Christ from his conception to his ascension is painted in greate draughts [drawings] and placed in gilt frames on both sides the Chappell, and at the East end, and to supply a void place the story of Michaell and the Dragon is set up in a frame as the rest.

The roofe is painted in a skie collour and set full of gilt starrs, at just distances are fastened in golden letters through the whole roofe *Jesus Christus Dominus Noster* short writ. Above the Altar is a gilt sunne with great light beames and a dove in the middest richly guilt, on the Northside neere the Altar and soe likewise in the outward chappell is there an open place into two little chappells (wch before Dr Beales coming thither were schollars chambers) wch are hung with red and greene hangings wth Altars at the east end of each covered.[125]

At the west end are a paire of organs set up by Dr Beale, in the wainscot of wch is a hollow place capacious enough for an image just above the entrance into the Chappell.[126]

An inventory of 1642 fills out the picture. The pictures of Christ, sixteen of them, were 'hangings'. The cloth on the communion table was red velvet, and in addition the chapel possessed two rich cloths of gold and silver, and one damask cloth, edged with silver lace. There was good plate, the gift of Lord Burleigh and 'Mr Cecil'. The chapel possessed twenty-two service books in folio, and ten in quarto. In both the side chapels there were 'hangings of red and green serge, of half a yard broad, with white and green lace, round about the chapel', and, in each, 'one table, covered with the same'.[127]

By 1641, the Fellows must have had misgivings about the new interior, no doubt made more acute by the arrest and imprisonment of Beale in August 1642. In 1643 they began removing the most provocative furnishings:

payed by Mr Heron the Ju. Bursar for taking down the pictures
and the organs and whiting the walls[128] . . . . . . . . . . . £2. 8s. 6d.

Dowsing's entry is incoherent, but probably indicates that he found some memorial inscriptions to reform – the chapel was a mid-thirteenth-century building, taken over from the suppressed Hospital of St John the Evangelist, and contained some pre-Reformation monuments. The thinness of his record suggests that much of the embellishment of eight years before had already been removed. However in January 1644, a few weeks after his visit, there is an entry in the accounts, probably referring to the removal of old glass and the insertion of quarries, which suggests he did find it necessary to order some glass down:

> Jan 20 [1643/4] to Dan. Maldon 220 quarries of glass and for 149
>     foot of old glasse which was taken downe ?leaded and soadared
>     [soldered][129] . . . . . . . . . . . . . . . . . . . . . . . . . . . 18s. 0d.

A further visit on Dowsing's part may be alluded to in March 1644, a time when he was in Cambridgeshire:

> For taking downe the Crosse over the bell Tower, March 22[130]  . . 4s. 0d.

The removal of crosses is, of course, commonplace throughout the Journal. In the third quarter of the same year we find the organ case going, perhaps to a place of safety:

> Paid to old Dowsy [this is not Dowsing] when the organ case was
>     taken away[131] . . . . . . . . . . . . . . . . . . . . . . . . . . . 6s. 8d.

The chapel was pulled down when Scott's new chapel was built 1863–69. The organ of Dowsing's time, which had been set up again at the Restoration, was sold to the Rector of St Mark's, Old Bilton, near Rugby, and placed in the chancel, where it may still be seen. A jumble of fragments of glass from the east window of the old chapel, mostly of the fifteenth century, may be found in the hall, and a similar mosaic in the tower.[132]

There are some pre-Reformation brasses in various states of repair, that to Nicholas Metcalfe (d.1539), Master until his resignation in 1537, with the superstitious words on the inscription carefully defaced. The present eastern choir stalls came from the old chapel, and their carved seated figures 'seem to have been renewed perhaps in the seventeenth century', and may have been the 'statues' recorded in the accounts. The college still possesses a large bible and prayer book of 1633, bound together in crimson velvet with the silver clasps and mountings, donated in 1636, no doubt the very item recorded as being on the altar in the report of 1641.[133]

'Mr Thorten', one of the three who watched Dowsing, was probably Thomas Thornton who became President on 5 February 1644 and was ejected later that year for refusing to take the Covenant, as was 'Mr Turwhit' (Thomas Tirwhitte, Tyrwhit or Thirlwhitte) who had been admitted as Fellow on 16 April 1622. Both of these gentlemen later spent time with the royal army. In contrast Samuel Peachie ('Mr Peche') was a survivor of the coming purge: Fellow from 1620–47, made Senior Dean just after Dowsing's visit, and admitted President on 25 January 1645. He may have provided a degree of moral support to Dowsing.[134]

13. 1643, King's Colledg, Dec. 26. steps to be taken, and one thousand superstitious pictures, the ladder of Christ, and theves to go upon, many crosses, and Jesus writ on them.[135]

The first stone for King's College chapel was laid by the Founder, Henry VI, on St James's Day 1446, but the structure was not completed until 1515, after which the famous stained glass was added.[136] The glass survived the Reformation and although the original altar was pulled down then, the steps up to it appear to have survived.[137] There was plenty for Dowsing to do.[138]

As discussed in chapter 4, there was a Puritan arrangement in the early years of the seventeenth century and possibly before, as shown in the plan of 1609 (Plate 23); but this arrangement underwent considerable change some years later, as the new liturgical fashion took hold, and the east end became fully clothed for the first time. During 1629–33 the chapel walls were covered in carved panelling, at the expense of Thomas Weaver, a Fellow of Eton. A litany table was in use by 1630, and for the communion table a velvet cushion and a 'purple velvet Communion Cloth with silk and gold fringes' (costing more than £27) were donated in 1628 and 1629 respectively, the latter probably replacing the green velvet purchased for a mere 18s. 0d. just thirteen years earlier.[139]

Very extensive reordering took place in 1633–34, when there was significant expenditure – more than £300 – on the altar, its surroundings and furnishings. The communion table was placed nearer the east end, against a screen erected across the chapel between the first piers from the east (see Plate 22, a nineteenth-century view of the chapel, for location of the piers). The original stone steps were repaired. Some £30 was spent on the 'floare' and 'rayles' about the altar, which, from a later description, was probably further raised on a single step. To furnish the table, some £60 was spent on new cloths, more than £50 on a 'bason' (alms-dish), and about £26 on two books, including their 'clasps and bosses'. At a cost of more than £70, damask hangings were purchased for the east end, and tapestries may well have returned round the north and south walls. Upholsterers were paid a further £7 for making *'les hangings et* footstools'. Six candlesticks were purchased for the altar in 1636: these, however, were made of tin, and cost a mere 5s.; two 'great tapers' for the communion table were purchased in 1639, for 6s.[140]

Thus in 1641 a fine Laudian interior was reported to Parliament:

> An high Altar with stepps which hath bene erected of late yeares upon wch the Colledge hath bene at great expence. Over the Altar is an hanging canapy of wood. Behind the Altar are hangings of redd and blew taffaty.

The Altar hath 2 or 3 Coverings, one to the ground, a footepace. On the Altar stands two faire bookes richly embossed, and the Bible, the other the Liturgy, a gilt bason on the Altar, two gilt Candlesticks and two tapers wch they sometimes light, sometime foure tapars burning upon the Altar. A raile enclosing the Altar. [141]

There follows a description of the choral services:

The service is sung wth the organ on holy dayes, confession, prayers, Creed etc and Cathedrall service on other dayes. wth Choristers and singing men at eight of the clock in the morning and at 4 at night, this hath bene used of old. A litany desk below the high altar, at which they kneel that sing the litany with their faces towards the east. Many things in their service not easily understood. [142]

At the bottom of the page is an additional note, in the same hand, showing that at King's the Provost, Dr Collins, was not slow to undo some of the recent changes: [143]

The Mr of this College Dr Collins, hath since this information was drawne, removed the Altar and placed it table wise within the rayles, taking away the candlesticks and bason, He hath likewise prohibited adoration towards the East, and standing that way at the Doxologie and Creed.

Dowsing visited the college more than two years later. Some nine months before his visit, in the first quarter of 1643, the college took down the organ (by then in the screen-loft): this coincided with similar precautionary removals at other colleges.[144] Although his Journal entry mentions just the steps and the east window glass, much other superstitious material remained, and we are left to piece together the extent of his activities from the college records and the surviving fabric. One immediate puzzle is that the college accounts show a payment to him in the second quarter of 1644 (25 March to Midsummer Day): 'Solut' magistro Dowzing 6s. 8d'.[145] The sum and the man go together, but the date, of course, bears no relation to the Journal date. Did Dowsing visit King's again, perhaps at the end of March when he was spending weekends in the town? Did he perhaps use a second visit to order the removal of the organ case, which was taken down in the quarter after this payment (at much the same time, in fact, as at St John's)?[146] Or is this summer payment merely a late record of his winter visit, the general disruption having delayed the writing up of the accounts?

The outstanding puzzle, however, is why did Dowsing not insist on the removal of the famous east window glass, highlighted in his Journal, especially if he paid a second visit. Dowsing's garbled notes indicate how struck he was by this window: crosses do indeed dominate the upper lights, with signs above each of the three representations of Christ's cross (INRI not JESUS, as he suggests); and there is, as he says, in the upper right hand light, a striking representation of the body of Christ being removed from the cross via a pair of long ladders (Plate 25).[147] Given Dowsing's explicit listing of the east window, how is it that it survives? When Westminster Abbey, Hampton Court chapel and the cathedrals of Canterbury, Worcester, Peterborough, Winchester, and Norwich all saw major destruction of glass, and when Dowsing was to spend the next four months keeping glaziers in business in parish churches, its survival is not likely to have been due to squeamishness or sentimentality on his part.

But the east window has *not* been damaged.[148] Perhaps the solution to its survival lies in the words of the Journal entry – 'to be taken'. Clearly, the job was not done on the day. It was left, and left at a time when the college was used for billeting soldiers. The *Querela* indicates that, not unusually, the military used the chapel to train in.[149] Could it be that the destruction of the glass would have incommoded the troops and was therefore neglected? There would be a pleasing irony in that. Or might it have been, as suggested in chapter 1, that the legality of Dowsing's action had been called sufficiently into question to throw him off course, causing a temporary blockage to his plans which he never rectified?

One possibility, then, is that, for whatever reason, pragmatic or political (and a variety have been suggested), the glass in the east window was simply left undisturbed.[150] Another possibility is that Dowsing was realist enough not to demand that the whole east window was replaced, but merely insisted on certain of the pictures being dealt with, and his Journal entry should be read as a rough and ready note of the most offensive images, which were then removed (and were replaced after the troubles); or were perhaps whitewashed. Something not dissimilar happened at Norwich, St Peter Mancroft where Christ has been removed from a window (barring his feet), and at Gipping, Suffolk where damage to the figure of Christ seems to be selective. Bishop Hall deliberately removed the heads from the figures in the glass of his chapel at Norwich, to save the bodies from spoliation, and similar cases are known elsewhere.[151] This is discussed further below, when we review the evidence in the accounts.

A final, more romantic, possibility is that the glass was hidden, as seems to have happened at Peterhouse, and elsewhere.[152] Dowsing records some glass in the east window, so it could not *all* have been removed; but it is notable that he does not mention the dominant presence of Christ in the window, so it is not entirely impossible that there had already been a *partial* removal. Blomefield about a hundred years later reported such a tradition, though the claim about the west window loses this report some credibility,

Table J2 *Expenditure on glass in King's College chapel, 1641–53*

*Dates are shown as modern calendar years (January to December) and quarters. However quarters start on quarter-days: so quarter 1 starts 25 December, not 1 January, etc.*

| | | | | |
|---|---|---|---|---|
| 1641: 2 | Payment to the glazier. Could be glass or roof lead (he handled both). | 9 | 08 | 02 |
| | Ditto | 13 | 16 | 02 |
| 1642: 4 | Lead solder and 'new glass' for '6 casements in le Library' | 0 | 06 | 01 |
| 1643: 1 | 'Taking down some glass in the chapel'. | 0 | 05 | 06 |
| | 'Taking down more glass in the east window' | 0 | 07 | 06 |
| 2 | '51 foote of glass newe leaded in le east window of the Chappel' | 2 | 11 | 00 |
| | To the same workman for 'two holes mending' | 0 | 05 | 00 |
| | To workmen for the same | 0 | 03 | 09 |
| 4 | To the glazier and another workman for 'slighting the chapel windows' | 0 | 02 | 00 |
| 1644: 1 | Work on the windows in the chapel | 12 | 03 | 00 |
| 4 | To repair windows of library [in side-chapel] | 1 | 02 | 09 |
| 1645: 3 | To repair window in the Vice-Provost's chapel | 4 | 03 | 04 |
| 4 | For [work on] a window in the Provost's chapel | 3 | 06 | 08 |
| 1646: 1 | To repair windows in the senior vestry and interior of library [in side-chapel]. | 0 | 14 | 03 |
| 1647: 1 | Work on library windows [side-chapel] | 0 | 16 | 06 |
| 1648 | — | | | |
| 1649 | — | | | |
| 1650: 1 | Feb to March: to repair glass in chapel | 21 | 13 | 00 |
| | For 114 iron bars for the windows | 5 | 10 | 03 |
| | To repair windows in chapel | 1 | 19 | 10 |
| 1651: 2 | To repair windows and lead-work on roof | 2 | 13 | 11 |
| 1652: 3 | Work on window in chapel | 1 | 06 | 02 |
| | Work on window in chapel | 1 | 13 | 00 |
| 1653 | — | | | |

King's College Mundum Book

as it is now accepted that the west window never contained painted glass before the nineteenth century: [153]

> The Windows are extremely beautifull of painted Glass, except the west Window, which was entirely defaced by the wicked rabble in the late Civil Wars; the other, being fortunately taken down and concealed, before that wicked Crew took it into their Heads, to make use of this House of God to train and exercise their Souldiers in, they contain the History of the old and new testament compleat, except that Part of it which was in the west Window.[154]

William Cole, writing a little later in the eighteenth century, also recorded the story that the glass was taken down in advance and hidden under the organ loft, though he did not believe it being 'well informed that they never were removed, except to be mended, since their 1st putting up'.[155] The first guide-book to the chapel, written in 1769, is also dismissive, though mistaken about the organ case:

> I know it has been commonly said, that all the Windows of the Chapel were once taken down and hidden through fear of Oliver Cromwell, lest he (in compliance with the fanatick opinions he professed) should destroy them as relicks of Popery; and that, through the confusion this occasioned, one of them (which it is pretended was the West Window) was either stolen or lost. But no such accident ever happened: though there was undoubtedly Visitors sent down by the Long Parliament to Cambridge; whose business it was to remove every superstitious ornament about the University. They indeed in pursuance of this commission, ordered the Organ★ at that time in use to be taken down, and sold the pipes, but offered not the slightest injury to the Windows: sparing them most probably at the intercession of Dr Whichcot, then provost [in fact, not until a year later]; who was promoted to that dignity by the Long Parliament. The image (over the South door, within the Choir) did not escape, as 'tis said, the hands of some furious enthusiast who, in a fit of religious frenzy, effaced an object so offensive to this sight.
>
> ★*Footnote*:... As to the outer case [of the organ], it was never taken down.[156]

The college accounts are intriguing, but do not enable us to decide between the three possibilities.[157] Indeed, they can be used to support any of them. In early 1643, at about the same time that the organ was being removed as a precautionary measure, the regular college glazier and his three workmen spent about two and a half days 'taking down' glass in the chapel, one of the records of payment explicitly mentioning the east window (see Table J2), and shortly afterwards there was significant expenditure putting glass into the east window. Ten man-days would not have been enough to remove everything, but the most inflammatory material could have been selected. Was the same glass put back, or replaced with uncontentious infill? The expression 'taking down' does not seem to be used of the glass at other times during the period 1641–54, and the date is exactly right for the hiding of objects likely to offend Puritan sensibilities.[158] It may also be significant that, unusually, the payments for 'taking down' are recorded in the accounts under the catch-all 'Necessary Expenditure', rather than under the routine listing of outgoings on the chapel.[159] On the other hand, the use of the expression 'taking down' may be merest coincidence, and the work itself routine, dealing with normal wear and tear; glass at this period needed fairly frequent re-leading.

There was in the final quarter of 1643, during the time Dowsing visited the college, an intriguing payment for 'slighting the chapel windows'; this took about two man-days, but it is quite unclear what it means. In addition there was a relatively large sum of £12. 3s. 0d. paid to the college glazier for work on the windows in the following quarter (Christmas term), at the start of 1644, suggesting that *something* might have been done then, immediately after Dowsing's visit. In the following years, except for the side-chapel windows discussed below, there was no further expenditure on glass until the relatively major work of late winter 1650–51, when more than £27 was spent in repair work, including payment for 114 iron window bars. This overall sequence of expenditure could be interpreted as partial precautionary removal in early 1643, and/or whitewashing and/or partial removal in late 1643 and 1644, followed (in any of those cases) by reinstatement some eight years later. Equally, the expenditure may simply represent an accumulation of running repairs: these typically totalled about £50 every ten years, and the total for our whole decade is of this order of magnitude.[160] Sadly, the matter of the east window glass simply cannot be resolved.

In contrast, the more accessible side-chapels have lost a considerable quantity of glass: might some of this damage have been at the hand of Dowsing or his contemporaries?[161] In support of this is a notable run of expenditure on repairing glass in these windows in the couple of years after Dowsing's visit (Table J2). Interestingly, one of these windows still had white-wash visible a hundred years later, though it was then said this had been put on at the Reformation.[162]

If the east window glass is a puzzle, the extent of other damage which Dowsing might have instigated, or nodded at, is a little clearer. There is no programme of repairs to the chapel furnishings until 1651–52, seven or eight years after his visit, when there are repairs to the organ loft (probably where the organ had been removed before he arrived) and to the chancel pavement, where he had ordered steps removed.

*1651 quarter 1*
Paid George Ashley for repairing the shields in the chapel  . . . . o  06  oo

*1651 quarter 4 – 1652 quarter 4*
Paid to George Woodruff for his and his servants' work about
    the screen at the east end of the chapel, together with nails,
    iron and glue . . . . . . . . . . . . . . . . . . . . . . . . . . . . . . I  10  00
Paid to the same for his and his servants' work about 'la roodloft'
    and in repairing those things which were broken during the
    time of the commission . . . . . . . . . . . . . . . . . . . . . . o  13  00
Paid to them for similar work . . . . . . . . . . . . . . . . . . . . . o  05  00
Paid to Thomas Parker for 400 'le paving tyles' in the cha-
    pel[Dowsing's work on the steps still unrepaired?] . . . . . . 12  07  06
Paid to him for his and others work in the chapel . . . . . . . . . 3  18  00
Paid to Jacobo Wisdom, painter, for his work in the chapel . . . . I  03  00
Thomas Grumball for his work about the east end of the chapel . . o  10  04
Paid John Adams for Meremio and his and his servants work on
    'le Rood-loft' in the chapel[163] . . . . . . . . . . . . . . . . . 3  04  07

There is also at this time an intriguing payment for the carriage of the chapel ornaments to London, and a few months later the chapel clerk, Jonathan Pyndar, is rewarded with one pound for 'repairing and keeping the chapel ornaments' (for just how many months or years had we guarded them, we are left wondering).[164]

Although Dowsing mentions only the steps and the glass, at the Restoration it was found necessary not only to purchase new hangings (at a cost of about £50), and (the evidence suggests) to lay a new floor of black and white marble within the altar rails, but also to put up new panel-work behind the screen, and to mend the altar at a cost of some £24. This may reflect significant damage, which could, of course, have been done by Dowsing, or by others before his arrival, or may perhaps have been the result of later hooliganism on the part of the soldiery who were quartered in the college (ten shillings was paid to soldiers who were 'like to be tumultous' in the chapel in late 1644).[165]

The fabric itself sends mixed messages. There are many superstitious survivals: the angel frieze in the choir, the corbel angels between the choir windows, the three figures over the south choir doorway, the depictions of God the Father, Christ and St George on the screen, and the representations of the four evangelists on the lectern. In the mid eighteenth century Cole recorded a parchment *Orate* to Provost Robert Brassie (d.1558), covered in horn, attached to a chantry door.[166] There is, however, some defacement of stone sculpture, notably an Assumption on the south-east doorway. In addition, there is damage to brasses, though not all can be attributed to

Dowsing and his contemporaries: for example, Robert Brassie (d.1558) has today lost a scroll, but this was still in place in the mid eighteenth century.[167] However, Robert Hacombleyn (d.1523) had lost his foot inscription plate by the mid eighteenth century,[168] and the brass of John Argentein (d.1507), appears to have been deliberately damaged as it had already lost its crucifix (but kept its *Orate*) when Cole described it in 1742; a further two shields have disappeared since then, reinforcing the point that without documentary evidence it is impossible to allocate blame for partial damage to brasses.[169] Quite clearly deliberate is the gouging through of the opening *Orate pro anima* and closing *cuius anime propicietur Deus* of the William Towne brass of 1496; as Cole put it, 'the beginning and end scratched out with a chisel'.[170]

So by no means all has been destroyed, either by Dowsing or by other excesses of enthusiasm of one sort or another in subsequent centuries.[171] Most importantly, although the east end has undergone major changes since Dowsing's time, the glass is still there to be wondered at.

## 14.  1643, Sidney Colledge, Dec. 30. We saw nothing there to be mended.

Like Emmanuel, Sidney Sussex was founded in Elizabethan times to train preachers, and under the hard-line Calvinist Samuel Ward, Master since 1610, was a well-known centre of Puritanism.[172] This was the college of Cromwell; and the college, too, of the Earl of Manchester, in charge of the Parliamentary forces of the Eastern Association, and the authority behind Dowsing's warrant.

The college chapel was fitted up (probably in 1602) from a ruined Franciscan building on the site, which was cleared of rubble and had its thatched roof repaired. To the discomfort of the Laudian wing of the church, the chapel, along with those of Emmanuel and Corpus Christi, was not consecrated; and it was (again, like Emmanuel) orientated north-south.[173]

Inside it was plastered and whitewashed, with a floor of stone, and had a wainscoted south end, surmounted with a carved coat of arms. The upper floor of the building was the library, and the ceiling of the chapel was decorated with plaster pendants, put up by the same builder who made those in the drawing room of the Master's lodge at Trinity. There were the arms of Queen Elizabeth in 'painted glasse in the great window at the upper end of the Chappel'. Hanging on the walls were two old iron candlesticks, and another 36 of brass were purchased in 1638 (and lasted for more than a hundred years – this was not a rich college). There is, of course, no sign of the altar candlesticks provided in many of the other colleges.

For furniture there was, unusually for a college chapel, a pulpit (as also at Emmanuel), with a velvet hanging and cushion; the pulpit was at originally movable, but after 1636 was fixed to the wall. There were three desks. The communion table, round which the college gathered, was provided with a choice of carpets. Presumably for routine use was an old one bought for 8*s.* 4*d.* in 1605; there was a cloth carpet of 'French Green', three yards long, costing £1. 12*s.* 0*d.*; and, probably saved for festivals, was a very expensive velvet carpet, fringed with gold, with the college arms and the initials of the donor in the centre. This was kept in its own box, and together with the pulpit hangings, cost £50. Also for the table there were two damask cloths, and three damask napkins, all with the college name on them. And, the gift of various donors, there was fine communion plate bearing the college arms, much of which has survived. [174]

Thus the chapel was not stark or unadorned, and for a college short of funds, had some rich appurtenances to worship. However it contained none of the aids to devotion associated with the Laudian movement, and had, of course, no overhang of medieval imagery: it is not surprising that Dowsing found there 'was nothing to be mended'.

One may speculate – in the complete absence, it must be admitted, of any evidence – that Dowsing had been there on business a few months before, for early in the morning of 13 September 1643 Parliamentary soldiers burst into the chapel and interrupted the Fellows during their service. This was on the day they were to elect a new Master, Samuel Ward having died, and it was feared that a Royalist candidate, a moderate supporter of episcopacy, might win by a majority of one. A Fellow was taken from the communion table and imprisoned, thus ensuring a victory for the more acceptable candidate. These were Manchester's soldiers, and if, as suggested in chapter 1, Dowsing was Provost-Marshall and in Cambridge, he would surely have known of the incident even if he had no direct hand in it. [175]

The incident suggests that a good number of the Fellows were less rigidly Calvinistic than Samuel Ward. Perhaps it was a generational divide. The actions of 'Mr Rodes', probably in his later thirties, would support this. These are recorded in the 1641 report to the Parliamentary Committee, which, as would be expected, is very brief, a few lines compared with the several pages devoted to Peterhouse, and contains no criticism of the furnishings of the chapel. But some changes were being introduced, or tolerated:

Some in this Colledge bow towards the Elements at the sacrament tyme. Mr Rodes sometimes Deane used some violence to bring the schollers to the observation of some rites, not in practise there before, as standing up at gloria patri and the Gospell and bowing at the name Jesus. [176]

This chapel was pulled down in 1776 and rebuilt in approximately the same position; the new chapel was remodelled in 1833, and altered, extended and refitted in the early twentieth century.[177] Nothing from the chapel of Dowsing's period survives.

### 15. Madlin Colledg, Dec. 30. We brake downe about 40 superstitious pictures, Joseph and Mary stood to be espoused in the windowe.[178]

Under the Mastership of Henry Smyth, Magdalene appears to have been little influenced by the events in other colleges, and the report of 1641 paid scant attention to the chapel.[179] Of its appearance it said only that 'the Communion table is set Altarwise and stands close to the wall', and went on to complain that 'the second service [communion service] is read there, towards which place many in the colledge bow, as also turnings towards the East upon severall occasions are practized'.[180]

The chapel, of medieval origin, was greatly reworked in the eighteenth and nineteenth century. Little appears to be known of the glass destroyed by Dowsing, though some armorial glass appears to have outlived his visit.[181] The east window, which presumably held the superstitious glass, was bricked up in 1754, and exposed, replaced and reglazed in the nineteenth century. The old glass now in the windows is almost certainly an import, collected by Thomas Kerrich, late eighteenth-century antiquary and President of the college.[182]

### 16. 1643, Christ's Colledg, Jan. 2. We pulled down divers pictures, and angels, and the steps. Dr Bambridg have promised to take them downe; *Orat. pro anima* on the brasen eagle.

*Marginal comment by Baker, transcribing the text:* NB These notes are in a bad hand, and neither good English or Latin.

Christ's was somewhat tardy in effecting Laudian reform. Its head, Thomas Bainbridge, was generally regarded as a Puritan. Perhaps Laud's proposed visit in 1635 concentrated minds, for by 1636 it was reported to Laud that 'their service is much reformed of late', although 'of the Organ (which they had) there is nothing left but a broken case'. Towards the end of 1636 and into 1637 there was considerable expenditure on the chapel, including the setting up of a new organ,[183] and the report of 1641 shows that some very unpuritan furnishings and ceremonial had been introduced:

> An high Altar wth steps and railes of late yeares erected, behind wch are rich hangings of blewe and pictures of Angells above the Altar.
> On the Altar stand two Candlsticks, two Tapers and a Bason.

> Adoration is directed towards the Altar and used by the greatest part, and turnings towards the east generally practiced at theire risinge up at gloria patri and other occasions, on surplice dayes they sing the sev[er]all parts of Divine service save the chapters, and in theire singing of hymnes and anthemes they use organs and sing alternation, Many things in theire service is performed non-intelligibly to men not acquainted wth pricksong. Schollers spend very much time in learning of pricksong… to the great losse of theire time and preiudice to theire studdies.[184]

But the change of political climate led to a quick retreat, for the report adds a postscript:

> Since this information was made the master of this Colledg Dr Bainbrigge hath taken away the railes, hangings, Candlesticks and bason, placeing the table according to Rubrick. He hath likewise prohibited adoration towards the East and standing that way.

The recently installed organ was taken down at around this time, and re-erected elsewhere in the college, to be put back in the chapel at the Restoration.[185]

Despite this early reformation, the new angels remained to catch Dowsing's eye. He also saw 'divers pictures' which may have been the 'hangings of blewe and pictures of Angells above the Altar', but may refer to the 'glass with imagery' (including a Saint Christopher) set up around the time of the chapel's completion (1510–11), and probably still in place at the time of his visit. The chapel was altered in the seventeenth and eighteenth century, but some pre-Reformation glass remains in the chapel's north windows, mainly of English monarchs, preserved by the terms of the Parliamentary Ordinance, but including a God the Father which may owe its current fragmentary condition to Dowsing (it may, however, not have originally belonged to the chapel).[186]

It seems that although Dowsing would have seen the communion table 'placed according to Rubrick' (ie table-wise), the steps themselves had not been removed. The current communion table is of the mid seventeenth century, and may therefore be the one referred to in the 1641 report, and seen by Dowsing.[187]

The medieval 'brasen Eagle' lectern referred to in the Journal remains (Plate 28). It bears, however, no sign of an inscription, nor obvious damage where one might have been filed away; the inscription was possibly attached rather than engraved.[188] Or it may be that there has been some slight mistranscription of the text and the final phrase should be read as listing two separate items: an *Orate* (from one of the brasses in the chapel) and a brazen eagle.[189]

## 17.  Emanuell Colledg. There is nothing to be done.[190]

That there was 'nothing to be done' is a reflection of the consistent Puritan bias of the 'pure house of Emmanuel' since its Elizabethan foundation. The chapel – unconsecrated, set north-south, 'plain in its neatness' – was whitewashed in 1587, and probably remained so. It was wainscoted, with 'seats thrice round about', and contained nine windows, with the arms of Queen Elizabeth 'in the greatest [window] at the end'. There were two reading desks, and a pulpit 'with a moveable ladder up to it', and 'a base of wood in the wall for the Howerglasse to stand on'. A seat was erected in the chapel for the Master 'to defend him from the wynd'.[191]

Early in the seventeenth century it was recorded that

> they receive the Holy Sacrament sittinge upon Forms about the Communion Table, and doe pull the Loafe one from the other, after the Minister hath begon. And soe the Cupp, one drinking as it were to another, like good fellows, without any particular application of the said words [this is my body], more than once for all. [192]

The 1636 report to Archbishop Laud confirmed the earlier picture, and cannot have pleased him: 'their seates are placed round about & above [to the liturgical east of] the Communion Table'.[193]

Not surprisingly, in comparison with many other colleges, little was spent on the chapel fittings during the 1630s, though under the Mastership of William Sandcroft (1629–37) there was some concern for more seemly communion furnishings: a new 'communion tablecloth' was purchased in 1630 (the old one was later recycled into six napkins for the hall!), another 'of Diaper' in 1634, and a 'carpet for the Communion table' and 'cushion for the pulpit' in 1635. So far so chaste, though further signs of a desire for beauty might be seen in the generous bequest of Sandcroft who in 1637 left £100 for the purchase of splendid new communion plate, still possessed by the college. [194]

Despite this long-standing and committed Puritanism, by 1636 an alumnus of the college was distressed to find 'cursed formalists' at the college, 'many of the fellows bowing at Jesus'.[195] The 1641 report confirms that college members were not immune to the attractions of Laudian ceremonial, and felt the pull of Peterhouse:

> Bowing towards the Communion table introduced and practised at ingresse and egresse out of the Chappell by two of the Fellowes without the Consent of the Colledge viz Mr Hall and Mr Holbech... Some few Schollers in the colledge have practised this bowing at ingresse and egresse wherein some of them have bene so p[er]emptory as that they would not easily forbeare upon the Masters prohibition and some still continue in the

practise of it... Some of the Schollers have received harme by theire frequent goeing to Peterhouse chappell contrary to the orders and government of the Colledge as appeareth by theire Novel gestures in the Chappell, as bowing at theire rising up at gloria patri or the Gospell, as also by crucifixes wch have bene occasionally discovered in two or three of theire Chambers by the Fellowes wch weekely visit Schollars chambers by course according to the colledg statutes.

As at Christ's and King's, the change in circumstances in the early 1640s encouraged a quick about-turn, for a note added later states:

Since this information was drawne Mr Holbech hath forborne bowing towards the Table, and Mr Hall professeth that he will forbeare because he sees authority against it.[196]

The chapel of Dowsing's time was converted first to a library (in 1678–79, following the completion of Wren's new chapel), and then to an additional dining-hall in 1932; it is now used chiefly as a meeting room and lecture room. During this twentieth-century work the screen separating the chapel from the ante-chapel was exposed, and more fully restored in the 1950s, but no other chapel furnishings of Dowsing's time survive in the college. The original pulpit is now in Trumpington church. The communion table of Dowsing's time may be the one previously in the ante-chapel, and at present on E staircase of the college.[197]

*Dowsing was dealing with the parish churches in Cambridge at the same time as the college chapels. However he records them separately. As discussed briefly in chapter 4, he seems not to have visited them in any particular order.*

18. 1643. At Peter's parish [St Peter], December 30, we brake downe ten popish pictures; we took 3 popish inscriptions for prayers to be made for their soules, and burnt the rayles, diged up the steps, and they are to be levelled on Wednesday.[198]

There are records of a number of lost inscriptions and brasses which could be the 'popish inscriptions'. In the eighteenth century it was recorded that 'the Altar is neither railed in nor on any ascent; nor are there any inscriptions either in the chancel or nave, tho' a great many stones for both. There is no painted glass of any sort in the windows'.[199] Dowsing's work had been done well.

This was a small, poor urban parish. The church had fallen into disrepair by 1760, and was rebuilt in much reduced form in 1781.[200]

19. 1643. Giles' parish [St Giles], December 30, we broke down 12 superstitious pictures, and tooke 2 popish inscriptions, 4 cherubims, and a dove for the high loft of the font, and a holy water fonte at the porch dore.

The church was rebuilt in 1875.

20. 1643. At Little Mary's [St Mary the Less], December 29, 30, we brake downe 60 superstitious pictures, some popes, and crucifixes, and God the Father sitting in a chayer, and holding a globe in his hand.

The original church of St Peter-without-Trumpington-Gate was appropriated to the use of the Bishop of Ely's scholars in 1284, giving the newly-founded college its name (now Peterhouse). The present building of 1352, with changed dedication to St Mary, continued to serve as the college chapel for almost another three centuries. In 1632 the college built itself a new chapel (see commentary on Journal entry 1), leaving the church largely for parochial use.

In 1639, in reply to the Bishop's enquiries, the churchwardens reported the 'chancel windows out of repaire' and 'no dore to the inclosure of the communion table'.[201] By this time Peterhouse had met most of the expenses associated with its new chapel, and had dealt with the ravages of the storms of Autumn 1636, and thus in 1637–38, by decree of the Master and Fellows, a portion of the college income was allocated to the restoration of the choir and altar of the parish church. In the following year other income was similarly set aside, and the sum topped up by donations for the east window from the Fellows, with Cosin, the Master, leading the way with a gift of £5.[202]

This funded an extensive building campaign. Surplus stone from the new college chapel was used to relay the pavement round the altar. The windows were repaired, with work to the east window alone costing more than £40, about half of which was on glass, the other half on stone and ironwork. A new roof was built, almost certainly the fine seventeenth-century roof over the three easternmost bays which was taken down by Scott in the late nineteenth century as beyond repair. There were major repairs to the internal and external fabric. Payments are recorded to masons, metalworkers, paviours, plasterers, carpenters and painters, the wage bill coming to more than £50, and the total bill to the college amounting to more than £100, not including materials already in stock.

What was the result of all this? We would expect Cosin, a leading exponent of ceremonial in worship, to ensure that the church was provided with an appropriate interior. That this was the case is confirmed by the report written a couple of years after completion of the work, in 1641. This describes, from an outraged Puritan viewpoint, the curacy of Richard Crashaw, author of *Steps to the Temple*, who was ejected from his Peterhouse fellowship soon after Dowsing's visit, followed by exile and conversion to Roman Catholicism. The Puritan account of his ministry gives an incidental description of the interior of the church:

> His [Crashaw's] practyses in little St Maryes, where he is curate, are superstitious. On every Sunday and on many holy dayes he hath a Communion, when the parish is both poore and of small extent: what this Implyes those know who are not ignorant of the popish doctrine of private masses. The church plate he hath exchanged for a covered bowle made after his owne devising: on the cup is the full portrature of the Christ with these words, *This is my blood indeede.* Soe likewise on the lipp of the Cover are these words, *This is my body indeed.* On the top of the cover is a Crosse. Before he officiates at the Communion he washes his hands in the vestry, where is a table set Altarwise towards the East, and puts on a fresh paire of shoes which are appropriated to the Altar. All the remainder of wyne after he hath made his low incurvation he drinks off and picks up the crummes which remaine of the bread.
>
> In his Catechise he told the people that God had set apart one part of the church and that was the place where the Altar stood, calling it *Sanctum Sanctorum.* And that he puts much holinesse in that place appeares from hence, that hee permitts not the clerke to come within the railes and hath converted a carpet wch cost £8 into a foot carpet to tread upon when offices are performed at the Altar. He requireth an offertory to be made by all that Communicate at the rayles, and gives mony to the poore people to offer with all. [203]

Such an interior may well have been decorated with images of one sort and another, as in Peterhouse chapel, and certainly Dowsing found a significant number of superstitious pictures; but it is impossible to say how many were recent and how many of medieval origin. Any new pictorial glass in the east window would have been at risk, and there is a hint of severe damage in the gift of £4 from the college in 1643–44 'pro reparacione templi', and in that of £2 from Catharine Hall in 1646–47, 'towards the reparation of Little S. Mary's'.[204] In line with the Parliamentary Ordinance, Dowsing left untouched a number of coats of arms, which were still in place in a chancel window early in the eighteenth century. By an oversight he also left amongst them an *Orate* to William Whittlesey (Master of Peterhouse at the time of the medieval rebuilding of the church), and a Trinity triangle with a *Pater non est Filius* – this, at least, was medieval glass. All this has now gone.[205]

Still surviving are two – more strictly, one and a half – brasses to former Masters of Peterhouse. One is the lower half of John Holbrook (d.1436) who now has just a fragment of inscription left: in the eighteenth century Cole recorded a great deal more, so Dowsing cannot be blamed for this removal. The other brass, probably to John Hawkworth (d.1500) has lost its foot inscription, and had done by Cole's time, though whether Dowsing was responsible for this is not known. There are records of further lost brasses and inscriptions.[206]

There are canopied niches both inside and outside the church which could have held 'some popes and God the father sitting in a Chayer' if they were not in the glass.

The font cover of 1632 remains (heavily restored earlier this century), a reminder of the 1630s drive for decency in church furnishings (Plate 29). The medieval font is decorated with later coats of arms, painted on the formerly blank shields, perhaps as part of the beautification of 1638–40.[207]

## 21. 1643. At Butal parish [St Botolph]. We dig'd down the steps, and beat down twelve popish inscriptions and pictures. Church-wardens, Mr. Morley, Mr. Wilson.[208]

In the churchwardens' accounts there is, as elsewhere, evidence indicative of work being carried out before Dowsing's visit. In 1642 there is a relatively small sum for

mending the steeple and all the glass windowes about the church . 17s. 6d.

However in 1638 £11. 18s. 0d. had been spent on 'new glazing all the windows' in plain glass, so there may not have been very much imagery remaining to be dealt with by this time.[209] Certainly, compared to some of the other Cambridge churches, Dowsing's description of what needs to be done is relatively restrained.

In 1643 there is an item 'for takeing up the steps in the chancell according to order'. This is for the sum of one shilling, representing one or two day's wage for a labourer, which may accord with the amount of work required. The churchwardens' accounts for the following year include small sums for windows which could be the result of Dowsing's visit

*1644*

| | | |
|---|---|---|
| For mending the glasse windows . . . . . . . . . . . . . . . . . . . . . | 0 04 | 00 |
| 18 quarres of new glass put in and 14 foote of glasse... . . . . . . . | 0 04 | 10 |
| Boards for the windows[210] . . . . . . . . . . . . . . . . . . . . . . | 0 01 | 08 |

Three bells survive here with forbidden inscriptions: *Sancte Apoline ora pro nobis* also *Sancte Andrea...* and *Sancta Margareta...*, an indication, confirmed elsewhere, that Dowsing was not greatly interested in bells.

In 1750 there was a 'fine ancient altar tomb with all the brasses reaved'.[211] In the north aisle there is a mutilated mid-fifteenth-century brass of the small figure of a priest and the indent of a figure in academic dress. Any or all of these could have had 'popish inscriptions'.[212] The splendid font casing and canopy of 1637 survives intact: it has no superstitious imagery, unlike the pelican covers of the same period in the Marshland (Plate 29). (If pelicans were superstitious – Dowsing left alone the one atop the font cover at Ufford in Suffolk, entry 247.)

## 22. 1643/4, January 1. Edward's parish [St Edward, King and Martyr], we diged up the steps, and brake down 40 pictures, and took off 10 superstitious inscriptions.[213]

In 1639 the churchwardens' reported that 'there are 2 steps in our Chancell to the Comunion table, wee have a decent raile of wood above the stepps without a cover as yet reaching cross from north to south, the pillars are so close that noe doggs cann get in'.[214] By the time Dowsing arrived the rail had gone (perhaps as early as 1641, as at Great St Mary's), but the steps still needed dealing with.

Little appears to be known of the glass in this church, though in 1639 it was reported to be 'in no place stopped up but well glazed'. In the early eighteenth century the east window contained the arms of Trinity Hall, which may have been a recent introduction associated with new arrangements for the altar, or may have been a survival of Dowsing's visit (arms were explicitly protected by the Parliamentary Ordinance); the glass was later replaced. One bell with *Sancta Anna ora pro nobis* remained and survived the recent rehanging. Numerous figure and inscription indents are still present. The pulpit, tangible reminder of some of the early Reformers, is back in the church after its sojourn at King's.[215]

## 23. 1643, January 1st, Alhallows [All Saints]. We brake downe diverse superstitious pictures, and eighteen cherubims. Mr. James church-warden.[216]

All Saints, in Trinity Street, was demolished in 1864. The churchwardens' accounts for the year 1643–44 survive under the names of Thomas James ('Mr James') and George Potter. The following items are of interest:

For taking down the crosse at the chancel end . . . . . . . . . . . o o1 o6
For the fee of him that had order for the glasse windows . . . . . o o6 o8

For writing a petition to the Earle of Manchester . . . . . . . . . 0 02 00
For cleaning the church after the prisoners being there . . . . . . 0 05 06
To the Glasier [217] . . . . . . . . . . . . . . . . . . . . . . . . . . 1 00 00

If the entries are in their correct order the taking down of 'the crosse' was
done before Dowsing's visit. It is not mentioned by Dowsing and may have
been done on the initiative of the parish, perhaps with the aim of making a
visible gesture which would placate the reformers.

The description 'of him that had order for the glasse window' is useful in
confirming the predominance of window breaking when 'superstitious
pictures' are given in the Journal, corroborated in almost every set of
surviving parish church accounts.[218] In this case some idea of the meaning
of 'divers' can be judged by the glazier's bill for £1.

## 24. Great Maries [St Mary the Great], 1643/4, December 27, and before 7th of January, Mr. Hawayward, church-warden.[219]

Dowsing records two visits to this church, on Wednesday 27 December
and 'before Jan 7th' (a Sunday).[220] He notes them in a single entry, which
simply reads 'Mr. Hawayward, Church-warden' – this refers to William
Howarde, joint churchwarden at the time.[221] At first sight the brevity of this
entry is inexplicable. St Mary the Great, the University church, thronged
alike by town and gown, was arguably the grandest parish church in the city,
and had been altered and beautified just four years earlier. Indeed, the
church's significance was such that the reordering and introduction of
ceremonial were specifically raised against Archbishop Laud at his trial.[222]
The church must surely have been a prime candidate for Dowsing's reforming zeal.

Yet no works of destruction are listed in his Journal, and to this day there
remain medieval superstitious pictures in the roof bosses (for example, a
priest kneeling before a crucifix) and cherubim in both the nave roof bosses
and north aisle corbels. On the other hand Cole, writing a hundred years
later, says that although Dowsing records no visit, 'I make no doubt but that
he made sad Ravage here by the Quantity of dismantled grave stones in
every part of the Church', and there are still numerous indents of pre-
Reformation brasses.[223] Did Dowsing do work here or not? Dowsing's
cryptic entry for this significant and highly visible church needs some
explanation.

Seven years earlier, in 1636, a critical (indeed, antagonistic) report on the
church had been provided to Archbishop Laud. Severe overcrowding was
reported, Great St Mary's being shared by town and university, and university sermons being a considerable draw.[224] The hustle and bustle, the

irregular orientation of the congregation (who, wherever they sat, all faced towards the pulpit in the centre of the nave), the presence of layfolk in the chancel, the pulpit blocking the view of the communion table at the east end, the minister reading the ante-communion service facing due *west* – all went strongly against the principles of controlled good order and public reverence which Laud was enforcing:

> The Service Pulpit is sett up in the midst, a good distance below the Chauncell, and looks full to the Belfrie, so that all Service, second Service [the first part of Holy Communion] and all… is there and performed that way…
>
> When the University comes in for the Sermon the chancell (the higher part of it) is filled with boyes and Townsmen, and… with *Townswomen* also, all in a rude heap betwixt the Doctors and the Altar.[225] In the Bodie of the ch. Men Women and Scholers thrust together promiscuously, but [for] the place onely before the Pulpit, *which they call the Cock Pitt*, and which they leave somewhat free for masters [Masters of Arts] to sitt in. The rest of the churche is taken up by the Townsmen of the Parrishe and their families, which is one reason among others that many Scholers pretend for not coming to this churche… [226]

On top of the crowding and (to Laudian eyes, at least) lack of decorum, the church itself was disordered and cluttered:

> a parte of it [the church] is made a Lumber House for the Materials of the Scaffolds [for the annual Commencement ceremony], for Bookbinders dry Fats, for aumerie Cupboards, and such like implements, which they know not readily where else to put. The West windows are half blinded up with a Cobler's and a Bookbinder's Shop… The Seats many of them are lately cooped up high with wainscot…[227]

These unsatisfactory arrangements had continued despite a recent re-ordering of the chancel. Probably in 1635 (the work does not seem to be well documented) a new communion table had been placed within rails at the east end. This was at the expense of the University.[228] To provide a decent covering, £3. 16s. 0d. had been spent by the parish on 'a green broad cloth for the communion table and silk fring for it, and for velvett for a cuschon and fring for the same'.[229]

A few years later, in 1639, little seemed to have changed from what was disapprovingly reported in 1636. In particular, the communion service was not always carried out in the approved manner, kneeling devoutly at the rails in the chancel:

> At the three great feasts, the table [is] brought in the body of the church by reason of the multitude of communicants… some receive the communion

in their seats... the ministers... face to the west... our minister doth not read the second service [communion service] at the communion table.[230]

A casual approach to the altar and its setting ('we have provided a man to keepe out doggs, but he is negligent in doing it') may not have been unusual in Cambridge, a town inclined to Puritanism. At Christmas the same year, in his report to the King, Laud complained that 'in most of the Chancels of the Churches in Cambridge, there are common Seats over-high and unfitting that place', and suggested that 'admonition' be tried, followed by a High Commission if that failed. The King agreed, annotating the report 'if faire meanes will not, power must redress it'.[231]

But change had already arrived at St Mary's. If in the first place it was triggered by Bishop Wren's instructions to deal with the faults reported to him earlier in the year, it received major impetus in November 1639, when John Cosin, Master of Peterhouse, became Vice-Chancellor of the University. Cosin was a leading exponent of good order, ceremonial and beauty in worship, and a leading hate figure for Puritans, not least for the elaborate services he had introduced at Peterhouse. He may well have written the unfriendly report on the church in 1636.[232] He knew what to do, and moved quickly, with a style perhaps midway between 'faire meanes' and 'power'. By December he had taken space in the nave of the church away from the townsfolk to make more room for members of the University; removed students and townsfolk from the chancel 'where some hundreds used to stand and heare', reserving it instead for 'doctors and such'; forbidden anyone 'to sitt on the pulpit staire'; cutt the pews about to make them uniform; imposed formal seating arrangements; restored a dress code for university members; and arranged for bouncers on the door to enforce the new regime. And he was at least allowing if not actively encouraging bowing to a cross in the church.[233]

The townsfolk protested at their loss of privilege. They would in 'no wise assent or approve of' what had been done, and insisted they would enter both church and chancel 'to serve God as they have done time out of mind of man'. A legal battle seemed likely. In the event, as we shall see, this was unnecessary.[234]

During his year in office Cosin was to spend more than £164 of university money on the church.[235] The parish paid virtually nothing, contributing a mere 1s. 0d. on 'mending the rayles before the communion table'. Some of the University's money was spent on decorating the altar with

a dresse of red and blew taffaty for the Altar (erected and railed in formerly by Dr Lany [Laney] and Dr Beale) wherein he [Cosin] hath placed two bookes covered with red velvet, providing a great Number of long Cushions [for kneeling on] of red and blew taffatie...[236]

In October 1640, Cosin spent more than £100 in providing a new screen

> at the entrance into the Quire the coronis [cornice] of wch on both sides is full of Crosses cut through the wainscot, from the middle of wch skreene ascends a great hollowe pile of wainscot cast into the forme of a pyramis and capacious enough for the receiving of an image. This is mounted to the topp of the Roofe where it is entertayned wth a sheild wch seemes to hover over it. [237]

What was this 'pyramis' (that is, a pyramid) which surmounted the screen? At Brancepeth church in County Durham, where Cosin was appointed to the living in 1626, he arranged for considerable woodwork to be introduced into the church. This included, probably in the 1630s, a screen with five gothic canopies, seemingly in imitation of the medieval reredos at Durham Cathedral, where he was prebendary. These might perhaps be described as a pyramids, so perhaps the object at St Mary's was a giant gothic canopy. Whatever the precise shape, Puritan lampoons of a few years later referred to the 'triple crown' (that is, a pope's crown) which Cosin erected at St Mary's, so it seems likely that the 'pyramis' had three stages.[238]

The Puritan author of the report in which these details are recorded was in no doubt as to the idolatrous purpose of these and other changes.

> What his reason for this, as also for there moving of the readers pewe from the middle of the Church to one side, and of barring schollers out of the upper part of the square, cannot be imagined unless that the Altar might with more conveniency be eyed at the tyme of Adoration. This is most certaine that since he trimmed up the Altar, and left the middle spaces of the Church for void the practice of incurvation [bowing in reverence] and kneeling towards the East hath bene much improved...[239]

Such 'innovations' had no place within the Puritan scheme of things. Within a year of this work, in September 1641, the House of Commons issued an order insisting on the removal of communion tables from the east end of churches, and the destruction of their rails.[240] Across the country the response to this was variable, but at St Mary's there is evidence of the rapid, and probably enthusiastic, compliance of the parishioners, as can be seen in the churchwardens' accounts for 1641–42

> payd for takeing downe the rayles and levelling the chancel . . . £2. 7s. 0d.

Yet at about the same time the churchwardens record expenditure for 'a bonefire at the King's returne out of Scotland and a bonefire on the King's birthday'. These accounts, bowing to Parliament yet celebrating the King, are a sharp testimony of the troubles of a community on the brink of civil war.

In 1641, then, the churchwardens responded briskly to the order from Parliament. But at some stage they were blocked, at least temporarily, by Dr Rowe, of Trinity College, which held the advowson.[241] The evidence is provided some years later by a sworn statement from the two church-wardens. One of them, Peter Collins, a grocer, said that

> being about to execute that Ordinance by taking away the Railes, and stepps, in the said Church the said Doctor Row, sent for this deponent and asked him, what he meant to doe, this deponent answered, he meant to execute the Ordinance of Parliament by laing the Chancell levill, and takeing away the stepps, whereupon he said this deponent had nothing to doe with the Chancell, and [it] went contrary to the Ordinance, and it was not the Parliaments meaneing that he should doe soe, and bidd this de-ponent doe noe more then he would answer, for he should heare of it hereafter and said, he would bring [claim] that there had been two stepps there by the space of forty yeares, and went away in a greate rage, threatening this deponent.[242]

The other warden was Stephen Fortune, haberdasher, a man active against Royalists. He confirmed the story, saying that 'Dr Row came to the church to this deponent, and thretened this deponent that if he went forward with the worke he would proceed against him, wheruppon this deponent did desist until he had further order from the Parliament'.

Whatever frustrations the Puritan churchwardens felt in 1641, within eighteen months there were new developments. By then Parliamentary troops were in Cambridge in some numbers, making a nuisance of them-selves, their noisy presence giving ample scope for Royalist propaganda.[243] It is from such a source (biased and unreliable) that we hear of the story of Master Cromwell ordering the tearing up of a prayer book at St Mary's:

> in the University Church... in the presence of the then Generall our Common-Prayer Book was torne before our faces... *M. Cromwell* encour-aging them in it, and openly rebuking the University Clerk who com-plained of it before his Souldiers. [244]

Cosin's 'triple crown' was set upon. According to the Royalists, this too was Cromwell's responsibility:

> multitudes of enraged Souldiers (let loose to reforme)... have ruined a beautifull carved structure in the universitie church... (though indeed that was not done without direction from... *M. Cromwell*)... [which] had not one jot of Imagery or statue worke about it.[245]

The events of early 1643 are clarified by a diary kept by Dr Dillingham.

|        | Mr. Crumwell come to Towne. |
|--------|------------------------------|
| Jan    | Dr Cosin's Screene at St Marie's defaced. |
| [Jan] 29 | The clarke set the 74 Psl to be sung before the sermon in the after-noone. |
| Febr   | The Pyramis at St Maries over the Doctors Seats quite pulled down.[246] |

The choice of Psalm 74 on Sunday 29 January is a telling detail. Sung at the University sermon, at one o'clock in the afternoon, it must have expressed the dismay of many Fellows at recent events: [247]

As men with axes hew downe trees,
   that on the hills doe grow:
So shine the bills and swords of those,
   within thy temple now.

The seeling [ceiling] sawn, the carved boords,
   the goodly graven stones;
With axes, hammers, billes and swords,
   they beat them downe at once.

The slow, slow, unaccompanied singing gave plenty of time to absorb the words of abandonment:

Yet thou no signe of helpe doest send
   our prophets are all gone:
To tell when this our plague shall end,
   among us there is none.

Not even Sternhold and Hopkin's bathetic versifying can hide the anguished plea:

Why doest withdraw thy hand abacke
   and hide it in thy lap:
O plucke it out and be not slacke,
   to give thy foes a rap.

Regard thy covenant and behold,
   thy foes possesse the land.
All sad and darke, sore worne and dole,
   our Realme as now doth stand.[248]

For all this, the screen, and just possibly the pyramid, seems to have survived (or was repaired and replaced), for William Cole wrote nearly a century later that 'the nave is separated from the chancel by a beautiful & lofty screen with a canopy and spire work, under the noble large arch'.[249]

About a month after these events, in March 1643, the House of Lords issued an order intended to protect the University from being 'plundered and spoiled'. It included the instruction that services 'be quietly performed and executed throughout all the said University according to the settlement of the church of England, without any trouble, let or disturbance, until the pleasure of Parliament be further signified'.[250] Was this, in part, a reaction to the troubles at Great St Mary's?

So by early 1643 the church and soldiery had between them removed some – perhaps all – of Cosin's innovations. Dowsing's visit came at the very end of that year, and the churchwardens' accounts for the year ending Easter 1644 provide evidence for this period. Considerable sums are recorded on the destruction of glass:

pd to King for glazing the windowes . . . . . . . . . . . . . . . . 1  00  00
pd to the glaziers for defacing and repairing the windowes  . . . . 7  00  00
pd to the overseer of the windowes   . . . . . . . . . . . . . . . 0  06  08
pd more to the glaziers for the windowes   . . . . . . . . . . . . 2  00  00
pd to King the glazier for mending the windowes [251] . . . . . . . 0  11  00

This glass would have been the surviving pre-Reformation glass, some of which is likely to have been of quality, having been glazed by James Nicholson, responsible for part of the King's College glass. However, in line with the Parliamentary Ordinance, and as at other churches visited by Dowsing, armorial glass seems to have been left untouched (it has since been lost). [252]

There are other relevant entries from the same period:

For taking down of the cross of the steeple and chancell  . . . . . 0  16  04
To the workmen when they were levelling the chancell  . . . . . 0  01  00
For taking downe the clothe in the chancell and the borde
   [communion table] [253] . . . . . . . . . . . . . . . . . . . . 0  02  06

Money was also spent on ensuring that the leader of the regional Parliamentary forces received a warm welcome:[254]

Pd for ringing the bell for a sermon for the Earl of Manchester  . . . . 7d.

There is evidence, then, that superstitious items were removed from the church at the expense of churchwardens inclined to Puritanism, and we have already seen that soldiers had removed Cosin's screen. What was Dowsing's role, if any? The 6s. 8d. paid to the 'overseer' in the above accounts is Dowsing's standard fee, frequently noted in his journal, and is a strong indication of his hand at work, although, as at All Hallows, he himself does not record its receipt on this occasion. It is interesting that at both these churches (and at Metfield in Suffolk)[255] this fee should be particularly associated with the glass – did Dowsing (or an assistant) inspect the glass and advise on which pictures were to be regarded as superstitious, and which could stay?

If Dowsing were involved, why did he not record some or all of this destruction in his journal? At all the college chapels and at all but two of the other churches in Cambridge he documents his own work of destruction, done on the spot; but for Great St Mary's he does no more than record the churchwarden's name. The glass, at least, cannot have all been done before his arrival, else his inspection would hardly have been necessary (unless, indeed, it was a final check on the work).

A possible explanation is that he took his fee and carried out some work in the normal way (including the removal of the two external crosses, so typical of his visits) but for some reason failed to record what he had done. Alternatively he may have left verbal instructions for work to be carried out, not troubling to make a note of what was required because he trusted the churchwarden, or was short of time, or thought he would be returning in the near future (as he did) and could trust his memory.[256] The visit took place immediately after the spat at Pembroke, and he may have been preoccupied in arranging for his second commission. The only other churches in Cambridge at which he records nothing are the undated entries for the two St Andrews, which from their position in the text may have been visited at about the same time as his visit to Great St Mary's.

But this is speculation. Dowsing may have been involved: but his presence was not necessary. The churchwardens were perfectly capable of cleansing their own church to meet the requirements of the Ordinance, seeing to the finishing touches some time the following year:

Pd to James Proste for putin out the pickture of S Marys[257] . . . . 1s. 6d.

None of this explains why they allowed some mediaeval imagery in the roof to remain untouched. Perhaps it was simply that they concentrated all their energies (and spent their neighbours' funds) on the removal of blatant superstition and popery, both pre-Reformation and contemporary. That took time, energy and cash enough, and it might have been politic not to peer upwards into the relative obscurity of a dark roof.

Today, in addition to the font of 1632, which survived the Commonwealth (Plate 29), there is in the church a table described as 'mid seventeenth century'.[258] Might this be that same communion table which went back and forth in the 1630s and 1640s, now standing as a quiet reminder of the transitions of the period?

25. 1643. Trinity parish [Holy Trinity], Mr. Frog, church-warden, December 25. We brake downe 80 popish pictures, and one
of Christ and God the Father above.[259]

The churchwardens' accounts of John Frogg ('Mr Frog') and Martin
Harper for 1643–44 do not record a payment of 6*s*. 8*d*. but the following
items are of interest:

For pullinge downe the crosses in the church . . . . . . . . . . . 0 03 00
To Henry Mucars (?) for taking downe glasse . . . . . . . . . . 0 01 06
To Mills for makinge cleane the walls . . . . . . . . . . . . . . 0 08 04
To Mucars (?) for mendinge the windowes . . . . . . . . . . . 0 08 02
[There follow a number of items for building materials for
   mending the church walls]
For pulling downe pictures in the church . . . . . . . . . . . . 0 08 02
[Further items follow for materials which could imply the lev-
   elling of the chancel]
To Daniell Maldin for glasse [260]. . . . . . . . . . . . . . . . . . 1 04 00

As at All Saints, (and in many places where churchwardens' accounts
survive), work was done which is not mentioned in the Journal, in this case
removing crosses in the church.

The glass was probably the remains of the medieval glass; a few years
previously the church had been somewhat dilapidated, and it had been
reported that the windows were 'halfe stopped up'. William Cole, writing
nearly a hundred years later, may have been reporting an oral tradition, or
may have been drawing his own conclusions from the entry in the Journal,
when he records that 'Will. Dowsing was in this church on Christmas Day,
1643 and broke all the windows in the church, which no doubt were very
valuable and numerous'.[261]

Given that Dowsing's visit was late in 1643, a few months after the
Parliamentary Ordinance was issued, and after the deadline had expired,
these accounts raise the question of how much was destroyed in advance of
his arrival. Items in accounts are not necessarily written in date order, but
much precedes the last and largest item for glass. This particular expense
might reasonably be directly connected with Dowsing's visit, but here some
caution is required, as in some parishes work on the glass took place some
time after he had left. As with St Mary the Great (previous entry), perhaps
All Saints (entry 23), and elsewhere (for example, Stowmarket, entry 103),
destruction by and at the cost of the parish may have had as much impact, or
more, than that actually wrought by Dowsing during his recorded visit – or
more was done during his visit than he recorded.

The cherubim supporting the roof of the nave and north transept remain intact (the south transept is modern).

## 26. Great Andrew's parish [St Andrew the Great]. 1643.

The church was rebuilt 1842.

## 27. Little Andrews [St Andrew the Less].

The church was heavily restored 1854–56.

Baker (only) puts this and the previous entry together on one line, suggesting they may have been part of a joint visit despite the fact that they are some considerable distance apart. Dowsing's blank entries are discussed briefly on page 144.

## 28. 1643. Michell parish [St Michael]. December 26. Jan. 28. We digged up steps, brake downe divers pictures.[262]

Dowsing was in Ipswich at the end of January, so the January date must be incorrect, probably a mistranscription.

The church was restored after a fire in the nineteenth century, and much altered by George Pace in the mid 1960s to form a parish hall for the parish of St Mary the Great. Cherubim survive, supporting niches in the south chapel. There is also (in the nave) a full-length portrait of Charles I shown kneeling in front of an altar. This was given to the church in about 1660, a few years before Dowsing's death; he would not have been pleased.[263]

## 29. 1643. Clement. December 21, and Jan. 1. We brake down 30 superstitious pictures, divers of the apostles, and pope Peters kies [keys].[264]

A reset section of inscribed wall plate survives with *Orate pro bono statu Thomas Brakin Armigire et Luce 1538* and another *Orate* alone. At the end of the seventeenth century, there was armorial glass to be seen in the windows, probably left untouched at Dowsing's visit.[265]

## 30. Jan. 2. Pullchers or Round parish [Holy Sepulchre], in Cambridge, Mr. Giffard, church-warden, George Harrison, Cunstable. We brake down 14 superstitious pictures, and diverse idolatrous inscriptions, and one of God the Father, and of Christ, and of the Apostles.[266]

Dowsing's pictures might have been in the pre-Reformation glass, which possibly survived until his visit. The church was much restored in the nineteenth century but a host of old wooden angels survive in the chancel and north chapel roofs and at a fairly accessible height.[267]

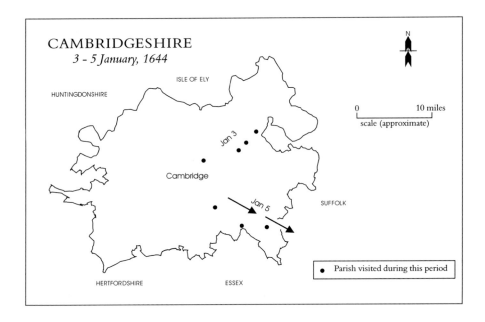

3–5 January. *On Wednesday 3 January 1644 Dowsing set out into the countryside. That day he visited four churches to the north-east of Cambridge. The following day he probably returned to Cambridge. On Friday 5 January he began the journey back to his home at Stratford St Mary in Suffolk.*

31. 1643. Diten [Fen Ditton], January 3. Cambridgeshire. We beat down two crucifixes, and the 12 Apostles, and many other superstitious pictures.

Iconoclasm is evident in the defaced cherubim on the font (holding shields within quatrefoil panels) and possibly in a spoiled medieval reredos with cherubim which was hidden behind panelling until the eighteenth century.[268] Samuel Collins, Provost of King's and Regius Professor of Divinity, was rector until he was ejected in 1644. The charges against him included ceremonialism and the fact that he

> set up an Altar in the Chancell at his owne cost and charges and Wainscoated the same and made a Canopy over it and rayled it about and Decked it with carved and painted pictures and made report that soe soone as he could get some spare money he would have it hung with curtains[269]

Were the 'carved and painted' pictures the ones Dowsing saw, or had these recent images already been taken down?

32.  At Little Swaffham [Swaffham Prior]. We brake down a great many pictures superstitious, 20 cherubims, and the rayles we brake in pieces, and diged down the steps.

There are two churches in the same churchyard – St Mary, and St Cyriac & St Julitta – the latter now being in the care of the Churches Conservation Trust. The two churches are an impressive and unusual sight, and it is surprising that they did not inspire or deserve individual comment in the Journal, though the entry could be read as embracing both churches (Cole assumed this). The day's work on 3 January was only four churches, and this may suggest another explanation, that a fifth, that is a second church at Swaffham Prior, was in fact despoiled, but omitted in error.

A third possibility is that it was not considered necessary to list both churches because one was derelict or unused and nothing was worth doing. Against this hypothesis is the fact that the 1638 bishop's visitation treated the two churches as though they were both active (though the fabric of St Mary's alone is mentioned).[270] In support of the hypothesis is the fact that Layer in his hunt for coats of arms about four years before Dowsing also only records one church.

The fact that three brasses with *Orate* inscriptions survived in St Mary's does strongly suggest that the other church, St Cyriac's, might have been the only one of the two visited by Dowsing. These surviving brasses commemorate Richard Water 1515, William Water de Reche 1521, and a civilian of *c.*1530.[271]

Cole's account of 1744 suggests that both churches were then reasonably sound,[272] though he found the chancels of both churches were in a similar state. St Mary's was 'in a slovenly manner, without any rails or Step to the altar,' and in St Cyriac's 'the Altar is neither rail'd nor on any eminence'. This supports the Journal report that 'the rayles we brake in Pieces, and diged down the steps'. Both naves were standing as late as 1805. The nave of St Cyriac's was completely rebuilt in brick between 1806 and 1812. St Mary's was greatly restored in 1887 and again later, and shows signs of having at some stage been open to the weather.

Raven recorded one bell in St Cyriac's with the name of Mary.[273]

Richard Peacock, vicar of St Cyriac's, was ejected in September 1644. He was accused, among other things, of being so drunk that he could not take prayers at a wedding, of speaking against Parliament and dissuading a woman from lending it money. And it was said that even after the rails had been pulled down, he continued his practice of reading the communion service from the communion table in the chancel.[274]

It is worth recording that, although one might have expected to find a link between churches visited by Dowsing and the subsequent ejection of ministers, none has been found, either in the selection of churches or the relative dates of visit and ejection. Dowsing seems to have visited churches without regard to the theology of the incumbent.

### 33. January 3, Burwell, 1643/4. We brake downe a great many superstitious pictures.

St Mary's is a large and wealthy church and surely deserving more than a single line entry. There is a carved black letter inscription over the chancel arch recording the benefaction which completed the nave roof, *Orate p[ro] a[n]i[m]ab[u]s joh[ann]is benet johane [e]t alicie ux...* which must be the most blatant *Orate* inscription in the county. That roof and its corbels are weighed down with cherubim and other doubtful images. How could Dowsing have missed these? Second thoughts... when I revisited this church in January it was almost impossible to see the inscription and roofs, even on a relatively bright morning. Dowsing was probably there late in the afternoon and the upper parts of the church would have been in darkness – bad light stopped play.

In the chancel the angels forming niche supporters have been renewed but the canopy angels are intact. The Wardeboys brass of 1542 has lost its inscriptions but retains most of its image of a praying abbot and the surmounting representation of the Resurrection.[275]

There was a second church, St Lawrence's, a stone's throw from St Mary's, which was still standing, though ruinous, a century later.[276] That it didn't even merit a 'nothing to be done' (as at Chattisham, below) suggests it was already abandoned. There was also a church little more than a mile away at Reach which was a ruin by 1744.[277] Again, the absence of any reference suggests abandonment by Dowsing's time.

### 34. 1643–4. Swaffham Bulbecke, in Cambridgeshire. 4 crucifixes and Christ nayled to them, and God the Father on one of them; and we brake downe a hundred superstitious pictures, and 2 crosses we took off the steeple, and 2 on the church and chancell. The two church-wardens Christopher Michell, and Martyn Appleyard, and James Lawrance have the tythes; we diged down their steps and 20 cherubims.

John Grange, that dwelt at the maner-house this summer, after he, and the other malignants, had bin drinking and laughing at round-heads, had his (house, I suppose) burnt downe at 10 a clocke in the morning. Witness Robart Cuttell, and many others.[278]

A good set of bench ends with fabulous beasts survives here but they are much mutilated. There is also a fifteenth-century chest with low relief carvings of the crucifixion, symbols of the Evangelists, the Resurrection and the Assumption on the inside of the lid. This must be a later acquisition, or hidden away when Dowsing arrived.[279]

This church provides a good example of how difficult it can be to piece together the history of brasses, and how much relies on luck. Dowsing makes no mention of superstitious inscriptions. However, Layer recorded three brasses a few years before Dowsing's visit, at least one of which included an *Orate* (Layer does not always trouble to record prayer clauses on inscriptions): *Orate pro animabus Elisab Graciae et Annae filiarum Roberti Blackwell.* A hundred years later, in 1743, Cole found none of Layer's three inscriptions in their correct place, but he did find the Blackwell brass in a chest in the church. With it was half the inscription from another of Layer's brasses, that to William Hamond, the piece including a prayer clause. By good fortune however, another antiquary (Beaupré Bell), visited the church a few years before Cole; Bell didn't look in the church chest, but he did find the *other* half of the Hamond brass *in situ*, this half having no prayer clause. Also *in situ* he found the third of Layer's inscriptions, again with a prayer clause. Both of these latter inscriptions must have disappeared from the body of the church in the few years before Cole's visit, and none of the three survive today. From all this we can be sure that Layer's three inscriptions survived Dowsing's visit, in the sense of having a continued existence, though for two of them his visit may have led to them being lifted in whole or in part from their slabs and thrown into the parish chest.[280]

John Grange has not been identified. As for the burning of the house (if it was a house – this might be some transcriber's interpolation) two of the surviving manors have substantial work of the medieval period (Mitchell Hall and Burgh Hall) and have certainly not been 'burnt downe'. Lordship Farm has a nucleus of the seventeenth or eighteenth century and could have been new built after being razed in 1643.[281] Robert Cuttell, Dowsing's witness to the burning, was involved in the sequestration of the Vicar, William Isaacson, who was ejected later in 1644 for being zealous for Bishop Wren and preaching obedience to him. Isaacson had not taken the Covenant and only once read a Parliamentary declaration, and then so that it could not be understood. [282]

35. Jan. 5, At Babarham [Babraham], in Cambridgeshire, 1643. We brake down three crucifixes, and 60 superstitious pictures, and brake in pieces the rayles.

The church was refurnished by the Bennets from 1665 onwards (when the missing 'rayles' were replaced in the style of the day).

Some years before Dowsing, Layer recorded a number of superstitious inscriptions in glass and brass which are not in the Journal. The glass inscriptions could be included in Dowsing's 'superstitious pictures'; perhaps he overlooked those in brass, or they had already gone, or he removed them but forgot to record the fact. Just one brass inscription was found by Blomefield in the 1720s, and this was in pieces in the church chest.

36. Jan. 5, 1643. At Linton, we took up 8 inscriptions, we beate downe 3 crucifixes, and 80 superstitious pictures, and brake the rayles, and gave order to deface 2 grave-stones, with *Pray for our souls*. [March 20.][283]

There are numerous brasses (now under fixed carpets) with removed or damaged inscriptions which could be the '8 inscriptions' taken up (see Plate 36). In particular, two brasses to members of the Parys family of 1538 and 1558 have just the opening words of the inscriptions removed. They had gone by 1684. Layer recorded these words before they went missing as *Of your charity Pray for the soules...* and *I Pray God have mercy of the soules of...*, so these might be Dowsing's '2 gravestones'.[284] There are no other examples of such selective obliteration in the county, except in Cambridge which has two examples (at St John's and King's, entries 12 and 13). It is notable that Dowsing's order here was to 'deface' the inscriptions, an expression he uses very infrequently, and nowhere else about brasses. The reference to 20 March is found in only one of our transcripts, but is probably correct, as Dowsing was in and around this area at that date (see entries 184–8), and this may indicate that he returned to Linton to check that this fussy and relatively time-consuming form of iconoclasm had in fact been carried out. The Parys family had held the manor from the mid fourteenth century. They were still in place at the time of Dowsing's visit, and were well-known recusants, so the brasses and their inscriptions would for them have represented a living tradition, and it seems reasonable to assume that they intervened to ensure minimum damage.[285]

Glass fragments survive in the south aisle, the remains, perhaps, of the '80 superstitious pictures'. There is a clock bell with the inscription *Sancta Maria ora pro nobis*.

Linton had a strong Puritan party. In the 1580s the vicar rejected the Prayer Book and refused to wear his headgear. His successor was presented for giving communion to the sick at home. By 1635 the Puritans had appointed a Scottish schoolmaster and in 1641 started a lecture at the weekly market. In 1642 they petitioned for Parliament to allow them to elect a 'godly preaching minister', but they got instead a Pembroke College Laudian, Roger Ashton, who obstructed the weekly lecture, substituting Laudian preachers. He was ejected in 1643 and the living sequestrated a year later. He was one of those who stood up to Dowsing in Pembroke chapel (Journal entry 2). [286]

## 37. At Horse Heath, January 5. We brake down 2 crucifixes, 6 prophets pictures Malachi, Daniel, Ezekil, and Sophany [Zephaniah], and 2 more, and 40 superstitious pictures.[287]

The prophets may have been on the lower panels of the screen (assuming two door panels which no longer exist). It is interesting that Dowsing should have regarded Old Testament figures as unsuitable for representation in church.

Like nearby Linton there was a Puritan tendency in the parish:

> The Wakefields, father and son, incumbents between 1589 and 1668, both lived in the parish. They possibly had Puritan tendencies: each was presented... for not wearing the surplice...[288]

In 1662 the churchwardens reported that 'in the late rebellious times, the inscriptions of brass were taken away, but by whom we know not'.[289] Had they never known Dowsing's name? Or is he innocent – there is no mention of brasses in the Journal. Possibly some anonymous band of soldiers had done the deed, or there may simply have been a failure of memory, or an unwillingness to drag up twenty-year-old grievances. Whatever the case, it emphasises the need for caution in putting the blame on Dowsing for missing and broken brasses (of which there are several in this church) not recorded in his Journal.

## 38. Jan. 5. At Withersfield [Withersfield St Mary], we brake down 3 crucifixes and 80 superstitious pictures.

The entry for Withersfield is repeated below (entry 46). See page 145 for a discussion of the significance of the duplication.

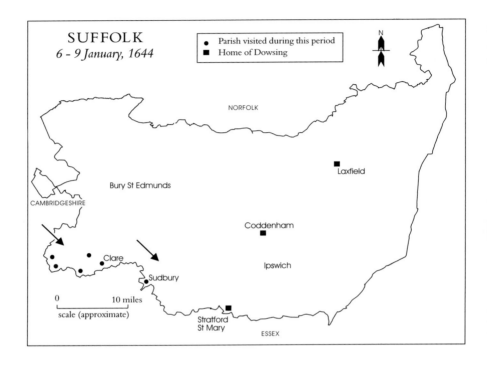

6–9 January. *Dowsing arrived in Clare, Suffolk on Saturday 6 January. Thomas Westhropp, one of his deputies, lived in Hundon, which he dealt with that day; perhaps he stayed the weekend with Westhropp.*

*He rested on Sunday as normal. His next entry is for the Tuesday 9 January, dealing with three churches in Sudbury (these Sudbury entries are out of chronological order). After the work on Tuesday there is silence for several days.*

39. Sudbury, Suffolk. Peter's parish. Jan. 9 1643/4. We brake down a picture of God the Father, 2 crucifixes, & pictures of Christ, about an hundred in all; and gave order to take down a cross off the steeple; and diverse angells, 20 at least, on the roof of the church.

The church dominates the centre of the town overlooking the market place, but is now in the care of the Churches Conservation Trust. During paving of the town in 1825, the remains of some painted angels were found, whilst some years later 'directly opposite the church, a large quantity of stained glass was found broken into very small pieces'.[290] The roof was renewed in 1695 and coloured in the nineteenth century, so that any damage done there was made good. The screen has eight figures in as many panels, ideals of Victorian values. The font, all gothic architecture, is perfect. The hood mould stops outside the north door have been savaged.

Here, as always, Dowsing distinguishes between what *he* does to images – 'brake down'– and what he orders *others* to do – 'take down'. (The only exception is at his return visit to Ufford (entry 247), where he muddles himself about his previous visit.) This may just reflect a turn of phrase, but it may perhaps be a careful sticking to the letter of the law, which ordered offensive images to be 'taken away' or 'removed', rather than 'broken'. For brass inscriptions, mostly done on the spot, he normally uses 'took up'.[291]

## 40. Sudbury, Gregory parish. Jan. 9. We brake down 10 mighty great angels in glass, in all, 80.[292]

This church is lit by large three-light windows, which makes it difficult to suggest where '10 mighty great angels' might have been accommodated. The font is architectural and undamaged, but the cover is almost as good as Ufford or Worlingworth and the eight canopied niches are vacant. The painted screen panel figures all face sideways, the nineteenth-century restorers wanting no one to think them original. Two interesting original panels do survive, one to Master John Shorn and just the canopy, head and inscription for St Audrey. Many fine matrices are totally brassless. Around the margin of the incised slab of *c.*1325 to Sieve, wife of Robert de St Quentin, wool merchant, at the east end of the south aisle, it is still possible to read most of a Norman French prayer to St Gregory for her soul. This slab was found in the late 1840s concealed beneath the flooring of the pews.[293]

The chief item of curiosa here, in a niche in the vestry, is the head of Simon of Sudbury, Archbishop of Canterbury and Lord Chancellor, and a local man, beheaded by Wat Tyler's rebels. This would have been the best sort of episcopal head to Dowsing.

While the chancel cross is obviously modern, that on the porch has every appearance of antiquity. West of the south porch the brasses of kneeling figures with prayer scrolls have all gone from the kind of table tomb rarely seen out of doors.

## 41. Allhallows [All Saints], Jan. 9. We brake about 20 superstitious pictures; and took up 30 brazen superstitious inscriptions, *Ora pro nobis*, and *Pray for the soul* etc.

Twelve angels may have been cut off the roof members at the point where they rest on the corbels. There are only three or four brassless indents (one including a Trinity), but in tiling the church floor other slabs may have been covered or discarded. There are six blank shields on the font bowl, and another held by an angel. All appear to have been chiselled flat. The west door to the tower had angels as hood mould stops: they are damaged. There are empty pedestals for nave and chancel gable crosses.

## 42. Suffolk. At Haveril [Haverhill] Jan. 6 1643/4. We brake down about a hundred superstitious pictures; and 7 fryers hugging a nun; and the picture of God, and Christ; and divers others very superstitious. And 200 had been broke down afore I came. We took away 2 popish inscriptions with *Ora pro nobis*; and we beat down a great stoneing cross on the top of the church.[294]

The '7 fryers hugging a nun' has always intrigued readers of the Journal, but has never been elucidated. Seven short-haired male figures and one veiled female could be a family group (see *Children on Brasses* by John Page-Phillips), perhaps in brass, or perhaps, as at St Matthew's, Ipswich, gild members on a screen. Dowsing's 'inscriptions' could be in a variety of media: the two popish inscriptions here, to the Turners in brass and the Gyffords in glass, were recorded by William Hervy in his pocket book at the 1561 Visitation.[295]

## 43. At Clare, Jan. 6. We brake down a 1000 pictures superstitious; and brake down 200, 3 of God the Father, and 3 of Christ, and the Holy Lamb, and 3 of the Holy Ghost like a dove with wings; and the 12 Apostles were carved in wood, on the top of the roof, which we gave order have taken down; and 20 cherubims to be taken down. And the sun and moon in the east window, by the King's Arms, to be taken down.[296]

In spite of the scale of Dowsing's activity here, the east window of the chancel still contains a good deal of glass older than the visit. Two horizontal rows of five heraldic panels include many fragments of the lost windows, but even the arms of five knightly benefactors to the church in 1617 and the Haberdashers are in poor order. Higher up the sun and moon roundels which Dowsing noted for destruction are still there, but much of the former and most of the latter are made up from other small pieces of yellow and gold glass, i.e., they were broken. The Royal Arms are gone; they were not proscribed until 1649, so may have survived the visit. The loss of the other arms is surprising, not only because the Parliamentary Ordinance which provided Dowsing's authority explicitly excluded 'any... coat of Arms... set up or graven onley for a Monument of any King, Prince, or nobleman, or other dead Person which hath not been commonly reputed or taken for a Saint', but also because many of the arms in this window were those of Elizabethan Puritans.[297] His '1000 pictures' has always seemed like exaggeration, and an estimate of the numbers of subjects (two in a tall light, even four in the east window) which could have been accommodated is worth making. Including the clerestory (assuming it was fully glazed, as at Melford), the total is about 186 and cannot exceed 200, the more believable number 'brake down'.[298] Much else was missed. In the south porch the hood mould stop angels over the inner door lost their heads, but the main corbel with the head of Christ is unscathed. The chantry screen on the south has many crowned MRs carved on the frieze, and rows of carved stone angels above the piers of the nave and chancel are undamaged. At least one brass was overlooked (though has since disappeared).[299]

## 44. Hunden [Hundon], Jan. 6. We brake down 30 superstitious pictures; and we took up three popish inscriptions in brass, *Ora pro nobis*, on them. And we gave order for levelling the steps.

Rebuilding here after the fire of 1914 will have obliterated some evidence, but the south porch bears testimony to thorough cleansing. The freestone decorations trimmed and then weathered all seem as flush as the flint and brick around them. Cautley describes the gable cross and base on a window sill as fourteenth century, but when did it come down?[300] There are carved stone heads at the top and bottom of wall shafts over the arcades, but where instead there are plain cubes of stone are they replacements or unworked originals? The font is plain but the piscina displays a mixture of damage and decay.

## 45. Wixo [Wixoe], Jan 6. We brake a picture; and gave order to levell the stepps.

There is nothing here to connect with Dowsing's visit.

## 46. Withersfield [Withersfield St Mary], Jan 6. We brake down a crucifix, and sixty superstitious pictures; and gave order for the levelling the steps in the chancel.

Two bench ends showing St George and the Dragon and St Michael weighing souls were surely missed here.

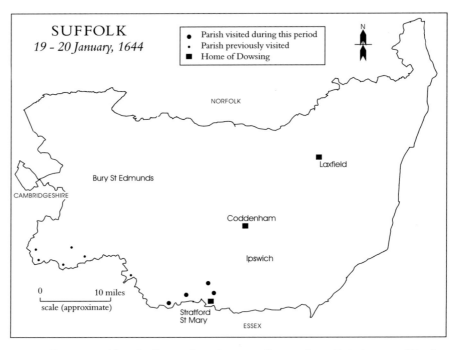

SUFFOLK
*19 - 20 January, 1644*

● Parish visited during this period
· Parish previously visited
■ Home of Dowsing

N

NORFOLK

■ Laxfield

Bury St Edmunds

CAMBRIDGESHIRE

Coddenham
■

Ipswich

0          10 miles

scale (approximate)

Stratford
St Mary

ESSEX

*19–20 January. After Sudbury, there is a gap for ten days. It is just possible that Dowsing was carrying out a reconnaissance of north Essex, but more likely that he had business at home, where he is next found. There was some very cold weather this January, and travel may have been unattractive.[301] Whatever the case, he dealt with a mere two churches on Friday 19 January, and two more the day after, both close to his home.*

47. Stoke Nayland [Stoke by Nayland], Jan. 19. We brake down an hundred superstitious pictures; and took up 7 superstitious inscriptions on the grave-stones, *Ora pro nobis, etc.*

Four brasses dating from c.1400 and 1408 (both to Tendrings), and 1425 and 1535 (both to Howards), and three fourteenth-century indents to two Peytons and a Roding would account neatly for the seven inscriptions taken up, though the two Norman French Peyton inscriptions, in separately inlaid Lombardic letters, are still easily legible.[302]

A great deal here was passed over. There are bosses in the stone vaulted south porch which should have been counted as superstitious, and the canopied niches on the doors there are still inhabited with saints and apostles. The font is in excellent order despite having the evangelists and their symbols on the eight panels; lower down there are shields with various forms of cross symbol – they do not look restored. In 1874 wall frescoes were found under plaster over the chancel arch and in St Edmund's chapel off the north aisle (where Peytons were buried). These had probably been dealt with as part of Tudor cleansing; they are not in evidence today.[303]

## 48. Nayland, Suff. Jan. 19 1643/4. We brake down 30 superstitious pictures; and gave order for the takeing down a cross on the steeple. We took up 2 popish inscriptions, *Ora pro nobis, etc.*

Many wealthy clothiers of the parish had their memorials here, mostly canopied brasses, and there are at least eight indents, some with whole or part figures, and two from which the marginal inscriptions have been selectively expurgated, by cutting and removal. On the other hand, the brass to Richard and Joan Davy (1516) in the north aisle with merchant's mark and complete *Orate* inscription is only worn, not damaged. Eight original screen panels remain, four with faces still intact. One clerestory window has enough early glass in an upper light to show that some of the thirty pictures may have been that high up.

Dowsing was to visit here again – see entry 117.

## 49. Houghton [Holton St Mary], Jan. 20. We brake down 6 superstitious inscriptions.[304]

The font here has suffered mutilation, shields and figures having been hacked off too thoroughly to show what was originally there.

## 50. Rayden [Raydon St Mary], Jan. 20. We brake down a crucifix, and 12 superstitious pictures; and a popish inscription, *Ora pro nobis.*[305]

Outside, there is a stoup in the south porch with its front knocked off in the usual rude manner. Of course, this could be Edwardian damage.

In the chancel, there are twelve main lights to the windows, matching Dowsing's count. The top lights of several of the windows still contain glass fragments of the broken 'pictures'. The brass inscription has been removed from beneath the damaged figure of a lady in butterfly head-dress, but another *Orate* inscription remains on the neighbouring slab. However, Blois, *c.*1660, could read both inscriptions, so Dowsing may not have achieved all he wished here, perhaps because John Mayor, rector here between 1631 and 1663, was not on his side.[306] He died in office, showing that he was prepared to conform at the Restoration; his last book had the title *Unity Restored to the Church of England.*

The architectural decoration of the north chancel recessed tomb, no
doubt used as an Easter sepulchre, has been hacked off. Was it adorned with
something offensive to the Puritan eye?

*22-28 January. On Monday 22 January Dowsing set off with renewed vigour, and
over the next six days he visited twenty churches, the bulk at the end of the week. Passing
through Coddenham, his old home parish, he made his way to the coast at Aldeburgh
then moved north as far as Kelsale, before making his way back home in a figure of eight
to Stratford, in time for Sunday. The return journey took him via Ufford, a place which
was to cause him problems.*

51. Barham, Jan. 22d. We brake the 12 apostles, in the chancell,
and 6 superstitious more there; and 8 in the church, one a Lamb
with a cross on the back; and digged down the steps; and took up 4
superstitious inscriptions of brass, one of them *Jesu, Fili Dei,
miserere*, and *O Mater Dei, memento mei*, – O Mother of God, have
mercy on me![307]

The new chancel roof in 1865 was set on stone corbels carved with large
male heads, ungainly Victorian substitutes for the figures of apostles

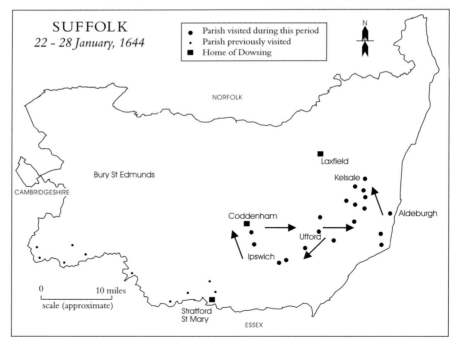

SUFFOLK
22 - 28 January, 1644

• Parish visited during this period
· Parish previously visited
■ Home of Dowsing

N

NORFOLK

Laxfield

Bury St Edmunds

Kelsale •

CAMBRIDGESHIRE

Aldeburgh

Coddenham •

Ufford

Ipswich

0        10 miles
scale (approximate)

Stratford
St Mary

ESSEX

which Dowsing removed. It is odd that he found four brass inscriptions objectionable, but left untouched the entire marginal fillet on the Southwell brass of 1514 with its *quorum animabus…* As elsewhere, his attempt to translate from the Latin ended in confusion. Hervy in 1561 recorded an inscription (now lost, perhaps at Dowsing's hand) on the canopied tomb of Catherine, wife of Richard Bothe, who died in 1446.[308] The canopy is still intact, sheltering the tomb chest of Richard himself (d.1477) with indents of his armoured figure and marginal inscription.

## 52. Clayden [Claydon], Jan. 22. We brake down 3 superstitious pictures; and gave order to take down 3 crosses off the steeple; and one off the chancell.

The stump of the chancel cross was shown in Henry Davy's etching of 1841, so what is there today is a replacement. There are eight angels at the corners and mid points of the sides of the tower-top, but these are all part of the rich Victorian embellishment of the church. The octagonal font is unusual in its design, in eight canopied niches four crowns and four angels holding shields on straps. The crowns are unscathed, but the angels have suffered and the devices on the shields are chiselled off.

## 53. Codenham [Coddenham], Jan 22. We gave order for takeing down 3 crosses off the steeple; and one off the chancell.

Here at Dowsing's own former parish church, where Matthias Candler was both sound Puritan and enthusiast for antiquities, the record mentions nothing but external crosses. However, the wall-post angels have been damaged (Plate 3). Candler lamented the loss of the brass inscriptions, destroyed because they were superstitious, but today no figures survive either. Hervy in 1561 gives two inscriptions: Edmund Jermy Esq., 1506 and Thomas Barnaby, priest (his arms shown) 1489.[309]

But much remains: the *Orate* inscriptions on the south clerestory parapet are still legible with an effort though the infilling flints are gone, reducing the legibility. There are crowned M's too (for Mary). The Trinity and IHS shields in the south porch spandrels are crudely carved and must be replacements. Inside the porch the hood mould stop ornaments have been renewed, presumably after damage. In the church the south aisle piscina shelf is now flush with the wall, so that the whole could have been cut back, infilled and plastered over. On the altar here is a fine alabaster crucifixion panel, found in 1774 in the roof of the curate's house (perhaps once the old vicarage), presumably where Candler or a predecessor hid it for safety.[310]

**54. Yke [Eyke], Jan. 23. We brake down 25 superstitious pictures; and took up a superstitious picture.**[311]

There are stumps of gable crosses on porch and nave. Symbols of the evangelists and four lions on the font are undamaged. Fragments of early glass are gathered in a south chancel window. Why did Dowsing 'brake down' some superstitious pictures and 'take up' another. Does the first refer to glass, the second to brass? The inscription is indeed lost from the brass memorial of John Staverton, baron of the exchequer (d.142) and his wife Margaret, and the heads of both figures have gone too. Four other 'popish' inscriptions here were recorded by the anonymous Chorographer about 1602.[312] Dowsing may not be admitting to all that was done here. However, in 1807, D. E. Davy noted part of the marginal inscription then remaining on the brass to Thomas Dalling, 'quondam Rector', but now lost: surprisingly, it was the part which might have been expected to be the first to go, his rubbing showing *cui[us] anime p[ro]picietur d[eu]s ame[n]*.[313]

On the way from here to Tunstall the tower of Rendlesham is passed on the left. Who could resist visiting? There are stumps of gable crosses in the three usual places, the work, no doubt of a Dowsing deputy.[314] The basin of the stoup at the entrance to the south porch has been patched up with brick. On the font the four shields held by angels have been carefully chiselled flat, as has the surround of the chancel piscina. The two angels supporting the pillow on the early-fourteenth-century sculptured monument to Sayer Sulyard, priest, have lost their original heads and the nineteenth-century replacements are both loose. The stone nave roof corbels, all figurative, were perhaps too high up to be damaged; or perhaps it was feared that they held up the roof.

**55. Dunstall [Tunstall], Jan. 23. We brake down 60 superstitious pictures; and broke in pieces the rayles; and gave order to pull down the steps.**

There are in all 29 lights in the glazing scheme; each could have held two pictures to make 58. Fragments of early glass are gathered in a north nave window. One brass indent remains in the paved floor.

Of porch and nave gable crosses, stumps remain. Fine Trinity and Passion shields are unharmed in the porch doorway spandrels, but the hood mould stops of the south door are missing. There is a stoup beside the door. The Norman font stands on a later pedestal with architectural decoration.

**56. Aldborough [Aldeburgh], Jan. 24. We gave order for the takeing down 20 cherubims, and 38 pictures; which their Lec-**

turer Mr. Swayn, (a godly man) undertook, and their Captain Mr.
Johnson.

The '20 cherubims' will have been accommodated on the nave roof beam
ends leaving two empty; or is Dowsing's arithmetic letting him down?
Three shields held by angels around the bowl of the font have been chiselled
flat, but the fourth, with symbols of the Passion, escaped, presumably
because, as at St Margaret's Ipswich (entry 82), that face stood against a
protective wall or column. The stem supporters were trimmed off so cleanly
that only plinths for their feet prove their former existence.

The 'Lecturer Mr Swayn' is probably John Swayne, born at Thorpe,
Yorks.[315] He was curate of Great Bentley, and vicar of Westleton 1626–41.
He was then appointed Lecturer at Aldeburgh, presumably in preference to
Maptid Violet, ejected as a scandalous minister.

'Capt. (Thomas) Johnson' of Aldeburgh commanded the town's train-
band in the Civil War and was a lay member of the fourth classis division,
mainly for Plomesgate hundred, meeting at Saxmundham. Johnson was
seven times Bailiff of the Borough, and his black ledger slab takes pride of
place in the centre of the chancel with his arms: a bend wavy between two
toads erect. His funeral in 1658 cost the Corporation 10 shillings for beer for
the soldiers.[316]

J. W. Darby in his 1827 church notes drew eleven brass indents. Although
the first part of an inscription to one Benet —, 1519 survives, with *Of your
charity Pray for the souls of...*, while the harmless half is missing, one senses
there was no lack of zeal for reformation here.

The accounts confirm that windows needed repair after Dowsing's visit,
and there is an earlier entry for 'worke and stuff to mende the floore in the
Chancell', suggesting that steps were taken up before Dowsing came.[317]

## 57. Orford, Jan. 25. We brake down 28 superstitious pictures; and took up 11 popish inscriptions in brass; and gave order for digging up the steps, and takeing of 2 crosses off the steeple, one off the church, and one off the [chancel], in all four.[318]

Dowsing records '11 popish inscriptions in brass': from eight surviving
brass memorials 1480 –*c.*1520 the inscriptions are completely missing; part
only of a ninth of 1580 was taken up. The strangest thing is that Dowsing
missed a Trinity on one memorial of *c.*1520 (Plate 35). The font, with *Orate*
inscription for the donors John and Katherine Cokerel running around the
step, also suffered less than would be expected. On the font, Christ was
headless in the Pieta panel when Francis Grose drew it in October 1775.

Modern restoration has replaced it. There was in 1775 (and is now) no dove to accompany God the Father holding his crucified Son, but there may never have been. [319]

Loder adds the word 'chancel' to complete the sentence in the Martin MS, but the chancel fell into ruin during the seventeenth century and probably had no east wall when Dowsing came. The porch still had a 'handsome' gable cross in 1775,[320] so the correct reading is: 'and takeing of 2 crosses off the steeple, one of the church and one of the *porch*, in all four', but not all that was ordered seems to have been carried out. Large shields with the Trinity and the Passion instruments on the porch seem to have been overlooked.

### 58. Snape, Jan. 25. We brake down 4 popish pictures; and took up 4 inscriptions of brass, of *Ora pro nobis*, etc.

J. W. Darby (1831) recorded the four empty brass indents: two of them plain inscriptions, one a man and wife with children and a shield, and the other what appears to be a large group above an inscription. None of these remain now as the floor is completely tiled and paved.

There is a carved stone Agnus Dei in the foliage trail along the top of the south porch. This and the Trinity and Passion shields in the spandrels of the opening (the latter similar to those at Tunstall) were spared by the visitors. On the south doorway, hood mould stops in the form of angels holding shields were not ignored.

The font, one of the most elaborate and beautiful in East Anglia, was not subjected to systematic cleansing, save that perhaps the scrolls running round seven panels may have been chiselled flat to remove inscriptions. The dedication inscription is still partially legible. Two members of the May family who gave it stand on either side of the Trinity; Richard has lost his head.

### 59. Stanstead [Sternfield], Jan 25. We brake down 6 superstitious pictures; and took up a popish inscription in brass.

There are shields in glass in the west tower window, but complete retiling has removed the empty brass matrix. Henry Davy (1847) shows the stump of a nave cross.

### 60. Saxmundham, Jan. 26. We took up two superstitious inscriptions in brass.[321]

The four lions and four angels holding shields (plain cross, Trinity, Passion and three crowns of east Anglia) around the bowl of the font are all in perfect order. An angel with scroll on the east respond of the south arcade is also undamaged. Higher up there are unusual furnishings at the north and south ends of the rood loft. On the north there are stone decorations including IHS and MR in good condition, but opposite there are still signs that a Lombardic letter inscription *SANCT[E] JOHANNES ORA PRO NOBIS* was obliterated with black paint. (The church is dedicated to the Baptist.) The nave roof seems to lack fourteen angels on the braces and the chancel twelve more. There is a single angel with scroll in early glass in the west tower window.

## 61. Kelshall [Kelsale], Jan. 26. We brake down 16 superstitious pictures; and took up 12 popish inscriptions in brass; and gave order to levell the chancell, and takeing down a cross.[322]

There is the stump of a gable cross on the nave. The Trinity and Passion shields in the spandrels of the south porch are unharmed. The flushwork keys of St Peter over the image niche in the gable must surely be modern.

The accounts survive, but the only indication of iconoclasm is the removal of the font some months later.[323] The font, which is unusually broad, shows random damage: two of the supporting lions, and the calf of St Luke, and two of the shields held by angels, are chiselled off, but on the other two the three crowns were left, and the three chalices only slightly affected.

## 62. Carleton [Carlton], Jan. 26. We brake down 10 superstitious pictures; and took up 6 popish inscriptions in brass; and gave order to levell the chancell.

The porch is featureless, but there is the stump of a gable cross on the chancel. Two separate brass figures lack their inscriptions, and the cross brass to John de Framlingham, founder of this chantry chapel to Kelsale in 1333, has only the indents of the separate marginal inscription letters.

## 63. Farnham [Farnham St Mary], Jan 26. We took up a popish inscription in brass.

There is the stump of a gable cross on the nave (as in Henry Davy's etching of 1844). Inside the south door, blocked to strengthen the south wall, there is stoup whose front has been knocked down. The thirteenth-century style is too plain to attract attention even if it is only actually as old as the seventeenth century. There is one brassless slab in the centre of the nave floor, perhaps as Dowsing left it.

64. Stratford [Stratford St Andrew]. We brake down 6 superstitious pictures.

> This church is unsafe to enter at present and the north porch so overgrown as to obscure its details.

65. Wickham [Wickham Market], Jan the 26. We brake down 15 popish pictures of angels and saints; and gave order for takeing 2 crosses; first on the steeple, 2nd on the church.[324]

> The '15 popish pictures of angels and saints' must include the badly defaced figures which support the early Tudor south chancel chapel roof. The sanctus bell on the east gable of the nave is surmounted by an iron cross, a replacement no doubt for Dowsing's '2nd on the church' (Plate 34). The font escaped damage as its decorations are entirely architectural.

66. Sudburne [Sudbourne], Jan. 26. We brake down 6 pictures; and gave order for the taking down a cross on the steeple; and the steps to be levelled.[325]

> As at Tunstall, Orford, Snape, and Kelsale (entries 55, 57, 58, 61), the large shields in the spandrels of both porches bear the symbols of the Trinity and the Passion and are no more than weathered. In his later visits, Dowsing took more notice of such items (see, for example, Ipswich, St Peter's, entry 76, and Blyford, entry 234).
>
> A substantial fragment of a stone gable (or steeple?) cross is housed in the canopied niche over the north porch entrance.

67. Ufford, Jan. 27. We brake down 30 superstitious pictures; and gave direction to take down 37 more; and 4 [40] cherubims to be takeing down of wood; and the chancel levelled. There was a picture of Christ on the cross, and God the Father above it; and left 37 superstitious pictures to be taken down; and took up 6 superstitious inscriptions in brass.[326]

> Ufford was revisited by Dowsing in late August (entry 247).

68. Woodbridge, Jan 27. We took up 2 superstitious inscriptions in brass; and gave order to take down 30 superstitious pictures.[327]

> The churchwardens' accounts record expenditure of 7s. 8d. for 'taking down the images' which will have included taking the heads off the figures in the rayed panels of the seven sacrament font and defacing the thirty screen-painted saints and apostles, enough to cross the entire width of the

church.[328] Craven Ord commissioned Isaac Johnson to record all the figures in water-colour *c.*1780. A nineteenth-century replica with 24 figures has the full inscription with prayers for the souls of the donors of the original: John Albrede, a twill weaver, who died in 1450 and Agnes his wife, died 1458. Fourteen of the original panels remain also, with enough of the inscription to show that the *Orate* and the saints' faces were defaced. To the north of the chancel under Thomas Seckford's table tomb lies the empty matrix of a fine canopied brass to a couple believed to be the Albredes; its mutilation accounts for one of the two brass inscriptions taken up.[329]

## 69. Kesgrave, Jan. 27. We beate down 6 superstitious pictures; and gave order to take down 18 cherubims, and to levell the chancel.[330]

If there were '18 cherubims', they may have adorned the beam ends of both nave and chancel.

## 70. Rushmere [Rushmere St Andrew], Jan. 27. We brake down the pictures of the 7 deadly sins, and the Holy Lamb with a cross about it, and 15 other superstitious pictures.

The Agnus Dei which Dowsing saw, no doubt in glass, also occurs on the reverse of the seal of Holy Trinity Priory, Ipswich, whose black canons held the advowson here and would have staffed the church; the device would have symbolised the link. It survived the iconoclast's visit to migrate in the 1880s from the east window here to fill the small two light window in the east wall of the north aisle at St Matthew's, Ipswich, presented by Dr William Partridge Mills: 'pattern work, with merely the Agnus Dei and sacred monogram in the upper part'. This and another window given by Mills have since been replaced, and the earlier glass lost.[331]

29 January – 3 February (map overleaf). *Having systematically covered a number of churches to the east of Ipswich, and rested on Sunday 28 January, on Monday Dowsing moved into the town itself, visiting four churches on the journey from his home. This Monday was perhaps the busiest he was to spend; he dealt with eleven churches to the south and west of the town. On Tuesday he finished off the town's eastern churches, then moved out to Playford, a village to the east. Why he should have done that is puzzling, for the remainder of the week was spent dealing with a number of villages to the west of Ipswich, starting with Great Blakenham, then working his way round to the south, no doubt returning home on Sunday 4 February. By the end of this week, apart from the ten-days gap in mid January he will have been on the go for more than six weeks, typically covering five or six churches a day.*

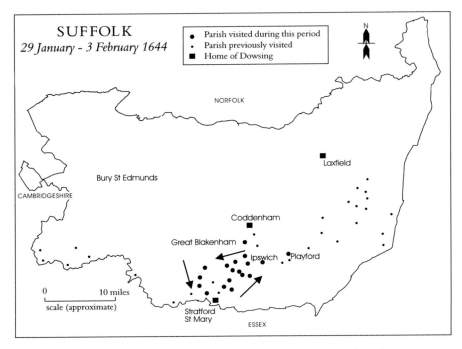

71. Chatsham [Chattisham], Jan. 29. Nothing to be done.

'Nothing to be done'. The Puritan Squire Daniel Meadows of Chatti-sham (1577–1651) will have seen to that, just as in July 1644 he saw to the ejection of Jeremiah Ravens, the Laudian vicar who had overspent parish funds on steps, rails and other trimmings.[332]

The hood mould stops at the south door have been removed, and the piscina is as plain as possible, its flat base without a drain.

72. Washbrook, Jan. 29. I brake down 26 superstitious pictures; and gave order to take down a stoneing cross; and the chancell to be levelled.

There is a cross stump on the chancel gable (nave and chancel are under one roof). The total number of window lights is 25, close enough to Dowsing's 26. The four lions around the font pedestal, and angels holding shields around the bowl, are in such good order that one suspects restoration. The shields are without emblems and two betray signs of new stone cut in.

73. Cobdock [Copdock]. Jan. 29. I brake down 150 superstitious pictures, two of God the Father, and 2 crucifixes; did deface a

cross on the font; and gave order to take down a stoneing cross on the chancell, and to levell the steps; and took up a brass inscription, with *Ora pro nobis*, and *Cujus animæ propitietur deus.*

Evelyn White found the font here very mutilated, but H. W. Birch in 1898, a few years later, wrote that it had been much restored.[333] New stone must have been let into the damaged panels to take the present high relief carving. Henry Davy (1842) shows no cross stump on the chancel gable.

## 74. Belstead. We brake down 7 superstitious pictures, five of the Apostles, and 2 others; and took up 4 superstitious inscriptions in brass, of *Ora pro nobis*, etc.[334]

William Hervy on his visitation in 1561 did record all four inscriptions removed by Dowsing. Of the four brasses, only the Goldingham slab remains, lacking a foot inscription and a lower smaller plate with, presumably, children. The three figures of John (d.1518) and his wives Jane and Thomasine, and two shields, survive. [335]

On the screen painted figures of saints have been unevenly mutilated, but the facial features have gone in every case. From north to south there are Saints Sitha, Ursula, Margaret of Antioch and Mary Magdalene; then two bishops, Lawrence, Stephen, Edmund and Sebastian, ten figures in all. Wodderspoon saw a saint's head in glass in a south aisle (*recte* nave) window, but that will have gone in the 1860s when a local firm glazed the only nave window.[336] The font must have suffered, because it has been recut.

## 75. Ipswich Stoke Maryes [St Mary Stoke]. 2 crosses in wood, and 2 cherubims painted; and one inscription in brass, with *Ora pro nobis*.

In 1870–71 Butterfield built a new nave relegating the medieval one to north aisle status, but it still has at least seven bays of its fine single hammerbeam roof, one spandrel decorated with the *Agnus Dei*. The heads of the hammer figures of saints and angels are replacements. Henry Davy's etching of 1839 shows a cross stump on the then chancel gable and a brick porch with five empty niches, two over three, and legible shields bearing the arms on one, and the crest on the other, of the same Lord Windsor whose chapel at Tendryng Hall was visited (see entry 118).

## 76. At Peter's, was on the porch, the crown of thornes, the spunge and nayles, and the Trinity in stone; and the rails were there, which I gave order to break in pieces.

The south porch has no adornments save lions sejant as hood mould stops and a small empty niche above the arched opening. There are no signs of the removal of the 'crown of thornes, the spunge and nails, and the Trinity in stone', indication that the porch must have been largely rebuilt in the nineteenth century.

Dowsing mentions no superstitious pictures, suggesting the glass was already down, and this is supported by the churchwardens' accounts for the period, which show expenditure on glazing. Nor does he mention steps, but there is expenditure on masons, bricks and tiles, which might be connected with lowering the chancel, perhaps before his visit; and shortly after the Covenant (thus probably in April) 'for paveing', perhaps tidying up after the earlier removal.[337]

*1643–44*

| | | |
|---|---|---|
| For glaseing the church . . . . . . . . . . . . . . . . . . . . . . . . | 2 | 08 | 00 |
| For five dayes worke to a mason & laborer at 3s. per day . . . . . | 0 | 15 | 00 |
| For 4 dayes worke to a mason at 2s. per day and for his labourer 3 dayes ½ at 12d. . . . . . . . . . . . . . . . . . . . . . . . . . . . . | 0 | 11 | 06 |
| For Fardinando Quinting for 1 M 1/4 brick & tyle [1250] . . . . | 1 | 00 | 00 |
| For charcoale for the glassyer . . . . . . . . . . . . . . . . . . . . . | 0 | 01 | 00 |
| For writing the covenant . . . . . . . . . . . . . . . . . . . . . . . . | 0 | 04 | 00 |
| For paveing 16 yds at 3d. . . . . . . . . . . . . . . . . . . . . . . . | 0 | 04 | 00 |
| For paveing 68 yds at 3d. per yard . . . . . . . . . . . . . . . . . . | 0 | 17 | 00 |

If steps and glass had been removed before Dowsing came, it is surprising that the rails had not also been removed, and also surprising that Dowsing did not break them up himself on the spot, his normal practice: perhaps his entry should be read as indicating that they had been removed already, and were being stored in the porch.

## 77. Mary's at the Key [St Mary at the Quay], Jan. 29. I brake down 6 superstitious pictures.

The seated figures carved from the wall-posts of the nave roof are mutilated as are those at St Margaret's. On the font the four panels with symbols of the evangelists are intact but the angels holding shields have suffered. One shield not defaced shows a lion rampant, presumably the arms of the donor, probably a Bigod. The badge of St Edmund (crown and crossed arrows) on another went unrecognised but the other two are chiselled flat.

## 78. St Mary Elmes [St Mary at the Elms], Jan. 29. There was 4 iron crosses on the steeple which they promised to take down that day, or the next.

'There was 4 iron crosses on the steeple…'. The Tudor brick tower of this church has four small polygonal corner turrets which are most likely to have been surmounted by the crosses. However on the painted panorama of Ipswich in 1600 (on the memorial of William Smart in St Mary le Tower church) the Elms church tower top is shown plain but for the turrets.

Also in the panorama, shown as a tall tapering column, is the 'stoneing cross' where the Norwich Road leaves the town (still Stoning Cross Street on Ogilby's map surveyed 1674). However, Dowsing seems to have used this term generally for any stone cross, even if it was not free standing – in all seven cases they were on the church rather than free standing.[338]

## 79. Nicholas, Jan. 29. We brake 6 superstitious pictures; and took up 2 brass inscriptions, of *Ora pro nobis*; and gave order for another, *Cujus animæ propitietur deus*; and there was the crown of thorns.[339]

The two brass inscriptions taken up must include that of William Style (d. *c.*1500) and Margery his wife, from which William's figure survives. But how did the foot inscription for the first William's parents, William Style (1475) and Isabel his wife (1490) escape notice, with its prayer: *q[uo]r[um] a[n]i[m]e* [sic] *requiescant i[n] pace[m]?* Their two figures and the foot inscription remain, but the reuse for a memorial of the 1820s of the part of the slab which includes indents for prayer scrolls and a Trinity shows that it had been cleansed of some at least of its superstitious parts before then.

It seems certain that the memorial brass of Wolsey's parents, Robert and Joan, was also despoiled by Dowsing. Matthias Candler of Coddenham wrote: 'Nov 13 1657 The sexton showed me a fine marble lying in the middle alley between the church doors, which he told me was placed there by Cardinal Wolsey for preserving the memory of his father and mother; the brass was taken away (he saith) about a dozen years since'. William Blois of Grundisburgh, perhaps three years later, wrote: 'a greate stone nigh the fo(n)t was for Card. Wolsyes Fath'r the butchers axe was upon it'. A prayer scroll could perhaps leave an indent which could be mistaken for a cleaver.[340]

At this church and at St Margaret's and St Stephen's (and nowhere else that is known of) the Royal Arms boards of 1660 were found in modern times to have other boards nailed to their backs bearing the device of the Prince of Wales feathers and the motto 'Ich Dien'. The painted designs, which can only be interpreted as a covert act of loyalty to the crown during the interregnum, however heraldically inappropriate, faced the back of the Royal Arms in each case.

80.  Matthew's, Jan. 29. We brake down 35 superstitious pictures, 3 angells with stars on their breast, and crosses.

D. E. Davy saw carvings in the north aisle roof in 1824 which were probably the 'angells' Dowsing saw; but they did not survive the widening of the aisle in 1877: 'the figures... bear shields before them, which have on them the instruments of our Saviour's Passion, viz., 3 nails, the cross and crown of thorns, the spunge and spear in saltire, three scourges, 2 and 1, etc., also the symbol of the Trinity'. Henry Davy (1841) shows a cross stump on the chancel gable. There are here two surprising survivals: the font has scenes from the life of Christ and the BVM in perfect order, as it was in Davy's time; it has never been suggested that the figures are recut. Secondly, six panels on the screen, four showing bishops, are only slightly damaged, which is surprising in view of Dowsing's anti-episcopal remarks at Polstead, Nettlestead and Benacre (entries 225, 240, 249). The others have groups of people, nine men on one and seven women on the other, probably members of the Gild of St Erasmus in the parish. Alexander Sparhawke of the parish by his will proved 1539 was to be buried in the chapel of St Erasmus, and left 20s. 'to the making of a parclose within the said chapel'. One of the episcopal figures holds what may represent the windlass with which the saint was disembowelled.[341] In the 1880s these panels formed the doors of a large cupboard in the vestry.

81.  Mary's at the tower [St Mary le Tower], Jan. 29. We took up 6 brass inscriptions, with *Ora pro nobis*, and *Ora pro animabus*, and *Cujus animæ propitietur deus*; and *Pray for the soul*, in English; and I gave order to take down 5 iron crosses, and one of wood on the steeple.[342]

Until the hurricane of February 1661, the tower was surmounted by a spire. Today only the arcades and some late monuments remain from the medieval civic church following the rebuilding campaign 1860–80.

This was the town church for Puritan Ipswich. Just a few years previous to Dowsing's visit, Ferdinando Adams, together with his fellow church-warden Titus Camplin, had been excommunicated for 'not taking downe the seates standing above the Communion Table in this Church, and railing in the Table Altar-wise against the wall, as he was injoyned'. Adams had previously refused to give up the keys to the church to Bishop Wren's visitation commissioners, verbally assaulting them, and confronting them with 'musketts charged, swords staves and other weapons'. Adams fled to New England, returning in 1640. Such Puritan resistance to Laudian reform was widespread in the town.[343]

It is possible to suggest rather more than six pre-Reformation brasses here which once had prayers in Latin or English. Of the survivors, none have superstitious inscriptions today; perhaps some were missing already when Dowsing came:

*c.*1320  Roger Le Neve – Norman French inscription still legible to Kirby in 1748;

1446  Margaret, wife of William Debenham, seven times Bailiff of the town – lost;

1460  Margaret Walworth, first wife of William Walworth, descendant of the Lord Mayor of that name – lost;

1479  Robert Wimbill, notary publick, Bailiff 1469–70 – figure extant, with prayer to the Trinity on a breast scroll unscathed, but other prayers in the main inscription already excised by 1744, leaving only his name and office;

1479  Elizabeth Wimbill his daughter, kneeling with beads and book – lost;

1487  Clemencia Walworth, second wife of William above – lost;

1488  John Walworth, son of William and Margaret – lost;

1512  Sir Thomas Sampson – lost;

1512  Thomas Drayll and two wives, bailiff seven times – figures and bracket extant;

1525  Thomas Baldry and two wives – figures only remain.

However, the inscription on the surviving brass of 1506 to Robert Wimbill, Alys his wife and her second husband Thomas Baldry, with an English prayer for their souls, is undamaged today, though the prayer scrolls above the figures are only partly remaining.[344]

The font survived intact also, perhaps an indication that it was stored away during the 'basin and stand' fashion. The Tower not only had powerful Puritan preachers, but loyalists biding their time.

## 82. Margarett's, Jan. 30. There was 12 Apostles in stone taken down; and between 20 and 30 superstitious pictures to be taken down, which a godly man, a churchwarden promised to do.

The churchwardens' accounts are incomplete, and there is no record of the 'godly' churchwarden in 1644, but in 1642–43 the two were Thomas Carter and Joshua Major and in 1645–46 Thomas Newton and James Hornigold.

'There was 12 Apostles in stone taken down'. There are seated wooden figures, carved from the wall-posts set on stone corbels, and it is probable that Dowsing mistook them for stone because they had been whitewashed. They are discussed below. Of the corbels themselves, only one was seriously damaged; the sixth corbel from the east on the north side has been repaired with a piece of stone spliced in and very crudely carved with a face and Ws. The hammerbeam angels, not mentioned in the Journal, have been roughly hacked off; they were replaced by 22 *trompe l'oeil* shields of arms in 1700.

Although the wooden figures are badly mutilated, for several of them enough remains to show which saints they represented (Plate 32). The scrolls they hold will have had painted phrases from the Creed which would have identified them decisively, but all that is long gone.

*North side numbering from the East:* 4: St Luke in a doctor's hat; 5: St John in mass vestments (tassels remain) holding a chalice; 7: St James the Less with a fuller's club; 9: St Peter with his key.

*South side:* 3: St James the Great in a large hat on which would have been a scallop shell; 5: A female saint, unidentifiable; 6: St Philip with three loaves; 7: St Paul with a sword; 8: St Simon holding a fish; 10: St Jude holding a ship.

Although the font is not mentioned in the Journal it suffered much (Plate 39). Angels held scrolls with legends relating to the sacrament of baptism, of which only one, with the inscription *sal et saliva*, remains intact – and that appears untouched. In the opposite compartment the angel has been removed (all but the wings, carved in low relief) but the stump has been recarved to form a simple cross on a small Calvary mound – of the two, the cross would have upset Dowsing more than the angel he knocked off. D. E. Davy's notes taken in 1826 and his plan made in 1832 explain the surviving angel.[345] At that time and no doubt earlier the font stood against the south side of the westernmost north arcade pier. Davy did not record the *sal et saliva* inscription as he surely would had it been visible, so it must have been against the pier, and the hidden position saved it from mutilation. The simple cross panel faced south across the nave.

The Ordinance to which Dowsing was working did not mention fonts; they were included in the second Ordinance, published in May, some months after his visit. But he would have felt free to remove superstitious images wherever they were found.[346]

## 83. Steven's [St Stephen], Jan 30. There was a popish inscription in brass, *Pray for the soul.*

Two *Pray for the soul* inscriptions in English are known to have been here: that for William Waller (d.1535) and his three wives was recorded by Henry Chitting, Chester Herald in the 1620s; the other was for William and Anne

33. Damaged external crosses. 33a (top left). The porch at Badingham, Suffolk (see page 319). 33b (top right). The chancel cross at Dennington, Suffolk (see pages 317–19). 33c (left). The gable cross at Kingston, Cambridgeshire (see page 257).

34. Damaged external crosses. 34a (top left). Gable cross at Wickham Market, Suffolk (see page 224). 34b (top right). Chancel cross at Blyford, Suffolk (see pages 298–9). 34c (bottom left). Possible stump of cross on parapet at Offton (see page 309). 34d (bottom right). Gable cross at Elmsett, Suffolk (see page 308).

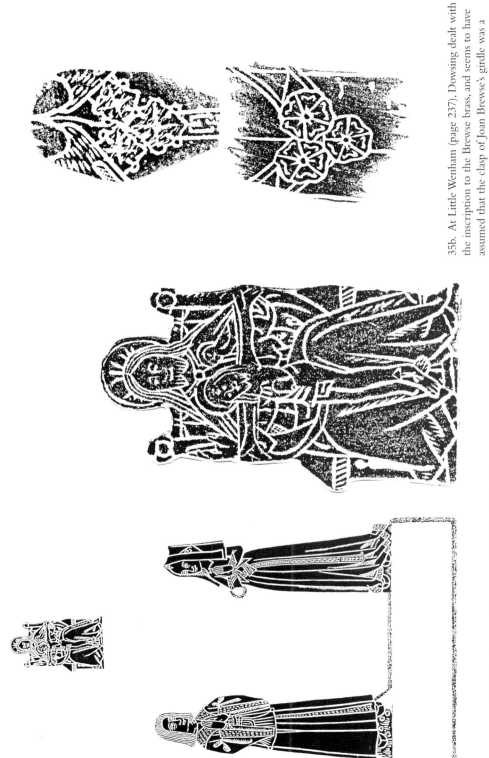

35b. At Little Wenham (page 237), Dowsing dealt with the inscription to the Brewse brass, and seems to have assumed that the clasp of Joan Brewse's girdle was a rosary (top). Compare with the undamaged brass in Christchurch Mansion, Ipswich (bottom).

35a. Brass at Orford church. Dowsing removed the inscription, but overlooked the Trinity (see page 221).

36. Brasses at Linton, Cambridgeshire to members of the Paris family, damaged by Dowsing (see pages 210-11). 36a (left). A snatched photograph (it is normally under fixed carpets) of the effigy of Nicholas Paris (1424), with inscription removed (shields not shown). 36b (below left). William Parys (1538/9), with prayer clause removed. 36c (below). Sir Philip Paris (1558) and first wife Margaret (1551), a Marian brass, also with prayer clause removed.

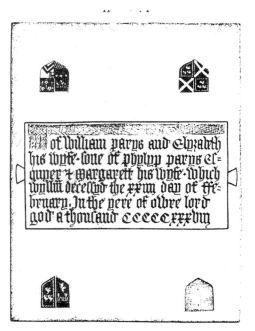

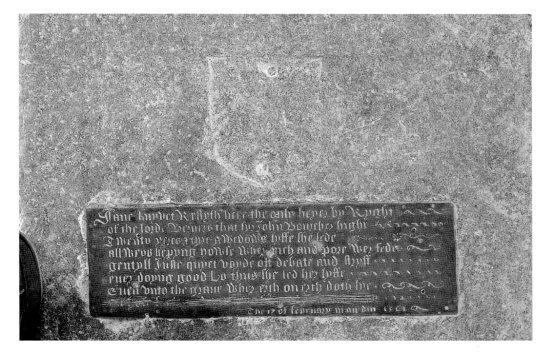

37a. Brass at Ashwellthorpe, Norfolk, to Jane Knyvett (d.1561) with an unacceptable phrase erased either by Captain Gilley or in advance of his visit by the Knyvett family (see page 112).

37b. Brass to John Smythe (1534) at Stutton, Suffolk, with damaged prayer clauses (see page 86).

38a. Brass at Metfield, Suffolk to John Jermy (d.1504) and Isabelle his wife. Dowsing met some resistance here (pages 315–16), but the brass was eventually dealt with – the opening prayer clause cut off, and the closing one defaced.

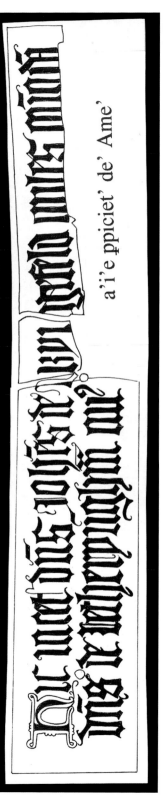

a'i'e ppiciet' de' Ame'

38b. Tracing of inscription (now lost) to Sir John Wingfield (d.1389) at Letheringham, Suffolk (page 252) showing how Dowsing's deputy removed just the prayer clause, but managed to break the rest of the inscription in doing so.

39. The font at St Margaret, Ipswich (see pages 231-2). This is badly defaced. One angel has later been replaced with a cross, which would not have pleased Dowsing.

40 (opposite). Little Wenham church, showing the wall paintings at the east end. It is probable that the figure of the Virgin Mary mentioned by Dowsing (page 237) is the painting to the north of the east window.

41 (left). Drawing published by Weever in 1631 of glass at Tendryng Hall chapel, now lost, showing the kneeling figure of a Howard (perhaps John Lord Howard). Dowsing visited here, and probably broke the glass (page 248).

42. Glass at Madingley church, Cambridge previously in the east end. This glass was listed by Dowsing (pages 254–5). The figure of Mary (detail below) has been damaged, as can be seen from the misfitting head.

43. The Stukeley monument (*c.*1636) at Madingley church, Cambridgeshire. As can be seen in the lower picture, the cherub faces have had to be replaced.

44. Some of the ten defaced figures, probably Dowsing's 'cherubim in wood', to be found in the ground-floor chamber of the tower of Madingley church, Cambridgeshire.

45. Kingston church, Cambridgeshire, visited by Dowsing in March 1644 (see page 257). 45a (above). The shadow of the rood, which may have been Dowsing's 'crucifix'. 45b (left). Dowsing ordered the chancel steps to be removed, and from the height of the piscina it seems that the floor has never since been raised.

46. Bourn church, Cambridgeshire (see pages 258–9 for Dowsing's visit). 45a (top). A modern cross on the old apex stone; the original was ordered down by Dowsing. 45b (bottom left). An angel in the chancel, one of a pair which Dowsing 'did down'. This one has since had its head replaced. 45c (bottom right). A carved panel of the Virgin and Child, which Dowsing also mentioned.

47. Trumpington church, Cambridgeshire (page 263). 47a and 47b (above). Glass images to St Peter and St Paul, largely complete, despite Dowsing's visit. 47c (left). The famous brass to Sir Roger de Trumpington had already lost its marginal inscription before Dowsing's visit.

48a. The base of the tower at Pampisford church, Cambridgeshire, showing the flushwork crosses on the buttresses (see page 274).

48b (above left). The tower of Ickleton church, Cambridgeshire, showing the flushwork cross above the belfry window (see pages 275–6). 48c (above right). Bench end at Ickleton showing St Michael weighing souls. Close examination shows that this has been damaged at some stage in its life, possibly by Dowsing.

Wimbill (d.1504), Anne (Rivers) his widow, and her second husband Thomas Alvard.[347]

**84. Laurence [St Lawrence], Jan. 30. There was 2 popish inscriptions, one with beades, and written *Ora pro nobis*.**

One of the 'popish inscriptions' will have come from the elaborate matrix in the chancel of the brass of Edmund Daundy, Bailiff, 1514. He gave the town its first market cross, and this church a chantry where Daundys and Wolseys (close relatives) were to be remembered. One reason for there being no superstitious pictures here was the extensive Edwardian cleansing ordered in 1547: 'ix glas wyndows of fayned storyse… to be glaced with whyght glas' costing twelve pounds. The communion rails had gone some years before Dowsing's visit, burned with broom faggots.[348]

**85. Clements, Jan. 30. They four days afore they had beaten up divers superstitious inscriptions.**

The churchwardens' accounts for this year survive, and show expenditure on glass. They also record the purchase of 'an Eyron and basin to baptyse children by the Deske Syde', an early example of what later became a widespread abandonment of fonts.[349] The font, which was thus made redundant, and perhaps stored away, is of exactly the same type as at neighbouring St Mary at the Quay, save that all four shields held by angels originally had religious emblems, and all are more or less effaced. One panel has the well-carved initials FS and IK, the churchwardens from Easter Monday 31 March 1662: Fitz Sample, baker and John Keeble, mariner. It is likely that they replaced the font, ordered the crocketted cover, and had font and cover painted a stone colour.

**86. At Helens, Jan. 30. Nothing.[350]**

The dominant influence of the Puritan activist, Samuel Dunkon, in this parish would account for there being nothing left to be done here. The elaborate decorations of the niche over the porch have been savaged, as have the heads and scrolls of angels in the spandrels of the opening. In the porch a fine stoup must also have been beaten down before the visit. Nothing else is pre-Victorian and even the font is gone – the one the Revd A. J. Deck reported to the Parkers in 1855 was plain and of wood, a rare sight indeed![351]

**87. Playford, Jan. 30. We brake down 17 popish pictures, one of God the Father; and took up 2 superstitious inscriptions in brass; and one *Ora pro nobis* and *Cujus animæ propitietur deus*, and a second *Pray for the soul*.**

John Sell Cotman's 1817 etching of the brass here of Sir George Felbrigg, 1400, (recorded before the clergy sold the canopy for scrap in 1838 to pay for a remounting of the figure), shows about one-third of the marginal inscription removed already, with no trace of the name but leaving prayers for the soul in Norman French.[352] The Journal entry mentions only Latin and English prayers for the soul; and there is evidence elsewhere that French prayers were generally overlooked by Dowsing and his deputies (for example, Letheringham, entry 127, and Brundish, entry 213).[353] J. W. Darby (1828) drew indents of two other brasses despoiled: one to a man, another to one with two wives and groups of children.

## 88. Blakenham, at the water [Great Blakenham], Feb. 1st. 1643/4. Only the steps were to be levelled, which I gave them eight days to do it.

The porch is of wood and has a canopied figure (probably the Blessed Virgin Mary and Child since this is St Mary's church) above the opening which looks more weathered than defaced. The font has emblems on the Passion theme, unusual in being spread between all four shields around the bowl: sacred heart surrounded by crown of thorns; nails, spear, and rod and sponge; and scourging pillar, rope, sword and (uncommonly) a cock crowing. They are in remarkably good condition. High up in a small circular east window in what may be old glass is IHS, but laterally inverted. In 1645, an elaborate alabaster monument with two large kneeling angels at the sides was erected in the north chapel in memory of Richard Swift, merchant of London. To make room for the organ the memorial has now been tucked away under the tower. This church was let off lightly.

## 89. Bramford, Feb. 1. A cross to be taken off the steeple; we brake down 841 superstitious pictures; and gave order to take down the steps, and gave a fortnight's time; and took up 3 inscriptions, with *Ora pro nobis*, and *Cujus animæ propitietur deus*.

The 841 pictures, like the 1000 at Clare, if in glass, would have taken so long to count that it would have saved time just to smash them. But the figure is bizarrely precise, and may merely be a witness to Dowsing's messy handwriting and blotched scratchings out.

There has long been a small spire on the tower here, so that the cross could have stood where the weathervane used to be until the 1987 hurricane brought it down. The wide niche low down in the west face of the tower with its elaborate groined vault may have housed a rood group, and if that had survived the Reformation could equally well have been the cross Dowsing wanted destroyed.

No indents remain from the three Latin inscriptions which were taken up. Sixteen roof angels are now headless.

## 90. Sproughton. We brake down 61 superstitious pictures; and gave order for the steps to be levelled, a fortnight's time; and 3 inscriptions, *Ora pro nobis* and *Cujus animæ propitietur deus.*

Darby (1828) drew indents of an inscription and shield, and a woman with foot inscription. Only the latter remains today, but there is a shield indent at the bottom of the composition.

Wodderspoon, gathering material for his proposed edition of the Journal, was rehearsing his purple prose when he wrote: 'angels evidently cast down from the roof... [an] axe... laid these wooden emblems low... headless, armless, reft and twisted'.[354] The roof was repaired in the 1860s, and the present angels must be replacements.

## 91. Burstall, Feb. the 1st. We took off an iron cross off the steeple; and gave order to levell the steps.

The south door hood mould stops are replacements for something savagely knocked off. Inside, the steps seem not to have been levelled in the high north chapel, probably because it is almost filled with the huge marble slab covering the vault of the Puritan Cage family. Edward Cage, twice Bailiff of Ipswich (d.1607), and his son William (d.1645), who was seven times Bailiff and who sat in eight Parliaments for the town, were both buried here. The font, octagonal on four thin and one thick central columns, was at some stage recarved to gothicise it. The panels are now flat, leaving mean corner pilasters looking rather ridiculous. This may imply cleansing. Modern angels in the nave roof presumably replace earlier figures.

## 92. Hintlesham, Feb. 1. We brake down 51 superstitious pictures; and took up 3 inscriptions, with *Ora pro nobis,* and *Cujus animæ propitietur deus;* and gave order for digging down the steps.

This church has plenty of large windows to hold fifty 'pictures'; there are early fragments in the upper lights of several in the north aisle. One large indent and two small ones account for Dowsing's three inscriptions. Traces remain of paintings on the north wall, probably the St Christopher reported some years ago.[355] There was no need to damage the heraldic shields around the font bowl, and nor did they, but the lions around the stem were targets.

The chancel, now up two small steps, still seems lower than the nave. The hood mould stops on the south and west doors into the building are completely missing.

## 93. Hadley [Hadleigh], Feb. 2. We brake down 30 superstitious pictures, and gave order for taking down the rest, which were about 70; and took up an inscription, *Quorum animabus propitietur deus*; and gave order for the takeing down of a cross on the steeple; gave 14 days.

The spire has a large, modern, cross below the weather vane. Three niches over the south porch door and one over the west door may have been emptied during an earlier reformation.

There are many indents, from any of which the single inscription might have come. The font is mainly architectural, with eight angels supporting the bowl; but these are well-carved replacements, betrayed by the contrasting colour of the stone.

## 94. Layham, Feb. 2. We brake down 6 superstitious pictures, and takeing down a cross off the steeple.

This tower has no cross now. Henry Davy's etching of 1846 showed the stump of a cross on just the nave gable; porch, nave and chancel are all provided with crosses now. The font, plain Norman, attracted no anger.

## 95. Shelley, Feb. 2. We brake down 6 superstitious pictures; and took off 2 inscriptions, with *Cujus animæ propitietur deus*.

Only the heraldry remains of an elaborate Tilney tomb on the north of the chancel, which may account for one of the inscriptions. Cautley suggested that the decorative oak-panelled canopied alcove to the west was a [late] Easter sepulchre.[356] With nothing beneath it, it looks like a pew in the wrong dimension, which perhaps accounts for its survival.

## 96. Higham [Higham St Mary], Feb. 2. We brake down 15 superstitious pictures in the chancell; and 16 in the church, (so called); and gave order to levell the steps in 14 days.

Restoration has left little here as old as the seventeenth century. There is only one indent, and the altar is up one step. Perhaps the south-east nave piscina has been trimmed flush with the wall. The font, all architectural in its decoration, is not damaged.

Presumably Dowsing's aside about the 'so called' church reflects his view that the word should be reserved for the People of God, rather than a building; or perhaps he was being scathing about what went on in this particular parish.

## 97. Feb. 3, Wenham Magna [Great Wenham]. There was nothing to reform.

So much is restored here, and the font is plain, that it is not possible to spot any damage done before Dowsing's arrival. But he missed one thing: the chancel pavement has fifteenth-century tiles which include many with the IHS monogram.

## 98. Wenham Parva [Little Wenham], Feb. 3. We brake down 26 superstitious pictures, and gave order to break down 6 more; and to levell the steps. One picture was of the Virgin Mary.

It is generally assumed that most or all medieval wall paintings had been whitewashed well before Dowsing's time, and sometimes covered with texts (as at Great Cornard and Mutford, entries 113 and 228); or had been defaced, as at Wilby (214).[357] Is it possible that some had escaped and were still untouched in the 1640s? Or might Elizabethan whitewash sometimes have been thinly applied, or have flaked and chipped after nearly a century, so that the pictures were again visible? Certainly by the eighteenth century, Cole was recording wall paintings at Comberton (146).

Unfortunately, Dowsing is little help on this, as he rarely specifies the medium in which his 'pictures' were executed. Only at Papworth Everard (141) does he state clearly that he is dealing with wall paintings. The only other evidence is here, at Wenham Parva, where the surviving wall paintings do include a representation (two, in fact) of the Virgin Mary, as specifically noted by Dowsing.[358] One is in the chancel, north of the altar, showing the Virgin and Child with two angels (only slightly damaged at her brow, and that could be plaster loss through time); to the south are three female saints with their attributes (Plate 40). The much larger St Christopher mural facing the south door is thought to have been overpainted so that the saint becomes Mary, providing a second representation of the Virgin and Child. Which version – if either – caught Dowsing's eye is unclear. The churchwardens would no doubt have whitewashed them after his visit, if they were the offending items.

On the brass of Thomas Brewse (d.1514) and Joan his wife almost half the marginal inscription fillet offended and was removed, but why have the three flowers forming the clasp of Joan's girdle also been vandalised (Plate 35)? Perhaps Dowsing imagined it was part of a rosary.

99. Feb. 3, Capell [Capel St Mary]. We brake down 3 superstitious pictures; and gave order to take down 31, which the churchwarden promised to doo; and to take down a stoneing cross on the
outside of the church, as it is called.[359]

Henry Davy's etching of 1842 shows a finial on the nave east gable and a
cross stump on the chancel; there are now gable crosses on both nave and
chancel, the latter looking the older.

100. Feb. 3. We were at the Lady Bruce's House, and in her
chappel [Little Wenham Hall chapel], there was a picture of God
the Father, of the Trinity, of Christ, and the Holy Ghost, the clo-
ven tongues; which we gave order to take down, and the Lady
promised to do it.

This is the only one of the several private chapels Dowsing visited which
survives (see entries 118, 119, 167). 'Lady Bruce' was the widow of Sir John
Brewse who died aged 47 in the first year of the Civil War.[360]

This gem of a vaulted late-thirteenth-century chapel could most easily
have accommodated Dowsing's 'pictures' as wall paintings, above the entrance doorway and on the western sections of the north and south walls.
The damage to the projecting sill below the piscina and sedilia, and to
narrow vertical courses at the north-west and south-west corners of the
chapel, look like iconoclasm until it is realised that when panelling and pews
were inserted such adjustments would be necessary.[361] On the central roof
boss is a three-quarter length figure of Christ in a vesica with the right hand
raised in the act of blessing; it is undamaged, so perhaps Lady Brewse did not
rush to do all of Dowsing's bidding.

*5–6 February. Sunday 4 February was a day of rest. It may be significant that it was
on this Sunday, when Dowsing was on the point of leaving Suffolk, and when his
initial tour in that county may have convinced him of the enormity of the task, that we
have the earliest evidence of his appointing a deputy, Thomas Denny (discussed page
67). Perhaps he initially authorised Denny to inspect those churches with deadlines
falling due during his absence (see entries 88, 89, 90, 93, 96).[362]*

*On the Monday he made his way back to Cambridgeshire, journeying to Bury
St Edmunds the first night. Whilst there did he perhaps stay with the Moody family, at
the suggestion of Thomas Westhropp (the deputy with whom he probably lodged on
6 January) who married a Moody a few years later?[363] Dowsing arrived just north of
Cambridge on Tuesday 6 February, his earlier visits that day showing signs of rush as he
broke his travels.*

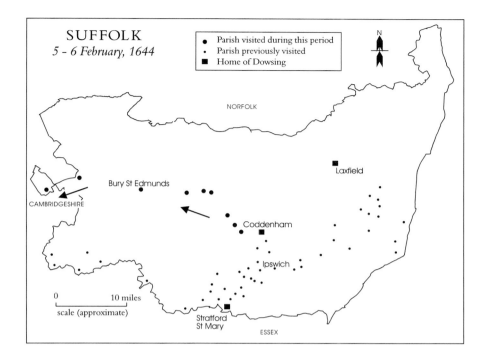

SUFFOLK
5 - 6 February, 1644

- Parish visited during this period
- Parish previously visited
■ Home of Dowsing

N

NORFOLK

Laxfield

Bury St Edmunds

CAMBRIDGESHIRE

Coddenham

Ipswich

0     10 miles
scale (approximate)

Stratford
St Mary

ESSEX

101. Nedham markett [Needham Market], Feb. 5. We gave order to take down 2 iron crosses on the chappell, and a stoneing
cross.

There is the stump of a stone cross on the chancel gable, and a replacement cross of iron on the nave. High up on buttresses on both sides of the
church are prayers still legible, e.g. *Christ ihs have merci on us*. One longer one
over the south chancel door should have been cleansed: *Pray we all for grace /
for he yt have holpe ys place / god reward he for her ded [deed] / & heve[n] may be her
mede [meed, i.e. reward]*.

The window at the north-east corner of the chancel is glazed with
fragments of medieval glass gathered here. The roof angels are of 1892 and
the shields held by angels on the corbels, all with symbols of the passion,
must be part of the same restoration.

102. Badley, Feb. 5. We brake down 34 superstitious pictures;
Mr. Dove promised to take down the rest, 28; and to levell the
chancell. We took down 4 superstitious pictures, with *Ora pro
nobis*, and *Cujus animæ propitietur deus*.[364]

William Dove was the principal inhabitant of this hamlet apart from Edmund Poley Esq. at the Hall[365] whose recent – and thus not superstitious – ancestors' brasses (1613, 1615 and 1633) were respected while four English inscriptions to earlier forebears, recorded by William Hervy in 1561, were taken up.[366] Darby (1827) drew the four indents.

103. **Stowmarkett, Feb. 5. We gave order to break down about 70 superstitious pictures; and to levell the chancel, to Mr. Manning, that promised it; and to take down 2 crosses, one on the steeple, and the other on the church as it is called; and took off an inscription, of** *Ora pro nobis.*[367]

William Manning was churchwarden and a leading citizen at Stowmarket, which for parish organisation was linked with nearby Stowupland, without a church of its own until 1843. Henry Davy's etching of 1842 shows stumps of crosses on the gables of nave and chancel. The roofs are modern and unadorned and damage to the porches and entrance doors seems to involve as much erosion as vandalism. The octagonal font with four crosses and four niches around the bowl is probably modern. The canopied tomb chest in the east bay of the north arcade which has lost all its brasses is probably the memorial of Margaret Tyrell of Gipping (died *c.*1470) and her thirteen children.[368] Two MR and two IHS carvings in stone on each face of the canopy have been chiselled flat. On the upper part of the memorial to William Tyrrell (d.1641) and his wife, a short inscription in gold letters has been obliterated. Surely there was nothing for Dowsing to reform on this, one of the newest memorials he will have seen on his tour. But in Mary's reign the Tyrrell family had been active against Protestants, and they remained conservative in religion: perhaps the inscription did contain something to annoy the Puritan.[369]

The vicar of the church from 1628–55 was Thomas Young, tutor and friend of Milton, and one of the five writers of *Smectymnuus*, a violent pamphlet against episcopacy.[370] Not long after Dowsing's visit, Young was made Master of Jesus College by the Earl of Manchester.

The churchwardens' accounts at Stowmarket have survived only in various partial transcriptions. Those for 1643–44 match Dowsing's account well, though, as so often they show expenditure for items not recorded by him (carvings on the stalls, and Peter's keys on the spire). It is impossible to tell whether this is work carried out before he arrived, careless note-taking on his part, or a burst of enthusiasm on the part of the churchwardens after he had gone.

For our part [half share of the cost, Stowupland paid the other
  half] for lowering of the chancell . . . . . . . . . . . . . . . . o 04 06
Item for takinge downe the pynacle crosse . . . . . . . . . . . . . o 01 03
Item to Mr Pettitt for blotting out the crosse keyes on the spire
  [St Peter's keys; this would seem to be extra to Dowsing's re-
  quirements] . . . . . . . . . . . . . . . . . . . . . . . . . . . o 00 08
For beatinge downe the pictures in the glass windowes of the
  churche & for cutting off the images of the endes of the
  stooles and the cross on the east end of the church . . . . 4 days' wages
Laide out for the towne paide to Fyler for glassinge where the
  pictures were battered . . . . . . . . . . . . . . . . . . . . . o 16 00

Dowsing would be displeased to see that the spire, replaced in 1994 by a
lighter modern construction, now has as a prominent feature the keys of
Peter in gold.

The year following Dowsing's visit the accounts show that the organ was
taken down, and the vestments sold – both in line with the Parliamentary
Ordinance of 1644.

Item received of Phillipp Enfeild for the halfe p'te of the organe
  pipes . . . . . . . . . . . . . . . . . . . . . . . . . . . . . . 1 01 06
Item received for the halfe p'te of two surplices and a tippetto . . o 09 03

## 104. Wetherden, Feb. 5. We brake 100 superstitious pictures in S[i]r Edward Silliard's eile; and gave order to break down 60 more; and to take down 68 cherubims; and to levell the steps in the chancell; there was takeing up 19 superstitious inscriptions, that weighed 65 pounds.

The south aisle ('Silliard's eile') is that of the Sulyard family, notorious
recusants. The aisle was begun by John Sulyard (d.1488) and his 'IS' in
ligature can still be seen on the richly decorated exterior stonework. A cross
there is still unscathed; the Marian pot of lilies on the south-west corner
buttress of the south porch is damaged, but its neighbour is not.

Here and at Walberswick the churchwardens weighed the brasses taken
up; 65 pounds must have included figures as well as inscriptions. William
Hervy in 1561 recorded nine inscriptions to Tyrrells and Sulyards which
would account for some of the nineteen.[371]

It seems almost certain that Dowsing was responsible for the damage to
the monument of the recusant Sir John Sulyard (d.1574), whose marginal
inscription defiantly ended *cuius anime propitietur Deus*: this has been partially
erased.

In the eighteenth century Thomas Martin described some of the fragmentary glass which survived Dowsing in both nave and aisle, including donor inscriptions with the objectionable elements removed. What remains is now collected in the upper part of the chancel east window.[372]

All the roofs are extremely fine medieval work, sensitively restored in the nineteenth century, when new angels were introduced, presumably into the spaces vacated by Dowsing's '68 cherubim'.[373]

105. Emswell [Elmswell], Feb. 5. We brake down 20 superstitous pictures; and gave order to break down 40 and above, and to take down 40 cherubims. We took up 4 superstitious inscription[s], with *ora pro nobis.*

J. W. Darby recorded four inscription indents on his visit in 1827, as well as a cross brass marginal inscription indent. Blois in about 1660 wrote of the cross brass: 'And a stone for Mr J. Brampton rector de Wolpett [Woolpit] *qui hanc capelle[m] etc'.*[374] Just the name and office survived the iconoclasts; would it be right to infer that they had trimmed the brass of any offending words?

The font is in perfect order except that a bird and an animal supporter around the pedestal are headless. Eight screen panels have the ugliest modern painted figures to be seen anywhere in the county; what is underneath? There are 36 main window lights and 20 more in the clerestory. In the roof 12 figures which stood on stone pillar tops under wooden canopies have gone completely.

106. Tostick [Tostock], Feb. 5. We brake down about 16 superstitious pictures; and gave order to take down about 40 more; and to levell the steps. We took a superstitious inscription, with *Ora p[ro] nobis.*

The stoup outside the porch door is filled in, and crowned MR and IHS in flushwork on the porch buttresses look maltreated. The font bowl has floral motives; if iconoclasts recognised two green men peering out on two panels they did nothing about them. The hammerbeam roof figures, ten under canopies, were beheaded, and there may have been ten angels higher up on what are now bare brace ends. There is some old glass in the east window; in all there are 29 window lights. A few bench end finial figures are mutilated, but as most are animals the iconoclasts may not be to blame.

107. Bury St Edmunds, Feb. 5. Mary's parish. Mr. Chaplin undertook to do down the steps and to take away the superstitious pictures.

'Mr Chaplin' was Thomas Chaplin, Esq., J. P., who given his views (discussed below, next entry) might have been relied on to make a thorough clearance; but, outside, the north porch still has its stoup, and the *Orate* inscription to its benefactors John and Isabella Notyngham (he died 1437) over the entrance arch. The ceiling of John Baret's chantry has the unobjectionable 'Grace me govern' on scrolls; the prayers on scrolls around his cadaver effigy are legible, but by Dowsing's time the memorial had been turned round, so most of the inscription was invisible to him, facing the wall, and therefore also unobjectionable. The foot inscription on the brass of Jankyn Smyth has been removed, as has the marginal inscription on the table tomb of the Carews (1501), but that on the Drury monument remains with its *orate* and *cuius animabus* injunctions. The bowl of the font is in a rather sorry condition, but this is not iconoclasm: the original carvings on the font were hacked off in 1783 and replaced by painted shields, which were in turn removed in 1928. The incomparable roof carvings, including many angels, were not molested.

108. James's parish. Mr. Moody undertook for.

'Mr Moody' was Samuel Moody, Esq., whose daughter later married Thomas Westhropp of Hundon, one of Dowsing's deputies (see chapter 6). Both Moody and Chaplin above were listed in the first category of lay members of the Bury classis, the eleventh division; they were also committee men for taking evidence against scandalous ministers.[375]

109. Kentford, Feb. 6. We gave order to take down a cross and other pictures.

The entire walls were covered with paintings here, but they have been fading badly. The large painting of the three living and three dead opposite the south door has been restored, but all the other paintings in the church seem to have been covered over, or may simply have disappeared.[376]

110. Feb. 6. At Newmarket they promised to amend all.

They may have promised; but Abraham Darby's notes on the church (made in the 1820s) mention at the east end of the south aisle 'carved and gilt' *Orate pro a[n]i[m]a thome wydon qui has sedes fieri fecit a[nn]o d[om]ni 1498.* So not all was amended.

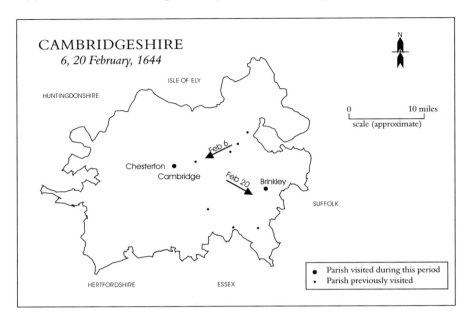

6–20 February. *The 'missing' fortnight, between 6 February and 20 February, is discussed in chapter 1. Dowsing may well have been visiting north Cambridgeshire.*

111. Feb. 6. At Chesterfield, we gave order to take down 14 crosses on the steple, and 2 on the porch; we brake down 40 superstitious pictures, and gave order to take down 50 more at least, and to levell the steps in the chancell.

Probably Chesterton, St Andrew, but a hard ride from Newmarket and Kentford on the same day. Newmarket may have been dealt with hurriedly to allow time for the journey, and was left with no more than a 'promise' by the locals 'to amend all'.

As discussed by John Morrill, it is likely that Dowsing visited Chesterton on his way to Cambridge to begin a further tour in the two week period which is missing from the Journal.[377] He would not have approved of the churchmanship there:

Richard Watts, vicar since 1630... was a confirmed Laudian. He placed the communion table altarwise and railed it in, and insisted until 1642 that parishioners should come to the rails to take the sacrament. The villagers later complained that he read half the service from the chancel and could hardly be heard in the nave... In the 1640s he proved a zealous royalist, obstructing Parliamentary propaganda, and objected in 1643 to fasts at

Christmas. Although ejected in 1644 he was still living in the village in 1650.[378]

It is difficult to see how the 'steple' could have had '14 crosses' in an architectural sense. These must have been applied, wooden or iron, crosses, or perhaps decorative stonework in the fabric of the tower (as at Pampisford and Ickleton, entries 181 and 183).

A number of beastly and human bench ends survive and there are many cherubic roof corbels. Those in the north aisle are easily accessible (those in the south are modern).

Probably during this period, 'the book of Canons was taken away with the Hood and surplice', as reported by the churchwardens in 1662, though it is impossible to know if this was related to Dowsing's visit.[379]

**112. February 20 [?29]. Brinckly [Brinkley].** I took down two superstitious inscriptions in brass, *Orate pro animabus*, and *Cujus animæ propitietur deus*, and *Pray for our souls* the second inscription; and I brake 10 superstitious pictures, one of Christopher carrying Christ on his shoulders, and gave order for taking down 2 more in the chancell, and to levell the chancell.[380]

Small fragments of old glass survive, including Christ crucified and two small angels. The picture of St Christopher was probably in the glass, though it might just have been a wall painting (see discussion under Little Wenham, entry 98). The indent of what is almost certainly one of the 'inscriptions in bras' may be seen – the three-figure brass of William Stutfield, which has only the indent where one of the figures and the inscription should be. Layer records this inscription, *Orate pro animabus Willm Stutfield*.[381] The inscription ends: *quorum animabus propicietur deus. Amen.* Two for the price of one?

*20–23 February (map overleaf) On Tuesday 20 February, Dowsing reappeared at Brinkley in Cambridgeshire. From there he travelled back into Suffolk, covering a cluster of villages in the south-west of the county. He gives the impression of slowing down as he travels back home, finishing the week's work on Friday. The entries are slightly out of order.*

**113. Cornearth Magna [Great Cornard], Feb. 20.** I took up 2 inscriptions, *Pray for our souls*; and gave order to take down a cross on the steeple; and to levell the steps. John Pain, churchwarden, for not paying, and doing his duty injoyned by the Ordinance,

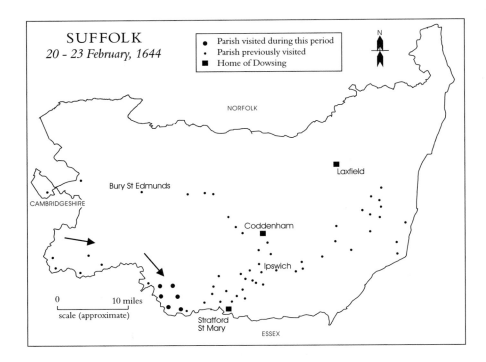

I charged Henry Taner, the Constable, to carry him before the Earl of Manchester.[382]

The steeple is still without its cross, and there are stumps of gable crosses on nave and chancel. Two niches on the west tower wall were probably empty before Dowsing came. Shields only remain on a tomb chest in the chancel which may account for one inscription taken. There were wall paintings here, some overpainted with Elizabethan texts which would have given Puritan visitors no offence; but modern hands have covered them all completely.[383] The font bowl shields are armorial and in good order, but the stem is new, perhaps indicating that the supporters were badly battered.

This is the only recorded instance of Dowsing using the power of arrest granted by the Earl of Manchester in his second commission.[384] Henry Tanner (the Constable) was rated at 11s. 0d. for ship money, indicating that he was comfortably off. John Pain is not listed in the ship money records.[385]

This and the following entry are duplicated later (entries 121, 122). See pages 144–5 for a discussion of the significance of the duplication.

114. Little Cornearth [Little Cornard], Feb. 20. There were two crosses, one in wood, and another in stone, which I gave order to

take them down; and I brake down 6 superstitious pictures. Had no noble.

There are no indents and a plain roof. The font shields are all armorial and in good order.

The noble had been a coin worth 6s. 8d., so was the colloquial expression for half a mark. The duplicate entries for the Cornard parishes disagree about whether Dowsing received payment or not.

115. Newton [Newton All Saints], Feb. 21. William Plume, churchwarden, and John [Shrive] Constable. I brake down 4 superstitious pictures, one of Christ, and 6 in the chancell, one of Christ, and of the Virgin Mary; and to see the steps levelled.[386]

Traces of extensive wall paintings remain in the nave, as does good heraldic glass in the five-light east window and four other two-light chancel windows. The font has nothing but architectural decoration. William Plume, the churchwarden, was rated at 5s. 10d. for Ship Money, and John Shrive at 3s. 6d.

116. Assington, Feb. 21. We brake down 40 pictures, one of God the Father, and the other very superstitious; and gave order to levell the chancel; and to take a cross off the steeple. Constable, James Springes.

There is no cross on the tower today. One head, a hood mould stop to an image niche in the south aisle east wall, has been knocked off, the other slightly damaged. The brass of an armoured figure and wife has lost its inscription, but Dowsing mentions nothing of the kind. There are still carved figures of angels, lions and birds (symbols of the Evangelists?) in the tracery of the south doors. The font is modern.

James Springett was rated at 13s. 6d. for Ship Money.

117. Nayland, Feb. the 21st. Henry Hall, Henry Campin, churchwardens; Abraham Vangover, Constable. Churchwardens promised the 6s. 8d. within a week.[387]

Dowsing had been here before, on 19 January (entry 48). This is one of just two churches for which he records a return visit – the other is Ufford (entries 67 and 247). He may also have returned to Linton and Sotterley (entries 36 and 224).

Henry Hall was rated for Ship Money at 4s. 0d., Abraham Vangover at 10s. 0d.[388]

118. Mr. Thomas Humberfields's or Somberfield's [Tendryng Hall chapel, Stoke by Nayland]. I brake down nine superstitious pictures, and a crucifix, in the parish of Stoke. He refused to pay the 6s. 8d. This was in the Lord Windsor's chappell.

This was the chapel of Tendryng Hall. Henry, Lord Windsor of Braden-ham, Buckinghamshire, acquired the estate by marriage.[389] 'Thomas Hum-berfield' was presumably bailiff or steward. Candler writes of him in dis-paraging terms: 'Thomas Umfrevile, sonne of Thomas Umfrevile whom some thinke to be of an ancient family; he was a Taylour and raised an estate which before was come to small matter, levied in Stoake 1655'.[390]

This chapel had much earlier attracted the attention of reformers: in 1531–32 'John Seward of Dedham overthrew a cross in Stoke park and took two images out of a chapel in the same park, and cast them into the water'. Shortly before Dowsing, Weever recorded a window with the kneeling figure of a Howard with a heraldic tabard over his armour (Plate 41).[391]

The hall and chapel were demolished about 1786 when Soane built a new hall for the Rowleys.

119. Feb. 23. At Mr. [Capt.] Watgraves [Waldegrave's] chappel, in Buers [Smallbridge Hall chapel, Bures St Mary], there was a picture of God the Father, and divers other superstitious pictures, 20 at least, which they promised to break, his daughter and ser-vants. He himself was not at home, neither could they find the key of the chappell. I had not the 6s. 8d. yet promised it. And gave order to take down a cross.[392]

Dowsing seems to have met his match!

Sir William Waldegrave's will of 1524/5 mentions an altar and alabaster images in the chapel within his mansion, but only one wing now remains after demolition of the rest of the house.

120. Buers [Bures St Mary], Feb. 23. We brake down above 600 superstitious pictures, 8 Holy Ghosts, 3 of God the Father, and 3 of the Son. We took up 5 superstitious of *Quorum animabus propitietur deus*; one *Pray for the soul*. And superstitious in the win-dows, and some divers of the apostles.[393]

This church had a chapel on the north side to Our Lady of Pity and a Jesus chapel on the south of the chancel which was also the Waldegrave mau-soleum. There were far more Waldegrave monuments here before the restorers got to work, but a few remain. The stoup in the south porch seems to have been overlooked, but although the heraldic shields on the font bowl are pristine (but coloured) the supporting evangelical symbols were knocked about.

The worst signs of iconoclasm are to be seen on the large table monument on the north side of the chancel opening into the vestry, no doubt to provide an Easter sepulchre as at Melford. Two large corbels above the chest once supported something spectacular, now lost. The angels supporters were damaged and one has no head. But this was done eighty years before, in 1559, by Puritan radicals, leading to furious denunciations and a Star Chamber case.[394]

121. Cornearth Magna [Great Cornard], Feb. 20. I brake down and took 2 superstitious inscriptions of brass 1st *Orate pro animabus* & 2d in English *Pray for our souls*, and gave order to levele the steps. John Prince churchwarden to answer, and Henry Turner Constable.[395]

122. Feb. 20, Cornearth parva [Little Cornard]. I brake down 6 superstitious pictures and gave order to take down 2 crosses one wood the other stone 6s. 8d.

This and the previous entry repeat numbers 113 and 114 above. See the discussion at the end of chapter 10.

26 February – 1 March (map overleaf). *The previous entries bring us up to 23 February, a Friday. On the following Tuesday, 26 February, Dowsing dealt with Glemsford, to the west of the parishes dealt with over the previous few days. During this week an unnamed deputy (probably Thomas Denny) is recorded at work in east Suffolk. We do not know whether the deputy was acting alone, or under supervision.*

*For some reason, the following entries have Dowsing's payment of 6s. 8d. routinely recorded (for discussion, see appendix 10).*

123. Glensford [Glemsford], Feb. 26. We brake down many pictures; one of God the Father. A picture of the Holy Ghost, in brass. A noble.

Darby's notes show no brass indent of a Trinity, which he would have recorded if the stone remained in 1831. No early glass survives in any window, and the roofs are either modern or unadorned by other than decorative work. The niches on the south porch front are probably more weathered than damaged. The font is remarkable for the variety of panel

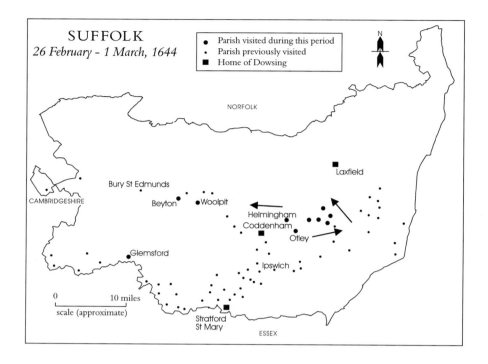

SUFFOLK
26 February - 1 March, 1644

- ● Parish visited during this period
- · Parish previously visited
- ■ Home of Dowsing

N

NORFOLK

CAMBRIDGESHIRE

Laxfield

Bury St Edmunds

Beyton    ●Woolpit

Helmingham
Coddenham
Otley

Glemsford

Ipswich

0        10 miles

scale (approximate)

Stratford
St Mary

ESSEX

subjects and the selective damage they have suffered. From the north-west clockwise: two chiselled flat; large head bearded and crowned; eagle of St John; Virgin enthroned, the throne beside her empty; winged lion of St Mark; angel with Passion instruments on a shield (defaced); mitred head, all virtually unscathed except as mentioned.

124. Otteley [Otley], Feb. the 27th. A Deputy brake down 50 superstitious pictures; a cross on the chancel; 2 brass inscriptions; and Moses with a rod, and Aaron with his mitre, taken down; and 20 cherubims to be taken down.—6s. 8d.[396]

This is the first mention of a deputy. It was probably Thomas Denny, as discussed in chapter 6. Dowsing records him as being active over the next few days, but he – like the other deputies – may well have been visiting churches since earlier in the year.

Only the stump of the cross of the chancel gable remains, but a large plain stone cross has been let into the east wall below it. The font, not mentioned in the Journal, has been much mutilated: lions' and angels' faces, and the shield devices, chiselled off. Only fragments of the rood screen remain; its panels will have accounted for ten or twelve pictures. The heads of twenty angels were hacked off the five arch-braces with hammers. The upper tier of ten had been carved from the whole hammers, those below were fixed to the lower ends of the wall-posts. The shields on the chancel roof-structure bear the letters of a suitably Puritan injunction: P and RE on the north and PA and RE on the south (PREPARE!). The fact that the middle shields on each side restore two of the devices taken off the font (the Trinity triangle and the Instruments of the Passion) betrays the Victorian date of these adornments.

Moses and Aaron were probably placed either side of a commandment board in the chancel. Although a common practice later in the seventeenth century, references before the Civil War are rather scarce. There were example at Castle Camps parish church (entry 189), at Norwich Cathedral and Exeter Cathedral (the latter installed in 1639), and at Sutton's Hospital in the Charterhouse, where the preacher was removed by the House of Commons for this and other innovations. It seems that St Mary Overy, London may have had the pair in place as early as 1624. Although not saints, they all had to go. Perhaps the implied emphasis on law and priestly sacrifice was not attractive to more extreme Calvinists. [397]

## 125. Mulleden [Monewden], Feb. 27. He brake down 6 superstitious pictures; and gave order to levell the steps in 20 days.— *6s. 8d.*

This much restored church has three empty image niches over the brick porch entrance, a wooden gable cross on the chancel, and an unusual fifteenth-century font with nothing more elaborate than eight blank shields suspended from fleurons around the bowl.

## 126. Hoo, Feb. 27. A superstitious inscription of brass, and 8 superstitious pictures brake down; and gave order to levell the steps in twenty days.— *6s. 8d.*

The 'superstitious inscription of brass' was to Thomas Hoo, citizen and grocer of London, 1413. It was just that – an inscription with no image. The indent is at the east end of the nave, covered by carpet. Somehow the brass survived, though with the extreme end snapped off (perhaps during removal from the indent), for early in the early eighteenth century it was recorded that

At the upper end of the Church there lies a Gravestone, which had an Inscription on Brass in a Church Text belonging to it, whereof a fragment remains in the Custody of Robert Naunton of Letheringham Abbey Esquire as followeth:

*Hic jacet Thomas Hoo quondam...*
*London, qui obiit 12 die Septem...*
*MCCCXIII, cujus A[n]i[m]e properi...*[398]

Thirteen window lights are plenty to have housed eight 'pictures'. The font bowl has a rose on one face and seven defaced figures, all but one holding a shield. What was on each determined the extent of mutilation: a crown on one and a lion rampant on another passed scrutiny, leaving four others – a just legible Trinity triangle and three totally erased. The four lions sejant around the stem are perfect.

## 127. Letheringham, Feb. 27. He took off three popish inscriptions of brass; and brake down 10 superstitious pictures; and gave orders to levell the steps in 20 days.— *6s. 8d.*

Until 1789, when it was demolished and a new east wall put across the nave, the chancel was full of monuments and brasses of the Bovile, Wingfield and Naunton families. Now little remains.

However the monuments and brasses are well documented and it is possible to work out the damage caused by the deputy sent here by Dowsing. Perhaps because it was his first day of duty, he showed maximum restraint. Apart from the steps, and pictures, probably in glass as elsewhere, only those parts of the three brass inscriptions necessary to remove the prayers for the soul in Latin or English were cut away, leaving the remainder of the inscription behind (Plate 38b). As elsewhere, others in Norman French were passed over. Thus, from a dozen brass memorials, less than half a square foot of metal was removed.[399]

## 128. Easton, Feb. 28. He brake up one inscription of brass; and 16 superstitious pictures; 3 crosses he gave order to take down; and to levell the steps in 20 days. This was at Eason— *6s. 8d.*[400]

The porch gable cross base holds the replacement; bare chancel and nave gables give nothing away.

The brass inscription is lost for a figure in armour of about 1420; Hervy saw it in 1561 and wrote 'John Broke of Eston died in 1426'.[401] The position of Dowsing's sixteen pictures can be suggested: top lights in excellent early glass remain above fourteen main window lights, and the remaining two were no doubt in an opening blocked to house the large mural monument to G. R. S. Nassau, Esq. (d.1823). The early font is totally plain.

129. Kettleborough [Kettleburgh], Feb. 28. In the glass, 6 super-stitious pictures; gave order to break them down, and to levell the steps in 20 days.— 6s. 8d.

The font bowl here, with angels holding shields with heraldic charges and more angel supporters lower down, escaped damage; in contrast, the pedestal supporters, certainly four lions sejant and perhaps four wildmen, are all chiselled off without trace. There are obvious places in the nave roof for fourteen angels, now taken by rather mean shields. Sixteen main window lights could easily have housed six 'pictures', and there are frag-ments of early glass in some of them.

130. Helmingham, Feb. 29. Brake down 3 superstitious pictures; and gave order to take down 4 crosses; and 9 pictures. And Adam and Eve to be beaten down.— 6s. 8d.

The tower parapet has on all four sides the kind of finial which could have carried crosses (as at Wilby today, entry 214). The porch and chancel gables both have cross stumps. 'Adam and Eve' may have been woodwose finials on the porch, as there are suitable pedestals.

The font is too perfect with tell-tale signs of restoration. There is no early glass in any of the 26 window lights.

131. Woolpitt, Feb. 29. My Deputy. 80 superstitious pictures; some he brake down, and the rest he gave order to take down; and 3 crosses to be taken down in 20 days.— 6s. 8d.

This church would have taxed the strength of most destroyers, so rich are its decorations. The nave gable cross stump remains. The hood-mould stop angels at the south porch opening are headless, but the crowned angel central boss in the porch vaulting is intact. There is much old glass in the top sections of the 38 main window lights and the 20 more in the clerestory. The rank upon rank of roof angels, much restored, can be counted: 66 in the nave, 32 in the north aisle and 30 in the south. The bench end finial figures are almost unculled.

132. Bayton Bull [Beyton], March 1. He brake down 20 pic-tures. And the steps to be levelled in 20 days.— 6s. 8d.[402]

Until the early eighteenth century the Bull Inn was used as part of the name of this village on the Ipswich to Bury St Edmunds road.[403]

The cross stump on the nave gable looks original. Mere cubes of stone form the hood mould stops on south porch and south doorway. There are 25 main window lights.

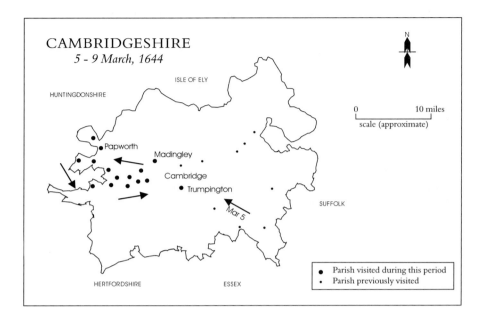

CAMBRIDGESHIRE
5 - 9 March, 1644

ISLE OF ELY

HUNTINGDONSHIRE

N

0          10 miles
scale (approximate)

Papworth

Madingley

Cambridge

Trumpington

Mar 5

SUFFOLK

HERTFORDSHIRE          ESSEX

● Parish visited during this period
· Parish previously visited

5–9 March. *The previous entry, in the name of Dowsing's deputy, was for Friday 1 March. By the following Tuesday Dowsing is in Cambridgeshire. Over the next three weeks he systematically dealt with the southern part of the county, starting in the west, moving to the south and then east. During this three week period he averaged nearly five churches per day, working five days per week, Tuesday to Saturday. He was often within ten miles of Cambridge, rarely as far as fifteen, so it is just possible that he returned each night; but the tours are loops and give the impression of an outward bound journey followed by a return, so it is more likely that he spent each night on the road.*

*A few of these entries are out of chronological order. In particular, entry 148, for Trumpington is dated Tuesday 5 March, and should therefore be first in the sequence. This church is the only one visited that day. It is just to the south of Cambridge, and this may indicate that Dowsing fitted it in as he arrived from Suffolk. The following day, Wednesday 6 March, he began a major tour to the west of the town, starting at Madingley, and working his way to the county boundary at Papworth Everard where he dropped south, before returning to Cambridge.*

133. March 6, 1643/4. Maddenley [Madingley]. John Ivett and Theodore Wictham [*sic*], church-wardens, Edward Dantry, Cunstable. There was 31 pictures superstitious, and Christ on the cross, and the two theves by him, and Christ and the Virgin Mary in another window, a Christ in the steple-window, order'd and

the steps to be leveled, and 14 cherubims in wood to be taken down, which promised to be taken down.

A number of reset pieces of glass survive here including a crucifixion (which was still in the east window in William Cole's time but which was moved to the chancel south window in the 1870s), a Virgin and Child with John the Baptist from a larger design, Mary with her head apparently replaced, and two roundels with emblematic figures. All predate the seventeenth century (Plate 42).[404] These almost accord with Dowsing's list of pictures of 'Christ on the cross… and Christ and the Virgin Mary'.

Even more interesting are ten defaced wooden figures, each about 600 mm tall, which are mounted in the ground floor chamber of the tower (Plate 44). These appear to be the figures from the wall-posts of an earlier roof and are almost certainly a majority of the '14 cherubims in wood' referred to in the Journal. They are among the most significant artefacts of the iconoclasm in Cambridgeshire.

In the chancel is a wall monument to a child, probably Elizabeth Stukeley (d.1636). The design has a reclining babe below a crown and flanked by winged cherubs (Plate 43). The cherubs and the crown have been severely damaged, and although not claimed by Dowsing, must have suffered during his visit or the subsequent compliance of the parishioners.

Madingley enjoyed a kind of stability during the interregnum, in that their priest continued to serve. The visit of 'souldiers' is however recorded in the response to Bishop Wren's Visitation of 1662:

> The book of canons was taken away by the souldiers together with hood and surplice… our railes were carried away… The people as yet receive the sacrament in the church [ie the nave] ever since the table was removed and the rails carried away.[405]

As Dowsing recorded none of this, it could refer to earlier, perhaps less organised, iconoclasm. Or his recording may have been selective.

## 134. March 6. Hardwicke. Thomas Howell and Robart Adams, Cunstables, and William Ivatt, church-warden. There was 10 superstitious pictures, and a cross on the church, which we appointed to be taken downe, and the steps to be levelled. Received but 3s. 2d.[406]

A few years before Dowsing's visit, Layer recorded one *Orate* inscription in glass which is not mentioned in the Journal but which had been lost by Cole's day, some one hundred years later. Was this one of Dowsing's superstitious pictures? [407]

Blomefield recorded three bells (all replaced in 1797), and on the third, *Sancta Maria ora pro nobis.*[408]

The rector of this parish was Edmund Mapletoft, whom Dowsing had encountered in argument at Pembroke College. A non-resident, he was ejected in 1644, after being accused of popish practices ('alter worship, east worship, and dopping [that is, ducking or bowing] worship'), and a Puritan successor installed. Robert Adams, one of the constables named by Dowsing, testified against him.[409] In 1639, three years before Mapletoft took over, this had been one of the few parishes in rural Cambridgeshire without communion rails or steps; communion was received by people in their seats. Ironically, William Ivatt (or Iratt) was churchwarden then, too, and was charged with making a rail and raising two steps for the table.[410]

135. March 6. Toft. Will. Disborugh, church-warden, Richard Basly, and John Newman, Cunstable. 27 superstitious pictures in glass, and ten other in stone, three brass inscriptions, *Pray for the soules*, and a cross to be taken off the steple (6s. 8d.) and there was divers *Orate pro animabus* in the windowes, and on a bell, *Ora pro nobis anima Sanctæ Catharinæ.*

The church was much rebuilt in 1863 and 1894.

Some fragments of ancient glass survive in the east window. Before Dowsing's visit, Layer recorded two *Orate* inscriptions in glass, one of which was accompanied by a picture of the donor at prayer, but he does not refer to any superstitious brass inscriptions. By the mid eighteenth century Blomefield found 'all the Brass Plates are pulled off'. Two of Dowsing's three brass inscriptions may be identified with indents in the nave and south aisle.[411] Dowsing's 'ten other in stone' may include a fifteenth-century alabaster altar piece of which two almost complete figures and some fragments survive in the chancel, where they are set into a panel in the south wall. They were discovered at the restoration of the church.

The bell inscription was probably ordered to be removed but, if so, the order was never executed, as the second still bears the inscription *Sancta Katerina Ora Pro Nobis.*

As at Hardwick, Kingston and Caldecote there was a strong Puritan preference in the parish:

> Puritan ideas had already taken root in Toft by 1638 when several of the parishioners [including William Disborough and John Newman] petitioned against Bishop Wren. In the same year it was reported that a number of parishioners had induced the curate to remove the communion table into the body of the chancel. Two men were excommunicated for refusing to

take the oath to the articles… In 1644 (the rector) was ejected by the Earl of Manchester… [412]

136. March 7. Kingston. Richard Glinister and Francis Gilman, church-wardens, (3s. 4d.), Francis Cockaram and John Anywood, Cunstables. We brake down a crucifix, seven *Ora pro nobis,* and gave order to levill the steps in the chancell, and to take downe 18 cherubims in stone and wood, and we tooke off a crosse of stone on the chancell.[413]

This is one of the most interesting Cambridge entries as far as visible evidence is concerned.

The levelling of the chancel appears to have been a substantial task. The piscina is at an exceptional height above the present single chancel step (see Plate 45 for this and other items at this church).

The '18 cherubims in stone and wood' are also identifiable with some certainty. The stone figures are no doubt the ten roof supporters which have been thoroughly defaced. This is an unusual example of the complete spoiling of angelic corbels at such an inaccessible height. The wooden figures were probably supporters to the aisle and/or chancel roofs where the wall-posts have lost their lower portions (the south aisle roof is renewed).

The 'crosse of stone on the chancell' was probably the gable cross. The ancient apex stone remains under a modern St Andrew cross.

The crucifix referred to by Dowsing may have been in the east window glass. But it is tempting to wonder whether the rood – or, more likely, its ghostly shadow – had somehow survived over the chancel arch, suspended below a tie beam, where the silhouettes of the cross and the rood figures today stand out as gaps in the wall painting. The rood figures appear to have been supported on surviving stone brackets, and were therefore three dimensional, and the mural painting, which consists of six angelic supporters to the rood, were painted round this grouping.

The bell is inscribed *Ave Maria.* This may be a later acquisition, or – as it seems he was not very interested in bells – it was ignored by Dowsing.

The destruction here was probably achieved with the help of the local people, as there was a strong Puritan leaning in the parish, many petitioning against Bishop Wren in 1638. Of the two constables and two churchwardens named by Dowsing, certainly two and perhaps three testified against Cuthbert Pearson, the rector, when he was ejected not long afterwards on the grounds that he had observed ceremonies and had preached in support of the king.[414]

137. March 7. Caldecot. Thomas Lily, church-warden, and Thomas Burnet. 20 superstitious pictures, and a crucifix, and a picture of Christ.

The third bell is inscribed *Ave Maria;* this may be a later acquisition, or it was passed over by Dowsing. The porch gable cross is missing and a stoup in the south porch has been defaced.

Again, the pastoral background is of interest:

> Thomas Sanders, presented in 1638, was an uncompromising royalist and Laudian. He was a 'constant practiser of ceremonies and innovations'; he had railed in the communion table, bowed to the east end at the name of Jesus, and told those who refused to take the sacrament at the rails: 'You are all damned, you are none of this congregation'. He said that papists were the king's best subjects and read the king's proclamations, but refused to read those of Parliament.

Sanders left 'in fear of his life in *c.*1643' and was ejected as a scandalous minister in 1644, with both Lily and Burnet testifying against him. The manner of his going helps to put Dowsing's activities in context:

> The liturgical books were scattered, the holy table removed from the church to a private house for domestic use, the font overturned and the poor box broken. George Biker, who was not in holy orders, became minister.[415]

The chancel was rebuilt in 1859 and the rest of the church is heavily restored.

138. March, 7. Boorn [Bourn]. Will. Phipps, George Newman, Cunstables, John Disher and John Peast, church-wardens. We did downe 2 angells, and took a superstitious inscription in brass, and one of the Virgin Mary, and divers other popish pictures, and gave order to take down two crosses on the steple and on the chancel.[416]

The '2 angells' could refer to bench ends in the chancel; there are two presently, one has been fully renewed, the other has a new head only (Plate 46). The 'inscription in brass' could refer to one of two surviving indents in the nave (male and female figures with attached inscription) or north tower aisle (a priest).[417] The cross on 'the chancel' probably refers to the gable where a modern cross sits on an old apex stone.

In the south transept there are two carved wooden panels of the sixteenth century.[418] One depicts the Virgin and Child (Plate 46) and the other an emblematic figure (St Helen?). These might be the survivors of a more extensive collection described as 'the Virgin Mary, and divers other popish pictures'.

Layer recorded one *Orate* in glass which is not mentioned by Dowsing, unless it is amongst his 'popish pictures'.[419]

## 139. March, 7. Cackston [Caxton]. Christopher Linsy, Miles Robarts, church-wardens; Henry Toms, Cunstable. A cross to be taken off the steple, and 2 popish inscriptions, one *Cujus animæ propitietur deus*, and the steps to be levelled, and a cross on the steple, and one on the church, and 20 superstitious pictures.[420]

The '2 popish inscriptions' could well refer to brass indents in the chancel – one a figure with inscription plate and the other a priest with a banderole issuing from his mouth. These may be the brasses to members of the Cretyng family which Layer recorded in the decade before Dowsing, but which have now disappeared.[421] One was inscribed *Orate pro animo Johannis Cretyng cuius animae propicietur deus*.[422] Or possibly Dowsing was referring to the *Orate* inscription which Blomefield found, one hundred years later, in the east window of the north aisle – perhaps the work was never carried out.[423]

Two stone roof supporters to the nave roof in the form of cherubim survive. These appear to be decayed rather than defaced.

It is odd that the 'cross on the steple' is mentioned twice in the same sentence – evidence, perhaps, that we are looking at Dowsing's rough notes.

## 140. March, 7. Eltesly [Eltisley]. Edward Smith, John Barfoot, church-wardens, Philip Woodward, Cunstable. A popish image, Christ carried by Christopher, and 4 other pictures.

The chancel has been rebuilt and the church much restored. Layer recorded a brass to Richard Monford, *Orate pro anima...* [424]

John Barfoot and Philip Woodward both signed the 1640 petition against Bishop Wren, indicating that they were antagonistic to the Laudian changes of the 1630s.[425]

John Disbrowe – later Major General – married Oliver Cromwell's sister Jane here, in 1636. The Disbrowes owned the rectory and in 1645 made Henry Denne vicar. He was a Baptist who had previously been imprisoned for his opinions. [426]

141. March 8. Uper Papworth [Papworth Everard]. (6*s.* 8*d.* promised.) The four Evangelists in the chancel painted on the walls, Matthew, Marke, etc. In the church 2 angells painted on the walls, and Abraham offering up Isacke. Left a Warrant with Robert Hamon, Overseer.[427]

This is an exceptional entry, the only occasion in the Journal which refers to images 'painted on the walls'. Were these medieval, or part of a more recent scheme of Laudian beautification? The scriptural subjects could be either, though Abraham sacrificing Isaac is an unusual topic for a medieval mural painting, at least among surviving examples.[428] But as late as 1639 the long-standing incumbent had not introduced even the basic Laudian requirement of steps up to the altar, so it is most unlikely that the wall paintings were a contemporary enhancement.[429]

The term 'overseer' could mean many things (Dowsing himself is described as one in the Great St Mary's accounts). The Hamonds seem to have been a well established local family. George Hamond was vicar 1581–99, and Robert Hamond, married in 1624 and thus in his middle years at Dowsing's visit, may have been Overseer to the poor.[430] The second Parliamentary Ordinance, published two months after Dowsing's visit, gave these Overseers joint responsibility with churchwardens for ensuring the work of destruction was carried out.

What was the warrant that Dowsing left with Hamond? He uses the term in a similar way at Covehithe (entry 226). It may perhaps have acted as an indemnity to parish officers nervous that their parishioners would later hold them personally liable for the work of destruction. Conceivably it was in the form recorded at the end of the Journal (page 321) leaving Hamond formally in charge of work in this church, and maybe also in neighbouring Graveley, not recorded by Dowsing. If so, Hamond is the only Dowsing deputy identified in Cambridgeshire, in contrast to Suffolk where ten are known.

The present church is almost entirely of 1850.

142. March 8. Croxton. John Suton, Cunstable, John Lyne, church-warden. A crucifix we brake, and the rayles, and brake 20 superstitious pictures; one crucifix, and 2 crosses to be taken downe, one in the steeple, and another in the highway. Upon the bell *Sit Munus Domini.*[431]

The wardens' accounts for Croxton have been lost relatively recently but Revd W. Simons in his description of the church records the Dowsing entry and states that 'This visit is confirmed by the churchwardens' accounts, who paid the officers 6/8 and spent money at this time on lime and glazing'. John Lyne, one of the wardens at Dowsing's visit, had previously signed the petition against Bishop Wren, indicating his anti-Laudian sympathies.[432]

The fifth bell still has the inscription recorded by Dowsing: *Sit Nomen D[omi]ni benedictum* (Dowsing's attempted transcription is nonsense). The cross 'in the Highway' may be the much restored cross in the churchyard on the north side of the church. The Parliamentary Ordinance included crosses in 'any open place'.[433] But why destroy this cross and not the churchyard cross at Little Gransden, (next entry)?

Some sixty years before Dowsing's visit, Edward Leeds acted for Bishop Goodrich in destroying altars and other superstitious items in the Ely diocese.[434] The Leeds dynasty occupied the adjacent hall for two and a half centuries from 1573, and the Leeds arms appear on the shields borne by startling timber angels in the roof. The date of the angels is a puzzle because the roof was repaired or reconstructed in 1659 (date on tie beam) but the angels look medieval and would be uncharacteristic for the mid seventeenth century – or for 1573. Yet if they were in place in 1643 it is difficult to imagine how they escaped Dowsing's attention, unless the non-superstitious decoration on their shields led him to disregard them.

There are cherubim also on the tomb of Edward Leeds (d.1589) which have escaped unscathed. Some glass of the fifteenth and sixteenth centuries survives, mostly fragmentary except for a roundel (north aisle) illustrating the death of Ananias. There are numerous brass indents with provision for inscriptions which might be expected to be mentioned by Dowsing.[435] Over the north door is a reset carving of the Virgin and Child, which is probably a later purchase.

## 143. March 9. Grandesden Parva [Little Gransden]. Will. Rowning and Edward Higny, church-wardens; Branson Peter, Cunstable. The steps and 43 cherubims we gave order to take down, and 2 angells, and 11 superstitious pictures we brake downe.[436]

The church was greatly restored in the nineteenth century. It is difficult to see where 43 cherubim could have been, other than in the glass. In this entry both 'cherubims' and 'angells' are used, and the distinction is not clear. Generally, Dowsing uses 'cherubim' for roof angels, though he is not always consistent.

One bell is inscribed *Sancte Necolane Ora Pro Nobis.* Its partner has the inscription apparently removed. It is not claimed by Dowsing, and we do not know whether it was in the church in Dowsing's time.

The politics of church fabric and worship at this time bore heavily on Gransden, the national turbulence mirrored in microcosm:

> By 1638, in obedience to Bishop Wren, the communion table had been mounted on steps at the east end and railed round. In 1644 William Dowsing came to level the steps and destroy the surviving carved angels and superstitious pictures. The benefice was contested. When it fell vacant in 1643, Wren, then in prison, instituted John Tolly, Fellow of Peterhouse presented by his father, Jon Tolly, butcher, of London to whom Wren had in 1642 granted the next two presentations. The younger Tolly was an ardent royalist, who filled his college rooms with ornaments considered to be popish, and therefore lost his fellowship. So the Parliamentarians installed Thomas Perry instead. In 1650 Wren named the voluminous royalist poet and divine, Joseph Beaumont, to succeed Tolly and on Beaumont's resignation in 1663 replaced him with Gibson Lucas. The benefice, however, remained in the possession of Thomas Jessop, who was minister there by 1650, and secured presentation to it from the Protector in 1654. Jessop anticipated the Restoration by receiving priests' orders from a wandering Irish bishop in 1659, and held on through every revolution until his death in 1700. [437]

## 144. 1643/4. March 9. Stow [Longstowe]. Will. Peck and Isaack Gad, church-wardens, and John Wodnell, Cunstable; we brake down 12 cherubims, and the steps be levelled, and a crosse to be taken downe by Aprill 9.[438]

All but the tower was rebuilt 1864–65. An ancient bell survives with the inscription *Sancte Paule Ora Pro Nobis*.

## 145. March 8. Nether, or Little Papworth [Papworth St Agnes], 2 angells.[439]

Rebuilt 1848–54.

## 146. 6s. 8d. March 9. Cumberton [Comberton]. We brake downe a crucifix and 69 superstitious pictures we brake down, and gave order to take down 36 cherubims, and the steps to be taken down by March 25.[440]

Dowsing's 'cherubims' were almost certainly figures decorating the eaves plate friezes of the north aisle and nave. Those of the nave have completely disappeared, but in the north aisle the sad remains of the damaged angels can be seen, and are important visible remains of the hand of Dowsing (Plate 32).[441] There were probably 40 cherubim in the original design.

Layer, writing shortly before Dowsing's visit, recorded a number of *Orate* inscriptions in glass which are not claimed by Dowsing (unless they fall within his 'superstitious pictures'):

> The windows of this church both below and above were made by the chiefe inhabitants of this towne as appeareth by inscriptions with the portratures of themselves their wives and children kneeling thereupon depicted.[442]

A few fragments of ancient glass survive. A figure of St Barbara and a wall painting of St Christopher existed in Cole's time (eighteenth century), but have now gone. There is a good collection of bench ends here which include two restored angels in the chancel.

## 147. One Pari[s]h (Triplow) utterly defaced.

This is a marginal note in Baker's manuscript only. 'Triplow' has been scored through, though it might be a ill-managed attempt at underlining, following Baker's custom with other place-names in the Journal. The defacing might refer to what happened (or had already happened) at Thriplow, or (more likely) the illegible state of the entry which Baker was copying, perhaps because it had been deleted. Dowsing's visit to Thriplow is recorded a little later in the Journal, on 13 March (entry 155).

## 148. March 5. Trumpington. 3 superstitious pictures, the steps to be levelled, which Mr. Thomson, to whom we gave order to do it, refused.

The small number of only '3 superstitious pictures' is somewhat puzzling given the survival of many fragments of old glass including largely complete figures of St Peter and St Paul. In 1639, James Thompson, (no doubt Dowsing's 'Thomson'), farmer of the rectory, was to 'unstop the chancel windows', maintenance of the chancel being a liability he took on with the rectory. If he had them glazed with plain glass, this would help to explain Dowsing's small haul. Dowsing's refusal to impose his will is interesting. The Thompson family was important locally: their arms are to be found above the front entrance of nearby Anstey Hall.[443]

There is still in the church the brass of Sir Roger de Trumpington, but missing its inscription (Plate 47) which was not recorded by Layer, so had probably gone before Dowsing. Layer did record the now lost brass of Agnes Perneys (d.1509).[444] Dowsing mentions neither of these. Under the tower is the base of a churchyard or village cross with an *Orate pro animabus* inscription (compare with Croxton, entry 142). Prior to 1980 there was a bell dedicated to the Trinity.

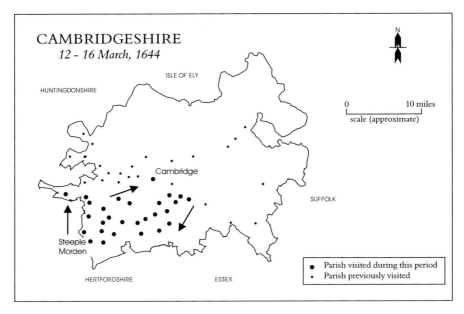

CAMBRIDGESHIRE
*12 - 16 March, 1644*

ISLE OF ELY

HUNTINGDONSHIRE

0        10 miles
scale (approximate)

Cambridge

SUFFOLK

Steeple
Morden

HERTFORDSHIRE        ESSEX

• Parish visited during this period
· Parish previously visited

12–16 March. *For the second week of his Cambridgeshire tour, starting on Tuesday 12 March, Dowsing began by dropping south from Cambridge, then spent the week tracing a ragged clockwise loop round the south-west corner of the county, turning at Steeple Morden to return to the town from the west on Saturday.*

## 149. Shelford [Great Shelford]. March 12. Edward Fuller and Olivir Carter, church-wardens; William Dalison and Avery Howling, Cunstables. The steps to be levelled by Jesus Colledge, a crucifix in chancel, and 34 superstitous pictures there; and 58 pictures, and two crucifixes, and 12 cherubims to be taken down, and 2 superstitious inscriptions.[445]

Despite the '12 cherubims to be taken downe' many survive as decoration to the roof, the capitals of the tower arch, east responds of the arcades and the niches over the south door. Inside the south porch, vaulting bosses survive, including a pelican. There is no way to match the '2 superstitious inscriptions' to existing indents or records of lost brasses, of which there are several.[446]

The rectory was appropriated to Jesus College in 1506.[447]

## 150. Little Shelford (6s. 8d.). March 12. Three superstitious inscriptions, steps to be levelled by the minister, 2 crosses, one on the steeple, 2 crucifixes, and 30 pictures.[448]

The 'three superstitious inscriptions' could relate to some of the many indents and lost brasses.[449]

There is a remarkable survival here. Niches are built into the two eastern corners of the south chapel and both have defaced or decayed angel supporters. The south east niche is the largest and it retains all but one of the angels decorating the canopy. Sheltered by that canopy is a complete figure of a bearded saint which has such presence as to invite vandalism. Why was it left? (In the other niche is an alabaster female figure which is not *in situ* and which appears to be weathered.)

The 'minister' was Gilbert Wigmore (d.1683), rector from 1641 to 1665. He owned the manor.[450]

151. (5s.) Stapleford, March 12. Three popish inscriptions, 20 superstitious pictures, and 2 crosses, which the church-wardens promised to take downe.[451]

The '3 popish inscriptions' could relate to surviving indents of lost brasses.[452]

152. March 13. Hauxton. Will. Reynolls and Robart Briant, church-wardens. Cunst. Thomas Stidman. Steps, and crucifix, and one inscription of brass, and steps to be levelled. Three popish pictures.[453]

The 'one inscription of brasse' may have been the brass to John Colvin which was recorded by Layer not many years before Dowsing's visit as *Orate pro anima Johannis Colvin...*, but remains now only as an indent.[454]

There is a thirteenth-century wall painting of Thomas Becket in a niche on the south side of the chancel arch; but this will not have been one of Dowsing's 'popish pictures' as it would not have been visible to him, having been walled up in the fourteenth century and only rediscovered in 1860.[455]

153. Harston. We brake down 12 superstitious pictures, and took up a brass inscription, and required Richard Bull to level the steps in the chancell, being parson of the parish, and the church-wardens to take down a cross off the steple.

The 'brass inscription' probably relates to a lost brass to John Clowe which was recorded by Layer.[456]

The Bull family of Hertford acquired the lease of the rectory some time after 1600. It was Robert Wallis who was incumbent here, from 1626 until his death sixty years later, at the age of 86.[457] But Bull would probably have stood in the place of the parson as regards responsibility for the chancel, as at

Hinxton, Ickleton and Great Abington (entries 182, 183, 185), and Dowsing may have been using 'parson' as a personal shorthand. The same probably applies at Newton (next entry) and Foxton (entry 157).[458]

154. (6s. 8d.) Newton, March 13. John Lambert and Nicholas Freall, church-wardens, and Will. Starling, Cunstable. We brake down 7 superstitious pictures, and a crucifix, and gave order to Robert Swaine to level the steps, being parson there.[459]

Robert Swan owned the rectory but was not the parson.[460]

155. (4s.) Triplowe [Thriplow], March 13. Timothy Blackman and Thomas Pharoh, church-wardens, and John Gooding, Constable. We brake about 100 superstitious pictures, and gave order to take downe 18 cherubims, and a crosse off the steple, and to levell the steps.[461]

The '18 cherubims' were almost certainly part of the nave roof, as there are 18 wall-posts, all of which have had their supporting figures – probably 18 cherubim – removed. As for Dowsing's 'superstitious pictures', there remained much ancient glass depicting saints and other subjects when Cole visited 100 years later, but this has since been lost.[462] There are numerous indents and records of lost brasses.[463]

156. Foulmyre [Fowlmere], March 13. John Man, Thomas Dove, churchwardens, and Ma. Hicks and John Spilman, Cunstables. 60 superstitious pictures, and 2 crosses to be taken downe. The 12 Patriarchs and 3 cherubims, and the steps to be levelled by John Moreden, parson and minister.[464]

The '12 patriarchs' could have been on the rood screen. A few years before Dowsing, Layer recorded many *Orate* in glass which are not explicitly mentioned in the Journal, but may be the 'superstitious pictures'.

The parson was John Morden, who, amongst other things, 'usually played bowls on Sundays'. He 'seems to have been on bad terms with some parishioners and 14 of them in 1644 testified against him and his Laudian sympathies'. Two of the witnesses against him were John Man and Thomas Dove, the churchwardens recorded by Dowsing.[465]

157. Foxton, March 13. Edward Rayner, Cunstable. We brake down 20 superstitious pictures, and gave order to break 20 more,

to take downe 2 crosses, and Mr. John Wildbore, parson, to levell the chancell. There was 2 pictures of Christ.[466]

Foxton has some interesting forbidden things. On the nave roof west tie beam, as plain as a pikestaff, is the image of a priest with a rosary. In the chancel, cherubim decorate the roof, but their fragmentary state is reminiscent of the north aisle at Comberton (entry 146). A number of the original bodies survive intact.

William Vaughan was vicar here 1630–56; perhaps John Wildbore had rights over the rectory, as was the arrangement at Harston (entry 153).[467]

158. Shepered [Shepreth], March 13. Mr. Edward Hailes. We brake downe 16 superstitious pictures, and a crucifix, and gave order to take downe a crosse.

Much rebuilt and restored. Edward Hailes has not been identified.

159. Melborne [Melbourn], March 14. William Alling and Benjamin Medcafe, churchwardens, and Francis Ratford and Timothy Adkison, Cunstables. 60 superstitious pictures, one of Christ, and a crosse on the steple, and steps to be taken by Will. Browne.

That the steps were taken is supported by Cole's journal of a century later. He found that 'the altar is neither railed in nor on any ascent but stands in a most slovenly manner in the midst of the chancel'.[468]

There are gilded angel boss decorations to the nave and chancel roofs which appear to be of *c.* 1500. Six sculpted heads support the purlins at the ends of the nave, representing Peter, Paul, God (east), a king, an angel, and a bishop (west). These may predate Dowsing and could have survived because they were inaccessible. At the end of last century, part of an inscription survived in the east window of the north aisle.[469]

William Brown was a gentleman of the parish, no doubt from the local land-owning family of the same name.[470]

Benjamin Metcalfe was the man who encouraged the Ship Money riot at his village in June 1640, when the villagers 'fell upon the said bailiffs and sheriffs men with stones and staves, and hedge-stakes and forks, and beat them, and wounded divers of them, and did drive them out of the highway into a woman's yard for their safeguard, and were forced for safeguard of their lives to get out of the town a backway, which notwithstanding some 30 or 40 able men and boys pursued them above a quarter of a mile, stoneing them and driving the bailiffs into a ditch, where some of their horses stuck fast, and the said multitude got some of the bailiff's horses and carried them away, and would not redeem them without money'. Later Benjamin (and Timothy Adkison, the Constable recorded by Dowsing) signed the 1640 petition against the 'Tyrannicall courses and Administrations of Dr Wrenn, Bishop of Ely'.[471] His son, also Benjamin, became a corporal in Cromwell's Ironsides, returned to the village in about 1651 and formed a Baptist church there. Young Benjamin's mother, old Benjamin's widow, was fined in the 1660s for not taking the sacrament at the parish church, so she probably attended the Baptist meeting.[472] Dowsing would have had moral support from that quarter, at least.

### 160. Meldrith [Meldreth], March 14. 60 pictures, and a cross on the steple, and 2 pictures of Christ.[473]

Layer recorded two *Orate* inscriptions in glass, now gone, and there are many indents and records of lost brasses.[474] However, the nave roof is supported by stone cherubim, and in the chancel south window a figure of St John survives intact.

The stone base of the cross was discovered in an orchard more than a hundred years ago, completely buried by time. It was of Barnack stone, the same as early thirteenth-century work in the church.[475]

### 161. March 14. Whadden [Whaddon]. Will. Walls, Cunstable, Will. Rutterforth. 6 superstitious pictures in the chancell, and 14 in the church, and 2 superstitous inscriptions in brasse, *Quorum animabus propitietur deus*, and a crosse on the steeple, which the Cunstable and church-wardens promised to take downe.

The brass inscriptions mentioned by Dowsing cannot be definitely identified from the number of indents which exist. These include a brass to John Descallers which had *cuius anime propicietur deus. Amen.*[476]

### 162. March 14. Basingborne [Bassingbourn]. 8 superstitous pictures in the chancell, 40 in the church, one brass inscription, *Quorum animabus propitietur deus*, and a crosse, which was promised to be take downe, and to take downe the steps.[477]

This entry records very little for a large and important church.

The indent of the 'brass inscription' cannot be certainly identified, but Layer recorded two *Orate* inscriptions. That to John Turpin of 1468 is given as *quorum animabus propicietur Deus* which corresponds almost exactly with Dowsing's claim. William Cole noted that the communion rails were taken by the rectory farmer to fence his hogyard.[478]

In the chancel, head stops to labels and masks to brackets have been defaced.

## 163. March 14. Litlington. We brake downe 6 superstitious pictures, and gave order to take a crosse on the steple.

There is a fine angel-borne font but the angels have been defaced, perhaps by the parishioners who apparently harboured Puritan feelings: in 1638 (as elsewhere) they were ordered to receive communion in the chancel.[479]

On a nave tie beam, there is a brass boss depicting the rood, which was salvaged from an earlier roof. Like the Foxton priest it may have simply been too difficult to get at. There are many indents and records of lost brasses.[480]

## 164. Shengey cume Wende [Wendy], March 15. A cross on the chancell, and the steps to be levelled. Robart Stoughton on [?of] Basingborne, Sequestrater.[481]

The church was decayed and unsafe in 1638 and demolished in 1734 when a faculty was obtained for rebuilding.[482] The second church was demolished in 1867 and a new church built only to be demolished in 1950.

The sequestrator was probably the Roger Stoughton who signed the 1640 petition against Bishop Wren. He may have been the Roger Stoughton of Bassingbourn who died in 1690 with a clear Puritan conscience, leaving a sum for bread to be given to the older men of Bassingbourn so long as the mass was not restored to parish churches.[483]

The minister at Wendy during 1625–63 was Seth Parvy, member of the Cambridge classis in 1650 and thus a man after Dowsing's own heart, so the reference to sequestration cannot refer to him.[484]

## 165. March 15. Abington [Abington Pigotts]. We brake downe 16 superstitious pictures, and gave order to take downe crosses off the steple, and to levell the steps.

There are many indents and records of lost brasses.[485]

On the three-decker pulpit there are carved wooden panels, including one of the Virgin and Child dated 1621. This is not in its original position and, if it were in the church at the time, may have been a 'superstitious picture'.

Pretty cherubim survive in the upper tracery lights of two nave windows. They fit the elongated lights perfectly and are true survivals of Dowsing's visit. The roof is supported on particularly attractive stone angel corbels.

166. March 15. Steple Morden [Steeple Morden]. John Siss-imer, Cunstable, and John Gatward, churchwarden. 9 supersti-tious pictures. We brake downe 3 superstitous inscriptions on brasse.[486]

The '3 superstitious inscriptions on brasse' cannot be positively identified but there are numerous indents. Before Dowsing's visit Layer visited this church, but recorded no superstitious inscriptions. The chancel had been pulled down shortly after 1625, after the steeple fell on it.[487]

167. At Shingey [Shingay], a chapell of Mr. John Russel's, there was a crucifix, and 3 of the Mary's, with her Children, and 12 pic-tures more.

John Russell, third son of Francis, Earl of Bedford, held the manor.[488] The church was pulled down in 1697 when a new chapel was built by Lord Orford. That too is now lost.

168. Todlow come Pincots [Tadlow], March 15. 4 superstitious pictures, and a crosse on the church, Richard Smith, church-war-den and Cunstable.

At St Giles (previously St John the Baptist) a fifteenth-century bell survives with the inscription *Sancte Andrie Ora Pro Nobis*.

169. Gillen Morden [Guilden Morden], March 15. The next Lent a crosse to be taken downe, and the steps leveled.

Another very large church with rich trappings, such as the chapels which form part of the screen, but very little recorded. There are many indents and records of lost brasses. [489]

170. East Hatly [East Hatley], March 15. Francis Blacke, Cun-stable, and Will. Heden, church-warden. Two popish inscrip-tions, *Quorum animabus propitietur deus*. And 2d, *Orate pro animâ*, and *Cujus animæ*, etc. A crosse on the church, and 2 angels to be taken downe.[490]

This church was heavily restored in 1847 and is now derelict. A two figure brass with the male figure and inscription missing which was moved from here to Hatley St George may be one of the 'popish inscriptions'. There are other indents, including one to a priest which may be the other.[491]

171. Hungerly Hatley, or St George Hatley [Hatley St George], March 15. George Price, Constable, George Squire, church-

warden. We brake down 10 superstitious pictures, and a picture of Christ, and the steps to be levelled by John Skelton, minister, and there was written over a coat of arms: Will. St George gave a hide of land in Haslingfield, with his daughter to be nun in Clarking-well, in the time of King Henry II; which we burnt.

'Hungry' Hatley was probably so called because of its poor soil.[492] The church was greatly restored and rebuilt in 1892.

The long-established St George family were recusants, which may have aroused Dowsing's antagonism to an ancient inscription. They possessed the advowson, a further cause of friction.[493]

John Skelton – described in 1639 as 'a frequenter of our alehouse' (to which 'he confesseth') – held the benefice until his death in 1665.[494]

## 172. Gamlingay. March 16. 3 superstitious pictures and a cross to be taken downe, which the church-warden promised to doe.[495]

Very little is reported for a large, rich church (which still has a ban-ner-stave locker). In the accounts for 1644 there is an item 'to the glazier for mending the church windows 7s. 0d'. This is consistent with the removal of a small number of pictures and their replacement by plain glass. There is no item for the common Dowsing fee of 6s. 8d, but this is absent in some two-thirds of churchwardens' accounts of parishes where Dowsing is known to have visited (see appendix 10).[496]

Only 'a cross to be taken downe' when there are (or were, as can be seen in old photographs in the church) gable crosses on chancel, porches and transepts. The present chancel cross appears to be ancient. Perhaps Dows-ing's cross was on the tower; or perhaps the churchwarden broke his promise.

There are cherubim corbels in the chancel and bishops' heads on the arm rests of the chancel stalls. There are also cruciform slits on the tower parapets (the easiest way to get many crosses on the tower) which may however be later. There are many indents and records of lost brasses. Layer recorded two brasses with superstitious inscriptions to members of the Palmer family.[497]

## 173. Crawden or alias Croyden. Crawden com Clopton [Croy-don], March 16. 2 crucifixes, and seven superstitious pictures. Church-wardens, Ar. Gad., Simon Hall, Cunstable.

The chancel was rebuilt in 1685 and perhaps the church was in poor condition in 1644, accounting for the small amount of work done here.

174. Wimple [Wimpole], March 16. Thomas Banes, Cun. Robart Finch and Henry Chapman, church-wardens. There were 40
superstitious pictures, and a crucifix, and 2 superstitious inscriptions, one, *Pray for the soul of,* etc. and 2 pictures of the Holy Ghost
in brass, one of the Virgin Mary.

> One of the 'superstitious inscriptions' could relate to the remains of a
> two-figure brass *c.*1535, which has lost the male figure and inscription.[498]
> The church was mostly rebuilt in 1749 and later.
> At least one of the churchwardens (Henry Chapman) signed the 1640
> petition against Bishop Wren, and it is not surprising that the steps and rails
> introduced in the late 1630s should have been removed before Dowsing's
> arrival.[499]
> Joseph Loveland, rector in 1641, was ejected in 1644 on charges of
> Royalism, non-residence and card playing. He was restored in 1660 and
> remained until 1695.[500]

175. Orwell come Malto [Orwell], March 16. Robart Fayr-
childe, Tho. Coldecott, church-wardens; John Godfrey, Cunstable. We brake down 16 pictures in the church, and gave orders
to take down 4 more; could not come at a crosse, to be taken off
the steeple within 3 weeks, and 28 pictures in the chancel.[501]

> Layer found an *Orate* inscription in the chancel glass which ought to have
> merited a Journal entry; or was it included in the '16 pictures'? There are
> indents and records of lost brasses.[502]
> A very fine fragment of a carved crucifixion with Christ and St John
> survives in the south aisle but I doubt that this was ever on the steeple since
> it looks as though it has always been indoors. Presumably this was victim of
> an earlier attack since Dowsing does not claim it.
> A chapel existed at Malton in 1638 on the site of a church demolished in
> 1509. This appears to have been missed or ignored by Dowsing.

176. March 16. Barton Cum W [Barton]. All the superstitious
were taken down with the glass, and hide up by the church-warden, and the stepps digge up, but not leveled.

> Barton, St Peter (the W for Whitwell). No ancient glass survives here
> despite being 'hide up'. An extensive programme of wall painting survives –
> presumably whitewashed before Dowsing, probably long before.

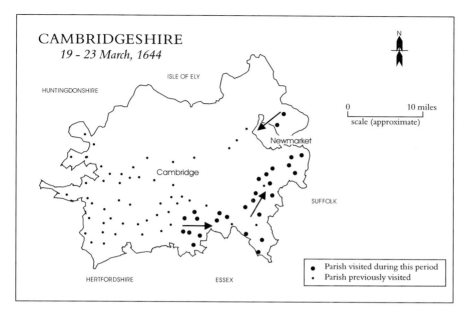

*19–23* March. *For his final full week in Cambridgeshire (Tuesday to Saturday), Dowsing again began to the south of Cambridge, but this time worked his way round to the east, looping round to finish north of Newmarket.*

177. Sawston (6s.) March 19. 5 superstitious inscriptions, *Orata pro animabus*, *cujus animæ propitietur deus*, and *Pray for our souls*, and a crucifix in the chancell, and some 16 superstitious pictures, [? in all 110].[503]

There are many indents and brasses. Two in particular may be linked to Dowsing's visit. On the wall in the south aisle is the indent of two shrouded figures with the inscription plate removed. Nearby is the indent of a kneeling priest with a caption scroll.[504]

In 1665 the steps in the chancel were to 'be made as formerlie'; as Dowsing does not mention them, they must have been dug up before his arrival. The glass windows in the church needed mending, perhaps where his sixteen pictures had been.[505]

178. Gillden Morden [Guilden Morden], March 15. Will. Chamberlaine John Warbis, church-wardens; Thomas Celis, Cunstable, a cross to be taken down, and steps leveled.[506]

This is a repeat entry (see entry 169). The significance of this and other repeat entries is discussed on pages 144–5.

179. Wittford [Whittlesford], March 19. Will. Colt, churchw. and Mihill Knight, Thomas Ward, and Bennet Bacock, Cunstables. A crosse on the chancel, and 3 superstitious pictures, and a popish inscription, *Pray for our soules*, and the Lambe in glass with a cross over it.[507]

Presumably the fine alabaster altar-piece fragments are the result of earlier iconoclasm since Dowsing does not mention them.

One Thomas Ward, probably the Constable recorded by Dowsing, signed the 1640 petition against Bishop Wren's innovations.[508]

180. Peter's Duxford [Duxford, St Peter], March 20. 2 crosses to be taken down, one off the steple, another off the chancell, which was promised to be done.

The cross 'of the chancell' was probably the gable cross. The old apex stone remains but now supporting a modern cross. In the north aisle there are two niches with generally intact angel supporters.

George Chamberlain, presented to the living by Cambridge University in 1642, was captured at the siege of Hereford and his living was sequestered. In 1650 he was expelled from his fellowship at Trinity for refusing to subscribe to the Engagement. He was restored in 1660.[509]

181. Pamsford [Pampisford]. March 19. Will. Hodgine and John Osborne (3*s*. 4*d*.) church-wardens, and Henry Litten, Cunstable, and Rich. Loden. We gave order to level the steps to Theophilus Turrell, and the cross to be taken off the steple, and two crosses off the side of the steple, and the windowes to be done up; 16 superstitious pictures we brake down, and one on the church.[510]

The 'two crosses of the side of the steple' could refer to two flushwork crosses, one on each of the west-facing buttresses (Plate 48). If so, the order was not carried out (as at Ickleton, entry 183).

Dowsing's expression 'done up' may simply be a cross-fertilisation between 'done down' and 'beaten up'; but in 1639 the windows were said to be decayed, so a more positive interpretation is possible (though this would be the earliest recorded use of the idiom by some twenty years). Cole found six female saints in glass, including St Etheldreda, some of which were partly damaged.[511]

Theophilus Tyrell of Bartlow owned the rectory from 1641 to 1707.[512]

182. Hinxton. (5s.) We brake downe 23 superstitious pictures, and gave order to take downe a cross off the steple, and the Lady Hinde to level the steps.

There are glass fragments remaining, but in 1639 two of the chancel windows had been 'stopped up', so the glass was clearly not in pristine condition even before Dowsing's arrival. The nave gable cross was missing in the 1920s, as shown on a sketch in the church. By 1742 the de Skelton brass (1416) had lost the prayer clause of its marginal inscription.[513] However, angels survive as decoration to the capitals of the south aisle responds.

Lady Barbara Hinde held the head lease of the rectory estates, which was leased from the Bishop of Ely, from her husband's death in 1633 until 1648.[514] She was responsible for the chancel and so responsible for levelling the steps.

The Puritan proclivities of the incumbent here had previously surfaced in 1638 when he was presented for not using the cross in baptism and refusing to wear a surplice.[515]

183. March 19. Ickleston [Ickleton]. We brake down 3 crucifixes, 60 superstitious pictures, and to take 2 crosses off the steple, and one off the church; to the Widow Rolfe to levell the steps in the chancell.[516]

In the eighteenth century, Cole reported:

> on it [the church] a large Spire, covered over with lead; on the top of wch was I was informed by the Rev: Mr Say the present Vicar & who has been so these 53 years [since 1689], was a large leaden Cross, wch the rebels in Oliver's time obliged the Parish to take down, or threatened to set fire to the Church, wch to prevent was performe'd accordingly But they could not so easily take down, or perhaps they would not have escaped, 2 neat large Crosses patonce [fleury, with bulbous limbs] of black flint on the outside of the Tower…

If this report is accurate (and the errors and accretions that can accumulate in a hundred years should not be underestimated) the church may have been visited before Dowsing by those of a more violent temperament – elsewhere in the Journal his unwillingness to use force is noticeable, as, for example, at Ufford (entry 247). If so, the high steeple cross had been taken down before his visit, leaving his '2 crosses of the steple'; these refer to two flint flushwork crosses on the east and south sides of the tower between the bell openings and the string course below the parapet. In that case, his 'one [cross] of the church' could relate to a cross either on the south porch or chancel gables; in each case the apex stone is older than the present cross (Plate 48).

There are two important survivals in this church. The first is an extensive programme of wall paintings which must have been whitewashed over before Dowsing. The other is the famous poppy head of St Michael weighing souls which appears to be a remarkable survival being eminently breakable and distinctly angelic (Plate 48). However, after a close examination I suspect that it is not medieval; certainly the head and wings are not of the same build as the body.

The 'Widow Rolfe' was probably the widow of Robert Rolfe, farmer of the rectory in 1639. She and her husband had been chastised at the bishop's visitation of that year for sitting together in church. She may have been related to Augustine Rolfe, who was vicar here 1660–78.[517]

184. March 20. 1643. Duxford St Johns. 2 superstitious inscriptions, *Pray for the soules*, and *Cujus animæ*, and 2 crosses to be taken downe, one off the steple, and the chancell levelled by Mathew Rayner, tenant to Dr. Love of Benet Colledge; 50 pictures we brake downe, one of Christ.

Now in the care of the Churches Conservation Trust. The chancel remains level. A bell of 1564 survived until well into this century with the inscription *Jubilemus Deo salutari nostro*.

The Rayners were a leading local family of land-owners. As Matthew Rayner was required to tidy up a seat in the chancel in 1639, he was probably farmer to the rectory.[518] For Dr Richard Love, Master of Corpus Christi (sometimes 'Bene't') College, see Journal entry 6, and our subsequent commentary.

185. March 20. (6s. 1d.) Abington Magna [Great Abington]. Richard Amy, church-warden, Thomas Smyth, James Hind, Cunstable. We brake 40 superstitious pictures, 2 crucifixes, and a cross on the steple to be taken down, and the steps to be levelled by Mr. Mihil! Dalton of Wrat.[519]

Michael Dalton of West Wratting was owner of the Great and Little Abington rectories.[520]

186. Abington Parva [Little Abington], March 20. Will. Amey and Samuell, Beuis, church-wardens, and Daniell Warde, Cun-

stable, for not taking diverse superstitious pictures, and an inscription on the windowes, and a cross of[f] the steple.

In both of the Abingtons the incumbents retained their livings through the 1640s despite ejections elsewhere. At Little Abington, Roger Wincoll held on 'despite his poverty, company-keeping and', (by 1650), 'imbecility'. At Great Abington, Henry Taverner opposed Parliament and frequented ale houses yet escaped eviction.[521] The entry for Little Abington is not entirely clear, but suggests Dowsing was recording non-compliance. He does not mention rails or steps, so these probably had been removed, perhaps not surprising given that William Amey, churchwarden, had earlier indicated his dislike of Laudian innovation by signing the 1640 petition against Bishop Wren. So too had Richard Amy (a relative?), across the way at Great Abington. Is it coincidence that members of the Amye (another spelling!) family at Great Abington were to be presented for nonconformity after the Restoration?[522]

187. **Hildersham.** A cross on the steple to be leveled, and a cross on the church, which the church-wardens promised to take downe, and brake downe 16 superstitious pictures.[523]

Four important brasses survived Dowsing's visit. All have now lost their inscriptions, and the banderoles of the (now stolen) Paris brass of 1427 which almost certainly bore *Orate* inscriptions have also gone. That Dowsing did not mention any inscriptions suggest that they had been removed before his visit. Given this, it is surprising to find that the Robert Paris brass of 1408 and the Henry Parice brass of 1466 both have blatant depictions of the Trinity as crucial elements of their design.

The church was greatly restored in the nineteenth century.

Henry Smith held the living throughout the Interregnum, being described as an orthodox and godly Divine.[524]

188. **Bartlow, March 20.** We brake down a crucifix, and a Holy Lamb, and 10 superstitious pictures, and gave order to take downe three crosses in stone, and to level the steps.[525]

Two of the 'three crosses in stone' could be the porch and nave gable crosses which are now modern on old apex stones. There are many glass fragments in the chancel tracery. Three ancient bells survive with superstitious inscriptions.[526]

John Baker, rector from 1643 was ejected from the living in April 1644; he was a staunch Royalist and had refused the Covenant, had threatened parishioners who attended elsewhere and was accused of drinking, swearing and scandalous conduct. His immediate predecessor was Robert Mapletoft, with whom Dowsing argued at Pembroke (entry 2).[527]

189. Castle Comps [Castle Camps], March 21. John Georg, Cunstable. We brake down 9 superstitious pictures in the church, and 7 in the chancell, and the steps to be leveled, and a crosse to be taken downe off the church. In the towne dwell in the castle Sir James Reynolds.

The 'crosse' could be the south porch gable cross which is only a stump. However, old crosses survive on the nave and chancel.

The Laudian vicar Nicholas Grey not only had a new communion table made and turned altar-wise and railed in, but he had pictures set up in the chancel with Moses and Aaron and cherubims, which might have provided some or all of Dowsing's '7 in the chancell'. (For a discussion of Moses and Aaron, see under Otley, entry 124.) Grey and his curates preached in favour of ceremonies and read the service in the chancel facing east 'toward the east window' (which might have provided further pictures for Dowsing) and read out Royal but not Parliamentary declarations and orders. Grey had a woman excommunicated for not coming up to the rail to be churched. He was ejected in 1644 (and replaced by a schoolmaster from Linton), became headmaster of Tonbridge School, and was restored in 1660, the year he died.[528]

Sir James Reynolds was lessee of the manor until 1646.[529]

190. March 21. Sudly, or City Comps [Shudy Camps]. (3s. 4d.) We brake downe 7 superstitious pictures.

There is no obvious location for the seven superstitious pictures – no glass fragments, nor any of the usual possibilities such as damaged brasses.

A puzzling survival here is at the west end, outside. In the spandrels of the west window arch are two figures about 1ft 6ins tall. To the north a mother and child and to the south a figure in armour. These are in poor condition, but are more legible in an illustration in Palmer's *Monumental Inscriptions.* Cole describes them as the Virgin and Child and St George.

191. West-Wickham. We brake down eight superstitious pictures in the church, one a crucifix, and one the Virgin Mary with Christ in her arms, and 6 in the chancell, and gave order to levell the steps in the chancell, and to take down a cross on the church.[530]

There is a broken cross on the chancel gable.

192. West Wratting. (*6s. 6d.*) March 21. We brake down 6 superstitious pictures, and a crucifix, and gave order to level the steps, and take downe a cross off that church.

In 1639 two steps of 'freestone or paving tile' had been ordered for the altar by Bishop Wren; by 1663 he was back in position, and having to order the 'steppes in chancel to be made up as formerly'.[531] The nave gable cross is missing.

193. Balsham, March 21. (*3s. 4d.*) We brake divers superstitious pictures, one crucifix, and gave order to take down a cross on the church, and to take down another on the steple, and to level the steps of the chancell within a month.

This is a big church with relatively little done. The survival of the Sleford brass of 1401 in the chancel may suggest that the order to level the chancel was ignored (the chancel was arranged more or less as at present when William Cole visited in 1754).[532] Both the Sleford and Blodwell brasses are exceptionally complete yet both bear popish inscriptions and many superstitious motifs. The chancel stalls have some intact cherubim but the misericords are de-nosed.

194. Weston Colvell [Weston Colville], March 22. (*6s.*) 3 superstitious pictures, *Cujus animæ propitietur deus*, and one *Pray for the soule*, and the 12 Apostles, and superstitious pictures, and a crosse on the porch, and the steps to be leveled in the chancell.

The Leverer brass of 1427 has lost its inscription, which Layer recorded as *quorum animabus propicietur deus*.[533] As for the 'cross on the porch', an old apex stone remains but no cross.

195. Carleton cum Wilingham [Carlton], March 22. (*3s. 4d.*) A crosse on the steple promised to be taken down, and we brake diverse superstitious pictures.

In earlier editions of the Journal, such as that of Cheshire, there is confusion about 'Willingham'. It is not the parish to the north west of Cambridge.

The 'steple' has been demolished. It contained two bells inscribed with the name of Mary.[534]

196. Barrow Grene [Burrough Green], March 22. (*6s. 8d.*) We brake down 64 superstitious pictures and crucifixes, and Joseph

and Mary stood together in the glasse as they were espouzed, and a crosse on the top of the steple, which we gave order to the church-wardens to take downe.[535]

The minister here, Thomas Wake was ejected from the rectory in 1644 on evidence of unseemly behaviour and Laudian attitudes. Just eleven witnesses bore testimony against him (the small number was not unusual), claiming:

> He was a notorious drunkard and common quarreller, pulled off his gown to fight, had fought with beggars, joined in beer and cakes at houses in the parish... [procured] company of women suspected of lewdness. [536]

197. Westly [Westley Waterless], March 22. We brake down 8 superstitious pictures, and gave orders to take down a crosse off the porch, and gave orders to the minister to levell the steps. Minister Gregory.[537]

The porch has gone. Layer, some years before Dowsing, recorded two superstitious inscriptions (since lost), which were not recorded by William Cole a century later, yet not claimed by Dowsing.[538]

Robert Gregory, the minister, was in post from the turn of the century until 1647. In 1617 he donated £14. 15s. 0d. to a new charity for the poor of the village, which survived in operation at least until 1975.[539]

198. Dalingham [Dullingham], March 22. We brake downe 30 superstitious pictures, 2 of them crucifixes, and gave order to take downe a crosse off the church, and to level the steps.[540]

Layer recorded an inscription on wood, *Ave mater Anna plena melli carna mater matris poli Regis atque soli* and an *Orate,* which are not mentioned by Dowsing. The *Orate* remained in Cole's day, in the mid eighteenth century.[541]

199. Steehworth [Stetchworth], March 22. We brake divers superstitious pictures, and gave order to take

Dowsing's entry tails away. Layer, a few years before Dowsing, recorded two *Orate* inscriptions which are not claimed by Dowsing but which had disappeared by Cole's time, in the middle of the next century – perhaps the words missing at the end of Dowsing's entry refer to these. At the east end of the south aisle there is a fine niche with an intact angel supporter. This has survived despite being accessible.

Raven found one bell with *Sancta Margarita ora pro nobis.*[542]

200. Wood Ditton, March 22. We brake down 50 superstitious pictures and crucifixes, and the Virgin Mary written, *Oh Mother of God have mercy on us.*[543]

There are fragments of an alabaster altar-piece which was probably destroyed at an earlier date. Wooden cherubim survive in the south porch despite being relatively accessible. Two bells are dedicated to Mary.[544]

201. Cartling [Kirtling], March 23. (3*s.* 4*d.*) 3 superstitous pictures, and 14 angells in the chancell, on the roof, which the Lord North's man promised to take of, and the windowes broken down, were new made.[545]

Dudley, Third Lord North (1581–1661) of nearby Kirtling Towers (now destroyed) owned the rectory, and the church acted as the family shrine. Amongst other achievements, he was the 'discoverer' of Tunbridge Wells. His daughter-in-law was cousin to the Earl of Manchester.[546]

It is difficult to imagine the 14 angels 'on the roof' in the chancel because there are no obvious points, such as wall-posts, for their connection. Wherever they were, it is highly unlikely that they were recent introductions, given Lord North's religious views (he petitioned the King against innovations in religious practice) and stretched financial position.[547] The windows 'new made' were probably the south aisle windows; that aisle is of seventeenth-century date, given the style of the windows.

202. Ashley, March 23. Onely a crosse on the top of the church.

There are four church sites including the existing nineteenth-century church in Ashley. The old St Mary's church, also in Ashley, was abandoned by Dowsing's day except for burials, and the ruined church at Silverley was out of use by the end of the sixteenth century. Dowsing probably visited a timber framed chapel in Ashley, which was demolished in the 1950s.[548]

203. March 23. Cheaneley [Cheveley]. (6*s.* 8*d.*) There were five superstitious pictures, one of Christ, many more were taken down afore, and there were two stoning crosses which we gave order to take downe.[549]

There are many indents in the church and Layer recorded one superstitious inscription which might have been expected to be mentioned – perhaps they too had been removed 'afore'. Raven found the inscription *Sancta Anna ora pro nobis* on the second bell.[550]

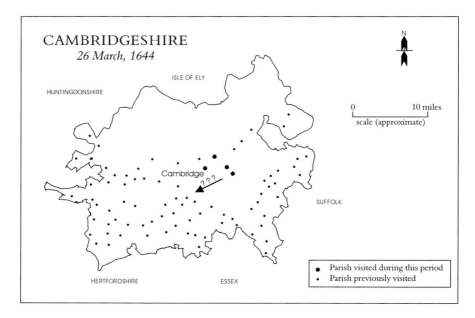

CAMBRIDGESHIRE
*26 March, 1644*

ISLE OF ELY

HUNTINGDONSHIRE

0                10 miles
scale (approximate)

Cambridge

SUFFOLK

• Parish visited during this period
· Parish previously visited

HERTFORDSHIRE                ESSEX

204. Chepengam cum Badlingham [Chippenham]. (3*s.* 4*d.*) March 23. 2 superstitious pictures, *Orate pro animabus*, and divers other superstitious ones in the window.[551]

There is an indent, which could have provided the *Orate*, though Layer did not record one a decade before Dowsing's visit. The porch cross is missing and the carved faces on the portal have been damaged. Raven recorded bells dedicated to St Mary and St Margaret.[552]

205. Snaylewell [Snailwell], March 23. A cross on the steeple, and steps to be levelled, and six superstitious pictures, a cross, and diverse brass inscriptions, 4 in all, and many superstitious pict.[553]

There are two indents in the north aisle and one in the chancel which could be the source of some of the 'diverse brass inscriptions'. The roof here has large figures of bishops on the hammer beams. These are defaced. The wall-posts have no terminating figures and have probably had angels removed. The third bell is inscribed *Sancte Petre ora pro nobis*.[554]

*26 March. Once again, Dowsing took Sunday and Monday as a weekend, presumably in Cambridge. On Tuesday 26 March he set out again to the east, but this time recorded entries for just one day. He may have been dealing with churches which lack of time made him pass by a few days earlier. It is possible that this was the start of another full week's tour, of which only the first day was recorded – his next entry is a week later, for Wednesday 3 April. If this was a week's tour, he might have been circling round to the south and west of the town, where a cluster of churches have no record in the Journal, or have been moving into north Cambridgeshire. See chapters 1 and 3 for discussion of the unrecorded churches in Cambridgeshire.*

206. Teversham, March 26. I broke a crucifix in the chancell, and there was Jesus written in great capital letters on six arches in the church, and in 12 places in the chancell, and steps there, the pavements digged up. The 6 Jesus in the church I did out, and six in the chancell, and the other six I could not reach, but gave orders to do them out. There was one side of the altar written Phil. ii.10. and on the other side, Psalm xcv. *Come, let us worship and kneele*, etc. and four suns painted; within the first writt, God the Father; and in the second, the Son; and in third, the Holy Ghost; and in the 4th, Three Persons and one God.[555]

Matthew Wren, who built Peterhouse college chapel, was vicar of Teversham 1615–35, later becoming Bishop of Ely (1638), when he was a strong enforcer of Laudian ideals in parish churches. Whilst vicar here, he took an interest in the physical condition of his church, writing in 1625 to the Chancellor of Ely about the need for roofing work to be done, to stop 'the rayne pouring in', together with glazing and other works.[556] It seems from Dowsing's description that he introduced 'High Church' (the term is an anachronism) decoration into the building. The reference he chose from Philippians to place at the side of the altar was 'at the name of Jesus, every knee should bow', matching his choice from the Psalms, kneeling at communion being one highly-charged point of difference between Puritans and those of Wren's churchmanship.

'Do them out' seems an odd term to apply to wall painting, but if they were 'done out', today the word 'Jesus' again decorates the chancel cornice, restored in the nineteenth century at the instruction of the Revd C. Drake.[557]

Raven recorded bells with *Sancta Katerina…* and *Sancta Maria ora pro nobis*.[558]

207. March 26, Stowe come Quie [Stow cum Quy]. There was superstitious inscription of brasse, *Orate pro animabus*, and *Cujus animæ propitietur deus*, and 8 superstitious pictures of wood, and the steps to be leveled.[559]

The 'superstitious inscription of brasse' could relate to any one of a number of incomplete brasses and indents, though the Anstey brass with its great number of offspring retained its *orate pro animabus…* inscription until the mid eighteenth century.[560] A very pretty font survives with angels supporting the bowl. These are not defaced. Two angels in the chancel have been defaced.

## 208. March 26. Wilbraham Parva [Little Wilbraham]. Were two crucifixes, and I brake downe 4 superstitious pictures, and gave order to take down 11 more.[561]

The porch gable cross is missing and may have been one of the 'two crucifixes'.

A brass to William Blakwey of 1521 retains an *Orate* inscription. Cole found 'an old shattered grey marble which formerly had a brass plate, and a handsome black marble slab which had a squarish brass for an inscription towards the head of it which was torn away'. [562]

An angel decorates the north-west respond and is intact despite being within reach. Three other angel corbels also survive. There are three loose wooden angels removed in 1850 from the ancient roof, which have much in common with those listed as destroyed at Madingley (entry 133).

The vicar, John Mundy, was ejected, with something over a dozen of his parishioners testifying against him. In one witness statement there is the authentic voice of an ancient grudge, building up to a climax of accusation in the final phrase:

> the said Mr Munday did 5 or 6 years since speake to this deponent in the Church, he being one of the Churchwardens, to provide a Rale for the Communion table but this deponent making noe hast[e] to provide the same the said Mr Munday told this deponent that if he did not provide a Rale, he would suffer for it, he said there were Rales at Greate Wilbraham and other Townes, where upon this deponent procured a Rale to be bought and sett up, at the upper end of the Chancell, according to his direction, which cost 31s. yet the said Mr Munday afterwards not being content therwith, he caused these Rales to be plucked up, and set up another paire more costly, which was done to the greate charge and cost of his parishioners, they being very poor, which former Rales did afterwards serve at Little Shelford.[563]

## 209. March 26, Wilbraham Magna [Great Wilbraham]. 13 superstitious pictures, a crosse to be taken off the steple, and the steps to be levelled, which were promised to be done.

In 1663 the east window, the north and south chancel windows, and others in the church were wholly or partly 'stopped up with brick', a cheap and quick response, perhaps, to Dowsing's removal of glass.[564] Cole's drawing of the mid eighteenth century shows the church with a substantial cross on the steeple.

*There are no further entries for Cambridgeshire. As discussed in chapter 3, Dowsing had worked his way through almost every church in the south of the county. After these exertions, there is silence for a few days. On Sunday 31 March he bought a Parliamentary sermon, of which he was an avid collector, which may mean he was back on home territory by then, unless it was an opportunistic purchase in Cambridge.[565]*

3–10 April. *Dowsing's Journal picks up again in Suffolk, but this time not at Ipswich but near his old home of Laxfield. This tour, starting on Wednesday 3 April and finishing the following Wednesday, is the last of his week-long systematic trawls.*

*He records the company of a deputy on the first day, probably Francis Verdon, accompanying him for the week as they made their way over to the coast, at Covehithe.[566] During Saturday they dealt with Beccles church. This was the home of Francis Jessup, another deputy; Dowsing may have stayed with him over the weekend, as the churches dealt with on Monday 8 April lead away from Beccles to pick up at South Cove, close to where work had finished on Saturday (Covehithe).*

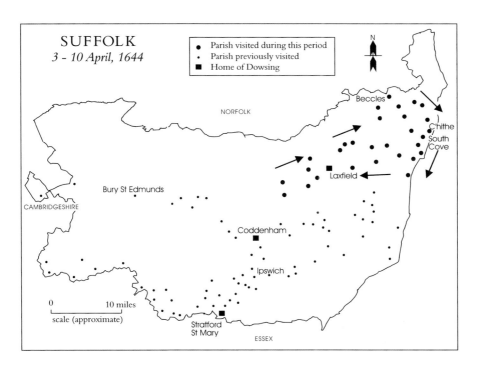

210. Kayfield [Kenton], April the 3d. A Deputy brake down divers, which I have done.[567]

Dowsing's meaning is unclear. So too is the identification of the parish. Both our authorities (Martin and Duck), have 'Kayfield' here, a place which unfortunately does not exist. No doubt this is an error in transcription. In the margin of his manuscript Martin has queried whether it was Laxfield; but this is unlikely, given the work Dowsing found to do at Laxfield on 17 July.

If one has faith in Dowsing's capital 'K', then Kenton would be the most likely identification. Then the deputy's work here would have surely included breaking the top edge off the square brass of John and Elizabeth Garneys, 1524, and removing the head (and right arm) of Christ crucified. The similar composition for Nicholas and Anne Garneys at Ringsfield, 1600, avoided religious iconography, and thereby, damage (entry 243).

Another possible identification is Ashfield, assuming that Dowsing's florid capital 'A' looked like a 'K', and that the 'h' of 'Ashfield', written in a seventeenth-century hand with a loop below the line, was misread one hundred years later as a 'y'. However the churches of Ashfield St Mary (and Thorpe St Peter nearby) were both in ruins in the seventeenth century, so this identification is unlikely.

211. April 3, Bedingfield. I brake down 14 superstitious pictures, one of God the Father, and 2 doves, and another of St Catherine and her wheel; and gave order to take down 3 stoning crosses on porch, church, and chancel.

On each level of the double hammerbeam roof there are fourteen bare hammer ends; the lower tier certainly appears robbed of adornment. The nave and chancel gable cross stumps are witness to what was done here, but the porch has been re-roofed.

212. Tanington [Tannington], April 3. My Deputy brake down 27 pictures, 2 were crucifixes, which I brake off part.

There is a huge modern cross on the chancel gable and a stump on the south porch. Font and roof are plain, except for a painted rood canopy of honour where some IHS have had to be recoloured. There are 26 window lights which may correspond with the 27 'pictures'. Because the bench end finials included small figures involved in the sacraments they, too, had to go.

**213. Brundish, April 3. There were 5 pictures of Christ, the 12 Apostles, a crucifix, and divers superstitious pictures. The vicar have 2 livings.**

The porch stoup has had its front broken down. There are 27 main window lights, many with old glass in the upper tracery. A fragment of the rood screen dado (in the tower) shows, under thick green paint, the marks of damage inflicted while effacing the faces of figures. The brass to Esmound de Burnedisshe, parson of Castre, *c.*1360, in mass vestments has its Norman French inscription overlooked as usual.

The 'minister with two livings' was Edmund Evans (1584–1645). A graduate of St Catharine's, Cambridge, he was ordained in 1608, and had no alternative but to hold Brundish as the Chapel of Ease to Tannington from 1609 until he died. His name heads the list of those signing the Solemn League and Covenant on vellum at Brundish in 1643, showing to that extent his sympathy with the Parliamentary cause.[568]

**214. Wilby. 4 superstitious pictures. April 4. 30 we brake down; and gave order to take 10 more, and the steps to be levelled; and the whip, and pincers, and nayles, that was at Christ's crucifying; and the Trinity, all in stone.[569]**

The nave roof has no decoration, but there are eight large replacement angels in the south aisle roof. The wall painting of St Christopher has had the heads of the saint and the Christ child obliterated, presumably in Tudor times. Some windows have the top lights complete still, but fragments of figure glass have been salvaged and replaced to show the quality of what was lost. The font has evangelists and apostles, only slightly damaged. The figures on bench ends (including the seven sacraments) have been treated quite unevenly – some are complete, some mutilated, and others gone altogether. John Agate points out that some figures are duplicated so that original and restoration can be compared, but he asks how 'new' in fact is new?[570]

Not being present on the font, one would expect to find the remains of Dowsing's Instruments of the Passion and the Trinity triangle on stone shields on the south porch, a most elaborate piece altogether. But apart from a shield with an undamaged plain cross (held by an angel in the inner volute of the entrance arch) there is not even the space for such shields on the exterior. A prominent MR on the porch plinth escaped damage. At the midpoints of the sides of the tower parapet there are four crosses of the sort Dowsing ordered down elsewhere; these must be later (Victorian?) additions – or replacements – here at Wilby.

215. Stradbrook [Stradbroke], April 4. 8 angells off the roof, and 8 cherubims in wood, to be taken down; and 4 crosses on the steeple; and one on the church; and one on the porch; and 17 pictures in the upper window; and *Pray for such out of your charity*; and organs, which I brake.[571]

The nave roof which was restored 1871–72 has no gaps where angels might have been cut down. The four crosses on the steeple may have heightened the slender corner turrets or been supported half way along each edge of the parapet. By the 'upper window' Dowsing meant the main chancel light, but J. C. Ryle paid for a new window and its glass in 1879, and nothing of Dowsing's time is evident.

This is the first of only two occasions on which Dowsing mentions organs (the second is at Ufford in late August, entry 247) and here he is rather jumping the gun – organs were not on the list for destruction in the Parliamentary Ordinance to which he was working, and were not proscribed until May 1644, when a further Ordinance was passed. But perhaps this organ was decorated with unacceptable images. The churchwardens' accounts for Walberswick also show organs coming down in April, shortly after Dowsing's visit, but they might simply have been anticipating the inevitable – it may be significant that they noted that the sale was carried out 'with the Consent of the paryshners'. At Stowmarket the organs came down in the year *after* Dowsing's visit. Other churches visited by the deputies also removed organs some time after April 1644.[572]

216. Nether, or Linstead Parva, April 4. A picture of God the Father, and of Christ, and 5 more superstitious in the chancell; and the steps to be levelled, which the churchwardens promised to do, in 20 [days]. And a picture of Christ on the outside of the steeple, nayled to a cross, and another superstitious one. Crosses on the font. [Will. (*M.S. blotted*) is curate.][573]

This was the home parish of Francis Verdon, deputy to Dowsing, who was probably accompanying him on this trip.[574]

The church here is a humble building but none the less delightful. The window mullions are of brick, there is a timber-framed filling between nave and chancel, and there has probably never been a tower, only a bell-cote. On the font, angels hold shields with three crowns, the Trinity and the Instruments of the Passion; all three and the lions' and angels' heads are defaced. 'And a picture of Christ on the outside of the steeple, nailed to a cross, and another superstitious one' seems to be explained by examining the west wall of the church where two niches surround a small and roughly cut window opening which may have been made by excavating a third larger niche. Three niches could have held a rood group, the figure of Mary or John gone by the time Dowsing came. The survival of an external crucifix, ninety years after the Reformation, is of some interest.

'Will — Curate' was William Aldhouse, as at Linstead Magna (below).

## 217. Linstead Magna, April 5. Here was 2 superstitious inscriptions *Orate pro animabus*, and *Cujus animæ propitietur deus*. There was 2 crucifixes and 8 superstitious pictures, and 3d of Jesus in a window. And gave order to levell the steps, to Mr. Evered, Will. Aldice curate, drunkard Francis Evered.[575]

The church became ruinous; the tower remained until it was swept away in 1964. The font and one medieval bell are at St Augustine's, Ipswich, a modern church designed by H. Munro Cautley, diocesan surveyor and author of *Suffolk Churches and their Treasures*. Damage to the font (the same pattern as at Linstead Parva) is not quite the same. The heads of one pedestal lion and the two angels holding plain crosses on shields have been knocked off. The shields themselves are quite untouched, even those bearing the Trinity symbols and the Instruments of the Passion.

William Aldhouse (sometimes 'Aldus') was curate at the Linsteads from 1635 to 1649 as can be seen from his signatures and distinctive hand in the Register. He and Mary baptised their daughter Mary in September 1648; she died in 1649.[576] Unlike Evans at Brundish (entry 213), though Aldus writes out the Covenant and signs for those who can only make their mark, it may be significant that he does not subscribe himself.

'Drunkard Francis Evered' was a recusant of Linstead Magna Hall, and some of his property later fell into the hands of Jacob Caley and another.[577] In the church William Hervy drew good armorial glass for the Everards, but that has now gone – the arms of recusants may have got short shrift along with the 'images'.[578] Probably when Loder printed the Journal he had no wish to slander a local family and so he printed asterisks for 'drunkard'.

## 218. Cheston, or Chedeston [Chediston], April 5. 2 superstitious inscriptions, and 7 popish pictures, one of Christ, and another of St George. — 6s. 8d.

J. W. Darby drew some intriguingly complex brass indents here, but the stones have since disappeared.

There are still three stumps for gable crosses on nave, chancel and porch, as shown on Henry Davy's etching of 1848.

The east window and another in the chancel have early and undamaged heraldic glass. In the nave roof there are fourteen bare brace ends, and six and two half spaces in the chancel. On the shields held by four angels around the font bowl the Passion Instruments are perfect, but the plain cross, a cross molines and the Trinity are almost totally effaced.

The communion rails here are stylistically of the early seventeenth century (Plate 31). How can they have survived the iconoclast's visit? They fit the space within an inch or two, and have not been cut about, so there is no indication that they were brought here from another church at a later date. The problem (which occurs elsewhere, though not so acutely as here) is discussed in chapter 7 above.

219. Hallisworth [Halesworth], April 5. 2 crucifixes, 3 of the Holy Ghost, and a 3 of the Trinity altogether; and 200 other superstitious pictures and more; 5 popish inscriptions of brass, *Orate pro animabus*, and *Cujus animae propitietur deus*; and the steps to be levelled by the parson of the town; and to take off a cross on the chancel. And then the churchwardens had order to take down 2 crosses off the steeple.[579]

The 'parson of the town' was James Ashton, rector from 1616 – a Lancashire man, of St John's College, Cambridge.

The Chorographer recorded two brass inscriptions, one to Sir William Argentine, 1418, in the chancel and the other to William Claxton, Gent., 1539, in the south chancel chapel to that family.[580] Henry Davy's etching of 1844 shows no cross stump on the chancel gable.

Despite all the work of reformation listed, much was overlooked. Lions, wildmen and shields with the Trinity and the Instruments of the Passion on the font were ignored, as were similar shields on the north porch, which retains two seated angels and a cross on its parapet.

220. Redsham Magna [Great Redisham], April 5. A crucifix, and 3 other superstitious pictures; and gave order for Mr. Barenby, the parson, to levell the steps in the chancel. He preach but once a day.

'Mr. Barenby, the parson' who 'preach but once a day', was Henry Barnby (signs Barmby in the Register twice), son of Thomas Barnby of Beccles, shoemaker.[581] The refusal to preach more than once on a Sunday was often amongst the reasons cited for ejecting ministers from their livings at this time, although it was in conformity with the King's *Instructions* of 1633, which ordered afternoon sermons to be replaced by catechising.[582]

The font is too plain in style to have provoked damage.

221. Reginfield [Ringsfield], April 5. The sun and moon; and Jesus, in capital letters; and 2 crosses on the steeple we gave order to take down; and to levell the steps in 14 days.

If the sun and moon were in glass, as at Clare, there were no windows here of a height to set them off. 'Jesus in capital letters' was probably painted on the roof, as reported at Benacre, Covehithe, Dunwich, Bramfield and Ufford (entries 225, 226, 236, 238, 247); if the surviving examples at Ufford and Blythburgh (235) are typical, Dowsing may have meant by 'Jesus' the IHS symbol, regarded as the Jesuit's sign.[583] At Acton (a church not visited by Dowsing) the vicar had 'set up in his chancell the Jesuit's badge in gold, in divers places', and was ejected for his pains, but the ministers survived in post in at all but one of the churches listed above, so it seems likely that the roof painting at these churches was a pre-Reformation survival.[584]

There are plinths on the midpoints of the north and south parapets of the tower where Dowsing's crosses probably stood. On the font bowl, two angels hold plain shields, but their faces and those of two lions have suffered; others sejant against the pillar are perfect.

There is in the chancel the chastely plain monument to Robert Shelford, rector for 40 years until 1639, and author of *Five Pious and Learned Discourses* (Cambridge, 1635), not a work which would have won Dowsing's heart with its claim that 'the beauty of preaching… hath preached away the beauty of holinesse'.[585] Outside, below the east window, is a weathered stone to Shelford's successor until 1663, Nicholas Gosling 'Preacher of God's Word'. The pulpit and other panels not now *in situ* have inscriptions in letters of gold, some in Latin. Are these the work of the (pre)Laudian Shelford or Preacher Gosling?

222. Beckles [Beccles], April 6. Jehovahs between church and chancell; and the sun over it; and by the altar, *My meat is flesh indeed, and My blood is drink indeed.* And 2 crosses we gave order to take down, one was on the porch; another on the steeple; and many superstitious pictures, about 40. Six several crosses, Christ's, Virgin Mary's, St George's and 3 more; and 13 crosses in all; and Jesus and Mary, in letters; and the twelve Apostles.[586]

This was the home of Francis Jessup, another of Dowsing's deputies.

Nave and chancel here have six and two bays respectively of continuous arcades. There is no chancel arch, so that 'Jehovahs' and 'the sun' between them must have adorned the screen in some way. Perhaps it was the Suffolk topographer Edmund Gillingwater who first noticed Dowsing's reversal of 'flesh' and 'meat', strange for one so well versed in the Scriptures. These would have been Laudian introductions; the rector, John Shardelow, was ejected, though no details of his churchmanship are available.[587]

There is no indication on the porch or the detached bell tower where crosses may have stood, but the roofs of the stair turrets could have accommodated crosses at their peaks. No damage was done to the fourteen crowned MRs around the frieze of the porch and the stair turret. The spandrel shields of the west door are defaced, but 'restored' in Henry Davy's etching of 1814.

## 223. Elough [Ellough], April 6. We brake down 12 superstitious pictures; and the steps to be levelled; and a cross to be taken down off the chancel, which they promised to do.[588]

Twelve of the twenty main window lights will have held 'pictures'. The replacement crosses now on nave and chancel gables here are large enough to be seen at a great distance. The font is too plain to have attracted iconoclasm. Only the pre-Reformation brasses have suffered: one completely removed and the inscription and shield below another taken up.

The Solemn League and Covenant, written on vellum and taken here on 3 March 1644, is in Craven Ord's Suffolk Collections at Ipswich.[589] Christopher West, clerk and minister, and Robert Richmond, churchwarden, head the list of signatures. They will have co-operated with the work of the visitors.

## 224. Saterly [Sotterley]. There was divers superstitious pictures painted, which they promised to take down; and I gave order to levell the steps; and to break in pieces the rayles, which I have seen done; and to take off a cross on the church.

Some of the 'divers superstitious pictures' painted will have included the twelve figures on the screen dado. Their total repainting is a sign that the originals were badly damaged. There are signs that in the seventeenth century scrolls and brackets had been attached to the upper parts of the screen, deprived of its tracery.

In two nave windows, and with every appearance of being original, are a head of Christ and an Agnus Dei.

The font has received odd treatment. The angels around the bowl hold shields: a plain cross, a Trinity triangle, Instruments of the Passion, and one plain. Nothing is damaged or defaced, but, as at Aldeburgh, of the lions and probably wildmen around the base, only the stumps of their pedestals remain.

Large decorative replacement stone crosses now grace the nave and chancel gables.

Dowsing must have returned to this church (perhaps the same day) to have seen that the rayles were 'done'. Nayland, Ufford, and possibly Linton are the only other examples in the Journal of a church being revisited (entries 48, 67, 36). As is pointed out in chapter 6, it is likely that many of Dowsing's later visits were checking up on the earlier work of the deputies, or dealing with difficult cases.

225. Benacre, April 6. There was 6 superstitious pictures, one crucifix, and the Virgin Mary twice, with Christ in her arms, and Christ lying in the manger, and the 3 Kings coming to Christ with their presents, and a Katherine nice [twice] pictured; and the priest of the parish [—] *materna Johannem Christi guberna, O Christ govern me by thy mother's Prayers!*—And three Bishops with their mitres; and the steps to be levelled within 6 weeks. And 18 Jesus's, written in capital letters, on the roof, which we gave order to do out; and the story of Nebuchadnezzar; and *Orate pro animabus*, in a glass window.[590]

Dowsing's Latin here let him down again!

This interior was given a Georgian reordering and new furniture, thus obscuring what was done by the visitors. One medieval feature which escaped alteration in either century was the north door where spandrel shields still bear the symbols of the Trinity and the Passion. The plain Norman font will have attracted no attention.

The rector at Benacre, whose name is a blank or a smudge in the manuscript, was William Raymond, of Peterhouse, ordained in 1619.[591] He held Benacre with Blyford (visited a few days later, entry 234). On 8 November 1645 he was ejected from Benacre rectory and succeeded by Thomas Woods.[592] When Raymond's will was proved, in 1647, he was described as clerk, of Wenhaston.

Henstead church, which should have been visited en route from this church to the next, has been so heavily restored that any clues to iconoclasm are lost.

226. Cothie [Covehithe], April 6. We brake down 200 pictures; one pope, with divers cardinals, Christ and the Virgin Mary; a picture of God the Father, and many other, that I remember not. There was 4 steps, with a vault underneath, but the 2 first might

be levelled, which we gave order to the churchwarden to do. There was many inscriptions of Jesus, in capital letters, on the roof the church, and cherubims with crosses on their breasts; and a cross in the chancel. All which, with divers pictures that we could not reach in the windows neither would they help us to raise the ladders. All which, we left a Warrant with the Constable to do, in fourteen days.[593]

Sometimes 'Cohyth', even 'Coethey' in contemporary documents; Gardner comments in 1754 that it is usually 'Cothie' in the county.[594]

The building of a smaller place for worship in 1672 in the south-west aisle necessitated some demolition and all but the tower has since fallen into picturesque ruin, completely obscuring any iconoclasm. Here, as at Walberswick (entry 233), the tiny parish will have been given an almost impossible task of reglazing a huge church, so that Dowsing, more than elsewhere, is indirectly responsible for what we see today. The worst fear now is that in less than a century the encroachments of the sea will carry off what remains. The record of destruction here is perhaps the fullest account which survives of the splendours of the original church.

## 227. Rushmere [Rushmere St Michael], April the 8. We brake 9 superstitious pictures; and gave order to levell the steps, in 20 days, to make their windows; and we brake down a pot, for holy water.[595]

'We brake down a pot, for holy water': there is still a usable stoup inside the south door, but another in the porch which is flat bottomed, perhaps a tidying-up of a broken one. Shields held by angels around the font bowl have been chiselled flat, but from the evidence which remains they carried a plain cross, Trinity, Passion, together with a cross molines which should have been recognised as heraldic and spared. One brass inscription has been reaved in a tapering slab. There is one step at the chancel and another before the altar. Wall paintings can just be discerned in the jambs of two nave windows.

## 228. Muttford [Mutford], April 8. We brake down 9 superstitious inscriptions of Jesus; 2 crosses on the steeple; and the steps to be levelled.[596]

The tower top here is octagonal, and the parapet could have taken crosses at any corner. The font panels, almost certainly showing the seven sacraments, are chiselled flat, and the pedestal lions are badly damaged, but the

*Orate* inscription around the top step is complete except for a small replace-ment stone which would have borne the words *pro ani[mabus]*. The remain-der is legible. Of the donors Thomas and Elizabeth de Hengrave, she was first to die in 1402.[597] The wall painting of St Christopher was partly painted over in the seventeenth century by the Lord's Prayer and the Creed in a large, ugly frame, now blackened into illegibility.

229.  Frostenden, April 8. 20 superstitious pictures, one crucifix, and a picture of God the Father, and St Andrew with his cross, and St Catherine; 4 cherubims on the pulpit; 2 crosses on the steeple; and one on the chancel. And Mr. Ellis, an high Constable, of the town, told me 'he saw an Irish man, within 2 months, bow to the cross on the steeple, and put off his hat to it'. The steps were there to levell, which they promised to do.[598]

Henry Davy made an etching of the church in 1848 which shows the stump of the chancel cross. The stone vaulted porch has a pelican in its piety as the centre boss, undamaged, but the other carvings in that roof have all suffered. There is a stoup inside the south door.

Dowsing's description of '4 cherubims on the pulpit' suggests painted panels on a 'wine-glass' pulpit. When D. E. Davy visited in 1807 the pulpit was 'modern, of oak', and it is of that pulpit that parts remain today, made up into a large chest.[599] The font has only quatrefoils and shields and is undamaged. Dowsing's anecdote here explains that it was the reverence shown to crosses which encouraged their proscription.

The Ship Money Returns do not survive and 'Mr Ellis' has not been identified.

230.  Coe [South Cove], April the 8. We brake down 42 supersti-tious pictures in glass; and above 20 cherubims; and the steps we have digged down.[600]

Sixteen 'cherubims' probably adorned the arch-braces of the roof, but there would be room for no more (perhaps Dowsing miscounted). On the font bowl, badly damaged, symbols of three Evangelists are recognisable, but the angel of Matthew is cut back to what looks most like a group of arms or tools (not Instruments of the Passion which will have been on one of the four totally effaced shields held by as many angels). The bowl now rests on a plain stone column (perhaps a trimmed section of pier from Covehithe?).

In the early nineteenth century there were traces of a doom painting, but that is now gone.[601] D. E. Davy visiting the church in 1807, 1826 and 1832 never recorded the fine painting of St Michael on the rood stair door, clear

enough indication that it had been obscured in earlier times. The archangel saint is identified with some fourteenth-century notable, perhaps a
Willoughby, by wearing gules a cross molines argent on shield and jupon.

## 231. Rayden [Reydon St Margaret], April 8. We brake down 10 superstitious pictures; and gave order to take down 2 crosses, one on the chancel, and another on the porch. Steps we digged up.

There are large replacement crosses on nave and chancel gables, but the
porch cross must have been very roughly removed, since the gable is
repaired in brick.

## 232. Southould [Southwold], April 8. We brake down 130 superstitious pictures; St Andrew; and 4 crosses on the four corners of the vestry; and gave order to take down 13 cherubims; and to take down 20 angels; and to take down the cover of the font.[602]

Towards the 130 superstitious pictures we can see 36 defaced screen
panel paintings: 12 angels across the north aisle, 12 apostles across the nave
and 12 prophets, most badly scraped, across the south aisle. It is odd that St
Andrew was mentioned specially, but his saltire cross does mark him out
next but one north of the chancel opening. The '20 angels' taken down from
the roofs (not in Martin's transcript of the Journal) are replaced by good
modern carvings: six pairs in the nave and four pairs in the chancel.

The seven sacrament scenes on the font were chiselled off more completely than elsewhere (though shadows remain). The font cover has been
replaced (in 1935) with one in the 'Ufford' style. Here there was no-one to
defend the original Southwold cover as stoutly as at Ufford (entry 247).

The '4 crosses on the 4 corners of the vestry' are the most puzzling entry.
Perhaps the parvise chamber was used as vestry in the 1640s; the porch
battlements could certainly have accommodated crosses; in fact one adorns
the higher stair turret at the north west corner today, and on Henry Davy's
1824 engraving two and a stump can be discerned, with one probably the
fourth at the north. These, like the bold inscription over the south entrance
'+SCT.EDMUND.ORA.P[RO].NOBIS+' must have escaped removal.

Gardner (*Dunwich*, 204) uses truly purple prose to describe what was
done:

Here blind zeal, ignorant superstition, and obstinate bigotry, with united
force, wrought their spight, by defacing, not alone, angels, apostles, and
prophets, but likewise extending their malice, by breaking all the historical
faces in the painted windows, and in committing sacrilege by robbing the
gravestones of the brass plates, which bore monumental inscriptions to the

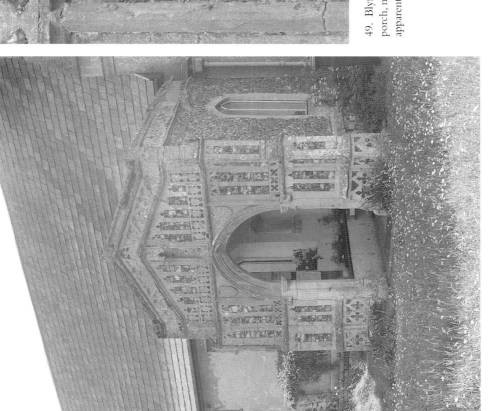

49. Blyford church, Suffolk. Dowsing particularly commented on the cross on the porch, now gone, and on the Instruments of the Passion and the sign of the Trinity, apparently untouched. See pages 298–9.

50. Blythburgh church, Suffolk, visited by Dowsing 9 April 1644 (pages 299-300). The images show the porch before and after its early twentieth-century restoration.

51. Blythburgh church, Suffolk, the image of God the Father on the east gable, overlooked by Dowsing.

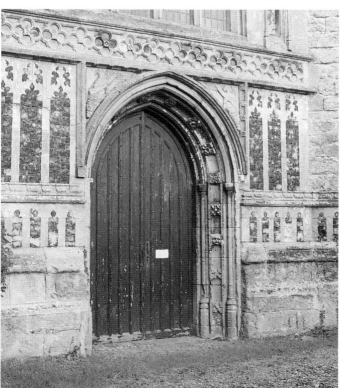

52. Laxfield church, the birth-place of Dowsing, and visited by him in July 1644 (see pages 302-3). 52a (above). The porch where he ordered the cross down (now replaced) and two 'pictures' in stone – if those were the angels, they appear not to have been touched. 52b (left). Dowsing's 'steeple's end', where he saw two angels in stone (in the spandrels of the doorway).

UFFORD

53. The famous medieval font cover at Ufford, Suffolk, spoken of rudely by Dowsing (pages 305-7), here drawn by Isaac Johnson (1754-1835). In the first published edition of the Suffolk part of the Journal, readers were directed to Johnson's drawing of 'this venerable remain of Antiquity'.

54a (above). The chancel roof at Ufford, showing the stencilled lettering criticised by Dowsing (pages 305–7).

54b (left). The pelican at the top of the font cover. Victorian roof angels can also be seen.

55. A seventeenth-century drawing of the lower lights of the east window glass at Ufford, now lost, perhaps broken down by Dowsing. The drawing shows coats of arms and Latin inscriptions inviting prayers for the donors.

56. The font at Nettlestead church, Suffolk, showing images mentioned by Dowsing (page 307) but apparently undamaged.

57. The north door at Somersham, Suffolk, containing a number of images which Dowsing wanted removed, despite their obscurity and small size (pages 307-8).

58. The receipt given by John Crow, one of Dowsing's deputies, to the churchwarden at Risby, Suffolk (see page 82).

59. The south door at Barking, Suffolk, showing, in the two lower panels above, the capital M's (for Mary) which Dowsing wanted removed (pages 309–10).

60. Barking, Suffolk, visited by Dowsing in August 1644 (pages 309-10). 60a (above left). Glass in a north aisle window, showing a Catharine wheel. 60b (above right). The eastern jamb to the window, also showing Catharine wheels amongst the decorations. 60c (below). Fragments of glass high up in the south clerestory, with an 'M' for Mary and a pair of scales from a Judgement scene. These are the remnants of what was probably a full scheme of glazing.

61a. Buttress at Wetheringsett, Suffolk, showing flushwork crosses (see page 311).

61b. A bench end at the rear of Dennington church, with the IHS symbol chiselled off following Dowsing's visit (see pages 317-19).

62. Ixworth, Suffolk, three photographs of the damaged bell inscriptions. Top and middle, bell 4, damage to *Sancta* and *Maria*; bottom, damage to bell 5. See page 381.

63. The east window at East Harling, Norfolk, removed from the church and later restored (see pages 113, 391), a reminder of what has been lost elsewhere.

64. Detail from the east window at East Harling, Norfolk, showing the Assumption of the Virgin Mary (see page 117). Although the image is complete, the surrounding glass is something of a jumble, perhaps due to its removal and later replacement.

memory of the dead, and erazing others; whereby one may conclude, that the paintings on the ceilings would have had no more favour shown them, if they had been as easily come at.

## 233. Walberwick [Walberswick]. Brake down 40 superstitious pictures; and to take off 5 crosses on the steeple, and porch; and we had 8 superstitious inscriptions on the grave stones.

The churchwardens' accounts record Dowsing's arrival with his 'troopers' (the only surviving accounts to name him or mention soldiers). The confirmation of the date is very pleasing, and the accounts themselves are informative (they are given more fully in appendix 8):

Pd that 8 of Aprill 1644 to **Mr Dowson** that cam w'th the troopers to o'r church a bout takinge downe of Images & Brasses of grave stones . . . . . . . . . . . . . . . . . . . . . . . . . . . . . . . . . 0 06 00
pd that day to others for taking up the Brasses of the Stones before the **officer Dowson** came . . . . . . . . . . . . . . . . 0 01 00
And the next day to Edwards and Pretty [carpenter] taking down 26 Cherubs . . . . . . . . . . . . . . . . . . . . . . . . 0 06 10
Received the 26 of Aprill 1644 of John Trappit, with the Consent of the paryshners, for 2 Bellowes, and wooden Stofe [stuff] from the Organs . . . . . . . . . . . . . . . . . . . . . 0 06 08
Received this 6 of January 1644/5 [nine months later] from out of the church 40 li weght of brasse which Nurse the glasyer of Sou[thwo]ld offered 3d 2ob per li [3½d. per pound weight] per me John Barwicke . . . . . . . . . . . . . . . . . . . . . . . 0 11 08
Paid to John Prety the 7 of March 1650 for Rashing out [erasing] the King's Arms in our Church . . . . . . . . . . . . . . 0 01 00

From these payments we can see that the church knew of Dowsing's arrival in advance, and that the work carried on after he left. There is a good match between his record and that of the churchwardens (images and brasses) but he is alone in noting steeple crosses (perhaps they were easy and cost nothing to knock down), and the wardens chose to take down cherubim not listed by Dowsing. On the mid points of the tower parapet sides there are small fleur-de-lys standing where the four crosses will have been, and Henry Davy in 1826 showed the plinth for the porch cross. The font has received the usual treatment: crosses on shields held by angels around the bowl hacked off, and stem figures somewhat mutilated. The organs went a few weeks after Dowsing's visit, and after a further nine months the wardens raised 11s. 8d. by selling off the brass to the glazier, not restricting themselves to chiselling off parts of inscriptions when money was badly needed to mend the windows. Davy sketched 18 brass matrices remaining at his visit, but of even greater interest in view of the phrase 'inscriptions on the gravestones' are three surviving Tudor inscriptions cut in stone (1532, 1534 and 1535) to mariners each given his mark (probably a net-mark), and Davy saw another similar slab under the tower. Most of the words *Of your charity pray* and *on whose soules may God have mercy* are carefully obliterated. These interesting slabs lie under fixed carpets which may also cover some brass indents of which only fifteen can be counted today.[603]

The damage done by the iconoclasts drove the parishioners to hire a Meeting House early in the Interregnum, repairing the church as well as they could afford in 1662 and 1663, later to settle for the same sort of reduction as at Covehithe – a small place of worship 20 by 64 feet at the west end of the south aisle. The Royal Arms, 'rashed out' in 1650, were not restored to view until 1674. Gardner enjoyed drawing on the church-wardens' accounts to write vividly about the fate of this church:

> When the nation was involved in the flames of the yet to be lamented Civil War, the sacrilegious faction viewing this fine church, defaced all the imagery, robbed the gravestones of the brass plates, broke down the organs, erased the King's Arms, and let the whole fabrick run to ruin; substituting a meeting-house, pawned the communion plate, and the church was destitute of an episcopal minister, continuing in a deplorable condition till after the King's Restauration; but then the visitors inspecting in to the state thereof, the Churchwardens were cited to appear at the ecclesiastical courts, where they were enjoyned to put the buildings into good repair, and provide books, and other things convenient.[604]

234. Blyford, April 9. There was 30 superstitious pictures; a crucifix; and the 4 Evangelists; and the steps promised to be levelled, and begun to be digged down. A cross on the chancel they promised to take down; and a triangle on the porch, for the Trinity; and 2 whips, etc. Christ and a cross all over the porch.[605]

*Marginal note in Martin's transcript*: In a window Andrews Cross &c in margent [margin] of MSS wch I could not read.

The stump of the 'cross on the chancel' remains (Plate 49). On the north porch the two shields which Dowsing saw – 'a triangle on the porch, for the Trinity, and 2 whips, etc'. – have the usual Trinity and Instruments of the Passion, but they are only weathered, with no signs of deliberate damage. To Dowsing the spear and sponge were 'whips'. Over the porch entrance there is an empty niche, perhaps for an image of Christ, and there are stumps, perhaps of crosses, on the gable and both sides, which may all explain 'Christ and a cross all over the porch'.

Two brass memorials, an inscription and shield, and a female figure and inscription, had been 'reaved' before the Chorographer arrived here in about 1602.[606] Davy sketched both indents in 1828.

235. Blyborough [Blythburgh], April 9. There was 20 superstitious pictures[;] on the outside of the church 2 crosses one on the porch and another on the steeple; and 20 cherubims to be taken down in the church, and chancel. And I brake down 3 *Orate pro animabus*; and gave order to take down above 200 more pictures, within 8 days.[607]

A photograph of *c*.1900 shows the stump of the porch cross and an image niche over the doorway roughly infilled (Plate 50). The two seated angels at each end of the parapet look genuine enough but surely cannot be. The church's dedication to the Holy Trinity is still celebrated in the seated figure (without cross and dove), much weathered, on the chancel gable, where Dowsing seems to have overlooked it (Plate 51).

Until unthinking people in the 1930s replaced it with a bulky stone lighting rose, there was another God the Father, remaining from a Trinity group, on a boss in the porch roof. Kirby drew it for an engraving in 1748. Around it was almost the same *Orate* inscription as the one still partially legible around the base of the font, and to the same benefactors, John and Katherine Mason, buried in their porch. The font panels, probably because they showed the seven sacraments, were chiselled completely flat (although it is said that 'shadows remain' for two of the sacraments).[608]

Gardner claimed 'Here are 27 grave-stones without inscriptions, and all deprived of their plates'. Davy sketched 23 brass matrices remaining in 1825, and a few more can be counted today. There are two puzzling survivals: the excellent wooden figures in niches along the front of the choir pews (they are not restored – Suckling showed them in the north east chancel aisle in 1848);[609] and the cross made of rectangular marble tiles set in the brick floor, with much of *Orate pro animabus* legible but the names worn out by passing feet, which could have been dug out in minutes.

The 'pictures' (glass) which Dowsing removed will have included the history of St Anthony, the bequest of Robert Pinne in 1457, which he requested be inserted next to the window of St John the Baptist. Only a few scattered saints and ecclesiastics remain in the tracery today, but Dowsing should not be blamed for everything – losses are known to have continued through the nineteenth century.[610]

The large nave roof angels here face east and west in the centres of the principal rafters. Twelve remain where there may have been twenty; only the two end bays at east and west lack them. Tales of iconoclasts' attempts to shoot them down were refuted when shot found in the angels' wings was found to be the kind used to clear sparrows from the church in the eighteenth and nineteenth centuries. If the angels were too high up to be taken down it is no wonder that the ceiling is still peppered with stencilled IHS.

236. Dunwich, April 9. At Peter's parish. 63 cherubims; 60 at least of Jesus, written in capitall letters, on the roof; and 40 superstitious pictures; and a cross on the top of the steeple. All was promised by the churchwardens to be done.

St Peter's in the lost town's market place was engulfed by the sea in 1702.

237. Allhallows [All Saints, Dunwich]. 30 superstitious pictures; and 28 cherubims; and a cross on the chancel.[611]

Erosion of the cliff over the years 1904 to 1919 led to the 150 foot long church becoming heaps of flint and rubble on the beach. Now the last tombstone in the churchyard has gone, taken for safety to the new church's yard. Most of one non-superstitious inscription brass of 1576, stolen from the ruins in 1770 for John Ives, came back to the modern St James church in 1927. Two fragments of the indent of a fourteenth-century military figure were recovered from the sea by divers in 1972 and 1979, the Norman French inscription still legible.[612]

238. Bramfield, April 9. 24 superstitious pictures; one crucifix, and a picture of Christ; and 12 angells on the roof; and divers Jesus's, in capital letters; and the steps to be levelled, by Sir Robert Brook.

The roofs are both ceiled, so no wooden structure is now visible. The unusual mural painting in the recess in the north nave wall, a cross with four attendant angels, must have been whitewashed. There were also in 1874 (but not now) traces of many other wall paintings including a conversion of St Paul with two angels, and a Doom over the chancel arch.[613] The elaborate rood screen has imagery all over it, but perhaps the visitors were in too much haste to spot it. 'Sir Robert Brook' has no entry in the Ship Money Records for Bramfield, but is listed for Yoxford and Blythburgh.[614]

239. Heveningham, April 9 and 10. 8 superstitious pictures, one of the Virgin Mary; and 2 inscriptions of brass, one *Pray for the souls* and another, *Orate pro animabus.*

The Chorographer recorded two inscriptions on brass (now lost), but, contrary to Dowsing's record, both were in Latin.[615]

The porch gable bears the stump only of a cross. Two fonts (the other from neighbouring Ubbeston) are both architectural in decoration and perfect. The six main nave lights all have old glass in the tracery lights. Fourteen figures stand under canopies on the wall plates; it is not easy to see whether they are whole or restored. There will probably have been two rows of fourteen angels in the double hammerbeam roof.

*15 April & 17 July. Now things more or less grind to a halt. Dowsing visited more than 200 churches in the four months following 19 December, when he received his commission. Over the following five months he visited hardly more than thirty. Possible reasons for this slow-down are discussed on page 22, above. April continued well enough, with three visits close to his Stratford home, on Monday 15 April. Was he on the way back to Cambridge? There is then a gap of three months, until on Wednesday 17 July a single visit is recorded to Laxfield, the parish where he was born and brought up.*

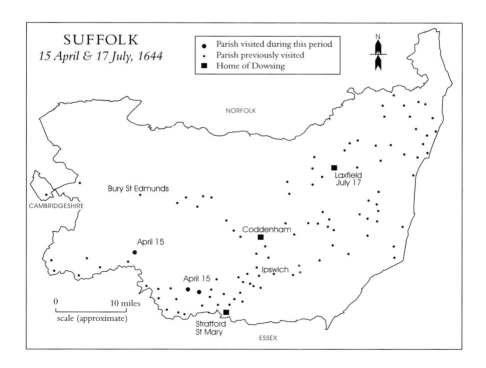

SUFFOLK
15 April & 17 July, 1644

● Parish visited during this period
· Parish previously visited
■ Home of Dowsing

N

NORFOLK

Laxfield
July 17

Bury St Edmunds

CAMBRIDGESHIRE

Coddenham

April 15

Ipswich

April 15

0        10 miles
scale (approximate)

Stratford
St Mary

ESSEX

240. Polstead, April 15. 45 superstitious pictures; one of Peter with his keys, 2 Archbishops with mitres on his head.— 6s. 8d.[616]

Confirmation that there were fine pictures to be broken here comes from glass fragments gathered in two windows, one in the north porch and another on the south side of the chancel. The latter include two sheep and a mitred figure with cross staff, so probably not Peter. There are 34 main window lights not counting those in the clerestory, well on the way to Dowsing's 45. A fragment of a wallpainting on the north wall of the nave also shows a bishop.

The only brasses, a priest of *c.*1430, and a family of *c.*1490, lack their inscriptions. The thirteenth-century font, the bowl rebuilt in brick in 1961 on the original corner and central columns, is unlikely to have had decorations to attract attention, but the headgear of the king and bishop on the north door hood mould corbel have suffered at some time.

241. Boxtead [Boxted]. We had 6 superstitious pictures.

In the north-east Poley chapel there are fragments of the broken pictures, the best the head and shoulders of a king. The complete shield of Felton is post-Restoration, and the font plain. The nave roof angels carry shields with the date 1885 lest any should take them for medieval. The Sir William Poley of Dowsing's time, married to the sister of the moderate Puritan antiquary Sir Simonds D'Ewes, will have been co-operative but protective of what was almost an estate church. D'Ewes probably erected the elegant marble pedigree of the Poleys in their chapel; he died in 1650.

242. Stanstead, April 15. 5 superstitious pictures.

At this much restored church, only fragments of glass canopy work remain to confirm Dowsing's record. The south porch gable has the stump of a cross and a stoup with its basin broken down; three large Victorian gable crosses adorn nave, chancel and vestry.

243. Laxfield, July 17 1644. Two angells in stone, at the steeple's end. A cross in the church; and another on the porch, in stone; and 2 superstitious pictures on stone there. Many superstitious inscriptions in brass, *Orate p[ro] animabus,* and *Cujus animae propitietur deus.* A picture of Christ, in glass. An eagle, and a lion, with wings, for two of the Evangelists; and the steps in the chancel. All to be done, within 20 days; the steps, by William Dowsing, of the same town.

'William Dowsing', the iconoclast's nephew, will have been relied upon to do his duty.[617] It is worth looking in some detail at the church where the iconoclast himself was born and brought up.

By 'Two angels in stone at the steeple's end' is meant angelic figures in banded robes holding scrolls in the spandrels of the west doorway (Plate 52). 'Another (cross) on the porch, in stone; and 2 superstitious pictures on stone there'. Now the cross on the south porch is considerably truncated (presumably saved and reinstated later) but the two seated angels at the corners of the parapet look well enough. There are empty niches below, and lower still the Passion and Trinity shields held by angels are defaced.

Inside, the seven-sacrament font is badly damaged (after which it was completely plastered) but is not mentioned in the Journal.[618] 'An Eagle, and a Lion, with wings, for 2 of the Evangelists' probably refers to bench ends, for there is a headless eagle, and several more badly damaged finial figures on the north side of the nave.

In front of the chancel arch lie two Dowsing memorials, one with a brass inscription in Roman capitals to William Dowsing's grandfather William, who died in 1614 aged 88 (Plate 2), and a black marble ledger slab for Sybille, wife of William Dowsing (the nephew), died 1676 aged 68, with the impaled arms of *Dowsing* (Arg a fess vert between two lions passant sable) and *Green*.

21–23 August (map overleaf). *There is then a further silence until a return to the old levels of activity in late August. On Wednesday 21 August Dowsing visited churches to the east of Ipswich, including the troublesome Ufford; and on Thursday and Friday he dealt with a number of churches to the west.*

## 244. Trembly [Trimley St Martin], Aug. 21, 1644. Martyn's. There was a fryar, with a shaven crown, praying to God, in these words, *Miserere mei deus*; which we brake down; and 28 cherubims in the church; which we gave order to take down, by Aug. 24.

The roof with accommodation here for '28 cherubims' is long since replaced. Like Swaffham in Cambridgeshire, the two churchyards here (St Martin's with St Mary's) have never been divided by more than a ditch. St Mary's may have been too dilapidated for Dowsing to visit it; at different times both buildings have needed substantial rebuilding.

## 245. Aug 21 Brightwell. A picture of Christ, and the Virgin Mary, that we brake down; and the 12 Apostles painted, in wood; and a

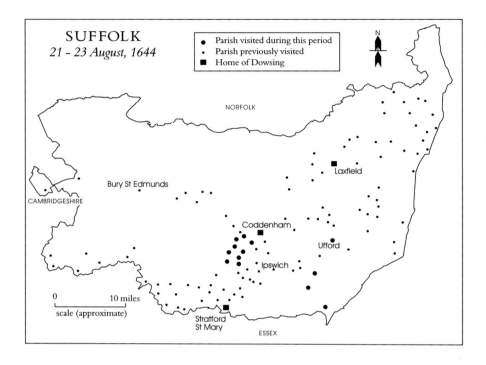

holy water font; and a step to be levelled; all which we gave order
to be broke down, and steps to be levelled, by Aug. 31.

Dowsing's reference to a 'holy water font' is a little surprising, as the fine
octagonal fourteenth-century font here has decoration which is sheerly
geometrical, and escaped unscathed. The Parliamentary Ordinance of 1644
used the term 'holy water font' explicitly to refer to baptismal fonts, which
were no longer to be used (and were to be defaced), so Dowsing may simply
be recording that one was still in use, without necessarily implying that it
required images to be removed. But at the church of St Giles, Cambridge he
used 'holy water font' of a stoup in the porch (entry 19), so here and in
some of the immediately following entries he may have been referring to
something other than the font, such as the piscina, which in the present
church is a plain opening, and probably a seventeenth-century tidying-up of
something broken earlier.

This church, almost in ruins, received a chaste if eccentric restoration in
1656 at the hands of Thomas Essington of Brightwell Hall. He placed

unusual monuments here to his children and one at Coddenham to Matthias Candler, Dowsing's one-time minister, who recorded Essington's work. If the 'picture of Christ, and the Virgin Mary' were glass figures, as is likely, they were reinstated in an east window of 1911 to the memory of a Curate of the parish.

246. Levington, Aug. 21. The steps only to be levelled, by Aug. 31. And a double cross on the church.

Henry Davy's etching of 1840 shows the stump of the a chancel gable cross. At the time the nave roof was slightly higher, so there may have been a second cross on its east end. The font shields are heraldic, yet at some time a heavy blow has landed on the north side. The brick tower, dated 1636, was almost new when Dowsing came.

247. Ufford, Aug. Where is set down what we did, Jan. 27 '30 superstitious pictures; and left 37 more to brake down'; and some of them we brake down now. In the chancel, we brake down an angel; 3 *Orate pro anima*, in the glass; and the Trinity in a triangle; and 12 cherubims on the roof of the chancel; and nigh a 100 Jesus—Maria, in capital letters; and the steps to be levelled. And we brake down the organ cases, and gave them to the poor and the rayles likewise we gave the poor. In the church, there was on the roof, above an 100 Jesus & Mary, in great capital letters; and a crosier staff to be broke down, in glass; and above 20 stars on the roof. There is a glorious cover over the font, like a pope's triple crown, with a pelican on the top, picking its breast, all gilt over with gold. And we were kept out above 2 hours, and neither churchwardens, William Brown, nor Roger Small, that were injoyned these things above 3 months afore, had not done them in May, and I sent one then to see it done, and they would not let him have the key. And now, neither the churchwardens, nor William Brown, nor the Constable James Tokelove, and William Gardener the Sexton, would not let us have the key in 2 hours time. New churchwardens, Tho[mas] Stanerd, Thomas Stroud. And Samuel Canham, of the same town, said, 'I sent men to rifle the church'; and William Brown, old churchwarden, said, 'I went about to pull down the church, and had carried away part of the church'.[619]

Weever's description of the church, written earlier in the century, explains why the churchwardens were nervous about allowing Dowsing in, and gives valuable detail about the organ:

> This is the most neatly polisht little church (that I have looked into) within this diocese. The roofe whereof, & other parts of the Quire, being curiously engraven with sundry kindes of workes of pictures, all burnisht with gold. The organ case, whereupon these words, *Soli Deo Honor et Gloria*, are carved, & gilt over, is garnished & adorned in most costly manner. The Font, & the cover of the same, is without compare, being of a great height, cut & gloriously depicted with many Imageries consistent to the representation of the holy Sacrament of Baptisme, as also with the arms of the Ufford, Earles of Suffolk, whose principale habitation was in this Towne.[620]

'In the chancel... 3 *Orate pro anima*, in the glass', says Dowsing. Of this a coloured drawing survives, made after 1634 (Plate 55).[621] The four lights commemorated John Jenny, rector in 1480 and his Willoughby and Jenny relations. The top half of each light held their figures while below there were coats of arms above Latin inscriptions.

Dowsing's angels are still in the chancel, six along the wall plate on each side, twelve in all: although those in the two eastern bays are either replacements or heavily stained, at least eight of the twelve look original. If he originally saw 40 wooden cherubim in the roofs (see the entry for 27 January, number 67), then these twelve, a further 18 blank spaces at the foot of the nave wall-posts, and 8 spaces on the braces now occupied by large Victorian replacements, would have made 38, close enough to 40 for a man in a hurry. The '100 Jesus and Maria in capital letters' still decorate the roofs of nave and chancel in profusion; there is no indication that these stencilled IHS and MR have been repainted (Plate 54).

In his *Suffolk and Norfolk*, M. R. James explains that when Dowsing describes the font cover as 'glorious' he means vainglorious or pretentious, in line with his comment that it is like a pope's crown (Plates 53 and 54). Nevertheless, only the images which formerly filled its niches have been removed. The font itself, perhaps because the shields carried only painted heraldry (matches of Ufford), did not suffer.

Dr James again helps by elucidating those puzzling quotations from Canham and Brown. He points out that they were referring to Dowsing but in quoting them himself, 'he' becomes 'I': 'WD sent men to rifle the church' and 'WD went about to pull down the church'. The uncooperative men of Ufford saved all they could, and really got under the iconoclast's skin.

Most of the protagonists in this incident can be identified from Ship Money records.[622] Respectable men, but although they defended their church they were not blind to the shortcomings of their rector since 1621, Richard Luffkin, whose 'house was plundered in the great rebellion' (save one silver spoon hid in his sleeve!), and 'Isaac Wells, a true blue Protestant served the cure'. When Luffkin was charged at Bury in October 1643 with being 'a common swearer, a cold preacher who objected to other ministers occupying his pulpit', Roger Smallage – Dowsing's 'Roger Small' – was among the witnesses against him. So here was a man prepared to act against his rector, but not prepared to follow Dowsing's bidding in his church. Restored in due course, Luffkin preached on the Sunday before he died in 1678, aged 110 years, if his successor and son-in-law's entry in the Register is to be credited. [623]

## 248. Aug 22, Baylham. There was a Trinity in a triangle, on the font, and a cross; and the steps to be levelled, by the minister, in 21 days.[624]

The Trinity on one shield held by an angel, and the cross and instruments of the Passion on another, have been rather half-heartedly chiselled off, but the mason has gone on to take away the faces of the angels, and those of all eight lions, four round the bowl and four round the base.

## 249. Nettlestead, Aug. 22. An inscription in the church, in brass, *Orate pro anima*; and six of the Apostles, not defaced; and St Catherine with her wheele; and 9 superstitious pictures more, 2 with crosier staves, with mitres; and the picture of St George, St Martyn, and St Simon.[625]

The only brass, a small figure in armour of *c.* 1500, inscription gone, lies in the centre of the nave. No early topographer visited the church to record the inscription and William Blois in about 1660 was too late. Some of the apostles and saints complained of here may have been painted on the panels of a screen of which no trace remains, though the font, with much lively carving, has some of the features listed (St Catharine with her wheel, and a mitred head), but is undamaged (Plate 56). The busts of Thomasine Sayer (*née* Lea, sister of Thamar Dowsing, WD's first wife), and her first husband, remain from a mural monument which has lost its frame.

## 250. Sumersham [Somersham]. The same day. A cross in the glass, and St Catherine with her wheele, and another picture in the glass in the church; & 2 superstitious pictures in the window;

and a holy water font in the church; and on the outside of the chancel door, *Jesus. Sancta Maria. Jesus.*

The 'holy water font in the church' might mean the piscina, which is plain but undamaged. The font itself is completely plain, and probably modern – was its predecessor damaged? Dowsing also recorded 'on the outside of the chancel door, Jesus, Sancta Maria, Jesus'. The North chancel door has the remains of a crowned MR in the hollow chamfer at the top, angels next below on either side, and crowned IHS below both, all chiselled off to different extents (Plate 57).

## 251. Floughton [Flowton], Aug. 22. A holy water font in the chancel.

It was not unknown for fonts to be placed in the chancel,[626] but in this case the 'holy water font in the chancel' probably means the piscina, which has had the protruding shelf trimmed off flush with the south wall. Perhaps it was supported by a figure corbel.

## 252. Elmsett, Aug. 22. Crow, a Deputy, had done before we came. We rent apieces there, the hood and surplice.

John Crow's receipt survives, discussed in chapter 6 (see Plate 58). He was perhaps asked to visit this church because George Carter, rector here and at Whatfield, was later prosecuted by his Elmsett parishioners as a scandalous minister; but Dowsing came after Crow to see what had been done. Perhaps he had knocked off the chancel cross (Plate 34).

Surplices did not appear in the Parliamentary Ordinance to which Dowsing was originally working; they were added to the list of banned items in the second Ordinance, of May 1644. At Madingley the hood and surplice were 'taken away' by soldiers, date unknown; at Stowmarket, visited in February, they were sold by the churchwardens some time in the year following Dowsing's visit; here the new Ordinance bit hard – they were 'rent apieces'.

It is implied in some commentaries that the plastering over of the shallow arches on the square Norman font was done to save the font from iconoclasm, but such a plain design could arouse no passions. The bowl of the stoup in the porch was knocked down, presumably 'done before we came'.

If the three-sided altar rails on their square platform are Laudian (that is, pre-1640), then their survival may have something to do with the ambiguity over Carter's fate. Although his sequestration from the living was ordered in 1646, the Registers bear his signature up until his death in 1649. By then rails may have seemed less objectionable.

253. Ofton [Offton], Aug. 22. There was a holy water font in the chancel; and the steps; and some crosses on the outside of the church, and chancel; and we gave order to deface them. We gave order to have them all defaced, and 2 more in a window in the church; and 2 stone crosses on the top of the steeple. All which, we gave order to mend all the defaults, by Saturday come seven-night. At Ipswich, at Mr. Coley's.

'There was a holy water font in the chancel…'. The piscina is very plain and undamaged, but there is a stoup near the south door which Cautley believed to be twelfth-century.[627] It could have been moved, since it is poorly installed, but it has suffered no obvious damage. Of the '2 stone crosses on top of the steeple' one can see what may be the stumps' bases half way along the north and south parapets, and the 'crosses on the outside of the church, and chancel' have also gone (Plate 34).

The font, finely carved and with lively lions, has three angels holding plain shields; the fourth holds a shield with a crown and two arrows for St Edmund, all allowed to remain.

After visiting seven or eight churches that day, Dowsing stayed at Ipswich with Jacob Caley of St Margaret's parish (for whom see appendix 4).

254. Barking, Aug. 21 There was St Catherine with her wheele. Many superstitious pictures were done down afore I came. There was Marias on the church door.

Amazingly we can make a strong case for St Catharine having the window in the north aisle which is embellished inside and out by terracotta arabesque work of Italian origin. As similar window mullion decorations are found at Shrubland Old Hall and at Henley and Barham churches, the accepted date is early in the mid 1520s, and the benefactor Sir Philip Booth (or Bothe) Kt of Shrubland. What makes the Barking window the most lavish and interesting are the low relief foliage trails inside, where there are Catharine wheels at regular intervals on the splayed jambs to the aisle. There are two circular designs in glass in the top lights, one closely resembling the wheels in terracotta. All this is illustrated in Plate 60.

The Bothe inheritance of Shrubland came through marriage with a Catherine Oke, and the Bothe crest was a Catharine wheel, so perhaps for two reasons Bothe's favourite saint was Catharine of Alexandria. At Barham he improved an Oake chantry and mortuary chapel for the family and there and at Barking (but not at Henley) had Catharine altars where it would be natural to find the saint herself in stone, wood or glass.

It is probable that the 'pictures… done down afore I came' were in the glass – fragments of a last judgement and crowned M's are still to be seen in the clerestory windows (Plate 60). Just possibly they were medieval murals, poking through earlier whitewash, and still under whitewash in 1927.[628]

'There was Marias on the church door', and there still are (Plate 59). The south door is faced externally with 20 carved panels in five rows of four. The second from the top incorporates the MR's, one filling the lower half of each panel. The three on the left have been partly chiselled down but are still legible; the fourth has been renewed by carving in relief, including the provision of small capitals in the loops of the large letters to spell the whole of MARIA. A dedicatory inscription, presumably because it requested prayers for the donors of the door, has also been obliterated. Painted above the opening is a framed text which looks contemporary with the damage: *Open to me ye Gates of Righteousness: I will go into them & praise the Lord Ps. 118 v. 19.* Their door was cleansed.

255. **Willesham [Willisham], Aug. 22. An holy water font in the chancel; the steps were levelled; and had been so once afore, by a Lord Bishop's Injunction; and by another Lord Bishop after commanded; testified to me, by him that saw it done, by Mr. John Brownbridge.**

This church is completely rebuilt, so that it is impossible to discover what Dowsing meant by the 'holy water font in chancel' here. There is an unscathed fifteenth-century font.

Little is known of 'John Brownbridge' (Brownrigg), who died in 1661,[629] but his son Robert married a daughter of Daniel Meadows of Witnesham, sturdy Puritan stock.[630]

256. **Damsden [Darmsden], Aug 23. Three crosses in the chancel, on the wall, and a holy water font there; and the chancel to be levelled by Saturday sevennight after.**

This church was completely rebuilt in 1880, but D. E. Davy (1827) noted 'a stoup at the East side of the South door of the Nave under the porch' and 'a piscina in the south wall'.[631]

26–30 August. *During the week Monday 26 August to Friday 30 August, Dowsing visited thirteen churches. He was probably based at his old home, Laxfield. There is no sense here of a coherent tour: each day an independent cluster of churches was dealt with. During this week, and for the remainder of the Journal, the visits give the impression of*

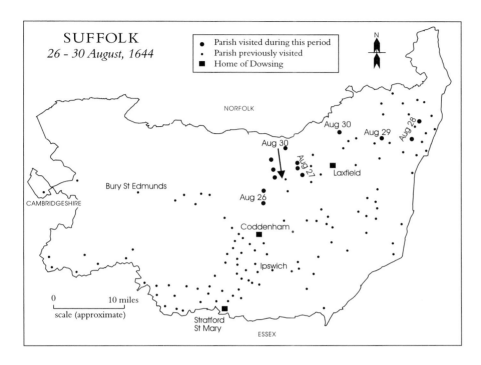

SUFFOLK
26 - 30 August, 1644

- • Parish visited during this period
- • Parish previously visited
- ■ Home of Dowsing

N

NORFOLK

Aug 30
Aug 29
Aug 28
Aug 30
Aug 27
Laxfield

Bury St Edmunds

CAMBRIDGESHIRE

Aug 26

Coddenham ■

Ipswich

0   10 miles
scale (approximate)

Stratford
St Mary

ESSEX

*being to places which had failed to comply, perhaps parishes which had previously been visited by a deputy.*[632]

257. Wetheringsett, Aug. 26. 19 crosses. 16 about the arches of the church; and 3 on the porch; a picture on the porch, a triangle for the Trinity, to be done. Thomas Colby, and Thomas Eley, churchwardens. Constables, John Suten, and John [Genkthorne].[633]

The south porch has the stump of one cross top centre and pedestals for two others at each side, so this fits Dowsing's record. With only a four-bay arcade there is no room for 16 crosses 'about the arches' without filling spaces still occupied by undamaged masons' marks. Dowsing was no master of architectural terms, and by arches he could have meant the five buttresses on the north side,[634] each of which has three simple crosses in flushwork in line on the vertical face, totalling fifteen, but there are three more on a south west buttress (Plate 61). If the flints were ever removed (rather than 'daubed') they have been replaced since. There is no niche for 'a picture on the porch' on the south porch, but an empty one above each of the two west tower openings, the first into the open Galilee, the other into the nave.

The churchwardens are known from the Ship Money records – solid middling citizens, as so often.[635]

258. Mickfield, Aug. 26. 2 crosses. And the glass to be made up by Saturday come three weeks. And 10s. to be p[ai]d to the poor within that time; and the rest afterwards. — 4s. 6d.

This today is one of the saddest churches in the county, disposed of for secular use but now virtually abandoned. One can crawl through a small square hole made in the north door by earlier intruders. With a south porch tower the nave and chancel have gables for three stone crosses, and of each a stump remains. There is no coloured glass in the windows, many broken by vandals. The stoup inside the south entrance is whole.

*Note*: Since writing this, the local authority has secured the building, which is in a very dangerous condition, and entry in the manner described is no longer possible.

Ten shillings was a fine rather than a fee. The Parliamentary Ordinance stated that a fine of 40s. 0d. was to be paid to the poor: here, in addition to paying Dowsing his fee of 4s. 6d., the churchwardens seem to have negotiated payment of the fine by instalments, the first payment of 10s. due within three weeks.

259. Horham, Aug. 27. In the chancel a holy water font; and the steps to be levelled; and there was the 4 Evangelists; and a part of a crucifix; and divers angells, 8; and other superstitious pictures; and *Orate pro animabus*. And on a grave stone, *cujus animae propitietur deus*. All which I brake [took] up; and gave 20 days to levell the steps, and make the windows. And in the church, *Orate pro animabus*; and divers superstitious pictures; and a triangle on the font; and a superstitious picture. — 6s. 8d.[636]

The chancel piscina has been rebuilt using several new pieces of clean cut stone to patch up the damage. The font has had the low relief carvings removed from all four shields, as well as the faces of the angels holding them. The heraldry on one of them, normally overlooked by Dowsing (following the Parliamentary Ordinance), was here chiselled off. It is impossible to tell which shield had the Trinity symbol.

260. Allington [Athelington], Aug. 27. In the chancel was Peter pictured, and crucified with his heels upward. And there was

John Baptist; and 10 more superstitious pictures, & Paul and another superstitious picture in the church.– 5s.[637]

The church is dedicated to St Peter, and his figure with the key (the right way up) is one of twenty fifteenth-century carved bench end saints totally unscathed. Twelve window lights are large enough, and the correct number, to have accommodated the ten figures alongside the Peter and John Baptist mentioned; there are no signs of a former screen. The font panels contain cusped geometric patterns including a saltire cross (undamaged). The roof is plain.

261. Wallingworth [Worlingworth], Aug. 27. A stone cross on the top of the church; 3 pictures of Adam on the porch; 2 crosses on the font; and a triangle for the Trinity, on stone; and 2 other superstitious pictures; and the chancel ground to be levelled; and the holy water font to be defaced; and steps levelled in 14 days. Edward Dunstone, and John [blank] Constables. [Will. Dod] and Robert Burmant, churchwardens.— 3s. 4d.[638]

The reference to '3 pictures of Adam on the porch' can only mean that figures of three wildmen stood along the top; crowned MR and IHS on the south porch are undamaged. The font does indeed have '2 crosses and a triangle for the Trinity, in stone' all held by angels and almost totally unscathed. This font may have been one of those plastered over, rather than chiselled clean. The font cover, second only in magnificence to Ufford, was surely hidden away.[639]

262. Holton by Halesworth [Holton St Peter], Aug. 29. 2 superstitious pictures in the church; and I H S the Jesuit's badge, in the chancel window; promised by the minister, Mr. William Pell.

The east window installed in 1899 restores the IHS device in glass two-fold: in the topmost light, and beneath the Christ in Glory. The Jesuits' devotion to Jesus led them to use IHS on title-pages and in paintings, and Puritans such as Dowsing saw it as a sure sign of popery – but the Jesuits were not unique in its use and it was never their formal badge, though even Davy, taking notes at Metfield, referred to it thus.[640]

Two memorials formerly on the south side of the church had been plundered of their brasses by 1602.[641]

'William Pell minister', probably of Clare College, intruded at Corton to replace James Utting, was ejected as a scandalous minister in 1644; he was perhaps afterwards vicar of Tonge, Kent where he died 1672.[642]

263. Wangfurd [Wangford St Peter and St Paul], Aug. 28. 16 superstitious pictures; and one I brake. 14 still remain; and one of God.[643]

This church was virtually rebuilt by the Rous Earls of Stradbroke in the heaviest high Victorian style, obliterating what had been done earlier. Before 1834 Isaac Johnson drew the font here, showing it to be plain enough to survive unscathed. Henry Davy's etching of 1847 shows the stump of a cross on the nave gable. The only surviving early glass, effigies of Saints Peter and Paul in a north aisle window, were rescued beforehand by the local schoolmaster antiquary Hamlet Watling, but what happened to them later (he died in 1908) is unknown.[644]

264. Wrentham, Aug. 28. 12 superstitious pictures; one of Saint Catherine with her wheele.

The tower base flushwork frieze (of shields alternating with sacred hearts in crowns of thorns) defeated the reformers' zeal. Henry Davy's etching of 1848 shows stumps of gable crosses on nave and chancel.

There is a stoup inside the south door, and the font bowl is supported on a section of column (compare South Cove, entry 230). The east window has some good earlier armorial glass showing that the Ordinance of restraint was obeyed, but how did the visitors miss St Nicholas (the patron saint) in a north aisle window?

265. Hoxne, Aug. 30. 2 stone crosses on church, and chancel; Peter with his fish; and a cross in a glass window, and 4 superstitious ones. The Virgin Mary with Christ in her arms; and cherubims wings on the font. Many more were brake down afore.

There are now stone crosses on the south porch, the nave and the chancel east gables.

There is known to have been a lady chapel with a pieta, thought to have been situated at the east end of the north aisle. Robert Barker left a bequest to it in his will proved 1479 and Thomas Aisbye in 1517 requested burial before 'Our Lady of Pity'.[645] Was this, as might be expected, a carving, or pictured in glass (or both)? If in glass, it could easily have survived until Dowsing's arrival.

The oddest entry here is the objection to 'cherubims wings on the font'. Indeed there are four angels in large panels and eight others act as corbels to the bowl, with wings overlapping slightly. None of the two dozen wings are damaged, but some heads are knocked off, and the evangelical symbols in the other main panels are by no means perfect. There were once wall paintings here: David and Goliath, St Paul in the stocks, a Crucifixion, and a Resurrection. [646]

266. Eaye [Eye], Aug. 30. 7 superstitious pictures in the chancel, and a cross; one was Mary Magdalen; all in the glass; and 6 in the church windows; many more had been broke down afore.

At the west door the niches for Saints Peter and Paul are empty, perhaps since the Reformation. This large and nowadays sumptuously furnished church seems to have caused Dowsing little trouble; as he remarked, 'much had been broken down afore'. Not a trace of early glass remains.

Were the fourteen screen figure saints covered over? They have probably had some restoration, but much original paint remains. An evangelical restoration committee in 1868 wished to remove the screen, but the architect John Collin saved it. The nave roof hammer saints are his, replacing damaged ones, and also the font. In 1932 Sir Ninian Comper more than made up for the iconoclasm of the sixteenth and seventeenth centuries.

267. Ockold [Occold], Aug. Divers superstitious pictures were broke. I came, and there was Jesus, Mary, and St. Lawrence with his gridiron, and Peter's keys. Churchwarden promised to send 5s. to Mr. Oales, before Michaelmas. 5s. p[ai]d m[emo-ran]d[um].[647]

It is suggested in chapter 6 that 'Mr Oales' is Alexander Ouldis of Thorndon, acting as deputy for Hartismere. The porch here is stuccoed and the font plain, so there are no remaining clues to what was done.

268. Russingles [Rishangles], Aug. 30. Nothing but a step. The pictures were broke afore.

The church is now in private hands and one cannot get in. The repainted church sign, old enough now to be scarcely legible, says 'The Old Church Studios'. There is a very solid and square-sectioned modern chancel gable cross. Apparently there are a few fragments of early tracery glass in a nave south window

269. Mettfield [Metfield], Aug. 30. In the church, was Peter's keys, and the Jesuit's badge, in the window; and Mary on the top of the roof. I. for Jesus, H. for Hominum, and S. for Salvator; and a dove for the Holy Ghost, in wood; and the like in the chancel; and there, in brass, *Orate pro animabus*; and the steps to be levelled,

by Sept. 7. Mr. [blank] Jermin, the Gent. in the town, refused to take the inscription, as the churchwarden informed, whose name is [blank].[648]

In the porch the wooden lierne vault has a Trinity as the central boss, from which all but the seated figure of the Father and the lower limb of the cross in front of his legs is gone. Here one dove 'in wood' must have been hacked away. The canopy of honour at the east end of the nave has its original painting, with crowned MR or IHS in each of sixteen panels; only two have been badly defaced.

'Mr Jermin' who 'refused to take the inscription' was Thomas Jermy, Esq., eldest son of Sir Thomas, K.B. The churchwarden who reported him to Dowsing was either Stephen Lilly or William Welton. Thomas Jermy died in 1652 without issue and had an altar tomb against the north wall of the chancel which by D. E. Davy's time (early nineteenth century) had been taken down and the broken slab laid in the floor.[649] There, hidden under carpets, it has every appearance of a ledger slab; the name is twice spelt Jarmy and the single arms of Jermy within a wreath are carved in bas relief.

Immediately to the south (and also hidden) is the slab with brasses which Thomas defended, as it commemorated his forebears, John and Isabelle Jermy (John d.1504). In the event, the left hand quarter of the inscription plate was cut away to remove the *Orate pro animabus*, but the final *quorum animabus propicietur deus amen* was marked around with two grooves and then merely defaced (Plate 38). The surviving portion was relaid inverted in the wrong part of the indent, but this has now been put right. The dexter shield only remains beneath, showing Jermy impaling Wroth – presumably a first marriage. In William Hervy's rough notebook kept on his 1561 Visitation the lost sinister shield is shown to have been Jermy impaling Hopton quarterly, for Isabelle was daughter of John Hopton Esq. of Blythburgh.[650] The angels on the font hold Jermy lions on shields, but these are totally undamaged (following the Parliamentary Ordinance).

The churchwardens' accounts record the standard fee of 6s. 8d. for inspecting the glass – but it is paid not to Dowsing, but to his deputy, Verdon. No fee is recorded in the Journal (which is somewhat erratic in this respect), but the evidence would support the suggestion that Verdon visited first and collected the fee, and Dowsing followed at a later date.[651] The accounts (given more fully in appendix 8) flesh out the details of the destruction of the glass:

It' p'd to **Mr Verdin** for his fee for vewing o'r church windows . . o 06 08
It' p'd for beere when the glasiers did come to mend the windows . . . . . . . . . . . . . . . . . . . . . . . . . . . . . . . . . o 00 02

It' p'd for beere when the church windows were taken down  . . o o1 04
It' p'd for glasinge the church windows other charges  . . . . . . 5 05 08

The chief glazier who did the work here (and drank beer at the parish expense) was probably William Rochester, who had done repair work in earlier years at the church, or perhaps his son John (who took over the business). Three generations of the Rochester family were glaziers in north-east Suffolk, the wills existing of John of Halesworth (1617) and his son William of Bungay (1644) who was in turn succeeded by his son John.[652] The family worked at the churches at Metfield, Weybread and Loddon removing superstitious pictures and repairing the windows afterward, John taking over necessary work at Weybread from his father, William. These churches are all within ten miles of Bungay. Although neither of the two testators could place more than his mark on his will, they were prosperous enough to provide well for their dependants. John had a 'parlor house with chamber over' at Halesworth, and asked William to teach his brother Robert the craft when he came of age, and William was in a position to request to be buried within St Mary's church, Bungay, 'near Katherine my late loveing wife deceased'.

26, 28 September, & 1 October (map overleaf). *After the late August activity there is a further gap for a month, and then the Journal peters out with three entries on Thursday 26 September, Saturday 28 September and Tuesday 1 October. These visits are all based within striking distance of Dowsing's old home in Laxfield. Dowsing seems to have expected to go on working, setting a deadline of mid October for his two final churches. A possible reason for his ceasing activity is discussed on page 13, above.*

## 270. Dinnington [Dennington], Sept. 26, 1644. 10 angels in S[i]r John Rouse his ile, and 2 holy water fonts; and in Bacon's isle, 9 pictures of angels and crosses, and a holy water font; and 10 superstitious pictures in the chancel, and a holy water font, and 2 superstitious inscriptions of Christ; the spear and nayles, on two stools, on the lower end of the church; and a cherubim in S[i]r John Rouse his stool.[653]

'Sir John Rouse his ile' is clearly the south aisle, where there is a mural monument to Sir John's father, Sir Thomas (d.1603), and his wife, within the parclose at the east end. No light can be shed on the 'cherubim in Sr John Rouse's Stool [stall]', unless it occupied the obvious gap at the top centre of the elaborate canopied surround to the window lying south of the Bardolf tomb.

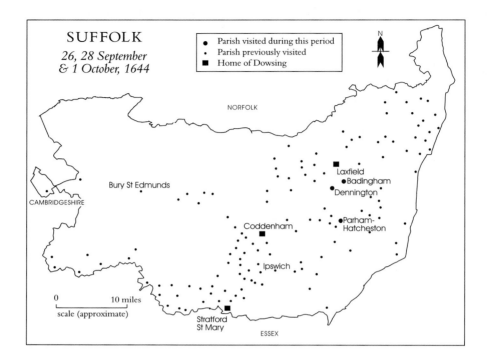

What Dowsing calls 'Bacon's isle' is presumably the north aisle. Nicholas Bacon Esq., of Dennington Place, paid £1. 4s. 0d. Ship Money in the parish and tax for four hearths in 1674, by which time he was a Knight of the Bath; his must have been the large family pew at the front on that side.

Dowsing has much trouble with holy-water fonts here. In both the north and south aisles there is a piscina and an aumbry, the shelf of the former broken off in 'Bacon's chapel', perhaps because it had an angelic supporter. In the chancel there are, surprisingly, two piscinas, both however in good order.

Careful examination of the lower parts of the back and sides of pews and benches at the west end of the church show exactly what is meant by '2 superstitious inscriptions of Christ; the Spear and Nails, on 2 Stools, at the lower end of the church', for two carved devices are hacked off but legible: a crown of thorns over a cross, and IHS on a shield (Plate 61); two more are completely effaced. Low down and gloomy, tucked away at the back of the church, these are perhaps the most hidden and unexpected, and thus in some ways the most satisfying, remnants of Dowsing's Suffolk visits. It is, too, worth peering behind the radiators along the entire range of seat backs at shields holding the rustic letters 'W S B S' (the last reversed – what do these stand for?) and 'D tun D tun' (for the town), and for damage on the ends of the benches arranged to fill the NW and SW corners of the nave.

The churchwardens' accounts survive and are particularly full.[654] Glass had been removed and steps levelled in the year ending Easter 1644 – that is, *before* the visit recorded in the Journal:

> Item laid out to one Smyth a glasier of Laxfield for 7 score and 7 foote of new glasse & 24 foote of old glasse & 6 score and 10 quarrells of glasse about repayringe the church windowes being much decayed and for collouring stuffe & for doeinge out inscriptions commanded by authority to be done . . . . . . . 6 01 06
> more to him for levelling of the chancell & some other work about the church . . . . . . . . . . . . . . . . . . . . . . . 0 03 04

In the year ending Easter 1645, further work is done on the glass, and the standard fee of 3*s*. 4*d*. is paid – but, as at Metfield (entry 269), not to Dowsing, but to his deputy, Verdon:

> paid to **Francis Verden** when he came with commissions from the Earl of Manchester to search for scandalous pictures . . . 0 03 04

No fee is recorded in the Journal (as also at Metfield), and the evidence would support the suggestion, made in chapter 6, that Verdon visited first and collected the fee, and Dowsing followed at a later date. A fuller transcript of these accounts will be found in appendix 8.

## 271. Badingham, Sept. 28. The steps to be levelled in the chancel; and 16 superstitious cherubims with crosses on their breast, all to be done, by the churchwardens, by the 13 of October.

No levelling of the steps in the chancel here would do much to lower the altar, for the church is built on rising ground and the nave aisle climbs 25 inches from west to east. In the nave roof there are 16 corbel angels holding shields which must be original, and 16 hammer-end angels with scrolls which look modern; they probably replace the '16 superstitious cherubims with crosses on their Breasts' which had to go (Plate 32). Although not mentioned in the Journal, the seven-sacrament font is considerably damaged, and the cross on the porch has been replaced (Plate 33).

## 272. Parham Hatchston [Hacheston], Oct. 1. There was 21 cherubims with wings, in wood; and 16 superstitious pictures, and popish saints; with a duple cross in the church; all and the representation of the Trinity on the font; and the spear & nailes, that [Christ] was pierced and nailed with; and 3 crosses, all in

stone; 4 superstitious pictures in the chancel and a cross all in glass; and the steps to be levelled, by Mr. Francis Warner, by Oct. fifteenth. All to be done.

Dowsing's 'Parham Hatchston' referred to today's Hacheston, south of Parham, (whereas the present Hasketon was known as 'Woodbridge Hacheston').

The nave roof here pre-dates the addition of a south aisle, as evidenced by the empty slots under the hammers above the arcade arch tops, where wall posts and braces had to be removed to avoid remaining useless and unsightly. The number of places where angels could be accommodated is thus reduced, and all are filled with small shields with painted arms, the displays here and at Parham the work of J. W. Darby when curate, probably in the later 1820s. From this it is possible to deduce just where there were '21 cherubims with Wings, in wood'.

Of the '16 superstitious pictures, and popish saints', ten paintings of saints with much damage, particularly to faces, are left on the fragments of the screen arranged around the font, which has been more savagely damaged than the Journal specifies. The 'double cross in the church' is probably a reference to the unusual timber-framing of the partition between nave and chancel, which could not be removed without structural damage to the building and would certainly seem like a 'double cross' if the shadowing from the original rood was superimposed.

An alabaster of Thomas putting his hand into Christ's side survives undamaged, and there is a good stone cross on the chancel gable, perhaps a replacement. The large fourteenth-century niche with three pedestals for a rood group on the west face of the tower might have suffered at a visit not recorded in the Journal, or been cleared of imagery in the previous century.

Francis Warner (1603–1658) was noted as 'Esq.' and rated at a fairly substantial £1. 10s. 0d. for Ship Money. There are several black marble ledger slabs at Parham for members of this gentry family.

## 273. Thomas Umberfield of Stoke [Tendryng Hall chapel, Stoke by Nayland], refused to pay the 6s. 8d. A crucifix; and divers superstitious pictures. Feb. 2 [*recte* 21].[655]

A stray duplicate of entry 118. See pages 144–5 for a discussion of the significance of the duplication.

*The following appears at the beginning of the transcripts of the Suffolk portion of the Journal. It is discussed in chapter 6.*

William Dowsing substitutes Edmund Blomefield of Aspall Stoneham Edmund Mayhew of Gosback & Thomas Denney Mr. Thomas Westhrop of Hunden, a godly man and Thomas Glamfield of Gosbrock Francis Verden for Wangford, Suthelmham, Blything, Bosmere, Sudbury, Clare, Fordham, Blacksmere, and would have had Hartsmere.

And Francis Jessop of Beccles for Lothingland and Muttford hundred, and Bungay, Bliborough, Yoxford and Ringshall.[656]

*The following entry appears at the end of transcripts of the Suffolk portion of the Journal. It is discussed in chapter 6.*

February 4. By Vertue of a Warrant directed to me from the right Honourable the Earl of Manchester I do hereby depute and appoint you T. D. in my absence to execute the sayd Warrant in every particular, within the County of _ _ _ _ according to an Ordinance of Parliament therein mentioned and power given unto me by the said Warrant as fully as I myself may or might execute the same. In witness whereof I have hereunto set my hand and seale.[657]

# Appendix 1

# William Dowsing: his immediate family

*Trevor Cooper*

A full, and essentially correct, genealogy of William Dowsing (WD) is provided in White's edition of the Journal.[1] It has not been thought worthwhile to reproduce it here.

WD's ancestry is there traced back to the his great-great-grandfather, John Dowsing, yeoman of Laxfield, who died in Edward VI's reign. The eldest son of John Dowsing was another John, whose eldest son was William, the iconoclast's grandfather; there is a brass to William in Laxfield church (Plate 2). Of the several children of the elder John Dowsing, one was Wulfran Dowsing, who was a witness in the conviction of John Noyes for heresy in 1557.[2]

The eldest son of WD's grandfather William was also named Wulfran, WD's father. Wulfran married Joan in 1582 at Laxfield. Their first-born was Simon, and after a gap they proceeded to produce a number of daughters at dangerously close intervals. In 1596 WD was born, followed by a brother Robert not long after. Wulfran died in 1607, seven years before his own father, and was buried at Laxfield; Joan, his wife, survived another 25 years.

WD married twice, first Thamar (whose sister Thomasine has a memorial in Nettlestead church), then Mary. WD's marriages and children are summarised in chapters 1 and 2.[3]

WD's eldest brother, Simon, was heir when their grandfather died in 1614. He is described as 'gentleman'. He married Prudence and in 1611 their first child, William was born. He was, of course, WD's nephew, and is mentioned in the Journal (Laxfield, entry number 243). This William, also a gentleman, married Sybille, who died in 1676. Her black marble memorial slab is in Laxfield church, under a carpet. Their only daughter and heir was Margaret, who died in 1707 and is buried under an altar tomb in the churchyard of Pulham St Mary, Norfolk.

# Appendix 2

# A possible portrait of William Dowsing

*Trevor Cooper*

In 1904 two portraits were noted as being owned by Dr Charles Biden, then living in Cratfield, Suffolk.[1] One portrait was recorded as being of 'John Smith of Studhaugh in Laxfield' (Plate 10).

The other was said by the owner to be of William Dowsing: 'this portrait has been handed down as a representation of William Dowsing of Laxfield, the Iconoclast, from whom its present owner [Dr Biden] is descended'.[2] This rather poorly painted portrait is the frontispiece of this volume.

By 1930 Dr Biden had moved to 'The Villa', Laxfield, and in June of that year he showed his portrait of William Dowsing to a group of visitors from the Great Yarmouth and District Archaeological Society. It made something of an impression: 'the face was not harsh and repellent, but sedate and serious, as of one intrusted with a solemn mission'.[3]

On Dr Biden's death two months later, both portraits passed to the Ipswich Museum, following his desire that they should have 'a local home'. Dr Biden's two nieces, acted as administrators to their uncle's estate. Unfortunately Hilda Biden muddled the two surnames in her first letter to the museum (so the portrait of John *Smith* became John *Dowsing*, and vice versa), and this was to have severe consequences.[4]

The comments in her letter expose the nature of her error. Thus 'William' Smith is 'notable only for the bequests he made in favour of Laxfield's poor'. In fact it was one *John* Smith who bequeathed land for the poor of Laxfield.[5] She explains, too, that 'John' Dowsing is 'the man who under Cromwell was responsible for much of the defacing of church monuments'. Attentive readers of this volume will know otherwise.

A letter from Hilda's sister a couple of days later silently used the correct names, and in her subsequent letter Hilda Biden herself spoke of 'William Dowsing' and 'John Smith', commenting 'the Christian names may be transposed – I cannot remember at the moment which belongs to whom'.

Despite this, the damage had been done, and the accession catalogue of the Ipswich Museum records the portrait of John Smith as John Dowsing, and the painting has been on display under this latter name. Similarly the portrait said by Biden to be of William Dowsing (our frontispiece) is catalogued as being of William Smith; this painting is not on display.[6]

Is the portrait reproduced in the frontispiece actually of William Dowsing? The frame (not shown in our picture) has been loosely dated to the later seventeenth or early eighteenth century, so is of little help. The image is of a man probably in his sixties, apparently wearing a curly brown wig, with a brown coat with large buttons down the front, and 'falling' lawn bands. The wig – if it is a wig, and not badly painted hair – places the picture as later than 1663, when Dowsing would indeed have been in his late sixties.

Otherwise the picture is hard to date, as it is badly executed, and the clothing provincial and unfashionable. In reproduction the falling bands perhaps look more narrow than in the original painting, where close examination of the poor brush-work shows them being wider than the sitter's face and neck by a couple of inches each side (thus wider than those worn by members of the professions in the eighteenth century). Bands of this style can be found through much of the latter seventeenth century. The ensemble bears a resemblance to the everyday clothing worn by the carved 'Little Man of St Albans' (on display in the north presbytery aisle of the cathedral), undated but usually assigned to *c.* 1680 (Plate 11). Similar clothing, probably rather unfashionable, is worn by the Puritan 'youth in his converted state' illustrated in Benjamin Keach's *War with the Devil*, of the mid 1670s (also Plate 11).[7]

So the dateable elements of the painting are probably consistent with it being Dowsing, though on first impression it undeniably 'feels' a little too late.[8]

One complication with Biden's identifications is that John Smith of Laxfield bequeathed bread for the poor in 1718.[9] The portrait shown in Plate 10 dates from the mid seventeenth century, and so cannot be of this John Smith, though it might, of course, represent an earlier man of the same name. One is tempted to wonder whether the identifications became accidentally switched as the pictures passed down the family, in which case any dating problems would disappear for both portraits – the earlier would be William Dowsing, the later, John Smith.

In the end, the question is one of Biden's credibility. At the extreme the possibility has to be faced that the names attached to the paintings were the product of Biden's imagination, together, perhaps, with his claim to be a lineal descendant of Dowsing. On the face of it, this is unlikely. He was in his early forties when he first went on record about the portrait, in professional life a surgeon, and at some stage in his life a County Councillor, and Chairman of Laxfield Parish Council. Someone who met him once as an elderly man recalled him as 'charming'.[10] There is, in short, no substantive evidence of eccentricity in someone whose life seems to have been the epitome of turn-of-the-century respectability. The crux, of course, is whether Biden did descend from Dowsing, and this claim we have not been in a position to test.

All we can say, bypassing the muddle generated at the time of accession, is that the portrait shown in the frontispiece was in 1904 owned by a professional gentleman who claimed lineal descent from William Dowsing, and who said it had been handed down to him as a representation of the iconoclast. Whether this face is indeed that of a cleanser of churches is a judgement each must make for himself.

*Since this was written, the Ipswich Museum has corrected the error which occurred at accession, and the possible portrait of William Dowsing has been displayed at Christchurch Mansion under that name.*

# Appendix 3

## Dowsing's collection of Parliamentary sermons

### John Blatchly

William Dowsing owned a set of printed sermons preached before Parlia-ment, as discussed by John Morrill in chapter 1. He acquired the set individu-ally over a long period. According to his recorded purchase dates he bought the first on 15 January 1641, and the last on 5 June 1646. He often wrote the date of purchase and first reading near the top edge of the title page and those dates that have survived being shaved by the binder are shown in Table A3.1. It will be seen that Dowsing read most of them within a few weeks of purchase. He purchased sermons in considerable numbers in 1643, but only four during the period of his church visits; perhaps he was too busy.

Dowsing had his collection bound in six volumes on 9 October 1646. They were put in fairly systematic order, and cased in reversed calf stamped with the initials W and D on either side of a thistle. Somehow or other this fastidious man was able to total the cost of all the sermons in each volume, though the only price on a title page (in pencil in a hand other than his) is a penny higher than his noted price. He paid between 3d. and 7d. per sermon, usually 5d. Perhaps he was offered a regular purchaser's discount.

When the volumes were rebound early this century they were mis-numbered. The original volume number is to be found (imperfectly legible owing to the resewing) on the fore-edges (which shows that any trimming was done by Dowsing's binder rather than since), and also on his manuscript contents leaf which remains in four of the six volumes (all but the original volumes 3 and 6).

Table A3.1 *The organisation of Dowsing's set of Parliamentary sermons*

| Present volume number | Dowsing's original volume number | Number of sermons in volume | Date range of sermons | Date when Dowsing re-read the volume | Contents of volume |
|---|---|---|---|---|---|
| IV | 1 | 31 | 1640–42 | 29 Dec – 12 Jan 46 | *First Volume of Fast Sermons preached before the House of Commons.* Before these are bound seven later sermons. |
| VI | 2 | 27 | 1642–43 | 12 – 30 Jan 46 | *Second Volume of Fast Sermons preached before the House of Commons.* The sermon of William Spurstow (21 July 1643) is out of order, bound in first. |
| V | 3 | 30 | 1643–44 | 31 Jan – 14 Feb 46 | *Third Volume of Fast Sermons preached before the House of Commons.* |
| III | 4 | 30 | 1644–46 | ? – 28 Feb 46 | *Continues the series of Fast Sermons.* The sermon of Daniel Evance (28 January 1645/6) is out of order, bound in first. |
| I | 5 | 22 | 1644–46 | 26 Feb – 7 Mar 46 | *Sermons preached before the House of Lords.* The sermon of George Gillespie (27 August 1645) is out of order, bound in first. |
| II | 6 | 31 | 1640–46 | 14 – 28 Dec 46 | *Sermons of Thanksgiving.* The sermon of John Gauden (29 November 1640) is bound in first, though not a Thanksgiving Sermon. |

Dowsing's library, including the sermons, passed to his eldest son and was sold at his death in 1704.[1] The sermons were donated to Ipswich Town Library in 1725 by William Mathews, perpetual curate of St Margaret's. [2]

In the published history and catalogue of the library (to which this appendix may be regarded as a supplement) the modern volume numbers are used to describe the sermons, and these numbers are used elsewhere in this book.[3] In the remainder of this appendix the sermons will be referred to by Dowsing's original volume number in Arabic, and the modern volume number in Roman.

## Dowsing's reading habits

Dowsing, when at his most meticulous, makes two annotations, one at each end of a sermon (Plate 5). His first entry gives the date of purchase and the second the date of reading, usually followed by one or two references to Scripture which are quite standard (see below). He uses month numbers rather than names, treating March as the first month of the year.

Taking as an example the third sermon in volume 2 (VI), with the letter to Newcomen on the first blank recto:[4]

*Title Page:*
Will'. Dowsing. a. 1643.m.2.d.25.5d.
[means bought for 5*d.* on 25 April 1643]

*Above the FINIS on page 61, the last:*
I.R. this Serm: 1643.m.3.d.2.3. 2 Tim.2.7. Rev.1.3. W.D.
[means I read this sermon 2-3 May 1643]

In this case he gives both of his standard references, 2 Tim. ii.7 and Rev. i. 3:

Consider what I say; and the Lord give thee understanding in all things.

Blessed is he that readeth, and they that hear the words of this prophecy, and keep those which are written therein: for the time is at hand.

Other texts occasionally quoted after reading are John xiii.17; Ps. xxxiii.1-3; Ps. lxxii.14; Isaiah lxii. 1, 2, 6, 7.

The letter to Newcomen, copied onto the sermon, is dated 6 March 1643/4, but the sermon itself was not bought until 25 April. This can only be explained by the copy being a later transcript, made after 25 April. The sermon before this, which seems by its reference to Musselburgh to have sparked the idea of writing to Newcomen, tantalisingly had the purchase date on the title page shaved in the binding, but the reading date is 28 April 1643. This is after the date on which Dowsing drafted the letter, but his eye may have been caught by

*Appendix 3*

Table A3.2   *The dates on which Dowsing purchased and read
the Parliamentary Sermons
(Shown in order of purchase date, year starting 1 January)*

| Vol.* | Posn in volume | Date of preaching | Date of purchase | Date of reading | Delay before reading (days) | Notes |
|---|---|---|---|---|---|---|
| 1 | 9 | 17-Nov-40 | | 28-Mar-41 | | |
| 2 | 2 | 25-Jan-43 | | 28-Apr-43 | | 1 |
| 2 | 10 | 31-May-43 | | 10-Sep-43 | | 1 |
| 1 | 8 | 17-Nov-40 | 15-Jan-41 | | | |
| 1 | 4 | 1-Apr-41 | 8-Sep-41 | 8-Sep-41 | 0 | |
| 1 | 13 | 23-Feb-42 | 18-Oct-42 | 9-Oct-42 | -9 | 2 |
| 1 | 12 | 23-Feb-42 | 18-Oct-42 | 10-Oct-42 | -8 | 2 |
| 1 | 6 | | 29-Oct-42 | | | |
| 1 | 7 | | 1-Nov-42 | 1-Nov-42 | 0 | |
| 1 | 28 | 30-Nov-42 | 17-Dec-42 | 18-Dec-42 | 1 | |
| 1 | 29 | 30-Nov-42 | 24-Dec-42 | 27-Dec-42 | 3 | |
| 1 | 22 | 27-Jul-42 | 2-Mar-43 | | | 1 |
| 1 | 14 | 30-Mar-42 | 7-Mar-43 | 8-Mar-43 | 1 | |
| 1 | 21 | 27-Jul-42 | 7-Mar-43 | 10-Sep-43 | 187 | |
| 1 | 19 | 29-Jun-42 | 21-Mar-43 | | | |
| 6 | 3 | 7-Sep-41 | 21-Mar-43 | 24-Mar-43 | | |
| 1 | 16 | 27-Apr-42 | 21-Mar-43 | 24-Mar-43 | 3 | |
| 1 | 17 | 25-May-42 | 21-Mar-43 | 25-Mar-43 | 4 | |
| 1 | 18 | 25-May-42 | 21-Mar-43 | 25-Mar-43 | 4 | |
| 1 | 25 | 28-Sep-42 | 21-Mar-43 | 26-Mar-43 | 5 | |
| 1 | 26 | 26-Oct-42 | 21-Mar-43 | 26-Mar-43 | 5 | |
| 1 | 15 | 27-Apr-42 | 21-Mar-43 | 24-Jan-44 | 309 | |
| 1 | 11 | 22-Dec-41 | 4-Apr-43 | 5-Apr-43 | 1 | |
| 1 | 23 | 28-Sep-42 | 4-Apr-43 | 5-Apr-43 | 1 | |
| 1 | 30 | 28-Dec-42 | 5-Apr-43 | | | |
| 1 | 31 | 28-Dec-42 | 5-Apr-43 | 4-Apr-43 | -1 | 2 |
| 1 | 23 | 31-Aug-42 | 11-Apr-43 | 13-Apr-43 | 2 | |
| 1 | 20 | 29-Jun-42 | 11-Apr-43 | 19-Apr-43 | 8 | |
| 2 | 3 | 25-Jan-43 | 25-Apr-43 | 2-May-43 | 7 | |
| 2 | 8 | 26-Apr-43 | 3-Aug-43 | 9-Aug-43 | 6 | |
| 2 | 9 | 31-May-43 | 23-Aug-43 | | | |
| 2 | 16 | 26-Jul-43 | 16-Sep-43 | 17-Sep-43 | 1 | |
| 6 | 13 | 18-Mar-44 | 31-Mar-44 | 4-Apr-44 | 4 | 3 |
| 3 | 4 | 28-Feb-44 | 12-Jun-44 | 14-Jun-44 | 2 | 3 |
| 6 | 15 | 9-Apr-44 | 14-Jul-44 | 12-Jul-44 | -2 | 2, 3 |
| 3 | 26 | 30-Oct-44 | 1-Nov-44 | 25-Nov-44 | 24 | |
| 3 | 24 | 22-Oct-44 | 6-Nov-44 | 23-Nov-44 | 17 | |
| 3 | 21 | 25-Sep-44 | 8-Nov-44 | 23-Nov-44 | 15 | |
| 2 | 20 | 27-Sep-43 | 31-Oct-45 | 27-Nov-45 | 27 | |

Table A3.2 (*cont*)

| Vol.* | Posn in volume | Date of preaching | Date of purchase | Date of reading | Delay before reading (days) | Notes |
|---|---|---|---|---|---|---|
| 3 | 25 | 30-Oct-44 | 31-Oct-45 | 8-Dec-45 | 38 | |
| 5 | 7 | 26-Mar-45 | 31-Oct-45 | 16-Dec-45 | 46 | |
| 4 | 13 | 30-Jul-45 | 1-Nov-45 | 6-Dec-45 | 35 | |
| 2 | 23 | 25-Oct-43 | 1-Nov-45 | 15-Dec-45 | 44 | |
| 2 | 22 | 25-Oct-43 | 4-Nov-45 | 8-Dec-45 | 34 | |
| 1 | 5 | 22-Apr-44 | 4-Nov-45 | 17-Dec-45 | 43 | |
| 6 | 25 | 22-Jul-45 | 15-Nov-45 | 29-Nov-45 | 14 | |
| 5 | 14 | 24-Sep-45 | 25-Apr-46 | 28-Apr-46 | 3 | |
| 4 | 19 | 26-Nov-45 | 4-Jun-46 | 9-Jun-46 | 5 | |
| 5 | 17 | 26-Nov-45 | 4-Jun-46 | 13-Jun-46 | 9 | |
| 4 | 26 | 25-Mar-46 | 4-Jun-46 | 15-Jun-46 | 11 | |
| 4 | 24 | 25-Feb-46 | 4-Jun-46 | 17-Jun-46 | 13 | |
| 6 | 28 | 2-Apr-46 | 5-Jun-46 | 9-Jun-46 | 4 | |

* Original volume number.

Sermons are only shown if either the date of purchase or the date of reading is noted on the sermon.

Notes:
1  The purchase date or reading date has been trimmed or torn away.
2  Reading date earlier than purchase date. The reason for this is not known (it might be a simple error).
3  Purchased and read during the period of the Journal.

the reference to Musselburgh, which is exposed on the back page, before he read the whole sermon. He could have owned and looked at the sermon any time after it was published – the preaching date was 25 January.

Dowsing is scrupulous in applying the errata to the text of the sermons. In one he notes his limitation: 'mended not ye Greek'. He is interested in the titles of the preachers, noting them beside the names in his manuscript contents lists: pastor, preacher, minister, and in a few cases, rector.

When the sermons were rebound, he read through them all again between 14 Dec and 7 Mar 1647, carefully recording the dates. Thus he records in volume 1 (IV):

I beg' thes Serm' 2d tyme 1646. Dece'b'.29 & end m.11 Jan. day.12. W.D. [29 Dec – 12 Jan 1645/6, after binding.]

It may be significant that he has John Gauden's sermon bound in as the first in his Thanksgiving volume 6 (II), although Gauden's is not officially designated as a Thanksgiving sermon at all. No popular account of John Gauden fails to mention this sermon against 'pictures, images, and other superstitions of popery' which he gave at his only opportunity to preach before the House of Commons, on 29 Nov 1640. Dowsing marks the passage 'some set up lying vanities, pictures'.

Dowsing's annotations show that he is pleased that in a sermon preached 12 March 1645, Richard Vines pleads for Cambridge University: 'that some expedient way be found for the easing of taxes and burdens, that Learning may not be starved; let not the Kingdome want both her eyes; to what purpose is it, that the University hath a wombe to beare, if she have no breasts to give suck?' [5] He had no objection to learning: his visit to the University the previous year had been to cleanse it, not destroy it.

## Dowsing's notes of a sermon

In a pocket at the back of volume 4 (III) is a manuscript on a single folded sheet in Dowsing's hand (Plate 6). This is singularly difficult to decipher – Dowsing's writing at its worst and blurred with age – but it appears to be a sermon outline. Was this a sermon preached by Dowsing, or something he had heard or read, noted down for discussion with his family? For some reason he thought it important enough to preserve.

It is too disjointed, and the illegibility creates too many gaps, to be worth printing in full. But there are some striking sections, reminders that Dowsing's iconoclasm was the outworking of a deep-rooted faith and piety, providing strength in times of trouble as well as of triumph. [6]

> Psa[lme] 136.26 Who remembered us in [our low estate] [*recte* Ps. 136.23]
> This psalme is a psa[lme] of prayse not for one but for many mercys of works of creation and works of p[ro]vidence... an exhortation to pray [to] God, God's method is to help his people when? no[ne] can helpe and they in a low estate...
> God's p[ro]vidence stand not on winds, his actions are not in [th]e creature but in his will... he deliver[s] not by a disciplined army but by a company of raw p[r]entises...
> God deliver in a low condition [tha]t mercy m[?ay] be advanced at a low condition, when he deliver his mercy shalbe worth [th]e giveinge God deliver in a low condition for [th]e confusion of his enemys... Hop[e] [th]e best breakfast but [th]e worst sup[er]. [7] God do by his enemys as [th]e Tu[rks] do by [th]e Jews... Thinke not [th]e worse of gods cause ?becous its lowe.

Its darke before day, [th]e greatest p[ro]mises whe[n] [th]e Church is
lowest we have [th]e greatest argume[n]t of gods love when we canot see
him, faith works not by sence… we are now in danger of surfet now we have
so ma[n]y mercys… now need to pray & morne to have o[u]r mercys sanctified, mercys like absolom, ready to seduce, we may have [th]e mercy & loose
[th]e comfo[r]t & use. God give mercys in an imp[er]fect way he bring his
people in to a wildrenes, they have thornes in ther eies [th]e English man is
sicke to late & well to soone let us not give ov[er] praying let us not live on
o[u]r ?stock… [th]e nobler [th]e being [th] tender [th]e afection, as mans
above all other creatures, mother tender to a child all its life[so] gods nature
is everlasting 2. his covena[nt] is everlast with ifs & ands, its absolute w[i]th
England & Scotla[n]d conditiall but to his Church everlasting… god love his
peeple when he chastise, & when he smile on his enemys he hates the[m] if
his wrath come on these countrys your unthankfullnes bring it…

Luk. 17.10 [i.e. unprofitable servant] most are like these ? they are but few
that returne to give god than[ks] & those are [th]e most contemptable…

Many are readyer to pray to god for fa[?vours]then to prayse him… take
notice of all gods deliverances…

# Appendix 4

# Jacob Caley: a Dowsing associate in Ipswich

## *John Blatchly*

Jacob Caley's name occurs in the Journal (mistranscribed as 'Coley') after the work at Offton, visited by Dowsing with seven other churches on that marathon of a day, 22 August 1644 (ending with Journal entry 253). Dowsing stayed with Caley overnight. It could be that Caley had done the long tour with Dowsing, for we know that business, of a kind possibly rather profitable to him, took him often to at least one of the Bosmere parishes visited that day, Flowton. In fact, as we shall see, he amassed a great many collecting offices in the early 1640s in Ipswich and the Hundreds of Bosmere, Claydon and Samford.[1]

Caley was a man of some local significance. He rose high in the Ipswich Corporation hierarchy.[2] His election in 1642 as one of the Twenty-Four, the common councilmen of the Borough, was surrounded in controversy, but his staunch Puritanism brought him through unscathed.[3] His next promotion, in 1644, was to Claviger, an office he held until in 1649 he became one of the Twelve, the Portmen, and Bailiff (joint Mayor). On 13 May 1645 he received an army commission,[4] and that November was chosen as one of the Puritan gentlemen to sit with the ministers under the Bailiffs and others on the second classis committee at Ipswich. He held various financial offices during this period.[5]

Some time after this Caley is found 'entering into the property' of Francis Everard at Linstead.[6] Everard is recorded as being a 'Drunkard' in the Journal (entry 217), but he may have earned the slur merely for being a recusant; the Everards had already paid dearly for their failure to conform.[7]

The County Committee for Suffolk to Committee for Compounding, *re* estate of Francis Everard states 2/3 = £3 per annum, former tenant Dawson,[8] marsh ground; much rent in arrear. Last Midsummer let it for £4 per annum [to] Capt. Jacob Caley & Capt. John Base who have entered into posses-sion.[9]

Caley served as a committee man for Suffolk and for Ipswich from 1644 until the committees were disbanded in 1657, and, with five others, was a Knight of the Shire in the 'Parliament of Saints' in 1653. Perhaps because of these wider involvements, Caley never held office in the Corporation again. It was September 1655 when he might next have served – as Justice (the Bailiffs and four other Portmen were the town magistrates) – but a letter in the Great Court Book signed by the Recorder and Town Clerk Nathaniel Bacon shows that the new Bailiffs could not agree between themselves over his appointment.

A month before Charles II was restored to the throne, an opportunity was taken to get rid of him altogether, at the Great Court held on 30 April 1660:

It is Agreed that Mr Jacob Calye shall be discharged of his Portmans place And of his attendance therein In regard that he the s'd Mr Calye hath not at-tended the services of this Town in his s'd Portmans place for severall years last past.[10]

Things became more difficult. In 1662 Sir Henry North and others meet-ing at Bury reported to the Attorney General a number of cases where they believed – or were prepared to claim – that collectors of public monies had misappropriated funds.[11] One complaint concerned Caley, who is alleged to have misappropriated the entire county levy for the second relief of Irish Protestants, perhaps £3000:

Jacob Caly of Ipswich June the 10th 1643 is chearged w'th the 2'd reliefe of the p[ro]testants in Ireland, payd by the chieffe Constables of Blackborn Hundred lyinge within the Franchis of Bury the sum'e of 160l. wch makes it apeare to us very p[ro]bable that he was Receiver of this tax, for the wholle County according to w'ch p[ro]portion he must stand chearged wth the receipt of the sum'e of 3000l. or thereabout.

Confirmation that he was indeed an official collector of moneys during the Civil War comes from other sources. Flowton was one of the parishes visit-ed by Dowsing the day he stayed with Caley (Journal entry 251), and in the Flowton Town Book, which includes churchwardens' and overseers' accounts as well as lists for other parish collections, Caley's name occurs often against large sums of money:[12]

Paid by Mr Thomas Bull, gent. [Constable of the parish] to Mr Jacob Caley for his 5th and 20th part £40.

*Weeklie assessment*

Chardged within the towne for 14 weekes assessment at 15s. a week, and paid to Mr Caley uppon the 26th December, and 27th Januarie, and 20th of February 1643 the somme of £10. 19s.

Paid to Mr Jacob Caley for tenne monthes paie from the 26th of March 1645 to the last of November 1645 the sum of £4. 10s. by month, which cometh unto £45.

*For horses and furniture in tyme of harvest*

Chardged within the same towne towards the settinge forth of a bodie of Horse by warrant from Mr Rewse, Julie the 22 1644 and paide to Mr Caley, the somme of £3. 2s. 8d.

*Paide for the Scotte*

Chardged within the said towne for the Scotte advance, and paid to Mr Jacob Caley, April the 6th 1645, the somme of £4. 10s.

More in August the 6th 1645 to him more for the Scotte the somme of £4. 10s.

*Monie lent uppon Tickette for the Scotte*

Paid to Mr Caley uppon an ordinance for the Scotte by Mr Tho. Bull, gent the somme of £7. 10s.

Paide to Mr Caley by Mr Crompton for the Scotte the somme of £3.

The total paid to Caley by the inhabitants of this small parish as detailed in these accounts amounts to £117. 11s. 8d. If he collected similar sums from all the 37 parishes in Bosmere and Claydon Hundred, and if he failed to pass the money on to the correct authority, the 1662 allegations would be understated.

# Appendix 5

# The Parliamentary Ordinances

*Trevor Cooper*

### *The Development of the Ordinances*

The first Order from the House of Commons regarding the removal of superstitious objects was made in September 1641. The genesis of this was a bill introduced on 5 February that year, which proposed the sending of commissioners into all the counties to deal with images, tables turned altarwise, crucifixes, ornaments and relics of idolatry.[1]

Little progress was made over the following months, but discussion was revived on 8 August: the House then declared that churchwardens had the right to take down communion rails. On 30 August the Commons resolved that 'churchwardens... do forthwith remove the communion table from the east end... and take away the rails and level the chancel, as heretofore they were before the late innovations', and a committee was appointed to draw up the terms of the Order. There was intermittent discussion of the details during the following week, during which a proposal that the Order should prevent all contempt and abuse of the Book of Common Prayer was shelved. With the wording agreed, on 8 September 1641 the House of Commons asked the Lords to consent to the Order.

The Lords debated it: whilst agreeing to the proposals for communion tables and images, they were not happy with banning bowing at the name of Jesus. On the following day they independently revived their much shorter and less draconian Order concerning the services of the church, which had been originally drafted on 16 January, and invited the Commons to assent to this. The Commons were not amused, and during the recess which followed a Commons standing committee responded by unilaterally publishing both Orders together, on 28 September 1641.[2]

Table A5.1 *Items forbidden under the terms of the Parliamentary Orders and Ordinances of 1641, 1643 and 1644*

| Item | Year of Order or Ordinance | | |
|---|---|---|---|
| | *1641* | *1643* | *1644* |
| Communion table (move away from east end)[1] | • | • | |
| Altars/tables of stone | | • | |
| Communion rails | • | • | |
| Raised chancels[2] | • | • | • |
| Crucifixes | • | • | |
| | | | |
| Crosses | | • | |
| Pictures of persons of Trinity | • | • | • |
| Images of Virgin Mary | • | • | |
| Other images of saints[3] | | • | • |
| Representations of angels | | | • |
| | | | |
| Superstitious inscriptions | | • | |
| Tapers, candlesticks, basins on Communion table | • | • | |
| Copes, surplices or other superstitious vestments | | | • |
| Roodlofts or roods | | | • |
| Fonts not to be used, to be defaced | | | • |
| | | | |
| Plate and others things used for worship which have cross, etc., on them | | | • |
| Organs and their frames and cases | | | • |
| Bowing at name of Jesus or towards east | • | | |
| Sunday sports and games | • | | |
| Preaching in the afternoon | • | | |
| | | | |
| Leave alone monuments, glass etc. of those not commonly reputed or taken as saints | | • | • |

1  1641: parish chuches only; 1643, all churches
2  1641: 'to their state before late innovations'; 1643: level 'same as was twenty years past'; 1644: no restriction
3  1643: 'other' saint; 1644: 'any' saint (rather than 'other' saint), so probably includes BVM

The matter was taken no further until the following February, when the Commons again resolved to bring in a bill based upon their Order. During the rest of 1642 the bill wended its way between the two houses. One notable additional clause, introduced by the Lords, was that commissioners in each county should be appointed by both Houses for the taking down of glass windows in churches; probably this was an attempt to manage the destruction, in order to avoid the excesses which had previously been seen, as for example at Chelmsford on bonfire night 1641 when the east window of the parish church had been smashed (including 'the Armes of the ancient Nobility and Gentry, who had contributed to the building and beautifying that faire structure'), and surplice and prayer book had been attacked.[3] In December 1642 the bill was amongst those for which royal assent was sought.

The Commons, not expecting such assent, continued to move forward. In April 1643 a committee was set up to receive information about monuments of superstition and idolatry. In June a new Ordinance was introduced, designed to replace the defunct bill; this was passed by the Commons in July, agreed by the Lords on 26 August, and passed on 28 August. This was the Ordinance referred to in Manchester's commissions to Dowsing.[4] Unlike the Order of 1641, it made no mention of bowing in church and Sunday sports, but added superstitious inscriptions to the list of banned objects. Nor was there any mention of county commissioners to supervise destruction, but at the end there was a caveat emphasising the need to leave alone images, pictures or coats of arms set up merely as a monument to any 'dead Person which hath not [been] commonly reputed or taken for a Saint'. This clause was lifted directly from the Edwardian Act of a hundred years earlier for 'putting away of divers Books and Images', but with two significant changes: the caveat in the 1643 Ordinance was not limited to tombs, but explicitly included glass; and it gave specific protection to coats of arms.[5] The inclusion of the clause, and the changed wording, were probably in reaction to earlier populism.

On 9 May 1644 a second Ordinance was issued. The first was republished with it.[6] The historical context of this second Ordinance is unclear. A need may have been felt to establish a clear legal footing for dealing with the copes and other material recently acquired from the royal chapels.[7] It is also possible that some of the additions reflect difficulties encountered on the ground by those seeking to carry out the earlier Ordinance: the inclusion of 'Overseers of the Poor' as responsible parties may reflect practical difficulties associated with Civil War disruption (see Journal entry 141 where Dowsing makes overseers responsible some time before the May Ordinance); the removal of any age restriction on levelling chancels might have been intended to avoid claim and counter-claim about the date of chancel steps (we know that Sir Thomas Knyvett saved his chancel by using the restrictions of the

1643 Ordinance, as did Dr Rowe at Cambridge);[8] the authority to demolish, rather than just deface, images, may have been deliberately introduced to increase freedom of action and completeness of cleansing; and the explicit permission to deface fonts and organ-cases (and perhaps angels) could be a response to arguments about whether such items were included in the terms of the first Ordinance. As the 1643 Ordinance was republished with the 1644 one, no significance should be attached to the items omitted from the latter.

Below are printed the 1641 Orders from both Houses, and the Ordinances of 1643 and 1644 (and see Plate 8).

## *Order concerning innovations (House of Commons)*[9]

*8 September 1641: promulgated 28 September 1641*

Whereas divers innovations in or about the worship of God have been lately practised in this kingdom, by enjoining some things and prohibiting others, without warrant of law, to the great grievance and discontent of his majesty's subjects; for the suppression of such innovations, and for preservations of the public peace, it is this day ordered by the Commons in Parliament assembled:

That the churchwardens of every parish church and chapel respectively do forthwith remove the Communion table from the east end of the church, chapel, or chancel into some other convenient place; and that they take away the rails, and level the chancels as heretofore they were before the late innovations.

That all crucifixes, scandalous pictures of any one or more persons of the Trinity, and all images of the Virgin Mary shall be taken away and abolished, and that all tapers, candlesticks, and basins be removed from the Communion table.

That all corporal bowing at the name of Jesus, or towards the east end of the church, chapel or chancel, or towards the Communion table be henceforth forborne.

That the orders aforesaid be observed in all the several cathedral churches of this kingdom, and all the collegiate churches or chapels in the two Universities, or any other part of the kingdom, and in the Temple Church and the chapels of the other Inns of Court, by the deans of the said cathedral churches, by the Vice Chancellors of the said Universities, and by the heads and governors of the several colleges and halls aforesaid, and by the benchers and readers in the said Inns of Court respectively.

That the Lord's Day shall be duly observed and sanctified; all dancing or other sports, either before or after divine service, be forborne and restrained, and that the preaching of God's word be permitted in the afternoon in the several churches and chapels of this kingdom; and that ministers and preachers be encouraged thereunto.

That the Vice-Chancellors of the Universities, heads and governors of colleges, all parsons, vicars, [and] churchwardens do make certificates of the performance of these orders; and if the same shall not be observed in any of the places aforementioned, upon complaint thereof made to the two next justices of peace, mayor, or head officers of cities or towns corporate, it is ordered that the said justices, mayor, or other head officer respectively, shall examine the truth of all such complaints, and certify by whose default the same are committed; all which certificates are to be delivered in Parliament before the thirtieth of October next.

## Order concerning the services of the Church (House of Lords)[10]

*Promulgated with the above*
That the divine service be performed as it is appointed by the Acts of Parliament of this realm; and that all such as shall disturb that wholesome order shall be severely punished according to law; and that the parsons, vicars, and curates in [their] several parishes shall forbear to introduce any rites or ceremonials that may give offence, otherwise than those which are established by the laws of the land.

## The Ordinance of 1643[11]

*Passed 28 August 1643*
An Ordinance for the utter demolishing, removing and taking away of all Monuments of Superstition or Idolatry

The Lords and Commons in Parliament taking into their serious consider-ations how well pleasing it is to God, and conduceable to the blessed Reforma-tion in his Worship, so much desired by both Houses of Parliament, that all Monuments of Superstition or Idolatry should be removed and demolished, do Ordain, That in all and every the Churches and Chappels, as well Cathe-dral and Collegiate, as other Churches and Chappels, and other usual places of publique Prayer, authorized by Law within this Realm of England and Do-minion of Wales, all Altars and Tables of stone, shall before the First day of November in the Year of our Lord God 1643. be utterly taken away and demolished; and also all Communion Tables removed from the East end of every such Church, Chappel, or place of publique Prayer, and Chancel of the same, and shall be placed in some other fit and convenient place or places of the body of the said Church, Chappel, or other such place of publique Prayer, or of the body of the Chancel of every such Church, Chappel, or other such place of publique Prayer: And that all Rails whatsoever, which have been erected near to, before, or about any Altar or Communion Table, in any of the said Churches or Chappels, or other such place of publique Prayer as aforesaid, shall before the said day be likewise taken away; and the Chancel ground of every such Church or Chappel, or other place of publique Prayer, which hath been within Twenty years last past, raised for any Altar or Communion Table to stand upon, shall before the said day be laid down, and levelled as the same was before the said Twenty years last past, And that all Tapers, Candlesticks and Basons, shall before the said day be removed and taken away from the Communion Table in every such Church, Chappel, or other place of publique Prayer, and neither the same, nor any such like shall be used about the same at any time after the said day: And that all Crucifixes, Crosses, and all Images and Pictures of any one or more Persons of the Trinity, or of the Virgin Mary, and all other Images and Pictures of Saints, or superstitious Inscriptions in or upon all and every the said Churches or Chappels, or other places of publique Prayer, Church-yards, or other places to any the said Churches and Chapples, or other place of publique Prayer belonging, or in any other open place, shall before the said first day of November be taken away and defaced, and none of the like hereafter permitted in any such Church or Chappel, or other places as aforesaid.

And be it further Ordained, That all and every such removal of the said Altars, Tables of stone, Communion Tables, Tapers, Candlesticks and Basons, Crucifixes and Crosses, Images and Pictures as aforesaid, taking away of the said Rails, levelling of the said Grounds, shall be done and performed, and the Walls, Windows, Grounds, and other places which shall be broken, impaired or altered by any the means aforesaid, shall be made up and repaired in good and sufficient manner, in all and every of the said Parish-Churches or Chappels, or usual places of publique Prayer belonging to any Parish, by the Churchwarden or Churchwardens of every such Parish for the time being respectively; and in any Cathedral or Collegiate Church or Chappel, by the Dean or Sub-Dean, or other chief Officer of every such Church or Chappel for the time being; and in the Universities, by the several Heads and Governors of every Colledge or Hall respectively; and in the several Innes of Court, by the Benchers and Readers of every of the same respectively, at the cost and charges of all and every such Person or Persons, Body Politique or Corporate, or Parishioners of every Parish respectively, to whom the charge of the repair of any such Church, Chappel, Chancel, or place of publique Prayer, or other part of such Church or Chappel, or place of publique Prayer doth or shall belong. And in case default be made in any of the Premises by any of the Person or Persons thereunto appointed by this Ordinance, from and after the said first day of November, which shall be in the year of our Lord God 1643. That then every such Person or Persons so making default, shall for every such neglect or default by the space of Twenty days, forfeit and lose Forty Shillings to the use of the Poor of the said Parish wherein such default shall be made; of if it be out of any Parish, then to the use of the Poor of such Parish whose Church is or shall be nearest to the Church or Chappel, or other place of publique Prayer, where such default shall be made; and if default shall be made after the first day of December, which shall be in the said year 1643, then any one Justice of the Peace of the County, City, or Town where such default shall be made, upon information thereof to him to be given, shall cause or procure the Premisses to be performed according to the Tenor of this Ordinance at the cost and charges of such Person or Persons, Bodies Politique or Corporate, or Inhabitants in every Parish, who are appointed by this Ordinance to bear the same.

Provided, that this Ordinance, or any thing therein contained, shall not extend to any Image, Picture, or Coat of Arms in Glass, Stone, or otherwise, in any Church, Chappel, Church-yard, or place of publique Prayer as aforesaid, set up or graven onely for a Monument of any King, Prince, or Nobleman, or other dead Person which hath not been commonly reputed or taken for a Saint: But that all such Images, Pictures, and Coats of Arms may stand and continue in like manner and form, as if this Ordinance had never been made.

## The Ordinance of 1644[12]

*Passed 9 May 1644*
An Ordinance for the further demolishing of Monuments of Idolatry, and Superstition.

The Lords and Commons assembled in Parliament, the better to accomplish the blessed Reformation so happily begun, and to remove all offences and things illegal in the worship of God, do Ordain, That all Representations of any of the Persons of the Trinity, or of any Angel or Saint, in or about any Cathedral, Collegiate or Parish Church, or Chappel, or in any open place within this Kingdome, shall be taken away, defaced, and utterly demolished; And that no such shall hereafter be set up, And that the Chancel-ground of every such Church or Chappel, raised for any Altar, or Communion Table to stand upon, shall be laid down and levelled; And that no Copes, Surplisses, superstitious Vestments, Roods, or Roodlofts, or Holy-water Fonts, shall be, or be any more used in any Church or Chappel within this Realm: And that no Cross, Crucifix, Picture, or Representation of any of the Persons of the Trinity, or of any Angel or Saint shall be, or continue upon any Plate, or other thing used, or to be used in or about the worship of God; And that all Organs, and the Frames or Cases wherein they stand in all Churches or Chappels aforesaid, shall be taken away, and utterly defaced, and none other hereafter set up in their places; And that all Copes, Surplisses, superstitious Vestments, Roods, and Fonts aforesaid, be likewise utterly defaced; whereunto all persons within this Kingdome, whom it may concern, are hereby required at their peril to yield due obedience.

Provided, That this Ordinance, or any thing therein contained, shall not extend to any Image, Picture, or Coat of Arms, in Glass, Stone, or otherwise, in any Church, Chapel, Church-yard, or place of publique Prayer as aforesaid, set up or graven onely for a Monument of any King, Prince or Nobleman, or other dead person which hath not been commonly reputed or taken for a Saint: But that all such Images, Pictures, and Coats of Arms may stand and continue in like manner and form as if this Ordinance have never been made; And the several Churchwardens or Overseers of the Poor of the said several Churches and Chappels respectively, and the next adjoyning Justice of the Peace, or Deputy Lieutenant, are hereby required to see the due performance hereof. And that the repairing of the Walls, Windows, Grounds, and other places which shall be broken or impaired by any the means aforesaid, shall be done and performed by such person and persons as are for the same end and purpose nominated and appointed by a former Ordinance of Parliament of the Eight and twentieth of August, 1643, for the utter demolishing of Monuments of Superstition or Idolatry.

# Appendix 6

# The Earl of Manchester: a biographical note

On 19 December 1643 William Dowsing was commissioned by the second Earl of Manchester to remove superstitious material from churches in the Eastern Association, with consequences which will be familiar to readers of this book. The following note is based on the life of Manchester by Bertha Porter in the *Dictionary of National Biography* supplemented by more recent work.[*]

Edward Montagu (Plate 9), the future second Earl of Manchester, was born in 1602, and educated at Sidney Sussex College, Cambridge. In the mid 1620s he represented Huntingdon in Parliament.

In 1623 he attended Prince Charles in Spain, and was created a knight of the Bath at Charles's coronation in 1626. Later that year he was raised to the House of Lords with the title Baron Montagu of Kimbolton, becoming known by the courtesy title of Viscount Mandeville later that year when his father, Henry Montagu, became (the first) Earl of Manchester.

Despite his contacts at court, Edward leaned towards a moderate puritanism, through the influence of his second wife, daughter of the second earl of Warwick, whom he married in 1626 (his first wife had died a year earlier). In the early sittings of the Long Parliament he became an acknowledged leader of the Puritan party in the Lords, meeting often with Pym, Hampden, Fiennes and St John. In July 1643, he was one of the ten peers nominated to sit as lay

[*]*Editor's note*: I am grateful to John Morrill for comments on an earlier draft of this appendix. Any errors remain my responsibility.

members in the Westminster Assembly of Divines, intended to provide a new framework for church government, worship and discipline.

In September 1642, two months before he succeeded to the Earldom, he took command of a regiment of foot in Essex's army, and was soon involved in fund-raising for the army and negotiation between his and the king's party. In early August 1643, on Cromwell's insistence (the two men knew each other well), he was appointed major-general of the Eastern Association (Norfolk, Suffolk, Essex, Cambridgeshire, Hertfordshire, Huntingdonshire and, more loosely, Lincolnshire). By the end of that month he was besieging King's Lynn, and after its capitulation joined Cromwell and Fairfax in the siege of Bolingbroke Castle. In October he accepted the surrender of the town of Lincoln.

On 22 January 1644 he was directed to 'regulate' the University of Cambridge, and a month later began ejecting suspect Fellows. He was also appointed to remove scandalous ministers in the Associated Counties, and committees were set up for the purpose, removing a substantial number of incumbents. Shortly before this (19 December 1643) he had commissioned William Dowsing, on the grounds that Parliament's Ordinance for taking down superstitious objects had not been obeyed. In addition to Dowsing's activities, Manchester's orders, rather than those of Parliament, are widely cited by churchwardens throughout the Eastern Association as the trigger for their taking down glass and other imagery.

In February 1644 Manchester became a member of the newly-formed Committee of Both Kingdoms, the central executive arm of the Anglo-Scottish war effort. By April his army was again seeing service, monitoring the movements of Prince Rupert, and retaking the town of Lincoln in early May. Manchester then marched to join Lord Fairfax and the Scots, besieging York. At this stage the Committee suggested the formation of a government excluding the king. Cromwell, then Manchester's lieutenant-general, was probably keen; Manchester and his colleagues rejected the suggestion.

Manchester fought at Marston Moor on 1 July 1644, and subsequently marched to Doncaster, then on to Lincoln, ignoring the wishes of his officers to blockade Newark, a Royalist stronghold. In early August, the Committee of Both Kingdoms urged him to march against Prince Rupert, but he argued the difficulty of the exercise, and it was not until the beginning of September 1644 that he finally got underway, reaching Reading at the end of that month. He stayed there several weeks, despite urging from the Committee, only moving to Basingstoke in mid October, where he was joined by the armies of Essex and Waller.

At the second battle of Newbury (27 October 1644), Manchester delayed launching his attack, almost certainly providing the opportunity for the king to avoid annihilation. At the council of war on the following day Manchester argued against Waller's and Cromwell's advice to pursue the king. He then failed to take Donnington Castle, and the king was able to return to withdraw the cannon he had left there.

This lack of energy and commitment was probably deliberate policy on Manchester's part. In November he made clear his opposition to the war: 'If we beat the king 99 times he is king still, and so will his posterity be after him; but if the king beat us once, we shall all be hanged, and our posterity be made slaves.' On another occasion he indicated that the war should be settled by 'accommodation' rather than by military victory.

Following these lost opportunities, Cromwell used the Commons as a platform to charge Manchester with neglect and incompetence; Manchester returned the compliment in the Lords. The arguments subsequently shifted from the actions of individuals to the need for a unified command structure, ultimately leading to the New Model Army and the resignation of their commissions by Manchester, Essex and others in April 1645. Significantly, forty of Manchester's officers had previously petitioned for his continuance, worried that his removal would 'breed a great confusion amongst them by reason of the differences between the Presbyterians and Independents': a sign of things to come.

Manchester continued to play a major role, dealing with the University of Cambridge, attending the Committee of Both Kingdoms, and frequently acting as speaker of the House of Lords. In 1646 he played an important part in negotiations with the king, and in the dispute between England and Scotland. The following year he was exploring options for settlement with the king. He strongly opposed the king's trial, and retired from public life when the formation of a commonwealth grew inevitable. In November 1651 he lost the Chancellorship of the University or Cambridge for refusing to take the Engagement, which required him to promise to 'adhere to' the 'government of this nation for the future in way of a Republic, without King or House of Lords'.

He took an active part in bringing about the restoration of the monarchy, and, as speaker for the House of Lords, welcomed the king on his arrival. At the coronation he bore the sword of state, and was made a knight of the Garter. He was involved in the trial of the regicides, apparently inclining to leniency. Thereafter he received many other honours and responsibilities. In 1667 he became a Fellow of the Royal Society.

He died on 5 May 1671, and lies in Kimbolton Church, in the old Huntingdonshire.

From the description of contemporaries, he appears to have been a generous and gentle character. One speaks of him as 'a soft and obliging temper, of no great depth, but universally beloved, being both a virtuous and a generous man'. His objectives during the Revolution were peace, a constitutional monarchy, and puritanism within established religion: his military lethargy arose in the period when the destruction of all three seemed an inevitable outcome of continued war against the King. It was easy to begin a war, he frequently said, but no man knew when it would end, and a war was not the way to advance religion.

Although intellectually a Puritan, his desire for compromise and settlement is often apparent. On the one hand he had a Congregationalist appointed to the vicarage of his home parish, Kimbolton; on the other, he was prepared to argue publicly the case for a moderate episcopacy and liturgy. Here stouter presbyterian Puritans felt he was urging them a step too far.

Why did he license Dowsing and others to remove superstitious ornaments from churches? His responsibility for ejecting scandalous ministers was set centrally; but as far as we know it was Manchester's personal decision to authorise individuals such as Dowsing to cleanse churches. As John Morrill has emphasised (chapter 1), the Parliamentary Ordinance did not require this, and Manchester did not have the legal authority to impose it. Did Manchester share Dowsing's belief that this cleansing would be pleasing in the sight of God, and would lead to a speedier resolution of the conflict? Or did he feel the need to placate one section of his army, of whom Dowsing was a representative member? Or was he, as Dr Sadler has suggested in chapter 5, concerned that matters would get out of hand through local enthusiasm, so that he saw the appointment of Dowsing, a man with a penchant for lists and regulations, as a means of stabilising the situation? We simply do not know.

# Appendix 7

# Dowsing's commissions
# from the Earl of Manchester

*Trevor Cooper*

Dowsing received two commissions from the Earl of Manchester. The first was issued on 19 December 1643. This survives only in a contemporary official copy in the Suffolk Committee Book (Plate 12).[1]

A Commission from the Earle of Manchester

Whereas by an Ordinance of the Lords and Com'ons assembled in Parliam't beareinge date the 28th day of August last it is amongust other thinges ordained th't all Crucifixes Crosses & all Images of any one or more p'sons of the Trenity or of the Virgin Marye & all other Images & pictures of Saints & supersticious inscriptions in or upon all & every the s'd Churches or Cappeles or other place of publique prayer Churchyards or other places to any the s'd Churches or Chapells or other place of publique praier belonginge / Or in any other open place shoulde before November last be taken away & defaced as by the s'd Ordinance more at large appeareth And whereas many such Crosses Crucifixes & other supersticious images & pictures are still continued within the Associated Counties in manifest Contempt of the s'd Ordinance. These are therefore to Will & require you forthw'th to make your repaier to the severall Associated Counties and put the s'd Ordinance in execution in every p[ar]ticular hereby requiring all Mayors Sheriffes, Bayliffes Constables headburoughs & all other his

Ma[jes]ties Officers & loveinge subiects to be ayding & assisting unto you whereof they may not faile at there perills. Given under my hand & seale this 19th of December 1643.

[Signed] Manchester

To Will'm Dowsinge gen.
& to such as hee shall appoint.

Dowsing's second commission survives in the original, signed by Manchester (Plate 13):[2]

These are to authorise and require you to bring before me all such heads of Colledges Deanes or Subdeanes of Cathedrals Churches or Chapples and Churchwardens as shall refuse upon the sight heerof o'r admonition given by you or your assignes under hand & seale To levell the stepps of all Chappels or chancells in the associated Counties of Essex Norf[olk] Suff[olk] Hertford Cambridge, Huntington & Lincolne acccording to an ordinance of parlia[men]t in that behalfe, and you are likewise to bring before me all such person or p[er]sons as shall oppose or contemne you or your assignes in the execuco' of the ordinance of parlia[men]t made in that behalfe or that shall ut[t]er disgracefull words [sic] speches against any of the member[s] in parlia[men]t & for the beter execution heerof require as well all Collonels Captanes & their officers as allso all Cunstables & other his Ma[jes]ties officers and loving subjects to be ayding & assisting unto you wherefore they may not fayle given under my hand & seale this 29th Decemb[e]r 1643

[Signed] Ed Manchester

To Will' Dowsing and such
as he shall apoynt

# Appendix 8

# Parish records

*John Blatchly collected the records for Suffolk, Norfolk and Essex, Robert Walker for Cambridgeshire, and Trevor Cooper for Huntingdonshire, Hertfordshire and Lincolnshire.*

This appendix contains evidence of iconoclasm from parish records for the period 1643–45 for the counties of the Eastern Association.

Unless otherwise stated, these records are of churchwardens' accounts, which account for the bulk of the entries. Other items are included, such as vestry minutes, diary entries, and extracts from correspondence.

We have included all the churchwardens' accounts which we found, whether or not they contain any evidence of iconoclasm (all but three do). In many cases the years immediately preceding 1643 were also examined. Summary accounts have been excluded, as they do not contain enough detail to be helpful.

Our dating convention is described on page xxi above. Churchwardens' years usually ran from Easter to Easter.

As discussed in appendix 11, costs associated with the signing of the Covenant can be useful in dating entries: it was typically signed in April, May or June 1644.

For ease of reference and comparison, sums of money have been expressed in a standard format: pounds, shillings and pence (rather than, for example, 'twenty-five shillings' or 'fifteen pence'), using arabic numerals, tabulated with leading zeroes.

To put the expenditure in context, as discussed in appendix 12, the daily wage for a craftsman might be between 1s. 0d. and 2s. 0d. per day, for a labourer about half that. Expenditure of £1 would, we estimate, pay for a glazier to replace approximately 30 square feet of glass.

## CONTENTS

Entries are in order of parish within county., as follows:

★ An asterisk against a parish indicates it is recorded in the Journal, and the entry number is then given.


## 1. CAMBRIDGESHIRE

★ CAMBRIDGE, ALL SAINTS (Journal entry 23)　　　　　　　　CRO P20/5/1

Extracts from the churchwardens' accounts of Thomas James and George Potter for 1643–44:

For taking down the crosse at the chancel end . . . . . . . . . . . . . . . . . . . 0 01 06
For the fee of him that had order for the glasse windows . . . . . . . . . . . . 0 06 08
For writing a petition to the Earle of Manchester . . . . . . . . . . . . . . . . . 0 02 00
For cleaning the church after the prisoners being there . . . . . . . . . . . . . 0 05 06
To the Glasier . . . . . . . . . . . . . . . . . . . . . . . . . . . . . . . . . . . . . . 1 00 00

★ CAMBRIDGE, HOLY TRINITY (Journal entry 25)　　　　　　CRO P22/5/2 & 3

Extracts from the churchwardens' accounts of John Frogg and Martin Harper for 1643–44:

For pullinge downe the crosses in the church . . . . . . . . . . . . . . . . . . . 0 03 00
To Henry Mucars (?) for taking downe glasse . . . . . . . . . . . . . . . . . . . 0 01 06
To Mills for makinge cleane the walls . . . . . . . . . . . . . . . . . . . . . . . . 0 08 04
To Mucars (?) for mendinge the windowes . . . . . . . . . . . . . . . . . . . . . 0 08 02
[There follow a number of items for building materials for mending the
　church walls]
For pulling downe pictures in the church . . . . . . . . . . . . . . . . . . . . . . 0 08 02
[Further items follow for materials which could imply the levelling of the
　chancel]
To Daniell Maldin for glasse . . . . . . . . . . . . . . . . . . . . . . . . . . . . . . 1 04 00

★ CAMBRIDGE, ST BOTOLPH (Journal entry 21)　　　　　　　CRO P26/5/1.

1642
mending the steeple and all the glass windowes about the church . . . . . . . . 0 17 06
1643
for takeing up the steps in the chancell according to order . . . . . . . . . . . . 0 01 00
1644
For mending the glasse windows . . . . . . . . . . . . . . . . . . . . . . . . . . . 0 04 00

18 quarres of new glass put in and 14 foote of glasse... . . . . . . . . . . . . . o 04 10
Boards for the windows . . . . . . . . . . . . . . . . . . . . . . . . . . . o 01 08

★ CAMBRIDGE, ST MARY THE GREAT (Journal entry 24)  CRO P30/4/2

1641–42
payd for takeing downe the rayles and levelling the chancel . . . . . . . . . . 2 07 00

1643–44
Entries relating to glass (quoted in Venables, 'S. Mary the Virgin', 285, and Sandars, *Great Saint Mary's Church*, 88–92, but we have been unable to locate these entries in the original manuscript):
pd to King for glazing the windowes . . . . . . . . . . . . . . . . . . . . 1 00 00
pd to the glaziers for defacing and repairing the windowes . . . . . . . . . . 7 00 00
pd to the overseer of the windowes . . . . . . . . . . . . . . . . . . . o 06 08
pd more to the glaziers for the windowes . . . . . . . . . . . . . . . . 2 00 00
pd to King the glazier for mending the windowes . . . . . . . . . . . . . . o 11 00

Other entries for the year (seen by us in the original):
For taking down of the cross of the steeple and chancell . . . . . . . . . . . o 16 04
To the workmen when they were levelling the chancell . . . . . . . . . . . o 01 00
For taking downe the clothe in the chancell and the borde[communion ta-
ble] . . . . . . . . . . . . . . . . . . . . . . . . . . . . . . . . . o 02 06
Pd for ringing the bell for a sermon for the Earl of Manchester . . . . . . . . o 00 07

1644–45
Pd to James Proste for putin out the pickture of S Marys . . . . . . . . . . . o 01 06
In later years there is considerable expenditure on glass.

★ CROXTON (Journal entry 142)  Originals lost. See extracts in *Transactions of the Cambridgeshire and Huntingdonshire Archaeological Society*, 5 (1930), 285.
'This visit [of Dowsing] is confirmed by the churchwardens' accounts, who paid the officers 6/8 and spent money at this time on lime and glazing'.

★ GAMLINGAY (Journal entry 172)  CRO P76/5/22

1644
to the glazier for mending the church windows . . . . . . . . . . . . . . . . o 07 00

LANDBEACH  CRO P104/1/1
The following entry appears between those for 14 June 1644 and 22 Sep 1644.
Item payd Goodman Mulldon for mendin the wendoes . . . . . . . . . . . . 2 00 00

## 2. ESSEX

BRAINTREE  D/P 264/8/3 fol. 143
Vestry decision: 4 March 1643/4
It is agreed that Go. [Goodman?] Write shall take downe the Crosse upon the top of the steeple & the Churchwardens are to give him 25s. for his paynes. he is to doe it before the 13th day of this Instant m[on]the. he hath Rec' 2s. 6d. in earnest & p[ar]te of payment.

BROMLEY, GREAT                                              ERO(CO) D/P 103/5/4

The account of John Stow and Daniell Church, Churchwardens of the parish of Much Bromley made, given up to the minister and p'rishioners the 26th day of May 1645 for the yere past as followeth:

The following entries occur after April 5 [towards the end of the account, and therefore 1645, unless there has been an error]

| | | | |
|---|---|---|---|
| for 17 foote new glasse | 0 | 09 | 11 |
| for 6 foote new leaded | 0 | 01 | 06 |
| for 4 foot repayred | 0 | 00 | 06 |
| for mendinge all the rest of the glass about the church | 1 | 05 | 00 |
| for 35 pounds of solder | 1 | 12 | 01 |
| for the plumers worke | 0 | 17 | 06 |
| for his diet eight dayes | 0 | 04 | 00 |
| for a help for him 5 dayes | 0 | 03 | 04 |
| for half a load of woode | 0 | 03 | 00 |
| more payd to Mr Dewden when he broke the glass in the church | 0 | 03 | 00 |
| more for 6 foote new glasse | 0 | 03 | 06 |
| for mendinge glasse | 0 | 00 | 06 |

This is about a year later than the campaign in Suffolk, and one entry from each of the three preceding accounts are illuminating:

| | | | |
|---|---|---|---|
| 1642 to Muntsaw for glaseing | 0 | 05 | 06 |
| 1643 to mending the church windowes | 0 | 05 | 06 |
| 1644 for Ingrosing the Covenant | 0 | 04 | 06 |

There are no Dewden or Dowden wills in ERO.

CHELMSFORD                                          ERO(CH) D/P 94/5/1/305, 307

June 24th [at top left] The Accompt of Samuell Joynour, William Payne & Daniell Bullock, churchwardens of Chelmsford and the hamlett of Moulsham 1642. [The date of 1642 is misleading, as the accounts mention the Covenant, which will have been signed in 1644, probably in April, May or June.]

| | | | |
|---|---|---|---|
| It' pd for taking downe pictures and setting up new glass in the window | 5 | 00 | 00 |
| It' pd Toby Fuller for 2 barrs of Iron for the porch windows | 0 | 02 | 06 |
| It' pd the Lord of Manchesters Servt. | 0 | 06 | 08 |
| It' pd for taking downe the crosse | 1 | 01 | 00 |
| It' pd for parchment & writing the Covenant | 0 | 05 | 06 |
| It' pd Johnson to white the church, and remove and take off pictures from the Funt | 0 | 07 | 00 |
| It' pd for glewing the Funt | 0 | 05 | 00 |
| It' pd for paynting the Funt in oyle | 0 | 11 | 00 |
| It' pd Johnson for mending the foote work of the Brasses in the midle Ile | 0 | 04 | 00 |
| It' pd for glazing the chancell window | 4 | 00 | 00 |
| It' pd for taking down images | 4 | 00 | 00 |
| It' pd for glass new and repayred | 2 | 12 | 09 |
| It' pd the Plummer to mend the defaults in the lead | 0 | 16 | 00 |

There had been riotous behaviour at this church on bonfire night 1641, with damage to the east window (see page 339 above).

EARLS COLNE

Diary entry of the incumbent Ralph Josselin for 1641 (Macfarlane, *The diary of Ralph Josselin*). This is part of a retrospective summary from 1616 until August 1644, when Josselin began to keep the diary regularly.

This Michaelmas upon an order of the House of Commons to that purpose wee took down all [images] and pictures and such like glasses: thus this winter passed away a time of hopes, and yet sometimes feares, but the King being returned out of Scotland Jan. 5, 1641: he attempted the house of Commons in case of the 5 members; but being disappointed he packed away from the house and came to them not to this houre: Aug. 8. 1644 and in Feb. following the Q went over beyond seas.

EASTON, GREAT                                     ERO(CH) D/P 232/8/1

The accounts are sporadic in their coverage and only in two undated sets are there items which may be relevant. The second more interesting extract has considerable expenditure on bells (not shown here), but unfortunately it has not been possible to date the extract by reference to Deedes & Walters, *Church Bells of Essex*. It does look as though iconoclasm had made the large expenses below necessary in about 1643.

Bill of Accounts of John Andrews Churchwarden
Imprimis Layd out for glazing . . . . . . . . . . . . . . . . . . . . . . . . . . . . 0 13 08
Accounts of John Pennington, Valentine Longe, Richard Skinner and Robert Maye
Imprimis paid to the glasier [eight times the last glazing bill] . . . . . . . . . . 5 06 08
Item payd to the plummer . . . . . . . . . . . . . . . . . . . . . . . . . . . . . 1 14 04
Item payd to the carpenter . . . . . . . . . . . . . . . . . . . . . . . . . . . . 13 07 00
Item payd to the mason & tyler . . . . . . . . . . . . . . . . . . . . . . . . . . 2 03 00

HAM, WEST                                        ERO(CH) D/P 256/5/fol. 12

Jerome Raustone gen', Wm Salter yeoman and Thomas Mortimer Butcher Church Wardens of Westham Easter 1643 to Easter Tuesday 1644

Paid unto the Masons for defaceing Images . . . . . . . . . . . . . . . . . . . . . 0 12 06
Paid for 3 doz. of Mr Perkin's Catechismes . . . . . . . . . . . . . . . . . . . . 0 03 04
Paid for taking up of brasse popish peices by an Order from the Parliament . . 0 06 08
Paid to the Ringers for ringing on Gunpowderday . . . . . . . . . . . . . . . . . 0 16 06
Paid to Prentice the bricklayer for defaceing of more Images . . . . . . . . . . . 0 04 00
Paid to Thomas Wager for takeing downe of some popish pictures in the
    glasse windowes in obedience to an Ordinance of Parliament and for set-
    ting up new glasse in the roome thereof . . . . . . . . . . . . . . . . . . . 1 16 00

HORNCHURCH                                       ERO(CH) D/P 115/5/1/305, 307

The Accompt of William Gibbs and Thomas Moyse Churchwardens for the period April 12 1642 to 8 April 1645 (Thomas Man Vicar)

For Taking Downe the crosse of the Steeple by comand from the Earle of
    Manchester . . . . . . . . . . . . . . . . . . . . . . . . . . . . . . . . . 2 05 00
Payd to John Bush the Glazier b'ys Bill due . . . . . . . . . . . . . . . . . . . 2 13 00
For taking up of Sup'stitious inscripcons of brasse and beating downe other
    things according to an order from the Earle of Manchester . . . . . . . . . . 0 07 00

To William Dawys the Glazier upon Byll for worke done to the Church
windows . . . . . . . . . . . . . . . . . . . . . . . . . . . . . . . . . 3 11 00

In the previous set of accounts there is the following payment:
John Bushe the Glazier for quarter of a yeare looking to the glasse windowes
ended 6 March 1642 . . . . . . . . . . . . . . . . . . . . . . . . . . . 0 13 00

LATTON                                                          *Essex Review*, 17, p.85

Lady Altham of Mark Hall writes on 26 March 1644 that the Cross on the steeple is taken
down and 'the sanct belly' [presumably sanctus bell] also taken away.

NAVESTOCK                            ERO(CH) D/P 148/1/1 (*Essex Review*, 4 (1895), 223)

Samuel Fisher, Vicar, who made his last entry in the first Register 24 March 1643/4, made
this note on the first page:

A note of such Brasse as was taken of
the stones in Navestocke Chancell, Anno 1644.
Jo. Everton Armigeri Co'ferarii Henry 6th
Obiit 6° die Aug. Anno 4° Edwardi Quarti.
Jo. ffurman Vicar obiit 26° Aug. 1512.
Agnes Seed uxor Roberti Seed and Ro.
Marsie Vicar March the 23. 1562.
Phillip Lentall Esquire and Parnell his
wife August 25. 1549.

NEVENDON                                                      *Essex Review*, 42 (1933), 62–7.

David Foulis, a Scot, was rector here 1653–1662. In the Register he gives a long list of repairs made by him to the church and parsonage with dates. In 1660 he repaired the chancel,
paved the floor, mended the walls, had them whitened within, rough cast them without,
and glazed the windows which were broke by the visitors of the Presbyterian Long Parliament, 'which did cost him ten pounds'.

SAFFRON WALDEN                               ERO(CH) D/P 192/5/3 fol.[1644–5]

Churchwardens' receipts July 1643–June 1644
Received of John Pam[m]ent for the brasses that were taken of the grave
stones by an Ordenaunce of Parliament, which wayd 7 score 18lb[about
4½d. a pound, cf 3½d. at Walberswick, Suffolk] . . . . . . . . . . . . . . 2 19 00

Payments, same period:
It' paid August the 20th to John Ramsher for mending the lockes th[a]t the
souldiers broak . . . . . . . . . . . . . . . . . . . . . . . . . . . . . . 0 01 01
It' paid Aprill 9th to Achell Shelford for takeinge down the crosses and the
Images in the church & to his helpe[r]s . . . . . . . . . . . . . . . . . . 2 17 06
It' paid to the man that came to view the Church from the Parliament . . . . . 0 10 00
Various payments to John Gibbs for glass of £5. 1s. 6d., 22 March 1643/4; and
£1. 3s. 0d.; and for wooden bars for windows (2s.) but the reason is not
specified.
It' paid… to John Newman for mending the Chest w'ch the souliers broake
up twice . . . . . . . . . . . . . . . . . . . . . . . . . . . . . . . . . 0 01 03
It Aprill 12 paid for Wrightinge of the Covenant and Parc[h]ment . . . . . . . 0 01 06

Receipts Sept 1648–Oct 1651:
Recayved of John Pamente for bell mettle and for the brasse Egle sould  . . . . o 10 00

Despite the sale of the brasses, eight figure brasses of 1480 to 1530 survive which were recovered from Audley End and restored to the church earlier this century (*Essex Arch. Soc.
Transactions* N.S. VII, 240–43). Achell Shelford has no will, but there are other Shelford
wills in the area.

WALTHAM HOLY CROSS                             ERO(CH) D/P 75/5/1 fol. 113

The accompt of John Alcock, churchwarden from May 1643–May 1644

pd Goodman Simons for taking downe the Crosse and nayles for the lead  . . . o 02 08
pd Wm. Aymes who came with a Commission from my Lo: of Manchester to
    Demolish Idolatrous pictures et'  . . . . . . . . . . . . . . . . . . . o 04 00
pd Goodman Candler for writing the Covenant  . . . . . . . . . . . . . . . . o 05 00

Inventory of ornaments of the church etc. by John Alcock:
Everything as the previous year 'except only the bookes of Common prayer which were
rentt peeces by the souldyers'.

1644–45:
pd for iron for the windows  . . . . . . . . . . . . . . . . . . . . . 1 18 10
pd James Clibon for glasseing  . . . . . . . . . . . . . . . . . . . . 1 07 00

1645–46:
It' to James Clibon for Glaseing the Church windowes as by his bill appears  . . . 9 00 00
It' to Amell Wood for 2 barre of Iorne waighing 6lb & 1/2 . . . . . . . . . . . . o 02 02
It' to him for 6 barres of Iorne waighing 23lb and nailes . . . . . . . . . . . . o 07 08
It' to fitt a barre of Iorne for a window . . . . . . . . . . . . . . . . . . . . o 00 02

There is a William Ames in *DNB* (d.1662), who was an officer in the Parliamentary Army.
Previously a Baptist minister, he later became a Quaker. Attempts to follow this possible
identification up in the Quaker literature failed because it only deals with his spiritual development, not his Civil War record, but what is known makes it unlikely that he is the William Aymes mentioned in the accounts.

WEALD, SOUTH                                      ERO(CH) D/P 128/5/1

The accounts of Brentwood and Upland churchwardens

fol. 84 account for 1643
Payd for taking of the Crosse . . . . . . . . . . . . . . . . . . . . . . o 04 04
fol. 85v
Paid to the Carpenter for taking Downe the pertic[i]on in the Church . . . . . o 04 00

The removal of rood-lofts was enjoined in the second Parliamentary Ordinance of May
1644.

WRITTLE                                           ERO(CH) D/P 50/5/1

Accounts of Thomas Robinson & Thomas Casbolt Churchwardens for the yeere 1642 tyll
Michellmas 1643

Receipts:
R' for an ould Cubbord & 4 slabbs . . . . . . . . . . . . . . . . . . . . o 04 04
R' for the ould Com[m]unio[n]table and a slab  . . . . . . . . . . . . . . . . o 05 00

Layd out:
Pd to Charles Clarke for mending all the glass wyndowes . . . . . . . . . . . 4  19  00
Pd to Bass for worke he did to the wyndows when the glase was mended . . . . 0  03  04
to Charles Clarke for mending the glase in the Church for halfe a yeere at
    Michellmas 1643 . . . . . . . . . . . . . . . . . . . . . . . . . . . . . . . 0  10  00

The accounts from 1644 onwards have been lost.

## 3. HERTFORDSHIRE

ASHWELL                                                            HERO D/P 7/5/1
1641
It payd to thomas russill for takinge out of glass and puttinge in new in the
    roome of it . . . . . . . . . . . . . . . . . . . . . . . . . . . . . . . . . 0  04  00

Nothing relevant in 1642

Layd out the years 1643 by us John ?Sill and Thomas Plomer and the year 1644 as followeth

[Two thirds of the way down]
It. Payd to Thomas Russill in pt. for glasinge of the church windowes  . . . . . 4  14  05
[five entries later]
It. Payd to Thomas Russill the last year for meninge of on window . . . . . . . 0  01  04
[About 25 entries for the year, totalling £16. 5s.8d.]

Layd out in the year 1645 and in the year 1646 by us John Sill and Thomas Plomer as
followeth and in the year 1648 [there are no accounts for 1647]:

It payd to Thomas Russill more for mending of the windowes the last year as
    apears by his note  . . . . . . . . . . . . . . . . . . . . . . . . . . . . . 1  05  00
[About nine entries for the year, totalling £2. 13s. 1d.]

1649
Payd to Russell for glassing the windowes . . . . . . . . . . . . . . . . . . . 5  05  00
[and later]
It payd to Baart Russell for the steepell window . . . . . . . . . . . . . . . . 1  11  00
It to Tho. Russell for glassing the ?western windows . . . . . . . . . . . . . . 0  08  00

BALDOCK                                                            HeRO, D/P12/5/1

Accounts dated simply 1643, probably referring to the period Easter 1643 to Easter 1644

Item for pulling downe the glasse in the church by Manchesters comand . . . . 0  03  04

BISHOP'S STORTFORD                                                 HERO, D/P21/5/2
(The accounts run from one Easter Monday to the next)
1641–42
Paid to John Eve for mending the glasse wyndowes of the church . . . . . . . . 1  00  00
[Some general building work, and expenditure on the Protestation]
Paid to John Eve for taking downe the glasse in the church windowes by
    comand and putting up new  . . . . . . . . . . . . . . . . . . . . . . . . . 0  18  00

1642–43
Paid to Eve for making up the glasse windowes which was broken downe by
    comand . . . . . . . . . . . . . . . . . . . . . . . . . . . . . . . . . . . 0  08  09

1643–44
Paid to John Eve for glazying the churchwyndowes due before the last
  accompt [this is the first entry for the year]. . . . . . . . . . . . . . . . . . . . . 1 00 00
Paid to Jo: Warman for worke he did in the churche . . . . . . . . . . . . . . . 0 00 02
Paid to John Warman for cutting the barres in the church wyndowes . . . . . . 0 02 00
Paid to John Tyler for mending the church rayles & for tymber & nayles [in
  this case the rayles may have been external fencing] . . . . . . . . . . . . . . 0 06 00
Paid to Tho: Warman for worke he did in the church . . . . . . . . . . . . . 0 00 02
[then other entries]
Paid to John Pegrome for worke & stuffe to mend the church wyndowes . . . . 0 11 07
Paid to John Eve for glazing the church wyndowes . . . . . . . . . . . . . . . 1 13 04
[then a few other entries]
Paid for 300 of paving tyles [for the chancel perhaps?] . . . . . . . . . . . . . 2 01 06
Paid for the charges when we went to take the covenant . . . . . . . . . . . . . 0 06 00
Paid for taking downe the crosse & for putting the wearthercocke uprighte &
  for ironwork . . . . . . . . . . . . . . . . . . . . . . . . . . . . . . . . . . 3 03 04
[then a few other entries]
Paid to the Earle of Manchester his officer . . . . . . . . . . . . . . . . . . . 0 01 06
Paid to Tyler for mending the church rayles [probably the fence] . . . . . . . . 0 00 04

1644–45
Paid to John Eve for one yeares & a halfe glazing the church . . . . . . . . . . 1 10 00
Paid him for 21 foote of new glasse . . . . . . . . . . . . . . . . . . . . . . . 0 12 03
[There is other building work in the this year and the previous year, not matched in
1642–43]


ST ALBANS , ST PETER                                      HERO, D/P93/5/2

The accounts run from Easter to Easter

1641–42
A large number of entries for glazing work on the windows, straddling 5 November. In
addition:
Paid to Daniell Smith for 2 days worke in the church for plastering and laying
  paving tyles [perhaps after removal of rails?] . . . . . . . . . . . . . . . . . . 0 02 08
Paid John ?Lawrence for bread and beere for the wringers for wringing when
  the Bishops were put beside their ?wotes in the house of Lords . . . . . . . 0 03 02

1642–43
Extensive building work. Some expenditure on glass. Payment for drawing up the petition
against Anthony Smith their minister. Later in the year, payment for drawing up a petition
to prevent the Bishop of Ely from 'putting in a vicar'.

1643–44
The following are interspersed amongst other entries, including some for general building
work
Paid James Campion for mending the church windows . . . . . . . . . . . . . 0 15 00
[a payment dated 5 November follows immediately]
For mending the glas in the church hows windows . . . . . . . . . . . . . . . . 0 03 00
To James Campion for mendinge the church windows . . . . . . . . . . . . . 0 06 00

To Anthony Kent for mendinge of 2 pounds of ould glasse and putting in 12
    new quareys . . . . . . . . . . . . . . . . . . . . . . . . . . . . . . . . o 03 04
Payd to Gilber[t] Spencer for ingrosinge the covenant into the parchment
    roule . . . . . . . . . . . . . . . . . . . . . . . . . . . . . . . . . . . . o 02 06

1644–45
Immediately after an item dated 29 June 1644:
Payd to the man that came to take up the popish sentences from of the graves
    and windows . . . . . . . . . . . . . . . . . . . . . . . . . . . . . . . . o 05 00
To Samuell Ellement to helpe him to cute them of . . . . . . . . . . . . . . o 00 06
Later in the year:
Paid for pavinge tiles & briks [perhaps for the chancel] . . . . . . . . . . . . . o 06 06

THUNDRIDGE                                 HERO D/P1 10/5/1

The accounts of William Bennet churchwarden from the 4 day of March 1643 to April the 8 day 1647

These are very crude, scrappy, brief accounts. The single entry for all of 1643 is as follows:
March the 20th Payd out for Glasinge the church windows . . . . . . . . . . o 08 00

## 4. HUNTINGDONSHIRE

BUCKDEN                                         HURO 2661/5/1

Accounts for the years 1643–45

Paid to the glayser for mending the Windoes in the yeare 1643 . . . . . . . . . o 09 10
Paid to James Hawyer for yron barrs for the windoes . . . . . . . . . . . . . . o 02 00
Paid to William Laurance for Morter and his Dayes worke about the Windoes
    and wood for the glayser . . . . . . . . . . . . . . . . . . . . . . . . . . o 03 00
Spent on the glayser and William Laurance when they were Mending the
    Windoes . . . . . . . . . . . . . . . . . . . . . . . . . . . . . . . . . . . o 01 06
[then some unrelated entries, including expenditure for Whit Sunday 1644
    and on the Covenant]
Paid for Two Bushells of Lyme to mend the glasse Windoes . . . . . . . . . . o 01 00
Paid to John Longland the Smith for yron Barrs which was used about the
    Church windoes . . . . . . . . . . . . . . . . . . . . . . . . . . . . . . . o 11 11
Paid for wood for the glayser . . . . . . . . . . . . . . . . . . . . . . . . . . o 06 09
[then one unrelated entry]
Paid to the Glaysesr for mending of the Church Windoes . . . . . . . . . . . 5 14 00
[by far the largest sum for a number of years]
Spent on the Glayser . . . . . . . . . . . . . . . . . . . . . . . . . . . . . . o 01 04
[then one unrelated entry, dated 5 November 1644]
Paid to William Laurance for mending of the glasse windoes with Morter,
    and for wayting on the glayser . . . . . . . . . . . . . . . . . . . . . . . o 10 00
Paid more to John Landell for wood for the glayser . . . . . . . . . . . . . . . o 00 06
Paid for measuring of the glasse Windoes about the Church . . . . . . . . . . o 00 08

As far as dates can be judged, there is no similar expenditure in 1645.

PAXTON, GREAT                                                             HURO 2119/3

Accounts appear to cover two years from Easter 1643.

Payd for tacking downe the glase of the Church windowes . . . . . . . . . . o o1 10
[Then Easter communion costs and expenditure on the Covenant, so this is 1644]
Payd Christopher for glaseing the Church windowes . . . . . . . . . . . . . 2 17 00
[this is a very major expense, dwarfing other items; later entries cover Midsummer and
Michaelmas, so still presumably 1644]

STAUGHTON, GREAT                                                      HURO 2735/5/1

There are entries related to the Covenant; immediately following the entry for 5 November 1644 is:

Paid to the glasyer for mendinge the Church windowes . . . . . . . . . . . . . o 11 6

This is the only expenditure on glass in the years 1642–44.

WARBOYS                                                               HURO 2795/5/1

Too fragile to consult. May contain relevant accounts.

The vicar of Warboys, John Bowen, was ejected under Manchester (Matthews, *Walker Revised*, 207).

# 5. LINCOLNSHIRE

## BOOTHBY PAGNELL

According to Hebgin-Barnes, *Stained Glass of Lincolnshire*, 'the Royalist rector Sanderson…
noted that the apostles in the chancel windows… had been "defaced and broken by the soldiers in the late warres"' (p. xli). No date for this event is given.

LOUTH, ST JAMES                       LA, LOUTH ST JAMES, 7/5, fols. 142–68

1641
There are a large number of small sums on unspecified work. About one third of the way
through the year:
To Kiswick for one dayes work about the communion Table & laying at the
    new bridge two peeces of wood . . . . . . . . . . . . . . . . . . . . . . . . . . o o1 06
A little later more than four pounds spent on the windows, including:
One Window Barr . . . . . . . . . . . . . . . . . . . . . . . . . . . . . . . . . . . . . o 00 05
[One unrelated entry]
3 foote of new glasse . . . . . . . . . . . . . . . . . . . . . . . . . . . . . . . . . . . o o1 06
6 score & 2 foote of glasse put into new leade . . . . . . . . . . . . . . . . . . 1 10 06
588 quaryes of glass putt in the windows . . . . . . . . . . . . . . . . . . . . . 2 17 04
There is other work, including the bells, clock and seats, then later in the
    year:
To Mawborne for 8 window barres weiging 12 Ca halfe . . . . . . . . . . . . o 04 08
To Mawborne for 3 window bars . . . . . . . . . . . . . . . . . . . . . . . . . . . . o o1 06
For 1 foot of glass put into new leades . . . . . . . . . . . . . . . . . . . . . . . . o 02 06
For 28 [??quarries] of new glasse . . . . . . . . . . . . . . . . . . . . . . . . . . . . o 02 04
For a ii [??or 11] foote of new glasse . . . . . . . . . . . . . . . . . . . . . . . . . o 05 06

1642
Some expenditure (a pound or so) on glass

1643
To John Elis for the windows mending May the 30 . . . . . . . . . . . . . . o o5 oo
[immediately follows entry dated May the 26 1644]

This is the only entry for repairs to windows this year, and, unusually, is buried amongst expenditure on normal church life – festivals and wine for communion.

1644
Begins with two entries for midsummer, then:
To Will Harrison for taking downe the cross over the south porch . . . . . . . o oo o8
[Then several other entries, including Michaelmas activities]
To Will Harison for mending the southwest windows . . . . . . . . . . . . . o o7 oo
To Mawborne for 2 [c?]ramps for the aforesaid windows . . . . . . . . . . . o oo o4
To Will Harrison for mending the walles about the south porch and a bushell
    of lyme     . . . . . . . . . . . . . . . . . . . . . . . . . . . . . . o o2 o6
[these last three consecutive]
Later (after 5 November):
To Jo: Ellis and Will Deane for mending the glass windowes about the church
    and the lead on the south queare . . . . . . . . . . . . . . . . . . . . 1 16 o4
To Mawborne for making fowerten barres for the windowses of old yron . . . o o2 o1
For five bares of new yron . . . . . . . . . . . . . . . . . . . . . . . . o o2 o6
Then some Christmas entries, followed by:
To Rob: Barrat for 3 dayes worke about the seates in the church and queare,
    and nailes idem    . . . . . . . . . . . . . . . . . . . . . . . . . . o o4 o8
Item to Will Deane and [word smudged] when he tooke done the glasse in
    the north west windows . . . . . . . . . . . . . . . . . . . . . . . . o oo o7
[the last two are consecutive]

## 6. NORFOLK

### ASHWELLTHORPE

In Schofield, *The Knyvett Letters, 1620–1649*, published by the Norfolk Record Society from the originals in BL Add. MS 42,153, there are two letters (p. 131, 146) from Sir Thomas Knyvett to his wife Katherine at Ashwellthorpe referring to the expected visit of Parliamentary agents to the church of All Saints in their parish, where the windows contained coats of arms of the Knyvett family (see Blomefield, *History of Norfolk*, V, 161). In the Knyvet-Wilson collection in NRO, there are two further letters; these are from Katherine to her husband, dated just before and after the second from Sir Thomas (NRO, KWL 259, 260).

*Thomas Knyvett to Katherine Knyvett 21 March 1643/4*
Concerning what I wrote formerly to you about the church windowes, you given [*sic*] me very good reason to let them alone, only thus, if you could finde out a man that had some sckill in Armory to take a note of the Coate Armes in the severall windowes, I showld be

very gladd. My cosin Browne of Sparkes, I thinke, would doe it for me if you sent to him, And then let them take ther fortune.

*Katherine Knyvett to Thomas Knyvett 11 April 1644*
My dearest
… my lord of Manchester had sent up to the parliament for order for the sequestration of your estate and Mr Holls in particular…

*Thomas Knyvett to Katherine Knyvett 11–14 May 1644*
I have sent you an ordinance concerning monm'ts & church windowes. I wish Mr Gallyerd would cause the church wardens to take downe the superstitious things in the windowes According to this ordinance, & preserve the coats of Armes by vertu of the same command, else perhapps thay may suffer together by violence.

*Katherine Knyvett to Thomas Knyvett 16 May 1644*
I must tell you our superstitious glas in the church windows and the brase upon the graves are going up most vehemently, the visiting captaine said he never came into a church wher he saw so much. 'Twill cost you a good sume the new glasing your chaple which truly shalbe let alone till winter; poor Mr Gallard grones at that which fales to his share to reforme; the ordinance of parliament which you sent downe hath preserved the steps att the altar which were sentenced to be taken away. Now tis time to lett you know I am Dear boy thy faithfull loveing wife K K

AYLSHAM                                                                                    NRO, PD 602/70

1641
paid to Christopher Tompson for takinge upp the rayles . . . . . . . . . . . . 00 01 02
1642: summary only; 1643: missing; 1644: nothing relevant.

BALE                                                                                          NRO, PD 550/36

There are detailed accounts for the relevant years but they contain nothing about a visit, or sums of a size for work on the church which implies reglazing etc.

BANHAM                                                                                    NRO, PD 552/15

1643 (presumably Easter 1643 to Easter 1644)
It' to Thomas Rawth for a boshill of lime and bringing of it from Thetford for
    sand to fasten the panes of glass in the church windoes . . . . . . . . . . . 0 01 04
It' to Cracknell of Diss for glasing work at the Church when the Imagerie
    Glass was taken downe by order from the Parliament, by the view and
    apointment of Mr Gillie of Hopton in Suff: being imployed by the Parlt.
    for the same purpose . . . . . . . . . . . . . . . . . . . . . . . . . . . . 2 13 01
It' given to the glaser and his man to drink when they began and when they
    mad an end of glasing . . . . . . . . . . . . . . . . . . . . . . . . . . . . 0 00 08

BESTHORPE                                                                              NRO, PD 309/34

Between the years 1640 and 1648 there is only one account, that of James Howes, church-warden for 1643, in which there are two interesting items; for the second, compare Fritton below.

For glasinge the Church windowes & for Irons . . . . . . . . . . . . . . . . . 0 10 08
Layd out when the townsmen w't to Norwich to pout the articles before the
    Lord of Manchesters Committee for our expencis . . . . . . . . . . . . . . 0 03 00

BRESSINGHAM                                                        NRO, PD 111/69

1644

Item paid vij of May to Captaine Gilley by the towne for the viewing of the
  church for abollishing superstitious pictures . . . . . . . . . . . . . . . . o  06  oo
Item paid to John Nun for 2 dayes work and for taking down of glas and pictures about the church and the letters about the bells . . . . . . . . . . . . o  03  04

Blomefield writes that the re-glazing of the windows after this reformation came to
£2. 6s. od., and that, though several of the windows were lost, some were preserved and put
up in the hall windows, as the emblem of the Trinity, St John the Evangelist, St Catharine,
the Virgin and St Margaret, together with the arms of Verdon &c. The glass came back to
the east window of the church at the expense of the rector in 1736, Humphry Clayton. The
church suffered much, for in 1664, £54 11s. 8d. was raised by rate to put it in order, and to
buy its ornaments of which it had been spoiled. (Blomefield, *History of Norfolk*, I, 70.)


DENTON                                                            NRO, PD 136/58

Apr 164? for the year last past.

[The Protestation was issued in May 1641 (see e.g. Cox, *Parish Registers*, 198–200) suggesting that these accounts ran from Easter 1641 to 1642, and that the missing figure in the date
is a '2'. The visitors mentioned here are therefore not connected with iconoclasm of
Dowsing's period.]

It'm for the dinners of six of us at the taking of the p'testac'on at Stratton and
  o'r horses . . . . . . . . . . . . . . . . . . . . . . . . . . . . . o  o6[cut away]
It'm paid to the vissiters . . . . . . . . . . . . . . . . . . . . . . . o  o1[cut away]

1643

Account of Rob't Gowen for the Breaking up of the Church . . . . . . . . . . o  06  08

1644

William Birdbanke and Thomas Primrose churchwardens
It'm disbursed for a seat for the commissioners at Ha[r]l[e]ston . . . . . . . . o  oo  06
It'm disbursed to Thomas Primrose for the new gat at the church-yard and
  for beating down the picters in the church and for Gowen a post and rayle
  and for a planck of his owen in the trench . . . . . . . . . . . . . . . . o  08  06


DERSINGHAM                      KING'S LYNN MUSEUM, DERSINGHAM FILE[1]

Folk-lore: Cromwell [stationed at Lynn under Manchester during the siege] 'rode into the
church and saw to the knocking out of windows and scratching out of Flemish art on
screen'. The note on which this tale is recorded continues: 'Mr Lee found broken glass
under window by digging. Few bits put in window in 1878'.


ELMHAM, NORTH                                                    NRO, PD 209/155

The originals are too fragile to be examined at all, and the transcript by the Revd A.G.
Legge, PD 209/478 (the original of which was soaked in the Library fire and at the time of
writing is being dried at Harwell) has only been partly published (*East Anglian Notes and
Queries (New Series)*, 9, 273), with no extracts between 1640 and what follows.

1648 [*sic*, but must be 1644 new style]
Layd out for the visitors Comeing to the Church . . . . . . . . . . . . . . . . o  06  08

Pd for the takeing downe the Crosses . . . . . . . . . . . . . . . . . . . . . . . o oi o6

Note that *East Anglian Notes and Queries (New Series),* 12, 52 mistakenly quotes repair figures for North Elmham which actually apply to Bressingham.

## FERSFIELD

Blomefield writes: 'The Church was purged of superstition by the rebels, who defaced the carvings of the heads of the seats with their swords, and hacked the [wooden] effigies of the Boises [they survive]. What few brasses there were, were all reaved, and several arms broken out of the windows, and the altar rails pulled down. The Evidences, King's arms &c were taken down previously by Mr Piddock, Churchwarden, who justly returned them at the Restoration'. (Blomefield, *History of Norfolk*, I, 112.)

## FRITTON                                                          NRO, PD 71/46

1643–44

Ite' for glasinge the windowes in the Church . . . . . . . . . . . . . . . . . 1 o8 oo

It' to Mr Sayer for writinge the answers to diverse gen[er]all Art[icl]es sent
   by the Earle of Manchester to our towne, twise over, and our accomptes
   writing . . . . . . . . . . . . . . . . . . . . . . . . . . . . . . . . . . o o5 oo

## GARBOLDISHAM                                                    NRO, PD 197/64

Nothing relevant in 1643 or 1644.

## HARDWICK                                                        NRO, PD 437/14/10

The Accompt of John Bardwell Churchwarden for the yeare 1643 and untill the 19 day of May 1644

Item Layd out to the visiter for revewing of the church . . . . . . . . . . . . . o o6 o8

Item Layd out to John Smith & Robt Rudlond for pulling downe the Picktors
   in the Church . . . . . . . . . . . . . . . . . . . . . . . . . . . . . . . . o oi o2

## HARLESTON

(Redenhall with Harleston, the church at the former and a chapel at the latter)

1644

May 4th for writing out the covenant . . . . . . . . . . . . . . . . . . . . . . o oi oo

May 14th for taking downe the crosses from the ends of the Chapell . . . . . . o oo o8

for takeing downe the pictures within the Chapell & defacing others . . . . . . o oo o9

There be fyve things are thowght each of them to make the Inventions of men very vnconvenyent & burthensome and soe not to be vsued.

fyrst. yf ther be noe necessarye vse of them.

second. yf they swerue from some patterne w'h may be had in such things in scripture.

third. yf they be thinges have bene or are abused to superstitions.

fourth. yf they have significac'on put vppon them by men.

fyft. yf they be fraudulous in the vse of them.

yf any such thinge bee at pr'sent in the Church, or happen to be hereafter; avoyd the vse of them w'th as mvch convenyency as may be vale.

1650

It'm, for taking downe the late King's arms & sending to Denton . . . . . . . . o oi oo

HARLING, EAST                                                    NRO, PD 219/58

Gaps for 1642 and 1643 but two sets of accounts made up on separate dates in May 1644 by Abraham Tuffield churchwarden:

May 9th 1644

It' paid to the glasser goodman Chapman for reparing of the wendowes . . . . 4 10 00
It' for the crase [?cross] taken downe . . . . . . . . . . . . . . . . . . . . 0 12 02
It' paid to Captine Gelle . . . . . . . . . . . . . . . . . . . . . . . . . . . 0 06 08
Lower down and in another hand:
Robert Baxter Barres for the windowes and welding some others . . . . . . . . 0 06 07
Humphrey Baxter for some more . . . . . . . . . . . . . . . . . . . . . . . . 0 09 05
John Whidby for making some from his own Iron . . . . . . . . . . . . . . . . 0 01 02

May 13th 1644

Expended at Thetford when I went to take the oath & covenant . . . . . . . . . 0 00 08

According to Blomefield the east window glass survives because it was removed to the Hall. 'Charles Wright, Esq. [the Wrights were lords of Herling's Manor at the time] lately glazed the east chancel window with ancient glass that he found in his house, which formerly came out of this window, and contains the principal passages of the New Testament from our Saviour's incarnation to his crucifixion'. (Blomefield, *History of Norfolk*, I, 332.)

KING'S LYNN                                                      NRO, PD39/74

On 15 November 1643 there is a payment for ringing the bells for the Earl of Manchester's visit.

Accounts of Robert Calthrop and Jonas Scott, Churchwardens, Wed the 21th of February 1643/4[2]

Whereas according to an Ordinance of both houses of Parliament of the 28th of August last past The Church Wardens of the Churches of St Margarett and St Nicholas within the parish of King's Lynn aforesaid have begunn to take downe the superstitious and offensive painted Glasse in the Windowes of the said Churches. Wee the parishioners of the said parish whose names are subscribed being Assembled this present Day about the raising of moneys for the repayring & setting up of white Glasse in the Roome of such painted glasse as is or shall be taken downe, According to the said Ordinance doe Unanimouslie Agree consent and Order That there shall be forthw'th Rated and taxed the sume of one hundred pounds for the beginning of the worke. And whereas this is a President w'ch wee never had the like of before, and the Chardge is like to be very great, wee therefore doe agree according to auncient Presidents that the said Rates or Taxes shall be as well upon all houses lands and Tenements within the said parish of King's Lynne As allso upon all the able Inhabitants of the said parish, for towards the Chardge & disbursements to be necessarily expended in the premisses. And it is further agreed, that if any of the Inhabitants shall refuse to pay their Taxes That then Mr Percevall and Mr Toll our Burgesses of the parliament are interated [*sic*] to take the pains to procure order from the parliament to compell them to pay the same. And wee doe declare that this shall be noo future President to make all the parishioners of St Margarette Liable to reparicion of St Nicholas Church. And lastly we appoint and Authorize the Churchwardens of both Churches aforesaid together with the persons here under named to be Assessors in this behalfe, viz.

Nathaniel Maney)     Alderman
Edward Robinson)                [and 16 others]

And we doe further Agree and order that the said Assessors or the maior part of them hath power to doe this worke
Edmund Hudson Maior
John Brady / Jno Revett . . . . . . . . . . . . . . . . . Churchwardens of St Nicholas
Robert Calthrop / Jonas Scott . . . . . . . . . . . . . . Churchwardens of St Margaret

Fryday the 20 of Dec 1644
... this forgoing order shall not stand or be of any force as a President for after times to make any Rate Levie or Taxation...
John Maye Maior
Valentine Walton [brother-in-law of Cromwell, and future regicide; at this time Governor of Lynn, it being a Garrison]

1645
To Mr King defacing superstitious Epitaphs [with other work] oo 10 02

1647 13th August
And whereas it appeares that there remaines in Arreare of the late assessment made for taking downe and repairing againe the windowes where ther was superstitious glasse it is therefore ordered that at the next Hall Collonel Valentine Walton shall bee intreated to have the assistance of some of his soldiers to helpe to collect the said Arreares w'ch is £38:09:09.

LODDON                                                                      NRO, PD 595/19

1642 [Mention of the Covenant in the entries indicates that the date at the head of these accounts is misleading.]

Laide out to Rochester, the glaser, defasinge of the Images in the Church . . . . o 06 oo
Laide out to Thomas Randandall [*sic*] for writinge Covenant . . . . . . . . . . o o1 oo

For Rochester the glazier, see our commentary on the Journal entry for Metfield (number 269).

NORWICH, ST BENEDICT                                                          NRO, PD 191/23

Account of Richard Puckle and Henry Tompson churchwardens Easter 1643 to Easter 1644

For glaseing the church windowes . . . . . . . . . . . . . . . . . . . . . . . . 02 10 06

The previous year only 12s. 4d. was spent on the windows.

NORWICH, ST GREGORY                                                          NRO, PD 59/54

Account of Nicholas Carre gent. and Nicholas Denny churchwardens for the year Easter 1643 to 1644

Two large sums, £4. 2s. 10d. and £6. 3s. 3d. spent on mending windowes and associated costs of what has been destroyed and must be repaired. Interesting items included: 'a Booke for the vowe iiijd', 'candles, bread and beere' for the glasiers, also the sum of 12s. 10d. for 'mending holes with the old painted glass'. A whole case of glass was needed, its carriage extra. Blomefield (iv, 273) records that in 1577 'a glazier paid 5s. for taking the images out of the windows'.

NORWICH, ST JOHN MADDERMARKET                                                NRO, PD 461/48

The Account of Thomas Baret and Joseph Danyell churchwardens for the year ending April 1643 (possible error here, as the date is given as 'ut supra')

To the painter for glasse windows [obliteration of what offended?] . . . . . . . o 01 06
To Symond Reade glasser . . . . . . . . . . . . . . . . . . . . . . . . . . . . . o 19 00
For a feirkin [firkin, a cask] of glasse . . . . . . . . . . . . . . . . . . . . . . . . 1 05 00
For mending the glass in the lower windowes . . . . . . . . . . . . . . . . . . . 3 15 00
More for mending the upper windowes . . . . . . . . . . . . . . . . . . . . . . 7 13 00

NORWICH, ST LAURENCE

Blomefield writes:

In 1636 the church was repaired, and the alter rails set up at above 70 li. expense, and in
1643 they were pulled down, and the chancel floor levelled, and the fine painted glass windows defaced, as appears by his entry in the parish book, 'laid out to Goodman Perfett for
the putting out of the superstitious inscriptions in the church windows and the pulling
down of crucifixes 1s. 8d'. (Blomefield, *History of Norfolk*, IV, 264.)

NORWICH, ST MARY COSLANY                                      NRO, COL 3/4 T130/A

Easter 1643 to Easter 1644

paid the glasier for mending the church windows . . . . . . . . . . . . . . . . 2 01 00

Earlier cleansing here came in Edwardian times according to the inventory of church goods
taken in Norwich in 1547–52: 'It' payd for the glasying of fyften windows with new glass in
the church and chancell xvij li' (*Norfolk Archaeology*, 6, 363–78). This is consistent with the
small cost incurred a century later.

NORWICH, ST PETER MANCROFT                                      NRO, PD 26/71(S)

1642
To Ducket for takeing downe images at the font . . . . . . . . . . . . . . . . . o 01 00

Account of Mr Edward Burman Alderman and Mr John Uttinge Alderman for the year
Easter 1643 to Easter 1644
Given to 3 glasers to drink when they were at work three dayes about the
      churche . . . . . . . . . . . . . . . . . . . . . . . . . . . . . . . . . . . . o 01 00
Pd to the Ringers when the Earle came into towne 26 August 1643 . . . . . . . o 03 04
Pd for a case of glasse to mend the windowes . . . . . . . . . . . . . . . . . . 1 15 04
Pd to Grew the glasier upon his bill date the 14 Decr 1643 . . . . . . . . . . . . 3 18 00

1644–45 *(extracted by Dr Julie Spraggon, to whom we are grateful)*
Pd to Rutter the glaser for glaseing at one time . . . . . . . . . . . . . . . . 11 10 00
Pd to Rutter more the 28 Febr 1644/5 . . . . . . . . . . . . . . . . . . . . . . . 1 00 00
Pd to William Rutter the glasier the 8 of Mch 1644/5 . . . . . . . . . . . . . . . 5 05 00
Pd to William Rutter the glasier 19 May 1645 £6 and 30s before which makes . . 7 10 00
Pd for mending the glasse about the church . . . . . . . . . . . . . . . . . . . 2 05 00
Pd for days work and stuff done by the glasier in 1644 & 1645 as appears by
      his bill . . . . . . . . . . . . . . . . . . . . . . . . . . . . . . . . . . . . 9 02 00

The following is an entry at the back of the churchwardens' accounts (fol. 157) dated
21 January 1645 *(noted by Dr Julie Spraggon, and quoted in her 'Iconoclasm', 109)*

Special rate agreed towards repaire of glasse windowes according To an ordynance of
parl[iament]. Made for the demolishing of all sup[er]stitious pictures in glasse winders &
other popish trash ther.

1645–46

Recd for 3cwt 2qu 4lb of old lead came out of the glasse windowes . . . . . . . 1 13 00
Pd to Ducket and his boy 4 dayes' worke for altering the desk . . . . . . . . . . 0 16 02
Pd for collouringe the Deske . . . . . . . . . . . . . . . . . . . . . . . . . . . . 0 04 00
Pd for takeing down the Crosse on the Steeple . . . . . . . . . . . . . . . . . . 0 19 00

1651 4 May

It was agreed that the Two brasse Eagles [£13. 2s. 6d.] and the organs [£2. 16s. 2d.], and old
iron, and other old thinges that are not usefull shall be sold, and the best made of them; and
the money thereof comeing shall be towards the payment of John Greeve the Glazier and
the Widdowe Nixon.

1660s: In her 'Iconoclasm', 109, Dr Spraggon notes that in the early 1660s Rutter was again
employed for glazing about the church, being paid £1. 10s. 0d. for work in 1660–61 and
another £4. 12s. 0d. in 1663–64.

NORWICH, ST SAVIOUR                    NRO, SMALL ACCESSIONS 11.9.70 shelf R154D

These accounts show income only, for whole years, Easter to Easter, with the objects of a
year's collection detailed in the heading. The totals decline markedly from 1641–42 to
1642–43 and 1643–44, and the latter, the most likely year for the making good of damage
done, drops the purpose 'church reparacions' from the title. The indications are that such
cleansing as this church needed was done very promptly, even in advance of the 1643 and
1644 Ordinances.

NORWICH, ST STEPHEN            *East Anglian Notes and Queries (New Series)*, 8, 378–9

1642–43

Whiting the church . . . . . . . . . . . . . . . . . . . . . . . . . . . . . . . . . 3 10 00
Taking down the rails and levelling the chancel where the rails had stood
For carrying earth out of the church for bread and beer for the workmen

1645–46

Received from the feofees of the parish houses for the repair of the church
  windows . . . . . . . . . . . . . . . . . . . . . . . . . . . . . . . . . . . . . 6 00 06

SWAFFHAM                                                NRO, PD 52/72

The account of Henry Vincent churchwarden from 5 November 1643 to 3 November
1644

It'm p'd to Mr Gylly w'ch came to view the Church windowes by the Earle of
  Manchesters warrant . . . . . . . . . . . . . . . . . . . . . . . . . . . . . . . 0 06 08

Despite Gilley's visit, the only sums which can be connected with subsequent repairs are:
To Edward Chapman [cf the glasier at East Harling] for glasing the church
  windowes . . . . . . . . . . . . . . . . . . . . . . . . . . . . . . . . . . . . . 1 05 00
Iron worke . . . . . . . . . . . . . . . . . . . . . . . . . . . . . . . . . . . . . 0 05 06

TOFT MONKS                                              NRO, PD 594/38

1643–44

Laid out to Ruselles the Glaysher for taken down of the painted glase . . . . . . 0 01 06
Laid out to Ruselles the Glasher for mending of the north window [rest illegible]

TUDDENHAM, EAST                                                    NRO, PD 447/49

Summary accounts only, but totals laid out in different years may be significant: in the years
to April 1642, 1643 and 1644 they are about £6, £25 14s. 6d. and £10 respectively. Either or
both of the last two ought to contain any major repairs to glass etc.

WALSHAM, NORTH                                                  NRO, MF/RO461/4

1642
payd to Xtopher Overton the glasier for xxxvii dozen & nyne quarrells of
    glasse at viij d the dozen . . . . . . . . . . . . . . . . . . . . . . . . . . . . . . 1 05 02

Labour and materials for this reglazing cost a total of . . . . . . . . . . . . . . 3 02 02

1643 Thomas Thirkle and Andrew Roose
Payd to Christopher Overton for glase sold [of ancient?] workemanshippe . . . . . . . ?
Payd for the covenants, writeing and parchment . . . . . . . . . . . . . . . . . 0 03 00

Given the mention of the covenant in the second set of accounts, the accounts must be for
the years beginning Easter 1642 and 1643 respectively. It suggests that this Norfolk parish
was quite forward in removing glass, and may not have had (or required) a visitor.

YARMOUTH, GREAT                                                    NRO, Y/C 39/2

Year ending the feast of St Michael the Archangel 1643 [29 September]
Fourth Quarter
Item for 2 Quire of paper to make bookes for takeing mens names that tooke
    the new covenant . . . . . . . . . . . . . . . . . . . . . . . . . . . . . . . . . . 0 01 03
Item paid to the Glasier for worke done about the church the whole yeare . . . 8 10 00

There is something odd about the date of the above entries, as the Covenant was taken in
early Spring 1644

Year ending the feast of St Michael the Archangel 1644
First Quarter
for the windowes . . . . . . . . . . . . . . . . . . . . . . . . . . . . . . . . . . 1 00 00
Third Quarter
more for takeing downe the crosses upon the church . . . . . . . . . . . . . . . 0 03 00
Fourth Quarter
Item payd for 6 hundred paveing tyle at vs per hundred . . . . . . . . . . . . . 1 10 00
Item for 6 loades of stones and old stuffe & for carting them . . . . . . . . . . . 0 04 00
Item for 8 bushells of haire at 5d per bushell . . . . . . . . . . . . . . . . . . . 0 03 04
Item paid to William Miller [who wrote the accounts] for 4 daies tymes in
    overseeing the worke of takeing downe the steppings of the Alter . . . . . . 0 05 00
Item payd for Rushes for the church . . . . . . . . . . . . . . . . . . . . . . . . 0 01 02
Item paid to Elvin the carter for carryin the muck out of the new werke . . . . 0 06 08
More to William Matchet [the sexton] for making cleane the chancell . . . . . 0 02 00
More to Presse the mason for takeing up a gravestone & laying it againe . . . . 0 01 00

## 7. SUFFOLK

In Suffolk the deanery is shown after the parish name. See chapter 6 for the likely distribution of deaneries amongst the deputies appointed by Dowsing.

★ ALDEBURGH, Orford Deanery (Journal entry 56)        SRO(I) EE1/I2/2

Chamberlains' accounts

1643
John Beale for worke and stuff to mende the floore in the Chancell . . . . . . . 0 01 06

1644
Paid Mr John Bence money that he laid out for glazing worke at Church as
    per bill appeareth  . . . . . . . . . . . . . . . . . . . . . . . . . . . . . 3 04 02

BARDWELL, Blackbourn Deanery        SRO(B) 2113/1/1

Edmund Craske, John Sillott, Thomas Wyndout and Charles Doe, wardens for the town 2 Nov 1643 to 2 Nov 1644

7 February Item p'd to the glasier, Mason, Joyner and other workemen for
    worke done in the Church, about pulling downe the ymages defaceing the
    pictures in glasse & wood and other work there done as doth appeare by a
    bill of perticulers thereof nowe shewed unto us . . . . . . . . . . . . . . 5 11 05
Item paid to John Cobb for 5 dayes worke which he spent in helping the said
    workmen then at 8d. the day . . . . . . . . . . . . . . . . . . . . . . 0 03 04
Item given then to the glasiers boy . . . . . . . . . . . . . . . . . . . . . . 0 00 06

It is worth noting that Dowsing was not far from here, at Newmarket and Kentford, the day after this bill was presented. However the work paid for took at least five days, so was not instigated by Dowsing, though may have been carried out in advance of a feared possible visit by him.

BOXFORD, Sudbury Deanery        SRO(B) FB77/E2/3

No accounts entered by Mr Allyn and Martin Gage, churchwardens for 1643

Laid out by Martin Caboll & Samuell Carter churchwardens for the year 1644

Item to Edward Coper for glasinge the church . . . . . . . . . . . . . . . . . 0 09 06
Item to two glasier/stone men  . . . . . . . . . . . . . . . . . . . . . . . 0 02 00
Item to Edward Coper for glasinge the vestrye . . . . . . . . . . . . . . . . . 0 02 00
Item laid out to Petit for work . . . . . . . . . . . . . . . . . . . . . . . . 1 01 00
Item laid out for Brick & masons worke . . . . . . . . . . . . . . . . . . . . 0 15 06

In 1645 £4. 6s. 6d. was spent on similar work.

BREDFIELD, Wilford Deanery        SRO(I) FC27/E1/1

Churchwardens John Bennett junior and William Partrydge: Disbursements for the year ending 7 April 1645

Layd out for glassing the church . . . . . . . . . . . . . . . . . . . . . . . 0 06 00
Layd out for glassing of the chanchell . . . . . . . . . . . . . . . . . . . . 0 09 06
Layd out for visiting fee . . . . . . . . . . . . . . . . . . . . . . . . . . . 0 06 08
Layd out for Paveing the chanchell . . . . . . . . . . . . . . . . . . . . . . 0 02 08

BUNGAY ST MARY, Wangford Deanery                                    SRO(L) 116/E1/1

Accounts of Samuell Style gent & Robte Birkingshawe Churchwardens 1643–1644

It'm to Jesopp for Veiwinge the Church by order from the Earle of Manches-
ter . . . . . . . . . . . . . . . . . . . . . . . . . . . . . . . . . . . . . . . . . . . . . . . . . . . . . . . . . . o 06 08
It'm to Robte Spence for stoninge the place where the grate [railing]was . . . . o 02 06
It'm more to him for takinge downe the Organs & makinge upp the place
with brick & lyme . . . . . . . . . . . . . . . . . . . . . . . . . . . . . . . . . . . . . . . . . . . . o 03 00

COTTON, Hartismere Deanery                                         SRO(I) FB161/E1/2

Account of Andrew Parker one of the churchwardens made 12 Apr 1645 for the year past

I'm laid out for taking downe the pictures . . . . . . . . . . . . . . . . . . . . . . . . . 2 10 00

CRATFIELD, Dunwich Deanery                                   SRO(I) FC62/A6/184, 185

The Account of William Aldus one of the Churchwardens for the year ending 23 March
1643/4

Laid out to Robert Smyth the glaser & to Ruben Tallowing [sometimes
Tallant, sexton] for helpinge of him . . . . . . . . . . . . . . . . . . . . . . . . . . . 1 00 00
Laid out for takeinge up of the pavements and throwinge downe of the stepes
in the Chancell . . . . . . . . . . . . . . . . . . . . . . . . . . . . . . . . . . . . . . . . . . . . . . o 03 00

The accoumpt of John Williams being one of the churchwardens for the yeere 1644 March
24th. [The account of the other churchwarden for the same year has the name John Smith
of Norwood added to the defective heading in a later hand.]

It' paid to Robert Smyth the glasser for Glassing of the church windowes in
part the soome of . . . . . . . . . . . . . . . . . . . . . . . . . . . . . . . . . . . . . . . . . . . 3 15 01
It' paid to Simond Warne for taking downe the crosses of the church & stepell . . o 03 00
It' paid to Simond Warne for a frame for the ordinance of p'lement for the ob-
servation of the sabboth day . . . . . . . . . . . . . . . . . . . . . . . . . . . . . . . . . . o 01 00
It' payd the glaziers [probably the other part of the bill] . . . . . . . . . . . . . 3 10 00
It' payd to Mr Varden for his fee . . . . . . . . . . . . . . . . . . . . . . . . . . . . . . . . . o 06 08

A manuscript copy of the oath to be taken by those subscribing to the Solemn League and
Covenant, undated and unsigned, is preserved in SRO(I), FC62/A3/1.

* DENNINGTON, Hoxne Deanery (Journal entry 270)                    SRO(I) FC112/E1/1

Account of Robert Downynge Church warden for the year ended 22 April 1644

Item laid out to one Smyth a glasier of Laxfield for 7 score and 7 foote of new
glasse & 24 foote of old glasse & 6 score and 10 quarrells of glasse about
repayringe the church windowes being much decayed and for collouringe
stuffe & for doeinge out inscriptions commanded by authority to be done . . . 6 01 06
Item to Richard Parker [the sexton] for 18 dayes worke in helpinge the glasier
& morteringe up the panes . . . . . . . . . . . . . . . . . . . . . . . . . . . . . . . . . . . . o 09 00
More to him for levelling of the chancell & some other work about the
church . . . . . . . . . . . . . . . . . . . . . . . . . . . . . . . . . . . . . . . . . . . . . . . . . . . . . o 03 04
It'm for lyme to use about the church . . . . . . . . . . . . . . . . . . . . . . . . . . . . . o 01 09
It'm to William Trowell for sand . . . . . . . . . . . . . . . . . . . . . . . . . . . . . . . . . . o 00 04
To Roger Briggs for iron barrs for the church windowes and for other work as
by his bill appeareth . . . . . . . . . . . . . . . . . . . . . . . . . . . . . . . . . . . . . . . . . . o 02 00

Account of Roger Holbacke & John Smyth churchwardens for the year ending 7 April 1645

paid to Francis Verden when he came with commissions from the Earl of
    Manchester to search for scandalous pictures . . . . . . . . . . . . . . . . . 0 03 04
Laid out to the glasier for 10 new panes of glasse . . . . . . . . . . . . . . . . 0 18 08
more to him for 52 new quarrells of glasse . . . . . . . . . . . . . . . . . . . 0 04 04
Given to Richard Parker for 3 dayes worke in helping of them & for making
    cleane the church . . . . . . . . . . . . . . . . . . . . . . . . . . . . . 0 03 00
Item laid out for beere for them . . . . . . . . . . . . . . . . . . . . . . . . 0 00 06

EARL SOHAM, Loes Deanery                 SRO(I) FC119/E1/1

The Accompt of Henry Bardwell one of the Churchwardens for the yeere of ou' Lord:
1643

layd out for nayles when the Church windows were glased . . . . . . . . . . . 0 00 06
layd out for 16 pound of Iron for bares for the windows of Church . . . . . . . 0 08 00
for my work when the Church windows were glased . . . . . . . . . . . . . . . 0 07 00
to John Kame when he tooke doune the Images of the Church . . . . . . . . . 0 02 00
and for my owne worke in defacinge & takings doune . . . . . . . . . . . . . 0 01 06
to John Kame for takinge the alter dune & my owne worke . . . . . . . . . . . 0 05 00
to Thomas Denny for his worke done then . . . . . . . . . . . . . . . . . . . 0 [torn]
layd out att Woodbrige when wee tooke the covenant . . . . . . . . . . . . . 0 01 00

ELMHAM, SOUTH, ST MARGARET, South Elmham Deanery    SRO(L) FC141/E1/1-18

The Accompt of Robert Headly Churchwarden from the 22th [*sic*] of Aprill 1644 to the 7th
of Aprill 1645

It' layd out to one Vardinge for the church 17th of May . . . . . . . . . . . . 0 03 04
It' to the glaser for the church windows the 6th of June . . . . . . . . . . . . 0 16 00

FRAMLINGHAM, Loes Deanery             SRO(I) FC101/E2/26

Churchworkes etc. 1644

August 10th to Mr Francis Verdyn as halfe a fee for visiting the church by
    E: Manchesters warr. 3s. 4d. & a pint of sack 8d. . . . . . . . . . . . . . . 0 04 00
Sept 4th to John Adkins for removing the organs . . . . . . . . . . . . . . . . 1 10 00
For glew, aqua vitae & nayles 6d & a skin to mend bellowes . . . . . . . . . . 0 01 00
To Tho. Ladd & Jo. Morrice each 2 dayes to help hym about the removall of
    the orgaines & setting them up againe . . . . . . . . . . . . . . . . . . . 0 04 00
Following year:
26 May 1645 Bason 4s. 4d. & Iron frame 3s. 6d.

HARTEST, Sudbury Deanery

Archdeaconry of Sudbury Proceedings, ante 1700 (not located in the original, but this
deposition reprinted in *East Anglian Notes and Queries (New Series)*, 10, 326–7).
From a deposition oath of Ambrose Dister made to the Allegation articles taken 13 December 1664:

To the first article 'that he the said Dister being Churchwarden of Hartest did pull down or
cause to be pulled down the Font of the said Church out of fear & by the colour of an Order
of some of the Earl of Manchester's soldiers lying then in and about Hartest'.

To the second article 'that he hath none of the materials of the said font in his custody nor ever coverted any stone or any other part of the lead or other materials beonging to the said font to his use or ever did enrich himself sacriligiously or is sacriligiously enriched by any of the utensils or materials belonging to the said font of Hartest'.

★ IPSWICH, ST CLEMENT, Ipswich Deanery (Journal entry 85)          SRO(I) FB 98/E3/1

The Acounte of Daniell Bowell and Robert Ellis Church wardins for the p'rish of Clements in Ipswich 1643

| | | | |
|---|---|---|---|
| For glassing the windowes | 2 | 03 | 00 |
| payd for an Eyron and basin to baptyse children by the Deske Syde | 0 | 06 | 02 |
| payd for the covenante writing and parchment | 0 | 03 | 00 |
| payd the carpender for planks and worke done to the church | 0 | 07 | 00 |
| payd the masons at severall tymes for worke done to the church and church wall | 2 | 05 | 00 |
| for lyme and mortar | 0 | 10 | 00 |
| payd for briks for church and church wall | 0 | 11 | 00 |

★ IPSWICH, ST PETER, Ipswich Deanery (Journal entry 76)          BL ADD MS 25344

1643 John Cole tanner and Robte Harvye churchwardens

| | | | |
|---|---|---|---|
| For makeing a new stoole & altering 2 stooles and the worke to the joyner | 3 | 14 | 00 |
| For glaseing the church | 2 | 08 | 00 |
| For 22 bushells of lyme | 0 | 11 | 00 |
| For five dayes worke to a mason & laborer at 3s. per day | 0 | 15 | 00 |
| For 4 dayes worke to A mason at 2s. per day and for his labourer 3 dayes 1/2 at 12d. | 0 | 11 | 06 |
| For Fardinando Quinting for 1M 1/4 brick & tyle [1250] | 1 | 00 | 00 |
| For the Wid: Cason for 140 brick | 0 | 02 | 04 |
| For 3 bushells lyme | 0 | 02 | 00 |
| For lath nayles & tile pynes | 0 | 01 | 06 |
| For making cleane the church | 0 | 05 | 06 |
| For charcoale for the glassyer | 0 | 01 | 00 |
| For 2 payre of Joynts | 0 | 05 | 00 |
| For beere for the workmen at severall tymes | 0 | 02 | 04 |
| For an hour glasse | 0 | 00 | 08 |
| For writing the covenant | 0 | 04 | 00 |
| For paveing 16 yds at 3d. | 0 | 04 | 00 |
| For paveing 68 yds at 3d. per yard | 0 | 17 | 00 |
| For 2 loads stones | 0 | 01 | 06 |
| For carrying the stones | 0 | 01 | 06 |
| For 4 Loads of sand and gravel | 0 | 04 | 00 |

1644 Manuell Sorrell and John Cole tanner churchwardens

| | | | |
|---|---|---|---|
| For A new bason for the water to baptise | 0 | 02 | 06 |
| For an Iron frame and paynting it | 0 | 03 | 00 |
| For A forme for the children to stand upon to be catechised | 0 | 01 | 02 |

Although there is no mention of a visit in 1643 the sums spent on building work have no parallel in other years of the same period. These items are commented on in *East Anglian Notes and Queries (New Series)*, 1, 278.

★ KELSALE, Dunwich Deanery (Journal entry 61)          SRO(I) GB 9:976/2

Churchwardens accounts April 1644–April 1645

Paid Thomas Maninge for a bason . . . . . . . . . . . . . . . . . . . . . . . . . . o 03 06
Paid for a Directory book . . . . . . . . . . . . . . . . . . . . . . . . . . . . . . o 01 06
Paid to Robert Moose for takeinge downe the Font . . . . . . . . . . . . . . . . o 00 06

LOWESTOFT, ST MARGARET, Lothingland & Mutford Deanery

Original register in NRO and illegible microfilm copy in SRO. Our transcript from Lees, *The Chronicles of a Suffolk Parish Church*, 166.

Extract from register quoted on page 80.

MELLIS, Hartismere Deanery          SRO(I) FB123/E1/1

May 24th 1644 Accompts of Robert Warne & William Holmes churchwardens for two years last past ending 22 Aprill last past

Robert Warne

Layd out for glaseinge the church windows . . . . . . . . . . . . . . . . . . . . 1 15 00
Layd out for lyme . . . . . . . . . . . . . . . . . . . . . . . . . . . . . . . . . o 00 04
Layd out to the Erle of Manchesters commissioners . . . . . . . . . . . . . . . o 06 08
Layd out in expenses with the glasers . . . . . . . . . . . . . . . . . . . . . . . o 00 04

William Holmes

Layd out w'th the glasers when they came to take the worke . . . . . . . . . . . o 00 04

Phillippe Baker churchwarden for the year ending Appr. 1645

In primis for clearing the glasse & glaseing . . . . . . . . . . . . . . . . . . . . 2 03 00
It'm for taking the crosses downe & spent on the glasiers . . . . . . . . . . . . o 01 06
It'm for mortar for the glasiers . . . . . . . . . . . . . . . . . . . . . . . . . . o 01 00
[The organ pipes sold for 16s.]

MENDLESHAM, Hartismere Deanery          SRO(I) FB159/E7/76

William Seaman April 1644–April 1645

28 April Layd out to John Lord for yrons for the Church . . . . . . . . . . . . o 02 00
30 April pd Stone the glasare as app'r by his bill . . . . . . . . . . . . . . . . . 2 14 05
11 June layd out to Joseph Petter for worke about the Church and chimes & 3
   dayes to help the glasier & for yrons . . . . . . . . . . . . . . . . . . . . . o 06 00
more to him for making clean the Church & strewinge . . . . . . . . . . . . . o 02 00

★ METFIELD, Hoxne Deanery (Journal entry 269)          SRO(I) FC91/E1/1

Summarised in *PSIA* XXIII, (1938) 128–147.

Stephen Lilly and William Welton [joyner] churchwardens in 1644

It' p'd for beere for the glasiers . . . . . . . . . . . . . . . . . . . . . . . . . . o 00 04
It' p'd for takinge downe the glasse in the Church windows . . . . . . . . . . . o 01 06
It' p'd for beere when we put out the glasse . . . . . . . . . . . . . . . . . . . . o 01 02
It' p'd the glasers for losse of ther worke one day . . . . . . . . . . . . . . . . . o 02 00
It' p'd to Mr Verdin for his fee for vewing o'r church windows . . . . . . . . . o 06 08
It' p'd for beere when the glasiers did come to mend the windows . . . . . . . o 00 02
It' p'd for beere when the church windows were taken down . . . . . . . . . . . o 01 04
It' p'd for glasinge the church windows other charges . . . . . . . . . . . . . . 5 05 08

It' p'd to Wm Welton the joyner for worke about the church . . . . . . . . . . o o5 o5
It' p'd the Smith for bars and nayles for the church windows . . . . . . . . . . o o7 o4
It' p'd the plumer for solder & lead and his wages

In 1631 William Rochester the glaser was paid for '17 skore quarels of glas besides our old glas'. 'Edwards the Smith for 11 bares of eyon & spikens for the glas windows at Church'. For detail of the various work needed on the east window in 1647–57 see *Proc. Suffolk Inst. Arch.* XXIII, 136. For Rochester, see Journal entry for Metfield (number 269).

MILDENHALL, Fordham Deanery                                          SRO(B) EL110/5/1,3,5,6
The churchwardens' accounts have a gap from 1603 to 1644 inclusive.

Simpson's *History of Mildenhall*, 31 has the following:
But a fiercer onslaught from Puritan fanaticism [than that of the mid-sixteenth century] awaited the remaining decorations of the interior. In 1651[?], the faces of the figures under the roofs of the aisles were destroyed, and the parish officials of that day soothed the bigotry of the period by hiring a man at the cost of a shilling a day, to deface and destroy all symbols of papish superstition, as this beautiful sculpture and high artistic skill of the fifteenth century was termed by the ignorant fanatics of that age. A total destruction of what was left of the stained glass windows was accomplished for the same reason, and the wantonly deformed Church remained as such.

PEASENHALL, Dunwich Deanery                                          SRO(I) FC67/E1/1

1641–42
Organs and rails removed

1643–44
[February] payed for helpe to take downe the sayntes bell . . . . . . . . . . . . o oo o4
payed to Meres of Halesworth for glasing the church . . . . . . . . . . . . . . . 1 o9 oo
payed to the mason for 2 dayes work abought the glasse windowes of the
    church . . . . . . . . . . . . . . . . . . . . . . . . . . . . . . . . . . o o2 o6
payed for parchment & for writtinge the Covenant . . . . . . . . . . . . . . . . o o2 o1

Dowsing was at Kelsale in the same Deanery on 26 January.

RISBY, Thingoe Deanery                                              SRO(B) FL618/4/1
An exercise book with material pasted in, including original Bishop's Transcripts. It has a receipt for a fine stuck into it which shows John Crow's almost illiterate signature. It is reproduced as Plate 58.

xxii Maij 1644
Recd of Grigorie Woods gent Church Warden of Risbie vjs viijd allowed out of 40s Forfeited for not takeing away and demollishing of popish Pictures & Crosses in & upon the Parrish Church of Risbie aforrsayd & Chancell of the same according to an Ordinance of Parliamt the Residue of the 40s is to be distributed to the Poore of the Parrish of Risbie aforesayd.

                                                                    Iohn Crow

SOMERLEYTON, Lothingland & Mutford Deanery
Wentworth MSS: Journal of Sir John Wentworth of the Hall, died 1651; original MSS not located, quoted in Suckling *History and Antiquities of the County of Suffolk*, Vol. II (London, 1848):

For fynes levied we never had any, only Thomas Manby, the churchwarden, that time being, paid to Francis Jessop, Quarter-Master to Captain William Browning [*sic*], the sum of 6 shillings and 8 pence for certayne painted glasse, being in the church windows.

STONHAM ASPAL, Bosmere Deanery                                    SRO(I) FB 22/E1/1

1642 The account of John Catchpole and Thomas Searles churchwardens

It' for gress for the bells and taking downe the Imags [on the tower?] . . . . . . 0 00 10

1643 The accompt of Thomas Searles and Edmond Blomfeild [one of Dowsing's Deputies] Churchwardens

This year routine repairs to the windows cost 15s.6d. The last transactions with Jeremy Holt, ejected 10 May 1645, occur in these accounts.

1644 The accompt of Edmond Blomfeild & John Hart Churchwardens

It' for taking down the Scandalous pictures . . . . . . . . . . . . . . . . . . . . . . 0 11 02
It' for our Dinners when wee tooke the Covenant . . . . . . . . . . . . . . . . . 0 02 10
It' for the Glasier for the Church . . . . . . . . . . . . . . . . . . . . . . . . . . . 9 00 00
It' to Richard Raynolds for helpinge the Glazier . . . . . . . . . . . . . . . . . 0 09 06
It' to Anth'y List for Lyme & sand for the Glasier . . . . . . . . . . . . . . . . . 0 02 00
[John Swayne who replaced Jeremy Holt appears this year.]

1645
It' for a bason & a frame for it . . . . . . . . . . . . . . . . . . . . . . . . . . . . 0 04 00

★ STOWMARKET AND STOWUPLAND, Stow Deanery (Journal entry 103)
The latter was a hamlet (with no church) of the former, where was there were two medieval churches, St Mary and SS Peter and Paul. When the latter was demolished about 1546 the remaining church became St Peter and St Mary. Both town and hamlet had churchwardens who kept separate accounts; most expenses and sums received were shared equally. All that survives in Ipswich SRO(I) is a parish account book for Stowupland 1618–1713 FB221/A2/1, which includes the accounts of the Stowupland churchwardens for the 1640s. The only items of expenditure below for which the original exists, in that volume, are the last, relating to the organ pipes and items of clerical dress. Fortunately there are quotations by Hollingsworth in his *History of Stowmarket* from documents at that time in the chest at Stowmarket, but since lost, and Wodderspoon in his extra-illustrated Journal [Bodley MS Top. Suff. d.19] gives transcripts which resemble Hollingsworth's entries, and more; he too must have had access to originals now lost. What follows are relevant extracts from these primary and secondary sources. We have not attempted to collate them.

*Hollingsworth p. 163:* ?1642 Stowmarket [but the Journal has this ordered 5 February 1643/4]
For our part [half share of the cost] for lowering of the chancell . . . . . . . . . 0 04 06
[Stowupland would have paid the other half]

*Wodderspoon:* Stowupland 23 April 1644
The accompt of Willm Heywood and John Hubbard for the year now ended [23 April 1644]
28 Dec [1643]
Item for takinge downe the pynacle crosse . . . . . . . . . . . . . . . . . . . . . 0 01 03
Item for cutting of the Images of the ends of the stooles & beating downe the
    pictures in the glass windowes of the Church . . . . . . . . . . . . . . . . . 0 02 02

Item charges at Ipswich about the Nationale Cov[enant] write[ing] . . . . . . o o3 o4

*Hollingsworth p.166*: John Hubbard and John Keble churchwardens
For beatinge downe the pictures in the glass windowes of the churche & for
cutting off the images of the endes of the stooles and the cross on the east
end of the church . . . . . . . . . . . . . . . . . . . . . . . . . . . . . 4 days' wages

*Wodderspoon*: from 'loose papers' John Hubbard and John Keble churchwardens
Item for cutting downe the crosse on the pynacle . . . . . . . . . . . . . . . o o2 oo
Item to Mr Pettitt for blotting out the crosse keyes [*Hollingsworth*: on the
spire] . . . . . . . . . . . . . . . . . . . . . . . . . . . . . . . . . . o oo o8

*Hollingsworth*: Stowmarket 1643
Laide out for the towne paide to Fyler for glassinge where the pictures were
battered . . . . . . . . . . . . . . . . . . . . . . . . . . . . . . . . . o 16 oo

*FB221/A2/1*: Stoweupland
The accounts of John Hubbard and John Keble of Howegate churchwardens for the year
ended 8 April 1645
Item received of Phillipp Enfeild for the halfe p'te of the organe pipe . . . . . . 1 o1 o6
Item received for the halfe p'te of two surplices and a tippett . . . . . . . . . o o9 o3


UGGESHALL, Dunwich Deanery
Bod. MS J. Walker c.1, fol. 271; see also Holmes, *Suffolk Committees for Scandalous Ministers*,
79–80.

The incumbent of Uggeshall, Lionel Playters, was ejected in Summer 1644. About sixty
years later his son wrote a brief note of what happened, including the following description
of the de-Laudianising of the church:

That before the Sequestration aforesaid so had & obtained [*sic*], Henry Crowfoot and others by the assistance and councill of the said Sequestrators did pull up the railes in the
chancell of Ugshall church & tooke the brasses from several gravestones & levelled the east
end of the Chancell & in levelling thereof they did take up a pott of nere two hundred
peeces of gold which they did carry away which the said Lionell did make challenge to and
in or nere which place the said Lionell had interred severall chilldren & buried the said pott
of money there himself.

[The three sequestrators were Thomas Crowfoot, Nicholas Anderson, William Ellis. All
three of these were also witnesses against Playters, and presumably from his parish, as no
doubt was Henry Crowfoot. There is no reason to doubt the broad thrust of this second-
hand account, though it seems from the contemporary case book of the Committee which
ordered Playters' sequestration that the churchwardens had removed the rails on a previous
occasion; in response, Playters 'gave out some threatninge speeches' against the churchwardens and 'required them [the churchwardens] to have them forthcominge at their
perills', which may mean that he enforced replacement of the rails, until their final removal
by 'Henry Crowfoot and others'.]

★ WALBERSWICK, Dunwich Deanery  (Journal entry 233)          SRO(I) FC185/E1/2
A chapelry of Blythburgh where the Walberswick parish books were kept. The running
head of the Walberswick section in Gardner's *History of Dunwich* reads 'Blythburgh', so
everything has conspired successfully to confuse historians into thinking these are the
accounts for Blythburgh.

Pd that 8 of Aprill 1644 to Mr Dowson that cam w'th the troopers to o'r
    church about takinge downe of Images & Brasses of grave stones . . . . . . 0 06 00
Pd that day to others for taking up the Brasses of the Stones before the officer
    Dowson came . . . . . . . . . . . . . . . . . . . . . . . . . . . . . . 0 01 00
And the next day to Edwards and Pretty [carpenter] taking down 26 Cherubs . . 0 06 10
Received the 26 of Aprill 1644 of John Trappit, with the Consent of the
    paryshners, for 2 Bellowes, and wooden Stofe [stuff] from the Organs . . . 0 06 08
Received this 6 of January 1644 [nine months later] from out of the church
    40 li weght of brasse which Nurse the glasyer of Sou[thwo]ld offered 3d
    20b per li [3½d. per pound weight] per me John Barwicke . . . . . . . . . 0 11 08

The following are of interest:

Paid to John Prety the 7 of March 1650 for Rashing out [erasing] the King's
    Arms in our Church . . . . . . . . . . . . . . . . . . . . . . . . . . . 0 01 00

1663
Paid for glaseing the church, to John Eade . . . . . . . . . . . . . . . . . . 5 00 00
Paid for drink with the glasers . . . . . . . . . . . . . . . . . . . . . . . . 0 01 00
Paid for cooules [coals] and broume for the glasers . . . . . . . . . . . . . . 0 02 03
Paid for lime and heare [hair] for the Church . . . . . . . . . . . . . . . . . 0 03 08
Paid for Irons, to John Robaordes, for the Church . . . . . . . . . . . . . . . 0 05 06

1674
It' for the King's-Arms, with a frame, & the brenging whome, and put it up . . 1 01 06

WATTISFIELD, Blackbourn Deanery              SRO(B) FL668/5/9/72

Wm Hassell and John Wyard Towne wardens chosen 29 Nov 1644

August 23 p'd the glassye for his worke for the church for lead & glasse as
    appeares by his bill . . . . . . . . . . . . . . . . . . . . . . . . . . . 4 11 06
This is the only considerable sum spent on such work in the period. Unless the dating of
the document heading is wrong (if, for example, this were retrospective for 1643–44) then
this might reflect very delayed repairs to earlier iconoclasm.

WENHASTON, Dunwich Deanery            SRO(I) FC189/E5/8

25 Apr 1641 to 10 Apr 1642
Sums for glazing total . . . . . . . . . . . . . . . . . . . . . . . . . . . . 0 18 11

10 Apr 1642 to Easter 1643
To glazing Nov 6 . . . . . . . . . . . . . . . . . . . . . . . . . . . . . . 0 06 00

Easter 1643 to Easter 1645
Ite' Layde out to the men w'ch cam to breake downe the pictures in the glasse
    windowes . . . . . . . . . . . . . . . . . . . . . . . . . . . . . . . . 0 05 00
Ite' Layde out to removinge of the topp of the funte & orgaines out of the
    church . . . . . . . . . . . . . . . . . . . . . . . . . . . . . . . . . 0 00 06

Easter 1645 to Easter 1646
To a mason for paving the church . . . . . . . . . . . . . . . . . . . . . . . 0 02 06
To Thomas Mannocke for glazing . . . . . . . . . . . . . . . . . . . . . . . . 0 06 04

WESTLETON, Dunwich Deanery                                    SRO(I) FC63/E1/1

The accounts survive for 1643–44, 1644–45 and 1645–46 and show little total income and expenditure in any of them:

|          | Income   | Laid out |
|----------|----------|----------|
| 1643–44  | 2  13  07 | 1  09  00 |
| 1644–45  | 3  14  07 | 2  00  01 |
| 1645–46  | 1  02  00 | 1  05  06 |

In the last year the first item of expenditure is the largest of any in those years by far:

Imprimis for mendinge the glass winddows . . . . . . . . . . . . . . . . . . . . . . . 0 15 00
Item paid to Savadge for iij new Iron boults used aboute the Church
windowes . . . . . . . . . . . . . . . . . . . . . . . . . . . . . . . . . . . . . . 0 02 00

WEYBREAD, Hoxne Deanery                                    SRO(I) FC99/E1/1

1639–40
Item to Rochester for pluming the church leads and glazing . . . . . . . . . . 1 00 06

John Fulcher and Richard Meene churchwardens to 8 June 18 Ch. I, [i.e. 1641–42]

It'm to Rochester for takeinge downe scandalous pictures in the church
windowes & for new glasinge the same . . . . . . . . . . . . . . . . . . . . . 0 16 00
It'm for wood to John Greene that Rochester used . . . . . . . . . . . . . . . 0 01 00

John Barbar and John Tuthill churchwardens to 25 April 19 Ch. I, [i.e. 1642–43]

Item for our charges at Laxfield at the returne of the names of the person subscribing to the order of Parlia' . . . . . . . . . . . . . . . . . . . . . . . . . 0 02 00
Item for our charges at Laxfield when we received Instructins concerning the
weekly collection for the Parl' . . . . . . . . . . . . . . . . . . . . . . . . . 0 02 00

The accounts of James Meene junior and Samuell Meene Churchwardens to 24 April Ch. I, [i.e. 1644]

Item to Rochester for glazing the church windowes . . . . . . . . . . . . . . 0 07 00
Item to a sheete of Parchment and for wrighting the covenant in it . . . . . . . 0 02 06
It'm to Mr Verdin [sic] for demolishing and taking away onlawfull things
upon our church windowes, and in other parts about our church being
authorised hereunto by the Earle of Manchester . . . . . . . . . . . . . . . 0 05 00

Items sold in 1651
Two brasses w[or]th 3s. 6d. & also for the little bell in the chest wh' was then
sould . . . . . . . . . . . . . . . . . . . . . . . . . . . . . . . . . . . . . 0 05 06
So much lead as cam to 1s. 6d.

For Rochester the glazier, see our commentary on the Journal entry for Metfield (number 269).

★ WOODBRIDGE, ST MARY, Wilford Deanery (Journal entry 68)        SRO(I) FC25/E1/1

Henry Usherwood churchwarden for 1643
The end of the year:
For taking down the images . . . . . . . . . . . . . . . . . . . . . . . . . . 0 07 08
To John Furness for making the iron for the basin . . . . . . . . . . . . . . . 0 02 00
1658
Much work done on church in anticipation of the restoration.

# Appendix 9

# Bell damage in Norfolk and Suffolk

## *John Blatchly*

This appendix gives details of deliberate damage to inscriptions on bells in Suffolk and Norfolk. The information is discussed in chapter 6, where the sources of information are given. Parishes are presented in alphabetical order within county.

★   ★   ★

## 1. SUFFOLK

BRADFIELD ST CLARE, Thedwastre deanery
Damage to the inscription on the first bell of three, Bury made, *c.*1510. The defaced inscription read:

> + Sancta : Maria : Ora : Pro : Nobis.

IXWORTH, Blackbourn deanery
Damage to inscriptions on two pre-Reformation bells.

STANTON ALL SAINTS, Blackbourn deanery
Damage to inscription on the first bell of four, a Bury bell of Roger Reeve. The defaced inscription read:

> + : Sancta : Maria : orapronobis :

Oddly enough, the second and third bells which had prayers to St Barbara were not touched.

WESTON MARKET, Blackbourn deanery
Damage to pre-Reformation inscriptions on bells 2, 3 and 4 noted by D. E. Davy.

## 2. NORFOLK

### BRADENHAM, WEST
Rather as at South Lopham the inscription on the first bell has the two words in brackets filed off:

+ [Virginis] Egregie Vocor Campana [Marie]

This damage was recorded by L'Estrange, but the original evidence was lost when the bell was recast in 1938.

### BRESSINGHAM
The damage to the inscriptions on the first and second bells was not sufficient to render them illegible, but nothing at all remained on the third (the second and third were recast in 1922).

1: SANCTUS JOHANNES ORA PRO NOBIS

2: SANCTA ANNA ORA PRO NOBIS

### COSTESSEY
The third bell here is from an unidentified church, bought second-hand from Osborne of Downham in 1800. A cross and 'Petrus' have been removed, leaving just:

Ad Eterne Ducat Pascua Vite

The other four bells were made in 1656 and 1657.

### HARDWICK
The memorandum of Dr Shuckford, rector here, 16 September 1743, records that the inscription on a split bell, then being recast and rehung, was AUE GRACIA PLENA. Perhaps Gilley removed the word 'MARIA'.

### LOPHAM, SOUTH
Inscriptions on bells 2 and 3 damaged; on the fifth only the middle word remains from:

[+ Virginis Egregie] Vocor [Campana Marie]

### PULHAM, ST MARY THE VIRGIN
Pre-Reformation inscriptions on bells here said by L'Estrange to be erased, but no details given under the entry for that church. Only the fourth bell is pre-Reformation, and Paul Cattermole thinks it a casting fault rather than iconoclasm.

### ROCKLAND ALL SAINTS
The fifth bell at Norwich, St Michael Coslany was bought second-hand in 1841 from Rockland All Saints. The bell is damaged, the word 'Ora' erased, leaving:

+ Sancta Maria _____ Pro Nobis

### SHIMPLING
The first bell here has been sold, so that bells 2 and 3 said to be damaged by L'Estrange have become numbers 1 and 2.

1: + Fac Margareta : Nobis Hec Munera Leta

by Richard Brasyer I (probably 1466)

2: + Missus de Celis : Habeo Nomen Gabrielis

probably by the second Richard Brasyer
Isaac Pennington, Regicide, lived here and would have wished the church cleansed.

## STOW BARDOLPH
Damage was done to early 17th century inscriptions on bells 3 and 6 by filing off about half the letters but no complete words. Here no Popery needed to be expunged. This rather sets the damage here apart from that along the Norfolk–Suffolk border. With a little more ingenuity no doubt the letters left could have carried suitable Puritan sentiments.

3: [+] NON : VE[RB]O : SED : [V]OCE : [R]ESO[NA]BO : [D]O[MI]N[I] : LA[VD]E[M] . 1601.

6: [CA]E[L]O[R]V[M] - - CHR[I]STI - - [P]LACEAT - - TIB[I] - - RE[X] - - [S]ONO - - [I]ST[E] - - 1612

## THARSTON
Pre-Reformation inscriptions on Bells 3 and 4 damaged by most of the letters being filed off leaving on 3 just 'NOS' and 'MERIT' and on 4 'alen' of Magdalen.
Thomas Trunch, intruded into the vicarage here, influential also at Wacton.

## TIVETSHALL ST MARGARET
The inscription on the fourth bell damaged by erasure of the words in brackets:

+: SCE : [EDMUNDE] : PRO : ME : [INTERCEDE] :

## WACTON, GREAT
Pre-Reformation inscriptions on Bells 2 and 3 mostly filed off. A photograph by Paul Cattermole shows part of the familiar:

AVE MARIA GRACIA PLENA

but the first 'A' of Gracia to the 'NA' of Plena has been totally removed.

# Appendix 10

# Discovering visitors
# in churchwardens' accounts

## *Trevor Cooper*

Despite Dowsing's tally of more than 250 churches, he visited fewer than half the parish churches in Cambridgeshire and Suffolk, and none in the other counties of the Eastern Association. For churches outside his Journal, church-wardens' accounts are a prime source of evidence for the period, although they typically survive in only a few percent of cases for the crucial years 1641–45.[1] This appendix explores what information they can yield about iconoclasm and iconoclasts. The results are used in chapters 6–9.

Unfortunately, the surviving accounts are not very helpful in checking whether Dowsing forgot to record any churches he visited: first, because so few accounts survive, and secondly because churchwardens do not always trouble to record the names of visitors. In fact, for one reason or another Dowsing's name rarely appears anywhere in parish records even in churches he did visit. He is named by churchwardens just once;[2] and though his name appears in another type of document (a receipt) at Risby, it is only as an absent Captain to his deputy Crow – and then he is put down as 'Browning'.[3] His name appears nowhere in the parish records of Cambridgeshire, despite his widespread activity there, although his surname (but not his Christian name) are preserved in Royalist propaganda.[4] Nor does his name appear in parish records in other counties. Indeed, if his Journal had not survived, and we relied on parish records, the Great Destroyer would be Verdon, with six mentions in Suffolk, followed by Captain Gilley in south Norfolk, with four.[5]

The paucity of parish records emphasises the importance of the Journal as a primary source for iconoclasm of the period. Of the more than 250 parish churches which Dowsing visited, just fifteen (6%) have surviving parish evidence. For almost all the others, the Journal is the *only* evidence of icono-clasm during this period, and without it there would be no record of what was damaged, by whom, or when.[6]

## Types of evidence in churchwardens' accounts

Where accounts have survived, we find three types of evidence for iconoclasm (see Table A10.1). Sometimes there is payment to an external agent (a 'visitor'), often, but by no means always, 6s. 8d. Somewhat surprisingly, of the fifteen sets of accounts which survive for churches in Dowsing's Journal, in only six is there such a payment. The other nine accounts record no such payment – the visitor is invisible. The point is important, because it means that, without the Journal, we would not have known that an external agent arrived at those churches to promote iconoclasm, even though the accounts survive.

This invisibility is rather peculiar. If Dowsing was routinely charging a fee, why does its payment not always appear in the accounts? Part of the answer is probably that the fee is sometimes there, but not explicitly identified. For example, in the accounts at Cambridge, Holy Trinity there is a payment 'for pulling downe pictures in the church 8s. 2d.', and this sum, 1s. 6d. more than what Dowsing typically charged, might have been – or have included – his fee. At Baldock in Hertfordshire the typical half-fee of 3s. 4d. is paid out by the churchwardens, for 'pulling downe the glasse in the church by Manchesters comand'; a visitor may have brought the Earl's command and taken the normal half-fee, or the command may have been issued in writing and the work given to a local labourer – it is impossible to say.

But it should not be assumed that a fee was charged at every church. For one thing, the Parliamentary Ordinance said that enforced removal of mate-rial after 1 December 1643 should be at the expense of the parish, and Dowsing may have charged for his visit only when he had to do some work on behalf of the parish. Charging on this basis would explain the lack of fee at some churches, such as Ipswich, St Peter's (76) and Gamlingay (172), but not at all (such as Kelsale, entry 61). Unfortunately the Journal is of little help in deciding whether this was in fact Dowsing's policy, as its records of fees are sporadic and erratic (which could be due to its history of transcription).[7]

An alternative possibility – that Dowsing and other visitors saw themselves as fining churches for full or partial non-compliance – is suggested by the receipt given by Crow, one of Dowsing's deputies (page 82), which shows that he regarded the 6s. 8d. as a reduced version of the fine of forty shillings set by Parliament. Sir John Wentworth at Somerleyton also regarded the sum as a fine, for not having dealt with the glass (appendix 8). So it may be that churches where a genuine effort had been made were not charged; perhaps Dowsing and his colleagues took *ad hoc* decisions affected by how hard the parish had previously tried to fulfil the Ordinance, how poor it was, and the persuasiveness and godly character of the churchwarden or other representative.

A final intriguing possibility is that Dowsing normally charged, but was willing to take brass for the war effort in lieu of cash. This fits well enough with eight of the nine examples of invisibility, particularly nicely so at Walberswick (233) where he *did* charge and where it was the parish who later sold the brass.[8] Taken as a whole, our evidence, though rather sparse, suggests that more than one of these explanations might have applied.

Although these nine accounts for churches visited by Dowsing record no payment to a visitor, all have *some* evidence of iconoclasm. Five have payments for destruction, typically payments for taking down glass, and this payment for iconoclasm constitutes the second type of evidence, here occurring in slightly under a third of the cases. The third and weakest form of evidence is where the accounts merely show payment for significant repair and replacement. Such payments can be indicative of destruction, but do not prove it. Payments of this nature are recorded at the remaining four churches which Dowsing visited.

Thus in the accounts of these fifteen Journal churches, which we *know* were visited, we find slightly over one third (6) recording an external agent visiting the church,[9] a third (5) describing destruction with no mention of a visitor, and the remainder, about a third (4), merely showing repairs. In considering accounts outside the Journal, the relative unlikelihood of finding mention of payment to visitors needs to be borne in mind – when there is a visitor, the experience of the Journal churches suggests there is only a one in three chance (very approximately) of finding evidence for this in surviving accounts. And the accounts themselves survive in a small percentage of parishes – five or six percent in Suffolk, for example. Assume for a moment that one hundred churches outside the Journal were all visited by an agent: then on average one might expect to have just six sets of accounts surviving today, only two of which might mention a visitor. If one was a little unlucky, it could be fewer than this.

In Suffolk, for example, there are seventeen churches outside the Journal for which accounts survive (Table A10.1). All of these show one of the three types of evidence for iconoclasm, and the evidence has broadly the three-way split we would expect if all seventeen had been visited. As these parishes are not recorded in Dowsing's Journal, any visitor was presumably one of Dowsing's deputies, as discussed in chapter 6. The other counties of the Eastern Association are discussed in chapters 8 and 9, and the pattern of evidence is similar, suggesting that visitors were present in all counties.

Table A10.1 *Number of cases of each type of evidence for iconoclasm in churchwardens' accounts,[1] 1643–44, by county*

| County | Type of evidence of iconoclasm | | | | |
|---|---|---|---|---|---|
| | *Visitor* | *Damage* | *Repair* | *None* | *TOTAL* |
| Suffolk – in Journal | 3 | 3 | 3 | 0 | 9 |
| Suffolk – not in Journal[2] | 8 | 5 | 4 | 0 | 17 |
| *Suffolk – TOTAL* | *11* | *8* | *7* | *0* | *26* |
| Cambs – in Journal[3] | 3 | 2 | 1 | 0 | 6 |
| Cambs – not in Journal | 0 | 0 | 1 | 0 | 1 |
| *Cambs – TOTAL* | *3* | *2* | *2* | *0* | *7* |
| Essex[4,5] | 4 | 4 | 1 | 0 | 9 |
| Herts | 2 | 1 | 2 | 0 | 5 |
| Hunts | 0 | 1 | 2 | 0 | 3 |
| Lincs | 0 | 1 | 0 | 0 | 1 |
| Norfolk[6] | 6 | 4 | 3 | 3 | 16 |
| *All Counties – TOTAL* | *26* | *21* | *17* | *3* | *67* |

The columns show the number of accounts with a given quality of evidence for iconoclasm during 1643 and 1644. For any one set of accounts, only the highest grade of evidence is listed. So if one set of accounts shows evidence both of a visitor being paid and evidence of deliberate damage, only the first of these is counted above.

1. Summary churchwardens' accounts have been excluded, as they do not include relevant evidence.
2. Thomas Denny appears in the accounts of Earl Soham, Suffolk his home parish. If we had not known from other sources of his association with Dowsing, he would not have been categorised as a visitor. For purposes of strict comparability this entry is placed under 'Damage' rather than 'Visitor'.
3. The accounts for Croxton, Cambridgeshire have been lost, but apparently recorded payment of 6s. 8d. to a visitor. These accounts are included in the above.
4. The accounts for Writtle, Essex have been included. They survive only to September 1643, but include glass repairs.
5. The decision of the vestry at Braintree, Essex has been included (the churchwardens were to pay).
6. Norwich, King's Lynn and Great Yarmouth accounts have been excluded, as being special cases.

# Appendix 11

## The chronology of iconoclasm outside the Journal

### Trevor Cooper

The legal chronology for our period begins on 28 August 1643, with the Parliamentary Ordinance for the 'utter demolishing, removing and taking away of all Monuments of Superstition or Idolatry'. Parishes were supposed to comply by 1 November, after which they could be fined; after a further month, on 1 December, a Justice of the Peace could enforce the Ordinance.

Dowsing was commissioned some three weeks after this final deadline, on 19 December; the bulk of his activity was complete by April 1644, though he continued to make occasional forays until October 1644. In May of that year, soon after the time his Journal starts to peter out, Parliament found it necessary to issue a second Ordinance.

As made clear in Dowsing's commissions, many parishes in the Eastern Association had failed to meet Parliamentary deadlines. To correct this situation, we know that Dowsing began work in December 1643. When were his deputies, and the visitors to other counties in the Eastern Association, active? – were they cleansing churches in parallel with him, or did they arrive on the scene later, perhaps when the enormity of the task became apparent? Did the second Ordinance of May 1644 have any impact on levels of activity?

In assessing how parishes reacted, we encounter a difficulty with church-wardens' accounts (the most common form of parish record), in that they normally only record the *year* when expenditure was incurred, and not the exact date. For these accounts the year typically ran from Easter to Easter, when new churchwardens were elected. Thus the year starting Easter 1643 and ending Easter 1644 encompassed the passing of the Ordinance, the deadline for compliance, and the majority of Dowsing's iconoclasm. When no

Table A11.1 *Number of churches with recorded iconoclasm: by year*
*(Churches visited by Dowsing are omitted)*

| Year (Easter to Easter) | Visitor recorded | Iconoclasm, but no mention of visitor |
|---|---|---|
| 1643 – 1644 | 9 | 10 |
| 1644 – 1645 | 12 | 4 |

Both this and the following table omit Great Bromley (visit recorded April 1645, perhaps in error), and Swaffham (year ran from November to November). The Cratfield accounts run from 24 March: they have been treated as though they run from Easter.

precise date is given it can be difficult to relate the expenditure in one parish to what was happening on the wider stage, although expenditure is often given in the order in which it was incurred, and this can be helpful.

Let us deal quickly with the special cases of Norwich, King's Lynn and Great Yarmouth – special because, as discussed in chapter 8 above, these Norfolk towns acted on their own initiative. Norwich set up a committee in January 1644, Great Yarmouth had taken down glass by then, and King's Lynn got under way a month later. Of these three towns, then, only Great Yarmouth may have acted as quickly as the Ordinance required; the other two delayed until early 1644.

The tables (A11.1 and A11.2) summarise the evidence for the date of iconoclasm outside these three towns, for all the counties of the Eastern Association. The first table shows that churchwardens were recording iconoclasm before and after Easter 1644, regardless of whether the accounts mention a visitor. The second table analyses the nineteen cases, representing four counties, where the churchwardens' accounts do provide a precise date for damage, or enable us to pin it down reasonably accurately.[1] At just two of these are there signs of any effort to act in time for the November deadline.[2] The remainder record damage ranging in date from February 1644 to August that year.[3] The overall impression is therefore one of activity from early 1644 through to mid or late summer, with no distinction between churches which record a visitor and those which do not.[4]

This overall range of dates matches what we know of the work of individual visitors beside Dowsing. Captain Gilley is found at work before Easter 1644 and in May; Francis Jessup is also found working before Easter 1644 and again in June; Verdon is most probably the deputy who accompanied Dowsing in early April, and is recorded again in May and in August.[5]

Table A11.2 *Number of churches with dated iconoclasm: by month*
*(churches visited by Dowsing are omitted)*

| Year | Month[1] | Number of churches with iconoclasm |
|---|---|---|
| 1643 | November | 2 |
| | December | 0 |
| 1644 | January | 0 |
| | February | 2 |
| | March | 2 |
| | April | 1 |
| | May | 8[2] |
| | June | 2 |
| | July | 1 |
| | August | 1 |

1 Where there is a range of possible months, the latest.
2 Half of the eight visits in May are those of Captain Gilley.

The most likely interpretation of the evidence is that iconoclasm did not get firmly under way until early 1644 and that there was probably little if any agent activity after late Summer 1644 (when the latest of the visitor payments occur: this assumes that the date of the visit to Great Bromley is anomalous, and is not part of the general pattern). This is more or less the period when Dowsing was active, and lends useful support to the notion that he was the instigator, or a typical representative, of what was happening elsewhere in the Eastern Association.

# Appendix 12

## How much glass was destroyed?

### *Trevor Cooper*

How much glass was removed in 1643-44 in East Anglia? One way to answer this question is to use Dowsing's records. Although he is sometimes teased about the huge number of 'pictures' he records, it is only at three parish churches that his numbers approach the incredible,[1] and here they might anyway be mistranscriptions, perhaps the result of his botched and blotched attempts to correct his notes.

In the majority of parish churches his numbers are quite reasonable, as shown in Table A12.1. This indicates how frequently Dowsing recorded a given number of pictures. For example, at 51 churches he recorded between 1 and 9 pictures. It can be seen immediately that in the majority of his churches he records fewer than 30 pictures.[2]

The table uses these figures to calculate the percentage of Dowsing's churches having different numbers of pictures destroyed. For example at nearly one fifth of his churches (18%) he records no pictures at all. At 20% he recorded between 1 and 9 pictures. By adding up the first five rows, we can see that in about three-quarters of his churches (77%) he records fewer than 40 pictures. If one believes that sometimes when he records no pictures this is down to inefficiency on his part, rather than a deliberate null return, the overall picture does not change greatly – in this case 77% of churches have less than 45 pictures (extreme right hand column of table).[3] From his own figures, then, we can see that Dowsing was responsible for the destruction of a few tens of stained glass pictures in each typical church, with about a quarter of his churches having more than this, in some cases substantially more.[4]

How are we to visualise this? The number of pictures in a single window varies enormously. The famous surviving east window at East Harling

Table A12.1 *Frequency distribution of 'pictures' in Dowsing's churches*
*(i.e. number of Journal entries where Dowsing records a given number of pictures)*

| Number of pictures recorded by Dowsing[1] | Number of Journal entries where Dowsing records this number of pictures | | | |
|---|---|---|---|---|
| | *Including* Journal entries where Dowsing does not mention pictures | | *Excluding* Journal entries where Dowsing does not mention pictures | |
| | No.[2] | %[3] | No.[2] | %[3] |
| 0 | 44 | 18 | — | — |
| 1–9 | 51 | 20 | 51 | 25 |
| 10–19 | 57 | 23 | 57 | 28 |
| 20–29 | 26 | 10 | 26 | 13 |
| 30–39 | 15 | 6 | 15 | 7 |
| 40–49 | 15 | 6 | 15 | 7 |
| 50–59 | 5 | 2 | 5 | 2 |
| 60–69 | 11 | 4 | 11 | 5 |
| 70–79 | 3 | 1 | 3 | 1 |
| 80–89 | 5 | 2 | 5 | 2 |
| 90–99 | 2 | 1 | 2 | 1 |
| 100–199 | 9 | 4 | 9 | 4 |
| ≥ 200 | 6 | 2 | 6 | 3 |
| *TOTAL* | *249* | *100%[4]* | *205* | *100%[4]* |

The table includes private chapels, but not college chapels.

1  Where Dowsing uses 'diverse' we have assumed 10 pictures; where 'many', we have assumed 20 pictures.
2  The number of churches at which Dowsing recorded the given number of pictures.
3  The percentage of the relevant churches which this number of churches represents.
4  Rounding errors mean that this column does not total exactly 100%.

(Norfolk) has five lights each containing four pictures, with space in the upper lights for another twenty or so smaller images (Plates 63 and 64). This dramatic and imposing window would thus have provided Dowsing with some forty 'pictures', a reasonably typical number.[5] Smaller windows, or those done to a different school of design, would hold fewer pictures, nine or even fewer.[6] We may assume, then, that in the majority of his churches Dowsing was destroying all the pictorial glass in a few typical windows, or in one rather good east window. In about a quarter of his churches he was destroying two or three times as much as this, or more.

This is to some extent an underestimate of the amount of glass destroyed at the time, because, as Dowsing make clear, in many cases some glass had been dealt with before his arrival. For example, at Haverhill (Journal entry 42) he says that '200 [pictures] had been broke down afore I came'.[7] This means that his own score is less than the total amount broken during the period.

Another approach to estimating the amount of glass destroyed is to look at the money spent on making good the damaged windows. In the note at the end of this appendix it is argued that each £1 spent on glaziers' repairs probably paid for about 30 square feet of glass (though it is emphasised how approximate this figure is). In Table A12.2 we show the amount spent on glass repair at those individual churches where we have records,[8] again sorted into ascending order.[9] This expenditure is for glaziers only: we have ignored iron bars, cramps, stone-work and suchlike.

This table show that some three-quarters of churches spent less than £6 (equivalent to 180 square feet, say), whilst the bottom half of the churches spent less than £2. 10s. 0d. (75 square feet).[10] The middle 50% of the churches spent between £1 and £5. 19s. 11d. (between 30 and 180 square feet). These figures too, are probably an underestimate, as they ignore expenditure after 1645.

If the whole window was having its glass replaced, and we assume, for the sake of argument, a typical aisle window to be three lights totalling 6 feet wide and 9 feet high, then this would suggest a few windows per church being filled with new glass. Or we may assume that a typical glass image occupies something between three and ten square feet, which would imply that most churches were having a few tens of pictures replaced with plain glass.

In a quarter of the churches, the amount was much greater than this, the most extreme example being King's Lynn where £100 was spent, equivalent, perhaps, to 3000 square feet – surely a complete reglazing.

It is pleasing that, despite the approximations and assumptions involved, the two approaches give reasonably similar answers, and allow us to assume that typical churches had glass equivalent to several full windows destroyed at this time; in some churches, the amount that went was much greater.

Table A12.2 *Frequency distribution of expenditure on replacing and repairing glass*
*1643–45 in parish churches in the Eastern Association*
*(i.e. number of churchwardens' accounts recording a given amount of expenditure)*

| Amount spent | Square footage[1] | Number of accounts[2] | %[3] |
|---|---|---|---|
| ≤ £0.19.11 | ≤ 30 | 13 | 25 |
| £1 – £1.19.11 | 30 – 60 | 7 | 13 |
| £2 – £2.19.11 | 60 – 90 | 8 | 15 |
| £3 – £3.19.11 | 90 – 120 | 2 | 4 |
| £4 – £4.19.11 | 120 – 150 | 3 | 6 |
| £5 – £5.19.11 | 150 – 180 | 6 | 12 |
| £6 – £6.19.11 | 180 – 210 | 4 | 8 |
| £7 – £7.19.11 | 210 – 240 | 3 | 6 |
| £8 – £8.19.11 | 240 – 270 | 2 | 4 |
| £9 – £9.19.11 | 270 – 300 | 2 | 4 |
| ≥ £10[4] | ≥ 300 | 2 | 4 |
| *TOTAL* | | *52* | *100* |

1  The estimated square footage of glass replaced, based on the assumption that £1 expenditure paid for 30 square feet; see text.
2  The number of churches with churchwardens' accounts recording this level of
   expenditure.
3  The percentage of our sample which this number of churches represents; rounding
   errors mean that this column does not total exactly 100%.
4  Omits King's Lynn (expenditure of £100).

## *A note on the cost of replacing glass in East Anglia, 1643–45*

The cost of replacing glass in East Anglia in 1643–45 can be obtained almost
immediately from our churchwardens' accounts which quote the price per
square foot of new glass. New glass cost 7*d.*, or sometimes 6*d.*, per square
foot.[11] This would imply about 35 or 40 square feet of glass would be obtained
for each £1 of expenditure.

In some cases, glass quarries were used. These seem often to have cost 1*d.*
each, on one occasion dropping to 8*d.* the dozen.[12] Each £1 of expenditure
might therefore have bought between 240 and 360 quarries. Quarries are
diamond shaped, with typical corner-to-corner measurements of 6 inches by

4 inches. Thus twelve quarries would cover about one square foot, and something between 20 and 30 square feet of coverage would be obtained for each £1 spent.

(A comparison with modern prices is of interest. Today one might pay £60 per 12 bespoke quarries, which is (very approximately) one-half day's wages for a skilled worker. In East Anglia in 1644 a glazier seems to have cost between 1s. 0d. and 1s. 6d. per day,[13] so the equivalent for half a day would be between 6d. and 9d., which would indeed buy up to a dozen quarries at the price of 8d. per dozen – a pleasing correlation.)

The complicating factor is how much labour was included in these standard costs. On the most likely reading of the evidence, these costs may have included actual fitting, though it is difficult to be certain. However, even if not, it seems that fitting costs may have been a relatively small extra charge. For example at Louth, the total bill for inserting 588 quarries suggests that labour of 8s. 4d. may have been added to the basic cost of £2. 9s. 0d. to reach a total of £2. 17s. 4d. Thus labour seems to have added some 17% to the bill in this case. If labour was not normally included in the standard charge for quarries, a 20% uplift might therefore be a reasonable estimate to allow for it. Then each £1 spent on quarries would buy between 16 and 24 square feet, including labour for fitting, instead of the 20 to 30 square feet quoted earlier.

The position is similar in the cases where the glass is measured in square feet. At Dennington, for example, the expenditure of £6. 1s. 6d. included (probably) labour to fix both 171 square feet and 130 quarries. If we assume that material and labour for the quarries cost 13s. 0d. (using an uplift of 20% on the basic cost of 1d. per quarry to allow for labour), then the 171 square feet of glass cost £5. 8s. 6d. overall.[14] Again the labour uplift is quite small, and suggests that £1 of expenditure paid for about 30 square feet, rather than the 35 to 40 square feet mentioned earlier.

In summary, each £1 of expenditure might buy anything between 30 and 40 square feet of glass, or between 16 and 30 square feet of quarries, the range depending on the base cost and one's assumptions about labour. For this appendix we have assumed taken a middle value, that £1 covered 30 square feet.

# Appendix 13

# How many brasses were damaged?

## Trevor Cooper

This appendix compares antiquaries' reports of the seventeenth and eighteenth century to estimate what proportion of monumental brasses had their inscriptions lifted by William Dowsing and his colleagues, and how many were left untouched.[1] The rate of brass destruction across different counties of the Eastern Association is also compared.

The results are summarised in Table A13.1. The first part of this appendix explains how the results were calculated, and the second part comments on individual counties.

The work presented here was carried out after the bulk of the book was settled, and has not been seen by the other contributors. Consequently the results are not fully integrated into the earlier chapters. They are, however, incorporated into the discussion of brasses in chapter 7, and into the discussion of individual counties in chapter 9.

It is important to appreciate that these results are tentative, and need to be tested by those who can spend more time tracking down the history of individual brasses. This requires wider use of the documentary sources for individual counties, including full use of manuscript sources, as this study has largely been restricted to printed accounts. It also needs a thorough local knowledge of the monuments themselves.

### Principles

The ideal way to find out how many brasses were damaged during 1643 and 1644 would be for an antiquary in a given county (the 'early' antiquary) to have noted a random sample of brasses and their inscriptions in 1642, and for the same brasses to have been systematically investigated for damage in 1645 (by the 'later' antiquary). Then, if the sample was large enough and truly random, the proportion of brasses which had not been damaged in the intervening few years could be estimated (the 'surviving' brasses – in this appendix we will use 'surviving' to mean 'surviving to be recorded by the later antiquary', whether or not the brass survives today).

In practice there are a range of difficulties with this approach. The antiquaries taking the early 'sample' visited as much as forty years before Dowsing, so some damage or destruction may have taken place after their visit but before he arrived. Furthermore, the sample collected by these individuals was probably not random (for example, Weever's collections seem to have been biased towards churches in towns, and the Chorographer's towards brasses to be found in chancels). It is also worth noting that, unlike later antiquaries, the early ones typically record only a small proportion of inscriptions, and our sample size is therefore usually quite small, reducing the statistical reliability of the results. In a very small number of churches, however, the early antiquaries collected rather large numbers of inscriptions; this can be a problem, for if these few churches happened to be visited, or happened to avoid iconoclasm, it could swing the overall averages unfairly; we have dealt separately with these cases. We have also excluded very major towns as the pattern of iconoclasm in these towns (for example, Norwich)[2] does not necessarily match the county as a whole, and each would require a special study.

A further complication is that the early antiquaries did not always distinguish terribly clearly between brasses, other forms of monuments, and inscriptions in glass; nor can we always be sure when they are describing a single brass with multiple inscriptions. On top of this, one of our early sources, Weever, is sometimes inaccurate, so some of his brasses seem to disappear simply because they were never there.

We are not interested in later brasses, as these did not contain prayer clauses, and therefore have ignored brasses later than 1540. Unfortunately the early antiquary did not always record the date; in this case, we discard his record. (It is important not to fill in missing dates using the later antiquary, because this would bias the results towards survival. It would be possible to fill in missing dates from a third, independent, source, though for reasons of time we have not attempted this. It would increase the sample size significantly.) As a final irritant, one cannot always rely on earlier antiquaries to say whether or not there was a prayer clause, so it is difficult to assess whether or not brasses with prayer clauses suffered differently from those without.

So much for the early antiquaries. In most cases, there was then a considerable gap after Dowsing's visit – up to a century – before a later antiquary

Table A13.1 *The survival rate of brass inscriptions from the first half of the seventeenth century to the first half of the eighteenth century*

| County | 17c antiquary | | 18c antiquary | | Comment |
|---|---|---|---|---|---|
| | *Name & when operating*[1] | *No. of brass inscr's*[2] | *Name & when operating*[3] | *Percent of brass inscr's surviving (approx)*[4] | |
| Cambs | John Layer, (1630s) | 60 | William Cole, (1740s) | 15% | South of county has high rate of destruction. Few examples to north of county. |
| Suffolk | Choro. (c.1600) & JW (1631) | 68 | Thomas Martin, (1720s onwards) | 20% | High rate of destruction, including in north of county (supporting idea that much of Suffolk visited). Earlier antiquary (Blois, 1660) found more surviving, so much disappeared between 1660 and 1720s onwards. |
| Herts | JW (1631) | 62 | Nathaniel Salmon (1728) | 30% – 35% | High rate of destruction. Examples widespread so whole county probably visited. |
| Essex | JW (1631) | 50 | Nathaniel Salmon (1740) | 30% – 40% | High rate of destruction. Examples widespread so whole county probably visited. |
| Norfolk | Choro. (c.1600) & JW (1631) | 105 | Francis Blomefield, then Charles Parkin (1739–1775) | ?50% – 75% | Evidence hard to interpret – Blomefield and especially Parkin may have silently used earlier Choro & JW records. Results perhaps show iconoclasm in south, little in north. |

This table summarises the rather complex evidence in the appendix.

1 This column gives the name of the seventeenth-century antiquary, and the date at which he collected or published his records. In this column 'Choro.' is the anonymous Chorographer (for whom see the Bibliography), and JW is John Weever, whose *Ancient Funerall Monuments* was published in 1631.

2 This column shows the number of brass inscriptions with dates of 1540 or earlier recorded by the antiquary or antiquaries in the previous column. Undated brasses have been ignored.

3 In this column the name of the eighteenth-century antiquary is given, together with the date at which his records were published (or, in the case of Martin, collected).

4 This column shows what percentage of the specific inscriptions recorded in the early seventeenth century were in place to be recorded by the later antiquary.

re-examined this original selection of brasses at all systematically. This means, of course, that any damage to the original sample may have been due to wear and tear, accident or vandalism, and not to deliberate iconoclasm. A further problem is that some later antiquaries are more interested in genealogy than in recording the precise state of monuments, so will quite happily quote the earlier antiquary without saying they are doing so. As discussed below, this is a particular problem in Norfolk. This biases apparent survival rates upwards.

Sometimes a later antiquary is not quite as systematic as he might have been, and overlooks a brass which we know from other sources happens still to be extant today: on these occasions, one must treat the brass as 'not surviving', otherwise we would again bias the survival rate upward (because there is no equivalent correction for non-surviving brasses).

Finally, it would be useful to know whether effigies survive even when inscriptions have been lost. The problem is that, when a brass has lost its inscription, identifying it from the remaining effigy or the arms alone requires careful, painstaking work. We have not attempted this.

In short, the sources do not make this type of numerical analysis very easy. Someone else carrying out the same work would certainly emerge with different numbers. But they would probably not be radically different: the broad pattern of results is likely to be reasonably robust.

The results can be used to explore patterns of survival across an area, and this is the thrust of this appendix. It is tempting to use them to ask whether individual churches suffered iconoclasm, but very great care must be taken in doing this, as the survival rate for an individual church will be the result of many chance factors. For this reason, before discussing individual churches in this appendix, the possibility that the results occurred by chance has first been assessed statistically.

We have looked at Suffolk and Cambridgeshire, where Dowsing visited, and compared the results with Norfolk, Hertfordshire and Essex. Most space is devoted to Cambridgeshire where the materials are more amenable, and where the comparison between the north and south of the county and the Isle of Ely is of some interest.

## Results

In Cambridgeshire and the Isle of Ely, Layer recorded 35 churches with brasses of the appropriate date (see Bibliography for Layer and other antiquaries). It is unfortunate that 29 of these, almost all of them, are for the south of the county. The sample in the north of the county, and the Isle of Ely, is thus too small to analyse formally (though the results are consistent with the suggestion that Dowsing did visit the north, where 1 of 8 inscriptions survived, and did not visit the Isle of Ely (2 of 3)).

In the south of the county, just 8 out of 60 Layer inscriptions survived to be found by Cole, and 2 of these were lingering in a church chest (Babraham (Journal entry 35), Swaffham Bulbeck (entry 34)), whilst at Linton (entry 36) and Hinxton (entry 182) the inscription survived but the prayer clause had been removed. This would suggest that in the area known to be covered by Dowsing, the loss rate of inscriptions was more than 80%.

This is an enormous rate of loss. Is it reasonable?[3] To check this, we looked at Cole's records for every church (not just those for which Layer had made notes) to see how many completely empty indents he recorded, how many effigies (or coats of arms) surviving but without inscriptions, and how many brasses with inscriptions. There are problems with this approach, but it will give an indication.[4]

In looking at the results, we must first deal with two churches, Isleham and Girton, with 9 and 8 surviving inscriptions respectively, an exceptional number (Table A13.2). These two (discussed in depth in chapter 3) are the only churches in the county with more than 4 inscriptions surviving in Cole's day, and alone they account for nearly one third of the surviving inscriptions. They are clearly outliers (in the statistical sense), and should be excluded from the general analysis, otherwise the history of survival in these two churches alone will have an inordinate effect on the overall result.

With these two excluded the results are clear cut. Cole found an estimated 37 brasses with inscriptions in Cambridgeshire, 39 effigies and/or coats of arms *without* inscriptions, and 173 empty indents. Brasses with their inscriptions thus formed a mere 14% of the whole. This figure is remarkably close to our estimate that more than 80% of the inscriptions mentioned by Layer had

Table A13.2 *The nature of brass survivals in Cambridgeshire,*
*based on the records of William Cole*

| | Churches | Inscrip's | Effigies | Indents |
|---|---|---|---|---|
| **Isle of Ely (excluding Ely)** | | | | |
| Wilberton | 1 | 4 | 2 | 0 |
| Haddenham | 1 | 3 | 0 | 2 |
| March | 1 | 3 | 0 | 1 |
| Wisbech | 1 | 1 | 0 | 4 |
| Rest of Isle of Ely | 23 | 2 | 0 | 2 |
| *TOTAL Isle of Ely* | *27* | *13* | *2* | *9* |
| **North Cambs.** | | | | |
| Isleham | 1 | 9 | 0 | 1 |
| Girton | 1 | 8 | 1 | 0 |
| Rest of North Cambs. | 27 | 10 | 3 | 56 |
| *TOTAL for North Cambs.* | *29* | *27* | *4* | *57* |
| **South Cambs.** | | | | |
| Churches in Journal | 79 | 4 | 8 | 13 |
| Churches not in Journal | 11 | 23 | 28 | 104 |
| *TOTAL South Cambs.* | *90* | *27* | *36* | *117* |
| *TOTAL Cambs.* | *119* | *54* | *40* | *174* |
| *Ditto, excl. Isleham & Girton* | *117* | *37* | *39* | *173* |

Table A13.3 *Brass inscriptions in Suffolk surviving to 1660*

|                                                      | In Journal? | |
| ---------------------------------------------------- | --- | --- |
|                                                      | *Yes* | *No* |
| Number of churches in sample[1]                      | 15  | 18  |
| Number of inscriptions recorded by 17c antiquaries   | 37  | 31  |
| Number of these inscriptions surviving to 1660[2]    | 19  | 14  |
| Approximate percentage surviving                     | 50% | 45% |

1  Three churches with exceptional numbers of brasses are dealt with separately and are not included in the above analysis (see text).

2  That is, survived to be recorded by William Blois and/or Thomas Martin.

disappeared by Cole's time. Clearly, by the 1740s, the great majority of brasses in Cambridgeshire had indeed lost their inscriptions.

Furthermore, the figure of 14% surviving brasses applies across Cambridgeshire, regardless of whether or not the church appeared in Dowsing's Journal, as one would expect if Dowsing visited the whole of the county. In the Isle of Ely, however, the pattern is very different. As shown in Table A13.2, three churches have very high rates of inscription survival, Wisbech has a low rate, and there are virtually no other indents or effigies amongst the remaining churches. This would suggest that there were rather few brasses in the Isle to start with (or, possibly, all had been cleared in an earlier reformation and the indents removed), and no major programme of iconoclasm occurred to remove the inscriptions in the 1640s, exactly as suggested in chapters 1 and 3.[5]

We can carry out one further cross-check, though its full interpretation will have to wait until we have examined the Suffolk evidence. Table A13.2 shows that in Cambridgeshire overall, the 119 churches for which we have data (more or less all in the county) shared a total of 249 inscriptions, effigies and empty indents, which is about 2 per church on average. Dowsing visited nearly 100 churches in Cambridgeshire, and it follows that if he had recorded every single brass in the same way, and if they had all been in existence, then he would have reported about 200. In fact, the number of brass inscriptions he mentions is a little over 60, rather less than we might have expected. One reason for the discrepancy is that a good number of brasses would already have been damaged or destroyed well before he arrived on the scene, either through age or iconoclasm, and thus be of no interest to him. The second reason will become clear once the Suffolk evidence has been examined.

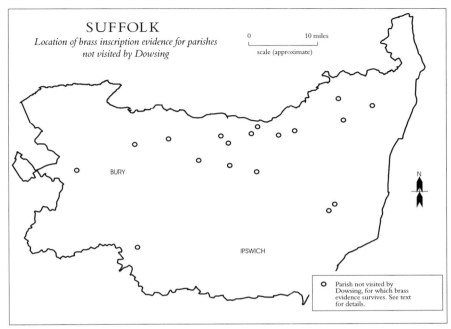

*Map A13.1* Suffolk: the location of brass inscription evidence for parishes not visited by Dowsing. See text for details.

In passing, it may be worth pointing out that in the majority of churches Dowsing visited, he did not record brass inscriptions – only in about a third of his churches does he mention them.

So much for Cambridgeshire. In Suffolk, we have two later antiquaries: William Blois who visited in about 1660, and Thomas Martin, active in the second quarter of the eighteenth century.[6]

Three of the 36 churches in our sample each had an exceptionally large number of brasses. These need to be separated out, otherwise the fate of just a few churches could affect the overall averages.[7] The results for the remaining 33 churches are shown in Table A13.3. Between them these churches had 68 inscriptions recorded by the earlier antiquaries. In the 15 churches visited by Dowsing, roughly 50% of the brasses survived. That is, even when a church is known to have been visited, only about one half of the inscriptions were damaged. It is striking that a very similar figure obtains for the 18 churches *not* in Dowsing's Journal most of which are spread over north Suffolk (see Map A13.1). As far as north Suffolk goes, these results tend to confirm the

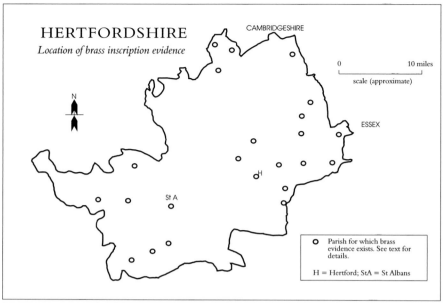

*Map A13.2*  Hertfordshire: the location of brass inscription evidence. See text for details. Note that one church is not shown, as its location could not be established with certainty.

suggestions made in chapter 6 and appendix 14 that much of Suffolk was visited by deputies, and that the majority of churches were dealt with.[8]

There is one further startling and important result. If we ignore the work of Blois, who visited twenty years after Dowsing was active, and only use the records of Martin, who visited nearly one hundred years after Dowsing, then the number of surviving inscriptions drops dramatically, down from about 50% to about 20%. In other words, whilst about 50% of inscriptions were lost in the 1640s, a good number more – perhaps 30% of those in place before 1640 – were lost between about 1660 and 1720 onwards. Churches underwent heavy reordering during this time, and burial in church became more popular, so perhaps this is not too surprising. This does, however, mean that the results in other counties will need to allow for 'natural wastage' running at, say, 30% between 1660 and the first half of the eighteenth century.

This, of course, is the second reason for the low number of inscriptions (about 60) recorded by Dowsing in Cambridgeshire, discussed earlier. In Suffolk he was noticing and destroying perhaps 50% of brass inscriptions then in existence, so in Cambridgeshire we should not have expected him to record more than 100 at most, rather than our initial estimate of 200, and even that would assume that every brass was in good condition before his arrival, which

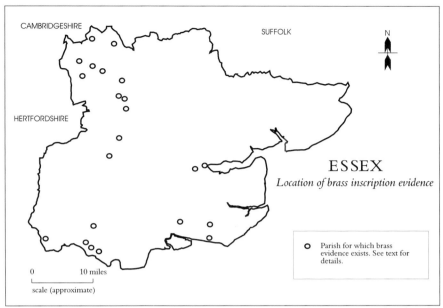

*Map A13.3* Essex: the location of brass inscription evidence. See text for details.

we know not to have been the case. His actual count of 60 now makes more sense.

We cannot do the same analysis in Suffolk, because we do not have the equivalent of Table A13.2 for Suffolk, but it is still worth comparing Dowsing's count in each county. In Cambridgeshire he found about 60 inscriptions in 100 churches, averaging 0.6 of an inscription per church. In Suffolk he found approximately 200 inscriptions over about 150 churches, about twice as many per church. However this figure is inflated by two particular churches (Sudbury, All Saints and Wetherden, entries 41 and 104) and the number of brasses would drop to about 150 if they were excluded, about 1 per church. This is still higher than Cambridgeshire. It is not known whether this difference is significant.

For Suffolk, then, our best estimate is that some 50% of inscriptions were lost during the 1640s, and a further 30% during the next 80-plus years.

In Hertfordshire, we have results for 23 churches, plus 3 churches in St Albans.[9] These 23 churches had 62 inscriptions recorded by Weever. Most churches in Weever's sample had no more than three inscriptions recorded by him, and most churches had lost some or all of them by the time of our later antiquary, Nathaniel Salmon.[10] Thus of the original 62 inscriptions,

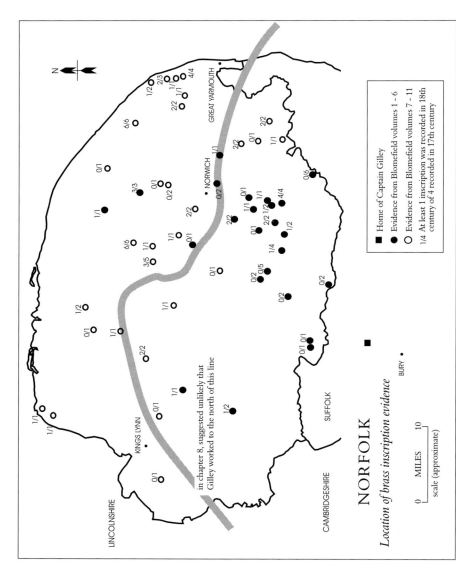

N

6/6

1/2  2/3
2/2  1/1
4/4

GREAT YARMOUTH

0/1

3/3  0/1
0/2

2/2
1/1
0/1

2/2  0/1
1/1

NORWICH
0/2  1/1

6/6  1/1
3/5

1/1
0/1

0/1

2/2

1/2

0/1  0/1
0/1  0/1

0/1

1/1

1/1
1/1

KINGS LYNN

0/1

0/1

in chapter 8, suggested unlikely that
Gilley worked to the north of this line

1/2

2/2  0/1
1/1  1/1
2/2  1/2
4/4
0/1
1/4
0/2  0/5
0/2

0/6

0/2

0/1  0/1

LINCOLNSHIRE

NORFOLK

*Location of brass inscription evidence*

SUFFOLK

BURY  ∎

CAMBRIDGESHIRE

■ Home of Captain Gilley

● Evidence from Blomefield volumes 1 - 6

○ Evidence from Blomefield volumes 7 - 11

1/4 At least 1 inscription was recorded in 18th
    century of 4 recorded in 17th century

0   MILES   10

scale (approximate)

*Map A13.4  Norfolk: survival of brass inscriptions from seventeenth to eighteenth century. See text for details.*

Table A13.4 *The survival of brass inscriptions in Norfolk*

| | Churches in sample | Inscriptions | | |
|---|---|---|---|---|
| | | $17c^2$ | Surviving[3] number | Surviving %(approx.) |
| *Early Blomefield, south of county*[1] | 22 | 42 | *15–20* | *40% – 50%* |
| South of county | 27 | 53 | 23–29 | 45% – 55% |
| North of county | 25 | 52 | 38–40 | 75% |

1  Volumes 1–6 of Blomefield's *History*; the south and north of the county are defined by means of the likely territory covered by Clement Gilley. See Map A13.4.

2  The '17c' inscriptions are those recorded by Weever and the Chorographer before 1640.

3  As elsewhere in this appendix, by 'survive' is meant 'were recorded by later antiquary', in this case Blomefield's *History*.

something between 17 and 22 survived to be recorded by Salmon (the uncertainty arises when Salmon implies that an inscription is present, but then quotes Weever). Overall, then, about 2 out of every 3 brasses were lost between the 1630s and the 1720s, over much of the county (see Map A13.2).[11]

In Essex, there are 50 inscriptions in Weever's sample, spread among 22 churches over much of the county (shown in Map A13.3). Of the 50 inscriptions, between 16 and 19 survived to be recorded by Salmon, our later antiquary, representing a loss rate somewhere between 60% and 70%. This is the same as Hertfordshire, itself not far removed in rate of loss from Suffolk and Cambridgeshire, supporting the suggestion made in chapter 9 that Hertfordshire and Essex suffered systematic visitation.[12]

In Norfolk we run into difficulties with our later antiquary, Blomefield. In the earlier volumes of his *History of Norfolk* it is usually – though not always – clear whether an inscription survives or is copied from earlier sources; after his death the work was taken over by Parkin and a hack writer, who did not have access to his materials, and there is considerably less certainty, the later volumes in particular giving no real impression that a church has been inspected. This has been dealt with in two ways. First, we have estimated a minimum and maximum rate of survival, the difference being those cases where survival is ambiguous. Secondly, in map A13.4, which shows the minimum estimated surviving number of inscriptions, we have distinguished between the earlier, and probably more reliable, volumes of the *History*, and those that came later.

The parishes dealt with in the first six volumes of Blomefield's *History* are mainly to the south-east of Norwich, part of the territory covered by Captain Gilley (see chapter 8). This is unfortunate, as the unreliability of the later volumes makes it difficult to compare north with south. As shown in Table A13.4, there are 22 churches in these early volumes for which we have early records of inscriptions, and which lie within 'Gilley territory' (that is those shown in dark dots on the map, below the line dividing north from south); in these churches, something between 15 and 20 of 42 inscriptions survived, representing some 40% to 50%.[13] If we widen the net to include all the churches within 'Gilley territory' including those within later volumes of Blomefield, then, the number rises somewhat to something between 45% and 55% survival, possibly because the later volumes overstate survival.[14] In the north a much higher percentage, 75%, are recorded as surviving in the *History*, but it is not certain whether this is an inflated figure, arising from the *History* simply quoting the early antiquaries without acknowledgement. It is note-worthy that the overall pattern matches our argument in chapter 8 that the north of the county was not visited, and also corresponds with our assessment in Suffolk that some 30% of brasses disappeared through natural wastage in the period, though the general uncertainty about this evidence reduces its force.

In summary, we have shown that Essex and Hertfordshire lost almost as many inscriptions as Cambridgeshire and Suffolk, and that the data suggests that about 50% of inscriptions were lost in the 1640s, with a further 30% in the subsequent century. The evidence for Norfolk is less clear cut, but would support a north-south divide, with the south being visited, the north not. There are many remaining questions – for example, the survival rate of effigies, whether French inscriptions were overlooked (this is certainly the impression one gains), whether or not brasses without prayer clauses were handled roughly, and how common it was to remove the prayer clause only.

To reiterate: this is exploratory work, open to criticism and correction. As such, 'Should any Man, in such an Undertaking, aim at Perfection; to walk in the Dark without stumbling, it were to invoke the Fury of Criticks…', as Nathaniel Salmon says of the work of his predecessor in Hertfordshire, Sir Henry Chauncy. He also points out (and this is less encouraging) that Chauncy's fate was 'to have his Usefulness and his Beauties over-looked, and the Hawk's Eye of all Mankind employed to spy out his Defects'.[15]

# Appendix 14

# How many churches in Suffolk were visited?

*Trevor Cooper*

In Suffolk, churchwardens' accounts of the 1640s survive in greater quantities than in other counties in East Anglia. In particular, there are seventeen sets of accounts for churches not in Dowsing's Journal (we will refer to these as 'non-Dowsing' churches). As discussed in appendix 10, all seventeen of these churches were probably visited by external agents intent on enforcing iconoclasm. This appendix considers what conclusions for Suffolk as a whole may be drawn from this sample, taking particular account of the risk that these seventeen churches may be a biased sample, and may therefore not be representative of the county as a whole. The results are used at the end of chapter 6.

In other counties, the smaller numbers of surviving accounts means that it is not possible to generalise across the county as a whole. To put this another way, although in other counties the surviving accounts all indicate iconoclasm, it is conceivable that iconoclasm was not particularly common, and that by pure chance the churchwardens' accounts survived in churches where it occurred.

In Suffolk, with seventeen sets of accounts, this is not credible. It is in the highest degree unlikely, for example, that only ten percent of non-Dowsing parishes in Suffolk suffered iconoclasm, and that *by pure chance* each one of our sample of seventeen happened to come from that ten percent of parishes.

There are two ways to explain the fact that all seventeen accounts indicate iconoclasm. One possibility is that iconoclasm was common amongst all classes of church. Then we would, of course, expect to find it recorded in all or most surviving accounts.

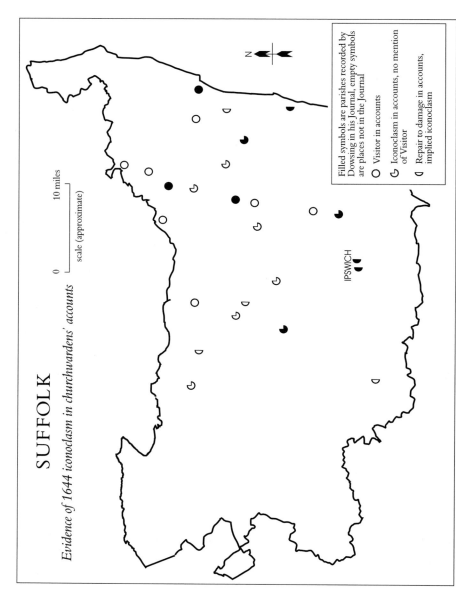

# SUFFOLK

*Evidence of 1644 iconoclasm in churchwardens' accounts*

Filled symbols are parishes recorded by
Dowsing in his Journal, empty symbols
are places not in the Journal

O  Visitor in accounts

G  Iconoclasm in accounts, no mention
   of Visitor

⌐  Repair to damage in accounts,
   implied iconoclasm

IPSWICH

N

0                    10 miles

scale (approximate)

*Map A14.1*  Surviving churchwardens' accounts in Suffolk, and their evidence for 1644 iconoclasm.

Alternatively, iconoclasm might have been relatively *uncommon*, but tended to occur at churches where the accounts subsequently survived. Perhaps, for example, visitors tended to select town churches because they were richer or easier to get to, *and also* town churches were more efficiently organised during the disturbances of the 1640s, and more systematic in the preservation of records in the succeeding centuries. Or perhaps a parish where the living was impropriated to an institution such as a Cambridge college might be more likely to preserve its accounts, *and also* might attract Laudian incumbents, or have preserved the stained glass in the chancel, and thus be more likely to be visited. In either case, surviving accounts would tend to record iconoclasm, not because it was particularly common, but because iconoclasm and survival of accounts shared the same underlying cause.

We need to decide between these two hypotheses before we can generalise from the surviving accounts.

On balance, the evidence in Suffolk is against the second hypothesis (that survival of accounts for the early 1640s goes hand in hand with iconoclasm). Firstly, a necessary part of the second hypothesis is that some churches were more liable to be visited than others. There is no evidence for this being the case, and some evidence against it. Dowsing himself did not select parishes, and found work to do at most churches, whatever their size, so there is no reason to suppose that different classes of church suffered different degrees of iconoclasm. In particular, he did not select parishes according to their church-manship. Similarly, for those three visitors (Gilley, Jessup and Verdon) for whom we have more than a single church, the impression is also of undifferentiated coverage. The same is true of the pattern of mutilated brasses found in Hertfordshire. Thus, we have evidence against the view that some churches were more likely than others to suffer iconoclasm, and this alone is sufficient to discount the second hypothesis.[1]

Secondly, an essential ingredient of the second hypothesis is that surviving accounts of the 1640s are strongly biased towards one class of church. Recent work by Andrew Foster has shown that the survival of accounts is probably never entirely random,[2] and is probably affected by a range of factors. This is a complex area, and in what follows we scout round it with a certain caution.

We have looked at three factors. First, we have explored the size of community being served by the churches with surviving accounts in Suffolk, and there is indeed a small bias towards larger communities. But the sample still retains a very good mix of small and large settlements, and it would not be reasonable to claim that the slight overweighting of towns explains the survival of accounts.[3]

Secondly, the surviving accounts are not biased towards parishes with Laudian vicars, so churchmanship is not an explanatory factor.[4]

Finally, we should also have examined the patronage of the surviving parishes, the nature of the impropriation (if any), and the size of living, and compared it with the pattern across Suffolk as a whole, to see whether or not the seventeen surviving non-Dowsing accounts are biased in any of these respects. Time has not permitted this.

It is, however, suggestive that almost all of our surviving non-Dowsing accounts are from the east of the county (see Map A14.1). Some factor must have been in play during the 1640s to create this bias. The excellent *Historical Atlas of Suffolk,* shows several east-west divides which would be worth further exploration as explanations. One which stands out is the pattern of vicarages and impropriated church livings in 1535, where the east clearly predominates (Bury Abbey to the west possessed over sixty livings, but did not impropriate them).[5] It turns out that the surviving churchwardens' accounts are somewhat overweight in impropriated livings, to an extent that is unlikely to be due to chance. However it is not clear whether impropriation *itself* made survival more likely, or whether some other factor makes survival more likely in the east of the county, which happens to be the area with a high proportion of impropriations. In either case, although there is some bias here, nearly a half of our surviving accounts are from livings which were not impropriated,[6] so this cannot be a particularly important factor linking survival of accounts to iconoclasm.

In short, although the survival of churchwardens' accounts in the 1640s in Suffolk is not entirely random, we have not found any strong biases, and where there is bias, no class of church is excluded (except those in very small communities).

Given this, and the fact that there is no evidence that there was selection of churches, the first hypothesis is more likely: that churches of different types all had similar chances of being visited, and those that were visited were not to any material extent more likely to have accounts preserved during the early 1640s than other churches.

Seventeen is a reasonable sample size for our purposes, and, as we have shown, the selection is fairly random, largely the result of history's lucky dip (though weighted towards the east of the county). Making an assumption of effective randomness, and using standard statistical tests, we can say that very probably more than 70% and virtually certainly more than 40% of churches in east Suffolk suffered iconoclasm during the period, and that much of it was instigated by external agents. In west Suffolk, too few accounts survive to have the same level of certainty, but those which are extant also show iconoclasm.

It seems that, in Suffolk, a church which survived the 1640s unscathed may well have been in the minority, perhaps a rather small minority.

# Appendix 15

# Long after Dowsing: forgery and pastiche

## *John Blatchly*

Such has been the fascination with William Dowsing and his doings since the subject became popular with antiquaries that there have been many attempts to embroider accounts of his work in East Anglian churches. One has only to address a local history society in the eastern counties on the Civil War period to be given a taste of the folklore which has grown up around the name Dowsing. Question time soon degenerates into a series of stories about men in steeple hats and long cloaks, troopers, horses, even Cromwell himself, his head and his remains, church treasures hidden away in lofts, subterranean tunnels dug in advance of visitors, and so on.

Antiquaries have not been slow to take up the challenge, and two nine-teenth century forgeries in print are described here as a warning to the unwary. The first has been widely quoted as authentic. The second would have been of value if genuine.

### *Jessup's record of his Gorleston visit*

To Francis Jessup of Beccles, William Dowsing allocated the deanery of Lothingland with Mutford, and the four parishes, Bungay, Blythburgh, Yox-ford and Ringshall. Jessup's visits are not recorded in the Journal, but he is mentioned in other genuine records at Lowestoft, Bungay and Somerleyton.[1]

Dowsing's previous editor, Evelyn White, printed a long first-person account of Jessup's supposed activity at the parish of Gorleston in his 1885 edition of the Suffolk Journal. Without saying where he found it or question-ing its veracity, he gave it this introduction:

The doings of this man at Gorleston, surpasses everything of the kind on record, and the account given here, is an example of the thoroughness, which, alas! characterised so much of the work done by these sacrilegious invaders of the churches of East Anglia.[2]

Several writers have since quoted Jessup's supposed diary entry for Gorleston. It is reproduced at the end of this appendix.

It was M. R. James who in 1906 exposed it as a forgery.[3] He showed how it could be split into 35 separate phrases each culled from almost as many different church entries in the Suffolk Journal. The forger had, for the most part, moved steadily through the Journal in search of his material; only two clauses had no exact equivalent in Dowsing, and in one of these the use of the term 'brasses' was a sure sign of a comparatively modern hand at work. James guessed that the origin of the spoof must have been fairly recent, and hoped that his readers would help him trace the culprit. But no-one did respond to the Provost of King's.

In researching the history of the piece it was not difficult to find two printed sources earlier than Evelyn White's which quote parts of the Gorleston 'entry'. The first appearance was in C. J. Palmer's *History of Great Yarmouth,* 1856, and then later in an account of the paper on the church read by John Bately of Gorleston at a British Archaeological Association visit.[4]

Paul Rutledge, then archivist of the Norfolk and Norwich Record Office, suggested the most likely perpetrator: a Gorleston man dangerously active in the 1830s, whose fanciful drawings of antiquities including a Druidical stone circle 'formerly in the parish' had misled antiquaries and archaeologists of the time. He was William Elsom Randall, described as 'Gentleman' in census returns and directories, a bachelor living with his widowed mother Dorcas in High Road, Southtown, a hamlet of Yarmouth adjoining Gorleston.[5]

The three bulky volumes of his collections, which contain about 1400 folios on assorted scraps of paper, take a good deal of wading through, not least because Randall was endlessly repetitive; he seems to have been in the grip of an obsession to make much of little (or nothing) about the parish of his birth.[6] But there in Egerton MS 2130 at page 358 in Randall's own hand on half a sheet of notepaper is the bold imposture: 'Francis Jessop's Journal Gorleston 1643', and at the foot of the passage 'v[ide]. Journal p. 36'.[7] The first phrase 'In the chancel as it is called' is an inserted afterthought, sure sign that Randall was creating rather than copying. He managed one clever touch, but only one. He included the 'Bacon's aisle' reference from Dennington (twice), probably obscure to Randall at that church, but entirely appropriate at Gorleston where on the north side there are remnants of at least two Bacon memorials including an early-fourteenth-century military brass bearing the arms of Bacon.

Despite expressing increasing scepticism about Randall's collections in a series of letters,[8] Palmer claimed to believe in them in his 1856 *History of Yarmouth* and, as we have seen, quoted the offending entry. By the 1870s, however, when his three-volume *Perlustration of Great Yarmouth* appeared, he expressed his serious reservations about Randall and the veracity of most of his manuscript collections. Palmer died in 1882 when Evelyn White will have been starting work on his edition of Dowsing's Journal; there was no one left to warn him against quoting Randall's 'transcript', which he presumably copied in full from the original.

### A fake letter mentioning Dowsing

The following letter, if authentic, would have provided important evidence that Dowsing appointed a deputy in Norfolk.

The letter was printed without preamble, reference or further comment in the second edition of the anonymous *Sketches for an Ecclesiology... in Norfolk*, (Norwich, 1846).[9] The author of this rare and slight work was the Revd [Richard] Caddy Thomas, a founder member of the Norfolk and Norwich Archaeological Society, who held the living of Brandiston, Norfolk about 1845–1850.

Tristram Craske to Mr Sheriff Tofts at Norwich

Coulshill [Coltishall], May 27th 1643

Sir—'Tis true what Phineas Puckle told of the scandalous minister at Belagh [Belaugh], and his unpurged mass-house. That godly man, to whom went the Earl's warrant for Norfolk, hath substitutes less heavenly-minded than Master Dowsing's. Peradventure thou wilt move him to the *Ordinance* having more speedy execution. Master Sherwood, albeit his fasts, is bulky, and was fain leave his cloak and baldrick at a dwelling house below the hill whereon Belagh steeple-house standeth, perked like one of the idolatrous high places of Israel. And this also reeketh foully of Superstition.

King Edward of pious memory brake down the Virgin Mary with Christ in her arms in the place prelatics call the chancel, and took away divers popish vestments, cups, platters and candlesticks. In a window S. Michael remains, together with many idolatrous; on the floor three *Orate pro animas* [*sic*]. In the aisle we saw a picture of S. Helen. The screen hath twelve apostles, their faces rubbed out by a godly trooper from Hobbies [Hautbois]; he pulled down a stoning cross. Oh! Master Tofts, the loft yet standeth. Moreover the sexton saith this malignant will not use a desk as ordered in time of the Man's father. Your servant to command, &c.   Tristram Craske.

Much here is credible. Toft was indeed Sheriff, and was heavily involved in the work of destruction in the Norwich churches and Cathedral. Livewell

Sherwood was another alderman and activist. There were also genuine Norwich aldermen with the surnames Craske and Puckle.[10]

However they had common first names, and the International Genealogical Index for Norfolk has no *Phineas* Puckle or *Tristram* Craske.[11] Nor was a scandalous priest ever named at Belaugh. Furthermore, although the language of the letter is a good pastiche, to be credible the date should be 1644.

That it is a fake is indicated in a knowing review of the 1846 edition of Thomas's book: 'Again, we think that in a plain matter-of-fact guide, an imaginary dialogue is hardly in place; and an imaginary letter still less so'.[12] There is no other letter in the book.

The three brasses at the church are still unmutilated today. The figure of St Michael in glass was still there to be seen by Blomefield, and the screen was only taken down 'in the lifetime of persons recently deceased' (in 1846).[13] In a clever and amusing passage the survival of things which might have been cleansed but were not has been given a contemporary explanation.

It is perhaps more than a coincidence that the following year Thomas Carlyle printed 35 letters to Cromwell which had been sent to him by one William Squire of Norwich.[14] Carlyle, having published *Life and Letters of Cromwell* in two volumes in 1845, accepted the Squire letters, making them an appendix to the second volume of *Life and Letters* in subsequent editions up to 1871. About that time scholars began to debate the authenticity of the extra letters; it was Walter Rye who in 1887 provided irrefutable evidence that they were fabricated.[15] Amongst a mass of evidence, he demonstrated that the forger chose unusual Christian names far more frequently than was normal for the times, as in our letter above.[16] Rye showed that Squire was certainly a hoaxer, but was less sure whether he had the skill to forge the letters themselves. He suggests that it may have been a prominent Norwich antiquary, but does not name him. Perhaps Caddy Thomas wrote 35 letters to Oliver Cromwell as well as the one to Sheriff Tofts.

### Other works based on Dowsing's activities

*Babylon Bruis'd and Mount Moriah Mended*, a pastiche, was written by two Jesus College dons and published by Heffer of Cambridge in 1948. It is in quite a different category.[17] Its intention is only to amuse whilst making some pointed comments about contemporary church interiors, and that it does with style.

An earlier Master of Jesus, Arthur Gray, wrote a ghost story 'The Necromancer' which begins with Dowsing's visit. Over the pen-name Ingulphus he published *Tedious Brief Tales of Granta and Gramarye* in 1919.[18] The story accurately quotes Dowsing's notes on the college chapel from the Journal (entry 8) and the Latin history of the college by the contemporary Fellow Dr John Sherman. Then fiction takes over.

In 1990 Radio Cambridgeshire broadcast a short story, *The Breaker*, by Graham Chainey, following Dowsing as he gains entry to a college, argues with the Fellows, and starts to smash the glass.

## Text of Randall's Gorleston forgery

GORLESTON In the chancel, as it is called, we took up twenty brazen superstitious inscriptions, *Ora pro nobis*, &c.; broke twelve apostles, carved in wood, and cherubims, and a lamb with a cross; and took up four superstitious inscriptions in brass, in the north chancel, *Jesus filii Dei miserere mei*, &c.; broke in pieces the rails, and broke down twenty-two popish pictures of angels and saints. We did deface the font and a cross on the font; and took up a brass inscription there, with *Cujus animae propitietur Deus*, and 'Pray for the soul,' &c., in English. We took up thirteen superstitious brasses. Ordered Moses with his rod and Aaron with his mitre, to be taken down. Ordered eighteen angels off the roof, and cherubims to be taken down, and nineteen pictures on the windows. The organ I brake; and we brake seven popish pictures in the chancel window, – one of Christ, another of St. Andrew, another of St. James, &c. We ordered the steps to be levelled by the parson of the town; and brake the popish inscription, *My flesh is meat indeed, and my blood is drink indeed*. I gave orders to break in pieces the carved work, which I have seen done. There were six superstitious pictures, one crucifix, and the Virgin Mary with the infant Jesus in her arms, and Christ lying in a manger, and the three kings coming to Christ with presents, and three bishops with their mitres and crosier staffs, and eighteen Jesuses written in capital letters, which we gave orders to do out. A picture of St. George, and many others which I remember not, with divers pictures in the windows, which we could not reach, neither would they help us to raise ladders; so we left a warrant with the constable to do it in fourteen days. We brake down a pot of holy water, St. Andrew with his cross, and St Catherine with her wheel; and we took down the cover of the font, and the four evangelists, and a triangle for the Trinity, a superstitious picture of St. Peter and his keys, an eagle, and a lion with wings. In Bacon's isle was a friar with a shaven crown, praying to God in these words, *Miserere mei Deus*, – which we brake down. We brake a holy water font in the chancel. We rent to pieces a hood and surplices. In the chancel was Peter pictured on the windows, with his heels upwards, and John Baptist, and twenty more superstitious pictures, which we brake; and I H S the Jesuit's badge, in the chancel window. In Bacon's isle, twelve superstitious pictures of angels and crosses, and a holy water font, and brasses with superstitious inscriptions. And in the cross alley we took up brazen figures and inscriptions, *Ora pro nobis*. We brake down a cross on the steeple, and three stone crosses in the chancel, and a stone cross in the porch.[19]

# Appendix 16

# Questions

*Trevor Cooper*

This appendix lists some of the questions raised by the book. They vary in their fundamental importance, but resolving any of them would add to our understanding of Dowsing, and the editor would be delighted to hear of any information on these or related matters. He may be contacted care of the Ecclesiological Society, at the address on the reverse of the title page, or by email via the website associated with the book, **www.williamdowsing.org**.

★ ★ ★

Can 'Dowsing Farm' in Laxfield be linked to William Dowsing? Where was Dowsing's home in Stratford St Mary? (Chapter 2.)

What is the history of the two portraits discussed in appendix 2? Was Biden a direct descendant of Dowsing?

Why did Parliament think it necessary to pass a second Ordinance in May 1644? (Appendix 5.) What factors influenced its contents?

Why did Manchester commission iconoclasm? (Appendix 6.)

What happened to the original of the Journal? (Chapter 10.)

Why are there gaps in Dowsing's Journal – what was he doing? Did he remain a member of Manchester's army? Did he visit other counties? (Chapter 1.)

Who was George Longe, who accompanied Dowsing in Cambridge? (Journal entry 1.)

Can the work of Dowsing's deputies in Suffolk be identified in surviving church fabric? (Chapter 6.)

Did the visitors recorded by name in Essex have any connection with Dowsing, or were they reporting directly to Manchester? (Chapter 9.)

To what extent could powerful local figures influence the extent and nature of iconoclasm? Compare for example James Thompson (Journal entry 148) and the Knyvetts in Norfolk, recorded in chapter 8.

Were the certificates recorded in chapter 8 used to certify compliance with Manchester's requirements for the cleansing of churches? Are there others?

We examined many pre-1643 churchwardens' accounts, but not systematically (we were concentrating on 1643–45). Does a full examination throw any further light on 1640s iconoclasm? (Appendix 8.)

What proportion of brasses had their inscriptions removed in the early 1640s, and were the effigies normally taken away at the same time? (Chapter 7 and appendix 13.)

Under what circumstances, and during what periods, was it the practice to excise prayer clauses on brasses, leaving the rest of the inscription untouched? What is the documentary evidence? What other examples are there in the Eastern Association? (Chapter 7 and appendix 13.)

We have suggested that damage to gable crosses is limited to the period 1643–45. Is this true? (Chapter 7.)

Are there any documented or validated examples of fonts being deliberately defaced before the 1640s? When were fonts plastered? (Chapter 7.)

Are there other examples of damage to bell inscriptions in the Eastern Association? (Chapter 8 and appendix 9.)

What are the factors influencing the survival of churchwardens' accounts of our period, and do they affect our conclusions about iconoclasm in Suffolk and the loss of stained glass in East Anglia? (Appendices 12 and 14.)

Have we correctly estimated the quantity of stained glass removed at this time? How much, if any, of this glass was recent or recently re-installed? (Chapter 7 and appendix 12.)

In Essex, Hertfordshire, Huntingdonshire, and Norfolk, what does a fuller examination of church fabrics and surviving documentation say about 1640s iconoclasm? What happened in Lincolnshire? (Chapters 8 and 9.)

We have found evidence that Laudian clergy may sometimes have welcomed the presence of pre-Reformation imagery, and found it liturgically valuable (see, for example, chapter 7, section on glass). Was this frequent?

# Glossary

*This glossary provides a brief explanation of words which may be unfamiliar to the general reader.*

ALTAR-WISE   The positioning of the communion table parallel to the east wall of the church, so that its short ends faced north and south. Contrast with 'table-wise', where the long side is east-west. The location and position of the altar, together with the question of its being railed in and raised on steps, were major points of issue between the different wings of the church.

CHURCHMANSHIP A term used to acknowledge different views on such matters as authority, church order, the means of grace and public worship.

CLASSIS   A district assembly of representatives from local churches, forming the first tier (above the local church) in the Presbyterian form of church government. In the mid 1640s fourteen such groups ('divisions') were created in Suffolk. In this volume membership of a classis is used as an indicator of social status and religious inclination.

COVENANT   In this context, the Solemn League and Covenant, which was an oath committing those who took it to the reformation of religion in England and Ireland and to the further reformation of Scotland, including the extirpation of both papacy and prelacy, and to the maintenance of the liberties of Parliament (Plate 16). On 2 February 1644 Parliament ordered the Covenant to be taken by all men above the age of eighteen, with local Committees taking it themselves, then passing it down to parishes. It became a test of support for Parliament.

DEANERY   A subdivision of a diocese (a bishop's area of responsibility).

EASTERN ASSOCIATION   One of many military and administrative structures set up by Parliament from the autumn of 1642. By the end of 1643 the Eastern Association comprised the counties of Cambridgeshire, Essex, Hertfordshire, Huntingdonshire, Norfolk, Suffolk and (more weakly) Lincolnshire. Its headquarters was in Cambridge. Edward Montagu, second Earl of Manchester, took over command of the Association in August 1643.

EJECTION   See 'Sequestration'.

FELLOW   In this context, the senior members of a university college. In the seventeenth century, Fellows of university colleges tended to be younger men, a fellowship not normally being regarded as a career in itself but as an upward step in the ecclesiastical hierarchy.

GODLY   A Puritan term of approval, used in this book more or less as a synonym for 'Puritan'.

HUNDRED   A secular subdivision of a county.

LAUDIANISM   A cluster of beliefs associated with William Laud (Bishop of London 1628 and Archbishop of Canterbury 1633), and Richard Neile (Bishop of Durham 1617, Winchester 1627, and Archbishop of York 1632). Those beliefs included a strong emphasis on the divinely-instituted order of bishops and of a clear authority for the Church and its ordained ministers; the necessity of restoring to the Church much of the wealth and jurisdiction taken from it at and since the Reformation; a renewed emphasis on church fittings, including altars railed at the east end of churches on raised platforms; and a greater emphasis on the efficacy of the sacraments than of preaching as a means of grace. Believed by some also to include a rejection of strict Calvinist doctrines of double pre-destination and to embrace a belief that men and women could play a part in effecting or rejecting God's offer of salvation (known as Arminianism).

LECTURER   Someone contracted to give regular sermons, frequently of a Puritan persuasion.

ORATE   See 'Prayer Clause'.

ORDINANCE   The legislative instrument adopted by Parliament after the King's abandonment of London in the spring of 1642. An Ordinance was a Parliamentary bill that had passed all its readings in the two Houses but lacked the royal assent necessary to make it an Act of Parliament.

PRAYER CLAUSE   Many, though by no means all, pre-Reformation monuments and memorials contained a request to the reader to pray for the person commemorated. This was often the first clause, 'Pray for the soul...', or in Latin *Orate pro anima....* Often there would be a closing prayer clause, appealing to God for pardon, *cuius anime propitietur Deus.*

RECUSANT   In this context, one who rejected the Church of England and continued to practise as a Roman Catholic, incurring civil penalties.

SCANDALOUS MINISTER   A minister not approved of by the local Parliamentary committee charged with enquiring into the conduct of ministers of whom complaints were made. Religious or political views typically made a minister 'scandalous'.

SEQUESTRATION   In the context of this book, the expulsion ('ejection') of a Fellow of a college or of a 'scandalous minister' from his living, and confiscation of the income. In the case of a minister, one fifth of the income passed to his wife, to prevent absolute poverty. Under powers given him by Parliament in January

1644, the Earl of Manchester organised county committees in February and March to hear evidence and pass judgement, and appoint others in the place of those expelled. At the University of Cambridge about half the Fellows were expelled during March and April 1644.

SHIP MONEY  Rate traditionally applied to coastal towns for purposes of defence. The attempt of Charles I to extend it to inland towns and impose it annually without reference to Parliament provoked considerable opposition. In this volume the level of imposed tax is used to ascertain the social status of various individuals. Someone paying seven to ten shillings is likely to have been of middling means.

SIZAR   A poor student, paying his way by 'sizing' – performing tasks for the college (such as serving at table).

TABLE-WISE   See 'Altar-wise'.

VISITOR   Normally, someone carrying out a visitation, such as a bishop or a herald. In this book the term is frequently used to refer to Dowsing and his deputies, and others instigating iconoclasm on behalf of the authorities.

# Notes

CHAPTER 1 *William Dowsing and the administration of iconoclasm in the Puritan revolution*

1. For a diagram tracing the transmission of the Journal from 1643 to this edition, see Fig. 10.1.

2. As by Aston, *England's Iconoclasts*, 74–84; Phillips, *The Reformation of Images*, 185–8; Kingston, *East Anglia and the Great Civil War*, 330–33; Rowse, *Reflections on the Puritan Revolution*, 45–9.

3. An early transcriber reported that the Suffolk Journal had been 'found in the library of Mr Samuel Dowsing, of Stratford, being written by his Father, William Dowsing'. (Iveagh MSS 435; see chapter 10, above.) The library is that discussed above, pp. 5–10. The man here identified as the iconoclast was the William Dowsing of Stratford, whose 1668 will refers to lands near Laxfield and in Coddenham and Stratford and to his eldest son Samuel, to whom he bequeathed all his books and papers. Two genealogies confirm the picture: those of Matthias Candler, vicar of Coddenham, in 1655 (BL Harl. MS 6071 fol. 358; copy in Bod. Tanner MS 257, fol. 186); and a later one in BL Add. MS 19127, fols. 126v–127r. Many other William Dowsings have been pursued through the records on my behalf by Tim Wales and this William fits all the known facts, and no other William Dowsing fits any of them!

4. It is worth pointing out that he is not the William Dausonne of Stratford St Mary in Redstone, *Ship Money Returns*, p. 209 (Redstone's transcript says Dansonne, but the original – BL Harl MS 7542 fol. 99r– is better rendered Dausonne), as the signature of William Dauson occurs in the parish books there regularly. I cannot find Dowsing in the Suffolk subsidy rolls at any point in the reign of Charles I. He can be found in Stratford in the tax records for the 1660s (e.g. PRO, E179/257/7 Free and Voluntary Gift, 1661).

5. It was John Blatchly who pointed out that the William Dowsing of Laxfield (1596–1678) usually said to be the iconoclast could not be the man and who drew my attention to the will of William Dowsing of Stratford (d.1668). This is clearly the will of the iconoclast as a comparison of the hands in the various documents used below demonstrates. The following biography owes much to the perseverance, skill and determination of Tim Wales, who scoured the PRO, the British Library and the House of Lords Record Office in search of Dowsing armed initially with little more than the will. He made several crucial discoveries, especially Dowsing's name in an Essex petition of 1642 and he took the Dedham link further than I would and taught me its significance. The oft-repeated story (e.g. as told by H. Evelyn White in *East Anglian Notes and Queries, NS*, 7 (1897–98), 5) that Dowsing was the son of a Catholic appears to be based on sloppy genealogy. A Wolfran Dowsing was involved as churchwarden and as witness in the conviction and burning of John Noyes for heresy in 1557 (Foxe, *Acts and Monuments*, 474–5). In fact, John Blatchly tells me, Wolfran Dowsing was the younger brother of our William Dowsing's great-grandfather! (See appendix 1 for brief genealogy.)

6. He may be the 'William Dowe' who appears in the Coddenham subsidy for 1621 (PRO, E179/182/476).

7. SRO(I), FB37/D1/1–2. The baptisms of the first four children are nowhere

recorded. They may have been baptised at Baylham church, nearer to the Dowsing's home; the registers there before 1661 do not survive.

8. PRO, SP16/411/307.

9. For her death, see n.56 below and p. 31 above. Dowsing's name does not appear in the list of principal inhabitants in the Coddenham vestry book, started 31 December 1641 (SRO(I), FB37/A1/1; *ex info*. John Blatchly). His move appears to coincide with the decision of Thomas Waterhouse, curate and schoolmaster of Coddenham, to emigrate to New England (Tyacke, 'Migration from East Anglia', appendix II, xi).

10. HLRO, Petitions Box 1641–42, Essex petition to House of Commons presented 20 Jan 1642. See below, n.24. There was a tenant in his house at Coddenham in 1642 (SRO(I), FB37/A1/1: Vestry Book 1641–1708; see below, n.18).

11. Irritatingly the Stratford parish registers are missing for the crucial years from 1637 to 1653.

12. PRO, SP23/211 no. 201.

13. Holmes, *The Suffolk Committee for Scandalous Ministers*, 37–8. The depositions against Lindsell were taken in early 1644 while Dowsing was away from home, so his name does not appear amongst Lindsell's accusers.

14. The Dedham records are unusually complete, and had he lived on that side of the border would surely be found amongst them. ERO(CO), D/P/26/1/2 (parish registers); D/P/26/5/1 (churchwardens' accounts); D/Q/23/5/1 fol. 47 and D/Q/23/15/1 (Dedham Free School Records).

15. HLRO, Petitions Box 1641–42.

16. See appendix 7.

17. SRO(I), Archdeaconry of Suffolk Wills, IC/AA1/98/149.

18. John Blatchly is responsible for the identification. He found reference to an Edward Ives living in 1642 'then dwelling in the House of Mr William Dowsing neere Bayleham Mill'; and a Robert Hersham in 1661 who was 'a ten[an]t to Mr Dowsing neere to Baylham Mill' (SRO(I), FB37/A1/1: Vestry Book 1641–1708). See below chapter 2 n.9.

19. Hervey, 'Suffolk in 1674: Being the Hearth Tax Returns', 231. This assumes his widow had not moved to another house in Stratford following her husband's death. No earlier return for Stratford survives.

20. PRO, PROB 11/125 fols. 68r–69v.

21. There are three Tamars in the Old Testament: (1) the unfortunate wife of Onan who seduced Judah (2) the daughter of David, sister of Absalom, victim of an incestuous rape (3) daughter of Absalom, much admired for her beauty.

22. The annotations in his library include quotations in both. Arnold Hunt of Trinity College Cambridge has commented to me that 'it is clear from his style of annotation that he copied references out of the books themselves and not from a commonplace book, suggesting auto-didacticism rather than a university-trained habit of mind'.

23. Venn & Venn, *Alumni Cantabrigiensis, pt I, to 1751*, II, 63.

24. HLRO, Petitions Box 1641–42. The Dedham identifications are based on my transcriptions from the Dedham sources listed in note 14.

25. Robert Astie, for whom see *DNB*; Matthews, *Calamy Revised*, 18, and sources there cited.

26. In the Old Testament, Bezaliel was the son Uri, son of Hur, and (ironically enough)

was a skilled craftsman in metal, stone and wood, who was appointed by Oholiab to make the furniture of the tabernacle (Exodus xxi. 1ff; xxxv. 30ff).

27. Axon, *Oliver Heywood's Life of John Angier of Denton*, 32, 47–8, 96, 134, 136, 163n. Bezaliel was the perfect Puritan – even in the shortened form he preferred to use, Beza Angier!

28. HLRO, Petitions Box 1641–42.

29. ERO(C), D/Q/23/5/1 fol. 47 and D/Q/23/15/1 (Dedham Free School Records); Shaw, *A History of the English Church during the Civil Wars*, II, 388 (the elders were John Alefounder, Henry Fenn, Robert Salmon, Robert Webb, Clement Fenn, Bezaliel Angier – three of whom are referred to in Dowsing's will).

30. *Statutes at Large* (1829), v. 513–14 (16 Car. II, cap.1); v. 648–51 (22 Car. II, cap.1).

31. For the strength of Elizabethan Puritanism in the area, see the classic account of Patrick Collinson, *The Elizabethan Puritan Movement*; and for the continuities into the Jacobean and Caroline periods, see Tom Webster, *Godly Clergy in early Stuart England*.

32. See above, p. 11.

33. See chapter 10.

34. See, for example, the copy in Dr Williams's Library, London, of George Walker's *The Manifold Wisedome of God. In the divers dispensations of Grace by Iesus Christ* (1641), which is still in its contemporary sheep (Plate 4). William Dowsing's initials are stamped in gilt in the centre of each board, with a thistle between them. (I am deeply grateful to Mr Arnold Hunt for drawing this volume to my attention.) I am told by John Blatchly that the six volumes of Fast Sermons in Ipswich were thus stamped until clumsily rebound earlier in this century.

35. Marginalia in his copy of *Eikon Alethine* (1649), 75. See below, n. 50.

36. SRO(I), Archdeaconry of Suffolk Wills, IC/AA1/98/149. This reveals that he gave all his books to his eldest son except for this commentary, which he perhaps left to his wife to comfort her in her distress! For some interesting comments on Caryll's *Commentary*, see McGee, *The Godly Man in Stuart England*, 235–6.

37. Marginalia on a sermon in Dowsing's six-volume collection of Parliamentary Fast Sermons in Ipswich School (henceforth, *Parliamentary Sermons*, I–VI). *Parliamentary Sermons*, III, no. 8 (Cornelius Burges, *The Vanity and Mischief of the Thoughts of a Heart Unwashed*, preached 30 April 1645), title-page. See below, n.58.

38. Ibid.

39. See above p. 11 and below n.91.

40. Copy in Cambridge University Library, Syn.8.54.172.

41. Bod. Tanner 942 (2). Dowsing acquired the English translation by J. Veron, published in 1551.

42. The title-page only is in the photocopy collection in the Ames Collection of Title-pages in the British Library. I am grateful to Arnold Hunt of Trinity College, Cambridge and David Pearson of the British Library for assistance with this collection.

43. Dr Williams's Library, London, (3029.D.24).

44. Dowsing's copies of Robinson and Dighton are bound together with two other of his pamphlets in Dr Williams Library, London, (564.B.30). The title-pages with their characteristic comments are printed in Harris and Jones, *The Pilgrim Press*, plates 11–13.

45. Copy in the British Library, (C.12.d.1). This had been published in 1548 and

Dowsing acquired it in 1638. I am grateful to Patrick Collinson and Arnold Hunt for drawing it to my attention.

46.  *Parliamentary Sermons*, III, no. 5 (W. Goode, *The Discovery of a Publique Spirit*, preached 26 March 1645), p. 8. See n.58.

47.  Marginalia in his edition of Polybius, now in the Houghton Library at Harvard.

48.  Marginalia in his edition of *A Diamond Most Precious* (Folger Library), at p. 43. The work he calls *The Destruction of Troy* (*Parliamentary Sermons*, III, no. 8, p. 25) is almost certainly Sir Thomas Wroth's translation of Book 2 of the *Aeneid* (1620).

49.  Marginalia in his edition of *The History of Polybius the Megalopolitan* (1634), now in the Houghton Library at Harvard. See also *Parliamentary Sermons*, II, no. 9 (S. Marshall, *The Song of Moses*, preached 15 June 1643) p. 38.

50.  Marginalia in his copy of *Eikon Alethine* (1649), p. 75, transcribed by Deedes, 'Further portraiture of Dowsing'.

51.  From a reference in a letter drafted on the blank page of a sermon. But he might have been referring back to the previous sermon. See above, p. 11. The letter is drafted onto the imprimatur granted by Henry Elsynge, clerk to the Parliament, for the publication of Jeremiah Whitaker's *Christ the Settlement in Unsettled Times*. (*Parliamentary Sermons*, VI, no. 3. See below, n.58.)

52.  His marginalia show he owned editions printed in 1610 and 1641. For reference to a third edition, that of 1576, see *Parliamentary Sermons*, V. no. 21 (Lazarus Seaman, *Solomon's Choice*), at p. 41.

53.  *The History of Polybius the Megalopolitan*, copy in the Houghton Library, Harvard University. I am grateful to Paul Hopkins for transcribing the marginalia for me while the book was on sale at Sotheby's in 1988. The title-page and a memorial on the annotations can be found in the Sotheby catalogue for the sale of books on 21–22 July 1988 at lot no. 10. The translation of Polybius was by Edward Grimston, nephew of Harbottle, for whom see p. 11 above and n.92 below.

54.  Discussed in C. Deedes, 'Further Portraiture of Dowsing'.

55.  Ibid.

56.  Now in the Folger Shakespeare Library in Washington D.C. Dowsing noted: 'I r[ead] this booke 6, 7 June 1640, a month want 2 day after my wives death. I have cause to eat my bread with ashes' (referring to Psalm cii. 9). He clearly now needed to learn how to direct the servants!

57.  See the discussion by C. Deedes, 'A portraiture of William Dowsing'.

58.  These are the six volumes in the Old Town Library of Ipswich, which is kept in the Headmaster's study of Ipswich School. For its arrival there in 1725, see Blatchly, *A History of the Old Town Library of Ipswich*, 49. See also appendix 3 above. I owe an enormous debt of gratitude to Dr John Blatchly, former Headmaster of the School, for telling me about this collection and for making the sermons available to me in the Cambridge University Library in 1987 and again in 1991.

59.  One sermon is missing from 31 Mar 1642, together with nine of the ten published for the second half of 1642. My comparison of the remainder is against the list printed in Wilson, *Pulpit in Parliament*, 239–46.

60.  A total of 25 sermons before the Lords, mainly for the period from October 1644 to May 1646, and mainly bound together as volume I.

61.  Mainly bound together in volume II.

62.  E.g. *Parliamentary Sermons*, I, no. 4 (T. Hill, *The Right Separation Encouraged*, preached 17 November 1644) or *Parliamentary Sermons*, III, no. 22 (J. Caryl, *Heaven and Earth*

*Embracing*, preached 26 January 1646).

63. See appendix 3.

64. *Parliamentary Sermons*, I, no. 11 (S. Rutherford, *A Sermon*, preached 25 June 1645), p. 34.

65. Often these references are tangential, a thought association triggered by the author. A general discussion in a tract of the biblical terms for ministers of the gospel leads to the aside 'see Latimer's Judgement in dislike of the ye priest for a minister, *Acts and Monu*' (Dr Williams Library 564.B.30 (5), *True Modest and Iust Defence of the Petition for Reformation* (1618)). Down to 1641, Dowsing always gave page references to an edition of 1610; thereafter to an edition of 1641.

66. To take a random example: on the front cover of a sermon by Francis Cheynell, *Sion's Memento* (preached to the Commons on 31 May 1643), Dowsing wrote: 'nothing from Babylon to build Zion with p. 32; scandalous & ignorant to be kept from the Lord's Supper, p. 39, 31'. On the clerk's imprimatur to the previous sermon, which he clearly had also at his side (and this too was his usual practice) he had 17 index entries including 'Pope Joane a whore'; 'separation before reformation'; 'episcopacy *iure humano*'; 'Ambrose put Theodosius fro the sacrament'; 'Romish and English liturgy'; 'graven images to be burnt'; and 'Brownisme'. (*Parliamentary Sermons*, III, no. 9.)

67. Single or double lines; words of emphasis ('observe', 'consider', 'mark well') and a drawing of a hand with pointed finger (i.e. a pilcrow) at a key passage.

68. Dr Williams's Library, London, (3029.D.24).

69. Dr Williams's Library, London, (564.B.30 (3)), pp. 1, 10, 17, 70, 73; (564.B.30 (4)), p. 9.

70. W. Cowper (Bishop of Galloway), *Three Heavenly Treatises upon the eighth chapter of the Romanes* (1609, and many subsequent editions).

71. Dr Williams's Library, London, (564.B.30 (5)), pp. 54, 190, 162, 153.

72. An acrostic of the initials of Stephen Marshall, Edmund Calamy, Thomas Young, Matthew Newcomen, UUilliam Spurstowe, five ministers who attacked the institution of episcopacy in 1641.

73. *Parliamentary Sermons*, IV, no. 18 (O. Sedgwick, *England's Preservation*, preached 25 May 1642), at pp. 24–6. There were four such plots: idolatry, superstition, ignorance and 'idoll' [*sic*] ministry.

74. *Parliamentary Sermons*, V, no. 1 (S. Rutherford, *A Sermon*, preached 31 January 1644), title-page.

75. *Parliamentary Sermons*, IV, no. 9 (S. Marshall, *A Sermon*, preached 17 November 1640), title-page and p. 35; and cf. his comments in *Parliamentary Sermons*, V, no. 8 (J. Ley, *The Fury of War*, preached 26 April 1643), title-page and pp. 41, 43.

76. *Parliamentary Sermons*, II, no. 2 (J. Burroughs, *Zion's Joy*, preached September 1641), title-page and pp. 27, 39.

77. See above, p. 10.

78. *Parliamentary Sermons*, I, no. 5 (E. Calamy, *An Indictment against England*, preached 25 December 1644), title-page and pp. 11–12.

79. *Parliamentary Sermons*, III, no. 11 (R. Byfield, *Zion's Answers to the Nation's Ambassadors*, preached 25 June 1645), title-page and p. 34.

80. *Parliamentary Sermons*, I, no. 1 (George Gillespie, *A Sermon*, preached 27 August 1645), p. 15.

81. *Parliamentary Sermons*, II, no. 10 (T. Goodwin, *The Heart's Engagement*); *Parliamentary*

*Sermons*, II, no. 11 (J. Caryl, *The Nature, Solemnity, Growth, Property and Benefit of a Sacred Covenant*).

82. *Parliamentary Sermons*, V, no. 21 (L. Seaman, *Solomon's Choice*, preached 25 September 1644), title-page and at p. 41.

83. *Parliamentary Sermons*, III, no. 2 (J. Whincup, *God's Call to Weeping and Mourning*, preached 29 January 1646), title-page.

84. *Parliamentary Sermons*, I, no. 1 (George Gillespie, *A Sermon*, preached 27 August 1645), p. 15; *Parliamentary Sermons*, III, no. 17 (F. Taylor, *God's Covenant, the Church's Plea*, preached 29 October 1645); *Parliamentary Sermons*, III, no. 26 (F Cheynell, *A Plot for the Good of Posterity*, preached 25 May 1646).

85. *Parliamentary Sermons*, III, no. 14 (J. Lightfoot, (untitled sermon), preached 23 August 1645).

86. *Parliamentary Sermons*, II, no. 28 (Hugh Peters, *God's Doings and Man's Duty*, preached April 1646). See also his approval of John Maynard's analogy that 'if a man is constrained to cut off a limbe desperately infected with a gangrene, must he therefore part with a usefull member for every little inflammation and distemper'. Dowsing notes 'Liberty of conscience granted to ye godly hinder not restraint of other' (*Parliamentary Sermons*, III, no. 4 (J. Maynard, *A Sermon*, preached 26 February 1645), title-page and at pp. 27–8).

87. *Parliamentary Sermons*, III, no. 13 (T. Goodwin, *Hope Deferred and Dashed*, preached 30 July 1645), at pp. 26–7.

88. *Parliamentary Sermons*, II, no. 6 (E. Calamy, *The Nobleman's Passion*, preached to the House of Lords, 15 June 1643).

89. How different it would have been if he cited Psalm 32:1–3. 'Blessed is he whose transgression is forgiven, whose sin is covered… When I kept silence my bones waxed old through my roaring all day long'. He clearly does give psalm 33 as his source, but there are examples elsewhere of his misremembering citations – see below, chapter 5 n.9.

90. SRO(I), C5/13/12 (Ipswich Petty Court Book 1648-1652). I am grateful to Dr John Blatchly for this reference. For the 'Engagement Controversy', see Wallace, *Destiny his Choice* and his 'The Engagement controversy', Skinner, 'Conquest and consent', and Burgess, 'Usurpation, obligation and obedience'.

91. Just possibly a reference to Hooker's *Laws of Ecclesiastical Policy*; but more likely a reference to T. Parker's *De Politeia Ecclesiastica* (1620). I am grateful to Patrick Collinson for the suggestion.

92. Presumably Harbottle Grimston jun., MP and Recorder of Colchester (where Matthew Newcomen had been born, and where his brother Thomas was a controversial Laudian minister). See *DNB*.

93. For a discussion of the way Dowsing annotated his own books, see above, pp. 6–7.

94. 'Sir, Col. 4. 1. Yet for my part I suppose its not equall that any man should take any man's booke & pull it a peces with out consent; I say no more but to offer you to 1 Cor. 16.14 with Math. 7. 12. & desire you to view Mr Calam., Mr Perkins & old Mr John Carter of Suff. on the [smudged] & if you please let Mr Grimston know what the p'ty have wrote to you that owe[n] the booke'.

95. That is, John Foxe's *Acts and Monuments* (or *Book of Martyrs*). The edition in question is that of 1610, and Dowsing's previous sentence is a close paraphrase of Foxe.

96. The letter concludes: '… A[cts] & M[onuments] edit[ion] last vol. 2 page. 669 at the end. Sir the messenger is coming away, in the eve[r] lasting armes of god I leave you

hasted March 6 desiring your earnest pray[ers] for mee & mine & all the Israell of God, your loving friend the Lord's unwo[rthy] servant William Dowsing to Mr Newco'en of Dedha' W.D.' (*Parliamentary Sermons*, VI, no. 3 (Jeremiah Whittaker, *Christ the Settler in Unsettled Times*, preached 25 January 1643), blank recto of *imprimatur.*)

97. I am grateful to John Blatchly for drawing this to my attention. It was not until 25 April that Dowsing bought the sermon onto the blank front page of which he transcribed his letter, so he must have made this copy after the original drafting date of 6 March 1643. The transcription must have been made before the sermons were bound in1646, because the binder has shaved the right hand margin, and Dowsing has replaced some of the trimmed words in the left hand margin. See appendix 3.

98. PRO, SP28/13 part II, fol. 210r. I am grateful to Dr Gordon Blackwood for this reference. See also the probable reference to him in the accounts of Samuel Moody, Suffolk county Treasurer, for the year 1643: PRO, SP28/176 pt I, p. 31.

99. The accounts were drawn up in a secretarial hand (as was normal). By a cruel stroke of fate the bottom of the document, with the signature of the accountant, is torn off, leaving just the top of the capitals. Comparison of these part-strokes are inconclusive. I am greatly indebted to Tim Wales for comparing the document against the signature on the 1642 petition.

100. The document (PRO, SP28/13 part II, fol. 210r) shows that the accounts were presented to the committee of Accounts on 16 March 1644 and agreed, or cleared off, on 20 March. Dowsing would not have needed to be present for this process.

101. In the case of cathedrals, responsibility was laid on the Dean and Subdean and in university colleges upon the Heads and Fellows.

102. Firth and Rait, *Acts and Ordinances*, I, 265–6 (Ordinance of 28 August 1643); see appendix 5 for the text of the Ordinance.

103. The commission is printed in appendix 7 above.

104. Firth and Rait, Acts and Ordinances, I, 215–18 (Ordinance of 25 July 1644); I, 309 (Ordinance of 11 October 1643).

105. Ibid., 242 (Ordinance of 10 August 1643); cf. *Lords Journal* VI, 175–6.

106. *Hist. MSS. Comm.*, *8th Report, Appendix II*, p. 59.

107. Firth and Rait, *Acts and Ordinances*, I, 371–2 (Ordinance of 22 Jan 1644).

108. See appendix 5.

109. See appendix 7.

110. Lincolnshire is mentioned in Manchester's second commission to Dowsing; his first does not name counties individually. Lincolnshire's status within the Eastern Association was always marginal and contentious (see Holmes, *The Eastern Association in the English Civil War*, 97, 103, 105–9, 130–35; and Holmes, 'Colonel King and Lincolnshire politics 1642–1646', 451–83).

111. For a full account, see above, chapter 5.

112. I base this on a careful discussion with Alex Koller of Magdalene College, Cambridge, whose PhD on seventeenth-century stained glass is nearing completion. He thinks that it is unlikely that all the glass was carefully taken down and stored (it would have left traces in the college record); or that it was whited over. He thinks that Dowsing failed to check and that benign neglect took over as official policy. I agree with him. For a further discussion of the puzzling survival of the King's College glass, see commentary to Journal entry 13.

113. The suggestion is that of John Adamson of Peterhouse, Cambridge.

114. The reference to 'cathedrals' in the plural is worth noting. He is commissioned to undertake work in the Associated Counties of Essex, Norfolk, Suffolk, Hertfordshire, Cambridgeshire, Huntingdonshire and Lincolnshire within which lay the cathedrals of Ely, Lincoln, Norwich and Peterborough, none of which he was in the event to visit. But does the commission here indicate that the original intention had been the inclusion of two or more of those and therefore of their surrounding areas.

115. For this second commission, see appendix 7 (PRO, SP16/498 no. 98).

116. On this occasion, overseers of the poor as well as churchwardens.

117. Firth and Rait, *Acts and Ordinances*, I, 425–6 (Ordinance of 9 May 1644); see appendix 5 for the text of the Ordinance.

118. See above, p. 17.

119. The best discussion of Culmer is in Aston, *England's Iconoclasts*, 84–95. Culmer seems also to have attempted to remove stained glass and other images from his own parish church, but as incumbent rather than as visitor.

120. For example, three churches in Cambridge: All Saints, Holy Trinity, and St Botolph's. For churchwardens' accounts, see appendix 8 above.

121. For example, *Querela Cantabrigiensis*, 54–8, with its famous evocation of Dowsing as one 'who goes about the country like a Bedlam breaking glasse windows... [and] compelled us by armed souldiers to pay forty shillings a colledge for not mending what he had spoyled and defaced'.

122. Journal entries 1 and 2. For a discussion of the Cambridge entries, see p. 53.

123. The likeliest explanation is that one of the two Swaffham Prior churches (St Cyriac's and St Julitta's) was a ruin and in disuse. See the notes on the entry in the Journal, no. 32.

124. See Journal entry 247. He revisited Nayland in an attempt to collect his fee (entries 48, 117).

125. See pp. 85.

126. For example, during the period 27 February to 1 March 1644. Dowsing's deputies are discussed in chapter 6.

127. For example, Walberswick churchwardens' accounts: 'paid to Mr Dowson that came with the troopers to our church about the taking down of images and brasses off the stone'. See Journal entry 233, and appendix 8 for churchwardens' accounts.

128. Bury was 12 and Kentford 25 miles into his journey. See Journal entries 107–9.

129. See Journal entries 107–9.

130. Firth and Rait, *Acts and Ordinances*, I, 425–6 (Ordinance of 9 May 1644); see appendix 5 for the text of the Ordinance. The exception is the holy-water stoup damaged in Cambridge, St Giles on 30 December 1643 (Journal entry 19). Before the second Ordinance he dealt with crosses on the fonts at Copdock (73) and Linstead (216), but he would have regarded crosses as falling within the terms of the first Ordinance. Many fonts in churches visited by Dowsing have suffered deliberate damage at some time. See discussion in chapter 7.

131. Sixteen Cambridge colleges, 98 Cambridgeshire parish churches (including fourteen in Cambridge City), and 147 parishes in Suffolk.

132. Landbeach churchwardens' accounts, entry for 1644. I am grateful to Robert Walker for this reference. See above, p. 45.

133. My italics. *Ex info.* Robert Walker (see chapter 3). His source is Palmer, *Visitation Returns*, 92–4. For more on this, see above, pp. 45–6.

134. William Cole's inventory drawn up between the 1730s and the 1760s (printed in Palmer, *Monumental Inscriptions*).

135. (1) four volumes of the inventory drawn up by the Royal Commission on Historical Monuments for the City of Cambridge, West Cambridgeshire, and North-east Cambridgeshire; (2) Pevsner, *Cambridgeshire*, and (3) on personal visits to 72 parish churches. See discussion in chapter 3, above.

136. Pevsner, *Cambridgeshire*, 412.

137. Pevsner, *Cambridgeshire*, 503, 504, 430, 451.

138. Ibid., 419; Palmer, *Monumental Inscriptions*, 143–4.

139. Pevsner, *Cambridgeshire*, 496.

140. Journal entry 252. For Crow, see above, pp. 82–3.

141. Browne, *History of Congregationalism*, 154.

142. For a discussion of this, see final section of chapter 7.

143. See chapter 6.

144. His earliest trips were Stratford-based; his later ones Laxfield- or Coddenham-based or moving between the two.

145. Trevor Cooper has suggested an alternative: that throughout 1644 he remained an officer in Manchester's army, perhaps still Provost-Marshall, and that the gaps in the Journal can be correlated with Manchester's own absences on campaign. Thus Manchester – and more importantly his army – was quartered and inactive in the first three months of the year and then was ordered to attend a rendezvous to Aylesbury on 19 April, from whence he was instructed to move to the relief of York. He remained there until after the battle of Marston Moor (2 July 1644) and the surrender of York (16 July 1644). He then made his way back into the Association. Dowsing's Journal breaks from 15 April to 17 July. That means he would have left the Association with Manchester but returned after Marston Moor but before the fall of York. The later chronology is harder to fit together. The lack of any accounts of – or mentioning – Dowsing beyond those made up to 28 December 1643 and presented in the following March make this theory less likely, but it certainly cannot be ruled out.

146. See first part of chapter 8.

147. There is a possibility that the 'Mr Dewden' who visited Great Bromley in Essex in 1644 might be Dowsing, but it seems to me unlikely (ERO D/P/103/5/4, unfol.) See appendix 8.

148. HeRO, D/P21/5/2.

149. HeRO, D/P12/5/1.

150. For example: Chelmsford in Essex, 'by the Earl of Manchester's servant'; Hornchurch in Essex, 'by command of the Earl of Manchester'. For occasional references to the work of men sent 'from the Parliament' see Banham accounts (the parish visited by Captain Gilley) and those of Saffron Walden. The accounts will be found in appendix 8.

151. For that commission, see appendix 7.

152. Early transcripts of the Suffolk Journal reproduce the model commission after the last Journal entry, as in this edition (above, p. 321).

153. See John Blatchly's essay on the deputies, chapter 6.

154. See, for example, the entry from Besthorpe in Norfolk of the expenses of the men who travelled to Norwich to appear before 'the earl of Manchester's committee', and Fritton in the same county for a similar entry. The accounts will be found in

appendix 8.

155. See second part of chapter 8.

156. See discussion in chapter 9.

157. See commentary on Journal entries 1–16, *passim*.

158. For examples from the parishes of Bardwell, Cratfield, Mellis, Metfield, Weybread, see appendix 8.

159. See Ketton-Cremer, *Norfolk in the Civil War*, 253–5.

160. See Dowsing's own entry for his visit to Barton parish church (Journal entry 176), recording the glass being hidden before his visit.

161. Cautley, *Suffolk Churches*, 23.

162. Woodforde, *Norwich School of Glass Painting*, 203–6.

163. Scarisbrick, *The English People and the English Reformation*, 163–4.

164. Aston, *England's Iconoclasts*, 7.

165. Phillips, *The Reformation of Images*, 82–3, 89.

166. The phrase is Margaret Aston's, *England's Iconoclasts*, 20 and following.

167. For examples in glass, see Haverhill (Journal entry 42), Toft (135), and Whittlesford (179). At Toft he also ordered the removal of an inscription from a bell (*ora pro, anima S[anc]tae Catharinae*), though Robert Walker informs me that the inscription is in fact still intact.

168. Patrick Collinson has pointed out to me an awkward exception to this principle: the relentless Elizabethan vendetta against crosses and crucifixes. I am not yet in a position to account for this.

169. Journal entry 81. It has been maintained that Dowsing and his colleagues took great care to remove only the offensive words of invocation, leaving the commemorative plate itself. Blatchly, 'The lost and mutilated memorials of the Bovile and Wingfield families at Letheringham', 168–94, which shows that Dowsing's deputy removed just one square foot in different sections out of a total of fourteen square feet of brass, is a splendid case study. But while that may have been his intention, it often proved difficult not to pull off the whole inscription while trying to remove part. When William Cole made his tour of Cambridgeshire churches in the early eighteenth century he found some inscriptions in parish chests where they had been cast, broken in half, in 1644, as for example at Girton (Palmer, *Monumental Inscriptions*, 66). The removal of '19 superstitious inscriptions that weighed 65 pounds' at Wetherden (Journal entry 104) may indicate weighing in prospect of a sale. For an instructive example of a man troubled about 'popery' in the church but who stopped short of condemning such inscriptions, see Salt, 'Sir Edward Dering's attack on the ecclesiastical hierarchy', 34n. For further discussion of the partial removal of inscriptions, see final section of chapter 7 above.

170. See, for example, Evans, 'Malicious Damage to Brasses', 186–91; Norris, *Monumental Brasses*, 261–3. Inscriptions in Norman French were largely ignored by Dowsing, perhaps because he could not read them (*ex info*. John Blatchly).

171. I am grateful to Professor Diarmaid MacCulloch for pointing this out to me.

172. Morrill, 'The Church of England 1642–9', 109–10.

173. Journal entry 226.

174. It is also important not to see every damaged angel roof as his handiwork. The records also yield another warning. Dowsing has frequently been accused of having his troopers damage the angel roof at Blythburgh by shooting at it. But, John Blatchly tells me, 'in 1974, in the course of restoration work, the lead shot with

which the roof angels were peppered was shown conclusively to be of a type not used before the eighteenth century. The churchwardens' book for 1761 records: "to powder and shott to shoot jackdaws of the church and steeple'"!

175. *Ex info*. John Blatchly.
176. Fielding, 'Puritan opposition to Charles I'.
177. Hughes, 'Thomas Dugard and his circle'.

CHAPTER 2 *Dowsing's homes*

1. See, above pp. 2–5.
2. Ordnance Survey Reference TM 286 737, shown there as 'Dowsing Farm'. In 1751, one John Dowsing owned an estate lying somewhat to the south-west of this building (SRO(I) HD1620/7).
3. Fisher, *The Dowsing Farmhouse Panels*.
4. Foxe, *Acts and Monuments*, 474–5.
5. Ordnance Survey Reference TM 113 526.
6. Vestry Book 1641–1708, SRO(I), FB37/A1/1.
7. Browne, *History of Congregationalism*, 368, 493. Candler was instituted on 16 December 1629. Dowsing's first four children (Thamar, Nathaniel, Abigail and Elizabeth) are not recorded in the Coddenham register. They may have been baptised at Baylham church, rather nearer to Dowsing's home; the registers do not survive for this period. All but Elizabeth died as infants. In the Coddenham register the births are recorded of Thamar (born 3 December 1626, baptised 10 December); Anne (bap. 1 June 1629); Mary (bap. 1 May 1631); Samuel (bap. 23 May 1633) – it was Samuel in whose library the Journal was found at his death in 1703; Susan (bap. 20 August 1635, died an infant); Sarah (bap. 23 September 1637), mother allegedly died in childbed.
8. See also the correspondence in FB37/A2/2 between Munro Cautley and Montagu Benson in the 1930s: the alabaster was found in 'Jourdaines' opposite the church, and suggested to be Dissolution spoil from the Cistercian cell at Coddenham which may have included buildings on that site.
9. The Vestry meetings at Coddenham are recorded in Candler's hand between 1641 and 1663. He ordered fortnightly meetings beginning on 31 December 1641, and the book opens with a list of the principal inhabitants who should never miss without just reason. Dowsing is not in the list nor is he ever recorded as present, so he had left the parish by December 1641. He did sign the church rates in 1634 and 1635, and 'William Dewson' is found in the militia list of late 1638/early 1639 (new style). (Vestry Book 1641–1708, SRO(I), FB37/A1/1.) As noted earlier, p. 3 above, by 1642 there was a tenant in his house.
10. Bildeston register, Mr William Dewson and Mrs Mary Mayhew, 16 June 1647.
11. William (*c*.1647), Susan, Priscilla, Mary, Sarah (1653).
12. Hervey, 'Suffolk in 1674: being the Hearth Tax Returns', 231.
13. SRO(I), V5/5/ 3.1 & 3.2.
14. Holmes, *The Suffolk Committees for Scandalous Ministers*, 37–38.
15. In addition the porch has several shields with I and S both separately and an IS monogram. The fact that IS here stands for John Smithe, who paid for the porch, would probably be lost on Dowsing, though as Smithe died in about 1543 (will of that date, PCC 4 Pynnyng) and there is a brass with a (harmless) inscription to William Smithe (1586), the family may still have been remembered in 1644.

16. SRO(I), FB75, D1/2. A Samuel Dowsing, probably the iconoclast's son, was Overseer in 1690 and churchwarden in 1703 (*East Anglian Notes and Queries, NS,* 1, 172).

17. Candler's father William was a schoolmaster at Yoxford. Matthias himself matriculated aged 16 at Trinity College, Cambridge in 1620, took his BA four years later, but moved to Peterhouse before proceeding to MA in 1628, three years after being ordained at Norwich. He and his wife Anne (whose father, Peter Devereux, was rector of Rattlesden) had three sons and two daughters. (Parish registers, SRO(I), IC/AA2/12/75.) The eldest, Philip, was the seventh Master (in the first eight years of its existence) of Woodbridge School, and continued his father's antiquarian collections for the county. This Philip was in turn succeeded as Master by his son Philip in 1689.

18. The first edition of Edmund Calamy's *Account of the Ministers and others silenced...* states that Candler, Vicar of Coddenham from 1629, was ejected from the living there in 1662. A. G. Matthews in his modern edition (*Calamy Revised*) sets the record straight.

19. SRO(I), FB 37 D1/1. The Cromwellian register has not survived.

20. Matthews, *Calamy Revised*; Browne, *History of Congregationalism*, 163, 607.

21. Browne, *History of Congregationalism*, 610. Shrubland Hall was the home of Francis Bacon, the only one of the three chairmen who lived in Coddenham. The classis may not have met (Browne, 162).

22. See chapter 6.

23. Quoted in Candler's entry in Matthews, *Calamy Revised*.

24. Listed and described in Blatchly, *Topographers of Suffolk*, 10.

25. For Dowsing see appendix 1; for Blomefield p. 72.

26. BL Add. MS 155520.

27. Two shields show the arms of Gillet al's Candler on one (the family was recorded by Edward Bysshe on his 1664 Visitation of the county), and, in place of arms on the other, just the surname of his wife Anne, who was a Devereux. The two shields are joined by a ribbon inscribed 'The upright shall have dominion in the morning' and knotted about two palm leaves. A final inscription states that the monument was 'erected' (indication perhaps that it was always vertical) by Thomas Essington, Esq. and his wife Anne. Two Essington memorials to children who died young, delightfully unusual in design, are in the chancel of Brightwell church, which Essington restored from a ruinous condition in 1656.

CHAPTER 3 *Dowsing in Cambridgeshire*

1. Palmer, *Monumental Inscriptions*.

2. The location of William Cole's manuscripts is described in the Bibliography.

3. Matthews, *Walker Revised*. In addition the recent survey of *The Monumental Brasses of Cambridgeshire* was indispensable (Lack *et al.*, *Brasses*).

4. Frederick Varley suggested (mistakenly) that Dowsing may have concentrated on churches served by Laudians (*Cambridge during the Civil War*, 42–3).

5. Hutton, *Merry England*, 206–9; Wedgwood, *The King's War*, 285.

6. BL Egerton 2651, fol. 141 (printed orders of the Committee of the Eastern Association, 21 April 1643).

7. Within a day, the churches are not always recorded in the order in which they were probably visited. Thus the journey for 15 March would be shorter as Steeple

Morden to Guilden Morden to Tadlow. The entries for 3 January could also be out of order if Dowsing was not heading back to Cambridge, and should perhaps read Ditton, Swaffham Bulbeck, Swaffham Prior and Burwell.

8. Discussed in the commentary to the Journal, entries 11 and 24. Other examples of early destruction and removal are discussed in appendix 11, and in the commentary on the Journal (for example Cambridge, St Botolph's (entry 21) and Cambridge, All Saints (23)).

9. *Cambridge Transactions*, II, 566.

10. The petition is a mass of rural illegibility, making Spufford's analysis difficult to reproduce (Spufford, *Contrasting Communities*, 266–9). Amongst the more legible entries can be identified several churchwardens mentioned by Dowsing, and these are detailed in the commentary to the Journal, together with information from the minutes of the Committee for Scandalous Ministers. I am grateful to Trevor Cooper for identifying, and extracting from, both sources.

11. For the college chapels, see chapter 4 and individual entries in the Journal. For evidence of glaziers' bills, see appendix 8.

12. This is discussed in more detail in appendix 12.

13. See first part of chapter 8.

14. Blomefield, *Collectanea*, 126.

15. For example, see Coles' comment on Girton, above p. 45.

16. See for example Dry Drayton, discussed p. 45.

17. There is the possibility that in north Norfolk a certificate to Manchester confirming the compliance of the parish was regarded as sufficient, and that a visit was not required (see p. 117). This seems less likely in north Cambridgeshire, close to the centre of action, and where Dowsing saw the need to visit virtually every church in the south of the county.

18. The church guide book says that there was so much to be done there that Dowsing claimed double his usual fee. But this assertion is taken from an earlier guide in which no reference is given, and the author has since died. There are no churchwardens' accounts for this church in the CRO, nor are they held at the church.

19. Cole, BL Add. MS 5804, fols. 1–4.

20. Lack *et al.*, *Brasses*, 130–33; Palmer, *Monumental Inscriptions*, 251; Pevsner, *Cambridgeshire*.

21. Lack *et al.*, *Brasses*, 86.

22. Blomefield, *Collectanea*, 2.

23. Cole, BL Add. MS 5802, fol. 48.

24. Palmer, *Visitation Returns*, 96.

25. Palmer, *Cambridgeshire Villages*, 66–7, has no episcopal instruction regarding steps or rails, indicating that they were present in 1638; compare with Palmer, *Visitation Returns*, 112, recording the absence of both some thirty years later.

26. Blomefield, *Collectanea*, 172.

27. Blomefield, *Collectanea*, 6; Cole, BL Add. MS 5805, fol. 28.

28. Cole, BL Add. MS 5805, fol. 28.

29. CRO, P104/1/1. The entry appears between those for 14 June and 22 Sep 1644.

30. Term of abuse – apostate, runaway, vagabond.

31. Palmer, *Visitation Returns*, 92, 93, 94.

32. Lack *et al.*, *Brasses*, 162–71.

33. The RCHME unpublished notes say that the rails are of the early seventeenth

century; the listing inspector thought the same. Pevsner, *Cambridgeshire*, merely has 'Jacobean'. The communion table is of the same period, and both may have been part of a comprehensive refurnishing. There are similar rails at Chediston, Suffolk (Journal entry 218).

34.  Damage to the angel roofs of East Anglia deserves study. Some, for example Knapton in Norfolk, were clearly attacked, notably the lowest and most accessible layer of figures.

35.  However Cheshire, *Dowsing's Destructions*, 77, states that at Witcham, close to Ely, the broken cross from the nave roof lay in the churchyard from 1643 until 1896 when the Vicar repaired it and replaced it on its original site.

### CHAPTER 4  *The visit to Cambridge University*

1.  For his letter, see above, p. 10.

2.  Contemporaries might have labelled the movement 'Arminian' (a theology in opposition to Calvinism) but today this is not a widely familiar term, and may over-emphasise the significance of a particular theology of grace in binding the movement together. The term 'High Church', whilst evocative, is anachronistic and could be misleading. The role of Laud is still debated. (See, for example, Fincham, *Early Stuart Church*, 10 and *passim*; Davies, *Caroline Captivity*.)

3.  Quoted in Webster, *Godly Clergy*, 178.

4.  BL Harl. MS 349, fol. 141, published in D'Ewes, *Autobiography*, I, 142, quoted in Twigg, *University of Cambridge*, 35. Lazarus Seaman, a witness against Laud at his trial, also made the point that 'none of the innovations were known or used' some ten years previously; but he was to replace Cosin at Peterhouse, and is not an impartial witness (Prynne, *Canterburies Doome*, 73–4; Varley, *Cambridge during the Civil War*, 27; Twigg, *University of Cambridge*, 103–6).

5.  Heylyn, *Cyprianus Anglicus*, 314, 315, quoted in W&C, III, 517.

6.  John Smithson's plan, R.I.B.A. Drawings Collection, Smythson No. 1/4 (1) (previously AE 5/29). The plan is discussed by Chainey, 'King's College chapel delineated', 39–40, who places it about 1609.

7.  Chainey, 'East End', 144.

8.  See Journal entry 13.

9.  The plan is BL Harl. MS 3795, fol. 18 (previously fol. 23). It was first published in Prynne, *Canterburies Doome*, 122–4, and was reproduced in Staley, *Hierurgia*, I, 93–7, whence this copy is taken. It is also reproduced in Legg, *English Orders*, lxix–lxxi (I am grateful to Margaret Aston for this reference). There is a discussion of Andrewes' practice at the communion service, considering how his chapel and its appurtenances were used, in Welsby, *Lancelot Andrewes*, 127–30, based on Andrewes' *Notes on the Book of Common Prayer* (*Miscellaneous Works*, X, 141ff). Most recently, Nicholas Tyacke has reproduced the plan of the chapel and placed it in the context of Andrewes' developing thought and practice (Tyacke, 'Lancelot Andrewes'; I am grateful to Professor Tyacke for early sight of this article). Laud had been sent a copy of the plan of the chapel by Andrewes' household chaplain (Laud, *Works*, IV, 251), and at his trial it was thrown in his face by Prynne, who claimed that Laud agreed that from it he 'took his pattern of consecrating and furnishing churches, chapels and altars' (Prynne, *Canterburies Doome*, 121). Andrewes was an inspiration to others besides Laud, including John Cosin, at this time Master of Peterhouse (Tyacke, 'Archbishop Laud', 62–4); for example Andrewes' sermons and his notes on the

Prayer Book were transcribed by Cosin (*Works*, V, *passim*).

10.   For an old but still useful introduction to these changes, see Addleshaw & Etchells, *Architectural Setting*, 120–47.

11.   Letter from Edmund Stanford (in Benedict Zimmerman, *Carmel in England*, 1899, 58 quoted in Legg, *English Orders*, lvi).

12.   Quoted in Conybeare, *Cambridgeshire*, 218. The source is not given.

13.   See commentary on Journal entry 13, for King's.

14.   The following discussion of choral services and the introduction of organs is drawn from Payne, *Sacred Music*, 93–109. The evidence for a choir at Jesus is circumstantial (purchase of organ and service books).

15.   The writer of the pro-Royalist tract *Querela Cantabrigiensis*, John Barwick, was apparently an enthusiastic member of the St John's choir. (Barwick, *Life*, 10.)

16.   Christ's introduced an organ in late 1636 or early 1637, Queens' spent more than £114 on 'the Organs' in January 1637, and by 1641 Pembroke too had 'organs with anthemes' in the college chapel 'instead of the singing psalmes'. For Christ's, see Payne, *Sacred Music,* 103–5; for Queens', BL Harl. MS 7019, fol. 78 and further evidence discussed by Payne, *op. cit.*, 105–6; for Pembroke, BL Harl. MS 7019, fol. 81 (the only evidence) and discussion by Payne, *op. cit.*, 108–9. Writing some years later, Thomas Fuller recalled that in the academic year 1633/4 'the greatest alteration was in their [the college] Chappels, most of them being graced with the accession of Organs'. He comments that 'some took great distaste thereat, as attendancy to superstition'. (Fuller, *History*, 167.)

17.   Heylyn, *Cyprianus Anglicus*, 314, quoted in W&C, III, 517.

18.   Cooper, *Annals,* III, 280–83.

19.   Cooper, *Annals,* III, 282.

20.   Heylyn, *Cyprianus Anglicus*, 315, quoted in W&C, III, 517.

21.   See detailed discussion in the commentary on the Journal.

22.   The report of 1641 is BL Harl. MS 7019, fols. 52–93. It appears to have provided the basis for certain charges against Laud a few years later (Prynne, *Canterburies Doome*, 73–4). The report has been investigated by Dr Hoyle, whose work has been relied upon for its background and date (Hoyle, 'A Commons investigation'). In our commentary to the Journal we print the report's description of each college chapel: most of these descriptions are published for the first time. Those previously printed (and known to us) are: Peterhouse, discussed by Allan Pritchard in 'Puritan charges against Crashaw and Beaumont'; Caius, printed in Brooke, *Caius*, 122–3; and King's, in Chainey, 'East end', 146. The report, and other sources, are used by Hoffman to provide a summary of Cosin's work of beautification and enrichment at Cambridge in 'The Puritan revolution'. Dr Hoyle makes extensive use of the report in his unpublished thesis, (Hoyle, 'Near Popery', especially 212–17, 249–58), to which detailed reference is made in our commentary on the Journal. The thesis summarises the liturgical changes in the chapels, placing them in the context of the theological debates of the time, and has provided valuable background.

23.   BL Harl. MS 7019, fol. 79.

24.   There is no evidence that Dowsing saw the report.

25.   The declaration of 28 June 1641 is given in Cooper, *Annals*, III, 314, quoting from *CJ*, II, 191. It applied also to Great St Mary's. The order of 9 September 1641 is quoted in full in appendix 5.

26. Bod. Tanner MS 65, fol. 273, quoted in Hoyle, 'Near Popery', 258.
27. See p. 50.
28. On 17 February, following an appeal from some members of the University a few weeks before (*CJ*, II, 939, 969). Dr Dillingham records that on 4 March 'this day surplesses were left in all colleges in Cambridge' (BL Harl. 7048, fol. 38v). For Great St Mary's, see our commentary on the Journal, entry 24.
29. For the cessation of choral services, see Payne, *Sacred Music*, 159–71. King's and Christ's removed their Laudian altars in the early 1640s. King's, Peterhouse, Jesus, St John's and Trinity hid some of the offending items from their chapels. See our commentary on the Journal entries for these colleges for details.
30. For what remained in each college, see our commentary on the Journal.
31. Frederick Varley (*Cambridge during the Civil War*, 29–45) claims that Dowsing was *only* interested in Laudian furnishings in churches and college chapels. The Journal itself lends no support to this claim for the churches, and it is refuted by the evidence of churchwardens' accounts, and the remaining physical evidence of Dowsing's visits. In the college chapels recent Laudian changes do account for a substantial proportion of Dowsing's activities, but by no means exclusively so. It should be noted that Varley is unreliable elsewhere in his comments on Dowsing: in his claim that Dowsing broke rather little glass (see appendix 12), his assertion that the first commission is some sort of fake (Varley's argument is wrongheaded), his unsupported, and from our evidence quite mistaken, statement that Dowsing's deputies could not have visited all the Suffolk churches (see appendix 14), and his claim that Dowsing chose churches whose parishes had Laudian sympathies (Dowsing's churches have the average number of ejected ministers, and not the higher proportion which would be expected if Varley was correct).
32. St John's College records expenditure on 22 March for pulling down a cross, and King's College records expenditure between 25 March and Midsummer day to 'Magistro Dowzing'; Dowsing was at work in rural Cambridgeshire at the end of March, probably returning to Cambridge at weekends. See our commentary on the Journal.
33. Barwick, *Querela Cantabrigiensis*, 17–18. According to Varley, John Barwick left Cambridge in February 1643/4, so could have had first-hand knowledge of events up to that time (Varley, *Cambridge during the Civil War*, 8–11). Dowsing only records visiting one college hall (Queens', Journal entry 4).
34. See discussion page 144 above.
35. The Cambridge churches seem to have been visited in no particular order. Dowsing did not prioritise the three churches from which Laudian ministers were ejected (St Botolph's, St Mary the Less, and All Saints), nor were those churches where the living was held by a Laudian college dealt with any earlier than the other churches. (Matthews, *Walker Revised*; for rights of presentation, see VCH, III, 123–32.)
36. Batchcroft himself was ejected in 1649, returning in triumph in 1660. (Venn, *Caius College*, 119–21; Brooke, *Caius*, 127.)

CHAPTER 5 *The arguments at Pembroke*

1. For Dowsing's commission, and for the Ordinance, see appendices 7 and 5.
2. See above, p. 11.
3. Firth, *Cromwell's Army*, 282–3, 411.
4. Venn & Venn, *Alumni Cantabrigienses*, I, 147, 174; II, 129; III, 139, 412; IV, 159, 358;

Matthews, *Walker Revised*, 84.

5. For example, 10 August 1643, from impressment; 6 January 1643/4, exemption for individual members; 18 October 1644, from the Assessment for the relief of the British armies; 16 February 1647/8, from the relief of Ireland.

6. The phrase is John Morrill's (above, p. 17).

7. For Dowsing's status see above, pp. 2–5.

8. See above, p. 8.

9. For this paragraph, see Aston, *The King's Bedpost*, especially 26–36. The quotations are from II Chronicles xxxiv, 4 and II Kings xxi. 24. Dowsing's reference is an error or mistranscription, and should be to the *second* book of Kings, probably chapter 23.

10. I have used the 1635 folio edition of *Certaine Sermons or Homilies appoynted to be read in churches, in the time of the late Queene Elizabeth*, quoting from pages 12, 13, 23.

11. Frere, *Visitation Articles*, III, 9, 16, being items number 2 and 28 of the Royal Injunctions.

12. *The Prayer Book of Queen Elizabeth* (1559), 19.

13. John Cosin, for example, in his *Collection of Private Devotions*, identified as offenders against the second commandment 'they that fancie to themselves any likeness of the Deitie or frame and make any Image, either of God the Blessed Trinitie, or of God the Father, who never appeared to the world in a visible form'. He went on to include those who worshipped 'any image whatsoever, of Christ on the Cross, Angels, Idols or Saints'. Dowsing and his spiritual companions may have found common ground on his first four points but they were unlikely to concur with the following two points about 'they who are no due worshippers of God himself'.

14. Dowsing's notes describing his confrontation show a structural similarity with Francis Quarles's 'On Soloman and the Queen of Sheba'. The Queen travels to Solomon's court having heard of his fame. Once there:

> Th'arrived Queene has Audience; moves; disputes;
>> Wise Solomon, attends; replies; confutes;
> Sh' objects; he answers; she afresh propounds;
>> She proves; maintains it; he decides; confounds,
> She smiles; she wonders, being overdaz'd
>> With his bright beams, stands silent; stands amaz'd:

15. The legal status of Dowsing's commission is examined above, pp. 12–13.

16. Aston, *England's Iconoclasts*, I, 11, 15.

17. BL Add. MSS 15672; Matthews, *Walker Revised*, 77.

18. BL Thomason Tracts, E. 80 (1), 12 (Stephen Marshall, *The Churches Lamentation for the Good Man his Losse*, 1643).

19. The pamphlet is one of those which was not dated by Dowsing. The subsequent sermon was purchased by him on 31 January 1643/4 and read on 4 February.

20. The funeral was attended by the whole House of Lords.

21. BL Thomason Tracts, E. 80 (1), 12, 13, 126, 127.

22. It should not be assumed that illiterate sections of the population would automatically be excluded from written news. In a semi-literate society the habits shaped by an oral society were likely to co-exist with the presence of the written word, and it seems probable that those who could read would pass on the information to those who could not. A plaque on an inn in Hereford today records that someone was paid to read the newsbooks aloud there when they arrived from London. I owe this example to Jim Auty.

23. Wedgwood, *The King's War*, 256.
24. Holmes, *The Eastern Association in the English Civil War*, 108–9.
25. Mullinger, *University of Cambridge*, III, 287–288.

CHAPTER 6 *Dowsing's deputies in Suffolk*

1. George Longe accompanied Dowsing at Peterhouse (Journal entry 1), and possibly Caius (3), but there is no evidence that he was involved in any other visits. As discussed under the entry for Papworth Everard (141), it is just possible that Robert Hamon was given authority to deal with a few local churches.
2. Deputies are mentioned in the Journal on the following occasions: 27 February (entry 124) and 29 February (131) (in the period 27–29 February a number of visits are described in the third person, which occurs nowhere else in the Journal, no doubt indicating that a deputy visited those churches also); 3 April 1644 (210, 212), at the start of a long tour; 22 August (252), a visit to a church already dealt with by a deputy; 30 August (267), recipient of a fine.
3. Found at the end of the Suffolk Journal. See p. 321.
4. See chapter 8 for Norfolk, and chapter 9 for other counties.
5. See p. 321.
6. PRO, SP46/134 no. 284.
7. For this and other references to the classis in this appendix, see Browne, *History of Congregationalism,* appendix IV, 607–12.
8. See appendix 10.
9. Ship Money £1. 5s. 2d. For an explanation of Ship Money, see the Glossary.
10. Samuel and Hannah Stamphord (the ph no doubt 'f') of Cretingham and Rattlesden had two daughters: Lidia, baptised 1619, married to Edmund Blomfield, and Ann (two years older) to the minister John Swayne. (This is not the Swayn mentioned in the Journal at Aldeburgh.) When Samuel's burial at Rattlesden was entered into the register in June 1637, the minister added 'a gracious, holy man'.
11. Churchwardens' accounts and other documents relating to iconoclasm quoted in this essay are referenced in appendix 8. Unless otherwise stated, records of baptisms, marriages and deaths, and quoted wills, can be found at the Suffolk Record Office.
12. Bod. Tanner MS 180. For Candler, see above, chapter 2.
13. Bysshe, *Visitation of Suffolk*, 13 and 119 respectively.
14. Two of Edmund's older siblings, Stephen and Priscilla, were baptised in 1616. Edmund himself, christened in 1619, is omitted from the 1638 muster of able-bodied men, but at three years over the minimum age should have been included (Banks, *Able Men of Suffolk*), unless he was not able-bodied or was a 'trained man', or member of a 'trained band'. (The muster was a listing by parish of men between the ages of 16 and 60 in December 1638 and the following month. The muster was in the long tradition of militia, and had nothing to do with the impending strife. The hundreds of Lothingland and Mutford are missing.) Edmund married Lidia Stamphard in 1644 and they had seven children, Lydia, Robert, Edmund, Samuel, Priscilla, John and Barnabie, four of whom outlived their father when he died in 1669 aged 50, the same year as his mother and his son Edmund; his wife Lidia outlived him. His will is SRO(I), IC/AA1/99/162.
15. We are grateful to Susan Andrews, whose research helped piece all this together.
16. Ship Money 10s. 0d.

17. SRO(I)/IC/AA1/98/149. As Justice, William Blomfield conducted civil marriages at Bildeston, but not Dowsing's second marriage to Mary Mayhew (née Cooper) there in 1646.

18. Ship Money 4s. 10d. The Mayhews of Hemingstone and neighbouring Gosbeck appear in the 1664–68 Visitation (Bysshe, *Visitation of Suffolk*, 5). Edmund and Rebecca his wife, a daughter of Richard Cock, portman of Ipswich, had nine children in the 1630s and 1640s with names which could have inspired those of the Blomfields: Anne, Priscilla, Edmund, John, James, twins Richard and Lidia, Nathaniell and Samuell.

19. John was probably the eldest son of Robert Mayhew of Wilby, whose will was made and proved in the autumn of 1638. No firm link between the Wilby and Hemingstone Mayhews has been found.

20. Holmes, *Suffolk Committees for Scandalous Ministers*, 44, 46.

21. Taylor, *The Suffolk Bartholomeans*, 8 and (probably copying from Taylor) White, *Journal*, 10. Glandfield is not recorded in the Ship Money records nor the 1638 muster (Banks, *Able Men of Suffolk*) though he was in the right age-group for the latter.

22. Holmes, *Suffolk Committees for Scandalous Ministers*, 57, 59.

23. Ship Money £1. 7s. 6d. at Linstead parva.

24. *East Anglian Notes and Queries,* First Series, 3 (1869), 91.

25. Everitt, *Suffolk and the Great Rebellion*, 16, 79.

26. SRO(I), FC193/D1/1.

27. Further consideration of the statistics will be found in appendix 10.

28. See appendix 8. The taking down, repairing and immediate setting up of the organ is surprising, given that organs were instructed to be destroyed. Perhaps it was set up somewhere else, to avoid iconoclasm. A Howard was the original donor, so possibly Framlingham Castle was its home after 1644. It may later have been put back in the church: a pre-Reformation organ was recorded there in about 1660. The present organ case is late seventeenth-century, but erected over the front of the west gallery is a substantial panel from a much earlier instrument, probably the same one removed in 1644 and put back in the church by 1660. It contains beautifully carved cherubim. (MacCulloch & Blatchly, 'An early organ at Framlingham church'.)

29. See appendix 8.

30. Dunwich deanery, unlike Dunwich hundred, does not include the parish of Kelsale.

31. For the Scroope details see Weever, *Ancient Funerall Monuments*, 768–9. The Jettors suffered heavy fines for their recusancy.

32. See appendix 8 for reference.

33. Gillingwater, *Historical Account of Lowestoft*, 282.

34. In Spring 1644 Knyvett was in London (see p. 112). Was Rouse free at this time?

35. Extract from the parish register in Lees, *Chronicles*, 242–3.

36. He married Susan Clubbe, single, at Athelington. The Francis Jessup, tailor, who was married at Thrandeston in 1623, paid Ship Money of one shilling, and made his will there in 1679, cannot be our man.

37. See appendix 8 for reference.

38. *Monumental Brass Society Bulletin*, 48 (June 1988), 312–14.

39. Illustrated in Cautley, *Suffolk Churches*, 342.

40. Bungay is not recorded in the Ship Money records.

41. See Journal entry 238 for further details on Brook.

42.  The case of William Keeble, Rector of Ringshall, appearing before the Committee for Scandalous Ministers, makes interesting reading (Holmes, *Suffolk Committees for Scandalous Ministers*, 95–103).

43.  Ship Money 2s. 0d. at West Stow, where Crows flourished. The West Stow registers record the births of successive John Crows in 1569, 1625, 1627, and 1665, all but that of the deputy. He is listed as Jo: Crowe at West Stow in the 1638 muster list, and was thus at least sixteen years old at the time (Banks, *Able Men of Suffolk*). His wife Grace died in 1666, and John in 1670. His son John, born 1627, married another Crow, Dorothy, daughter of Theodore and Mary, of Ingham, at Westley in 1663.

44.  See above, p. 70. This is the only evidence that Crow moved from West Stow to Haverhill, and the coherent sequence of entries in the West Stow register (previous footnote) would suggest that, even if he did move, he was still based at West Stow. The Haverhill register is no help in clearing this up, as it does not begin until 1677 and after only four years of entries there is a gap until 1699.

45.  SRO(B) W1/127/109 (will) and In.3/16/147 (inventory). Westhropp appears under Hundon in the 1638 muster list (Banks, *Able Men of Suffolk*).

46.  See above, p. 70.

47.  Richard Almack told Wodderspoon by letter in 1844 that he possessed the original marriage settlement (Bod. Suff. Top. d. 19, fol. 61b). Margaret was baptised in 1622.

48.  There is no Thomas Denny at Earl Soham in the 1638 muster list, but there is one at nearby Marlesford (Banks, *Able Men of Suffolk*).

49.  See p. 321.

50.  See above, p. 67.

51.  Work was being carried out at nearby Mendlesham church in late April, suggesting that it too may have been visited some time before (see appendix 8).

52.  He is also found in the 1638 muster (Banks, *Able Men of Suffolk*).

53.  SRO(I), FB 155/E2/4.

54.  SRO(B), In.3/10/178. Alexander Ouldis married Ann, daughter of Peter Person, at Wherstead in 1638. Their sons Alexander and John christened children at Hoxne between their father's death and 1671, showing that the family base had shifted from Thorndon to the other side of Eye. Joan Corder suggests (personal communication) that Alexander may have been a member of the armigerous Oeils family, Huguenots from Brussels and merchants of London in the Visitation there of 1633. Such a background would certainly dispose Ouldis to sympathise with Dowsing's aims; the only clue to his religion in his inventory is slender: '3 great Bibells with some other small books' worth one pound.

55.  Did Dowsing in Stow deanery have special authority to include the Canterbury peculiar Hadleigh?

56.  The will of John Smythe asks for burial before Saint Sunday, (a still unresolved puzzle in hagiography). A year after his decease his grave was to be covered with a stone price 20s. 0d. (Registered copy of will at SRO(I), IC/AA2/12/75.)

57.  See appendix 14 for details of the argument.

CHAPTER 7 *Brass, glass and crosses: finding iconoclasm outside the Journal*

1.  Except where otherwise stated, all parish records used in this chapter will be found in appendix 8. Parishes referred to in this paragraph: Dennington, Metfield, Weybread, all in Suffolk; Banham, Swaffham, Bressingham, all in Norfolk; Great St Mary's and All Saints, both in Cambridge; Waltham Holy Cross, Essex.

2. Unnamed parishes referred to in this paragraph: Walberswick, Lowestoft, Somerleyton, all in Suffolk; St Albans, St Peter's, Hertfordshire.
3. See above, p. 15
4. Aston, 'Puritans and iconoclasm, 1560–1660' discusses this survival, the reasons for it, and the seventeenth-century Puritan reaction. I am grateful to Margaret Aston for stimulating and informative discussion of this and many other points.
5. BL Add. MS. 15672, fol. 8r.
6. White, *Century*, 6, 13.
7. White, *Century*, 42. Martin was parson both of Doddington (White has 'Dunnington') in Cambridgeshire and Houghton-Conquest in Bedfordshire. It is not clear which is here referred to. For his work at Queens', see the commentary to Journal entry 4.
8. See p. 137.
9. Holmes, *Suffolk Committee for Scandalous Ministers*, 78. In addition to the cases listed above, chance comments show that two other Suffolk churches, Ashbocking and Melton, had surviving medieval crucifixes in the east window (pp. 46, 64). In Lincolnshire, at Stamford, Jeremy Cole 'suffered a Crusifix in one of the Windowes of the Church' (Hill, 'Royalist Clergy of Lincolnshire', 87). Two examples in Northamptonshire are Lowick, where in 1644 the churchwardens paid for 'glazing of the windows when the crucifixion and scandalous pictures were taken down' (Marks, *Medieval Stained Glass of Northamptonshire*, xli), and St Peter's, Northampton which was criticised during the metropolitical visitation of 1637 for replacing the cross at the east end of the chancel with the town's arms 'as if it were the townes church and not Christs' (Webster, *Godly Clergy*, 218). The introduction of stained glass crucifixes may be what is referred to in the Nottinghamshire petition of 1641 where it was said that Laud's altar policy had introduced into parish churches 'crucifixes, or other superstitious images, upon, over, or about [the altar]' (*A Petition presented to the Parliament from the County of Nottingham...*, 12–13, quoted in Eales, 'Iconoclasm', 314).
10. The evidence from Lincolnshire is weak, hence six counties, not seven (Hebgin-Barnes, *Stained Glass of Lincolnshire*, xli; and see our parish records gathered in appendix 8). Some churches had taken prior action.
11. There are just three churches where the accounts record no visitors, no damage, and no repair. These are in Norfolk, and are dealt with by John Blatchly p. 115. It is likely that they were not visited, and did not carry out the work demanded by the 1643 Ordinance.
12. The accounts mention the location of glass as follows: chancel glass at Chelmsford (Essex), north-west and south-west glass at Louth (Lincolnshire), and north window glass at Toft Monks (Norfolk). Dowsing sometimes states that pictures are in the chancel or the church (i.e. nave), but usually only when there are examples of both locations in the same building.
13. Usually in the east window, but not always. On four occasions Dowsing gives the location of the crucifix. On three of these it is in the chancel, at Great Shelford (149), Sawston (177) and Teversham (206); on the fourth Dowsing seems to imply it is in the church [nave], at West Wickham (191). Dowsing distinguishes fairly carefully between 'cross' and 'crucifix'; our count is of the latter, unless he states that the cross contains a figure.
14. See appendix 12, which explains the methodology and emphasises the caveats.

15. See above, pp. 18–20 and 40ff.
16. See, for example, pp. 113 above.
17. Ladders at Ufford (247) and Covehithe (226). For examples of cherubim of wood or stone, or explicitly said to be in the roof, see Journal entries 56, 133, 136, 215, 272. For examples of a good match between the surviving roof and Dowsing's count, see Journal entries 56, 65, 69, 104, 124, 133, 136, 146, 155, 232, 247, 271. For examples of the few cases where 'cherubim' were definitely not roof angels, see 67, 75, 143, and 229. For roof angels referred to as 'angels' rather than 'cherubim', see 215, where Dowsing appears to distinguish between the two words, and 39, 201, and 238.
18. Based on the appearance of 'cherubim' in his record, ignoring those which are too few in number to be roof angels, or otherwise disqualify themselves, and including 'angels' where there are strong indications that they were in the roof.
19. Cherubim were overlooked by him at Cambridge, Holy Trinity (25), Burwell (33) and possibly Foxton (157). He overlooked cherub corbels and bosses at a few places, e.g. Chesterton (111), Caxton (139), Melbourn (159), Abington Pigotts (165).
20. There are a couple of other examples of his acting in advance of legislation. He mentions a font at Cambridge, St Giles (19) and an organ at Stradbroke (215), both visited before these particular items were proscribed by Parliament. It may be that it was imagery on these objects which caught his attention.
21. Ipswich, St Matthew's (80), Covehithe (226), and Badingham (271).
22. Sudbury, St Gregory (40).
23. At Wickham Market (65).
24. At Horseheath (37).
25. As at Aldeburgh (Journal entry 56), and possibly Cambridge, All Saints (23).
26. At Cambridge, St Mary the Great (24) where the churchwarden William Howarde was responsible; and at Bury St Edmunds, St Mary's (107), where Thomas Chaplin was left in charge.
27. *Proceedings of the Suffolk Institute of Archaeology*, 6 (1888), 318–19. I am very grateful to Susan Andrews, historian of Bildeston, for this intriguing reference.
28. There had been a running battle over the matter of basins for the preceding century, with frequent episcopal enquires and orders concerning their use instead of fonts (Wall, *Porches and Fonts*, 219–21; Davies, *Architectural Setting of Baptism*, 94–8). For replacement of fonts, see Cox & Harvey, *English Church Furniture*, 173–5.
29. Nichols, *Seeable Signs*, 81–9. I am most grateful to Ann Nichols for helpful discussion, and for clarifying the historiography of the font at St Peter Mancroft.
30. There was damage to a font *case* in Ashford, Kent in the early 1580s, probably one of wood painted with images (perhaps similar to that now at Thaxted, Essex). (Nichols, *Seeable Signs*, 86.) Robert Whiting, who has worked extensively on post-Reformation churchwardens' accounts well into the Elizabethan period, tells me that he does not recollect expenditure for removing images from fonts.
31. Nichols, *Seeable Signs*, 81, 85, 333 and personal communication.
32. Fryer, 'Seven Sacraments: Supplement', 98–100, 104–5, makes several errors in respect of this font (for example, in claiming that the sacraments were originally painted). In particular, although claiming to rely on the work of Flood, he ignores Flood's conclusion, which was based on his examination of the font during restoration, and on a deep knowledge of other seven sacrament fonts, that the initial removal of the carved images had taken place in the mid sixteenth century. Flood's

notes have not been published, and I am grateful to Ann Nichols for providing me with extracts. See also Nichols, *Seeable Signs*, 3, 85n., 345.

33.  In addition to the cases quoted, in Essex, Paul states that in 1638 the Archdeacon ordered that the font at Abbess Roding be painted to obliterate the carvings: this would be an early example of documented font defacement. Unfortunately Paul provides no reference. He reports that the carved decoration on the font is of foliage trails, circles and rosettes (the latter enclosing a whorl, sun and moon), with no other superstitious imagery, and it is surprising that this decoration caused offence, or if it did, that paint would have been sufficient to obliterate it; with the evidence available, it would be unwise to regard this as typical font defacement (Paul, *Essex Fonts and Font Covers*, 27).

34.  Known examples of East Anglian fonts being plastered include Alphamstone, Essex (plaster removed 1902); Belchamp St Paul, Essex (still with two panels obliterated); Brightwell (recorded with plaster by D. E. Davy in 1829); Elmsett, Suffolk; Falkenham (as for Brightwell); Great Maplestead, Essex (plaster removed 1930); Gresham, Norfolk (plaster removed in nineteenth century); Laxfield, Suffolk (plastered after partial damage); Pulham St Mary, Norfolk (plaster removed in nineteenth century, symbols of evangelists restored); Walsoken, Norfolk, possibly; Woodbridge, Suffolk (plastered after partial damage). (Paul, *Essex Fonts and Font Covers*, 23, 28; Cautley, *Suffolk Churches*, 33; Nichols, *Seeable Signs*, 89, 339, 340, 349; Tomlinson, 'Some Norfolk fonts', 223.) The lead font at Lower Halstow, Kent had its plaster removed as late as 1921 (Zarnecki, *Lead Fonts*, 14; I am grateful to John Vigar for this example). There is hardly any evidence available to date this practice, but the font at Norwich, St Peter Mancroft was plastered by 1740 and probably was not plastered when the carvings were defaced in 1642 (Fryer, 'Seven Sacraments: Supplement', 99). The case of Laxfield is particularly interesting, as *partially* damaged carvings have been plastered over. Dowsing visited this church after defacement of fonts was ordered by Parliament (Journal entry 243). He makes no mention of the font, so the carvings had probably already been dealt with, but whether many years before or only shortly before his visit, we do not know; nor whether the font had already been plastered or whether this happened at some later time, after the Restoration perhaps, when fonts made their way back into routine use. For an example of plastering-over of destroyed imagery on a larger scale, see Phillips, *Reformation of Images*, Fig. 18. However, as Simon Bradley (personal communication) points out, the early-nineteenth-century literature on church restoration is full of exhortations to scrape off whitewash to reveal carved detail, including purely decorative carving with no imagery. In the same way, the *plastering* of fonts may have been done at various times for the sake of tidiness, rather than in a mood of iconoclasm, as for example at Elmsett (Journal entry 252). (For some examples of whitewash on fonts, see Simpson, *Fonts, 11*, 38, 41, 49.)

35.  See appendix 5.

36.  W. Lyndwood, *Provinciale* (1679), p. 53, Lib. I, Tit. 10, *Archdiaconi*, notes i, k; *Provinciale*, *Constitutiones Legatinae* with new pagination, p 113, Tit. 17, notes g, h. For the similar responsibility of impropriators towards chancels, see Henry Spelman, *De non temerandis ecclesiis* (1676), pp. 22–3. I am grateful to Margaret Aston for these references.

37.  BL Add. MS. 15672, fol. 29r. For Ling see also Palmer, *Cambridgeshire Villages*, III, 41, 42. Dowsing encountered a flat refusal from James Thompson, farmer of the

rectory at Trumpington (entry 148). There was another recalcitrant rector at Great St Mary's, Cambridge (see p. 200). For an example at Panfield, Essex see White, *Century*, 16.

38. Davies, *Caroline Captivity of the Church*, 220, 242–3. An analysis of surviving responses to Matthew Wren's visitation questions in 1639 shows that, of 14 Cambridge town churches, only 1 was admonished for not having rails; and of 111 parishes in rural Cambridgeshire, only 9 were instructed to install them. The situation was different in the Isle of Ely, where 21 of 30 churches did not have rails. In 1644 Dowsing found rails at six Cambridgeshire churches (the rest had been removed before his visit), but unfortunately none of these six are amongst those which lacked rails in 1638, so we cannot check whether parishes had followed Wren's instructions to install them. However Dowsing does mention steps at some of the parishes which had been ordered to raise them in 1638 (for example, Hardwick (Journal entry 134) and Wendy (164)), confirming that parishes did comply with Wren's requirements. (Analysis based on visitation notes in Palmer, *Visitation Returns* and *Cambridgeshire Villages*.)

39. Although we (the various contributors to this book) have not looked at the matter systematically, I have the impression that the removal of rails is not always recorded in churchwardens' accounts, perhaps because the carpenter who removed them took them away in lieu of payment. As regards delays, procrastination in removal of rails is not necessarily indicative of the churchmanship of the incumbent. At two churches where Dowsing found rails, the incumbent was ejected (Swaffham Prior (Journal entry 32) and Linton (36)), so at these churches the vicar's churchmanship might have led to his preserving the rails. As discussed in the text, it was certainly possible for a determined minister to delay the removal of steps; the same would apply to rails – thus at Coveney in Cambridgeshire the minister 'did diswade the said parishioners from taking downe the Rales in their chappell'. (Matthews, *Walker Revised*, under Richard Peacock (p.85), Peter Smith (p.86), William Ling (p. 83), BL Add. MS. 15672, fol. 32v. For two further examples of ministers resisting the removal of rails see Hill, 'Royalist Clergy of Lincolnshire', 87, 103.) But at six other churches where Dowsing found rails, the incumbent was *not* ejected, and the delay in removing the rails at these churches was therefore probably not due to Laudian churchmanship on the part of the vicar. Notably, at Ufford it was the parishioners who resisted Dowsing. (Cambridge, St Peter's (Journal entry 18); Babraham (35); Tunstall (55); Croxton (42); Sotterley (224); Ufford (247). Ipswich, St Peter's (76) has an ambiguous reference to rails.) For a recent discussion of the attitude of parishioners of middle churchmanship to rails, see Maltby, 'By this book', especially p. 121.

40. I am grateful to Kenneth Fincham for helpful discussion of these points, which he has been investigating as part of a wider research project.

41. See above, p. 135.

42. There are unanswered questions both about the prevalence of *pre*-Laudian rails in churches, and their fate in the 1640s (Maltby, *Prayer Book and People*, 121–3; Cox, *Churchwardens' Accounts*, 104; Cox & Harvey, *English Church Furniture*, 17–19).

43. Dr Julie Spraggon, tells me that the inventories for two London churches, St Margaret Pattens and St Michael le Querne, record the rails as being stored in the belfry, in 1651 and 1648 respectively (see her 'Iconoclasm', 163–4). On page 142, she quotes an entry in the accounts of St Mary Aldermanbury in 1647–48, for

selling the 'old rales w[hi]ch were formerly about the Sacrament Table', indicating they may have been stored since the early 1640s. She also quotes the 1661 report at Brickhill Parva in Buckinghamshire: 'the rayles formerly enrayling the communion table were in the late unhappy times of distraccon taken downe and are now made use of by Richard Martin at the George in our towne for his private house' (Spraggon, 'Iconoclasm', 134). I am grateful to Dr Spraggon for helpful discussion during her research for her doctorate; her thesis appeared shortly before this book went to press.

44.   I am grateful to Matthew Winterbottom of the Victoria and Albert Museum for raising the possibility that these rails were built post-Dowsing in an out-of-date style by a local craftsman.

45.   Cox, *English Church Furniture*, 19. Pevsner, *North-East Norfolk*, has these merely as seventeenth-century.

46.   See above, p. 115.

47.   Some eighty of the parishes of the City of London have records for the time, though some are sparse and unhelpful. Of these, nineteen record the removal of steeple crosses. For this information I am grateful to Julie Spraggon; for details, see her 'Iconoclasm', chapter 4 and appendix IV. See also her page 147, which quotes the case of Maids Moreton church in Buckinghamshire, where the cross was forcibly taken down on 18 August 1643. For Cheapside cross, see Aston, 'Iconoclasm in England: official and clandestine', 183–5.

48.   See appendix 5 above. A gable *crucifix* was removed in October 1641 by Sir Robert Harley at Leominster, on the authority of the 1641 Ordinance (Aston, 'Puritans and iconoclasm', 116).

49.   Aston, *England's Iconoclasts*, 90.

50.   *Ecclesiologist*, 5 (1846), 16–18.

51.   See above, p. 81.

52.   Quoted in Bertram, *Lost Brasses*, 14. I am grateful to Jonathan Finch for helpful discussion of several of the points in this section. I am also in great debt to Philip Whittemore, who has collected a corpus of documented examples of destruction from all periods which it is to be hoped may be published at some time. I am extremely grateful to him for putting his materials at my disposal, and for much informative discussion, without which this section would have been very much slighter. Both he and Jonathan Finch kindly read and commented upon an earlier version of this section. Any remaining errors are, of course, my responsibility.

53.   See, for example, the discussion of the King's College brasses p. 185–6 above. Philip Whittemore has pointed out (personal communication) that those with authority could sometimes preserve brasses during this period. The brass at Wimborne Minster commemorating St Etheldred is thought to have been taken up and hidden, and the memorial to Thomas de la Mare in St Albans Abbey was supposedly turned on its face 'at the time of the troubles in the middle of the seventeenth century' (Clutterbuck, *History of Hertfordshire*, I, 67). At Llangyfelach, Glamorgan the brass has cut into its lower sinister corner a Latin inscription that says it had been saved from 'the rapacious hands of the sacrilegious' (Lewis, *Welsh Monumental Brasses*, 70–71).

54.   Harington, *A Briefe View*, 85. Pre-war descriptions of the Cathedral (before its destruction) indicate that almost all the brasses had been entirely removed.

55.   See above, p. 25.

56. Finch, 'Monuments in Norfolk', 304. It is Jonathan Finch's suggestion (personal communication) made later in the paragraph that anonymous brasses are more liable to further destruction.

57. As at Cople, Bedfordshire (Evans, 'Malicious damage to brasses', 187).

58. Norris, *Monumental Brasses: The Memorials*, I, 258–67.

59. Damage to *marginal* inscriptions may be less indicative, as casual snapping off can occur at any time and may not be easy to distinguish from selective removal (see, for example, the Argentein brass at King's, discussed p. 186).

60. It is also possible that defacement of the *images* on brasses, as distinct from inscriptions, was also a distinguishing feature of iconoclasm of the 1640s rather than earlier; but I have no documentary evidence to demonstrate this.

61. I am grateful to Julie Spraggon for this example and that of St James Garlickhithe (personal communication). Another example may be St Mary Woolnoth, where Dr Spraggon, in her 'Iconoclasm' (p. 147), quotes an entry from the 1642–43 accounts for 'defacing the superstitious inscriptions and cutting others in their stead that are not offensive'.

62. Marshall removed one inscription plate in its entirety and reused it in the production of another at Little Missenden, Bucks (Page-Phillips, *Palimpsets*, I, 22, 76; Lack *et al.*, *Monumental Brasses of Bucks*, 162–3). I am grateful to Philip Whittemore for this example and that of St Helen's Bishopsgate.

63. Evans, 'Malicious damage to brasses', 186.

64. The brass to William Markeby and his wife Alice at St Bartholomew-the-Less has had the prayer clause removed in very similar style. The accounts have no record of payment for this work. (*Monumental Brass Society*, Bulletin 80 (January 1999), 414.)

65. Noted by Philip Whittemore from a rubbing in the Collection of the Society of Antiquaries of London. Churchwardens' accounts are referenced in appendix 8.

66. See above, p. 112. Evans suggests that the two brasses at Cople, Bedfordshire may have been mutilated by Sir Samuel Luke of that village, but there is no documentary evidence (Evans, 'Malicious damage to brasses', 187).

67. I am extremely grateful to Philip Whittemore for ploughing through the many hundreds of aperture cards for these counties held by the Society of Antiquaries of London, a more tedious task than which it is hard to imagine.

## CHAPTER 8 *In search of bells: iconoclasm in Norfolk, 1644*

1. Ketton-Cremer, *Norfolk in the Civil War*, 253–5. The picture presented in this chapter now needs validation on the ground.

2. Parish documents referred to in this chapter will be found in appendix 8.

3. As well as the glass and bells, it may have been at this time that the bench-ends had their heads removed (Ted Mercer, churchwarden, personal communication).

4. Cattermole, *Church Bells and Bellringing: A Norfolk Prospect*, 30.

5. I am grateful to Ranald Clouston for the Suffolk examples, since J. J. Raven lists no damage in his *Church Bells of Suffolk*. Raven wrote 'to do justice to the Puritan regime there seems to have been little or no bell spoliation' [in Suffolk]. Davy's collections for Blackbourn deanery, where the four Suffolk examples are found, yield no examples of damage to bells since disposed of. Details of the Norfolk churches where bell inscriptions were damaged can be culled from John L'Estrange's *Church Bells of Norfolk* and Paul Cattermole has added to the list in correspondence. A list of the bell damage in Norfolk and Suffolk will be found in

appendix 9.

6.     That at Little Gransden, commented upon by Robert Walker in his commentary to Journal entry 143. For the general absence of inscription damage, see Owen, *Church Bells of Huntingdonshire*; Deedes & Walters, *Church Bells of Essex*; North, *Church Bells of Lincoln*; North, *Church Bells of Hertfordshire* (p. 203 of this implies that a pre-Reformation bell at Northaw had an inscription filed off, but the bell was destroyed in a fire in 1881 and it is impossible to check). For Cambridgeshire see chapter 3.

7.     At Toft (Journal entry 135) and Croxton (142), both in Cambridgeshire.

8.     Along the parapet the inscription can still be read when lit obliquely by the midsummer evening sun. There are no pre-Reformation bells at this church.

9.     Shown in the map attached to Kirby, *The Suffolk Traveller*.

10.    For location of these letters (here quoted in part), see appendix 8. Gallard survived in post to subscribe in 1664.

11.    Weever, Ancient Funerall Monuments, 815. It was also recorded by the Chorographer (Hood, *Chorography of Norfolk*, 79). The other brass recorded by the Chorographer was not to a Knyvett, so perhaps was not thought worth protecting in this way.

12.    Woodforde, *Norwich School of Glass Painting*, 42–68. See appendix 8 for accounts.

13.    This assumes that the churchwardens' year at that church followed the typical pattern, Easter to Easter.

14.    Ship Money £3. 19s. 2d. at Troston and 6d. at Ixworth Thorpe. For the muster see Banks, *Able Men of Suffolk*.

15.    Wills proved at the Archdeaconry Court in Sudbury, now at SRO(B): W1/86/44 and W1/93/94 respectively.

16.    BL Add. MS 19,079.

17.    Cotman, *Engravings of the Most Remarkable Sepulchral Brasses in Norfolk*; this was first published in 1819. The corpus of rubbings at the Society of Antiquaries of London yielded just three examples outside Norwich of deliberately damaged prayer clauses on foot inscriptions, a form of damage probably limited to the early 1640s (see above, pp. 103–5). They are at Hoe (brass to John Dunham (1467) and wife Alice and daughter Margery; closing clause removed); Poringland (Wm. Body (*c*.1500) and Edm. Canwold (1501); opening clause scratched out); Wells (Thos. Bradley, rector (1499), builder of the chancel; opening words scratched out). Those at Hoe and Poringland are within the arc of country covered by Gilley, the last is not: but the sample is too small for meaningful comment. In Norwich such damage is known at two churches: the Antiquaries corpus shows damage at St Stephen's (brass to Robert Burght, mayor, 1516), and St Andrew's (Robert Aylmer (1493), an early rubbing of which survives); and a further brass at St Andrew's, that to John Clark (d.1527) is recorded in the *Journal of the Norfolk and Norwich Archaeological Society,* 36 pt 1 (1936), 88, kindly drawn to our attention by Philip Whittemore. As regards inscriptions missing in their entirety, Greenwood and Norris list and illustrate a number in their *Brasses of Norfolk Churches*, but any geographical analysis requires careful comparison of antiquaries' records to ascertain the date of disappearance. See appendix 13 for an initial attempt at this.

18.    The Rector of Garboldisham, William Geast, was a convinced Laudian (Matthews, *Walker Revised*, 334–5).

19.    Unless they replaced rails which had been there many years. See p. 99.

20.    These churches are listed from Christopher Woodforde's *Norwich School of Glass*

*Painting* and King, *Stained Glass Tours around Norfolk Churches*.

21. Antiquarian accounts in H. L. Bradfer-Lawrence, *Norfolk Record Society*, 1 (1931).

22. Quoted in King, *Stained Glass Tours around Norfolk Churches*, 20.

23. The location map in King, *Stained Glass Tours around Norfolk Churches* gives the strong impression that the east and south of the county have least remaining glass.

24. The distribution map is based on Woodforde's *Norwich School of Glass Painting*, 172–3 (I am grateful to Trevor Cooper for this suggestion). The surviving pictures are usually in the tracery of the windows. It is worth pointing out that even where iconoclasm was rife, such pictures could survive (as at Norwich). We know that sometimes they were removed for safety and later reinserted, a possibility of which our map takes no account. This may explain the cluster south of Norwich, near to Ashwellthorpe where we know it was intended to remove the glass, and not far from Bressingham where this policy was carried out successfully. Nevertheless *on average* a higher proportion of Marian pictures are likely to have survived where iconoclasm was patchy or non-existent, and in general the map supports the other evidence adduced in the text.

25. Blomefield, *History of Norfolk*, III, 389ff. See also Spraggon, 'Iconoclasm', 107–12 for a discussion which became available after this chapter was written.

26. The churchwardens' accounts will be found in appendix 8, under 'Norwich'.

27. The spellings of these surnames have been corrected from Hardy (sometimes Cozens-Hardy) and Kent, *The Mayors of Norwich*. Other biographical detail in this section has been culled from the same work.

28. St Michael Coslany obtained a bell from Rockland, All Saints. See appendix 9.

29. The mayor in 1643 was John Thacker, woollen draper and hosier, a staunch Roundhead, but he left the work of iconoclasm to Toft, his sheriff.

30. *Bishop Hall's Hard Measure*, reprinted in Hall, *The Works of Joseph Hall, D.D.*

31. See, for example, Woodforde, *Norwich School of Glass Painting*, 209.

32. For Moses and Aaron, see the Journal entry for Otley in Suffolk (entry 124). We need not assume that everything put to the flames in Norwich market place was easily inflammable; lead would melt, and glass crack satisfactorily.

33. See above, n.17.

34. Much work had to be done on the east window after the Committee House explosion in 1647, as the accounts show. Mayor Utting's intervention indirectly caused the loss of the lecterns and organs, sold in 1651. (See appendix 8 for extracts from the accounts.) Since the above was written, Dr Spraggon has made a strong case that the glass was deliberately removed in 1644–45, stored, and replaced in the 1660s (see her 'Iconoclasm', 109–10).

35. The evidence of Samuell Carder [Carter?] in BL Add. MS 15,903, fol. 75. Davill went up to King's but graduated from Trinity, and christened two children at St Giles in 1639 and 1640. He is not listed with the ejected ministers of Norfolk in Matthews, *Walker Revised*.

36. Farrer, *Norfolk Monumental Brasses*, 66–7. The brass plates found by Farrer include one showing St Faith, Virgin and Martyr, from Horsham, St Faith, given refuge here at the Reformation. This plate, perfect when Cotman made his etching, disappeared later in the nineteenth century.

37. Blomefield, *History of Norfolk*, 11, 393.

38. The published accounts show no evidence of iconoclasm in the 1640s, or earlier (Beloe, *St Nicholas' Chapel, passim*).

CHAPTER 9 *Iconoclasm in other counties of the Eastern Association*

1. See his commission, appendix 7.

2. I am very grateful to Dr Bill Cliftlands for helpful discussion on iconoclasm in Essex, based on his thesis, 'Politics and religion'. I remain responsible for errors of fact or interpretation.

3. Cliftlands, 'Politics and religion', 149–50.

4. Davies, *Architectural Setting of Baptism*, 98.

5. Maldon Chamberlains' Account of John Stevens and James Starling, delivered January 1642/3 (ERO, D/B 3/3/306, quoted in Cliftlands 'Politics and religion', 145).

6. Here the Parliamentary Ordinance is given as the authority, rather than the Earl of Manchester, but the distinction between the two types of authority is not indicative of the presence or absence of a visitor. Compare the two descriptions of Captain Gilley at Banham and Swaffham (appendix 8). For accounts and other parish documents mentioned in this chapter, see appendix 8, unless otherwise stated.

7. Chelmsford, Great Bromley, West Ham, Hornchurch, Saffron Walden, South Weald, Waltham Holy Cross. The accounts at Writtle for our period stop at 1643 (they show repairs to glass), and those at Great Easton cannot be dated with certainty.

8. Chelmsford, Saffron Walden, and Waltham. Great Bromley has a visitor arriving in April 1645, which is so far out of line with the other evidence that it must be suspected that there has been an error with the dates, as with some of our other accounts of this period (perhaps because they were written up some time after the event, when times were quieter).

9. See appendix 10.

10. The surviving accounts in Essex are biased towards towns and away from rural parishes. The former are more likely to have been visited.

11. Braintree (vestry decision), Latton (letter), Navestock and Nevendon (notes in parish registers). Damage is recorded in the first three, a visitation in the last. See appendix 8.

12. This is particularly unfortunate given the possible split in loyalties between north-west and south-east suggested by Tyacke, *Anti-Calvinists*, 188–90. But see Webster, *Godly Clergy*, 153–4 for an alternative view.

13. Paul, *Essex Fonts and Font Covers*, 29, 86, 177, 222.

14. I am grateful to Philip Whittemore for this list. In addition to these, at Wivenhoe a pendant cross on the brass of Elizabeth, Countess of Oxford, 1537, has been partially obliterated (Evans, 'Malicious damage to brasses', 188–90).

15. RCHME, *Essex*, I, 5; I, 11; I, 15; III, 9; I, 106; III, 228; I, 179; I, 357. This cluster may be an accident of recording.

16. RCHME, *Essex*, IV, 67; I, 144; I, 321; *Ecclesiologist*, 5 (1846), 17. The RCHME photo of Tilty shows a cross strangely unweathered for its supposedly great age. Great Dunmow church (I, 117) is indexed as having just the base of a gable cross, but is recorded in the text as having a cross.

17. For an important general introduction to religious affairs in the county, see Holmes, *Seventeenth-Century Lincolnshire*, *passim*.

18. Collection of the Society of Antiquaries of London, searched by Philip Whittemore.

19. North, *Church Bells of Lincoln*.

20. Hebgin-Barnes (*Stained Glass of Lincolnshire*, xli) quotes just one report, by the

Royalist rector of Boothby Pagnell, Sanderson, who noted that the apostles in the chancel windows had been 'defaced and broken by the soldiers in the late warres'.

21.   The minutes of the Committee for Scandalous Ministers for Lincolnshire throw no light on organised iconoclasm (see Bibliography for reference).

22.   I used the handlist of churchwardens' accounts produced by Lincolnshire Archives. Of the six accounts listed, those for Algakirk, Broughton by Brigg, Kirton Lindsey and Witham on the Hill were either missing for the crucial years, or were summary accounts only. Those for Benington in Holland were fragile and could not be inspected, but are thought to contain accounts only for the year 1642 in the relevant period.

23.   LA, Louth St James, 7/5. See appendix 8 for the accounts.

24.   The church had railed in the communion table in 1635. Swaby, *Louth*, 146–7.

25.   *Ecclesiologist*, 5 (1846), 17. The surplice had disappeared by 1644: compare inventories for *c.*1641 and 1644, LA, Louth St James, 7/5, fol.139.

26.   Swaby, *Louth*, 148–9.

27.   In appendix 10 there is a discussion of the pattern of evidence which might be expected. At none of the three churches was the vicar ejected. It is notable that the Royal Commission Inventory, and parish histories in the Victoria County History, make not a single reference to iconoclasm.

28.   Heseltine, *Brasses of Huntingdonshire*.

29.   *Ex info.* Philip Whittemore.

30.   And at Brampton, but RCHME, *Huntingdonshire*, says these were brought from elsewhere (p. 25).

31.   PRO SP 16/466/23, noted by Fissel, *The Bishop's Wars*, 265–6. I am grateful to Margaret Aston for drawing this reference to my attention.

32.   See above, p. 104.

33.   Chauncy, *Hertfordshire*, I, 331; Cussans, *History*, I, 122. I am grateful to Eileen Roberts for these references and other information about remaining glass in the county.

34.   RCHME, *Hertfordshire*, 45.

35.   See appendix 10.

36.   Based on an approximates estimate of 115 churches in the county having medieval remains (the number estimated from Whitelaw, *Hertfordshire Churches*).

37.   The numbers in other counties are discussed in chapter 7.

38.   In the five north aisle windows of St Peter's, massed fragments of ancient glass have been grouped together.

39.   Of the 25 churches with prayer clauses removed, incumbents were ejected from eleven (44%). In the county as a whole, 63 churches had incumbents ejected. No exact count of the number of parishes in the county in the 1640s is to hand, but I estimate it at between 170 and 200, giving a figure for the overall proportion of incumbents ejected of between 30% and 40%. (Ejections analysed from Matthews, *Walker Revised*.)

40.   See above, p. 102.

41.   RCHME, *Hertfordshire*, 75, 166, 227.

42.   See above, p. 99.

43.   HeRO, Winterton 46351 quoted in Cliftlands, 'Politics and religion', 154.

44.   Nelson, *Ancient Painted Glass*, 100.

45.   For this and the following incident, see White, *Century*, 13, 17. These events must

have followed the Parliamentary Order of 1641.

46. HeRO, QSR 5: numbers 78, 82, 83, 141. I am grateful to Mr J. McIlwaine, archivist of the Diocesan Records, for bringing this case to my attention, and extracting the records.

47. Paske held many preferments, including being archdeacon of London.

48. The Earl of Salisbury said that the window had been 'lately built by him [Paske]' (Fissel, *The Bishop's Wars*, 265). I am grateful to Margaret Aston for this reference and helpful discussion of the incident.

49. Matthews, *Walker Revised*, 202.

50. Pevsner, *Hertfordshire*, 173.

CHAPTER 10 *The history of the Journal*

1. According to the *Gentleman's Magazine* (vol. 9, p. 108), which listed the book but did not review it, it was priced at 1s. 0d. The full title is: 'The Schismatics delineated from Authentic Vouchers with A modest Reply to Mr DANIEL NEALE'S Exceptions to the *Test Act* Addressed to that *Celebrated Historian* with an Appendix containing I. Some curious PRAYERS in the Time of the *Grand Rebellion*, copied from the Originals, and never before printed. II. *The Journal of Will. Dowsing, the famed Demolisher of Superstition,…*'. The first appendix contains a selection of prayers written by Mr George Swathe, minister of Denham in Suffolk, in 1641 and 1642. They are notable for their antipathy to King Charles, and Swathe's continued pleas to the Deity to deliver him from a range of domestic, agricultural and financial difficulties, some, it must be said, of his own making. In his footnotes Grey comments acidly on these rather bathetic prayers, quoting pointedly from *Hudibras*.

2. Rector of Houghton Conquest, and vicar of St Giles' and St Peter's, Cambridge, Grey is best known for his edition of Butler's *Hudibras*.

3. The first appendix was, 'copied from the originals'. Hence Grey's comment that the Journal was 'likewise' copied from the original. Grey invited the reader to examine the originals of the first appendix: 'The originals will be left in the Publisher's Hands for Six Months, to be perused by those who are desirous of comparing them with these extracts'. Grey did not repeat the offer for Dowsing's Journal, perhaps because he was not claiming to be providing extracts, and therefore could not be accused of bias, or because the Journal would cause no surprise.

4. The description of Dowsing as the 'famed' demolisher of superstition suggest his name was remembered in Cambridge.

5. One-time Fellow of St John's College, Cambridge, Baker left in manuscript a wide range of materials relating to the history of Cambridge. Many, including the Dowsing transcript, are now in the University Library.

6. Cambridge University Library, Mm. 1. 49 (Baker 38, No. 42) pp. 455–8, 471–3 (that is, in two sections). The creation of the transcript can be dated by the surrounding material to after 4 November 1738. There is another clue to the date. In his index, Baker describes his transcript as 'The Reformation or Prophanation of Churches in Cambridgeshire an. 1643. Since printed by Dr Grey an. 1739'. The second phrase is interlined with the first, showing that Baker added it later, almost certainly because he made his copy of the manuscript and indexed it before Grey printed it in 1739, then added the reference to Grey's publication at a later date. Baker's transcript, then, was made in late 1738 or early 1739, before Grey went into print. It is not surprising that both Grey and Baker should have handled the same

master copy as they were friends and correspondents. Grey planned to write a life of Baker, William Cole recording that 'Dr Grey told me very lately, that he had drawn up a life of him [Baker], which he designed shortly for the Press...' (BL Add. MS 5832, fol. 24). In fact it was left to Robert Masters to publish his *Memoirs of the life and writings of the late Rev. Thomas Baker, B.D.... from the papers of Dr. Zachary Grey,* Cambridge, 1784. Masters comments 'Dr. Zachary Grey... was intimately acquainted with the Subject... The last, though not the least of his [Baker's] friends... was Dr. Zachary Grey, the Collector of the Materials of this Life'. (Ibid, preface and 116.)

7.    The Baker manuscript was published with an introduction and some annotations by J. G. Cheshire as 'William Dowsing's Destructions in Cambridgeshire', in *Transactions of the Cambridgeshire & Huntingdonshire Archaeological Society,* 3 (1914). The Grey and Baker versions were printed in a comparative edition with an introduction and short commentary by A. D. Moule, *The Cambridge Journal of William Dowsing 1643,* reprinted from the *History Teacher's Miscellany,* 1926. There are small errors in both these editions.

8.    For example, Baker did not for the most part trouble to copy the biblical texts quoted by Dowsing during his visit to the Cambridge colleges; he omits the names of the churchwardens and others whom Dowsing made responsible; and fails to record their deadlines for carrying out the work. Nor does he mention the fees extracted. Other differences between the two can be explained as transcription errors or deliberate corrections on the part of Baker. For example Baker omits the entry for Caius College, perhaps because he decided to omit the second half of the argument at Pembroke, and his eye then skipped accidentally to Queens' College; he places King's College immediately after Trinity Hall, possibly as part of an attempt to put items in date order.

9.    He uses virtually identical language about Swathe's prayers (where the original manuscript was available for inspection) and Dowsing's Journal. Masters, an acquaintance of Grey, interpreted the word 'original' in its straightforward sense (Masters, *Corpus Christi,* 38).

10.   Grey noted that Baker's transcript was 'Since printed from John [*sic*] Dowsing's Journal (an original MS now in my custody) in the Appendix to a Tract intitled Schismatics Delineated. 1739 No. 2'. (Note in Grey's hand in BL Stowe 1057 fol. 47v. This comment of Grey's was also preserved by his son-in-law, William Cole of Ely in BL Add. MS 5832, fol. 24.)

11.   Grey is the last known possessor of the original manuscript, and it then disappears from sight. Trinity Hall, Grey's college, holds no papers or books of Grey's (personal communication from the Archivist), and his papers in the BL contain no sign of the Journal. Grey's books were dispersed very soon after his death, judging from two bookseller's catalogues held by the British Library. Neither catalogue appears to include a copy of *The Schismatics* and although a few manuscripts are listed, none seems to have any bearing on Dowsing. (*A catalogue of the libraries of the Rev. Zachary Grey... Tuesday, March 8, 1768,... By L. Davis and C. Reymers,* London, 1768; *A Catalogue of several Libraries... and a great number of curious single tracts and volumes of tracts, collected by the late Rev. Dr. Zachary Grey... Thursday, July 21, 1768... by L. Davis and C. Reymers,* London, 1768.)

      John Nichols says that Grey's son-in-law, William Cole of Ely (not to be confused with Dr William Cole, the eminent Cambridge antiquary) acquired a number of

Grey's manuscripts, and subsequently sold some (or all) of them to a bookseller, Thomas Burnham of Gold Street, Northampton, who in turn included them in a sale held in 1779. The only catalogue of Burnham's which I have located is of 1808, entitled *Cheap Books on Sale* (copy in BL). It is in two parts, very lengthy, giving the impression of being a complete stock list. It contains no manuscripts of relevance, and no copy of *The Schismatics*. John Nichols also says that he acquired from Burnham 'many' of Grey's papers, others being dispersed in London; Nichols lists five of Grey's manuscripts which he purchased from Burnham, including Grey's proposed 'Life of Baker'; but makes no mention of purchasing or possessing the Dowsing manuscript. (Nichols, *Literary Anecdotes*, II, 532–549; III, 673; V, 116; VIII, 415.)

    Nichols' library was partially dispersed after his death at two Sotheby sales in 1828, but the sale catalogues do not appear to include any of the five manuscripts (*A catalogue of the... library of the late John Nichols... April 16 1828*; *A catalogue... of the remaining portion of the topographical library of the late John Nichols Esq... 5th May 1828*; copies in BL). After the death of John Gough Nichols, the grandson of John Nichols, the rest of the latter's library seems to have been dispersed (Sotheby's sale catalogues 4 December 1874, 5 May 1879; marked up copies in BL). The first of these two sales did include one manuscript of Grey's, (item 990 'Memoirs of Robert Moss DD, Dean of Ely'), but neither of the sales appear to have any material relating to Dowsing. (Note that item 706 of the first sale, the intriguing manuscript 'Collections for the County of Cambridgeshire', is probably Cambridge University Library SSS 43/26, a heavily annotated copy of Carter, *The History of the University of Cambridge*.)

12.    Blomefield, *Collectanea Cantabrigiensia, or Collections relating to Cambridge, University, Town, and County,* Norwich,1750. Blomefield, educated at Caius College, Cambridge is best known for his monumental but incomplete *History of Norfolk* (discussed in the final pages of appendix 13, above). In *Collectanea* he quotes a few Journal entries, using the version of the Journal printed by Grey, rather than the Baker manuscript version (see, for example, the entry for Teversham, Journal entry 206, *Collectanea*, 184). Much of the *Collectanea* was based on material provided by Dr William Cole of Cambridge, who also provided Masters with the information about Dowsing which he used in his history of Corpus Christi (Stoker, 'Genesis of *Collectanea*', 376; Masters, *Corpus Christi*, 37).

13.    In 1753 Edmund Carter, in both his *County of Cambridge* and *University of Cambridge*, printed entries for Cambridgeshire from Grey's edition. Extracts from the Journal were also used by C. H. Cooper in his *Annals of Cambridge*, (1845), III, 364–7, who prints the entries for Cambridge town and University from Baker's manuscript.

14.    Joshua Kirby, *The Suffolk Traveller*. Canning's involvement with this edition was recorded by John Nichols (*Illustrations*, VI, 538; see also his *Literary Anecdotes*, II, 274 and VIII, 488).

15.    Kirby, *The Suffolk Traveller*, 39, 45, 49, 115.

16.    *The Journal of William Dowsing, of Stratford, Parliamentary Visitor, appointed under a warrant from the Earl of Manchester, for demolishing the superstitious pictures and ornaments of churches, &c. within the county of Suffolk in the years 1643, – 1644*, Woodbridge, 1786. There is an appreciative review (anonymous) in the *Gentleman's Magazine* (vol. 56, 422–4), but no indication of who had been Loder's editor. Like so many others in that journal, the review may well have been written by the editor John Nichols, who was the London distributor of Loder's books – this would explain the reviewer's

complimenting Loder as 'an ingenious provincial printer'. Loder's edition has formed the basis of all subsequent editions of the Suffolk portion of the Journal until this one. It was reprinted in 1818 by Loder's widow (second edition, *The Journal &c*, not in BL), and again in 1840 (as a supplement to Edward Wells, *Rich Man's Duty*, published by Parker, Oxford, afterward reissued by the publisher in separate form in 1844). Most notably it was reprinted with an extensive introduction and annotations by C. H. Evelyn White (ed.), *The Journal &c*, Ipswich, 1885. (This edition, complete with introduction and notes, was also published in *Proceedings of the Suffolk Institute of Archaeology and Natural History*, 6 (1885), 236–295.) White's edition reproduces Loder's text, (though his printer's eye skipped one line at Dennington, entry 270); on occasions his annotations and introduction are of value, but always need to be treated with care. The most recent edition I have located is of the early years of this century, *The Journal &c*, undated, with introduction and notes by J. Charles Wall, published by the Church Printing Company, London (not in BL; copy in Guildhall Library, London). This reprints White's text, including the error at Dennington. Wall's introduction and notes raise the emotional temperature, but add nothing to what had already been published. There is an interleaved edition of Loder in the Bodleian, with extra notes by John Wodderspoon (Bod. MS Top. Suffolk d.19).

17.    The existence of the Cambridge Journal was no doubt known to some of those who read Loder. Not long after Loder's edition was reviewed in the *Gentleman's Magazine*, a correspondent to that journal commented that 'The Journal of William Dowsing calls to mind the Journal of the same demolisher of superstition… printed at the end of Dr Zachary Grey's pamphlet'. The Revd James Ford of St Lawrence, Ipswich took the trouble to copy this remark into his copy of Loder's edition. (*Gentleman's Magazine*, July 1787, p. 593, col. 1; SRO(I), S 92 Dow.)

18.    SRO(I), HD 1538/435/1.

19.    'Honest Tom Martin' of Palgrave, in the north of Suffolk (where he was a somewhat indolent attorney), was a well known antiquary and amasser of manuscripts. His collections, mostly unpublished, provide valuable information about Suffolk churches. See *DNB*. Martin's name appears nowhere on the transcript, but his hand is very familiar to Suffolk historians.

20.    Edward Leedes was Master of Ipswich Grammar school 1712–37, having previously been Usher to his father Edward at King Edward VI Grammar School, Bury St Edmunds. He was vicar of Wherstead from 1718–44 where he was buried aged 60. Thus at any time between 1712 and 1744 he would have been 'of Ipswich'.

21.    William Dowsing the iconoclast left his books to his son Samuel. Samuel died in November 1703 (burial 13 November 1703, Stratford St Mary register). His half-brother William was executor (SRO(I), IC/AA1/133/79).

22.    Thomas Burrough was rector of Bradfield St George and vicar of Depden from 1710 until his death in 1732. He entered Corpus Christi College, Cambridge in 1697. He was the son of James, MD, of Bury and brother of Sir James, the Cambridge architect (see *DNB*) who was Master of Caius, Cambridge.

23.    The missing proper names and titles which have deliberate gaps are: 'Sudbourne' (Journal entry 66); 'Shrive' at Newton (115); the title 'Capt' for Waldgrave at Buers (119); 'Genkthorne' at Wetheringsett (257); 'Will Dod' at Worlingworth (261); 'Christ' at Hacheston (272). It is unlikely that all of these could have been filled in without access to another transcript of the manuscript.

24. Thomas Martin's mother Elizabeth was sister to Thomas Burrough.
25. Huse, who bought the manuscript, appears to be known as a bookseller only from a handbill of his which was printed in 1704, the same year in which he purchased Dowsing's library (BL Harl. 5946, 208). He is described in this advertisement as T. Huse, based at Exeter *Court* in the Strand, which stood right by Exeter 'Change [Exchange]. A number of booksellers rented space in Exeter Exchange, which was demolished about 1904 to make way for Aldwych.

   This is almost certainly the Thomas Huse who as a book*binder* was accepting apprentices from 1698 to 1712, the last being his son Joseph. (See McKenzie, *Stationers' Company Apprentices Records*.) Thomas's own apprenticeship is not recorded. He was probably the child baptised on 2 August 1668 at St Giles Cripplegate, making him 36 years old with a young son when he purchased Dowsing's library and had his handbill printed. One wonders, was the bookbinder trying to break into book*selling*?

   Although the handbill claims 'all these [books] were printed for, and sold by, T. Huse', the title pages of the BL copies of the first two of these books show them *not* to have been printed for Huse, but for Richard Smith (the third book does not name the publisher). Presumably Smith and Huse acted as business partners, shared the cost of printing, and had their own title pages affixed to their share of the books. Such arrangements are not unknown (e.g. Locke, *Human Understanding*, 1690).

   Smith had a bookshop, but he also regularly sold books at auction in Exeter 'Change, and it is possible that Huse passed Dowsing's library over to him for sale. Three of Smith's auction catalogues for our period have survived, one for 1704 and two for 1707 (13 November 1704, 25 February 1707, 20 October 1707; all in BL). They contain a few titles of books possessed by Dowsing; only one is of any scarcity and might reasonably be supposed to have been Dowsing's copy: *Sermons preached before the Long Parliament*, item 134 in the earliest catalogue, discussed by Professor John Morrill in chapter 1 (and see also appendix 3). It is possible, therefore, that Smith, as a business partner of Huse, handled some or all of Dowsing's library, though the evidence is slight.

   One can speculate further, though this time with the barest minimum of supporting evidence. In 1714 Smith published a book which the title advertised as being sold by J. Roberts, indicating that he knew the bookseller who twenty-five years later was to publish Grey's *The Schismatics*, which contained the first publication of the Cambridge portion of the Journal. As the *Schismatics* also contains another Suffolk manuscript of the Civil War (the prayers of George Swathe), it is at least credible that Huse purchased both the Journal and Swathe's manuscript whilst in Suffolk, passed both to his business associate Smith, who, after having been unable to sell them, in turn sold them on to Roberts, who published a number of books for Grey and might well have drawn his attention to this particular pair of items. This might explain why the appendix to the *Schismatics* which contains Dowsing's Cambridge Journal has its own title page as though it had been intended to publish it separately – perhaps Roberts planned this, but Grey realised he could use the material in his book; certainly Grey mentions the appendix just once in the body of the text in what reads like an inserted passage, an indication that its inclusion may have been an afterthought.
26. There is a slip of paper pasted onto the front page of the manuscript (and therefore added after the copy was completed) with a further note in Martin's hand: 'See

Masters hist[ory] of Bennet College for one William Dowsing a Great Reformer of Monuments painted Glass &c or Destroyer rather. page 38 &c'. ('Bennet' was an alternative name for Corpus Christi, Thomas Burrough's old college.) The book to which Martin is referring was published in 1753 (Masters, *Corpus Christi*). Martin's note must therefore have been written in 1753, or after that date. From Martin's phrase 'one William Dowsing', I interpret this as a slip he wrote to himself *before* he had encountered William Dowsing in the Journal, later pasting it onto the manuscript. This would imply that he had his copy of the Journal made after 1753, making it of a very similar date to Duck's transcript, discussed later in this appendix. (On the other hand, Martin refers to 'Mr Leedes... from whose copy my clerk transcribed this'; would Martin have referred to Leedes in this way if Leedes had been dead? – if not, then Martin had his copy made before 1744.)

27. Craven Ord, the antiquary, published a number of articles, but his main gifts to posterity are his collections relating to Suffolk, many now in the BL and more in HD1538/435 at the Suffolk Record Office. See *DNB*. Loder probably obtained the Martin transcript from Craven Ord and John Nichols, for whom he was the main agent for publishable Suffolk topographical material, particularly illustrations. See note following.

28. On the death of Thomas Martin the manuscript almost certainly went, along with many others, to John Ives (1751–1776) for whom see *DNB*. At the sale of his books and manuscripts in 1777, it would have passed to Craven Ord. It was sold in Craven Ord's sale in June 1829 (Evans of 93 Pall Mall, 25–27 June 1829, lot 605, £3. 13s. 6d.) to Payne the bookseller. The catalogue entry read: 'Suffolk Collections 4to Volume containing various papers, printed and manuscript. Among the manuscripts are an ancient transcript of Dowsing's Journal. Pedigree of the Seckfords, Loder's Collections for Woodbridge'. Subsequent owners were Thomas Phillipps (Phillipps 3866) and the Iveagh Collection at Elveden Hall (HD 1538/435/1). In 1987 it was purchased by the Suffolk Record Office, Ipswich, (SRO(I), HD 1538/435/1) as a result of public subscriptions and grants.

29. For example, the fine drawings Isaac Johnson made of the monuments at Letheringham, referred to on p. 10 of Loder's edition, are in Ord's elephant folio volumes, now in the British Library (BL Add. MS 8986 and 8987).

30. Soc. Antiq. MS 702. I am grateful to Philip Whittemore for drawing this manuscript to our attention. This is probably the copy at one time in the ownership of Charles Golding, nineteenth-century antiquary and bookdealer of Colchester. Golding wrote a note listing differences between his copy and Loder's printed version, and these variants match the copy in the Antiquaries' library exactly (*East Anglian Notes and Queries,* First Series, 1 (1864), 246). They were also noted without acknowledgement at the end of Evelyn White's edition of 1885 (p. 57).

31. *John Blatchly writes*: The highly distinctive hand of the Antiquaries' transcript is not that of any well known East Anglian topographer or antiquary. An important clue was that several other things besides Dowsing were of interest to the owner of the manuscript book, all of them centred on Ipswich and Colchester. In Ipswich, either St Lawrence's or St Peter's parish was the focus.

The preface to Thomas Gardner's *History of Dunwich,* 1754, was quoted in full in the manuscript book, so the subscribers' list to that work was combed for Ipswich purchasers. Surprisingly, there is only one Ipswich subscriber apart from six copies for Joshua Kirby who drew the illustrations. This single subscriber was John

Sparrowe, bailiff (joint mayor) a record thirteen times, unrivalled grandee of St Lawrence parish and sitter to Gainsborough, his house the finest pargetted building in East Anglia. A further point is that the Dunwich history, which has no named printer, may have been produced by William Craighton who also lived in the parish.

An examination of the St Lawrence parish books of the period settled the matter: in the Vestry Book and four Overseer's Books there are more than two dozen complete pages in the copyist's unmistakable florid script, and there and on parish deeds accessioned with them is the signature of Edward Duck, written often enough to confirm that the hand is his. And to complete the circle, Duck was churchwarden once with John Sparrowe and twice with William Craighton.

32. See the entry for Ufford (entry 247) where *The Suffolk Traveller* (p. 115) follows Duck in omitting mention of the altar rails, found in Martin's transcript. Of course, it is possible that the quotations in *The Suffolk Traveller* come from some third unknown transcript.

33. Gardner's work was illustrated by Joshua Kirby, himself author of *Historical Account of the Twelve* [Suffolk] *Prints*, 1748, which also missed several opportunities to quote Dowsing, had the Journal then been known to Kirby.

34. See Journal entry 232.

35. 'Here are 27 Gravestones without Inscriptions and all deprived of the Plates'. (Gardner, *Dunwich*, 125.)

36. Gardner, *Dunwich*, 204.

37. Was this related to the death of Leedes, and the presumed dispersal of his papers?

38. There is a line of contact to Loder from Duck via the Craightons, printers who lived almost next door to Duck, and were at one time joint churchwardens with him. On Craighton's death in 1761 he was succeeded in his printing business by his widow Elizabeth, and on hers, Charles Punchard took over, who had a brief partnership with Loder, dissolved in November 1773 when the latter went to Woodbridge to set up on his own.

39. Martin and Duck disagree on some 30 occasions. Six of these are the cases listed earlier where Martin has a blank and Duck does not. Many of the remainder are minor (for example, the substitution of 'pictures' for 'inscriptions'), and are easily explained by mistranscriptions. Where Martin and Duck disagree, Loder shows no particular preference, choosing Martin and Duck about equally.

Loder disagrees with *both* his sources about ten times, but with just one exception these can be explained as simple transcription error from Martin or Duck, or tidying them up. The exception is Buers (entry 119), where Loder adds a whole phrase not present in Martin or Duck. It is possible that Loder's editor or printer made a slip, or that Loder supplemented Martin's copy with a manuscript other than Duck.

40. This can be seen in his Cambridgeshire travels, where he respects the county boundary. The evidence for this is clear-cut on the east, where he never casually crosses into Suffolk. There is a risk of circular argument on the west and south of the county – we do not have a Huntingdonshire, Hertfordshire or Essex Journal, and so would not know if he had sometimes criss-crossed those borders during his Cambridgeshire trips. However the number of churches per day covered in Cambridgeshire whilst working to the west and south of the county never drops significantly, and there are no missing days, which combine to suggest that no excursions were made into neighbouring counties during that time.

41. George Longe was a witness on 21 December (entry 1). Crow is mentioned at Elmsett on 22 August (entry 252).

42. He records the names of those responsible far more often in Cambridgeshire than in Suffolk. This may be because his main visit to Cambridgeshire took place after the bulk of his Suffolk travels were over, when he had learnt the need for a fuller record. Or the presence of his deputies in Suffolk, or his local knowledge, may have made it less necessary to take a note of the names.

43. See above, p. 68.

44. See above, Journal entry 273.

45. See above, p. 67.

46. For example, Trumpington (entry 148) and Peters Duxford (entry 180).

47. See above, pp. 53.

48. Repetitions in, for example, Caxton (entry 139), Hauxton (152). Incomplete or mangled entries at Little Abington (186), Stetchworth (199), Kenton (210).

49. Withersfield (entries 38 and 46), listed under both Cambridgeshire and Suffolk (discussed later in this appendix); Cornard magna and parva (113, 114 and 121, 122), and Tendryng Hall chapel, Stoke by Nayland (118, 273), all in Suffolk; Gilden Morden (169, 178), in Cambridgeshire.

50. His comment at Covehithe (226) that there were many other pictures 'which I remember not' may indicate that he normally relied on his memory to write up each church, perhaps in the evening after the day's activities, or perhaps several days later. At Cambridge a number of entries are out of order by several days, indicating that at least this period of time must have elapsed before some of them were first written up (unless he was copying up later from disorganised slips of paper).

51. For example, in his duplicate entries for Cornard Magna, Dowsing recorded the Constable's name as first Taner, then Turner (entries 113 and 121).

52. Martin's transcript of the Suffolk Journal has 'SI' and 'SP'. It contains a marginal note in Martin's hand where he infers that these stand for 'Superstitious Inscription' and 'Superstitious Picture' respectively. Scribbled and not very distinguishable abbreviations would explain occasional disagreements between the transcripts, as at Holton St Mary (49); Eyke (54); Kelsale (61). These are all Suffolk entries, so it may have been Leedes who introduced the abbreviations, in his first generation transcript; however Baker appears to have retained the abbreviation in one case, though not legibly enough to be certain (All Saints, Cambridge, 23), which would suggest they were present in the original. The confusion over whether 'church' or 'chancel' is being referred to at Horham (259) may indicate that 'ch' was used as an abbreviation.

53. The evidence for poor handwriting in the Journal includes Baker's marginal note that 'these notes are in a bad hand' (Christ's College, 16); the fact that Baker could transcribe Mr Frog's name as 'Ewy' (Cambridge, Holy Trinity, 25); the impossible place name 'Kayfield' (210); and a host of minor variants between Baker and Grey who were working from the same manuscript (for example, 'seven' in Grey being read as 'and an' by Baker: entry for Kingston, 136). Dowsing's neat Italic may be seen in the marginalia of his books (e.g. Plate 5) and his hurried scrawl in Plate 6.

54. There is evidence against the view that unsorted notes on odd sheets of paper were what emerged from Samuel's library. First, both Grey and Baker (who, from what was said earlier, are likely to have been working from Dowsing's original) maintain virtually the same order of entries, despite their somewhat jumbled date order.

Secondly, Baker records what are almost certainly the position of page breaks by means of lines ruled across the page, indicating that he was working with a document already ordered into pages (these are recorded in the notes to our commentary on the Journal). Unfortunately he does not continue this practice all the way through, otherwise we might have been able to use the number of entries between page breaks to discover whether the manuscript from which he was working was organised chronologically or by county. Finally, there must be some doubt, too, that if Leedes were handling odd bits and pieces of text he would have described it as 'MSS'.

55. Besides that discussed in the text, there are various other clues to the original structure of the manuscript of the Journal, but all are tantalising and inconclusive.

For example, before the entry for Croxton (142), Baker includes the note 'Huntintonshire' [*sic*]. (In fact, Croxton is in Cambridgeshire, but that does not affect the argument.) What if the 'Huntintonshire' note were Dowsing's? Then this would be evidence that the original manuscript Journal did *not* separate out counties into separate manuscripts. Much more importantly, it would demonstrate that Dowsing recorded himself as having been to Huntingdonshire, even though he was mistaken about the county of this particular church. His visiting just one church in that county seems unlikely, but Baker would have included just this single 'Hunts' entry as it fell in the middle of a Cambridgeshire tour; he would not have troubled to record any more lengthy Hunts tours, as his primary interest was Cambridgeshire. The difficulty with this hypothesis is that Grey does not include the 'Huntintonshire' note in his printed version: this may be because he realised that Dowsing was mistaken about the county (which would not threaten our hypothesis), or because he recognised the annotation as being a later intrusion, and ignored it as not part of the original manuscript (which would). Conceivably the annotation is Baker's (mistaken) note to himself, in which case Grey would not even have seen it.

Another ambiguous clue arises from the entry for 5 January (entry 38). During transcription, Baker took particular care that the final entry for that day could be fitted onto the bottom of his page – the previous entry does not start on a new line as normal, but is continued on the same line as its predecessor, separated by a slash, to give a little more room for the final entry. This is the occasion of Dowsing's first entering Suffolk, and this change of county may have seemed a natural break point for Baker temporarily to end a page. This would suggest a *chronological* Journal, and not separate manuscripts for each county. On the other hand, it is a full month before Dowsing returns to Cambridge, and the size of that gap might equally have made it a natural break point for Baker, even if the original Journal had already separated Cambridgeshire out into a separate document.

Finally, the surviving text mentions the county name 'Suffolk' just three times – twice on the occasion of Dowsing's first entering Suffolk from Cambridge (on 6 January, entry 442), and the displaced entry for 9 January (39), and then again on 19 January (48) after a gap of ten days with no entries. One might hypothesise that the original manuscript was organised chronologically and had, for example, a brief Essex excursion between 10 January and 18 January and that the move back to Suffolk on 19 January was highlighted. Unfortunately, however, this elegant hypothesis is not supported elsewhere – there are no county names at any of the other county transitions later in the Journal. Indeed the fact that 'Cambridgeshire' is specified only at the initial entry into the rural county (3 January, entry 31), and that two of the three Suffolk designations occur at the first entry into that county on 6/9 January give some support to the alternative hypothesis – that there were separate manuscripts for each county, with the county name at the beginning of each. However, it is then difficult to explain the 19 January entry of 'Suffolk'.

56.  Grey however, recognising that Withersfield was in Suffolk ignored it when he printed the Cambridge Journal. There are other explanations. For example, if Dowsing transcribed the rough slips into separate county manuscripts he might accidentally have entered Withersfield twice, once under each county. This is not impossible, but requires not only a duplicate entry (which we know can occur) but some confusion on Dowsing's part about which county Withersfield belongs to – he would have entered it once in the Cambridgeshire section of his Journal, once in that for Suffolk. There is slight support for this possibility in the fact that the first occurrence of Withersfield (5 January, entry 38) is *not* flagged with the county-name 'Suffolk', which is reserved for the following day's entry.

57.  There were plenty of channels by which the existence of the two portions of the Journal could have been communicated between antiquaries in the two counties. Thomas Martin and Thomas Baker were themselves corresponding as early as 1718, a letter from Martin to Baker dated 27 October of that year surviving in the *Collectanea Buriensia* held at SRO(B).

58.  At least one author (Crouch, *Puritanism and Art*, 141) has suggested that the Journal may be grossly inaccurate and unreliable. The detailed evidence accumulated for this edition makes this view untenable.

*THE JOURNAL*

1.  Baker has 'Horscott' for 'Hanscott'; 'over the chappell door'; omits '& Porta Coeli'. Baker rules a line across the page after this entry, probably indicating a page break in the original.

2.  Hutchinson, *Memoirs*, 25, quoted in Twigg, *University*, 36. For Cosin's work of beautification elsewhere see Hoffman, 'The Puritan revolution', and the commentary on Journal entries 20 and 24.

3.  W&C, I, 42–3, 75–6; Walker, *Peterhouse*, 57, 127–8; Cosin, *Correspondence*, 223–4; Hoffman, 'The Puritan revolution', 97–9; Chainey, 'Lost stained glass', 78; Payne, *Sacred Music*, 94–100. As regards plate, there is a letter from Cosin's goldsmith mentioning a pair of candlesticks, a censer, and a flagon engraved with St Peter; these have gone, but a chalice and a flagon engraved with the Good Shepherd survive from Wren's time (Cosin, *Correspondence*, I, 223–4; Oman, *Church Plate*, 161, 206). W&C note that the *desiderata* quoted here is undated and assume it dates from around the time of the consecration of the chapel, but as printed in Walker it follows directly after a summary of 1634–39 expenditure; the later date is accepted by Hoffman. In 1632 seven windows still remained to be filled with painted glass, but the report of 1641 (quoted in the text) shows that Cosin had by then obtained at least two items from his wish-list (the marble front to the altar and the narrative paintings), and the remains of painted glass now in storage in the college suggest he achieved a third (see n.19 below).

4.  In July 1636 the chapel accounts included expenditure on two pairs of shoes and shoe strings (Hoffman, 'The Puritan Revolution', 98). Osmond quotes some Puritan doggerel of 1641 satirising (probably Cosin's) 'golden slippers consecrated' (Osmond, *Life of John Cosin*, 108).

5. *In quod cupiunt Angeli [prospicere]* – 'which things angels desire to look into', thus quoting St Peter in his own college (I Peter i.12). The Latin version of the New Testament from which this is taken has not been identified.

6. Cosin purchased a 'sencor' in July 1638, and used 'a little boat' formerly belonging to Bishop Andrewes to pour out frankincense. The college accounts for the chapel for 1643 show expenditure on rosemary, perfume and cloves. The purchase of frankincense and suchlike is recorded fairly widely in church accounts of this period but in most – perhaps all – cases this may simply have been to ensure that the church was, in George Herbert's words, 'perfumed' at great festivals (and one should bear in mind the belief that aromatics could clear the air of infection). The use of incense at Peterhouse was to some extent ceremonial, and was accordingly lampooned by Puritan writers. (Cosin, *Correspondence*, 224; Prynne, *Canterburies Doome*, 74, 123; Walker, *Peterhouse*, 55; Atchley, *Incense*, 369; Staley, *Hierurgia*, II, 175–180; Osmond, *A Life of John Cosin*, 82, 105–108.)

7. BL Harl. MS 7019, fol. 71. The background to this report of 1641 is discussed on p. 50 above. At the trial of Laud the innovations at Peterhouse received special attention; the details are virtually identical to those given in the 1641 report, and it seems likely that it was used as the basis for the accusations. One detail was added by his accusers, that there was 'a speciall consecrated Knife there kept upon the Altar, to cut the sacramental bread' (in fact the knife would at most have been blessed, not consecrated). (Prynne, *Canterburies Doome*, 73–4.)

8. College accounts, quoted in Payne, *Sacred Music*, 165.

9. Walker, *Peterhouse*, 58. For the roof, see RCHME, *Cambridge*, I, plate 25; Pevsner, *Cambridgeshire*, 79.

10. College Bursar's Rolls, extract kindly provided by Catherine Hall, who also provided some of the further extracts used later in this commentary.

11. Cole, BL Add. MS 5861, p. 260 (fol. 132v).

12. Hughes, *Catalogue*, xiii–xiv.

13. Inventory of 1650 in Peterhouse chapel MSS; BL Add. MS 5861, p. 260–62 (fols. 132v, 133r), p. 268 (fol. 136v); loose papers kept with Peterhouse chapel accounts.

14. Extract from college Bursar's Rolls, kindly provided by Catherine Hall.

15. This form of decoration can be seen today in the chapel ceiling at Gonville and Caius, and Pevsner, *Cambridgeshire*, suggests that the two chapels were originally alike in decoration.

16. The accounts are on a folded sheet tucked loosely into the book of chapel accounts. The relevant payments are on 6 & 8 June, 1638.

17. Fragments of glass of the same date as the east window remained in the side windows until 1855, and were then stored (W&C, I, 49n). After many years in a cellar the complete, and largely undamaged, panel from one of these windows is now on display in the Lubbock room: it is by the same artist as the east window, and may represent part of the subject of Christ washing the disciples' feet; significantly the section containing Christ did not survive. (RCHME, *Cambridge*, II, 157–8, 160.) We are grateful to Dr Roger Lovatt for drawing this to our attention, and arranging a visit, and for assistance with the college records.

18. RCHME, *Cambridge*, II, plate 215.

19. Blomefield, *Collectanea*, 157. Willis and Clark did not find significant sums spent on *replacing* the glazing in the college accounts. Thomas Walker provides an alternative explanation for the survival of the glass in *Peterhouse Men* (Pt. II, 283–4); he suggests

that the donor of the glass, Luke Skippon, was powerful enough to protect it. As pointed out by Steegmann, *Cambridge,* 53–4, quoted by Chainey, 'Lost stained glass', 78 n.66, Luke Skippon was the brother of Cromwell's general, Philip Skippon, which 'must have put the iconoclast Dowsing into a pretty quandary'. The implication is that in his Journal Dowsing simply turned a blind eye to the central crucifixion scene; this is, however, unlikely given the symbolic importance of Peterhouse chapel, and the wide degree of interest which developments there had aroused.

20. Barwick, *Querela Cantabrigiensis,* 17–18, quoted on p. 53 above. Soldiers were not an unusual sight in Cambridge colleges at this period, as they were frequently quartered there. Twigg, *University,* 144–6, summarises the evidence: soldiers are known to have been quartered at Pembroke, Peterhouse, Jesus, Corpus Christi, King's, Trinity, and St John's. Is it coincidence that these colleges were those at the forefront of Laudian reform?

21. Venn & Venn, *Alumni Cantabrigienses,* provides two candidates. One is George Long, admitted, at age 22, to St John's. Little is known of him. The other is the George Longe who was admitted Sizar at Trinity in June 1646, and in 1662 was ejected from his Staffordshire incumbency. His ejection, and later career, indicates that he might have been of a similar mind to Dowsing, but he was only fifteen or sixteen in December 1643, and seems a little young for the post of co-iconoclast; and he was from London, so there is no particular reason to suppose he would casually have been in Cambridge before his admission during those troubled times. Furthermore, if we are prepared to assume that Dowsing brought his assistant up from London then we lose any reason for searching for Longe amongst Cambridge alumni.

22. Walker, *Admissions to Peterhouse*; Venn & Venn, *Alumni Cantabrigienses*; Mullinger, *University of Cambridge,* III, 282–3, 403 n.5. Mullinger gives the Christian name of Francius as Adam; on Handscomb, Mullinger appears incorrect in his details.

23. We have followed Baker in inserting 'peril of idolatry *and the Queens Injunctions.* Others...'; Grey does not refer to the injunctions. Baker omits the paragraph headed 'More, Pembroke Hall'.

24. We are grateful to Jayne Ringrose, archivist of Pembroke, for commenting on an earlier draft of this section, and for rescuing us from an error regarding the college plate.

25. In 1628 the Master, Jerome Beale, removed whitewash from the chapel walls, perhaps to expose pre-Reformation wall paintings (Twigg, *University,* 18 n.45).

26. Attwater, *Pembroke College,* 70; Cooper, *Annals,* III, 283.

27. BL Harl. MS 7019, fol. 81.

28. Pictures painted on cloth are recorded at some of the other colleges (for example Peterhouse, Clare, Trinity College, St John's College); the possibility of prints is suggested by Laud's trial, in which the introduction of prints into his own chapel was held against him (Varley, *Cambridge during the Civil War,* 41–2).

29. W&C, I, 138; Chainey, 'Lost stained glass', 77.

30. In chapter 5.

31. Baker omits the entry for 'Keies Colledg'.

32. Batchcroft's predecessor, Gostlin, blocked Cosin's attempt to achieve a senior fellowship – he 'evidently thought him too much of a firebrand' (Professor Christopher Brooke, personal communication). Batchcroft himself voted with the Cal-

vinist and Puritan bloc (Twigg, *University*, 31 n.136, 34 n.153), but 'was not really a party man... [he was] a reed prepared to bend before the wind'. He retained his Mastership in 1644, when many others were ejected. Cosin was Fellow of Caius from 1620–24. (Brooke, *Caius*, 111, 122.)

33. See above, p. 50.
34. Twigg, *University*, 289.
35. Brooke, *Caius*, 122; W&C, I, 193–4; Venn, *Biographical History*, III, 161–4.
36. BL Harl. MS 7019, fol. 79.
37. Brooke, *Caius*, 114 n.43; but RCHME, *Cambridge*, I, 76 dates them to the early eighteenth century.
38. Blomefield, *Collectanea*, 102. We are grateful to Julie Spraggon for discussion about the 'letters of gold'.
39. Chainey, 'Lost stained glass', 75.
40. 'The roof is... inwardly arched and coloured with blue, beautified all over with cherubs' heads in rays of light' (Blomefield, *Collectanea*, 101, quoted by Brooke, *Caius*, 172). There was major work carried out in the period 1718–26, and Blomefield was a scholar at the college when the work was completed. It is not clear whether the cherubim had been restored before this date; Brooke, *Caius*, 113 n.41 says simply that the angels were restored after 1660. In Waterhouse's restoration of 1870 the blue and gilt background was stripped off the panels, so as to show the oak. (Venn, III, 165; RCHME, *Cambridge*, I, 74. See also W&C, I, 195.)
41. There is little chance of this being a case of Dowsing counting correctly (or of writing neatly enough to be legible), for there is a 1637 payment to the craftsman Woodrofe for 65 panels at 30s. 0d. each. As the ceiling is five panels wide this would imply that the ceiling then had thirteen rows of panels, or at least that thirteen rows were decorated. The ceiling today has seventeen rows of panels, the west screen having been moved a few feet to the west in 1870, and the ceiling extended – this patch of blank ceiling was filled in with more cherubim in 1981 when a new organ was installed. However, the two rows closest to the east end apparently had their cherubim removed in the early part of this century to provide a 'cordon sanitaire' between the clashing styles of the Laudian ceiling and the Victorian byzantine apse. Today, then, there are 75 angels on the ceiling (5 x 15). To confuse matters, however, in 1637 there was a separate payment for 'cherubins heads at the upper end of the chappell', so the original arrangement is not clear-cut, particularly as both of these entries in the accounts are phrased in a way which makes them appear to be variations from an original quote for work to be done – and as a further confounding factor, today's roof includes eighteen cherubim at the coving. (W&C, I, 194; RCHME, *Cambridge*, I, 74; Professor Christopher Brooke, personal communication.)
42. Twigg, *University*, 63, 243, 293; Mullinger, *University of Cambridge*, III, 293.
43. Baker has '*120* superstitious pictures'; omits 'pictures' after 'saints'. Baker rules a line across the page after this entry, probably indicating a page break in the original.
44. The following account is based largely on Twigg, *Queens' College*, 46, 143, 164, 273–5, 277–8, 384. See also Searle, *The History of Queens' College*, 515; W&C, II, 39–43; Twigg, *University*, 37 n.165. For the organ see Payne, *Sacred Music*, 105–6.
45. BL Harl. MS 7019, fol. 78.
46. W&C, II, 38.
47. Lack *et al.*, *Brasses*, 47; RCHME, *Cambridge*, I, plate 5.

48. W&C, II, 44.
49. See RCHME, *Cambridge* II, 172 and plate 226. We are grateful to Dr Walker, of Queens' College, for helpful comments on a draft of this section, and in particular for raising doubts about the antiquity of the angels! These uncertainties centre round the existence of an attic to the hall from at least the late seventeenth century, which might have been expected to interfere with the angels; the complete replacement of the roof of the hall above the ring-beam in 1846 (though the angels are let into the ring-beam, and might therefore have survived); and lack of mention of the angels in any college history before the mid twentieth century. One possibility is that one or two angels are original, with the remainder being nineteenth-century reproductions.
50. Baker has December *28th*; 'manifested' in place of 'maintained'; 'communion *plate*'; 'church' for 'civil act' (probably a slip of the eye, directly under 'church' in previous line); 'to break down' for 'we broake down'.
51. Cooper, *Annals*, III, 283.
52. St Catharine's College Muniments, L26, fol. 103r. This inventory was kindly extracted by Professor J. H. Baker. We are grateful to him for this, for examining the accounts (see following footnote), and for his comments on an earlier draft of this section
53. Jones, *St Catharine's College*, 22. The college accounts for 1636–42 do not include any items of significance relating to the chapel, with the possible exception of ten shillings spent on paving tiles, and the tantalising 'cariadge of the Communion plate from London', both occurring 1639–40 (L26, fols. 136v, 138r).
54. D'Ewes, *Journal*, 49, 59, quoted in Twigg, *University*, 49 n.45.
55. W&C, II, 87. The new chapel required the first act of Consecration since the Restoration (Browne, *St Catharine's College*, 157). There are panels of glass showing God the Father (1598) and another of St Paul (1600) in the hall, but these are continental, and unlikely to be original to the college (Chainey, 'Lost stained glass', 79).
56. Twigg, *University*, 28, 34, 51, 56, 101–2, 120; Jones, *St Catharine's College*, 94–8.
57. Baker has 'I Sa[muel] 19', with no verse number. We have inserted a full stop before the reference.
58. W&C, I, 289–91. The windows were given by individual benefactors, one, for example, containing a coat of arms and a religious poem, an acrostic on the name of the benefactor.
59. Cooper, *Annals*, III, 283, 294.
60. We are grateful to Catherine Hall, archivist of Corpus Christi, for extracting this inventory, and for her helpful comments on an earlier draft of these comments.
61. Twigg, *University*, 49.
62. Robert Tunstall or Tonstall. After 24 years as a Fellow he was ejected by Manchester in April 1644, but was reinstated in 1660, holding the post until his death in 1679. (Mullinger, *University of Cambridge*, III, 295; Twigg, *University*, 293; Venn & Venn, *Alumni Cantabrigienses*, IV, 273.)
63. The scriptural reference is a little odd, as it passes no judgement on Eli or the temple, merely observing that 'Eli the priest sat upon a seat by a post of the temple of the Lord'. It may simply be that Dowsing found Love seated in the church or chapel, and the reference was brought to mind. But a darker interpretation is possible: Eli allowed his sons to pervert their priestly office, and as a punishment the priesthood

was removed from his family line. It may be, however, that the reference is a mistranscription: Baker transcribed it as 'I Sa[muel] 19', without a verse number (a chapter with no obvious relevance), indicating how easily transcription errors could arise.

64. Stokes, *Corpus Christi*, 107.

65. Drummond, *Church Architecture*, 33.

66. Blomefield, *Collectanea*, 147.

67. Robert Masters, who wrote a college history in 1753. He comments: 'It is much to be wished that the master [Dr Love] had used his interest with Dowsing, whilst he was employed here in demolishing superstitious monuments, to have desisted from doing it in St Benedict's Church, where so many of his [the Master's] predecessors were interred: or if this could not have been obtained of the enraged rabble who assisted him in the execution thereof, that he [Dr Love] had at least preserved in writing what monuments of antiquity were then in it. *Footnote*: His tenant at Ickleton [*recte* Duxford St John's, Journal entry 184] assisted Dowsing in levelling the chancel there'. In his reference to an 'enraged rabble' Masters may be repeating oral tradition, or merely reflecting his own prejudices and preconceptions (Masters, *Corpus Christi*, 149).

68. The altar rails, and possible some of the panelling, went to Thurning Church, and 'two large oak Corinthian pillars which supported the altarpiece are to be seen in the drawing-room of Thurning hall'. Part of the wainscoting over the entrance to the chapel was at some date unknown made up into a pulpit for the church at Grant-chester, the central panel of which displays the arms of Dr John Jegon, which was the coat of arms nearest the President's stall in the chapel. (Bury, *Corpus Christi*, 14–15, 123.)

69. Baker has an illegible number of superstitious pictures, which might be seven; '*sent to them* a horse'; 'one hundred pound' for '300'; has 'Sonn', (whereas Grey reads his manuscript as 'Sunn', and puts an explanatory 'Son' in brackets); transcribes Latin inscription as *me tibi virgo pia gentier comendo maria*.

70. W&C, I, 281–5; *Church and Parish of St Benet*, 5.

71. Lack *et al.*, *Brasses*, 54.

72. Lack *et al.*, *Brasses*, 52–3; Cheshire, *Dowsing's Destructions*, 81n.

73. Masters, *Corpus Christi*, appendix, p. 10. He adds that removing the images cost 20s. 0d.

74. Baker omits the date. We have followed Baker, who has 'Boyleston'; Grey has 'Bogleston'.

75. Payne, *Sacred Music*, 101; Gray and Brittain, *Jesus College*, 73, 75, 76; W&C, II, 143; Hoyle, 'Near popery', 214.

76. *OED* gives 'septum' as a partition. The key to the plan of the private chapel of Bishop Andrewes lists 'the septum, with two ascents' (number 5. on the plan), and appears to be referring to the altar rails. Andrewes refers to the commandments in the communion service being read 'at the door of the septum', that is at the gate of the altar rails (Andrewes, *Notes on the Book of Common Prayer*, 141ff, quoted in Welsby, *Lancelot Andrewes*, 127 n.6).

77. BL Harl. MS 7019, fol. 80.

78. The organ was set up again at the Restoration, and then given to All Saints' Church, Jewry in 1790; that church was pulled down in 1864, and the organ is now at Little Bardfield in Essex. The case is supposed to be by Renatus Harris and some of the

pipework may be pre-Civil War. (Morgan & Morgan, *Jesus Chapel*, 192; Jesus College, A/C 1.3, p. 1030; Payne, *Sacred Music*, 161 n.4; Freeman, *English Organ-Cases*, 39; Diarmaid MacCulloch, personal communication.) We are grateful to Dr F. H. Willmoth for extracting references from the account books, and for helpful comments on an earlier draft of this section.

79.  W&C, II, 143 n.1(which has 'clearing', not 'cleaning', but this is probably a mistranscription); RCHME, *Cambridge*, I, 89.

80.  W&C, II, 141. Chainey, 'Lost stained glass', 76, traces the later history of the remnants of the glass.

81.  Jesus College, A/C 1.4, p. 24.

82.  W&C, II, 143.

83.  RCHME, *Cambridge*, I, 89, and plate 32.

84.  Sherman, *Historia*, 19.

85.  RCHME, *Cambridge*, I, plate 141.

86.  Mullinger, *University of Cambridge,* III, 301; Morgan & Morgan, *Jesus Chapel*, 194; Gray and Brittain, *Jesus College*, 81.

87.  W&C, I, 85, 86; Forbes, *Clare College*, 115.

88.  We are grateful to Dr Roger Schofield, college archivist, for confirming the point, and for kindly looking over an earlier draft of this section.

89.  Cole, BL Add MS 5803, fol. 8, quoted in Chainey, 'Lost stained glass', 74; see also W&C, I, 86. Cole reports five coats of arms remaining; as elsewhere, Dowsing had left these alone.

90.  BL Harl. MS 7019, fol. 84.

91.  Twigg, *University*, 63, 241.

92.  The date must be an error for 28 December; Baker omits it. Baker rules a line across the page after this entry, probably indicating a page break in the original.

93.  We are grateful to Margaret Farrar, archivist of Trinity Hall, for helpful comments on this section. The college accounts for this period are now too fragile to be consulted, but Crawley's silence suggests that they say little about the chapel in this period (Crawley, *Trinity Hall*).

94.  As David Hoyle points out (personal communication), Eden was a survivor, but something of an enigma: he was criticised in the report that went to Laud, yet sided with the Laudians over a controversial sermon in 1637; disliked by the writer(s) of the 1641 Puritan report, yet took the Covenant. His loyalties 'remained equivocal… He lent money both to the King and Parliament at different times' (Twigg, *University*, 34, 46). He died in 1645.

95.  Malden, *Trinity Hall*, 136–7. The college included laymen, who may also have been less bound up in religious controversy than the clerical Fellows at other colleges.

96.  BL Harl. MS 7019, fol. 85.

97.  Chainey 'Lost stained glass', 80; Crawley, *Trinity Hall*, 32.

98.  RCHME, *Cambridge,* II, 249; Lack *et al., Brasses*, 81–3; Blomefield, *Collectanea*, 105.

99.  Cullier's will was proved in 1657, so he probably died in office (entry in Venn & Venn, *Alumni Cantabrigienses).* The Venns misread Dowsing's note, assuming that it was the brass of 'Culiard' that Dowsing destroyed, and thus created a (virtually blank) entry for Culiard; the misunderstanding has been transmitted to Lack *et al., Brasses*, 81–3.

100. Baker has Turwhit, Peche, Roads as Fellows. This looks like a slip of the eye from St John's College, which in Baker's ordering of the entries, immediately follows

Trinity College.

101. Cooper, *Annals*, III, 282. We are grateful to Jonathan Smith for confirming references, and for helpful comments on an earlier draft of this section.

102. W&C, II, 575; Hoyle, 'Near popery', 213.

103. Hoyle, 'Near popery', 213; Tatham, *Puritans in Power*, 97. A pair of silver gilt flagons, donated by the Stuart brothers in 1636, are still possessed by the college (Cobb, *Trinity Organ*, 10; Gray & Swann, *Catalogue*, 1).

104. Tatham, *Puritans in Power*, 97; Rouse Ball, *Trinity College*, 90. In a later book (*Cambridge Papers*) Rouse Ball states, without giving his sources (and is followed by Trevelyan), that after Dowsing's visit the communion table was set up in the middle of the chapel without rails, the organ and hangings were removed, and certain figures painted on the walls of the east end were whitewashed. Rouse Ball also claims (again without giving his evidence) that there had been a crucifix on the altar. But this is in the highest degree unlikely at this date. Laud's use of a crucifix on the altar at the King's coronation at Westminster Abbey formed one the charges against him at his trial (he said it was part of the regalia), and it is inconceivable that if such an item had been introduced in a Cambridge college chapel it would not have been thrown in his face; it would, too, have appeared in the 1641 Puritan report on the colleges. Even at the coronation of the King in Scotland, the crucifix to which the bishops genuflucted was not on the altar, but was 'curiously wrought' on a tapestry behind it, whilst the King's chapel in Whitehall had a 'silver crucifix amaking to hange therein' (thus not on the altar) for the Spanish marriage of 1623. At first sight, Hollar (if he was the artist) shows soldiers removing a crucifix from a communion table in the famous 1642 print (see Plate 18), but on closer inspection it is being removed from a reredos behind the altar; similar reredoses appear in a Dutch engraving of the ratification of the Spanish marriage at the Chapel Royal (though McCullough points out that the Catholic ornament does not correspond with contemporary descriptions), and in an anti-Arminian print in a pamphlet of 1642 (though one wonders whether this was the original context of the woodcut). Perhaps they were based on reports of what was happening at places like St John's College, Journal entry 12. (Rouse Ball, *Cambridge Papers*, 96; Trevelyan, *Trinity*, 35; Prynne, *Canterburies Doome*, 473, 475, 487, 492; Lee, *Road to Revolution*, 129; *All the Memorable and Wonder Striking Parliamentary Mercies*, page 2 (reprinted in John Vicar's *Transactions* and *True Information*); McCullough, *Sermons*, 33–4 (for a better reproduction of the Spanish marriage, see Huray, *Music and the Reformation*, plate 10); Harbie, *Divi Arminii*, opp. title page.)

105. Cobb, *Trinity Organ*, 10 n.9.

106. BL Harl. MS 7019, fol. 77.

107. Cooper, *Annals*, III, 322; W&C, II, 576 n.3.

108. W&C, II, 576.

109. Thomas Comber, who was ejected in 1644 (Twigg, *University*, 296).

110. Quoted in W&C, II, 577.

111. Some glass was inserted in 1563–65, but would not have interested Dowsing, being mainly heraldic, all superstitious elements having been 'broken forth' in 1565; it survived until at least the eighteenth century (Chainey, 'Lost stained glass', 81).

112. Blomefield, *Collectanea*, 109.

113. W&C, II, 576.

114. Twigg, *University*, 303; Rouse Ball & Venn, *Admissions to Trinity College*, II, 262; Peile,

*Biographical Register,* I, 440–41.

115. We have followed Baker who has 'Thorten' (Gray has 'Therden'); '20 former, *the* last'.

116. For the election, see Twigg, *University,* 27.

117. BL Harl. MS 7019, fol. 74.

118. Payne, *Sacred Music,* 106–8.

119. Woodhouse, *S. John's College Chapel,* 9, based on college rental SB4.5, fol. 24 (top); SB4.5, fol. 49v. Baker (*St John's College,* I, 218) says that the new window was an east window. We are grateful to Malcolm Underwood, archivist of the college, for his helpful comments on an earlier draft of this section, for active help with the accounts and the references, and for untangling our confusion about dates.

120. W&C, II, 293–4; Crook, *From the Foundation,* 20–21; Baker, *St John's College,* I, 217; Hoyle, 'Near popery', 214. Baker says that the painting and pictures alone cost more than £100. The 'dove of glory' here and at Peterhouse were specifically mentioned in the charges brought against Laud: 'That in St. Johns and Peter House Chappels there were Pictures of the Holy Ghost in forme of a Dove' (Prynne, *Canterburies Doome,* 74).

121. D'Ewes, *Autobiography,* II, 112.

122. Quoted in Miller, *Portrait of a College,* 22.

123. BL Harl. MS 7019, fol. 75.

124. 'I H R N' may be the clerk accidentally muddling 'I H S' and 'I N R I'; or it may be a mistranscription of 'I C D N', the initial letters of what was painted on the roof.

125. The 'two little chappells' were the chantry chapels to Bishop Fisher and Hugh Ashton, which had been converted to secular use in 1561. Beale obviously converted them back. The 1641 report suggests that each chapel had an altar, which would be very surprising in an Anglican church of the period; however in the inventory discussed in the text they are simply described as tables. Little St Mary's had a similar table in the vestry. In 1644, following Beale's ejection, the chapels were again used for secular purposes. Fisher's chapel was subsequently restored to religious use, but not Dr Ashton's, which by 1848 served as the Master's pantry, and later as an outhouse for the lodge. (Woodhouse, *S. John's College Chapel,* 7–9, 15; Babington, *Hospital and Infirmary,* 27; Baker, *St John's College,* 153–4; our commentary on Dowsing's visit to Little St Mary's, above, Journal entry 20.)

126. BL Harl. MS 7019, fol. 74.

127. Woodhouse, *S. John's College Chapel,* 8, quoting BL Harl. MS 7047, that is, Baker xx, 253. Thomas Baker's mid-eighteenth-century portrayal of the chapel in Dr Beale's time corresponds closely with the above descriptions, and is probably based on the accounts and the inventory, which he preserved (Baker, *St John's College,* I, 217–8).

128. College rental SB4.5, fol. 226v.

129. College rental SB4.5 252v. Our interpretation (removal of old, replacement by quarries) is based on the analysis of the cost of glass in appendix 12. Woodhouse, writing in 1848, interprets this entry as referring to glass in the side-windows, presumably because when he was writing the old chapel was still standing, and there were many fragments of old glass still remaining in the east window, which he took to have remained untouched since Robert Taylor was 'set on work to place some old painted glass in the great window' in 1634. He may be correct, though he later says that 'the [east window] glass seems to have been placed there rather to save the expense of new plain glass, than to add any beauty to the window', and this may

be because the glass in the east window was replaced after iconoclasm, explaining the jumble. The armorial glass seems to have survived relatively unscathed, judging by the quantity described by Woodhouse. (Mullinger, *St John's College*, 129; Woodhouse, *S. John's College Chapel*, 9, 14, 17–20.)

130. See W&C, II, 294–5, quoting college rental SB4.5 fol. 256.

131. College rental SB4.5 fol. 252v. 'Old Dowsy' was not the iconoclast, his name appearing annually here and (if it is the same person) at King's as handyman. (Mullinger, *University of Cambridge*, III, 272 n.1, thus contradicting his earlier view in Mullinger, *St John's College*, 129; Graham Chainey, personal communication.)

132. Freeman, *English Organ-Cases*, 37; W&C, II, 308. RCHME, *Cambridge*, II, 191, 193; Chainey, 'Lost stained glass', 79. Chainey says that the figure of St John now in the hall is not original to the college.

133. Lack, *et al.*, *Brasses*, 59–60; RCHME, *Cambridge*, II, 191–2. The volume is recorded in the inventory as a 'Fair Bible in folio, covered with red velvet, with silver clasps and bosses, and ruled' (Woodhouse, *S. John's College Chapel*, 8, 15). Now in the college library, classmark Aa.4.40.

134. Matthews, *Walker Revised*, 81, 87; Twigg, *University*, 295; Venn & Venn, *Alumni Cantabrigienses*; Cheshire, 'Dowsing's destructions', 82 n.1.

135. Baker places this entry after the one for Trinity Hall.

136. In this discussion of King's College chapel we are greatly indebted to Graham Chainey, who has generously and enthusiastically put at our disposal his extensive knowledge of the chapel, its archives, and the sources for its history. This has smoothed our way enormously, and greatly enriched the discussion. Any errors of fact or interpretation are to be laid at our door.

137. The step immediately to the east of the stalls (the 'gradus chori'), part of the Founder's original plan, can be seen in the plan of 1609 (Plate 23; Plate 22 can be used for general orientation). However, the actual – as against intended – position of the pre-Reformation altar, and hence the original altar step(s), is not known. As shown in the 1609 plan, the two eastward bays were used for burials, and unlike the body of the choir, which had a fine marble floor, these two bays appear not to have been paved until 1611, when they were tiled. (Willis & Clark read the floor-tiling work as referring to the eastern bay only, and this affects their discussion. However, neither the way the entry is phrased, nor the number of tiles used, require this interpretation, and the 1609 plan, not available to them, contradicts it.) The pre-Reformation altar may therefore have rested on the original flooring in the third bay from the east, as at Trinity. If it were originally in this position in the third bay then the organ in the 1609 plan may be resting on the original altar platform, about sixteen feet square, with what may be a further step (or perhaps a dividing screen) to the east of it. (A step – 'le new footpace' – of seventeen feet, about the same width as the platform, is mentioned in 1611.) There is another possibility: we know that during the reordering of 1633–34 the table was moved from between the choir-stalls to stand in front of a screen at the junction of the first and second bay (this bay was, as we have seen, previously merely tiled, which would explain the large expenditure at this time on the 'floare'). At this time there were 'repairs' to the steps. It may well be that this position, between the first and second bays, was where the pre-Reformation altar had also stood, on its own floor surface over the burials: in this case the communion table that Dowsing saw was in more or less the original altar position, replaced on the original steps. The stone-work behind the wooden

panels indicates that the original builders intended (and may have built) two sets of steps; one, probably a single step for the altar, was at the junction of the first two bays and the other set (Scott in 1866 estimated four steps) began some six feet west of this junction. Now when Cole described the steps a hundred years after their post-Dowsing repairs, he spoke of the altar standing on one step, with three others 'at a good distance'. In similar vein Malden's guide book, published a little later, commented that 'you ascend it [the altar] by four steps'. There is thus a reasonable correspondence between (a) the steps of 1633, from the description of a hundred years later by Cole and Malden, and (b) the evidence of the stone-work for the original steps, and this suggests that the 1633 reordering reintroduced the pre-Reformation arrangement, placing the communion table where the altar had originally stood. (W&C, I, 369, 528 n.2, 529; Chainey, 'East end', 141–7; Malden, *King's College-Chapel*, 39.)

138.  It is noticeable that Dowsing does not mention the altar rails. They may have come down already, possibly removed for safety in advance. They would probably have needed to be three-sided in order to allow access to the eastern bay through the 1630s screen, and this is certainly what Cole's description of the later, post-Restoration, arrangement of the 1630s screen suggests, and also what James Gibbs assumed was required of a rebuild in 1724–27. If the rails did survive Dowsing's visit they are the ones now gracing Milton church, given to the church by the college in 1774 (see Plate 30). The rails have been crudely cut about to fit right across the chancel at Milton, and there is no joinery evidence of the previous (we presume three-sided) configuration. The rails have a design of open oblong panels with rails at right angles to the centre of each side joining the panel to the surrounding frame of sill, rail and posts. This motif can be traced back to the late sixteenth century but here it is accompanied by posts with obelisks as finials and other decoration – the frieze, the shell-like supporters to the posts and split baluster decoration – which, in our view, could take the date as late as the mid seventeenth century. (Chainey, 'East end', 147–8, and n.45.)

139.  This and the next paragraph: W&C, I, 523–5; Saltmarsh, *King's College*, 42; Hussey, *King's College Chapel*, 27–34; Chainey, 'East end', pp. 144–6. Chainey provides evidence that the organ was probably moved to its position above the screen in 1613; he also points out that until 1968 there were hooks on the choir walls, providing evidence for hanging tapestries.

140.  Despite the commitment to new chapel furnishings and appurtenances, the report written for Laud in 1636 found much to criticise in the way services were carried out (Cooper, *Annals*, III, 282).

141.  BL Harl. MS 7019, fol. 76.

142.  Ibid.

143.  Collins tended to vote with the Laudians. He was ejected in 1645 (Hoyle, 'A Commons investigation', 421 n.16; Twigg, *University*, 294).

144.  College Mundum Book, Nativity term 1642.

145.  Ibid, Annunciation term 1644. Of course, this may not have been WD.

146.  College Mundum Book, Baptist term 1644. For the Ordinance, see appendix 5. The organ was 'mended' in 1668, and 'a loftier' organ set up in 1674, itself replaced in 1688. The case retains carving (such as the corner satyrs) from the earlier organ of 1605, and such carving (and inscriptions such as those at Jesus College) must have provided another reason for Puritan distaste for organs in church (Hussey, *King's*

*College Chapel,* 31–4).

147. His comment on the thieves is probably just muddled note-taking, or mistranscription, or fading light, or short-sightedness. The upper central light has the thieves in their conventional position. The upper right-hand window (Plate 25) has the thieves' crosses already empty, and Joseph of Arimathea and a Roman soldier climbing ladders to retrieve the body of Christ, and it is remotely possible that Dowsing misinterpreted these two figures as thieves climbing up the ladder.

148. Wayment, *Windows, passim.*

149. Barwick, *Querela Cantabrigiensis,* 17.

150. That pragmatism may have saved the glass was also proposed by C. W. Scott-Giles in his *Sidney Sussex College,* 51. Other explanations are scouted and rejected in Chainey, 'Lost stained glass', 72–3, 76. Chainey himself inclines to the view (p. 76) that Manchester or Cromwell must have authorised the preservation of the glass, a proposal similar to that made by Leigh, *King's College,* 129–30 and by M. R. James ('The windows of King's College Chapel', 108*).* The first guide-book to the chapel, published in 1769, suggested that Provost Whichcote protected the glass: in fact Whichcote assumed the Provostship too late for this, though it is possible that he had influence as appointee before then *(*Malden*, King's College-Chapel,* 40).

151. Woodforde, *Norwich School of Glass Painting,* 211. For a Nottinghamshire example of faces being removed from windows, see Manning, *English Revolution,* 35. For examples of faces being deleted in other media, see Phillips, *Reformation of Images,* plates 20, 37, 38.

152. For Peterhouse, see above, p. 160. For other examples, see above, pp. 24 and 113.

153. Wayment, *Windows,* 1; Morgan, *Great West Window,* 5, 6.

154. Blomefield, *Collectanea,* 127. Sabine Baring-Gould, in his story *The Chorister,* has the glass taken down and hidden overnight by two men and eight choir boys, though he somewhat carelessly sets the whole incident six years too early, in 1637. His chorister hero, the fifteen-year-old William, is too perfect to live: he has a stressful 48 hours (during which the rough-necked soldiers are brought to tears by his playing of the organ), which ends when he is shot dead in his surplice by Cromwell's firing squad in front of the high altar, with the elegantly named Puritan, Zedechiah Pluckever (he of the 'rapidly-retreating' forehead), smirking in the background. In the book Baring-Gould claimed that he based the story on a true incident, but Graham Chainey has pointed out (personal communication) that he later admitted it was 'a hoax… a silly production which I trusted had been forgotten long ago' *(Cambridge Review,* 25 January 1924, 157).

155. W&C, I, 510, quoting Cole, BL Add. MS 5802, fol. 67. Antiquaries appear not to have taken much interest in the college accounts until rather later, so it is unlikely that the tradition was generated by the reference in the college accounts, discussed later, to 'taking down' the glass (Graham Chainey, personal communication).

156. Malden, *King's College-Chapel,* 40. As we now know from the accounts, the author is incorrect about the organ case.

157. Wayment, historian of the glass, assumes that Dowsing was not interested in destroying medieval glass and thus pays no attention to the detail of the accounts in this context (Wayment, *Windows,* 40). Willis and Clark discuss the accounts, but, again, not in detail (W&C, I, 513–14). Woodman follows Willis & Clark, but introduces some errors (Woodman, *King's College Chapel,* 247).

158. In 1591–92 and 1616–17 the glass in the north-west window was taken out and

repaired (RCHME, *Cambridge*, I, 124).

159. Expenditure on the chapel during our period is recorded under a heading devoted to the subject, which in the period 1641–54 had anything between three and twenty entries in a year. More or less the only expenditure not recorded under this heading in the 1640s is the 'taking down' of the glass in 1643 and the removal of the organ case in 1644, which are recorded under the catch-all 'necessary expenses', suggesting they were seen as exceptional items. This would lend weight to the idea that the taking down of the glass was not part of normal maintenance. On the other hand, the removal of the organ (as against the case) in 1643, surely an exceptional event, appears amidst other routine expenditure on the chapel.

160. Wayment, *Windows*, 40. Willis and Clark state that the sum of £178. 18s. 9d. was spent on releading and repairing glass in the late 1650s and early 1660s, which is large, but not dissimilar to the cost of major works carried out in the first and second decades of the following century, needed simply as a result of normal wear and tear (W&C, I, 513–14).

161. Wayment, *Side Chapel Glass,* 9–12; Wayment, *Windows*, plate 44.

162. Wayment, *Windows*, 122. Windows at Great St Mary's had been treated in the same way in the late sixteenth century (Bushell, *St Mary the Great*, 65).

163. College Mundum Book, 1651, 1652, 1653. Entries delatinised. The third entry mentions damage done at the time of the commission ('confracta sunt tempore Comission'). Probably this refers to Dowsing's commission from Manchester, but it may just be a reference to the commission set up by the Rump Parliament to ensure the universities subscribed to the Engagement (an oath of loyalty). Interestingly, a further sum of £2. 8s. od. was paid in Autumn 1652 to Dr Bolton (presumably Samuel Bolton, Master of Christ's College) as a reward for his expenses in 'delivering the college from the soldiers' (College Mundum Book, Michaelmas term 1652). The precise significance of this payment is not clear, though there must have been difficult relations with the soldiers around this time as Cromwell saw the need in July 1652 to command his troops not to quarter in the colleges, nor to 'offer any Injurie or Violence' to members of the University (Cooper, *Annals*, III, 452).

164. College Mundum Book, Annunciation and Michaelmas term 1652.

165. College Mundum Book, Michaelmas term 1644; W&C, I, 511–12, 525; Chainey, 'Lost stained glass', 72 n.10; Chainey, *King's Chapel*, 146–7.

166. Cole, BL Add. MS 5802, fol. 94. He recorded it in 1748. By 1769 it seems to have been in a less complete state (Malden, *King's College-Chapel*, 31) and had disappeared by 1829 (Graham Chainey, personal communication).

167. Cole, BL Add. MS 5802, fol. 92v. The scroll was referred to in the past tense by 1769 (Malden, *King's College-Chapel*, 32).

168. Cole, BL Add. MS 5802, fol. 86v.

169. Cole, BL Add. MS 5802, fol. 96v. The Argentein brass was taken up in the early nineteenth century and fixed on a loose board, the floor being boarded over, and was restored in 1896 (Graham Chainey, personal communication).

170. Cole, BL Add. MS 5802, fol. 78; RCHME, *Cambridge*, I, plates, 5, 160; Lack *et al., Brasses*, 32–6. As Cole explains, he has filled in the missing words in his drawing.

171. The destruction has continued into recent times. In the late 1960s a major reordering of the east end took place, involving changes to the original floor level and the destruction of many post-Reformation graves: there was no recording either of their position or the coffin inscriptions. In the 1980s the tomb slab to Wil-

liam Smith (d.1615) seems to have disappeared without trace when a vestry was refloored: although he was a former Provost of King's, it appears that his grave-marker was not allowed to stand in the way of progress.

172. We are grateful to Nicholas Rogers for extracting the chapel inventory of 1639 and for his helpful comments on an earlier draft of this section.

173. Wyatt, *Sidney Sussex College Chapel*, 1–2; Cooper, *Annals*, III, 283, 294.

174. Chapel Inventory, 1639, Sidney Sussex Muniments MR.31D, fols. 1–2; Wyatt, *Sidney Sussex College Chapel*, 2–3, 14–15; Wyatt, 'Building and Endowment', 51–2; W&C, II, 739; Scott-Giles, *Sidney Sussex College*, 22; Oman, *Church Plate*, 160–61. The Bishop of Bath and Wells, James Montagu, previously Master of the college, paid for the wainscot in 1612, and the coat of arms were his, impaled by those of his see. It is ironic that in the early years of this century, following the rebuilding of the chapel, services at the college became renowned for their High Anglicanism (Pyke, 'The new chapel of Sidney Sussex College').

175. Wyatt, *Sidney Sussex College Chapel*, 4; Twigg, *University*, 80–81.

176. BL Harl. MS 7019, fol. 84. 'Mr Rodes' must be Godfrey Rhodes, matriculated 1621, elected Fellow 1633, Treasurer of St Patrick's, Dublin, 1638 Dean of Derry 1640, d.1654 (Venn & Venn, *Alumni Cantabrigienses*, III, 447).

177. RCHME, *Cambridge*, II, 203, 204, 208.

178. Baker has plural 'windowes'.

179. Cunich *et al.*, *A History of Magdalene College*, 118.

180. BL Harl. MS 7019, fol. 83.

181. Le Neve records the 'King's arms' in the late seventeenth century; Blomefield 'Corbet impales Nevile' in a south window in the eighteenth. (BL Harl. MS 6821, fol. 53; Blomefield, *Collectanea*, 108).

182. *Ex info*. David Hoyle.

183. Cooper, *Annals*, III, 283; W&C, II, 207. The account books are not explicit about the nature of the expenditure on the chapel, and the accounts for 1639–45 have not survived (Peile, *Christ's College*, 160). For the organ, see *Payne, Sacred Music*, 103–5; Rackham, *Christ's College*, 229–30. We are grateful to Professor G. T. Martin for alerting us to the latter work, and for helpful comments on an earlier draft of this section.

184. BL Harl. MS 7019, fol. 83.

185. Rackham, *Christ's College*, 230–33.

186. Chainey, 'Lost stained glass', 74.

187. RCHME, *Cambridge*, I, 29.

188. There are some tiny holes by which an inscription might perhaps have been riveted.

189. The medieval eagle at Christ's is one of a series of which six now survive. This includes the one at Isleham church, Cambridgeshire, recovered from the fen in the mid nineteenth century. Might this have been a victim of 1640s iconoclasm? – William Cole mentions an eagle lectern at Fordham church, Cambridgeshire (next door to Isleham, so perhaps there is some confusion between the two) that had been 'buried in the sand during Oliver's usurpation', and eagle lecterns at Eton and Canterbury Cathedral were ejected or destroyed during the Civil War. At Maids Moreton in Buckinghamshire a note in the parish register for June 1643 says that 'a costly desk in the form of a spread eagle gilt, on which we used to lay Bishop Jewel's work [was] domed to perish as an abominable idle'. Other eagles were overlooked or ignored: Caius College had one, which was sold during the Commonwealth, in

1658, for £3, with which books were bought for the library. It had been donated in 1600, with a harmless inscription, and is not mentioned by Dowsing. Nor does Dowsing mention those at Trinity or Corpus Christi (the latter presumably Elizabethan, and thus not superstitious) which survived until 1722 and 1744 respectively. (Rackham, *Christ's College*, 243–4; Venn, *Biographical History*, III, 160; Graham Chainey, personal communication; the Moreton Parish Register note is quoted in Spraggon, 'Iconoclasm', 118, from Tennant, *Edgehill and Beyond*, 39.)

190. Baker rules a line across the page after this entry, probably indicating a page break in the original.

191. Cooper, *Annals*, II, 283; Stubbings, *Emmanuel College Chapel*, 1–6; W&C, II, 703. This section is largely based on the book on the chapel by Frank Stubbings. We are grateful to him for helpful comments on an earlier version of this section, and also to Professor Patrick Collinson for his comments.

192. W&C, II, 701. Laurence Chaderton, the Master from 1584–1622, said that communion was taken seated 'by reason of the seats so placed as they be; yet they had some kneeling also' (Shuckburgh, *Emmanuel College*, 35).

193. Cooper, *Annals*, III, 283. This was in contradiction to the Canons of 1604 and the King's regulations of late 1619, which required that in Colleges 'all the Communicants doe take the Communion kneeling' (Cooper, *Annals*, III, 130; Stubbings, *Emmanuel College Chapel*, 3).

194. Hoyle, 'Near popery', 215; Stubbings, *Emmanuel College Chapel*, 5. The plate is hallmarked 1637, and consists of three flagons, two 'basons' (alms-dishes), and two patens. There were further purchases that year of two communion cups with paten covers, and their old plate was disposed of. Oman (in his *Church Plate*, for example pp. 147, 160) warns against assuming there is any simple relationship between churchmanship and the gift of plate.

195. Noted by Samuel Rogers in March 1636 (Queen's University Belfast, Percy MS 7 ff. 106, 107; quoted in Webster, *Godly Clergy*, 178).

196. BL Harl. MS 7019, fol. 82. Thomas Holbeach and Nicholas Hall were later forced to give up their fellowships in a complex dispute about the original statutes of the college in which Parliament became involved. Holbeach returned to become Master of Emmanuel for five years, from 1675, and Vice-Chancellor 1677–78. He saw the new chapel completed and consecrated. (Twigg, *University*, 55–6, 291, 297; Mullinger, *University of Cambridge*, III, 215, 313; W&C, III, 707–8.)

197. RCHME, *Cambridge*, II, 274; Stubbings, *Emmanuel College Chapel*, 1, 2, 4. Although previous commentators have made the alternative suggestion that the communion table is the one now in the south aisle of St Edward's church, Cambridge, to which it was presented by the college in 1719, comparison with early inventories make it more likely that the table now in St Edward's in fact came from the Fellow's parlour, not the chapel (Frank Stubbings, personal communication).

198. Immediately before the entry for St Peter's, Grey introduces a sub-heading in brackets, 'Town of Cambridge'. For this entry, Grey has 'X popish inscriptions', we have used Baker's '3'. Baker has 'levelled *by* Wednesday'.

199. Lack *et al.*, *Brasses*, 72–4; Smith, 'St Peter's Church', 3, 4.

200. Smith, 'St Peter's Church', 5, 6.

201. Palmer, *Visitation Returns*, 36. Wren's visitation articles were printed in 1638, but the visitation did not begin until January 1639 (Fincham, *Visitation Articles II*, 150 n.9).

202. This and the following paragraph are based on the research of Catherine Hall, now

archivist at Corpus Christi, for whose willing help we are extremely grateful. The evidence is to be found in the Peterhouse Bursars' rolls for the years in question.

203. BL Harl. MS 7019, fol. 71.
204. Peterhouse Bursar's Rolls; W&C, I, 60 n.3.
205. Clark, 'St Mary the Less'; Chainey, 'Lost stained glass', 80–81; BL Harl. 6821, 57v. In the glass, Whittlesey was referred to as Bishop of Rochester, a post he held 1362–4; he was later Archbishop of Canterbury.
206. Cole, Add. MS 5803, fol. 57v; Lack *et al.*, *Brasses*, 69–71.
207. RCHME, *Cambridge*, II, 282; *Brief Description of the Church of St Mary the Less*, 5. The suggestion regarding the coats of arms is that of Catherine Hall. Two of the shields were not painted before 1966, probably because the font was placed in a corner when originally painted.
208. Baker has '*brake* down'.
209. *St Botolph*, 7.
210. CRO, P26/5/1.
211. Blomefield, *Collectanea*, 68.
212. RCHME, *Cambridge*, II, 268.
213. Baker has 'scriptures' for 'inscription', probably a transcription error.
214. Palmer, *Visitation Returns*, 6.
215. Palmer, *Visitation Returns*, 7; Cole, BL Add. MS 5834, fol. 201; Dawson, *Church of St Edward,* 10; RCHME, *Cambridge*, II, 273; *St Edward's Church,* 15.
216. After 'brake downe', Baker inserts an abbreviation in square brackets, probably reading '6 SPs', meaning '6 superstitious pictures'. Baker has '*8* cherubims'.
217. CRO, P20/5/1.
218. See the discussion in chapter 7, and detailed analysis in appendix 12.
219. Baker omits 'before', giving 'and 7th of January'.
220. We are grateful to Dr Thomas Cocke and Professor Christopher Brooke, who kindly read and commented upon an earlier version of this discussion of Great St Mary's. We remain responsible for any remaining faults.
221. CRO, P30/4/2.
222. It was held that, under his influence, 'in the University Church of St. Maries there was an Altar railed in, to which the Doctors, Schollers and other usually bowed'. (Prynne, *Canterburies Doome,*73–4.)
223. RCHME, *Cambridge*, II, 278; Cole, BL Add. MS 5810, fol. 33; Lack, *et al.*, *Brasses*, 66–8. In the late seventeenth century, Le Neve recorded no pre-Reformation inscriptions, so they might all have gone by then (BL Harl. 6821, fol. 55).
224. Bushell, *St Mary the Great*, 129.
225. Heads of colleges and other university dignitaries sat in stalls in the chancel. A gallery was built for them in 1610 but pulled down in 1617 at the King's command, presumably because it led to their turning their backs to the altar. (Bushell, *St Mary the Great*, 128–9; Cooper, *Annals*, III, 104.) Some idea of the layout may be obtained from the illustrations and plan in Binns and Meadows, *Great St Mary's.*
226. Cooper, *Annals*, III, 280–81.
227. Ibid. The bookbinder's shop was removed in 1768 (Bushell, *St Mary the Great,* 122).
228. The evidence is as follows. The response of 1639 to the bishop's visitation speaks as though the church already had rails (Palmer, *Visitation Returns*, 37), and the Puritan report of 1641 mentions in an aside that the altar had been 'erected and railed in

formerly by Dr Lany [Laney] and Dr Beale' (BL Harl. MS 7019, fol. 69; see above, p. 198–9 for full quote). Laney was Vice-Chancellor 1632–33, Beale 1634–35. Both were Laudians. The churchwardens' accounts for the decade show no expenditure in putting up the rails, suggesting that the University paid, as happened with the far more drastic reordering under Cosin in 1639. Neither is there mention of a new communion table in the accounts, but in 1635–36 a few shillings was spent on 'cutting the Communion Table' (CRO, P30/4/2), and in 1639 it was reported that 'the table which the bedles use was once our communion table' (Palmer, *Visitation Returns*, 37), which might suggest that the acquisition of a new table had led to the 'cutting' of the old to convert it for use by the beadles. In the inventories for 1640–41 and the following year there is a reference to *two* communion tables (down to one by 1647–49). The seventeenth-century communion table now in the church shows no sign of cutting. It may be worth noting that although in his work on the church, Sandars suggests that the chancel was wainscoted and 'adorned with spire-work' at about this time, this appears to be an error, this work having been carried out in 1663 (Sandars, *Great Saint Mary's Church,* 88; Bushell, *St Mary the Great,* 154).

229. CRO, P30/4/2.
230. Responses made by the churchwardens in 1639 to questions posed by Bishop Wren (Palmer, *Visitation Returns,* 37–8).
231. *Palmer, Visitation Returns,* 37–8; Twigg, *University,* 68–70; Cooper, *Annals,* III, 295.
232. Twigg, *University,* 37.
233. Cooper, *Annals,* III, 294, referencing Bowtell MS vi 2098; Hoffman, 'The Puritan revolution', 100; Bod. Tanner MS 157, fol. 97; BL Harl. MS 7019, fol. 69.
234. Collinson, 'Reformation or deformation', 43. We are grateful to Professor Collinson for a copy of his article before publication.
235. CRO, P30/4/2, p. 24; Hoffman, 'The Puritan revolution', 101. Cosin may not have obtained the permission of the heads of colleges before proceeding with this expenditure (BL Harl. MS 7019, fol. 69).
236. BL Harl. MS 7019, fol. 69.
237. Ibid. For the date of the erection of the screen, see the diary of Dr Dillingham, extracted by Thomas Baker: 'Oct. 1640. The New Screen at St Maries betwixt the Church and Chancel set up'. (BL Harl 7048, fol. 38v, was fol. 72.)
238. Hoffman, 'John Cosin's cure of souls', 73, 74, 77–8; Osmond, *A Life of John Cosin,* 105, 107. His church at Sedgewick has a similar arrangement; according to Hoffman, this is possibly of the same date, or perhaps a little later. The tester of his pulpit at Brancepeth had (until the recent fire) 'a profusion of towering pinnacle work above', in classical form, and this, too, is vaguely pyramidal (Cox, *Pulpits,* 108).
239. Cosin also knocked 'two door wayes through a mighty thick wall, to disable, probably, the Chancell from holding soe many schollers, by drawing downe the Drs seats lower' (BL Harl. MS 7019, fol. 69). These doors into the chancel were 'close to the east wall of the iles' (Bod. Tanner MS 157, fol. 97).
240. See appendix 5 above. Bowing to the communion-table at Great St Mary's (and at both the universities) was made non-obligatory in June of that year (Cooper, *Annals,* III, 314).
241. Bushel, *St Mary the Great,* 23.
242. The statements were made to the Committee for Scandalous Ministers in January 1644/5 (BL Add. MS 15672, fols. 48v, 49r). Stephen Fortune signed the petition

against Bishop Wren in 1640, and was 'a prominent member of the local committee for sequestration of royalists' goods'; the Fortune family were protestant non-conformists in the next reign. (Palmer, *Visitation Returns*, 76 and facing illustration; Twigg, *University*, 94.) 'Dr Row' was Cheney Rowe of Trinity College; he was ejected in 1644 (Twigg, *University*, 296; Matthews, *Walker Revised*, 86). The 'further order from Parliament' referred to, which allowed the work of clearance to proceed, was probably the Parliamentary Ordinance of 1643 – the accounts record the steps being levelled some time before Easter 1644 (see above, p. 202).

243. Twigg, *University*, 78–82.

244. Barwick, *Querela Cantabrigiensis*, 11. The words 'M. Cromwell' are in the margin. Although such dramatic incidents are the stuff of legend, the story should not be dismissed too quickly, for in the register of baptisms for the church alongside the entry for Edmund Porter (christened 1592) is the observation 'Was he not the parish clerk, when Cromwell ordered the Prayer-book to be torn?' (Venables, 'S. Mary the Virgin', 284 n.78). During the year ending Easter 1644 the church accounts record the need to buy a new service book: 'pd to Mr Porter for a service booke 6s 8d' (CRO, P30/4/2). At Peterborough Cathedral in April 1643 the soldiers under Cromwell's command are reported as destroying prayer-books (*Mercurius Rusticus*, chapter 5, 30, 33; Gunton, *Peterborough*, 99; both quoted and discussed in Payne, *Sacred Music*, 166); at Waltham Holy Cross the inventory for 1644 recorded that everything was as the previous year 'except only the bookes of Common prayer which were rentt peeces by the souldyers' (see appendix 8).

245. Barwick, *Querela Cantabrigiensis*, 17.

246. Transcribed by Baker: BL Harl. 7048 fol. 38v (was fol. 72).

247. Bushell, *St Mary the Great*, 123. University sermons offensive to the Puritans were still being preached as late as 1644 (Twigg, *University*, 93).

248. Sternhold and Hopkins, *Psalmes*, Psalm 74 (abbreviated). The church probably had no organ at this time (Bushell, *St Mary the Great*, 149). For the slow unaccompanied singing of this period, see Temperley, *Music*, I, 63, 91.

249. Cole, BL Add. MS 5810, fol. 39.

250. Cooper, *Annals*, III, 339.

251. CRO, P30/4/2, 62. Two similar entries on p. 61 have been crossed out.

252. Venables, 'S. Mary the Virgin', 270; Bushell, *St Mary the Great*, 64–5, 79; Chainey, 'Lost stained glass', 80. Despite having an unusually complete series of church-wardens' accounts, it is difficult to be sure how much pre-Reformation glass was still in place in 1643. Bushell claims that most of the medieval glass was lost in Elizabethan times, but his arguments are based on generalities. Images in glass were painted over in 1567–68, some were put out in 1569, and there were some remaining in 1638. (Foster, *Churchwardens' Accounts*, *passim*.) For armorial glass, Chainey quotes William Cole describing armorial glass surviving in the mid eighteenth century (Cole, BL Add. MS 5810, fol. 52).

253. Quoted in Venables, 'S. Mary the Virgin', 285, and Sandars, *Great Saint Mary's Church*, 88–92. We have been unable to locate these entries. The 'borde' is no doubt the communion table. It is referred to as such in the prayer books of 1549, 1552, 1559.

254. This may have been in December 1643: Dr Dillingham records on 14 December, 'Soldiers billeted in many colledges in the Town. The Earl of Manchester commander in chief for the Parliament [?is here]'. (BL Harl 7048, fol. 39, was fol. 73.)

Dowsing received his commission from Manchester on 19 December.

255. See appendix 8 above.

256. As discussed by John Morrill in chapter 1, it is only later in his iconoclastic career that Dowsing routinely left instructions for work to be carried out in his absence.

257. CRO, P30/4/2, 65. In 1645 the college accounts for Trinity record expenditure on removal of 'images' from the chancel of the church. As Trinity held the advowson and the appropriated revenues of the church, it was responsible for maintenance of the chancel. (Twigg, *University*, 127; Bushel, *St Mary the Great*, 22–6.)

258. RCHME, *Cambridge*, II, 279–80. Since Dowsing's time the church has been altered and restored on several occasions. The pulpit of Dowsing's period is probably that now in Orton Waterville church, near Peterborough (RCHME, *Cambridge*, II, 275–6; Bushell, *St Mary the Great*, 131).

259. Baker has 'Mr. Ewy' for 'Mr. Frog'. Dowsing's handwriting again!

260. CRO, P22/5/2 & 3.

261. Palmer, *Visitation Returns*, 38; Cole, BL Add. MS 5805, fol. 69. See also Chainey, 'Lost stained glass', 75.

262. Baker omits the second date.

263. RCHME, *Cambridge*, II, 286.

264. Baker has 24 December, which was a Sunday and is therefore not likely to be correct. Baker gives the final phrase as 'apostles, the Pope, Peter's kies'.

265. RCHME, *Cambridge*, II, 271; BL Add. MS 6821, fol. 53.

266. Baker has 3 January. Baker rules a line across the page after this entry, probably indicating a page break in the original. After this entry, Grey inserts a sub-heading in brackets, 'County of Cambridge'.

267. Adams, *Round Church*, 13, quoted in Chainey, 'Lost stained glass', 75; RCHME, *Cambridge*, II, 257; *Ecclesiologist*, 3 (1847), 21; *History of the Church of the Holy Sepulchre*, 12.

268. RCHME, *North-East Cambridgeshire*, 51.

269. Matthews, *Walker Revised*, 78; BL Add. MS15672, fol. 51v (I am grateful to Trevor Cooper for references to this latter manuscript, here and elsewhere). One of the complaints investigated by the sub-committee of divines appointed by the House of Lords in 1640 to consult upon innovations was 'making Canopyes over [the altar], with traverses of Curtains (in imitation of the Vaile before the Holy of Holyes) on each side and before it' (Legg, *English Orders*, lvii).

270. Palmer, *Cambridgeshire Villages*, IV, 71.

271. Palmer, *Monumental Inscriptions,* 239; Lack *et al.*, *Brasses*, 227–32.

272. Cole, BL Add. MS 5804, fol. 119, and 5807, fols. 9–13.

373. Raven, *Bells of Cambridgeshire*, 169.

274. Matthews, *Walker Revised*, 85; BL Add. MS 15672, fol. 6r. Accusations of drunkenness against scandalous ministers are common, and are perhaps merely a 'conceit' of the age, not to be taken literally (Maltby, *Prayer Book and People*, 75).

275. Lack *et al.*, *Brasses*, 18.

276. William Cole drew it: BL Add. MS 5804, fol. 103.

277. Cole, BL Add. MS 5804, fol. 117.

278. Baker has 'God the Father *over* one of them'; omits 'and', giving 'we diged down their steps. 20 cherubims'. He omits the words in brackets, probably indicating that they were inserted by Grey or some other interpreter of the text.

279. RCHME, *North-East Cambridgeshire*, 100.

280. Palmer, *Monumental Inscriptions,* pp. 160, 239, 262; Cole, BL Add. MS 5804, fols. 122–29.
281. RCHME, *North-East Cambridgeshire,* 107; Matthews, *Walker Revised,* 82; BL Add. MS 15672, fols. 26v, 69v.
282. Palmer, *Monumental Inscriptions,* 247.
283. Baker has '*brake* downe 3 crucifixes'; omits 'March 20'.
284. Lack *et al., Brasses,* 179–81; Notes taken by Sir Henry St George, Clarenceux on 11 July 1684 during his visitation of Cambridgeshire (SRO(I) HD1538/79); Palmer, *Monumental Inscriptions,* 231.
285. VCH, VI, 85; Spufford, *Contrasting Communities,* 314.
286. VCH, VI, 100. For Ashton, see chapter 5.
287. Grey includes 'Zephaniah', Baker omits it. We have followed Baker.
288. VCH, VI, 78.
289. CUL, Ely Records, B/9/1. I am grateful to Trevor Cooper for this reference.
290. Letter from the vicar, H. W. Wilkinson, dated 1843, in Bod. Suff. Top. d. 19 fol. 52 (Wodderspoon's interleaved copy of Loder's edition of Dowsing's Journal).
291. We are grateful to Margaret Aston for drawing this to our attention, and for other helpful discussion. Dowsing's vocabulary does not always make useful distinctions. For example, his use of 'we' and 'I' seems erratic, and is not indicative of whether or not he was accompanied on a particular visit (see, for example, entries 42 and 81).
292. Duck (probably smoothing the text) has '… in glass & about seventy small ones'; Loder agrees with Martin.
293. *Journal of the British Archaeological Association,* 3 (1848), 330.
294. Martin repeats 'and divers others', probably his own accident of transcription. We have followed Loder.
295. Hervy, BL Add. MS 4969, fol. 30v.
296. Loder and Duck have '*I* brake down 200'. Duck (probably smoothing the text) has '*about* a thousand'; 'three of God the Father and Christ and the holy Lamb and three of the holy Ghost…'; Loder agrees with Martin.
297. We are grateful to Diarmaid MacCulloch for this point. For the Parliamentary Ordinance, see appendix 5.
298. See appendix 12 above.
299. In 1786 Craven Ord took an impression of a brass scroll in the north aisle of the chapel, bearing the inscription *S[an]c[t]a trinitas unus deus.* He recorded that it was 'the only brass plate remaining at this time'. (SRO(I), HD 1538/68.)
300. Cautley, *Suffolk Churches,* 277.
301. Wedgwood, *The King's War,* 289. We are grateful to John Kington of the Climatic Research Unit, UEA, who has confirmed the bitterness of this winter, with much snow in January until it melted on or about the 21st (personal communication).
302. MacCulloch, *Chorography of Suffolk,* 84.
303. *Proceedings of the Suffolk Institute of Archaeology,* 4, 187.
304. Loder and Duck omit 'down'. Loder and Duck have 'pictures' in place of 'Inscription'.
305. Loder and Duck reverse this and the previous entry.
306. *Blois,* 176.
307. Loder and Duck have 'brake *down* the 12 apostles'. Loder, probably using editorial initiative, inserts a large X after Cross; Duck does not. Loder and Duck insert 'mei' after 'Miserere'.

308. Hervy, BL Add. MS 4969, fol. 52v.
309. Hervy, BL Add. MS 4969, fol. 53v. For Candler, see chapter 2. For discussion of damage to effigies, see pp. 101–3.
310. See above, p. 31.
311. Loder and Duck have 'inscription' for 'picture'.
312. MacCulloch, *Chorography of Suffolk*, 95.
313. MacCulloch, *Chorography of Suffolk*, 95–6; BL Add. MS 19,096 fol. 317r; BL Add. MS 32484.
314. See chapter 6 for a discussion of the extent of the deputies' coverage.
315. Sizar at Jesus, Cambridge in 1617, BA in 1621, MA in 1624, ordained Priest in 1621 aged 23. At Westleton, Mr Swaine for his ecclesiastical estate was rated at 10s. 0d., for his temporal living rated at 2s. 9d.
316. Browne, *History of Congregationalism*, 608–12. The funeral expenses are from the Aldeburgh Town Accounts, quoted by Ronald Blythe in his 1957 guide to the church.
317. For accounts, see appendix 8 above.
318. Loder omits 'one' after 'steeple'; Duck agrees with Martin. Loder and Duck have 'chancel', and we have followed them; Martin has a deliberate blank. Duck omits the final three words; Loder agrees with Martin.
319. Nichols, *Seeable Signs*, 322–3.
320. Grose, who was on tour in 1775 drawing and writing for his *Antiquities of England and Wales: (Suffolk)*. The last memorial put up in the chancel (1621) was moved into the nave a century later.
321. Duck reverses the order of this and the previous entry; Loder agrees with Martin.
322. Loder and Duck have *6* superstitious pictures.
323. See appendix 8.
324. Loder has 'one' in place of 'first'.
325. Loder and Duck have the place name, and we have followed them; Martin lacks the place name.
326. Loder and Duck have *40* cherubim.
327. Loder has 'took *up* 2 superstitious inscription'; Duck has 'broke down'.
328. See appendix 8.
329. For accounts, see appendix 8. Craven Ord's Suffolk collections are in BL Add. MS 8987.
330. Loder has 'We *took* down'; Duck has 'broke down'.
331. *Proceedings of the Suffolk Institute of Archaeology*, 7, 148–9. *Editor's note*: Harriet Blodgett has suggested that Samuel Beckett took from Dowsing's Journal the phrase 'nothing to be done' for use in *Waiting for Godot*. The evidence is somewhat weak: the fact that, in their different ways, both Beckett and Dowsing were iconoclasts. (Blodgett, 'Iconoclasm in Samuel Becket's Waiting for Godot and William Dowsing's *Journal*'.)
332. Holmes, *Suffolk Committees for Scandalous Ministers*, 40.
333. White, *Journal*, 42; *East Anglian Notes & Queries, NS*, 7, 273–4.
334. Loder omits 'five of', and 'superstitious'; Duck agrees with Martin.
335. Hervy, BL Add. MS 4969, fol. 58.
336. Wodderspoon, Bod. Suff. Top. d. 19, fol. 97.
337. Churchwardens' accounts will be found in appendix 8.
338. Haverhill (entry 42), Washbrook (72), Copdock (73), Capel (99), Needham Market

(101), Cheveley (203), and Bedingfield (211).

339. Loder has '*anima* (sic)'. Duck has '*animæ*', though this might just be misread as 'anima'.

340. Candler, BL Add. MS 15520, 19; *Blois*, 350. D. E. Davy in 1826 took the 'axe' idea seriously and drew an indent then near the south door to support it (Davy, BL Add. MS 19094, fol. 125).

341. Davy's notes in BL Add MS 19094, fol. 82. The Sparhawke will is SRO(I), vol. 13, fol. 107.

342. Loder and Duck have '*of* wood', and we have followed them; Martin has 'on wood'.

343. Prynne, *Canterburies Doome*, 102; Grace, 'Schismaticall and factious humours', 97, 115.

344. Blatchly & Northeast, 'Seven figures'.

345. Davy, BL Add. MS 19093, fol. 298ff.

346. For the Ordinances, see appendix 5.

347. *Proceedings of the Suffolk Institute of Archaeology and History*, 26 (1986), 101–14.

348. Wodderspoon, *Memorials of Ipswich*, 359–60; *East Anglian Notes & Queries*, Second Series, 1, 8; Grace, 'Schismaticall and factious humours', 113.

349. Churchwardens' accounts will be found in appendix 8.

350. Martin's clerk has written 'Helens' rather illegibly, and a marginal note 'St Helens' has been added in explanation. Loder has 'Elms, ?St Helens'; Duck has 'Mary Elms'.

351. Parker & Parker, *Ecclesiastical Topography, VII, Suffolk*, entry 189.

352. Cotman, *Engravings of the Most Remarkable Sepulchral Brasses in Norfolk*, pl. VI, p. 6.

353. See above, p. 103.

354. Wodderspoon, Bod. Suff. Top. d. 19, fol. 114.

355. *East Anglian Notes & Queries, NS,* 13 (1910), 87.

356. Cautley, *Suffolk Churches*, 310.

357. David Park, personal communication. A possible exception is Abingdon, Berkshire. In 1644 it was said of Christopher Newsted, the minister, that 'there being in his church at Abington the pictures of God the Father, and of purgatory, he caused to be raced [*sic*] out some Scripture which were upon the walle, shewing the unlaw-fullnes of them; and others to be put up falsely quoted, and aplied to justifie and maintaine them, as 1 Peter 3 19'. It looks as though a pre-Reformation doom painting, or something similar, was being pressed back into service; though even here it is possible that the offending picture was in glass, with the text on the wall beneath (BL Add MS 5829, fol. 19).

358. Dowsing's use of the phrase 'break down' looks a little odd applied to a wall painting, but he used the equally odd 'do them out' of the painted texts at Tever-sham (entry 206).

359. For the date we have followed Duck and Loder; Martin has 'Feb. 8' – no doubt a mistranscription.

360. She was a Peyton of Isleham.

361. Early twentieth century photograph, and J. W. Darby 1828 who mentions altar rails and 'fronts of seats'.

362. See above, chapter 6. We are grateful to Margaret Aston for this suggestion.

363. See above, p. 83.

364. Loder and Duck have '4 superstitious *inscriptions*'.

365. Dove: Ship Money £1. 6s. 1½d; Poley: Ship Money £2. 2s. 4d.

366. Hervy, BL Add. MS 4969, fol. 39.

367. Loder and Duck expand the phrase to 'promised *to do* it'.
368. Lillistone, *The Lady and the Abbot's Tomb*.
369. MacCulloch, *Suffolk and the Tudors, passim*.
370. See above, p. 8.
371. Hervy, BL Add. MS 4969, fol. 36.
372. *Fragmenta Genealogica*, 1903, 44–5.
373. We are grateful to Diarmaid MacCulloch for this and other information regarding the church.
374. *Blois*, 244.
375. Holmes, *Suffolk Committees for Scandalous Ministers*, 25.
376. See for example, *East Anglian Daily Times*, 1927, 23 November: 'Les Trois Rois Vie et Mort and Seven Deadly Sins'.
377. See above, pp. 18–20.
378. VCH, IX, 32.
379. Palmer, *Visitation Returns,* 99.
380. Our sources give two possible dates for the Brinkley visit. Grey gives 29 February, three days after the Monday visit to Glemsford (entry 123), and it could then be interpreted as Dowsing making his way back into Cambridgeshire; but three days (26–29 February) is excessive for a thirty mile journey with no other recorded activity – and if, to solve this problem, one surmises that Dowsing was assisting his deputy 27–28 February in mid Suffolk, then the distances again become problematic. Much more likely is that the Brinkley visit took place on Tuesday 20 February (the date as transcribed by Baker), which fits its position in the text (immediately before another visit made on 20 February). It is well over 30 miles from the Cornards which he also visited that day, and this would have made for a hard day's work, but not an impossible one.
381. Lack *et al.*, *Brasses*, 16; Palmer, *Monumental Inscriptions,* 221.
382. Loder has 'Henry *Turner*' (as does Martin in the duplicate entry 121*)*; Duck has 'Tanner'.
383. They were still visible in 1965 (*ex info.* Diarmaid MacCulloch).
384. See appendix 7 for the commissions.
385. Nor is John Prince, the version of the name appearing in the duplicate entry for this parish (entry 121).
386. Martin has a deliberate blank where Loder and Duck (whom we have followed) have 'Shrive'. Duck omits 'one of Christ, and 6 in the chancell' (probably a slip of the eye); Loder agrees with Martin.
387. Loder reverses this and the previous entry; Duck agrees with Martin. Loder and Duck have 'Hill' for 'Hall'; we have followed Martin.
388. Henry Campin does not appear in the Ship Money records, unless he was John Campen at Wiston, rated at just 9*d*.
389. He married Anne, daughter and heir of Sir Thomas Revett.
390. Candler, Soc. Antiq. MS 667. Humberfield (as 'Umfrevile Esq.') was rated £1. 10*s*. 0*d*. for Ship Money at Stoke, a substantial sum, and (surely the same man) 'Hummeville Esq.', 9*s*. 0*d*. at Polstead.
391. Foxe, *Acts and Monuments*, (J. Pratt's edition of 1870), IV, 707; Weever, *Ancient Funerall Monuments*, 775.
392. Where Loder and Duck have 'Cap$^t$', Martin has a deliberate blank. Duck has 'Walgrave'; Loder has 'Waldgrave'. The final sentence 'And gave order...' is from

Loder, and is not present in Martin nor in Duck.

393. Loder has 'inscription' in place of 'superstitious'; Duck has 'superscriptions'.

394. MacCulloch, *Suffolk and the Tudors*, 183–4.

395. Loder omits the body of this repeat entry for Great Cornard, simply cross-referring the reader back to the original entry, and he makes no mention of the repeat entry for Little Cornard. Duck omits both the repeat entries altogether, in line with his policy of tidying up.

396. Loder and Duck have 'cherubims to be *broke* down'.

397. Moses and Aaron were also seen as types of the relationship between monarch and clergy (Maltby, *Prayer Book and People*, 168). For Norwich cathedral, see above p. 121. For the example at Exeter cathedral, of which only the heads survived nineteenth-century reordering, see Bishop & Prideaux, *St Peter in Exeter*, 61; the original design is illustrated in Croft-Murray, *Decorative Painting*, I, 126. For Sutton's Hospital, see White, *Century*, 5. An engraving showing Moses and Aaron with the ten commandments was sold in 1624, 'taken out' (copied, presumably) from St Mary Overy, Southwark, London (Watt, *Cheap Print*, 246–8). It is noticeable that the title page for the Authorised Version of 1611 has the two figures in a setting not unlike an altarpiece. Rouse comments that the two figures appear in post-Reformation wall paintings (Rouse, *Medieval Wall Paintings*, 71). For general discussion see Addleshaw & Etchells, *Architectural Setting*, 161, and Aston, *England's Iconoclasts*, 78.

398. Blois recorded the inscription (presumably before the Civil War). The quotation is from Hawes' History of Loes (Pembroke College MS), p. 394. We are grateful to Diarmaid MacCulloch for providing these details about the brass.

399. Blatchly, 'Lost and mutilated memorials at Letheringham'.

400. Loder omits the final sentence.

401. Hervy, BL Add. MS 4969, fol. 59v.

402. Duck omits 'Bull'; Loder agrees with Martin.

403. As in the strip maps in John Ogilby's *Britannia* (1675), plate 73. The first edition of Kirby, *Suffolk Traveller* (1735) mentions the inn; the 1764 edition has plain 'Beyton'.

404. Cole, BL Add. MS 5805, fol. 63; VCH, IX, 176; RCHME, *West Cambridgeshire*, 179.

405. Palmer, *Visitation Returns*, 98.

406. Baker has 'cross *in* the church'; '*ordered* to be taken downe'; his final phrase is '*delivered out 3s. 2d.*'

407. Cole, BL Add. MS 5821, fol. 12; Palmer, *Monumental Inscriptions*, 229.

408. Blomefield, *Collectanea*, 12.

409. VCH, V, 103; Matthews, *Walker Revised*, 84; BL Add. MS 15672, fol. 24r.

410. Palmer, *Cambridgeshire Villages*, IV, 64.

411. Palmer, *Monumental Inscriptions*, 241; Blomefield, *Collectanea*, 11; Lack *et al.*, *Brasses*, 236.

412. BL Egerton MS 1048, fol. 24; VCH, V, 134.

413. Baker has 'and an' in place of 'seven'; 'ora pro *animabus*'; 'and the forme' in place of 'and we tooke'. His final clause is '*in* the chancell'.

414. The witnesses in question were named as Richard Anywood (Dowsing may have misremembered his Christian name, or it might be a different person), Francis Cockerill (Dowsing's 'Cockaram') and Richard Glinester (BL Add. MS 15672, fol. 20r). See also VCH, V, 119.

415. BL Add. MS 15672, fol. 16v; VCH, V, 25–6.

416. Baker omits the date; has 'two crosses *in* the steple'.

417. Lack *et al.*, *Brasses*, 14.
418. RCHME, *West Cambridgeshire*, 21.
419. Palmer, *Monumental Inscriptions,* 221.
420. Baker omits this entry altogether.
421. Lack *et al.*, *Brasses*, 84.
422. Palmer, *Monumental Inscriptions,* 222.
423. Blomefield, *Collectanea*, 30.
424. Palmer, *Monumental Inscriptions,* 225.
425. BL Egerton MS 1048, fol. 24.
426. VCH, V, 57.
427. Baker has 'Robert *Harrison'*.
428. Judging from the index to Keyser, *List*.
429. Palmer, *Cambridgeshire Villages*, IV, 69.
430. For George Hamond, see VCH, IX, 364. For the marriage of Robert Hamond on 18 April 1624, see the parish registers (CRO, open shelves transcripts).
431. Baker incorrectly inserts 'Huntintonshire' [*sic*] before 'Croxton' (for discussion, see above, n.55 to chapter 10). He has 'And over the bell' in place of 'Upon the bell'.
432. *Transactions of the Cambridgeshire and Huntingdonshire Archaeological Society*, 5 (1930), 285; BL Egerton MS 1048, fol. 24.
433. See above, p. 37.
434. VCH, V, 43.
435. Lack *et al.*, *Brasses*, 96.
436. Baker has *48* cherubims'; omits 'we' in 'we brake downe'.
437. VCH, V, 97.
438. Baker has an ampersand in place of '9', and the next entry, for Papworth St Agnes, runs straight on; the ampersand is probably a slip of the pen.
439. Baker has *9* March.
440. Baker has *6* cherubims; omits 'by March 25th'. Grey inserts a semicolon after 'pictures'.
441. RCHME, *West Cambridgeshire*, 50.
442. Palmer, *Monumental Inscriptions,* 224.
443. Palmer, *Cambridgeshire Villages*, IV, 73; VCH, VIII, 255.
444. Lack *et al.*, *Brasses*, 238.
445. Baker has 'Shelford *Magna'*; 'and 58 pictures, *a 2d* crucifix...'; omits the final 'and'.
446. Lack *et al.*, *Brasses*, 208.
447. VCH, VIII, 217.
448. Baker has '*a* crucifix, 30 pictures'.
449. Lack *et al.*, *Brasses*, 212–14. This misquotes the Journal to make it appear the brasses were to be levelled by the minister.
450. VCH, VIII, 222, 225.
451. Baker has '... crosses, the *churchwarden caused to be taken* downe'. After this entry Baker interrupts his transcription with some pages of other material.
452. Lack *et al.*, *Brasses*, 219.
453. Baker omits initial mention of the steps.
454. Lack *et al.*, *Brasses*, 150; Palmer, *Monumental Inscriptions,* 229.
455. Tudor-Craig, 'Wall paintings', 326–7.
456. Lack *et al.*, *Brasses*, 146; Palmer, *Monumental Inscriptions,* 229.
457. VCH, VIII, 191, 192.

458. For further discussion of this point, see above, p. 266. We are grateful to Margaret Aston for helpful discussion on this matter.

459. Baker has '*21* superstitious pictures'; 'Robert *Swan*'.

460. VCH, VIII, 196.

461. Baker has 'about 100 *cherubims and* superstitious pictures'.

462. Cole, BL Add. MS 5803, fols. 30–39.

463. Lack *et al.*, *Brasses*, 236.

464. Baker has '2 crosses to be taken downe *and* the 12 Patriarchs...'; 'Croden' for 'Moreden'.

465. VCH, VIII, 162; Matthews, *Walker Revised*, 85.

466. Baker has 'We brake 60 papre superstitious pictures, and gave order to break downe and take downe 2 crosses...'; was the word 'papre' his mistranscription of 'papist', or is this an example of paper prints and pictures being used to decorate a church? Baker omits 'of Christ' in the final sentence. The general impression is that his mind was wandering as he transcribed this entry.

467. VCH, VIII, 174. There was more than one John Wildbore at Cambridge during this period (Venn & Venn, *Alumni Cantabrigienses*).

468. Cole, BL Add. MS 5803, fol. 72.

469. Palmer, *The Puritan in Melbourn*, 11.

470. Palmer, *The Puritan in Melbourn*, 6; VCH, VIII, 72.

471. BL Egerton MS 1048, fol. 24.

472. Palmer, *The Puritan in Melbourn*, 9, 12–14, 17; Spufford, *Contrasting Communities*, 233, 279. I am grateful to Trevor Cooper for these references.

473. Baker has *62* pictures.

474. Palmer, *Monumental Inscriptions*, 234; Lack *et al.*, *Brasses*, 189. Steps were ordered to be built in 1639 (Palmer, *Cambridgeshire Villages*, IV, 68).

475. Palmer, *The Puritan in Melbourn*, 12n. and marginalia in BL copy.

476. Lack *et al.*, *Brasses*, 246; Palmer, *Monumental Inscriptions*, 244.

477. Grey has '8 superstitious pictures in the chancell, and *upon* the church'; in this case we have followed Baker. Baker has 'we promised' for 'which was promised'; he has the final word as 'steple'. Both these latter variants must be mistranscriptions.

478. Lack *et al.*, *Brasses*, 10; Palmer, *Monumental Inscriptions*, 220; VCH, VIII, 27.

479. VCH, VIII, 149.

480. Guide book; Lack *et al.*, *Brasses*, 182.

481. Baker has '*in* the chancell'.

482. VCH, VIII, 141.

483. BL Egerton MS, 1048, fol. 24; VCH, VIII, 96.

484. VCH, VIII, 141.

485. Lack *et al.*, *Brasses*, 3.

486. Baker has '9 superstitious pictures we brake down, & *30* superstitious inscriptions of brasse, & at Shingay'.

487. Lack *et al.*, *Brasses*, 193; Palmer, *Monumental Inscriptions*, 238; Palmer, *Cambridgeshire Villages*, IV, 71.

588. VCH, VIII, 125.

489. Lack *et al.*, *Brasses*, 192. As late as 1639 the parish was required to 'make another ascent to the communion table' (Palmer, *Cambridgeshire Villages*, IV, 63).

490. Grey read his text as *Orata*, and corrects it in a bracketed note. Baker (whom we follow) either read it as *Orate*, or silently corrected it.

491. Lack *et al.*, *Brasses*, 147.
492. Reaney, *Place-Names of Cambridgeshire*, 54.
493. VCH, VII, 99; V, 107, 110; Palmer, *Visitation Returns*, 78.
494. Palmer, *Visitation Returns*, 80, 87; VCH, V. 110.
495. Baker has 'churchwardens' in the plural.
496. CRO, P76/5/22.
497. Lack *et al.*, *Brasses*, 135; Palmer, *Monumental Inscriptions, 227.*
498. Lack *et al.*, *Brasses*, 260.
499. BL Egerton MS 1048, fol. 24.
500. VCH, V, 270.
501. Baker has 'gave order to take downe 4 more, we could not come out/at, & a cross to be taken off the steple'.
502. Palmer, *Monumental Inscriptions,* 235; RCHME, *West Cambridgeshire*, 191; Lack *et al.*, *Brasses*, 195.
503. Baker has '*The* superstitious inscription…'; he concludes with 'and some 16 super-stitious pictures ?&c'. Grey alone has the entry in square brackets. Grey comments on Dowsing's Latin: '*Orata* (for *Orate*, as before) *pro Animabus*…'; however Baker has transcribed the word as *Orate*.
504. Lack *et al.*, *Brasses*, 198–204.
505. Palmer, *Visitation Returns*, 127.
506. Baker omits this duplicate entry.
507. Baker has 'same' in place of 'Lambe'.
508. BL Egerton MS 1048, fol. 24.
509. VCH, VI, 216; Twigg, *University*, 303; Matthews, *Walker Revised*, 78.
510. Baker has '*crosses* to be taken of the steple'.
511. Palmer, *Cambridgeshire Villages*, IV, 69. For 'do up', see *OED*.
512. VCH, VI, 108.
513. For windows, Palmer, *Cambridgeshire Villages*, IV, 65; for the de Skelton brass, Palmer, *Monumental Inscriptions*, 82.
514. VCH, VI, 224.
515. VCH, VI, 111.
516. Baker has '*the* crucifixes'; 'and *brake* 2 crosses off'.
517. Palmer, *Cambridgeshire Villages*, IV, 66; VCH, VI, 243.
518. Palmer, *Cambridgeshire Villages*, IV, 61; VCH, VI, 211.
519. Baker omits 'to be', having 'the steps levelled by'.
520. VCH, VI, 9 and 193.
521. VCH, VI, 16.
522. BL Egerton MS 1045, fol. 24; Carlson, 'Churchwardens', 178.
523. Baker omits the number '16'.
524. VCH, VI, 68.
525. Baker has 'about 10 superstitious pictures'.
526. Raven, *Bells of Cambridgeshire*, 121.
527. VCH, VI, 34. For Mapletoft, see chapter 5.
528. BL Add. MS 15672, fol. 8r; VCH, VI, 46; Matthews, *Walker Revised*, 80.
529. VCH, VI, 46.
530. Baker has 'in the church, & a crucifix, & the Virgin Mary'.
531. Palmer, *Cambridgeshire Villages*, IV, 73; Palmer, *Visitation Returns*, 125.
532. Cole, BL Add. MS 5807, fols. 67–71.

533. Lack *et al.*, *Brasses*, 244; Palmer, *Monumental Inscriptions*, 243.
534. Raven, *Bells of Cambridgeshire*, 133.
535. Baker has '64 superstitious pictures and *one* crucifix'.
536. Matthews, *Walker Revised*, 87.
537. Baker has 'a crosse *at* the porch'.
538. Palmer, *Monumental Inscriptions*, 243.
539. VCH, VI, 181–2.
540. Baker has 'brake' for 'take'.
541. Cole, BL Add. MS 5820, fols. 86–8.
542. Palmer, *Monumental Inscriptions*, 238; Raven, *Bells of Cambridgeshire*, 167.
543. Baker has '3*0* superstitious pictures, *a* crucifix'.
544. Raven, *Bells of Cambridgeshire*, 139.
545. We have used Baker to end the final sentence. Grey has '… and were not made'.
546. Randall, *Gentle Flame*, 15, 67.
547. Randall, *Gentle Flame*, 19, 62.
548. Halliday, 'The churches of Ashley and Silverley'.
549. We have used Baker for 'stoning', where Grey has 'staring'.
550. Lack *et al.*, *Brasses*, 88; Palmer, *Monumental Inscriptions*, 223; Raven, *Bells of Cambridgeshire*, 134.
551. As his final phrase, Baker has 'superstitious on the windows'.
552. Lack *et al.*, *Brasses*, 92; Raven, *Bells of Cambridgeshire*, 135.
553. Baker ends with '&c' in place of 'many superstitious pict'.
554. Lack *et al.*, *Brasses*, 215; Raven, *Bells of Cambridgeshire*, 167.
555. Baker begins 'We broke 2 crucifixes'; he has 'pavement' in the singular.
556. Palmer, *Visitation Returns*, 137.
557. Cheshire, *Dowsing's Destructions*, 91n.
558. Raven, *Bells of Cambridgeshire*, 171.
559. Baker has the meaningless '… of brasse, orate pro animabis 2 cherubims & picture deus, and 8 superstitious'. Probably Dowsing's poor handwriting again, and perhaps a tired transcriber.
560. Lack *et al.*, *Brasses*, 219–22; Blomefield, *Collectanea*, 236.
561. Where Grey has '11 more', Baker has written a digit, scratched it out and replaced with '1 more'.
562. Cole, BL Add. MS 5821, fols. 20–21; Lack *et al.*, *Brasses*, 252.
563. BL Add. MS 15672, fol. 37v.
564. Palmer, *Visitation Returns*, 124.
565. See appendix 3.
566. See chapter 6, especially pp. 76–80.
567. Martin has two marginal notes in two different hands suggesting 'Laxfield'. Duck interprets Dowsing as saying 'and I have done the rest', which is a reasonable expansion.
568. SRO(I), FC89/A1/1.
569. Duck omits '4 superstitious pictures'; Loder agrees with Martin.
570. Agate, *Benches and Stalls*, 12.
571. Loder has '8 angells *off* the roof'; Duck has '*on* the roof'. Loder omits '8' before cherubims; Duck agrees with Martin.
572. See churchwardens' accounts for Bungay, Framlingham, Mellis and possibly Peasenhall (the date does not fit). The accounts will be found in appendix 8.

573. Loder and Duck have '20 *days*'. The final sentence appears in Loder (whom we have followed) and Duck, but not in Martin; Duck has it as 'William [blank] Suff is Curate'.

574. See chapter 6, especially pp. 76–80.

575. Loder omits the word 'inscriptions' in first sentence; Duck has 'inscriptions', but *20* of them. Loder and Duck both insert 'inscriptions' before 'of Jesus'. Loder is coy about the word 'drunkard', printing it as 'D ✶ ✶ ✶ ✶ ✶ ✶ ✶'; Duck agrees with Martin.

576. William Aldhouse (Aldus) was probably pensioner of Clare 1622, MA 1629, ordained Norwich in 1628. He signs the Register Aldus, but enters family events in the name of Aldhouse. It is coincidental (and potentially confusing) that another William Aldus, a Christ Church man, curate of Blaxhall, was ejected from Copdock in 1645 as a scandalous minister; he was reinstated at Blaxhall 1653 to 1680 when he died. His hand in the Blaxhall Register from 1673 (Copdock is lost) does not correspond with the Linstead man's Italic, even allowing for deterioration with age.

577. Ship Money: Francis Everard, Esq., £1. 17s. 0d., and 5s. 0d. more for his tithes, and 1s. 6d. at Linstead parva. Francis Verdon, 3s. 4d. as outsitter here. For Caley, see appendix 4.

578. Hervy, BL Add. MS 4969, fol. 77.

579. Duck reverses this and the previous entry; Loder agrees with Martin.

589. MacCulloch, *Chorography of Suffolk*, 73–4.

581. Sizar at Caius, BA 1628, ordained priest 1629, vicar here from 1631.

582. Fincham, *Visitation Articles*, II, 38 and *passim*. For other examples of complaints about once-a-day preaching, see e.g. White, *Century*, *passim*.

583. See commentary to entry for Holton St Peter (262). Dowsing was similarly casual at King's, describing 'INRI' as 'Jesus' (Journal entry 13).

584. For Acton, see White, *Century*, 34. Only at Bramfield was the vicar ejected (Matthews, *Walker Revised*, *passim*).

585. Shelford, *Five Pious Discourses*, 12.

586. Martin has April 16, no doubt a mistranscription; Loder agrees with Martin. Duck has 'church' in place of 'steeple'; Loder agrees with Martin.

587. Blatchly, *Topographers of Suffolk*, 25, where Gillingwater's manuscript note is reproduced; Walker, *Matthews Revised*, p. 344.

588. Loder omits 'down'; Duck agrees with Martin.

589. SRO(I), HD 1538/18 at fol. 120.

590. Duck reverses this and the previous entry; Loder agrees with Martin. Duck omits mention of the crucifix; Loder agrees with Martin. Loder and Duck read: 'and St Catherine *twice* pictured'. Loder, Duck and Martin all note that the word or words occurring after 'parish' have been blotted.

591. Pensioner at Peterhouse 1615, BA 1619, MA 1622.

592. Holmes, *Suffolk Committees for Scandalous Ministers*, 60–61.

593. Duck and Loder have plural 'Churchwardens'. Loder has 'divers pictures, in the windows, which we could not reach'; Duck follows Martin.

594. Gardner, *Dunwich*, 216.

595. Loder and Duck have '10' in place of '9'.

596. Loder and Duck have 'We brake down 9 superstitious pictures; and gave order take 9 superstitious Inscription of Jesus; 2 crosses on the steeple; and the steps to be levelled'.

597. Gage, *History and Antiquities of Hengrave*, 89.

598. Loder and Duck add 'with her wheel' after 'St. Catherine'.
599. BL Add. MS 19080, fol. 369r, and information from present churchwarden.
600. Duck reverses this and the previous entry; Loder agrees with Martin. Loder has *'took down* 42 superstitious pictures'; Duck has *'four* superstitious pictures'. Loder has *'about* 20 cherubims'; Duck agrees with Martin.
601. Bryant, *Churches of Suffolk*, II, 48.
602. Duck has *30* cherubim; Loder agrees with Martin.
603. BL Add. MS 19083, fol. 40ff.
604. Gardner, *Dunwich*, 160.
605. Martin has the marginal note quoted, and Duck supports Martin in a mention of the St Andrew's Cross in the window; Loder does not mention it.
606. MacCulloch, *Chorography of Suffolk*, 89; BL Add. MS 19080, fol. 122v.
607. Loder inserts 'one' after the first mention of 'pictures'; Duck agrees with Martin.
608. Nichols, *Seeable Signs*, 330.
609. Gardner, *Dunwich*, 125; Kirby, *Historical Account*, plate V, fig. 3; indents drawn in BL Add. MS 19080, fols. 103r–105v; Suckling, *History of Suffolk*, II, lithograph facing p. 154.
610. Woodforde, 'Blythburgh Church'.
611. Duck has *20* Cherubim; Loder agrees with Martin.
612. Cooper, *Dunwich*, 23–31; Blatchly, 'Indents from the seabed at Dunwich'.
613. *Proceedings of the Suffolk Institute of Archaeology*, 4, 455.
614. Yoxford £1. 5s. 0d.; Blythburgh £1. 2s. 6d and 10s. 0d. For Brooks, see above, p. 82.
615. MacCulloch, *Chorography of Suffolk*, 87.
616. This entry is difficult to make sense of. Duck tidies it to 'a Bishop with his mitre'; Loder has '… with his keys 2nd a Bishop's mitre on his head'.
617. He is rated at £1. 13s. 4d. for Ship Money.
618. Nichols, *Seeable Signs*, 340.
619. Loder and Duck agree in omitting 'and the Rayles likewise we gave the poor'. Loder has 'kept out *of the church*'; Duck agrees with Martin. Loder and Duck name the first new churchwarden as 'Stanard'. Martin (only) has 'Edmund Mayhew' in the margin.
620. Weever, *Ancient Funerall Monuments*, 754.
621. Plate 55 ( a folding sheet bound into BL Add. MS 4969, not Hervy's own work).
622. William Brown, 4s. 4d.; Roger Small[age], 17s. 0d.; James Tokelove, Constable [of Melton] 4s. 2d.; William Gardener, Sexton [of Melton], 2s. 0d.; Thomas Stannard, 2s. 0d.
623. Notes written by Jacob Chilton, Rector from 1721, starting a new book for the parish register with brief accounts of his predecessors; Maitland, *Story of Ufford*, 29–31.
624. Loder has no date; Duck has Aug 21.
625. Martin may have *9 superstitious pictures*: the manuscript is not clear. Duck and Loder have *3*.
626. White, *Century*, 38.
627. Cautley, *Suffolk Churches*, 300.
628. Harris, 'Medieval mural paintings'.
629. Brownrigg was rated for Ship Money at £1. 8s. 8d.
630. Bysshe, *Visitation of Suffolk*, 1.
631. BL Add. MS 19085, fol. 4.

632. For discussion of this point, see p. 85 above.
633. Loder and Duck have 'Suton'. Duck and Loder have 'Genkthorne' where Martin has a deliberate blank.
634. *OED* gives 'arch-buttress' as a flying buttress.
635. Thomas Colby, 11*s.* 0*d.*; Thomas Eley, 10*s.* 6*d.*; John Suton, 6*d.* No entry for Genkthorne.
636. Martin has 'brake took up'; Loder omits 'took' after 'brake'; Duck has 'broke and took up'. Duck has 'church' for 'chancel'; Loder agrees with Martin.
637. Loder ends '... John Baptist; and *10 more* superstitious pictures in the Church'; Duck agrees with Martin. Loder (unusually) omits mention of the 5 shillings; Duck, as often, also omits mention of this.
638. Loder and Duck have '*in* stone', not '*on* stone'. Loder has 'step' in the singular; Duck agrees with Martin. Loder has '*Edmund* Dunstone'; Duck agrees with Martin. Loder and Duck have 'Robert *Bemant*'. Duck, Loder and Martin all agree in having a blank after 'John'. Martin has a deliberate blank space where Loder and Duck have 'Will. Dod' and 'William Dod' respectively.
639. Only two of those mentioned can be identified from Ship Money records: 'Edmund Dunstone' is probably Edward Duston, an outsitter at Bedfield, rated for Ship Money at 2*s.* 6*d.*; 'Robert Burmant' is Robert Beamond an outsitter at Bedfield rated at 1*s.* 6*d.*
640. Thus William Prynne used the fact that John Cosin's *Book of Private Devotions* had IHS on its frontispiece as evidence that it was 'meerely Popish': 'Now what is this, but an undoubted Badge, and Character of a Popish, and Jesuiticall Booke… Looke into the Frontispiece of all Jesuits workes, you shall finde this stampe, and Impresse on them' (Prynne, *A Brief Survay*, 6). At St Bartholomew, Smithfield, London the 1643 Parliamentary Ordinance was noted in the parish book, and led to the immediate decision that the 'three letters in the pulpit cloth IHS should be put out'; the accounts record a payment of 15*s.* 0*d.* 'to the imbroderer for taking IHS out of the pulpit cloth, and imbrodered same again with other work' (Hulme, *Symbolism*, 52 n.3).
641. MacCulloch, *Chorographer*, 46 and 89.
642. Pell was Sizar of Clare 1625; BA 1628; MA 1633. For his ejection, see Holmes, *Suffolk Committees for Scandalous Ministers*, 68.
643. Duck has '29 August'; Loder agrees with Martin.
644. Tricker, *The Church of St Peter and St Paul, Wangford*.
645. NCC Wills: Barker, 198–200 Gelour; Aisbye, 40 Briggs.
646. *Gentleman's Magazine*, 1835, 420.
647. Loder and Duck have 'churchwardens' in plural. Loder does not have the memorandum about the money being paid (nor, as usual, does Duck).
648. Loder and Duck have '*many* on the top of the Roof'. Martin and Duck have 'Mr [blank] Jermin'; Loder omits the blank. Martin has '*on* the steps'; we have followed Loder (and Duck, who is forever tidying up) in omitting 'on'.
649. Martin, SRO(B), E2/41/8, vol ib, fol. 389 (16 September 1743).
650. Hervy, BL Add. MS 4969, fol. 67.
651. See chapter 6, especially p. 85.
652. John Rotchester [*sic*] of Halesworth, glazier, 1617: SRO(I), AA1/53/201; William Rochester of Bungay, glazier, 1644: SRO(I), AA1/82/93.
653. Loder and Duck omit the first '10'. Loder and Duck have 'Bacon's Isle', and we have

followed them; Martin has 'Barcon's Isle'. Martin has a marginal note '1644', possibly a transcription from the original, possibly his own note.

654. Churchwardens' accounts will be found in appendix 8. Those for Dennington are discussed in the context of the work of Dowsing's deputies in chapter 6.

655. Duck omits the entry altogether; we have used Loder's date (21 February), rather than Martin's (2 February).

656. Loder has the following variants from Martin: Edmond Blomfield, Aspell-Stonham, Gosbeck, Denning, Westhorp, Glanfield, Suthelham, Jessup, Lethergland & Shutford (for Lothingland & Mutford), Blithborough. Duck has the following variants from Martin: Aspall Stonham, Gosbeck, Dunning, Westhorp, Hundon, Glanfeild [*sic*] of Gosbeck, Frances Verdon for Waingford, Suthelham, Bosemere, Fordam, Jesup, Becceles, Lothingland Mutford and Bungay, Blythburgh.

657. Loder and Duck have '*by* the right Honourable'. Duck does not have the date; Loder agrees with Martin. Duck has no reference to 'T.D.', the text running continuously with no gap; Loder agrees with Martin.

APPENDIX 1  *William Dowsing: an outline genealogy*

1. White, *Journal*, 58–61.
2. See above, n.5 to chapter 1.
3. See above, pp. 3–4, 30–31.

APPENDIX 2  *A possible portrait of William Dowsing*

1. Edmund Farrer, *Suffolk Portraits (East)*, vol. 1 (manuscript, never published, held in SRO(I)). For current location of the paintings, see later in this appendix.

2. Walter Charles Biden, born at Southsea, Hants, 1863; educated at Charing Cross Medical College, University of London and University of Birmingham; surgeon at Charing Cross Hospital; one-time member of East Suffolk County Council, and Chairman of Laxfield Parish Council; in 1912 residing at the Lodge, Cratfield; died 1930. (Cox, *Cox's County Who's Who Series, Suffolk*, p. 13.) Birth registered at Portsea Island under the name of Charles Walter [*sic*] Biden, son of William Marks [*sic*] Biden (Chief Engineer in HMS 'Undaunted') and Eleanor Parry Biden, née Jones, of 12 Jubilee Terrace, Southsea; date of birth 22 April 1863. His great-great-niece, Mrs Caroline Excell, has kindly provided me with a family tree, from which it appears that Walter had an elder sister and three elder brothers (two doctors and a solicitor), and a younger brother (another doctor). The family tree takes the ancestry back to our Biden's grandparents. The transcript of Biden's will at Somerset House reveals nothing about the background to his paintings. I am grateful to surviving relatives of Dr Biden (none of them lineal descendants) for their help and enthusiasm in response to my initial cold contact.

3. 'Reminiscences of William Dowsing the iconoclast', *Proceedings of the Great Yarmouth Archaeological Society*, 1930. I am very grateful to Tom Mollard, librarian of the Norfolk and Norwich Archaeological Society, for locating a copy of the pre-war proceedings of their daughter branch in Great Yarmouth. It was this that first alerted me to the existence of a portrait of Dowsing, and Dr John Blatchly then followed up the clue and found the painting.

4. The three letters are in the files of the Ipswich Museum. The first letter is from

G. Hilda Biden, dated 29 December 1930. The second letter is from her sister, B. Biden dated 31 December 1930, and the third and final letter in the series is from Hilda, dated 22 December the following year, arranging collection of the portraits from the caretaker of her late uncle's house.

5.   John Smith of Laxfield bequeathed bread for the poor in 1718 (Page, *Supplement*, 409).

6.   John Dowsing (*recte* Smith) is catalogue 1931–126. William Smith (*recte* Dowsing) is catalogue 1931–127.

7.   I am grateful to Dr David Kelsall, Cathedral archivist, for information about the St Albans carving. For general discussion of clothing of the period see for example Ewing, *Everyday Dress 1650–1900*, 25–7; Cunnington & Cunnington, *Costume in the Seventeenth Century*, 140–41 and *passim*; Cole, *Collars, Stocks, Cravats*, 15–17.

8.   The wording of Farrer's entry in his *Suffolk Portraits* (see note 1 above) implies some uncertainty as to date.

9.   See note 5 above. For the dating of this picture, see *The Triumphant Image*, entry 18.

10.  Ena Biden (personal communication). The only hint of eccentricity in Dr Biden's character is that his nieces should not have known about (or, at least, not told the museum) their uncle's claimed lineal descent from Dowsing. It is perhaps also surprising that Biden, as the fifth rather than first child of his parents, should have held the portrait.

### APPENDIX 3 *Dowsing's collection of Parliamentary sermons*

1.   See above, p. 141.

2.   Mathews was born in Cambridge 1680, Emmanuel College 1696, LLB 1702, Deacon 1705, Priest 1712. He was perpetual curate at St Margaret's 1716–25, moving on perhaps when he donated the sermons. At the foot of Dowsing's contents list in volume 1 (IV), there is a note in his hand, referring to William Fairclough's sermon *The troublers troubled, or Achan condemned and executed* (preached 4 April 1641). Mathews comments: 'From this first sermon of Fairclough's, the Achans of Israel & the Troublers of Israel became a common Phrase in the mouths of the Seditious Preachers in the times following to signifye the King's Friends'.

3.   Blatchly, *Town Library of Ipswich*.

4.   Discussed on pp. 10–11 above.

5.   Volume 6 (II) number 22.

6.   I am grateful to David and Marion Allen for transcribing this. A query in front of a word indicates uncertainty as to its correct transcription.

7.   'Hope is a good breakfast, but it is a bad supper' (Francis Bacon, *Apothegms*, 36).

### APPENDIX 4 *Jacob Caley: a Dowsing associate in Ipswich*

1.   I am grateful to Frank Grace for assistance with the material in this appendix. I concentrate here on Caley's local activities, particularly those which might have a bearing on Dowsing: a broader account of his career will be found in the work of the History of Parliament Trust.

2.   The Caley family pedigree is recorded in Bysshe's Visitation of Suffolk, attested to by Jacob's signature and dated 1664. He died in 1680.

3.   The dispute in August 1642, just on the eve of war, was over whether the Twenty-Four could elect their own replacements, or whether it was a matter for the whole

body of freemen in the Great Court. Nicholas Philips and Caley had been elected by the Twenty-Four, but Philips leant towards loyalty to the King, as the epitaph on his ledger slab in St Margaret's church confirms. So his election was disallowed: Caley's not only stood, but he was put on a committee to investigate the affair.

4. SRO(I), HD36/A/145.

5. Frank Grace has found Caley in at least seven different 'collecting' roles from 1641 onwards, probably all of them before 1644.

6. Green, *Calendar*, pp. 418, 691, 693.

7. Henry Everard of Linstead was jailed at Bury for recusancy in 1579, and was repeatedly fined and had lands seized by the Crown (Pipe Rolls to 1592, then Recusant Rolls). The Everards were indicted often at Norwich Consistory Court and Assizes 1596–1616. Henry and his wife Ann had a son Francis (over nine years old in 1591) who could be the Francis in the Journal. The boy was indicted in 1591, and also in 1610 and 1615 when he was a 'sojourner' with William Everard and his wife Dorothy (née Waldegrave of Kenninghall).

8. Could this be Dowsing? – there are no Dawsons in the Ship Money Records.

9. John Base of Saxmundham was a Commissioner for Sequestrations in Suffolk from 1654.

10. The services referred to were held in the Tower church on Mondays, Wednesdays and Fridays when Bailiffs, Portmen and Common Councilmen were obliged to attend robed, processing in and out after proceedings which on occasion lasted up to three and a half hours.

11. It is possible that North was seizing an opportunity to get at Puritans, and that the true issue was one of indemnity rather than misappropriation.

12. SRO(I), FB21/A2/1. The quotations are from John Wodderspoon's published transcripts (*Antiquarian and Architectural Year Book*, 1831).

APPENDIX 5 *The Parliamentary Ordinances*

1. This account has been summarised from Shaw, *A History of the English Church during the Civil Wars,* I, 104–108, where a more detailed chronology will be found. See also Aston, *England's Iconoclasts*, 75–7, especially footnotes.

2. *A Declaration of the Commons in Parliament: made September the 9th 1641*, London, 1641.

3. *Mercurius Rusticus*, number 3, 18 quoted in Cliftlands, Politics and religion', 155.

4. See appendix 7.

5. 3 & 4 Edw. VI cap. X (1549).

6. *Two Ordinances of the Lords and Commons Assembled in Parliament for the Speedy Demolishing of all Organs, Images, and all manner of Superstitious Monuments... 9 Maii. 1644. Ordered by the Lords in Parliament...*, London, 1644. It was published on May 11.

7. The suggestion is that of Julie Spraggon (personal communication). She points out that in February 1643/4 the 'Copes, Surplices and other Chapel-stuff' from the Royal chapels were to be viewed, and that on 17 April the Commons were still requesting the Lords to agree to the sale of the copes. A week later, on 24 April, there was a proposed Ordinance in the Commons for the defacing of copes (out of which the May Ordinance may have developed). No such squeamishness had been felt the year before when copes from Lambeth Palace, Westminster Abbey and St Paul's had all been brought in, and ordered to be burned or converted to the relief of the poor in Ireland. This royal context might explain the somewhat puzzling reference in the

second Ordinance to roods and roodlofts, most of the former of which had surely gone from parish churches by the 1640s. The requirement in the Ordinance to deface copes and other items reads like an afterthought to the original requirement that they simply be not used, which lends support to the idea that a particular problem was being grappled with. (*Commons Journal*, III, 389, 422, 463, 486; see also III, 63, 110, 347, 368.)

8.   See above, pp. 112 and 200.
9.   Extracted from Gee & Hardy, *Documents*, 551–2.
10.  Extracted from Gee & Hardy, *Documents*, 553.
11.  Extracted from Firth & Rait, *Acts and Ordinances*, 265–6.
12.  Extracted from Firth & Rait, *Acts and Ordinances*, 425–6.

## APPENDIX 7 *Dowsing's commissions from the Earl of Manchester*

1.   SRO(I) HD 64/6, pp. 77–8. This commission was printed by Evelyn White in his edition of the Journal (pp. 6–7).
2.   PRO SP16/498/87. It has not previously been published. It is calendared in *Calendar of State Papers Domestic, Charles I, 1641–43* (1887), 509. Varley used the Calendar to publish an abbreviated version in his *Cambridge during the Civil War* (p. 36).

## APPENDIX 8 *Parish records*

1.   We are grateful to Elizabeth James for this reference.
2.   We are grateful to Elizabeth James for this reference also.

## APPENDIX 10 *Discovering visitors in churchwardens' accounts*

1.   Accounts will be found in appendix 8. Summary accounts are not detailed enough to give the sort of evidence that is required, and have been excluded from this discussion.
2.   At Walberswick.
3.   See above, p. 82.
4.   He is called *John* Dowsing.
5.   See chapters 6 and 7.
6.   The proportion of surviving accounts is a little higher for churches Dowsing visited than for those he did not. This is probably because he visited both Ipswich and Cambridge, and accounts in major towns have survived better than in rural areas.
7.   The Martin transcription of the Suffolk entries has the fees recorded, seemingly casually, in the margin. At Cambridge, All Saints (entry 23) and Walberswick (entry 233) the accounts record the payment of a fee, but there is no mention of it in the Journal.
8.   The case which does not fit is Cambridge, Holy Trinity (entry 25).
9.   In two churches (Metfield and Dennington, entries 269 and 270) the visitor is named and is not Dowsing, but one of his deputies, Verdon, who probably visited before Dowsing and took the fee. The thrust of the argument is unchanged.

## APPENDIX 11 *The chronology of iconoclasm outside the Journal*

1.   Braintree, Latton, Saffron Walden, Great Bromley, and West Ham (Essex); Bishop's Stortford, St Albans (St Peter's), (Hertfordshire); Bressingham, East Harling, Harl-

eston, and Ashwellthorpe, (Norfolk); Peasenhall, Bardwell, South Elmham, Risby, Lowestoft, Stonham Aspal and Framlingham (Suffolk). St Albans, St Peter's acted independently in November 1643 (see following note), and then received a visitor in June 1644. Two of the above churches (Bishops Stortford and Stonham Aspal) can have their iconoclasm dated because the event occurred between the Easter year-end and expenditure on the Covenant. Parliament ordered the Covenant to be taken (by all men above the age of eighteen) on 2 February 1644, with local Committees taking it themselves, then passing it down to parishes. One may normally reckon that parishes signed the Covenant in April, May or June 1644. In our area the accounts show that the Covenant had mostly been signed by Easter 1644 (21 April), with some parishes straggling into May.

2. St Albans, St Peter's in Hertfordshire, and West Ham in Essex.

3. The anomaly is the April 1645 visit to Great Bromley. This is so far outside the range of the other visits that it must have been of a different nature, or (more likely) an error in accounts written up some time after the event – such errors are found elsewhere. Not too much significance should be placed on the apparent burst of activity in May, half of which was caused by Captain Gilley and the accident of his being well-recorded. With so few records, it is likely that entirely spurious patterns will be found if the data is examined too closely.

4. By chance, all the precise dates for visitors fall after Easter 1644, and all the precise dates for iconoclasm with no mention of visitors fall before that date. Table A11.1 shows that it would be wrong to conclude that there were no visits before Easter 1644, or that iconoclasm without mention of visitors stopped at that date.

5. Gilley at Banham, Bressingham, East Harling (all Norfolk); Jessup at Bungay and Lowestoft (both Suffolk). Dowsing's tour with his deputy (probably Verdon) starts at Kenton on 3 April (Journal entry 210), and he is recorded at South Elmham and Framlingham in May and August respectively.

APPENDIX 12 *How much glass was destroyed?*

1. Buers (Journal entry 120), 600 pictures; Bramford (entry 89), 841 pictures; Clare (entry 43), 1000 pictures.

2. As discussed in chapter 7 (and assumed throughout this volume), the majority of Dowsing's 'pictures' were in stained glass. To make these counts, I have ignored mention of angels and cherubim as they were normally in the roof, but have counted all other occurrence of pictures unless it was clear they were not in the glass. College chapels were excluded, as were duplicate entries. All other entries were included, even where Dowsing comments that some glass had previously been removed. On about a dozen occasions he uses the phrase 'diverse', I have assumed this meant ten pictures; on the five occasions where me merely says 'many' I have taken this to be twenty; on the four occasions where he mentions pictures but gives no hint as to the number I have assumed ten. Taken together, these assumptions introduce a degree of doubt into about 10% of his entries.

3. The analysis was carried out separately and cannot be reproduced from the tables shown here.

4. We can be reasonably sure that Dowsing's 'pictures' are individual images, and not entire windows, because he quite often lists pictures by subject.

5. Woodforde, *Norwich School of Glass-Painting*, 45; Cautley, *Norfolk Churches*, 85.

6. Osborne, *Stained Glass*, 53.

7.  Other examples include Ipswich, St Clement's (Journal entry 85), Cheveley (203), Barking (254), Hoxne (265), Eye (266), Occold (267), Rishangles (268).

8.  King's Lynn is omitted, as the sum of £100 dwarfs that of any other church. The table shows expenditure in the churchwardens' years 1643-4 and 1644-5. There are four churches which have minimal expenditure in those two years, but do have large expenditure in the following year, and this expenditure has also been included. All accounts used in this appendix will be found in appendix 8.

9.  I assume that the churchwardens' accounts form a reasonably representative sample, a point taken up in appendix 14 with regard to Suffolk.

10. Strictly speaking I should have subtracted the average spent in the previous years on maintaining the glass, to arrive at an estimate of how much extra was spent in 1643-4. We do not have the data to do this, but those of us who have been collecting the parish records on which this analysis is based have found that expenditure on glass in 1643-5 is almost invariably much greater than in the previous few years.

11. Using the accounts for Bishop's Stortford, Hertfordshire; Great Bromley, Essex; Louth, Lincolnshire (appendix 8).

12. Using the accounts for Dennington, Suffolk; Louth, Lincolnshire; Walsham, Norfolk (appendix 8). I am very grateful to Ruth and Jonathan Cooke for information about seventeenth-century quarries, and also to Chapel Studios for help in this area. Quarries probably do not vary enough in size to spoil our estimates.

13. Evidence of glaziers' daily rates will be found at Buckden, Hunts; and Metfield, Suffolk (wasted time). The daily rates of other skilled tradesmen and unskilled labourers for comparative purposes will be found at Bardwell, Suffolk; Bressingham, Norfolk; Framlingham, Suffolk; Great Bromley, Essex; Ipswich, St Peter's, Suffolk; Louth, Lincolnshire; Norwich, St Peter Mancroft, Norfolk; Peasenhall, Suffolk; St Albans, St Peter's, Hertfordshire.

14. The argument is complicated slightly by the fact that a small proportion of the glass at Dennington was second-hand, so this particular piece of work was perhaps obtained slightly more cheaply than would otherwise have been the case. The figures imply a work rate of about 10 square feet a day (after allowing a day or two for the quarries). It has not been possible to obtain independent confirmation of the reasonableness of this figure, but it is interesting that glazing a chapel in the Tower of London in 1286 was done at the rate of something under 15 square feet a day, and this probably did not require the removal of any old glass. (Salzman, *Building in England*, 175–6.) In this analysis, I have ignored the evidence from Cambridge, St Botolph's, as it cannot be interpreted without knowing how much each square foot of glass cost without labour.

APPENDIX 13 *How many brasses were damaged?*

1.  I am grateful to Philip Whittemore and Jonathan Finch for reading an earlier draft of this appendix. It was Dr Finch's initial analysis of Norfolk brasses (based on research for his *Church Monuments*) which led me to undertake this work.

2.  See, for example, Williams, 'Brasses of Norwich Cathedral', for an example of localised brass iconoclasm. I am grateful to Philip Whittemore for this reference.

3.  Another reason for carrying out this analysis is that Layer might have been significantly biased – tending perhaps to record brasses which were particularly visible or accessible, and therefore more liable to suffer destruction, so that our rate of destruction is inflated and brasses as a whole have suffered lower rates of destruc-

tion than our figures would suggest. If the figure of 80% loss of inscriptions is correct, then Cole should record many, many indents and effigies without brasses, and relatively few inscriptions. If, however, Layer was selecting brasses which were particularly liable to destruction, then Cole's more systematic approach to recording should result in more equal numbers of the three categories. Another reason for carrying out this analysis is that Bertram quotes rather higher survival rates in his *Lost Brasses*, of the order of 60% for Bedfordshire, Berkshire, Oxfordshire, Surrey, and Sussex combined, and about 35% for Huntingdonshire (pp. 123–5), and I wanted to check that my figures were self-consistent.

4. First, indents may have disappeared by Cole's time; secondly we do not know whether he systematically recorded indents, though he gives the impression of doing so; thirdly some indents will be of post 1540 brasses, which are out of our scope. All of these factors could bias the results.

5. The survival of inscriptions shows more or less the sort of pattern one might expect if distributing 37 inscriptions randomly amongst 119 churches. Most churches have no inscriptions, 18 churches have 1 surviving inscription, 3 churches have 2, 3 churches have 3, and one church has 4. However, although the pattern of results is largely explicable by chance, there are four churches with more surviving inscriptions than one would expect by chance alone. Three of these are in the Journal, and are discussed in the commentary – Balsham (entry 193), Swaffham Prior, St Mary's (32), and Whaddon (161). The case of Fulbourn, a church not in the Journal, is discussed in chapter 3.

6. I used D. E. Davy's 37 manuscript volumes of topographical and historical notes, as he has systematically copied the church notes of previous antiquaries.

7. The first of these exceptional churches is Letheringham, visited by a Dowsing deputy (Journal entry 127), where John Blatchly has shown that prayer clauses were systematically mutilated. The second was Stoke by Nayland, visited by Dowsing (entry 47), where 6 of 12 inscriptions survived to be recorded by the later antiquaries. The third was Long Melford, where the reports of the antiquaries are not entirely clear, but it seems that of 14 inscriptions recorded before the 1640s, none survived to the early eighteenth century.

8. Although the average survival rate of inscriptions is the same for these 18 churches as for the ones known to have been visited by Dowsing, it is possible, of course, that only some of these 18 were visited. The only way to test this is to look at the pattern of survival. In the churches visited by Dowsing, we do not find a clear distinction between churches where everything survived and churches where nothing survived. Thus, in almost all these churches, there were 3 or fewer inscriptions in the initial sample, and the number that survived is anything between 0 and 3. This suggests that survival in an individual building was largely a matter of chance, rather than some churches being thoroughly cleared and others untouched. Exactly the same pattern occurs in the churches not visited by Dowsing, which does not prove, but strongly suggests, that they were subject to the same forces of destruction as the Dowsing churches. (In just one church with more than three brasses did all the inscriptions survive – Wingfield, not visited by Dowsing; but here there were only four brasses in the initial count, and the fact that all survived could well have been a matter of chance, the odds being about one in sixteen.)

9. Weever records inscriptions in three parish churches in St Albans. St Stephen's had 4 and St Michael's 2; none survived. St Peter's had 16 of which 9 are recorded by

Salmon, though it is not entirely clear whether in some of these he is quoting Weever.

10.  We were not able to use the work an earlier antiquary, Sir Henry Chauncy, who published his *Historical Antiquities of Hertfordshire* in 1700. He used paid assistants, who obviously used Weever as a basis for some of their records, sometimes correcting his errors and blanks (particularly missing months), sometimes not, so that one is never quite certain whether the inscription was actually in place at the time of their visit. Chauncy was, of course, more interested in the genealogy and history represented by the inscriptions than the physical status of the brass.

11.  Two churches stand out as an exceptions, and may not have suffered in the 1640s – Berkhamsted, with 4 out of 5 surviving (but 3 of the 4 may not have had prayer clauses), and 'Harden', with 3 out of 3 – but this survival rate in an individual church could be due to chance.

12.  One church, Maldon has a notable rate of survival, with all 4 out of 4 inscriptions surviving. This could be due to chance.

13.  In case others should wish to pursue Norfolk in more detail, these are my results for the survival of brasses: numerator is survivors, denominator is number in sample. Ashby 2/2; Ashwellthorpe 0/1; Attleborough 0/5; Blo Norton 0/2; Booton 1 or 2/2; Brampton 3/3; Buckenham, New 1/4; Burgh St Margaret 1/1; Clippesby 2/2; Ellingham 1/1; Ellingham, Great 0/2; Erpingham 1/1; Forncett St Peter 2/2; Fretenham 0 or 1/1; Gressenhall 1/1; Hardingham 0/1; Hellesdon 2/2; Hemsby 2/3; Holme by the Sea 1/1; Honingham 0/1; Hunstanton 1/1; Ingham 6/6; Ketteringham 2/2; Loddon 0 or 1/1; Narborough 1/1; Newton Flotman 1/1; ?Oby 1/1; Ormesby St Margaret 4/4; Raveningham 2/2; Redenhall 0 or 4/6; Raynham, East 1/1; Ringland 1/1; Rougham 2/2; Salle 6/6; Sculthorpe 0/1; Shelton 4/4; Shotesham St Mary 0/1; Snetterton 0/2; Snoring, Great 1/2; Sparham 3/5; Spixsworth 0/2; Stratton St Michael's 1/1; Stratton St Mary's 1/2; Surlingham 1/1; Thetford St Cuthbert's 0/1; Thetford St Peter's 0/1; Terrington 0 or 1/1; Trowse 0/2; Tibenham 1/2; Walsham, North 0/1; Winch, East 0/1; Winterton 1/2.

14.  Three churches have a major influence on these figures: Attleburgh, where it seems that 0 inscriptions survived out of 5; Redenhall where something between 0 and 4 survived out of 6; and Sheldon, where all 4 survived. However, removing these three churches leaves us with 19–21 survivals out of 38, still around the 50% mark.

15.  Salmon, *Essex*, 109.

## APPENDIX 14  *How many churches in Suffolk were visited?*

1.  For Dowsing's non-selection of churches in rural Cambridgeshire, see p. 36. In Cambridge and in Ipswich he dealt with every church. In Suffolk, he tended to work reasonably systematically in the east of the county, covering an area fairly completely; in the west his visits are more patchy. In Suffolk overall, the proportion of churches visited by Dowsing which ejected ministers is about the same as the proportion of ejections in the county as a whole – there were about 169 ejections in about 515 parishes, approximately one third; and of the 147 parish churches visited by Dowsing, 55 had an ejection, also about one third (data collected from Matthews, *Walker Revised*).

2.  I am very grateful to Andrew Foster for helpful discussion of this point. See his 'Churchwardens' accounts', 76–84, where bias in survival is usefully explored.

3.  In what follows, the first figures I quote are for the 17 non-Dowsing parishes.

These are followed in brackets by the equivalent result for all 24 surviving accounts, made up of the 17 plus the 7 parishes for which accounts survive which *were* visited by Dowsing, but excluding the two Ipswich churches (Ipswich is a special case). Based on the Hearth Tax returns of 1674, 3 of the 17 non-Dowsing parishes had between 26 and 50 heads of households (4 of the 24 parishes), 10 (11) had between 51 and 100 households, 2 (5) had between 101 and 200, 1 (2) had between 201 and 300, and 1 (2) had more than 300 (analysed using Dymond & Martin, *Historical Atlas of Suffolk*, page 46). There is therefore a bias towards larger settlements, in the sense that they are somewhat over-represented, but the sample contains a good mix of settlement size; only the very smallest settlements (between 1 and 25 heads of households) are not represented at all. The reasonable balance of these parishes between town and village is confirmed by examination of John Speede's 1610 map of Suffolk, where just 2 of the 17 non-Dowsing parishes are shown as towns (non-italic typeface on the map), and 15 are not (of the 24 parishes, 5 are shown as towns, 19 as not). Quite reasonably, Dowsing tended to include towns in his travels, so the figures in brackets in the above analysis are proportionally slightly higher than chance alone would suggest.

4. The seventeen non-Dowsing churches with surviving accounts have six ejections, the nine churches with surviving accounts which he did visit have three ejections. Over Suffolk as a whole, about one third of churches have their ministers ejected.

5. Dymond & Martin, *Historical Atlas of Suffolk*, map 31.

6. Of the 17 non-Dowsing parishes which have surviving accounts of the 1640s, 9 were impropriated. If parishes visited by Dowsing are included then there are 24 sets of accounts surviving (ignoring Ipswich, a special case), of which 14 had their livings impropriated. These figures are above average for the county as a whole: about one third of Suffolk livings were impropriated. (Analysis based on Dymond & Martin, *Historical Atlas of Suffolk*, 72–3.)

APPENDIX 15  *Long after Dowsing: forgery and pastiche*

1. See above, pp. 80–82.

2. *Proceedings of the Suffolk Institute of Archaeology*, 6 (1885–8), 243–4 or White, *Journal*, 10–11 (the book version).

3. *Notes and Queries*, 10th series, V (1906), 421–2.

4. *Journal of the British Archaeological Association*, 36 (1880), 435–41.

5. The Druidical circle is in BL Egerton MS 2132. Randall was 29 when he founded and edited the monthly *Gorleston and Southtown Magazine* during its brief existence from January to July 1831, using as pen-names 'R. E. W.' and probably both 'Romulus' and 'Remus'.

6. Randall died in 1855, and in 1863 someone arranged for the printing of a title page for the first of his volumes stating that Dorcas Randall was the compiler. She had died in July 1856, aged 87, and was buried at Gorleston. Whoever next acquired the collections must have been under the impression that it was her work rather than her son's. They were accessioned as Egerton MSS 2129–32 at the British Library in 1871. Few collections are less worthy to be there.

7. As with almost all Randall's meanderings, no reference is given.

8. Written to D. Gourlay, junior, between May and October 1855. The letters are in the front of BL Egerton MS 2132.

9. *Sketches for an Ecclesiology of the Deaneries of Sparham, Taverham and Ingworth in Norfolk*

(1845), 2nd edition 1846, p. 195. Caddy Thomas also wrote an undated *Ecclesiologist's Guide* to the churches of Brisley and other deaneries.

10.  See above, p. 119.

11.  All the surnames the perpetrator used can be found in Blomefield, *History of Norfolk*, III, 389.

12.  *The Ecclesiologist*, V (1846), 73.

13.  As Caddy Thomas points out on p. 194 of his *Sketches*.

14.  It was again Paul Rutledge who drew our attention to the Squire papers controversy of the 1870s and 1880s.

15.  Rye, W. (ed.), *Norfolk Antiquarian Miscellany,* III, ii, 402–23.

16.  Ibid, 407–8.

17.  Brittain, F. and Manning, B., *Babylon Bruis'd & Mount Moriah mended; being a compendiouse & authentick Narracion of the Proceedinges of the William Dowsing Societie...,* William Heffer & Sons, Cambridge, December 1940, price sixpence, and many later editions at one shilling.

18.  W. Heffer & Sons, Cambridge. Facsimile edition 1993, Ghost Story Press, London.

19.  BL Egerton MS 2130, page 258.

# Bibliography

The bibliography is in four parts:

1. Editions of William Dowsing's (WD's) Journal
2. Topographical collections and manuscript sources
3. Articles about WD and his family
4. Other printed works

## 1. EDITIONS OF WILLIAM DOWSING'S (WD'S) JOURNAL

*The history of the text of the Journal is discussed in chapter 10 above. The following is a list of transcripts and printed editions of the Journal. The list for each county is shown in chronological order.*

CAMBRIDGESHIRE

Baker's transcript, in manuscript: Cambridge University Library, Mm. 1. 49 (Baker 38, No. 42) pp. 455–8, 471–3 (that is, in two sections).

Grey, Zachary, *The Schismatics delineated from Authentic Vouchers*, 1739. (Published under the pseudonym 'Philalethes Cantabrigiensis'.)

Carter, Edmund, *The History of the County of Cambridge*, 1753. (Journal for rural Cambridgeshire.)

—*History of the University of Cambridge*, 1753. (Journal for town and university.)

Cooper, Charles Henry, *Annals of Cambridge*, III, 1845, 364–7. (Journal for town and university.)

Moule, A. C., *The Cambridge Journal of William Dowsing 1643*. (Reprinted from *The History Teachers' Miscellany*, 4, 1926.)

SUFFOLK

Martin's transcript, in manuscript: SRO(I), HD 1538/435/1.

Duck's transcript, in manuscript: Soc. Antiq. MS 702.

[Ord, Craven (ed.),] *The Journal of William Dowsing*, Woodbridge, 1786. Printed by and for R. Loder. There was a second edition in 1818, published by Loder's widow.

Wells, Edward, *Rich Man's Duty*, Oxford, 1840. (The Journal was a supplement to this work, and was reissued by the publisher in separate form in 1844.)

White, C. H. Evelyn (ed.), *The Journal of William Dowsing*, Ipswich, 1885. Also in *Proceedings of the Suffolk Institute of Archaeology and Natural History*, 6 (1885), 236–95.

Wall, J. C. (ed.), *The Journal of William Dowsing*, n.d. (*c*.1902).

## 2. TOPOGRAPHICAL COLLECTIONS & MANUSCRIPT SOURCES

*A number of topographical and other manuscript collections, mostly unpublished, were used in preparing this edition, and the following puts them in context. For further information on many of the topographers and their work, see Blatchly,* Topographers of Suffolk.

BLOIS, WILLIAM                                          SRO(I), GC 17:755, VOL. 3
Four MS volumes of about 1660 containing Suffolk notes by William Blois of Grundisburgh (1600–73). Volume 3 contains church notes, organised by parish.

BLOMEFIELD, FRANCIS
The Revd Francis Blomefield (1705–52), the celebrated author of *The History of Norfolk,* also published a description of Cambridgeshire in 1750 as *Collectanea Cantabrigiensia.* Much of the material was provided by Cole, for whom see below.

CANDLER, MATTHIAS                                          SOC. ANTIQ. MS 667
Of the seven extant Candler manuscripts, we make use only of the above (sometimes referred to as Conder MS, after a previous owner). There is a brief biography of the antiquary Matthias Candler (alias Gillet), 1604–63, in chapter 2 above.

CHOROGRAPHER
The anonymous chorographer was active between about 1600 and 1604, recording material for Suffolk and Norfolk. His manuscript for Suffolk was broken up and the entries widely dispersed; the original work is reconstituted in Diarmaid MacCulloch (ed.), *The Chorography of Suffolk,* Suffolk Record Society, 19 (1976). That for Norfolk was published in 1938 by Mrs Christobel Hood.

COLE, WILLIAM                                          BL ADD. MSS, (various)
The journals of the antiquary William Cole of Cambridge (1714–82), of the 1730s and 1740s, are helpful for Cambridgeshire. The references we give are the BL Additional Manuscript number, applying also to microfilm copies in the CRO.

COUNTY COMMITTEES FOR SCANDALOUS MINISTERS
The county committees heard evidence against local ministers in 1644. We have used the records of the hearings not only for information about ministers, but also to see how many of the churchwardens and others named by Dowsing acted as witnesses and accusers. The reports provide useful sidelights on the fabric and furnishings of the churches. We have used:

*Cambridgeshire*: BL Add. MS. 15672 (typed transcript in CUL Palmer B58);

*Essex*: early transcript by William Cole in BL Add. MS 5829;

*Lincolnshire*: Lincoln City Library, the book of Manchester's Committee for Scandalous Ministers, (transcribed by J. W. F. Hill, 'The Royalist Clergy of Lincolnshire', *Lincolnshire Architectural and Archaeological Society Reports and Papers*, NS2 (=OS44) (1938–40), 34–127);

*Suffolk*: (transcribed by Clive Holmes, *The Suffolk Committees for Scandalous Ministers 1644–1646*, Suffolk Record Society, 13 (1970)).

DARBY, REVD JOHN WAREYN                                                    SRO(I)
Transcriptions of monumental inscriptions in Suffolk (excluding Bury St Edmunds and Ipswich), made in the 1820s and 1830s by the Revd John Wareyn
Darby (1791–1846). The notes for each parish, on unbound sheets, are boxed by
hundreds.

DAVY, DAVID ELISHA (1769–1851)                          BL ADD. MSS 19077–113
Davy's important notes on Suffolk churches are included in his collections in the
British Library (Add. MSS 19077–247), and are available on microfilm in SRO(I).
They include transcripts from earlier antiquaries, including the missing volume
of Martin's notes.

DAVY, HENRY
Artist, etcher, and publisher, Davy (1793–1865, no relation to the above) published three books of Suffolk etchings, and nearly 200 separate etchings and
lithographs. We refer to his prints by subject and date; for a list of them all, see
*Proceedings of the Suffolk Institute of Archaeology*, 29 (1961), pp. 78ff.

HERVY, WILLIAM                                              BL ADD. MS 4969
This is the rough notebook which Hervy, Clarenceux King of Arms (d.1567),
carried on his Visitation of Suffolk in 1561, containing arms and inscriptions in
churches and houses.

'INNOVATIONS IN RELIGION'                          BL HARL. MS 7019, fols. 52–93
This report of 1641, entitled 'Innovations in religion and abuses in government in
the University of Cambridge', contains brief descriptions of the interiors of all but
one of the Cambridge college chapels, written from a Puritan perspective. Its
background is discussed briefly in chapter 4 above.

LAYER, JOHN
John Layer (1585?–1641), a lawyer, recorded monumental inscriptions in Cam-
bridgeshire in the early 1630s. Layer's notes are printed in William Palmer,
*Monumental Inscriptions and Coats of Arms from Cambridgeshire*, (Cambridge, 1932).

MARTIN, THOMAS                                              SRO(B) E2/41/8
Considerable use is made of the invaluable Suffolk church notes of Thomas
Martin of Palgrave, Suffolk (1697–1771), attorney's clerk and antiquary, and
previous owner of the manuscript copy of the Suffolk part of the Journal used as
the basis for this edition.

WODDERSPOON, JOHN                                      BOD. SUFFOLK TOP. d. 19
This is an interleaved copy of Loder's edition of the Journal, with extensive
manuscript notes by John Wodderspoon (1806–62), journalist, writer and artist.
This was for his proposed edition of the Journal which never came to fruition.

## 3. ARTICLES ABOUT WD AND HIS FAMILY

*The following articles provide background information. Many are short items, without formal titles. Their accuracy and value varies. For each volume of each Journal, the page number, author and subject matter of the piece is shown.*

*East Anglian Notes and Queries* (First Series)  (Samuel Tymms, ed.)
Vol. 1 (1864)
- 146   *George Rayson*  Pulham St Mary branch of Dowsing family
- 162   *H. Spelman*  A weak joke on the frequency of the Dowsing family name in Norwich
- 218   *John Gough Nichols*  Queries
- 246   *Charles Golding*  Variants in Golding's early manuscript version of the Journal (Edward Duck's transcript)
- 246   *George Rayson*  A Dowsing tomb in Pulham St Mary churchyard
- 259   *George A Carthew*  Dowsing memorials at Laxfield

Vol. 2 (1866)
- 256–8   *G.R.P.*   Laxfield register extracts
- 359–62  *G.R.P.*   Dowsing entries in Laxfield registers

*East Anglian Notes and Queries* (New Series)  (C. H. Evelyn White, ed.)
Vol. 1 (1885–6)
- 138   *J. J. Muskett*  The will of WD (brief discussion)
- 164   *Beckford Bevan*  John Crow, deputy of WD at Risby
- 172   *J. G. Brewster*  Brief note on mention of the Dowsings in recently published Stratford St Mary church guide
- 363   *Anon.*  Church goods at Laxfield sold 1547

Vol. 4 (1891–2)
- 302   *W.C. Pearson*  Lea of Coddenham (includes WD's first wife's baptism)

Vol. 5 1893–4
- 257   *H. W. Birch*  Glass left by WD

Vol. 7 (1897–8)
- 1–5   *C. H. Evelyn White*  Dowsing's visitation of Cambridgeshire (continued in Vol. 12)
- 17–19  *C. Deedes*  'A portraiture of WD' (discusses one of WD's books)
- 241   *H. W. Birch*  Dowsing at Belstead
- 307   *Anon.*  Brasses at Lowestoft overlooked by WD
- 10–11 (in a *Book Notices Supplement* at end of volume)
  *Anon.*  Review of Conybeare's History of Cambridgeshire noting errors about WD

Vol. 8 (1899–1900)
- 103   *Anon.*  Dowsing entries in Cambridgeshire registers
- 293   *Anon.*  William Dowsing of Laxfield paid £13. 6s. 8d. Subsidy c.1610

Vol. 9 (1901–2)
  133, 181 and 341
      *Anon.* Pewter basons for baptism; one survives at Rampton
Vol. 11 (1905–6)
  33      *C. Deedes* 'Further portraiture of WD as a student' (discusses another
          book owned by WD)
  320     *R. G. C. Livett* Parish registers of Bildeston (WD second marriage)
          William Blomfield of Wattisham conducting civil marriages there
Vol. 12 (1907–8)
  49–53, 71–3, 90–93
      *C. H. Evelyn White* WD's visitation of Cambridgeshire (continued
      from Vol. 7), not completed

*East Anglian Miscellany*
  3213 and 3222 (1910)
      *H. W. B. Wayman* Dowsing memorials at Friston
  8922 and 8926 (1933)
      *Charles Partridge* Commentary on WD's will
  8932 (1933)
      *Charles Partridge* Commentary on WD's collection of Parliamentary
      sermons
  9069 (1933)
      *W. M. Lummis* Discussion of WD's family at Coddenham
  9305 (1934)
      *V. B. Redstone* WD obtains judgement, probably for a debt, but execu-
      tion is delayed because he 'hath not taken the Ingagement'. He is acting
      on behalf of the estate of the late John Mayhew, his wife Mary's previ-
      ous husband. See next entry.
  9318 (1934)
      *John Booth* Provides the text of the Engagement from Journals of the
      House of Commons. '… I will be true and faithfull to the Common-
      wealth… without a King or House of Lords'.
  9715 (1936)
      *Charles Partridge* Charles Partridge hopes that some reader can tell him
      whether the Dowsings were on calling terms with his ancestor Robert
      Partridge, churchwarden at Stratford in 1669!

4. OTHER PRINTED WORKS

*This list contains nearly all printed works referenced in the text, including printed editions of the Journal. The main exceptions are books owned by WD, discussed by Professor Morrill in chapter 1. On the few occasions when a work is not listed below, full bibliographical details will be found in the text. The place of publication is not given if it is London.*

Adams, W. T., *The Round Church of Cambridge*, Cambridge, 1930.

Addleshaw, G. W. O. and Etchells, F., *The Architectural Setting of Anglican Worship*, 1948.

Agate, John, *Benches and Stalls in Suffolk Churches*, Suffolk Historic Churches Trust, [Ipswich],1980.

*All the Memorable and Wonder Striking Parliamentary Mercies Effected and Afforded unto this our English Nation within this Space of lesse than 2 Yeares Past, Ao 1641 & 1642*, n.d. (1642). A series of prints without text, possibly by Hollar.

Andrewes, Lancelot, *Notes on the Book of Common Prayer*, in J. Bliss (ed.), *Two Answers to Cardinal Perron and other Miscellaneous Works* (1854), being vol. X of Andrewes' *Collected Works* (J. Bliss (ed.), 1841–54).

Aston, Margaret, *England's Iconoclasts*, vol. I, Oxford, 1988.

—*The King's Bedpost: Reformation and Iconography in a Tudor Group Portrait*, Cambridge, 1993.

—'Puritans and iconoclasm, 1560–1660', in Christopher Durston and Jacqueline Eales (eds.), *The Culture of English Puritanism, 1560–1700*, (1996).

—'Iconoclasm in England: official and clandestine', reprinted in Peter Marshall (ed.), *The Impact of the English Reformation, 1500–1640* (1997), 167–92.

Atchley, E. G. Cuthbert, *A History of the Use of Incense in Divine Worship*, 1909.

Attwater, A., *Pembroke College*, Cambridge, 1936.

Axon, E. (ed.), *Oliver Heywood's Life of John Angier of Denton*, Chetham Society, n.s. 97, 1937.

Babington, C. C., *History of the Infirmary and Chapel of the Hospital and College of St John the Evangelist at Cambridge*, Cambridge, 1874.

Baker, T. *A History of St John's College*, (ed. J. E. B. Mayor), Cambridge, 1869.

Banks, C. A. (ed.), *The Able Men of Suffolk, 1638*, 1931.

[Baring-Gould, S.,] *The Chorister, a Tale of King's College Chapel in the Civil Wars*, Cambridge, 1854.

Barton, J., 'Notes on the past history of the church of Holy Trinity, Cambridge', *Cambridge Antiquarian Society Communications*, 5 (1879–80), 313–35.

Barwick, John, *Querela Cantabrigiensis*: *A Remonstrance by way of Apologie for the Banished Members of the Late Flourishing University of Cambridge*, Oxford, 1647.

Barwick, Peter, *The Life of the Reverend Dr John Barwick, D.D.... translated into English*, 1724.

Beloe, Edward Milligen (ed.), *Extracts from the Chapel Wardens' Accounts of St. Nicholas' Chapel King's Lynn from the Year 1616 to the Date of the Restoration of His most Sacred Majesty King Charles the Second*, King's Lynn (privately published), 1926.

Bertram, Jerome, *Lost Brasses*, Newton Abbott, 1976.

Binns, John and Meadows, Peter, *Great St Mary's: Cambridge's University Church*, Cambridge, 2000.

Bishop, H. E. and Prideaux, E. K., *The Building of the Cathedral Church of St Peter in Exeter*, Exeter, 1922.

Blatchly, John, 'The lost and mutilated memorials of the Bovile and Wingfield Families at Letheringham', *Proceedings of the Suffolk Institute of Archaeology and History*, vol. 33 pt. 2 (1974), 168–94.

—'Early fourteenth century indents from the seabed at Dunwich, Suffolk' *Transactions of the Monumental Brass Society*, 13 (1982 and 1983), 260–64 and 359.

—*Topographers of Suffolk*, Suffolk Record Office, 1988 (fifth edition).

— *A History of the Old Town Library of Ipswich*, Woodbridge, 1989.

'Whose were the "Several Hands" of the second *Suffolk Traveller?*', *Suffolk Institute of Archaeology and History Newsletter,* 42 (Spring 1996), 10–11.

Blatchly, John and Northeast, Peter, 'Seven figures for four departed: multiple memorials at St Mary le Tower, Ipswich', *Transactions of the Monumental Brass Society*, 14 (1989), 257–67.

Blodgett, Harriet, 'Iconoclasm in Samuel Beckett's *Waiting for Godot* and William Dowsing's *Journal*', *Notes on Contemporary Literature,* (Carrollton), vol. 20, no. 5 (i.e. issue 100) (November 1990), 6–7.

Blomefield, Francis, *Collectanea Cantabrigiensia, or Collections relating to Cambridge, University, Town, and County,* Norwich, 1750.

—*History of Norfolk*, (completed by Revd Charles Parkin), 11 vols., 1805–10.

*St Botolph, Cambridge: Guide to the Church*, 1961 (by G[oodman], F. R. and G[oodman], A. W.).

*A Brief Description of the Church of St Mary the Less, Cambridge*, Cambridge, 1938, (by E. A. B. B.).

Brittain, F., *A Short History of Jesus College Cambridge*, Cambridge, 1940.

Brooke, C., *A History of Gonville and Caius College*, 1985.

Browne, G. F., *St Catharine's College,* 1902.

Browne, John, *History of Congregationalism in Norfolk and Suffolk*, 1877.

Bryant, T. H., *The Churches of Suffolk*, 2 vols., 1912.

Burgess, G., 'Usurpation, obligation and obedience in the thought of the Engagement controversy', *Historical Journal* 29 (1986), 515-36.

Burton, Henry, *A Tryall of Private Devotions, or a Diall for the Houres of Prayer*, 1628.

Bury, Patrick, *The College of Corpus Christi and of the Blessed Virgin Mary,* Cambridge, 1952.

Bushell, W. D., *The Church of St Mary the Great*, Cambridge, 1948.

Bysshe, Edward, *The Visitation of Suffolk begun 1664 and ended 1668*, (ed. W. H. Rylands), Harleian Society, vol. 61 (1910).

Carlson, Eric, 'The origins, function, and status of churchwardens', in Margaret Spufford (ed.), *The World of Rural Dissenters, 1520–1725*, (Cambridge, 1995), 164–207.

Caroe, W. D., 'Canterbury Cathedral choir during the Commonwealth and after with special reference to two oil paintings', *Archaeologia*, 62 (1911), 353–66.

Carter, Edmund, *The History of the County of Cambridge*, 1753.

—*History of the University of Cambridge*, 1753.

Cattermole, Paul, *Church Bells and Bellringing: A Norfolk Prospect*, Woodbridge, 1990.

Cautley, H. M., *Suffolk Churches and their Treasures,* Ipswich, 1937. References are to this edition; later editions have different pagination.

Chainey, Graham, 'The lost stained glass of Cambridge', *Proceedings of the Cambridge Antiquarian Society,* 79 (1990), 70–81.

—'King's College chapel delineated', *Proceedings of the Cambridge Antiquarian Society,* 80 (1991), 38–61.

—'The east end of King's College chapel', *Proceedings of the Cambridge Antiquarian Society*, 83 (1994), 141–65.

Chauncy, Sir Henry, *The Historical Antiquities of Hertfordshire*, 1700. (2nd edition Bishop's Stortford, 1826, reissued in facsimile, Dorking, 1975, with new introduction.)

Cheshire, J. G., 'William Dowsing's destructions in Cambridgeshire', *Transactions of the Cambridgeshire and Huntingdonshire Archaeology Society*, 3 (1914), 77–91.

*Church and Parish of St Benet*, Cambridge, 1915. Signed W. G., C. S. (William Greenwood and C. J. Swann).

*Churches of Cambridgeshire and the Isle of Ely*, Cambridge (Cambridge Camden Society), 1845.

Clark, J. W., 'Annals of the church of St Mary the Less, Cambridge,' *Ecclesiologist* (October 1857), 272–87.

Cliftlands, Bill, 'The "well-affected" and the "country": politics and religion in English provincial society, *c.*1640–1654', (PhD thesis, University of Essex, 1988).

Clutterbuck, R., *History of Hertfordshire*, 1815–27.

Cobb, G. F., *A Brief History of the Organ in the Chapel of Trinity College Cambridge,* Cambridge, n.d. (*c.*1913).

Cocke, Thomas, 'Rediscovery of the Romanesque', in *English Romanesque Art 1066–1200* (Catalogue of the Romanesque Exhibition held at the Hayward Gallery, 1984).

Cole, Doriece, *Collars, Stocks, Cravats: a History and Costume Dating Guide to Civilian Men's Neckpieces*, 1972.

Collinson, Patrick, *The Elizabethan Puritan Movement*, 1967.

—'Reformation or deformation? The reformed church and the university', in Binns and Meadows, *Great St Mary's*, 24–47.

Conybeare, E., *A History of Cambridgeshire*, 1897.

Cooper, Charles Henry, *Annals of Cambridge*, III, 1845.

Cooper, E. R., *Memories of Bygone Dunwich*, Ipswich, 1931.

Cosin, John, *Collection of Private Devotions*, 1627.

—*Works*, (ed. J. Sansom), vol. V, Oxford, 1855.

—*Correspondence*, Surtees Society, 52 (1869).

Cotman, J. S., *Engravings of the Most Remarkable Sepulchral Brasses in Norfolk*, 1819.

—*Engravings of Sepulchral Brasses in Suffolk*, 1838.

Cox, Homersham, *Cox's County Who's Who Series: Norfolk, Suffolk, Cambridgeshire*, 1912.

Cox, J. C., *The Parish Registers of England*, 1910.

— *Churchwardens' Accounts from the Fourteenth Century to the Close of the Seventeenth Century*, 1913.

— *Pulpits, Lecterns and Organs in English Churches*, 1915.

Cox, J. C. and Harvey, A., *English Church Furniture*, 1908.

Crawley, Charles, *Trinity Hall: The History of a Cambridge College 1350–1975*, Cambridge, 1976.

Croft-Murray, E., *Decorative Painting in England, 1537–1837*, vol. I, 1962.

Crook, Alec, *From the Foundation to Gilbert Scott*, Cambridge, 1980.

Crouch, J., *Puritanism and Art*, 1910.

Cunich, P., Hoyle, D., Duffy, E. and Hyam, R., *A History of Magdalene College Cambridge 1428–1988*, Cambridge, 1994.

Cunnington, C. W. and Cunnington P., *Handbook of English Costume in the Seventeenth Century*, 1955.

Cussans, J. E., *The History of Hertfordshire*, vol. I, 1879–80.

Dawson, R. S., *The Church of St Edward, Cambridge*, Cambridge, 1946.

Davies, J. G., *The Architectural Setting of Baptism*, 1962.

Davies, Julian, *The Caroline Captivity of the Church: Charles I and the Remoulding of Anglicanism, 1625–1641*, Oxford, 1992.

Deedes, C., 'A portraiture of William Dowsing, the Parliamentary visitor, 1643/4', *East Anglian Notes & Queries (New Series)*, 7 (1897–8), 17–19.

—'Further portraiture of Dowsing', *East Anglian Notes and Queries (New Series)*, 11 (1905–6), 33–5.

Deedes, C. and Walters, H. B., *The Church Bells of Essex*, 1909.

D'Ewes, Simonds, *The Autobiography and Correspondence*, (ed. J. O. Halliwell), 1845.

—*The Journal of Sir Simonds D'Ewes*, (ed. W. H. Coates), Yale, 1942.

Drummond, A. L., *The Church Architecture of Protestantism: An Historical and Constructive Study*, Edinburgh, 1934.

Dymond, David and Martin, Edward, *An Historical Atlas of Suffolk*, third edition, Suffolk, 1999.

Eales, Jacqueline, 'Iconoclasm, iconography, and the altar in the English civil war', in Diana Wood (ed.), *The Church and the Arts* (1992), published for the Ecclesiastical History Society by Blackwell, 313–27.

Ewing, Elizabeth, *Everyday Dress 1650–1900*, 1984.

Evans, H. F. Owen, 'Malicious damage to brasses', *Transactions of the Monumental Brass Society*, 10 (1963–8), 186–91.

Everitt, Alan (ed.), *Suffolk and the Great Rebellion, 1640–1660*, Suffolk Record Society, 3 (1960).

Farrer, Edmund, *List of Norfolk Monumental Brasses*, 1890.

—*A List of Monumental Brasses remaining in the County of Suffolk*, Norwich, 1903.

Fell, John (ed.), *Paraphrase and annotations on all the epistles of St. Paul*, 3rd edn, 1703.

Fielding, John, 'Puritan opposition to Charles I: the diary of Robert Woodford, 1637–1641', *Historical Journal*, 31 (1988), 769–88.

—'Arminianism in the localities: Peterborough Diocese 1603–1642', in Kenneth Fincham (ed.), *The Early Stuart Church*, 93–113.

Finch, Jonathan, *Church Monuments in Norfolk and Norwich before 1850: a Regional Study of Medieval and Post-medieval Material Culture*, BAR British Series, 2000 (forthcoming).

Fincham, Kenneth (ed.), *The Early Stuart Church, 1603–1642*, 1993.

—'Episcopal Government 1603–1640', in ibid. 77–8.

—(ed.), *Visitation Articles and Injunctions of the Early Stuart Church*, vol. II, Suffolk, 1998.

Firth, C. H., *Cromwell's Army*, 3rd edn, 1992.

Firth, C. H. and Rait, R. S., *Acts and Ordinances of the Interregnum*, 3 vols., 1911.

Fisher, Sheila, *The Dowsing Farmhouse Panels*, Laxfield and District Museum, 1988.

Fissel, Mark Charles, *The Bishop's Wars: Charles I's Campaigns against Scotland, 1638–1640*, Cambridge, 1994.

[Forbes, M. D. (ed.),] *Clare College, 1326–1926*, Cambridge, 1928.

Foster, Andrew, 'Churchwardens' accounts of early modern England and Wales: some problems to note, but much to be gained', in Katherine L. French, Gary G. Gibbs and Beat A. Kümin (eds.), *The Parish in English Life 1400–1600*, (Manchester, 1997), 74–93.

Foster, J. E. (ed.), *Churchwardens' Accounts of St Mary the Great, Cambridge from 1504 to 1635*, Cambridge, 1905.

Freeman, Andrew, *English Organ-Cases*, 1921.

Frere, Walter Howard, *Visitation Articles and Injunctions of the Period of the Reformation*, vol. III, Alcuin Club Collections, 16 (1910).

Fryer, Alfred C., 'Fonts with representations of the seven sacraments: supplement', *Archaeological Journal*, 90 (1933), 98–103.

Foxe, John, *Acts and Monuments*, (eds. S. R. C. Cattley and G. Townsend), 8 vols., 1837–41.

Fuller, Thomas, *History of the University of Cambridge*, 1655.

Gage, John, *History and Antiquities of Hengrave*, 1822.

Gardner, Thomas, *History of Dunwich*, 1754.

Gee, Henry and Hardy, William, *Documents Illustrative of English Church History*, 1896.

Gillingwater, E., *Historical Account of Lowestoft*, 1790.

Grace, Frank, ' "Schismaticall and factious humours": opposition in Ipswich to Laudian church government in the 1630s', in David Chadd (ed.), *Religious*

*Dissent in East Anglia III*, (Centre for East Anglian Studies, Norwich, 1996).

Gray, A. and Brittain, F., *A History of Jesus College Cambridge*, 1960.

Gray, P. C. and Swann, I. J., *A Catalogue of the Silver Plate in the Possession of the Master, Fellows and Scholars of Trinity College, Cambridge*, Cambridge, 1956.

Green, M. A. E. (ed.), *Calendar of Committee for Compounding etc., 1643–1660*, 1889.

Greenwood, R. and Norris, M., *The Brasses of Norfolk Churches*, Norfolk Churches Trust, 1976.

Grey, Zachary, *The Schismatics delineated from Authentic Vouchers,* 1739. (Published under the pseudonym 'Philalethes Cantabrigiensis'.)

Grose, Francis, *The Antiquities of England and Wales*, 4 vols., 1783–97.

Gunton, Simon, *History of the Church of Peterborough*, 1686.

Hall, Joseph, *The Works of Joseph Hall, D.D.*, (ed. Revd Peter Hall), Oxford, 1837–9.

Halliday, Robert, 'The churches of Ashley and Silverley', *Proceedings of the Cambridge Antiquarian Society*, 73 (1984), 29–45.

Harbie, Thomas, *Divi Arminii Mactatorum Renata, et Renovata Petitio*, 1642.

Hardy, B. Cozens, and Kent, E. A., *The Mayors of Norwich 1403–1835*, Norwich, 1938.

Harington, John, *A Briefe View of the State of the Church of England as it Stood in Q. Elizabeths and King James his Reigne to the Yeare 1608*, 1653. Posthumous publication: Harington died in 1612. His grandson, John Chetwind, wrote the dedicatory epistle of 1652.

Harris, H. A., 'Medieval mural paintings', *Proceedings of the Suffolk Institute of Archaeology*, 19 (1927), 304.

Harris, R. and Jones, S. K., *The Pilgrim Press: a Bibliography and Historical Memorial of Books Printed at Leyden by the Pilgrim Fathers*, Cambridge, 1922.

Hebgin-Barnes, Penny, *The Medieval Stained Glass of the County of Lincolnshire*, Oxford, 1996.

Hervey, S. H. A. (ed.), 'Suffolk in 1674: being the Hearth Tax returns', *Suffolk Green Books*, vol. 11, no.1, 1905.

Heseltine, Peter, *The Brasses of Huntingdonshire*, Cambridgeshire Libraries, 1987.

Heylyn, P., *Cyprianus Anglicus*, 1668.

Hill, J. W. F. (ed.), 'The Royalist Clergy of Lincolnshire', *Lincolnshire Architectural and Archaeological Society Reports and Papers*, NS2 (=OS44) (1938–40), 34–127.

*History of the Church of the Holy Sepulchre or Round Church, Cambridge*, Cambridge, 1846.

Hoffman, John, 'John Cosin's cure of souls: parish priest at Brancepeth and Elwick, County Durham', *Durham University Journal*, 71 (1978).

—'The Puritan revolution and the "Beauty of Holiness" at Cambridge', *Proceedings of the Cambridge Antiquarian Society*, 72 (1984), 94–105.

Holmes, Clive (ed.), *The Suffolk Committees for Scandalous Ministers 1644–1646*, Suffolk Record Society, 13 (1970).

—'Colonel King and Lincolnshire politics 1642–1646', *Historical Journal*, 16, 1973, 451–83.

—*The Eastern Association in the English Civil War*, Cambridge, 1975.

—*Seventeenth-Century Lincolnshire*, Lincoln, 1980.

Hollingsworth, A. G. H., *The History of Stowmarket*, 1845.

Hood, Christobel M., *The Chorography of Norfolk*, Norwich, 1938.

Hopkins, H. E., *Holy Trinity Church, Cambridge*, Cambridge, 1977.

Hoyle, David, 'A Commons investigation of Arminianism and popery in Cambridge on the eve of the Civil War', *Historical Journal*, 29 (1986), 419–25.

—'"Near Popery yet No Popery": theological debate in Cambridge 1590–1644', (PhD thesis, University of Cambridge (D061943), 1991).

Hughes, Ann, 'Thomas Dugard and his circle: a Puritan-Parliamentarian connection', *Historical Journal*, 29, 1986, 771–94.

Hughes, Anselm, *Catalogue of the Musical Manuscripts at Peterhouse, Cambridge*, Cambridge, 1953.

Hulme, F. E., *The History, Principles and Practice of Symbolism in Christian Art*, 1892.

Huray, Peter Le, *Music and the Reformation in England 1549–1660*, 1967.

Hussey, Christopher, *King's College Chapel, Cambridge, and the College Buildings*, 1926.

Hutchinson, Lucy, *Memoirs of the Life of Colonel Hutchinson*, (ed. J. Sutherland), Oxford, 1973.

Hutton, Ronald, *The Rise and Fall of Merry England*, Oxford, 1994.

James, M. R., 'The windows of King's College chapel', in C. R. Fay (ed.), *King's College Cambridge*, 1907, 103–24.

—*Suffolk and Norfolk*, 1930.

Jeffs, Robin (ed.), *Fast Sermons to Parliament November 1640 to April 1653*, Cornmarket Press facsimile edition, 1970–71.

Jones, John, *The New Art of Spelling*, 1704.

Jones, W. H. S., *A History of St Catharine's College, once Catharine Hall, Cambridge*, Cambridge, 1936.

Josselin, Ralph, *The diary of Ralph Josselin*, (ed. A. MacFarlane), 1976.

K[each], B[enjamin], *War with the Devil*, 4th impression, 1676.

Ketton-Cremer, R. W., *Norfolk in the Civil War*, 1969.

Keyser, C. E., *A List of Buildings in Great Britain and Ireland having Mural and Other Painted Decorations…*, third edition, 1883.

King, David, *Stained Glass Tours around Norfolk Churches*, Norwich, 1974.

Kingston, A., *East Anglia and the Great Civil War*, 1897.

Kirby, Joshua, *Historical Account of the Twelve [Suffolk] Prints of Monasteries…*, Ipswich, 1748.

—*The Suffolk Traveller,… The Second Edition, with many Alterations and large Additions, by Several Hands*, 1764.

Lack, W., Stuchfield, H. M. and Whittemore, P., *The Monumental Brasses of Buckinghamshire*, 1994.

—*The Monumental Brasses of Cambridgeshire*, 1995.

Lake, Peter, 'The Laudian style', in Kenneth Fincham (ed.), *The Early Stuart Church*, 161–186.

Laud, William, *Works*, Oxford, 1847–60.

Lee, Maurice, *The Road to Revolution: Scotland under Charles I, 1625–37*, University of Illinois Press, 1985.

Lees, H. D. W., *The Chronicles of a Suffolk Parish Church* [Lowestoft St Margaret], Lowestoft, 1949.

Legg, J. Wickham (ed.), *English Orders for Consecrating Churches in the Seventeenth Century*, Henry Bradshaw Society, 41 (1911).

Leigh, A. A., *King's College*, 1899.

L'Estrange, John, *Church Bells of Norfolk*, Norwich, 1874.

Lewis, J. M., *Welsh Monumental Brasses*, 1974.

Lillistone, David, *The Lady and the Abbot's Tomb in the Church of St Peter and St Mary*, Stowmarket, Suffolk, privately published, 1990.

Locke, J., *Essay concerning Human Understanding*, 1690.

Loder, R. (publisher), *The Journal of William Dowsing*. See under Craven Ord.

MacCulloch, Diarmaid (ed.), *The Chorography of Suffolk*, Suffolk Record Society, 19 (1976).

—*Suffolk and the Tudors: Politics and Religion in an English County 1500–1600*, Oxford, 1986.

MacCulloch, Diarmaid and Blatchly, John, 'An early organ at Framlingham church', *Proceedings of the Suffolk Institute of Archaeology and History*, 37 (1989), 18–30.

McCullough, Peter E., *Sermons at Court: Politics and Religion in Elizabethan and Jacobean Preaching*, Cambridge, 1998.

McGee, J. S., *The Godly Man in Stuart England*, 1976.

McKenzie, D. F., *Stationers' Company Apprentices Records*, 1974, 1978.

Maitland, R. W., *The Story of Ufford*, Ipswich, n.d., (*c*.1934).

Malden, H. E., *Trinity Hall*, 1902.

Malden, Henry, *An Account of King's College-Chapel, in Cambridge*, 1769, reprinted 1973.

Maltby, Judith, 'By this book: parishioners, the Prayer Book, and the established Church', in Kenneth Fincham (ed.), *The Early Stuart Church*, 115–37.

—*Prayer Book and People in Elizabethan and Early Stuart England*, Cambridge, 1998.

Manning, Brian, *The English People and the English Revolution*, 1976.

Marks, Richard, *The Medieval Stained Glass of Northamptonshire*, 1998.

Masters, R., The *History of the College of Corpus Christi and the B. Virgin Mary (Commonly called Bene't) in the University of Cambridge from its Foundation to the Present Time*, 1753.

—*Memoirs of the Life and Writings of the late Rev. Thomas Baker, B.D. of St. John's College in Cambridge, from the Papers of Dr. Zachary Grey*, Cambridge,1784.

Matthews, A. G., *Calamy Revised*, 1934.

—*Walker Revised: being a Revision of John Walker's Sufferings of the Clergy during the Grand Rebellion 1642–60*, Oxford, 1948.

Millar, Oliver, *The Age of Charles I: Painting in England 1620–1649*, 1972.

Miller, E., *Portrait of a College*, Cambridge, 1961.

Morgan, D., *Great West Window*, 1996.

Morgan, I. and Morgan, G., *The Stones and Story of Jesus Chapel Cambridge*, Cambridge, 1914.

Morrill, John, 'The Church of England 1642–9', in John Morrill (ed.), *Reactions to the English Civil War* (1982).

—'William Dowsing: the bureaucratic Puritan' in Morrill *et al.*(eds.), *Public Men and Private Conscience, 173–203.*

Morrill, J., Slack, P. and Woolf, P. (eds.), *Public Men and Private Conscience in Seventeenth-century England*, Oxford, 1993.

Moule, A. C., *The Cambridge Journal of William Dowsing 1643*. (Reprinted from *The History Teachers' Miscellany*, 4, 1926.)

Mullinger, J. B., *St John's College*, 1901.

—*The University of Cambridge*, III, Cambridge, 1911.

Nelson, Philip, *Ancient Painted Glass in England*, 1913.

Nichols, John, *Literary Anecdotes*, 1812.

—*Illustrations of the Literary History of the Eighteenth Century*, 8 vols., 1817–58.

Nichols, A. E., *Seeable Signs: the Iconography of the Seven Sacraments 1350–1544*, Woodbridge, 1994.

Norris, Malcolm, *Monumental Brasses: the Memorials*, 2 vols., 1977.

North, Thomas, *The Church Bells of the County and City of Lincoln*, Leicester, 1882.

—*The Church Bells of Hertfordshire*, 1886.

Oman, Charles, *English Church Plate 1597–1830*, 1957.

[Ord, Craven (ed.),] *The Journal of William Dowsing, of Stratford…*, Woodbridge, 1786. Printed by and for R. Loder. There was a second edition 1818.

Osmond, Percy H., *A Life of John Cosin, Bishop of Durham 1660–1672*, 1913.

Owen, T. M. N., *The Church Bells of Huntingdonshire*, 1899.

Page, Augustine, *Supplement to the Suffolk Traveller*, Ipswich, 1847.

Page-Phillips, John, *Children on Brasses*, 1970.

—*Palimpsests: the Backs of Monumental Brasses*, 2 vols., 1980.

Palmer, W. M., *The Puritan in Melbourn, Cambridgeshire*, Royston, 1895. The copy in the BL (09009.aaa.12(1)) contains important marginalia, including references.

—*Documents Relating to Cambridgeshire Villages*, Nos. III and IV, Cambridge, April, June 1926.

—*Episcopal Visitation Returns for Cambridgeshire*, Cambridge, 1930.

—*Monumental Inscriptions and Coats of Arms from Cambridgeshire*, Cambridge, 1932.

Parker, John and Parker, James, (eds.), *The Ecclesiastical and Architectural Topography of England: Part VII, Suffolk*, Oxford and London (published by John and James Parker under the sanction of the Archaeological Institute of Great

Britain and Ireland), 1855.

Paul, W. Norman, *Essex Fonts and Font Covers*, Baldock, 1986.

Payne, I., *The Provision and Practice of Sacred Music at Cambridge Colleges and Selected Cathedrals c.1547–c.1646*, 1993.

Peile, J., *Christ's College*, 1900.

—*Biographical Register of Christ's College 1505–1905,* Cambridge, 1910–13.

Pevsner, N. (series ed.), *The Buildings of England,* volumes published by county, 1951–76.

Phillips, J. R., *The Reformation of Images*, Berkeley, 1973.

Pritchard, Allan, 'Puritan charges against Crashaw and Beaumont', *TLS*, 2 July 1964, 578.

Prynne, William, *A Briefe Survay and Censure of Mr Cozens His Couzening Devotions*, 1628.

—*Canterburies Doome*, 1646.

Pyke, C. S. B., 'The new chapel of Sidney Sussex College, Cambridge' in D. E. D. Beales and H. B. Nisbet (eds.), *Sidney Sussex College, Cambridge* (Bury St Edmunds, 1996).

*Querela Cantabrigiensis*: *see under* Barwick, John.

Rackham, H., *Christ's College in Former Days*, Cambridge, 1939.

Randall, Dale B. J., *Gentle Flame: the Life and Verse of Dudley, Fourth Lord North (1602–1677)*, Duke University Press, USA, 1983.

Raven, J. J., *The Church Bells of Cambridgeshire,* Cambridge, 1882.

—*The Church Bells of Suffolk*, Ipswich, 1899.

RCHME, *An Inventory... Hertfordshire*, 1910.

—*An Inventory... Essex*, 4 vols., 1916–23.

—*An Inventory... Huntingdonshire*, 1926.

—*An Inventory... City of Cambridge*, 3 vols., 1959.

—*An Inventory... West Cambridgeshire*, London, 1968.

—*An Inventory... North-East Cambridgeshire*, 1972.

Reaney, P. H., *The Place-Names of Cambridgeshire and the Isle of Ely*, Cambridge, 1943.

Redstone, V. B. (ed.), *Ship-Money Returns for the County of Suffolk, 1639–40*, Suffolk Institute of Archaeology, 1904.

Roberts, B. D., *Mitre & Musket: John Williams, Lord Keeper, Archbishop of York, 1582–1650*, 1938.

Rouse, E. Clive, *Medieval Wall Paintings*, fourth edition, Princess Risborough, 1991.

Rouse Ball, W. W., *Notes on the History of Trinity College, Cambridge*, 1899.

—*Cambridge Papers,* 1918.

Rouse Ball, W. W. and Venn, J., *Admissions to Trinity College, Cambridge,* II, 1913.

Rowse, A. L., *Reflections on the Puritan Revolution*, 1986.

[Ryves, Bruno,] *Mercurius Rusticus*, Oxford, 1646.

*St Edward's Church, Cambridge*, Cambridge, 1949.

Salmon, Nathaniel, *The History of Hertfordshire*, 1728.

—*The History and Antiquities of Essex*, 1740.

Salt, S. P., 'The origins of Sir Edward Dering's attack on the ecclesiastical hierarchy 1625–40', *Historical Journal*, 30 (1987).

Saltmarsh, J., *King's College: a Short History*, Cambridge, 1958.

Salzman, L. F., *Building in England down to 1540: a Documentary History*, Oxford, 1952.

Sandars, Samuel, *Historical and Architectural Notes on Great Saint Mary's Church, Cambridge*, Cambridge, 1869.

Scarisbrick, J. J., *The English People and the English Reformation*, Oxford, 1983.

Schofield, B. (ed.), *The Knyvett Letters 1620–1644*, Norfolk Record Society, 20 (1949).

Scott-Giles, C. W., *Sidney Sussex College*, Cambridge, 1975.

Searle, W. G., *The History of Queens' College*, 1867.

Shaw, W. A., *A History of the English Church during the Civil Wars and under the Commonwealth*, 2 vols., 1900.

Sheingorn, Pamela, *The Easter Sepulchre in England*, Kalamazoo, 1987.

Shelford, Robert, *Five Pious and Learned Discourses*, Cambridge, 1635.

Sheridan, William, *Several Discourses*, 1704.

Sherman, A. J., *Historia Collegii Jesu Cantabrigiensis A. J. Shermanno*, (ed. J. O. Halliwell), 1840.

Shoberl, Frederick, *Topographical and Historical Description of the County of Suffolk*, 1820. (Reissue of vol. 14, part I of E. W. Brayley and J. Britton, *Beauties of England and Wales*, 1813.)

Shuckburgh, E., S., *Emmanuel College*, 1904.

Simpson, A. E. (ed.), *History of Mildenhall*, Mildenhall, 1892.

Simpson, F., *A Series of Ancient Baptismal Fonts Chronologically Arranged*, 1828.

Skinner, Q., 'Conquest and consent: Thomas Hobbes and the Engagement controversy, in G. E. Aylmer (ed.), *The Interregnum* (1972), 79-98.

Smith, J. J., 'On St Peter's Church, Cambridge', *Transactions of the Cambridge Camden Society*, 1841, 1–8.

Spraggon, Julie, 'Puritan Iconoclasm in England 1640–1660', (PhD thesis, University of London, 2000).

Spufford, Margaret, *Contrasting Communities: English Villagers in the Sixteenth and Seventeenth Centuries*, Cambridge, 1974.

Staley, V. (ed.), *Hierurgia Anglicana*, 1902.

Steegman, John, *Cambridge*, 1940.

Stephenson, Mill, *A List of Monumental Brasses in the British Isles*, London (for the Monumental Brass Society), second edition, 1964.

Sternhold, T. and Hopkins, J., *The Whole Booke of Psalmes, collected into English metre…*, 1562 and many editions thereafter.

Stoker, David, 'The genesis of *Collectanea Cantabrigiensia*', *Transactions of the Cambridge Bibliographical Society*, 9 (1989), 372–80.

Stokes, H. P., *Corpus Christi*, 1898.

Stubbings, F., *Emmanuel College Chapel 1677–1977*, Cambridge, 1977.

Suckling, A. I., *History and Antiquities of the County of Suffolk*, vol. II, 1848.

Swaby, J. E., *A History of Louth*, 1951.

Tatham, G. B., *The Puritans in Power*, Cambridge, 1913.

Taylor, Edgar., *The Suffolk Bartholomeans: a Memoir of the Ministerial and Domestic History of John Meadows… Ejected under the Act of Uniformity from the Rectory of Ousden in Suffolk*, (2nd edition)1840.

Temperley, Nicholas, *The Music of the English Parish Church*, Cambridge, 1979.

Tennant, Philip, *Edgehill and Beyond: the People's War in the South Midlands, 1642– 1645*, Stroud, 1992.

Tomlinson, Harold, 'Some Norfolk Fonts', in Clement Ingleby (ed.), *A Supplement to Blomefield's Norfolk*, 1929, 205–36.

Trevalyan, G M., *Trinity College: An Historical Sketch*, Cambridge, 1983.

Tricker, R., *The Church of St Peter and St Paul, Wangford*, 1982 (church guide).

*The Triumphant Image: Tudor and Stuart Portraits at Christchurch Mansion, Ipswich*, Ipswich Museum, n.d. (mid 1990s).

Tudor-Craig, Pamela, 'Wall paintings', in Carola Hicks (ed.), *Cambridgeshire Churches* (Stamford, 1997).

Twigg, John, *A History of Queens' College, Cambridge 1448–1986*, Bury St Edmunds, 1987.

—*The University of Cambridge and the English Revolution 1625–1688*, Bury St Edmunds, 1990.

Tyacke, Nicholas, 'Migration from East Anglia to New England before 1660' (PhD thesis, University of London, 1951).

— *Anti-Calvinists: the Rise of English Arminianism, c.1590–1640*, 1987.

—'Archbishop Laud', in Kenneth Fincham (ed.), *The Early Stuart Church*, 51–70.

—'Lancelot Andrewes and the Myth of Anglicanism' in Peter Lake and Michael Questier (eds.), *Conformity and Orthodoxy in the English Church, c.1560–1660*, Woodbridge, forthcoming.

Varley, F., *Cambridge during the Civil War*, Cambridge, 1935.

VCH, *The Victoria History of the County of Cambridgeshire and the Isle of Ely*, (ed. L. F. Salzmann *et al.*), 9 vols., 1936–89.

Venables, E., 'On the church of S. Mary the Virgin, commonly called Great S. Mary's, Cambridge', *Transactions of the Cambridge Camden Society*, 3 (1845), 248–91.

Venn, J., *Biographical History of Gonville and Caius College,* Cambridge, 1901.

—*Caius College*, 1901.

Venn, J. and Venn J. A., *Alumni Cantabrigienses*, Part I, Cambridge, 1922–7.

Vicar, John *A Sight of the Transactions of these Latter Yeares*, n.d. (1646).

—*True Information of the Beginning and Causes of all our Trouble*, 1648.

Walker, Thomas, *Admissions to Peterhouse*, Cambridge, 1912.

—*A biographical register of Peterhouse men…*, 1930.

—*Peterhouse*, Cambridge, 1935.

Wall, J. C., *Porches and Fonts*, 1912.

Wallace, J. M., *Destiny his Choice: the Loyalism of Andrew Marvell*, Chicago, 1955.

—'The Engagement controversy: an annotated list of pamphlets', *Bulletin of the New York Public Library* 68 (1964), 384-405.

Watt, Tessa, *Cheap Print and Popular Piety 1550–1640*, Cambridge, 1991.

Wayment, Hilary, *The Windows of King's College Chapel*, 1972.

—*King's College Chapel, the Side Chapel Glass*, 1991.

Webster, T., *Godly Clergy in early Stuart England: The Caroline Puritan Movement c.1620–1643*, Cambridge, 1997.

Wedgwood, C. V., *The King's War: 1641–1647*, 1959.

Weever, John, *Ancient Funerall Monuments*, second edition, 1767. (First edition was 1631.)

Welsby, P. A., *Lancelot Andrewes 1555–1626*, London, 1958.

White, C. H. Evelyn (ed.), *The Journal of William Dowsing*, Ipswich, 1885. Also in *Proceedings of the Suffolk Institute of Archaeology and Natural History*, 6 (1885), 236–95.

[White, John,] *The First Century of Scandalous, Malignant Priests...*, 1643.

Whitelaw, J. W., *Hertfordshire Churches and other Places of Worship*, Harpenden, 1990.

Williams, J. F., 'Brasses of Norwich Cathedral', *Transactions of the Monumental Brass Society*, 9 (1952–62), 366–7.

Willis, R. and Clark, J. W., *The Architectural History, of the University of Cambridge*, Cambridge, 1886.

Wilson, J. F., *Pulpit in Parliament*, 1969.

Wodderspoon, John, *Antiquarian and Architectural Year Book*, (for 1831).

—*Memorials of Ipswich*, 1850.

Woodforde, C., 'The fifteenth-century glass in Blythburgh church', Ipswich, 1933, reprinted from *Proceedings of the Suffolk Institute of Archaeology and Natural History*, 21 part 3.

— *Norwich School of Glass Painting*, Oxford, 1950.

Woodhouse, F. C., *Some Account of S. John's College Chapel, Cambridge, its History and Ecclesiology*, Cambridge, 1848.

Woodman, Francis, *The Architectural History of King's College Chapel*, 1986.

Wyatt, T. S., *Sidney Sussex College Chapel: A Brief Account*, Cambridge, 1973.

—'The Building and Endowment of the College' in D. E. D. Beales and H. B. Nisbet (eds.), *Sidney Sussex College, Cambridge* (Bury St Edmunds, 1996).

Zarnecki, G., *English Romanesque Lead Sculpture: Lead Fonts of the Twelfth Century*, London, 1957.

# Index to objects and images in the Journal

References are to Journal entry number, not to page number. The index lists images and other 'superstitious' objects mentioned by Dowsing in the Journal; for discussion of these objects, use the General Index. For places in the Journal, see the list on page 151. For people mentioned in the Journal, see the General Index.

# General index

References are to page number, with the most significant references shown in bold. A more convenient list of Journal places will be found on page 151. To locate examples of church furnishings and furniture mentioned in the Journal, use the previous index, using this index for references to discussion of those items. Thus 'crosses' in the previous index lists Journal entries mentioning crosses; in this index it references our discussion of the topic.